DONNA HOWES 1993

Accounting – An Introduction

Accounting – An Introduction

Third edition

MA Faul
BCom(Hons) BEd CA(SA) TED
Professor in Accounting
University of South Africa

CWI Pistorius
MCom CA(SA)
Vice-Rector: Business Administration
University of Pretoria

LM van Vuuren
MCom CA(SA) ACMA
Director: Public Accountants' and Auditors' Board
Johannesburg

BUTTERWORTHS
DURBAN

Butterworth Publishers (Pty) Ltd
Reg No 91/05175/07

First Edition 1974
Second Edition 1981
Third Edition 1988
Reprinted 1990
Reprinted 1991
Reprinted 1992

ISBN 0 409 10006 4

Durban
8 Walter Place, Waterval Park
Mayville 4091

Johannesburg
108 Elizabeth Avenue
Parkmore 2196

Pretoria
301 Telkor Building, 270 Main Street
Waterkloof 0181

Cape Town
3 Gardens Business Village, Hope Street
Cape Town 8001

Acknowledgement:
The cover photograph of the HP-17B pocket calculator is used with the kind permission of Hewlett-Packard

Typeset by Positone Pinetown
Printed and bound by Interpak Natal Pietermaritzburg

PREFACE

The objective of academic career training is to equip the student with a knowledge of the fundamental theory and practice of his discipline and with skills in applying this knowledge. Thus more is involved than merely teaching a particular technique. An academically schooled student should be able to analyse a practical situation and apply the appropriate theory in order to find a solution to a problem.

The first edition of this work was published in 1974 to fulfil the long-felt need for a theoretically based introductory handbook on accounting for South African students. A second, improved edition appeared in 1981. In this, the third edition, the authors have brought the contents up to date with the latest developments in accounting and have adapted the presentation to meet the changing needs of educational institutions.

Directed primarily at first-year students in the economics and management sciences, the book serves as a basis and reference work for further study in accounting. The material is arranged so that it can be used selectively by students of management and other disciplines which require an orientation in accounting as a management tool.

The theoretical and conceptual approach is supplemented by an emphasis on the informational and reporting functions of accounting. An effort has been made to provide a comprehensive overview of accounting from the financial and management points of view, and to maintain a balance between an understanding of accounting procedures and the ability to interpret and use accounting information effectively.

Organisation of subject matter and use

The first four chapters cover the basic theory of accounting. These chapters, which have been completely rewritten, should form the basis of every accounting course.

The accounting process, which explains the fundamental techniques, is dealt with in chapters 5 to 9. These five chapters contain material essential to students wishing to become professional accountants, but of less importance to those requiring only an orientation for management purposes.

The concept of profit determination is introduced with reference to trading concerns in chapter 10. Every student of accounting should have a clear grasp of the principles of profit determination. More advanced profit determination problems in manufacturing concerns are dealt with in chapters 24 and 25.

Chapter 11, which has been rewritten, and chapter 12 deal with the design of accounting systems. More attention is devoted to computerised systems and these chapters are of particular interest to students wishing to become professional accountants and those interested in the development of management information systems.

Chapters 13 to 15 cover current assets. Chapter 15, which deals with inventory, has been adapted to conform with the requirements of AC 108.

Fixed assets and investments are dealt with in chapter 16, which has been adapted to conform with the requirements of AC 106.

Chapter 18, which has been rewritten, lays the foundation for financial reporting. Chapter 19, which deals with Generally Accepted Accounting Practice (GAAP), is new.

The accounting aspects of the various forms of organisation, including close corporations (chapter 22), are discussed in chapters 20 to 23. Chapter 23, which deals with the accounting aspects of companies, has been adapted to place greater emphasis on disclosure.

Chapters 24 and 25 provide an introduction to cost accounting and manufacturing concerns.

Chapters 26 to 28 deal with aspects of financial management. These chapters are of particular relevance to students of management. The examples of budgets in chapter 26 were developed with the aid of computerised spreadsheet programmes. The computer programmes, suitable for practical teaching purposes, can be obtained directly from the authors. Cash flow statements have been included in chapter 28.

The analysis and interpretation of financial information is dealt with in chapter 29. This chapter is of importance to all students of accounting.

Departmental accounts, branches, consignments and joint ventures are covered in chapters 30 to 33, which have been restructured.

The last three chapters of the book cover a few specialised topics not dealt with separately in the previous editions, namely non-profit organisations (chapter 34), incomplete records (chapter 35) and the effect of price level changes (chapter 36).

Questions and exercises

Due to a lack of space no questions and exercises are included in this book. The questions and exercises relevant to this work are contained in a separate book, namely *Accounting: An Introduction – Selected questions* by Faul, Reed and De Lange, Butterworths, 1988.

In this work the authors have perforce taken a stand on certain matters of principle, procedure and terminology. As far as possible such stands are motivated and, where necessary, alternative approaches and treatments are indicated. In view of the fact that this is an introductory text on the subject, lengthy academic arguments motivating any particular point have been omitted.

Comment which might result in improvements to future editions of this book is welcome.

Acknowledgements

This handbook, and especially this third edition, would not have been possible without the co-operation of colleagues at almost all the South African universities, who submitted meaningful comments and criticism. The authors wish to express their appreciation to each one who contributed in this way.

Our heatfelt thanks to the ladies who handled the word processing so professionally: Mrs Leonie Steyn and Mrs Anette Hechter. Our thanks, too, to Mrs Liesbet van Wyk and Miss Megan Hills of Butterworths for their dedication and professional handling of the editing of the book.

M A Faul
C W I Pistorius
L M van Vuuren

Pretoria
October 1988

CONTENTS

1

THE NATURE AND FUNCTION OF ACCOUNTING

The **AIM** of this chapter is to introduce you to accounting, a discipline of the economic sciences.

1.1 INTRODUCTION: TWO BASIC QUESTIONS

Everyone contemplating a study of accounting will probably ask two basic questions:

- ☐ What is accounting?
- ☐ Why should I study accounting?

The purpose of this book is to answer these questions in detail. In the first chapter certain guidelines for answering these questions are laid down. The guidelines also serve as a basis for the rest of the book.

1.2 THE NEED FOR FINANCIAL INFORMATION

1.2.1. The operation of the economic system

Economic activities in our society are carried on partly by private initiative and partly by the government. That section of the economic system which is carried on by private individuals, undertakings or institutions is referred to as the **private sector**, while that carried on by the authorities (ie the various government bodies) is referred to as the **public sector**.

Each undertaking or institution, whether it falls within the public or the private sector, has specific objectives. These objectives are always twofold, namely **functional** and **financial**. The **functional objective** relates to the production and distribution of goods or the rendering of services, whereas the **financial objective** refers to the financial position or the financial performance of an undertaking.

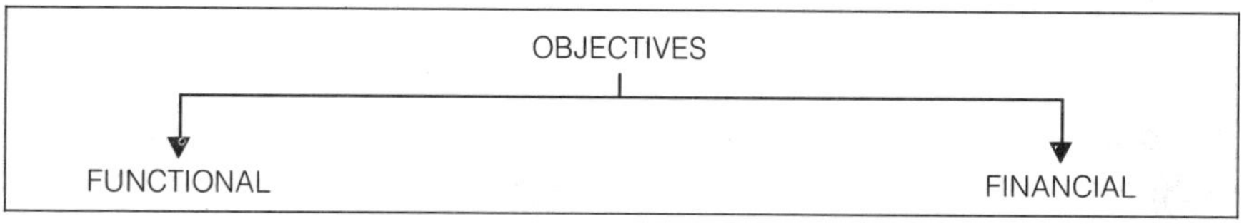

The economic system in South Africa's private sector functions on the principle that individuals or undertakings can own property which they can apply, at their own risk, to produce goods and services which in turn can be supplied to consumers at a profit.

Private business undertakings supply the majority of goods and services consumed by our society. **The objectives of these private undertakings are to maintain a sound financial position and to earn a realistic profit** from the production and/or distribution of goods or the rendering of services.

Besides the goods and services provided by private business undertakings, there are also numerous **services rendered without gain** by other institutions in the private sector, such as churches, clubs and associations. These institutions depend primarily on funds from the community. The main objective of such associations is to provide a service and in order to do so they need to maintain a sound financial position.

The public sector provides a range of essential services which are not provided by the private sector. Besides government administration departments, these include, *inter alia*, services such as security, education, health, transport, post and telecommunications, electricity, water and sewerage.

The authorities finance these services from funds obtained from the private sector in the form of taxes, levies or loans. The financial management function of the authorities is aimed primarily at containing the cost of services within the available income.

1.2.2 Information as a basis for decision making

Every economically active individual or institution, whether in the private or public sector, needs **financial information** to ensure that his or its financial objectives are attained.

Why is financial information necessary?

Specific actions are required from individuals in order that the objectives of an enterprise may be achieved. However, before an individual can act, he must first decide how he should act under the given circumstances in order to achieve his objectives.

Goal-orientated actions, such as those of a businessman wanting to achieve his profit objective, are not haphazard, but are preceded by rational decisions regarding the best action under the circumstances.

A decision is a choice between two or more alternatives. A decision must be rational in order to be meaningful and it must be justifiable in terms of the objective that is to be achieved. A decision can be rational only when the decision-maker has sufficient information concerning the matter on which he must decide and has examined this information thoroughly.

> Consider the actions of a trader who wants to sell goods at a profit. Before he buys his merchandise, he must determine the goods for which a market exists, the size of the market and what price people will be prepared to pay for the goods. Only then can he act by buying merchandise and selling it at a profit.

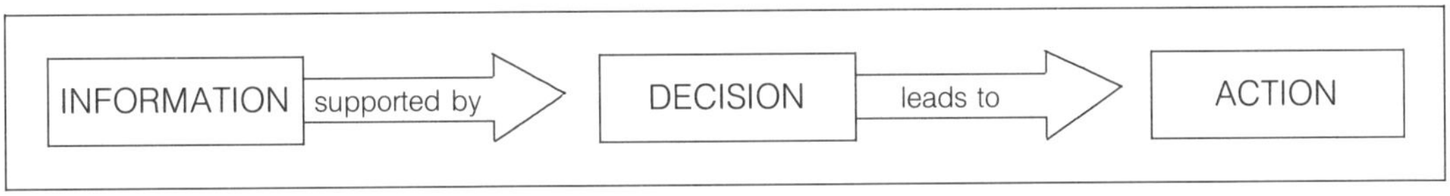

Consequently, in our society any person or enterprise with financial objectives must have information concerning the financial consequences of their economic activities. This information is the basis for purposeful decisions to regulate their economic activities.

> It is the responsibility of the accounting discipline to satisfy the need for financial information in an orderly manner.

We are now in a position to look more closely at the different decision-making processes in which financial information can be used.

1.2.3 Information as a basis for accountability

The means by which accounting provides financial information stems from the responsibility of the person to whom funds have been entrusted for a specific purpose, to account to the provider of those funds for the manner in which the funds have been applied. This responsibility is known as **accountability**, and is the way in which the supplier of funds exercises control over the application of his funds by other persons.

The entrepreneur or investor who invests funds in an enterprise, the donor who donates funds to an institution, or the taxpayer who pays taxes to the government all expect the enterprise, institution or authorities to account for the way in which the funds are applied and utilised.

Those who provide funds to business undertakings fall into two categories, viz **owners** and **creditors**. The interest of these two groups in an undertaking differs. Consideration will be given to the interest of the owners first.

The **owners** invest funds in an undertaking in order to share in its profits. In the modern economic system **management** and **ownership** of an enterprise are often separated, since in most large undertakings the owners are not directly involved in management.

The undertaking is managed by professional managers and staff who usually have little or no proprietary interest in the undertaking.

The **owners** delegate the management of the business undertaking to managers who are employed by the business. Therefore management has stipulated functions and specific objectives to achieve. As such, management is accountable to the owners for its actual performance.

Creditors lend funds to an undertaking and do not own the undertaking. Creditors are interested in the financial strength of the undertaking, because they want to ensure that repayment of their loan is not jeopardised and that earnings are sufficient to cover interest on the loan.

The concept accountability is not confined only to business enterprises. It applies equally to government as well as provincial and local authorities with respect to funds provided by taxpayers; to churches, societies and clubs with respect to funds contributed by members; to universities and research institutes with respect to the funds received from the State or private donors; and to all other institutions that use funds provided by outsiders.

> The concept accountability therefore embraces the responsibility of reporting past financial events.

1.2.4 Information as a basis for investment decisions

Investors invest funds in business concerns with the expectation of earning regular interest or dividends or of the potential capital appreciation of their investment.

Investment decisions concern whether or not an investment should be made in a particular concern, whether an investment in a particular concern should be reduced or increased or even withdrawn, comparisons of investments in different concerns and the timing of investment decisions.

Investors rate investments in terms of the return on the investment in relation to the cost or the value thereof.

> Therefore, in order to make investment decisions, investors and potential investors need information about the financial position and result of an enterprise in which they invest or intend to invest.

By virtue of its nature, accounting information is historical. Historical trends do, however, serve as valuable guidelines for future projections.

1.2.5 Information as a basis for business and management decisions

> The running and management of an enterprise require actions which are continuously dependent on financial information.

Management comprises primarily **planning** and **control** of the business activities of an enterprise. The manager requires continuous financial information about the activities of his business in order to set realistic objectives and to **plan** activities in such a manner that these objectives are achieved. For example, in order to achieve a specific profit, the manager needs to know the cost of production and sales revenue.

Control embraces the comparison of actual results with objectives as a basis for corrective action. The manager thus requires continuous information regarding the actual financial achievements of the enterprise in order to identify deviations requiring managerial action.

The sales manager, for example, will want to know how the sales of different products are progressing in different geographical areas; or the production manager will want to know the production costs for each type of product, and how these compare with budgeted costs.

Business operations embrace all the activities carried out in the course of managing an enterprise. The execution of financial activities requires financial information. Numerous business activities are dependent on accounting information. The debt-collecting department needs to know at all times the amount each client owes; the buyer must know at any particular moment what stocks are still available; and the treasurer must know the daily bank balance.

1.3 THE NATURE OF ACCOUNTING

> Accounting encompasses the identification, measurement and recording of occurrences which influence an enterprise's financial position and result; and the processing, communication, interpretation and application of the information derived therefrom.

Accounting is the 'language' of the financial world. Like any language it is a communication medium – an instrument for transmitting information. The distinction is, however, that a language is a general communication medium, whereas **accounting is a specialised medium for communicating financial information**. In the business world it is essential that financial information is truly and fairly presented. Often an absolute or high degree of accuracy is required of financial information. Users of financial information expect accurate and comprehensive information which cannot be provided by general spoken or written language. Accounting was developed to satisfy this specialised need.

Just as language is structured by means of grammar, so that it is uniform and therefore understandable to all users, so **accounting theory embodies a set of principles, methods, procedures and conventions**.

The existence of the **theory and practice** of accounting, which has developed over more than five centuries of practical application, is justified by the **usefulness** thereof. It satisfies the need for useful financial information regarding the activities of undertakings. This premise, which emphasises the benefit or utility of accounting, is referred to as the **utility concept**. Whether or not accounting is effective lies in the answer to the question: 'does it represent the position truthfully and fairly?' In other words, the utility concept is the key to the successful use of accounting.

1.4 DEVELOPMENT OF ACCOUNTING

1.4.1 Historical

The history of accounting bears constant witness to the fact that it developed in response to changing requirements for financial recording and reporting; these requirements in turn having been generated by constant changes, over the centuries, in economic, business and social conditions.

The particulars of transactions and financial relationships between different parties have been written up in the form of financial records since the dawn of civilisation, examples being Babylonian clay tablets and records from the Roman and Greek civilisations.

Our present system of accounting has its origins in Renaissance Italy. By the 12th century the bustle and extent of the wide-ranging trading activities engaged in by the Italian city-states had created the need for an effective system of financial recording which could accurately determine the results of large volumes of transactions involving several parties. Consequently, the double-entry system of bookkeeping, the basis of our modern accounting system, was developed.

During the Renaissance this system became known throughout Europe; by the 16th century it was standard practice in England, Germany and Holland. The first published description of the double-entry system appeared in Venice in 1494. Written by Luca Paciolo, it was entitled **Summa de Arithmetica Geometria et Proportionalita**.

The 18th century saw the emergence of another factor which exerted considerable influence on the development of accounting, namely the Industrial Revolution.

There was a tremendous increase in the nature and scope of manufacturing enterprises, trading activities and seafaring ventures and the financial services geared to these activities demanded an ever-increasing degree of accuracy of financial records in order that prices and profits might be determined. This led, in the 19th century, to the development of **cost accounting**, the field of accounting concerned with determining the cost of products and processes and specific objectives.

By the beginning of the 20th century, both manufacturing activities and marketing and administrative activities had become far more complicated and extensive and therefore effective methods of planning and control were essential. These needs led to the emergence, out of cost accounting, of management accounting, the specific function of which is to provide whatever financial information may be required by the management of the enterprise for the purposes of planning and control.

The influence of electronic data processing (EDP) on accounting has been of paramount importance in the second half of the 20th century. It should be borne in mind, however, that EDP is purely a technology which has produced a dramatic increase in the speed at which large volumes of data can be processed. Although it has influenced the utilisation of accounting information, it nevertheless has had no effect upon the theory. The computer has made accounting information more effective chiefly in that it is now more complete and more readily available.

1.4.2 The influence of the development of entrepreneurial forms

The development of accounting as a science has been greatly affected by the different forms of enterprise – first sole traders, then partnerships and finally companies – the reason being that once the business represents the interests of more than one owner, each individual interest must be separately determinable.

In the case of partnerships – a common form of business since the Renaissance – accounting must provide for the periodic and accurate determination of profits in order to allow for the regular distribution of profits to each partner.

A dramatic increase in the extent of business activities in the early 16th century made it impossible for sole proprietors to bear the entire financial burden. This led to the formation of **companies with limited liability**. In this type of organisation capital is provided by a number of shareholders whose share in the profit is proportional to their share in the capital. The company owns the assets and is liable for its own debts. Serious problems were encountered in this type of structure, primarily with respect to protecting the interests of shareholders not involved in the management of the company. As a measure against fraud and corruption, statutory regulations governing financial reporting were adopted as company law in Britain in 1844.

The regulation of accounting practice contributed greatly to improving the quality of financial reporting. Today it is standard practice to issue guidelines for financial reporting in the form of company legislation and stock exchange regulations. In South Africa companies are governed by the **Companies Act**, 1973 (Act 61 of 1973).

There is another form of enterprise in South Africa, namely the close corporation, which came into being on 1 January 1985 as a result of the Close Corporations Act (Act 69 of 1984).

1.4.3 The influence of the formation of groups

A trend towards company expansion, which was especially prevalent in the USA around 1870, led to large companies gaining a controlling interest in the shares of other companies and forming groups controlled by a single parent company. This resulted in a need for a means of reporting the financial position and result of a group of entities, excluding inter-group transactions. Therefore consolidated financial reports for groups of companies were developed. Current company legislation makes it obligatory for groups of companies to issue consolidated statements to their shareholders.

1.4.4. The influence of professional societies

The emergence and growth of the accounting and auditing profession in the 20th century undoubtedly constituted one of the most important phases in the development of accounting. The demands made on accounting by the rapid developments in the business world created a need for professionalism on the part of accountants and auditors. Two aspects were especially important, namely:

- ☐ the need for the formulation of generally accepted accounting practice
- ☐ standards of training and experience as prerequisites for admission to the accounting profession.

Professional societies were first formed in the mid-19th century. The formation of the Institute of Chartered Accountants in England and Wales in 1880, and of the Institute for Certified Public Accountants in New York in 1897, contributed considerably to the establishment of generally accepted accounting practice.

The first organised association of accountants in South Africa was established in 1894 with the foundation of the **Institute of Accountants and Auditors** of the South African Republic. The present-day organisation of the profession in South Africa consists of four provincial societies, namely the Transvaal Society of Accountants, founded in 1904, the Cape Society of Accountants and the Society of Accountants in the Orange Free State, both founded in 1908, and the Natal Society of Accountants, founded in 1909. Only members of these societies have the status of Chartered Accountant (SA) and only persons who have passed the Final Qualifying Examination of the Public Accountants and Auditors Board and have completed their period of clerkship are admitted to these societies. The South African Institute of Chartered Accountants serves as the co-ordinating body linking the provincial societies. One of the functions of the Institute is the formulation of recommendations on standard accounting practice in South Africa.

The year 1951 saw the promulgation of the **Public Accountants' and Auditors' Act**, 1951 (Act 51 of 1951), to govern the accounting profession in South Africa. This led to the foundation of the Public Accountants' and Auditors' Board, a body involved principally in registering accountants and auditors for public practice and maintaining professional discipline and training standards.

1.5 SPHERES OF APPLICATION OF ACCOUNTING

The following categories of accounting may be identified according to the nature of the information they supply:

- ☐ financial accounting
  and
- ☐ management accounting.

☐ Financial accounting

Financial accounting provides **external users** with financial information regarding the enterprise. These users include the owners and creditors as well as other institutions which have no direct financial interest in the enterprise, but nevertheless require the information for various reasons, for example, taxation or economic policy making. The principal objectives of external reporting are to facilitate accountability and investment decisions. Financial accounting provides interested parties with information concerning the enterprise as a **whole** in the form of annual **financial statements**. These statements contain information regarding the financial position of the enterprise and the result of its activities.

☐ Management accounting

Management accounting provides financial information regarding the enterprise for the benefit of **internal users**. These users are chiefly the internal management and business managers of the enterprise. The function of management accounting is to provide specific information about specific aspects of the undertaking's activities.

For example, management accounting provides information relating to the costing of production activities, budgets and budgetary control and cash flow control.

☐ Interaction between financial and management accounting

In practice these two aspects of accounting often overlap. Frequently, for example, the information needed for future planning by management will be extracted from the historical data contained in financial accounting reports.

Financial and management factors within an enterprise are both components of the same information system. The separation of the two sections is useful for teaching purposes, but in practice it is often difficult to classify a particular accounting application as exclusively financial or managerial.

1.6 WHY STUDY ACCOUNTING?

Now that accounting has been explained, the second question, 'why study accounting?', can easily be answered.

Knowledge of accounting is of benefit to:

- ☐ those persons who use the financial information supplied by the accounting process
- ☐ those persons who use accounting as a means of providing users with financial information.

Users of financial information need not necessarily be qualified accountants. However, everyone who makes financial decisions ought to have at least a superficial knowledge of accounting. This ensures that the decision maker understands the information in financial reports sufficiently to make rational decisions. The more involved the decisions regarding financial matters, the greater the knowledge required by the decisionmaker. For example, to determine the taxation implications of complicated transactions or to design a complex financial plan would require more than a superficial knowledge of accounting. Thus a knowledge of accounting enables a person to execute the financial planning of an enterprise more effectively.

The accountant who assumes responsibility for designing accounting systems, the processing of accounting information and the preparation and analysis of financial reports requires an in-depth knowledge of the theory and practice of accounting and related fields.

There is a wide variety of career prospects open to persons qualified in accounting.

A chartered accountant is, in accordance with the Public Accountants and Auditors Act, able to go into public practice. The most important functions of a chartered accountant in public practice are the independent auditing of the financial records and reports of an undertaking, the design and implementation of accounting systems, taxation work, estate planning, financial investigations and financial and management consultancy.

The accounting profession is highly thought of in the community and provides members with a great deal of security and job satisfaction. An accountant gains a sound understanding of all the activities in an enterprise during the performance of his normal duties. A qualification in accounting and, more specifically, a professional qualification provides an excellent opportunity to enter the world of business.

2

THE NATURE OF ACCOUNTING THEORY

The **AIM** of this chapter is to explain the elements of accounting theory.

2.1 ORIGIN OF THE THEORY

Anyone extracting financial information from an accounting report wants to be sure that he understands the content of the report and that the information is fairly presented. In practice this means that both the author and the reader of the report must agree on how the information should be compiled and presented.

If it is to be **comprehensible** and **reliable, accounting must be used in accordance with specific rules and regulations**. It would cause chaos of Babylonian proportions if each person used his own grammar and vocabulary – nobody would understand anybody else. Likewise, it is **essential that accounting is used according to generally accepted rules**.

The first prerequisite is that accounting should agree or conform with:

- ☐ the **basic truths** according to which our economic system functions
- ☐ the **current economic and business practices**
- ☐ the **applicable law** as embodied in legislative regulations or common law.

Consequently it is important that **uniformity is maintained in accounting practice**; in other words, a specific set of circumstances, wherever it may be encountered, should be dealt with by everyone in exactly the same way within the accounting process.

Accounting theory creates a framework which ensures that accounting practice complies with the requirements of conformity and uniformity. This theory is embodied in a set of principles, policies, methods, procedures and conventions.

The continuously increasing scope and complexity of our economic system requires a corresponding process of adaptation in accounting in order that the relevant information regarding economic activities may be recorded. It is essential that everyone involved in accounting should understand this process of adaptation; moreover, a prerequisite for such understanding is a grasp of not only the theory of accounting, but also the structure of that theory.

2.2 CONCEPTS AND POSTULATES

Accounting theory is based on a set of basic economic truths which are of a dual nature. **First, accounting theory is based on propositions generally accepted in the economic order of a particular society**. For example, consider the concept of personal ownership: a generally accepted tenet of our society is the exclusive right of every person to own things – they are his personal property and no one else's. This concept is a basic economic truth.

Second, the **basic economic truths have characteristics similar to those of natural laws in the sense that specific causes generate specific consequences**. If, for example, someone derives greater value from a transaction than what was put into the transaction, his net worth – his wealth – will have increased by the surplus amount. This, too, is a basic economic truth.

These economic truths are formulated as concepts and postulates.

A concept is a generally accepted view of a specific phenomenon, which is described in specific terms.

A concept usually embodies a single meaning, for example **debt**.

> The term 'debt' refers to the concept of an obligation that one party has to pay a sum of money to another party.

> A **postulate** is a **generally accepted hypothesis** or supposition of a specific condition or phenomenon, which serves as a basis for the formulation of principles.

A postulate usually describes the relationship between different concepts. For example, it is postulated that a person's financial wealth is measured by the value of his assets less the value of his liabilities. In this postulate three concepts are involved, viz financial wealth, assets and liabilities.

In the development of accounting theory, concepts and postulates serve as formulations of the basic truths or propositions upon which the theory is based. They do not attempt to prescribe the working of the accounting process, but are simply the foundation upon which the structure of accountancy is based.

> The regulations or guidelines for the functioning of the accounting process are based on concepts and postulates and are embodied in the applicable principles, methods, procedures and conventions.

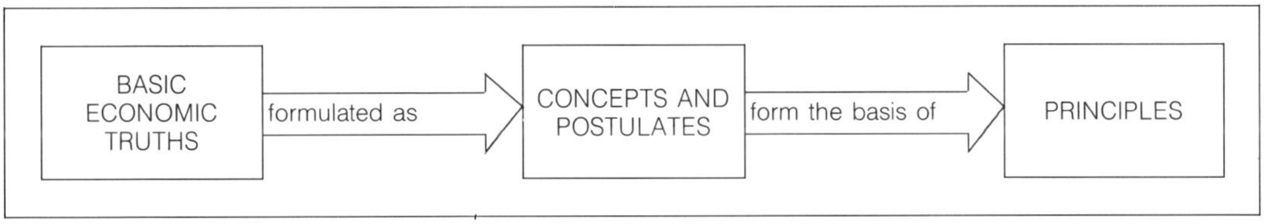

On the basis of the postulate of **financial worth**, we can define the following **accounting principle**:

> Financial position is represented by the following equation:
>
> ASSETS − LIABILITIES = NET WORTH

You need not be too concerned about the exact meaning of the principle – it is explained in detail further on in the chapter.

2.3 ACCOUNTING PRINCIPLES

> **The term principle refers to the fundamental basis according to which something functions or to a rule of conduct.**

According to this definition, it is possible to distinguish **two types** of principles. The first type comprises **absolute truths** such as natural laws.

> The principle governing the operation of a steam engine is an absolute truth. Steam, forced into a cylinder, moves a piston inside that cylinder; no man-made rule or law has the power to affect the pressure exerted by the steam upon the piston.

The **second** type of principle is a **generally accepted rule** laid down by society as a guideline for the conduct of its members.

> When someone says that he will not commit fraud on the grounds that it is against his principles, it means that he has accepted as a principle the generally accepted rule laid down by society – namely that it is wrong to deceive others – and has based his behaviour on that principle. The principle does not prevent him from committing fraud; but exposes him to the censure of society, if he does commit fraud.

Accounting principles fall within the second group of principles; they are **generally accepted rules developed from a basis of postulated circumstances, and serve as guidelines for accounting practice**.

2.4 ACCOUNTING POLICY

> **Policy is a guideline for dealing consistently with a recurring situation which, if it is dealt with in different ways, will have different outcomes**.

Thus the accounting policy of a particular enterprise consists of a set of decisions regarding how it **consistently** handles specific situations in the accounting process where alternative treatments are possible.

For example, an undertaking's policy may be to consider only tools costing more than R100 as assets and items costing less than R100 as expenses.

There are **three universal policies** that are vitally important in accounting. We have described these **policies** as universal because, **in specific circumstances, they are applied by all entities**.

These universal policies have, to some extent, characteristics similar to those of principles. Therefore they differ from other policies, where alternative approaches are possible in a given situation and where an undertaking can formulate its own policy in respect of choosing an approach best suited to its particular circumstances.

The three universal policies are:

- ☐ the policy of prudence
- ☐ the policy of consistency
- ☐ the policy of materiality.

2.4.1 The policy of prudence or conservatism

On the basis of the information available to them, and by applying sound judgement, accountants attempt to compile meaningful financial reports. In forming their opinions and making estimates they often deal with uncertainties. In such situations they always apply the policy of prudence. This means that where they deal with material uncertainties regarding which accounting policy to use, they will generally use the policy that is least likely to overstate assets or income.

> Where alternative procedures exist for the treatment of a transaction or event in the accounting process, the alternative chosen is that representing the more conservative approach of profit determination, according to the **policy of prudence**.

For example, income is not brought into account before it is realised in cash or in the form of other assets, the eventual cash realisation of which is reasonably certain. On the other hand expenses and losses are brought into account as soon as they become known, irrespective of whether the amount has already been paid or even determined with any accuracy.

Although prudence is a useful approach in doubtful circumstances, the misuse of this policy can result in incorrect and misleading financial statements. Prudence often conflicts with proper disclosures and consistency.

2.4.2 The policy of consistency

Within the framework of the principles, methods and procedures of accounting, there are numerous alternative ways in which specific transactions or events can be dealt with, often producing different results.

An enterprise which is continually buying raw materials during a period of rising prices can use different methods to determine the cost of raw materials consumed. It may use the first-in-first-out method and assume that the cheaper items bought first are also the items that are drawn from stock first. Alternatively the last-in-first-out method can be used. This assumes that the more expensive items bought last are drawn first from stock. The cost of raw materials consumed will be different for each of these methods.

If an undertaking were to adopt a different accounting approach for each item or for each period, specific transaction, or event, different bases would be used and the end results would be not only confusing, but also not comparable.

> The **policy of consistency** requires that once a specific basis, method, procedure or approach has been decided upon, it should always be followed. Should it become necessary to deviate from this policy, the fact should be disclosed together with the influence of the change in accounting policy on the financial result and position of the undertaking.

2.4.3 The policy of materiality

> According to the **policy of materiality**, transactions and events which are not material in relation to the nature and scope of an entity's activities need not be brought into account if the cost and difficulty in recording thereof are not justified by the resulting benefit.

The earlier example of the enterprise which recognised only items costing more than R100 as assets is an example of the application of the policy of materiality.

2.4.4 Disclosure of accounting policy

Because accounting policies apply to situations where alternative approaches are possible, it is important that an undertaking **discloses the accounting policies adopted in its financial statements**.

2.5 GENERALLY ACCEPTED ACCOUNTING PRACTICE

A chaotic situation would arise if each enterprise applied its own rules and interpreted accounting theory in its own way in its financial reporting process. To bring order into the accounting and reporting process, over the years the accounting profession has **developed an underlying basis for the measurement and disclosure of the results of business transactions and events**. This basis is the set of **suppositions, concepts, principles, methods and procedures which are collectively known as generally accepted accounting practice** (GAAP).

The existence of GAAP does not imply that all undertakings measure and report all their financial activities in the same way.

No two undertakings are alike and therefore a rigid set of measurements and reporting regulations would not be practical or even possible. The accounting profession developed GAAP as a general framework comprising the fundamental rules for measuring and reporting, but within which a degree of diversity is still possible.

2.5.1 The development of GAAP

The development of accounting standards has received much attention in recent years, not only in the United States of America, but also internationally.

In South Africa the South African Institute of Chartered Accountants (SAICA) has taken the lead through the formation of its Accounting Practices Committee. This body submits statements of GAAP to the Accounting Practices Board (APB) for approval after they have been prepared and exposed to interested parties for comment.

The APB consists of representatives from commerce, industry, the stock exchange and the accounting profession. Established in 1973, its main objective is: 'To bring about the acceptance of what the Board (APB) considers to be generally accepted accounting practice.'

2.5.2 Approach to the development of accounting standards

The Accounting Practices Board aims to identify the accounting standards which are desirable and consequently to limit the variety of available accounting practices without endeavouring to impose uniformity or a rigid set of rules for all circumstances. The aim is to set standards that are generally applicable, but which exclude undesirable alternatives.

The Companies Act, section 286(3) requires that 'the annual financial statements of a company must fairly present the financial position of the company . . . and the results of its operations in accordance with generally accepted accounting practice.'

The dominant requirement of the Companies Act is that of fair presentation. The existence of a **standard** is an aid to comparability as well as to fair presentation. However, compliance with a standard does not guarantee that fair presentation will be achieved. Although compliance with accounting standards is not prima facie evidence of fair presentation, such compliance is highly influential and persuasive. Consequently it is necessary to disclose any deviations by means of explanatory notes in the financial statements.

It is recognised that extraordinary circumstances can exist where GAAP cannot be strictly applied, since compliance therewith would not result in fair presentation – in other words compliance with GAAP would be misleading. Such circumstances arise in certain specialised industries which cannot be catered for in general statements.

2.6 METHODS AND PROCEDURES

A **method** is the orderly manner in which something is performed. A **procedure** is the sequence in which the steps are performed.

To ensure uniformity in accounting, specific methods and procedures are prescribed for recording and processing transactions and for the presentation of information.

The following is an example of an accounting method:

> The date, description and amount of each transaction are recorded in a journal in the numerical order of the source documents.

The following is an example of a procedure:

> Transactions are recorded in a journal and then posted to the general ledger.

The methods and procedures of accounting are discussed fully later in this book.

2.7 SUMMARY OF THE THEORETICAL STRUCTURE

The various theoretical aspects of accounting which have been discussed so far can be summarised schematically as follows:

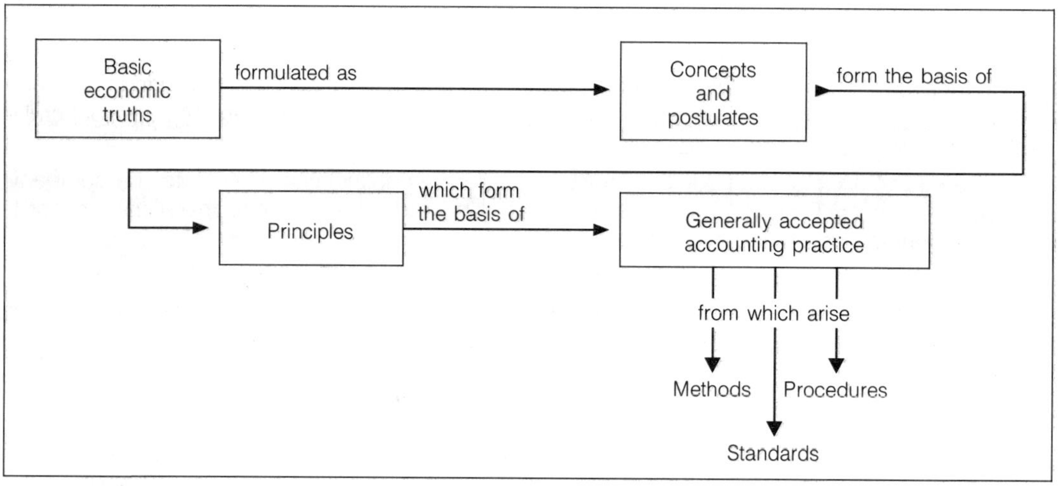

2.8 QUALITY OF FINANCIAL INFORMATION

The fact that generally accepted accounting practice is complied with, does not guarantee the **quality of financial information**. There is usually a variety of factors which influence the activities of an undertaking. Meaningful financial information can be produced only when those factors which may materially influence the quality of that information are identified and interpreted. In this the accountant's judgement plays an important role.

Because judgement plays such an important role, it is the accountant's responsibility to ensure that the quality of information in the financial statements is satisfactory.

The most important attributes of quality in financial information are:

- ☐ relevance
  and
- ☐ reliability.

Relevance pertains to the use that is made of the information. Reliable information reflects a reasonable image of the given situation.

These attributes of information are discussed in more detail further on in the book.

3

FINANCIAL POSITION

The **AIM** of this chapter is to explain the fundamental concepts and principles upon which the theory of accounting is based.

3.1 PRIMARY AIM OF ACCOUNTING

The primary aim of accounting is to measure and communicate two aspects of the financial activities of an entity, viz:

FINANCIAL POSITION
and
FINANCIAL RESULTS

This chapter looks at the development of accounting theory applicable to these two aspects. Each particular postulate will be reviewed in conjunction with the principles based thereon and the relationship between them will be defined.

This chapter also deals with the concept **financial position**, whereas the concept **financial result** is dealt with in chapter 4.

3.2 ACCOUNTING ENTITY

The primary objective of accounting is to provide information pertaining to the financial position and financial result of an entity.

> An entity is any independent economic unit, the financial transactions of which must be managed separately from those of any other unit.

Any specific set of accounting records and the reports resulting therefrom pertain to a specific entity. All transactions concerning the entity are recorded in the accounting records, and transactions which do not concern the entity are excluded. In the accounting process an accounting entity is dealt with as an independent unit, irrespective of the owner's or any other controlling interest therein.

If financial information is to be meaningful the entity to which that information pertains must be clearly defined. There must be no doubt in the mind of the user of financial information as to the exact nature of the entity concerned. Often, however, the division between entities is rather vague.

> Charles Small owns a chain of restaurants all trading under the same name. If the financial position of the chain must be assessed, then all the restaurants will be considered as a single entity. If, on the other hand, the financial position of each restaurant must be assessed, then each restaurant will be considered as a separate entity. If the financial position of only his restaurant business must be assessed, then Charles' personal assets and liabilities, such as his home and mortgage bond, will be considered separately from those of his business.

Thus the deciding factor in what is regarded as an accounting entity is the **extent of information** pertaining to a specific economic unit. When it is necessary to obtain information regarding a specific unit to the exclusion of any other unit or units, the unit concerned is treated as an accounting entity.

Most entities are defined by law – either by statute or common law; thus identification is usually quite simple. Entities include individuals or specific institutions such as societies, churches or business enterprises which can be registered as companies or close corporations. However, a point to be noted is that an accounting entity need not necessarily also be regarded as a legal entity. The criterion for regarding a unit as an accounting entity is not whether it has an independent legal existence, but whether separate financial information can be made available for the unit.

Four types of business entity are popular in South Africa, viz:

- ☐ sole traders
- ☐ partnerships
- ☐ close corporations
- ☐ companies limited by virtue of shares.

The same basic accounting principles and systems apply to all these entities. Therefore this book will concentrate on sole traders initially and the other entities will be discussed in later chapters.

3.3 ASSETS, LIABILITIES AND EQUITY

3.3.1 Elements of the financial position

The concepts **assets**, **liabilities** and **equity** are the elements which constitute the financial position of an entity. Consequently, the nature of these concepts will be analysed before the concept financial position is analysed.

3.3.2 The nature of assets

The term 'asset' refers to something which has value. A person considers as assets those of his possessions to which he attaches value.

Something has value when it can be utilised to yield further value: money has value because it can be exchanged for goods or services; land has value because it can be sold or utilised to produce income, and raw materials have value because they can be processed into products which can be sold.

The value of a thing to a person is determined by the value that person is willing to sacrifice for it. In accounting, the assets of an entity are taken into account at the value that the entity sacrificed in order to obtain those assets – in other words, the cost of the assets.

Before an asset can be brought into account as an asset of a specific entity, it must have the following characteristics:

- ☐ The entity must own the asset.
- ☐ It must have value.
- ☐ It must have been acquired for a measurable cost.

> Suppose that a local authority builds a dam to store water which can be sold to the public. The dam will be accounted for as an asset to the municipality, since it possesses value by virtue of the fact that it can produce value; it belongs to the local authority and has been acquired at a measurable cost. If it should rain and the dam is filled with water, is the accumulated water also an asset that must be brought into account? It does have value, because it can be sold and it does belong to the municipality.

However, it has not been acquired for a measurable cost. Therefore the answer to the question is NO, the water should not be accounted for as an asset – because the dam was filled with water at no cost to the municipality. Suppose, however, that it does not rain and the municipality is obliged to buy water from another dam higher up the river. This water will be brought into account as an asset because it has also complied with the third criterion, viz that it has been obtained at a measurable cost.

The assets of an enterprise typically consist of land and buildings, machinery and equipment, vehicles, furniture, raw materials, trading stock, investments, debtors (i e amounts owing to the business), cash, etc.

3.3.3 The nature of liabilities

The term **liability** refers to the concept **the debt** of a person who owes money to another person. The person to whom money is owed is called a **creditor**. The person who owes the money is called a **debtor**.

A person to whom money is owed = a creditor

A person who owes money = a debtor

No one ever wants to sacrifice value without *quid pro quo*. When someone attaches value to something, he is usually willing to exchange it only for something else of value. Consequently, if one person receives value from another person without giving value in exchange, but on condition that he will do so, the person who has not yet received value will hold the person who has received value liable for the value not yet received. Such an **enforceable obligation** to give value to another person is called a liability or **debt**.

DEBT = LIABILITY

Liabilities (or debts) are therefore legally enforceable obligations which an entity has to its creditors to pay specific amounts at specific times.

3.3.4 The nature of equity

The accounting term **equity** refers to the concept the **right** or **claim** of a person or another entity against an asset. A person has a **right** to an asset when that asset belongs to him or is rightfully his. Someone has **claim** against an asset when a debt owing to him must be liquidated from that asset.

3.3.5 The interests of creditors

A creditor has an **interest** in the assets of a debtor to the extent of the latter's debt. The creditor has the right to enforce settlement of the debt out of the assets of the debtor.

If Peter Small has assets of R30 000 and owes Charles Long R5 000, then we can say that Charles Long has an interest of R5 000 in the assets of Peter Small. In this case
Peter Small is the **debtor**
and
Charles Long is the **creditor**.

When we consider the assets of an entity it is important to know the extent of the **interest** of creditors in those assets.

If a creditor advances money to a debtor so that he can acquire an asset, we can also say that the creditor is **financing** the debtor's asset. The term **financing** therefore refers to the concept **making funds available**. The creditor, who has an interest in the asset, can thus also be described as a **source of finance**.

3.3.6 Owner's equity or net worth

The difference between a person's assets (what he owns) and his liabilities (what he owes) represents his **net worth**.

ASSETS − LIABILITIES = NET WORTH

Consider the following circumstances in which John Rose finds himself:

He possesses **assets** of	R100 000
His **liabilities** (ie debt to creditors) amount to	40 000
John Rose's **net worth** is therefore	R60 000

The net worth represents that portion of the assets to which **creditors** have no claim. It therefore represents the owner's interest in the assets. Thus **net worth** is also referred to as **owner's equity**.

NET WORTH = OWNER'S EQUITY

In the previous paragraph it was explained that **liabilities are legally enforceable claims against assets**. The creditors therefore have a first claim for settlement of the debt owed to them. The owner's equity is consequently the **resultant interest** of the owner in the assets, after the interest of creditors has been deducted.

From this it can be postulated that the **net worth** of an entity is the difference between the value of the assets and the liabilities.

The **owner's equity** therefore represents the extent of the entity's **net worth**.

ASSETS	−	LIABILITIES	=	NET WORTH or OWNER'S EQUITY

The owner's equity can also be regarded as the extent to which owners **finance** the assets of the undertaking. Owner's equity is therefore also a **source of finance**.

3.4 SOURCES OF FINANCE

We have seen that the various **interests** in the assets of an entity can be regarded as **sources of finance** of those assets.

If the entity owns **assets**, they must have been obtained from a specific source of funds. These funds were made available by parties having an **interest** in the assets – the owners to the extent of owner's equity and creditors to the extent of liabilities.

INTERESTS = SOURCES OF FINANCING

SOURCES OF FINANCING = OWNER'S EQUITY + LIABILITIES

3.5 FINANCIAL POSITION

In accounting it is postulated that the **financial position** of an entity is described **at a specific time** in terms of:

☐ the assets belonging to the entity at that specific time, on the one hand, and
☐ the interests in those assets, on the other.

You will also remember that we identified two types of assets:

☐ the interests of creditors
☐ the owner's equity.

The accounting report which represents the **financial position** is called a **balance sheet**.

It is important to note that the **financial position** is always measured at a specific **point in time**. It can be compared to a photograph – which represents a specific position at the specific moment when the photograph was taken.

John Smith is the owner of Excelsior Services which undertakes general household repairs and maintenance. Excelsior Services owns numerous items of equipment, such as lathes, electric drills and saws, hand tools, wheelbarrows and ladders. At any point in time, a number of clients owe Excelsior money for services rendered.

Assume that Excelsior owns the following assets at 31 December 19.1:

Equipment	R6 000
Amounts owing by customers	3 000
Cash in bank	1 000
	R10 000

We can now represent the financial worth as follows:

EXCELSIOR SERVICES
BALANCE SHEET AT 31 DECEMBER 19.1

ASSETS		OWNER'S EQUITY	R7 000
Equipment	R6 000		
Debtors	3 000	LIABILITIES	
Cash in bank	1 000	Creditors	3 000
	R10 000		R10 000

This illustration of Excelsior Services' financial position shows that at 31 December 19.1 it had assets of R10 000 and owed R3 000 to creditors. The owner's equity of R7 000 is the difference between the assets of R10 000 and the liabilities of R3 000. Note that the owner's equity is the resultant interest; ie the remaining interest after the **liabilities** have been deducted from the **assets**.

3.6 DUALITY PRINCIPLE

According to the **postulate of net worth** there is an interest in **all** the assets of an entity. **Creditors** have an interest to the extent of the **liabilities** and the remaining interest is that of the **owners**.

ASSETS − LIABILITIES = OWNER'S EQUITY

According to the **postulate of financial position**, the financial position of an entity is described in terms of the **assets** which it owns and the **interests** in those assets.

These two postulates form the basis for the **duality principle**.

Since the assets are always totally represented by the interests in them, **each transaction** will have a **dual influence** on the composition of the financial position in order to maintain the relationship between assets and interests.

This premise, which is known as the **duality principle**, is the **basic principle of accounting**. It forms the foundation on which the accounting system is based.

The equality of assets and interests is expressed in the **basic accounting equation**.

ASSETS = OWNER'S EQUITY + LIABILITIES

According to the duality principle, the financial position of an entity can be described in terms of the basic accounting equation and all transactions which influence the financial position should be recorded in such a way that the equation remains in equilibrium.

Refer again to the financial position of Excelsior Services as reflected in the balance sheet at 31 December 19.1 in paragraph 3.4.

According to the duality principle, in terms of the **basic accounting equation** the financial position of Excelsior can be expressed as follows:

ASSETS		OWNER'S EQUITY		LIABILITIES
Equipment R6 000 + Debtors R 3000 + Cash R1 000	=	R7 000	+	R3 000

The preceding discussion regarding the accounting entity, financial worth, financial position and duality principle can be represented diagrammatically as follows:

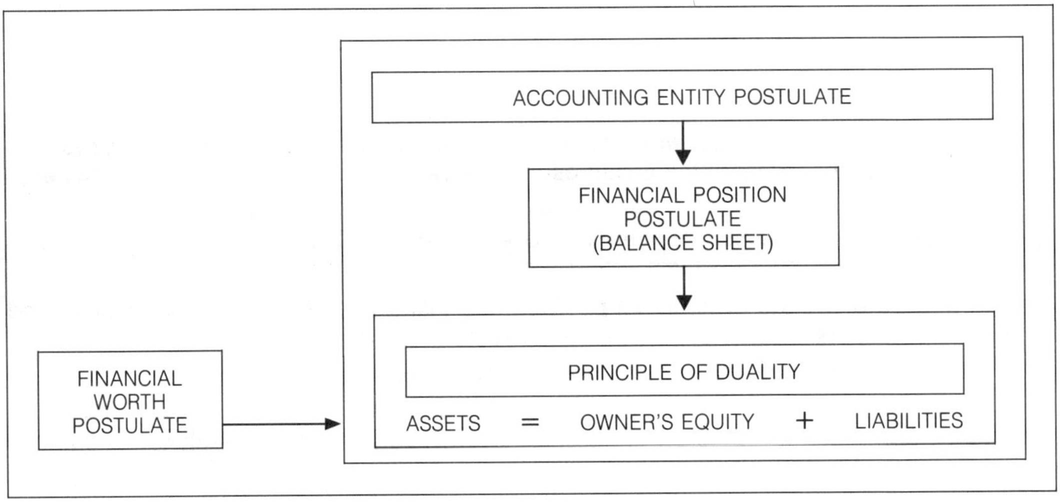

3.7 UNIVERSAL ACCOUNTING DENOMINATOR

The elements of an entity's financial position usually consist of a variety of assets and liabilities. If the financial position is to be described accurately and meaningfully, these assets and liabilities must be expressed in terms of a universal accounting denominator.

In our economic system, **money is the universal denominator** for all values.

Although money best fulfils the function of a universal accounting denominator, it has two main shortcomings.

In the **first place**, with money as the universal accounting denominator, only those factors measurable in terms of money can be brought into account in determining the financial position and result of an entity. This tends to limit the usefulness of information generated by the accounting process. The state of an entity's affairs can be influenced considerably by events which, because they cannot be expressed in terms of money, are not revealed by the accounting process. For example, the financial position of an enterprise as described by the accounting process gives no indication of the ability of its management, the quality of its products or its market-share. Thus a complete picture of the position of an enterprise's affairs cannot be drawn from accounting reports alone. The annual financial reports of large enterprises therefore usually include substantial additional, non-accounting information.

For example, a typical annual report issued by a large business enterprise will be accompanied by the chairman's report, discussing the enterprise's activities and achievements during the past year, and often also the prospects for the coming year.

The **second problem** arising from the use of money as a universal accounting denominator is the instability of the value of money. Like the value of commodities, the value of money is influenced by the forces of supply and demand, as well as various other factors. Inflation causes the value of money to drop in relation to the value of goods and services – in other words, goods and services become more expensive in monetary terms. This phenomenon radically affects the measurement and evaluation of financial position and result. In essence this means that the results of transactions concluded during a period in which the value of money was unstable are not always comparable and the information thus produced is often misleading.

A business purchasing a piece of land for R10 000, will record the transaction at R10 000. Ten years later the value of that land may have risen to R25 000, while it is still recorded at R10 000. This feature has serious implications when profit is determined. If a business is using minerals bought at R100 per ton when the price per ton has already risen to R150, then the business is sacrificing value of R150 while its accounting records show that value at only R100.

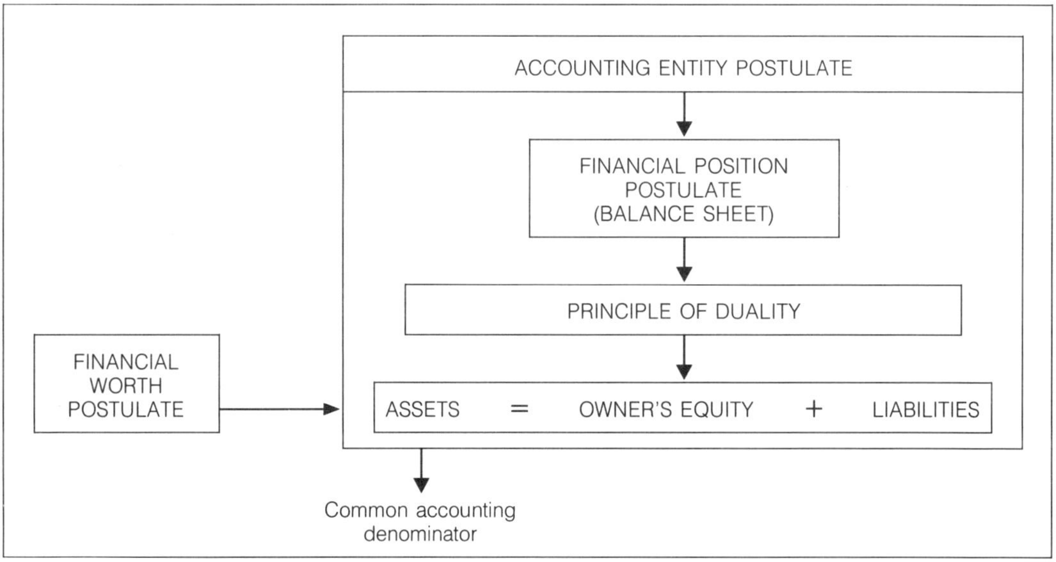

3.8 THE COST PRINCIPLE

According to the cost principle, assets are initially brought into account in the accounting process at the cost that the entity incurred in acquiring those assets.

The principles discussed thus far stipulate that transactions should be recorded in monetary values. However, the fact that a specific circumstance can be expressed in monetary terms does not determine the basis on which the amount concerned is to be recorded.

An analysis of the concept 'value' indicates clearly that it is essential to have a guideline for valuing assets for accounting purposes. We have already noted that the net worth of an entity is the difference between the value of the assets and the liabilities. However, since the concept value is subjective, it is necessary to formulate a guideline according to which value can be determined.

The monetary terms in which the **value** of goods or services is expressed, refers to the amount that will be paid for the acquisition of those goods or services. The two principal factors determining the value of a commodity are first, the need for that commodity, and second, the availability or shortage of the commodity; in other words the forces of supply and demand. Various other secondary factors, such as sentiment, also play a part. Value, therefore, changes according to the forces of supply and demand; the same goods or services can have different values for different people at the same time, or to the same people at a different time.

> A very thirsty person will be prepared to sacrifice more value – in other words pay a higher price – for water than someone who is not thirsty. During a drought, anyone who is affected by the shortage of water will be prepared to sacrifice more value to obtain water than he would during the rainy season when water is plentiful. People living in a desert will always sacrifice more value for water than those who live in an area where water is not scarce.

The **price** of something is the amount which is charged for it. In the case of something already bought, it is the amount paid. The **price** of an object is therefore an indication of the **value sacrificed** for the object **at the moment of buying**. The concept cost therefore denotes value sacrificed.

The **cost principle** requires that assets should be brought into account at cost, the **assumption being that value is equal to the cost at which goods or services were acquired**, in other words the price that was paid for them. Price is an historical fact and not subject to the different interpretations surrounding the concept value.

The cost principle, however, also has negative implications. If an asset, bought at a specific cost, changes in value during the course of time, the accounting records will no longer reflect the true value of that asset.

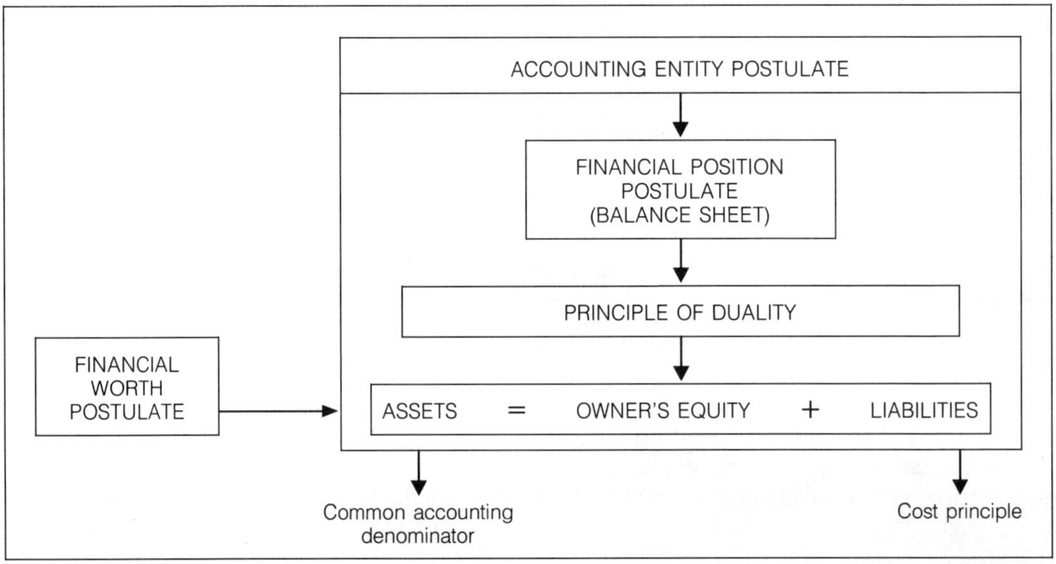

3.9 THE GOING CONCERN PRINCIPLE

The description of the financial position and financial result of an entity in terms of the basic accounting equation is based, according to the cost principle, on the principle that the entity will continue indefinitely with its activities, unless the facts indicate differently. A going concern acquires assets with the intention that they will be utilised in the entity's continuing activities rather than be sold immediately. It makes a big difference to the financial position of an entity if the going concern principle is not applied.

> Consider the situation of a retail enterprise on 31 December 19.1, which has merchandise acquired for R1 million in stock. The enterprise intends to dispose of the stock under normal circumstances over a period of four months for, say, R1,5 million. If, however, the enterprise was forced to dispose of the entire stock at 31 December, it would no doubt have to be sold for much less than R1 million. According to the going concern concept, the stock at 31 December would be shown at its cost of R1 million.

The possible loss that will have to be sustained by the enterprise if it has to dispose of all the stock at 31 December is not taken into consideration, since it is considered to be a going concern and as such the stock will be sold in the normal course of business. Similarly, any profit that may be made from the sale of the stock is not taken into consideration until such time as it is realised.

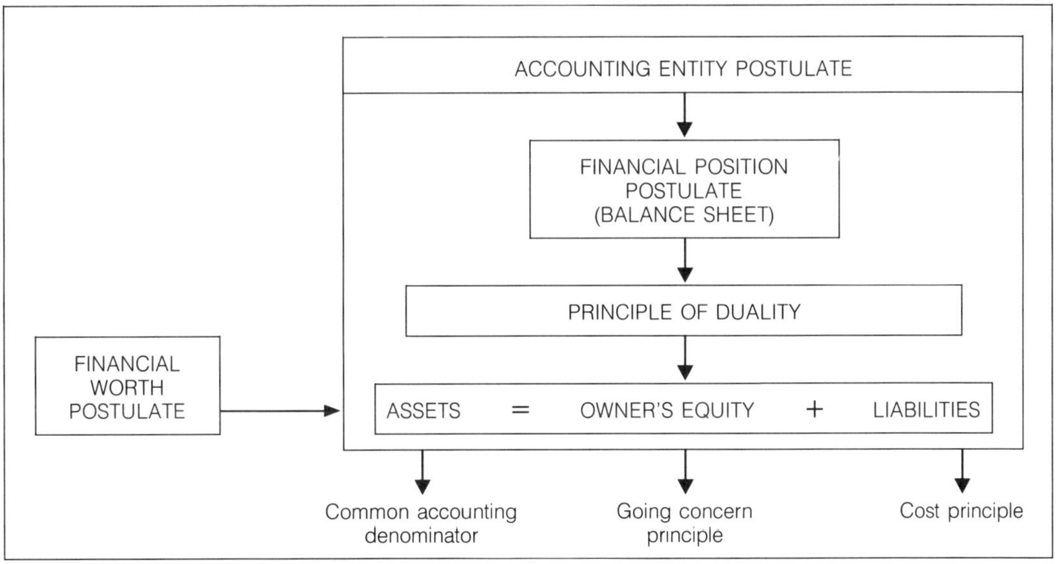

4

FINANCIAL RESULT

The **AIM** of this chapter is to explain the concept income and the principles derived therefrom.

4.1 THE FINANCIAL RESULT POSTULATE

In chapter 3 the primary purpose of accounting was identified as measuring and communicating two aspects of an entity's financial activities, namely **financial position** and **financial result**.

Financial position was discussed in chapter 3, and financial result is discussed in this chapter.

The financial objective of a trading concern is to maximise owner's equity. This is achieved by earning **profit** which is added to owner's equity.

The financial result of an enterprise's activities over a period, that is its profit or loss, is measured as the difference between the **value earned by the entity** and the **value sacrificed**.

An entity makes a profit when it earns a value greater than the value it sacrifices and it suffers a loss when it sacrifices a value greater than the value it earns.

The value that an entity **earns** is **income** and the values that it **sacrifices** to produce the income are **expenses**.

Therefore, in accounting terms **the financial result** is measured as **the difference between income and expenses**. **Profit** is also described as **net income**. The term **profit** is usually used by trading concerns, whereas service enterprises and associations not for gain generally use the term net income.

FINANCIAL RESULT POSTULATE → FINANCIAL RESULT

INCOME − EXPENSES = PROFIT

The financial result of an enterprise is depicted in an **income statement,** which shows the income earned and the expenses incurred in a period.

SPORTS CLUB
INCOME STATEMENT FOR THE YEAR ENDED 31 DECEMBER 19.1

Income		308 600
Membership fees received		
Less: Expenses		294 000
Salaries and wages	180 200	
Maintenance of sports fields	84 700	
Rent	10 000	
Municipal services	8 000	
Telephone	1 500	
Stationery and printing	6 000	
Auditor's remuneration	1 600	
Depreciation of equipment	2 000	
Net income		R14 600

4.2 THE INFLUENCE OF PROFIT/LOSS ON NET WORTH

Income increases and expenses reduce net worth. This implies that profit increases and losses reduce net worth.

Consider again the financial position of Excelsior Services on 1 January 19.1, and assume that services are rendered to a client for R1 000 cash. At the same time Excelsior pays R500 cash for wages and R100 for repairs to equipment. The **income** of R1 000 and the **expenses** of R600 will influence net worth as follows:

OCCURRENCE	ASSETS		NET WORTH		LIABILITIES
Initial situation	10 000	=	7 000	+	3 000
Cash received for services rendered	+1 000		+1 000		
Salaries paid	-500		-500		
Repairs paid	-100		-100		
Financial position	R10 400		R7 400		R3 000

The profit made by Excelsior Services can be calculated as follows:

INCOME	–	EXPENSES	=	PROFIT (or Net Income)
R1 000		R600		R400

In the basic accounting equation above, which describes the financial position of Excelsior Services, the **net worth** has been increased by the amount of the profit, R400, from R7 000 to R7 400.

4.3 THE FINANCIAL PERIOD POSTULATE

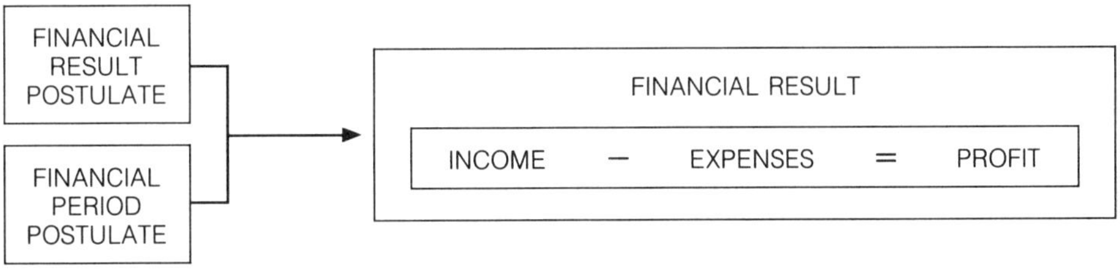

The going concern principle discussed in paragraph 3.9 states that the life of an economic entity is indefinite.

For purposes of reporting to interest groups for distribution of profits and for internal management, it is necessary that the financial result and financial position of an entity are measured at regular intervals during its lifespan.

The internal management of an entity is expected to give regular, periodic account of the financial result and financial position of the entity to its owners. A decline in the frequency and regularity of these reports will tend to produce a corresponding decrease in the degree of control exercised by the owners over internal management.

Another requirement of the owners is the periodic distribution of the profit earned by the entity. To facilitate regular profit distribution, profit must be determined and the financial position reviewed periodically. It is necessary to determine the amount of profit or loss and the amount that can be paid out to the owners, taking into consideration the current financial position of the entity.

Furthermore, for the purposes of internal management it is essential that the financial result and position of an entity are determined at regular intervals. This makes it possible for management to make timely judgements and to make decisions about future actions based on conclusions arising from those judgements. The intervals between successive determinations of financial result depend upon the requirements of the control process. Certain aspects of an enterprise's activities may necessitate the continuous measurement of the position or result, such as in the case of a large trading organisation. In other cases, the specific financial position or result need only be determined monthly or even annually.

For the purposes discussed above, the lifespan of an entity is divided into financial periods of equal length. At the end of each period:

- the financial result, that is the profit or loss for the relevant financial period, is ascertained from the **income statement**; and
- the financial position of the entity, that is the state of its assets, liabilities and owner's equity at the closure of the relevant financial period, is ascertained from the **balance sheet**.

A financial period, therefore, is the period for which the financial result of an entity is determined and at the end of which the financial position of the entity is also ascertained. All income and expense items which are accounted for in the financial statements for a specific period should be included in the income statement for that period. The financial history of an entity will therefore consist of a series of income statements reflecting the profit or loss for each separate financial period and a series of balance sheets showing the financial position of the entity at the end of each financial period.

This can be represented diagrammatically as follows:

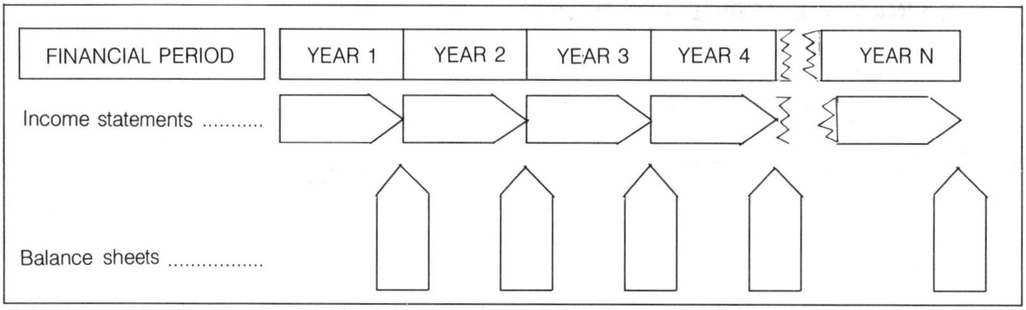

The financial result of Excelsior Services for January 19.2 and its financial position at 31 January 19.2 will be reflected as follows in its income statement and balance sheet:

EXCELSIOR SERVICES
INCOME STATEMENT FOR THE MONTH ENDED 31 JANUARY 19.2

Income		1 000
Less: Expenses		600
Salaries	500	
Repairs to equipment	100	
Net income		R400

BALANCE SHEET AT 31 JANUARY 19.2				
ASSETS		OWNER'S EQUITY		7 400
Equipment	6 000	Balance 31 December	7 000	
Debtors	3 000	*Add*: Net profit	400	
Cash	1 400	LIABILITIES		
		Creditors		3 000
	R10 400			R10 400

It is general practice, and obligatory as far as entities subject to legal regulations are concerned, that the financial result and position of an entity are determined at least every 12 months and communicated in the form of a set of financial reports to external interest groups. This period of 12 months, which ends on the same date each year, is known as the entity's **financial year**. Businesses are free to set the commencement of their financial year at a date convenient to the nature of their activities. Most enterprises observe a natural cycle in their business activities, some months being exceptionally busy and other months less so. Under normal circumstances, an enterprise will choose the closing date of its financial year to coincide with the end of the month in which activities are generally at a low ebb, and just before they are expected to increase. In practice, however, the closing date of a financial year generally coincides with the end of the tax year, that is the 12-month period over which the enterprise is taxed. The most common year-end dates are 31 December, 28 February and 30 June.

4.4 INCOME

Income is the value which in the normal course of business accrues to an entity in exchange for goods sold or services rendered or for placing its assets at the disposal of third parties.

It is necessary to distinguish between the terms income, gross income and net income. Gross income is the total income earned. Net income is the difference between gross income and expenses. Therefore net income is synonymous with profit.

The term income, as used in this chapter, refers to gross income. In practice, the term income is also sometimes used for net income.

Income can be earned in different ways. In a **trading enterprise** it arises from **sales**. **Professional persons**, such as doctors or accountants, earn income in the form of professional **monies** or **fees**. Income from investments is in the form of **interest** or **dividends**, and income from the letting of property is in the form of **rent**. The manner in which income is earned is usually indicated in the income statement.

Value which accrues to an entity as a result of the disposal of non-current assets is not recognised as income. The proceeds from the sale of trading goods will be recognised as income, since it is the objective of the enterprise to earn a profit from the sale of such goods. If, however, the enterprise sells the building in which it performs its activities, the proceeds will not be considered to be income; since it is not the objective of an enterprise to earn income from the sale of its fixed assets.

Income is recognised only when it has been earned and realised.

4.5 THE REALISATION PRINCIPLE

The realisation principle prescribes two conditions for the recognition of income. Income must be **earned** and it must be **realised** before it can be recognised.

Income is earned when the party giving value has completed its obligation towards the party receiving value. In the case of the sale of goods, delivery must have taken place. Delivery takes place when the risk of ownership has passed from the seller to the buyer – in other words when legal ownership has been transferred.

In the case of services, the rendering thereof must be complete before the income can be recognised. However, if a service is delivered over an extended period the income can be recognised periodically on that part of the service already accomplished.

Interest is usually earned proportionately over the period of a loan. Dividends are earned only when they have been declared by the relevant company.

The postulate underlying the concept profit and, therefore, also the concept income, is that profit must be available for use. The owner of the enterprise will wish either to pocket the profit or to reinvest it in the business. The manner in which the profit has been realised should not limit the possibilities for its application. We can compare profit with fruit picked from a tree; before the fruit is picked, it is not available for use. Similarly, as long as an enterprise has not sold the product it offers, no income has been earned. The fact that the enterprise has incurred costs in producing the product, and the fact that the product is ready for sale do not affect the matter in any way.

To be **realised**, income must be measurable and recoverability thereof must be reasonably certain.

When can value be utilised? The point at issue here is the degree of liquidity of the value received, in other words the acceptability of that value as a medium of payment. Cash is the most liquid form of value and the second most liquid form is a **claim on cash**, in other words something is sold on credit and the seller does not immediately receive cash, but receives a claim on cash which must be paid to him at a specific date. The longer the interval between the moment of sale and the moment of payment, the less liquid the claim on cash. For the purposes of determining the realisability of the income, debts which will be settled within 12 months are regarded as liquid. Income generated by cash or credit sales is therefore regarded as realised income.

Value derived from the sale of a product is not, however, the only value that can accrue to an enterprise. Assets can increase in value while in the possession of the enterprise. An enterprise owning land in an area in which property values are rising, will discover that its worth has increased considerably. However, this is not a realised increase, since the increase is inseparably linked to the asset. Therefore this unrealised increase in value is not regarded as income.

4.6 EXPENSES, COSTS AND LOSSES

4.6.1 Expenses

An entity incurs **expenditure** when it exchanges one value for another. An entity therefore incurs expenditure when it purchases goods or services. Expenditure can be incurred on **assets** or **expenses**.

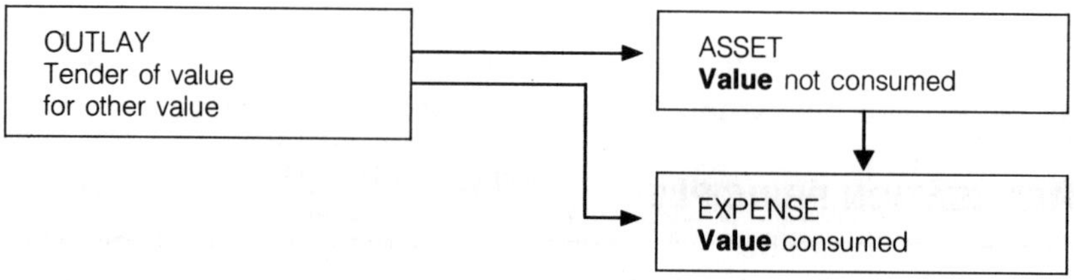

Expenditure on an asset includes the acquisition of value which has not been consumed. For example, an enterprise buys a machine for R100 000 cash. The value tendered is R100 000 cash. In exchange therefor a machine worth R100 000 has been acquired.

Conversely, an expense is an expenditure which has been consumed. Assume that an enterprise pays the municipality R500 for electricity. The enterprise has tendered R500 cash for value (electricity) which has already been consumed.

An asset, or phrased differently, the value of an asset, can also be consumed. That portion of the value of an **asset which has been consumed**, will also constitute an expense.

It is necessary to distinguish between the **use** and the **consumption** of assets. Certain assets are **used**, but are not necessarily consumed, for example the land on which trading activities take place. The land remains physically unchanged, irrespective of what is erected thereon. The fact that the ground is being used does not decrease its usefulness.

Assets with a limited lifespan, on the other hand, are **consumed**, and **that portion of the value which has been consumed is an expense**. We distinguish between two types of assets, namely:

- assets which are completely consumed or disposed of in a short period, such as raw materials, production materials and trading goods
- assets with a limited, yet relatively long lifespan, which are consumed in due course, ultimately becoming technically or economically worthless, such as buildings, machinery, equipment, vehicles, etc.

4.6.2 Costs and cost price

The term **costs** refers to expenses which are specifically incurred. Costs arising directly from the consumption of goods or services in the production process are product costs and constitute the cost price of the manufactured product. Although product costs (such as the cost of the use of equipment, raw material and labour) incurred during a specific period represent the utilisation or consumption of goods or services no sacrifice of value is involved, only the transformation of value from one form to another. Through the utilisation or consumption of equipment, raw materials and labour a new asset is formed, namely the manufactured product.

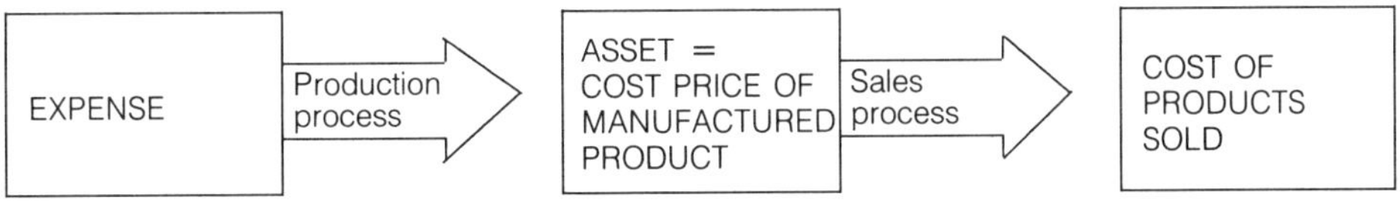

The value of the manufactured product is sacrificed only when the product is sold.

Costs not directly absorbed in the manufacturing process, but which represent a sacrifice of value as and when they occur, are termed **period costs**. These costs are called period costs because they are taken into account against income in the period in which they arise. **Product costs** are costs incurred in manufacturing the product; period costs include costs incurred in marketing the product, as well as the administrative and financing costs of the enterprise.

4.6.3 Loss

A loss is value lost. This can occur in several different ways. Costs incurred for no purpose are a waste and consequently a loss. If the costs that an enterprise incurs to earn income are greater than that income, the difference represents a loss, since it is value lost. Losses incurred in the normal business activities of an enterprise are called operating losses.

However, losses can also be incurred without any consumption having taken place. For example, a loss will be incurred if an asset decreases in value. One of the most important factors determining the value of any economically useful item is its potential earning capacity – in other words the value at which it can be resold, or the amount that can be earned from its usage. A vacant piece of property bought 10 years before for R20 000, in an area for which tremendous industrial development was forecast, could have a present value of only R5 000 if that development did not materialise and now the land is suitable only for agricultural purposes. This type of decrease in value does not, however, arise from consumption of the asset – it is a loss of a capital nature.

Losses are brought into account as soon as they become known, regardless of whether they are **realised**. This is an extremely important principle which can exercise a strong influence on the profit of an enterprise and which, because losses do not necessarily occur in conjunction with consumption, must be applied with great caution.

4.7 THE ACCRUAL PRINCIPLE

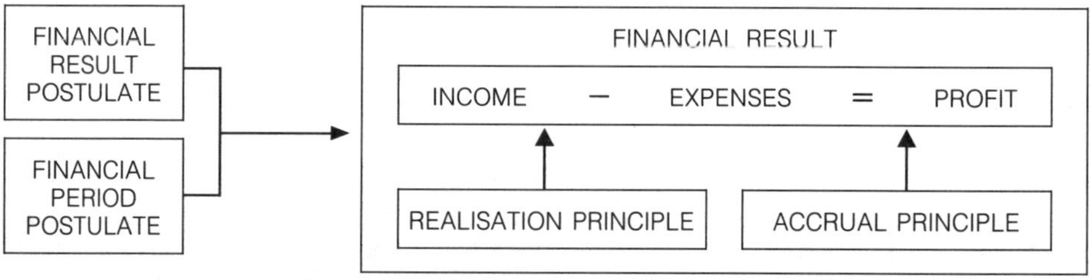

Profit for a specific period is the difference between value earned during that period and expenses incurred during the same period.

There is a difference between:

value received	and	value earned
	and between	
value tendered	and	value sacrificed.

The accrual principle states that, in calculating the profit for a specific period, only income earned during that period (regardless of when it was received) may be brought into account, and that only value consumed during that period can be brought into account as expenses (regardless of when payment was made) in the determination of profit.

It is possible for value to have been received but not yet earned, and *vice versa*.

Assume that, during January 19.2, Excelsior Services received an advance payment of R1 000 from a client for work to be carried out in February and March. During January, Excelsior received value of R1 000, but had not yet earned that value. According to the definition of income, the R1 000 cannot be regarded as income for January. Assume that half of the work is done in February and the other half in March. This means that R500 of the R1 000 received in January will have been earned in February and can consequently be regarded as income for February.

☐ **Value which has been received but not yet earned constitutes an obligation, and is therefore treated as a liability**

Cases where value has been earned but not yet received are common in business, for example all credit transactions fall within this category.

> Assume that during January Excelsior Services renders services to the value of R400 to a client, who only pays in February. Although the cash is only received in February, the income was actually earned in January, and will therefore be accounted for in January.

☐ **Value which has been earned but not yet received is treated as an asset**

Similar principles apply in the case of expenses. It often happens that payment is made in advance for goods or services which will be utilised or consumed only at a later date.

> Assume that on 1 January 19.2, Excelsior Services pays R2 400 in rental for the ensuing period of 12 months to 31 December 19.2. During January, only one-twelfth of the amount of R2 400 can be brought into account as an expense. The balance of R2 200 must be regarded on 31 January as a prepayment, which is an asset.

☐ **Expenditure on services or goods not yet consumed is treated as an asset**

Another common occurrence is that an entity incurs expenses through the utilisation or consumption of value, while payment for that value will be made only at some later date.

☐ **Value which has been consumed but not yet paid for is treated as a liability**

The effect of the accrual principle is that profit is measured as the difference between income and expenses actually incurred, and not as the difference between cash receipts and cash payments.

4.8 THE MATCHING PRINCIPLE

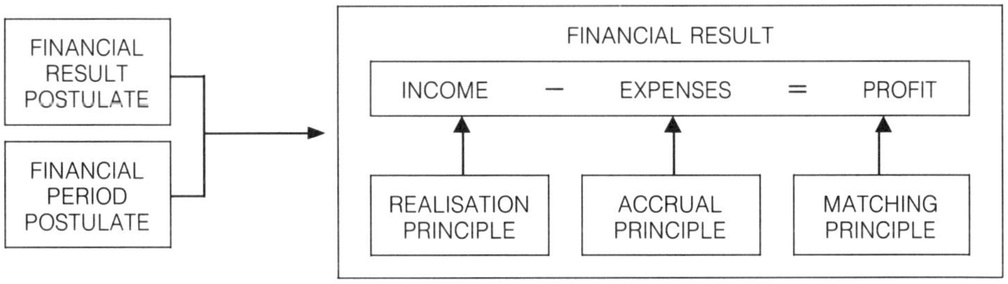

According to the matching principle, income and expenses incurred in generating income must be brought into account during the same financial period.

> Assume that during January a dealer buys goods to the value of R4 000, half of which he sells for R3 000 before the end of the month. The income of R3 000 from sales is related to only half of the goods that were acquired. Only the product costs of these goods which have been sold, in other words half of the R4 000 – that is R2 000 – can be taken into account against income.

The **period costs** for January, namely rental and electricity, although they do not contribute to the cost of the goods, are brought into account when profit is determined.

5

THE DOUBLE-ENTRY SYSTEM

The **AIM** of this chapter is to familiarise you with the basic analysis of transactions, how this affects items in the accounting equation, and how the results of a series of transactions can ultimately be reflected by means of financial statements.

5.1 REASONS FOR CHANGES IN THE FINANCIAL POSITION OF AN ENTERPRISE: TRANSACTIONS

According to the duality principle, every occurrence which affects an entity financially has a **dual influence on the financial position** and hence on the basic accounting equation, so that as a result the equation is always in equilibrium.

All economic behaviour occurs through **transactions**. A transaction is a mutual transfer of value between two parties. Other activities in the business are not necessarily transactions. For example, the appointment of an employee does not affect the accounting equation and therefore is not included in the accounting process.

Transactions are the primary input into the financial accounting process. By means of the accounting process transactions are classified, recorded and summarised and eventually the result is reported.

There are basically two types of occurrences which are dealt with in accounting:

- ☐ First there are transactions consisting of the transfer of value from one party to another.

The financial position of an entity is influenced by every transaction entered into with a third party.

This does not necessarily mean that every transaction will influence owner's equity, or, more specifically, that all income or expense items will increase or decrease owner's equity. Certain transactions only change the asset structure of the entity without simultaneously giving rise to income or an expense.

- ☐ Apart from transactions with third parties, there are also other events and circumstances which influence the financial position of an entity. Ageing, for example, can influence the value of an asset – and this does not involve a transaction with a third party.

Most businesses conclude a large number of transactions. Consider, for example, a retail chain store. The tremendous volume of transactions it engages in makes proper classification and summary essential if meaningful information is to result. **This is the task of the accounting process**. The process can take place in various ways – today most concerns use highly sophisticated computerised systems rather than manual systems.

In essence the fundamental structure of the accounting process remains the same, irrespective of the sophistication of a particular accounting system. Therefore the approach in the next few chapters is to explain the accounting process as applied in a simple manual system, the purpose being to establish a sound understanding of the fundamental aspects of accounting. Later on the more advanced aspects are emphasised.

5.2 THE WAYS IN WHICH THE FINANCIAL POSITION CAN CHANGE

For the sake of clarity, we can divide the circumstances influencing the financial position of an entity – and which must consequently be recorded – into the following:

- ☐ transactions which do **not** immediately influence income or expenses, that is they influence only assets or equity
- ☐ transactions which generate income or expenses
- ☐ other circumstances influencing the financial position.

Any transaction can influence the basic accounting equation, and thus the financial position, in any **one** of the following ways or in a combination thereof:

☐ An increase in an asset together with an **equal** increase in an equity item.

ASSETS	=	EQUITY
+		+

☐ A decrease in an asset together with an **equal** decrease in an equity item.

ASSETS	=	EQUITY
–		–

☐ One asset decreases while another asset increases simultaneously by an **equal** amount.

ASSETS	=	EQUITY
– +		

☐ One equity item decreases while another increases simultaneously by an **equal** amount.

ASSETS	=	EQUITY
		– +

Despite all these changes, the equation maintains its equilibrium.

Before a transaction is recorded, it must be **analysed** to determine its influence on the basic accounting equation, as well as its effect on specific asset and/or equity items.

In order to explain the various transactions which can occur and their influence on the accounting equation, the rest of this chapter illustrates a number of typical transactions concluded by Excelsior

Services during January 19.2 and provided an **analysis** of each transaction.

On 31 December 19.1, the financial position of Excelsior Services was reflected as follows by an accounting equation:

ASSETS						EQUITY		
Equipment R6 000	+	Debtors R3 000	+	Cash in bank R1 000	=	Owner's equity R7 000	+	Creditors R3 000
		R10 000					R10 000	

Any transaction entered into after 31 December 19.1 will influence the elements of this equation.

5.3 TRANSACTIONS AFFECTING ONLY ASSETS AND/OR EQUITY

In this section examples are given of transactions which influence the elements of the financial position and owner's equity, but which do not immediately generate income or expenses.

Example 5.1(1) An increase in an asset together with an equal increase in an equity item

☐ **Assets/owner's equity**

TRANSACTION	ANALYSIS
3 January 19.2 J Smith decides to increase his investment in Excelsior Services in order to expand his business He draws R2 000 from his personal savings account and deposits this sum in the enterprise's bank account	1 The asset **cash in bank** increases by R2 000 because more money is now available to the enterprise 2 **Owner's equity** increases by R2 000, since the owner has increased his interest in the enterprise by R2 000

	ASSETS						EQUITY		
	Equipment		Debtors		Cash in bank		Owner's equity		Creditors
☐ Previous balances	R6 000	+	R3 000	+	R1 000	=	R7 000	+	R3 000
☐ Influence of this transaction –					+R2 000		+R2 000		
☐ New balances –	R6 000	+	R3 000	+	R3 000	=	R9 000	+	R3 000
			R12 000					R12 000	

This transaction has **increased** both the assets and owner's equity by the same amount. Liabilities remain unchanged, since creditors are not involved in the transaction. The influence of the transaction can be represented diagrammatically as follows:

ASSETS	=	EQUITY
+		+

Note that after the transaction has been recorded, the totals on each side of the equation agree.

☐ **Assets/liabilities**

TRANSACTION	ANALYSIS
5 January 19.2 Excelsior Services buys additional equipment to the value of R1 000, on credit, from a creditor. The amount must be paid on 5 February	1 The asset **equipment** increases by R1 000 because the enterprise now owns more equipment 2 **Creditors** increases because the enterprise now owes more money to creditors

	ASSETS					=	EQUITY		
	Equipment		Debtors		Cash in bank		Owner's equity		Creditors
☐ Previous balances	R6 000	+	R3 000	+	R3 000	=	R9 000	+	R3 000
☐ Influence of this transaction –	+R1 000								+R1 000
☐ New balances –	R7 000	+	R3 000	+	R3 000	=	R9 000	+	R4 000
	R13 000						R13 000		

The additional equipment has increased the total assets to R13 000.

By comparison, creditors now have a total claim of R4 000. Owner's equity has not been affected by this transaction and remains unchanged at R9 000. The transaction can be represented diagrammatically as follows:

ASSETS	=	EQUITY
+		+

The only difference between this transaction and the previous one is that each transaction affected different elements of the equity. The accounting equation remains in equilibrium.

Example 5.1(2) A decrease in an asset together with an equal decrease in an equity item

TRANSACTION	ANALYSIS
10 January 19.2 Excelsior Services pays R1 500 cash in partial settlement of its creditors*	1 The asset **cash in bank** decreases by R1 500, because the enterprise now owns less money 2 The liability **creditors** decreases by R1 500, because the enterprise's debts have been reduced by that amount

	ASSETS						EQUITY		
	Equipment		Debtors		Cash in bank		Owner's equity		Creditors
☐ Previous balances	R7 000	+	R3 000	+	R3 000	=	R9 000	+	R4 000
☐ Influence of this transaction –					–R1 500				–R1 500
☐ New balances –	R7 000	+	R3 000	+	R1 500	=	R9 000	+	R2 500
			R11 500					R11 500	

**NB:* In all transactions involving cash, it is accepted that all cash received is deposited in the enterprise's bank account and that all payments are made (by cheque) from this account.

Payment to a creditor thus affects both assets (cash) and equity (creditors), each being reduced by the same amount. Owner's equity is not affected. The diagrammatic representation of the transaction is as follows:

ASSETS	=	EQUITY
–		–

TRANSACTION	ANALYSIS
20 January 19.2 Excelsior Services completes work for a client and receives R600 in payment for services rendered	1 The asset **cash in bank** increases by R600 because the enterprise now owns more money 2 **Owner's equity** increases by R600 because the enterprise has earned that amount of income
22 January 19.2 Services to the value of R400 are rendered to a client, who must pay his account on or before 22 February	1 The asset **debtors** increases by R400 because the enterprise is now owed more money 2 **Owner's equity** increases by R400 because the enterprise has earned that amount of income

	ASSETS					=	EQUITY						
							Owner's equity						
	Equipment	+	Debtors	+	Cash in bank	=	Capital	+	Income and expenses	+	Creditors	+	Loan
☐ Previous balances	R7 000	+	R2 200	+	R2 300	=	R9 000			+	R500	+	R2 000
☐ Influence of these transactions: Cash sales –					+R600				+R600				
Credit sales –			+R400						+R400				
☐ New balances –	R7 000	+	R2 600	+	R2 900	=	R9 000	+	R1 000	+	R500	+	R2 000
	R12 500						R12 500						

Through services rendered to clients the asset side of the equation is increased, because the assets 'cash' and 'debtors' increase. The equity side of the equation must also increase accordingly. Since liabilities (creditors and loans) are not affected by these transactions, owner's equity has to increase. This growth in owner's equity is called **income**. The diagrammatic representation of the transaction is:

ASSETS	=	EQUITY
+		+

Note that income is shown separately under owner's equity in the accounting equation. The purpose of this is to distinguish between the owner's investment in the enterprise (known as capital) and changes in his equity arising from other factors such as income and expenses.

Application of the realisation principle

This principle is discussed in chapter 4. In the transaction on 20 January income was earned for services rendered and cash was received. Income is earned, however, not only when cash is received.

As has already been seen, the **realisation principle** regulates the recognition of income.

The realisation principle:

- ☐ defines income as an inflow of assets (or value) (not necessarily cash) in exchange for goods or services
- ☐ requires that income is recognised (i e recorded in the accounting records as income) at the point that it is earned (generally it is assumed that income is earned at the point when ownership of the goods sold is transferred or when services are rendered)
- ☐ also requires that the income which is recognised must be measurable in terms of money or, if other assets are received in exchange for goods or services, the reasonable cash equivalent thereof.

In order to illustrate the latter situation:

On 22 January the enterprise renders services worth R400 to a client on credit. The asset which has been received in exchange is the **right** to claim R400 from the client at a later date. If the transactions on 20 and 22 January are compared, it can be seen that the only difference between them is the type of asset received (cash as opposed to debtors). The future settlement of his account by the debtor (as in the case of the transaction on 15 January) is merely an exchange of one asset for another. The receipt of cash from the debtor does not influence owner's equity. The income had already been recognised, according to the realisation principle, on the date on which the services were rendered.

Example 5.1(6) A decrease in an asset together with an equal decrease in owner's equity

Payment of the current operating expenses of the enterprise provides a typical example of this type of transaction.

TRANSACTION	ANALYSIS
26 January 19.2 Excelsior Services pays its employees' monthly salaries of R500 in cash	1 The asset **cash in bank** decreases by R500 because the undertaking now owns less money 2 **Owner's equity** decreases by R500 by virtue of the expense incurred by the enterprise

	ASSETS						EQUITY						
							Owner's equity						
	Equipment		Debtors		Cash in bank		Capital		Income and expenses		Creditors		Loan
☐ Previous balances	R7 000	+	R2 600	+	R2 900	=	R9 000	+	R1 000	+	R500	+	R2 000
☐ Influence of this transaction –					–R500				–R500				
☐ New balances –	R7 000	+	R2 600	+	R2 400	=	R9 000	+	R500	+	R500	+	R2 000
			R12 000							R12 000			

Both the asset and the equity sides of the equation decrease by the same amount. Thus:

ASSETS	=	EQUITY
−		−

Since liabilities are not affected by the transaction, owner's equity decreases and the equation remains in equilibrium.

Example 5.1(7) A decrease in owner's equity together with an equal increase in liabilities

TRANSACTION	ANALYSIS
28 January 19.2 A supplier carries out repairs to the value of R100 on equipment, the repairs being done on credit	1 **Owner's equity** decreases by R100 because the enterprise has incurred an expense 2 **Creditors** increase because the enterprise owes another R100

	ASSETS							EQUITY						
								Owner's equity						
	Equipment		Debtors		Cash in bank		Capital		Income and expenses		Creditors		Loan
☐ Previous balances	R7 000	+	R2 600	+	R2 400	=	R9 000	+	R500	+	R500	+	R2 000
☐ Influence of this transaction –									−R100		+R100		
☐ New balances –	R7 000	+	R2 600	+	R2 400	=	R9 000	+	R400	+	R600	+	R2 000
	R12 000						R12 000						

Assets are not affected by this transaction. Owner's equity has decreased and liabilities have increased. Thus schematically:

ASSETS	=	EQUITY
		− +

5.5 OTHER CIRCUMSTANCES WHICH CAN INFLUENCE THE FINANCIAL POSITION

As we have already noted, besides transactions with third parties, other factors can also influence the financial position of an entity.

One of the most common examples is the **depreciation** of assets in the course of time.

Example 5.2

Assume that the equipment used by Excelsior Services during January has an estimated lifespan of five years (60 months). If its useful lifespan was only one month, it would not be accounted for as an asset, but rather as an expense, the whole of which would have been brought into account against owner's equity in January. However, since it has an estimated lifespan of 60 months, only 1/60 of the cost of the equipment will be brought into account during January, as a **depreciation expense** against owner's equity. The calculation of depreciation on the equipment for one month is calculated as follows:

$$\frac{R7\ 000}{60} = R117$$

The influence of depreciation on the financial position may be illustrated as follows:

TRANSACTION	ANALYSIS
31 January 19.2 Depreciation on equipment amounts to R117 for the month	1 The value of the asset **equipment** decreases because it has been used during the month 2 **Owner's equity** decreases because an asset, against which he has a claim, has depreciated

	ASSETS						EQUITY						
							Owner's equity						
	Equipment		Debtors		Cash in bank		Capital		Income and expenses		Creditors		Loan
□ Previous balances	R7 000	+	R2 600	+	R2 400	=	R9 000	+	R400	+	R600	+	R2 000
□ Influence of this transaction –	–R117								–R117				
□ New balances –	R6 883	+	R2 600	+	R2 400	=	R9 000	+	R283*	+	R600	+	R2 000
	R11 883						R11 883						

*This amount therefore represents the net income of the enterprise for the financial period under consideration.

In this case both assets and owner's equity are reduced, while liabilities remain unchanged. Thus schematically:

ASSETS	=	EQUITY
–		–

Example 5.3

In terms of the accounting equation, the transactions of Excelsior Services for January 19.2 can be summed up as follows:

	CHANGE		ASSETS			EQUITY			
						Owner's equity			
	Assets	Equity	Equipment	Debtors	Cash in bank	Capital	Income and expenses	Creditors	Loan
1 *Transactions which do not generate immediate income or costs*									
January 19.2									
1 Initial balances			6 000	3 000	1 000	7 000		3 000	
3 Additional investment by owner, R2 000	+	+			+2 000	+2 000			
5 Purchase of equipment to the value of R1 000 on credit	+	+	+1 000					+1 000	
10 Pay creditors R1 500	−	−			−1 500			−1 500	
15 Receive R800 from debtors	+ −			−800	+800				
18 Transfer of R2 000 from creditors to loan		− +						−2 000	+2 000
2 *Transactions which generate income or expenses*									
20 Services rendered to client for R600 cash	+	+			+600		+600		
22 Services rendered on credit, R400	+	+		+400			+400		
26 Pay salaries to staff, R500	−	−			−500		−500		
28 Supplier repairs equipment on credit, R100		− +					−100	+100	
31 Depreciation on equipment for the month, R117	−	−	−117				−117		
Balances at month end			R6 883	+ R2 600	+ R2 400 =	R9 000	+ R283	+ R600 +	R2 000
				R11 883				R11 883	

5.6 THE SET OF FINANCIAL STATEMENTS

When reporting on the financial position and performance of an entity, no purpose would be served by furnishing a complete record of all transactions such as those given above in the basic accounting equation relating to Excelsior Services. Indeed, such a report would be cumbersome and impractical.

As explained in chapter 4, **periodic reporting of the financial position and performance of an entity is in the form of a set of financial statements**. This set of financial statements actually constitutes a summary of the information contained in the basic accounting equation, and consists of a **balance sheet** and an **income statement**.

A **balance sheet** is a statement which describes the financial position of an entity in terms of investment in assets, liabilities and owner's equity, **at a specific moment** in time. The fact that the balance sheet illustrates the financial position at a specific moment in time is important, since events after that date could alter the financial position. Consequently, **the heading** of each balance sheet states not only the name of the entity concerned, but also the relevant date.

The form of the balance sheet is based upon the accounting equation: assets = liabilities + owner's equity. Accordingly, assets are shown on the left-hand side and owner's equity on the right-hand side of a balance sheet. To illustrate this point, we transform the accounting equation relating to Excelsior Services on 31 January 19.2 into a balance sheet:

ACCOUNTING EQUATION OF EXCELSIOR SERVICES ON 31 JANUARY 19.2

ASSETS						EQUITY						
						Owner's equity						
Equipment		Debtors		Cash in bank		Capital		Net income		Creditors		Loan
R6 883	+	R2 600	+	R2 400	=	R9 000	+	R283	+	R600	+	R2 000
		R11 883						R11 883				

EXCELSIOR SERVICES
BALANCE SHEET AT 31 JANUARY 19.2

ASSETS		EQUITY		
Equipment	6 883	Owner's equity		9 283
Debtors	2 600	J Smith: Capital	9 000	
Cash in bank	2 400	Add: Net income	283	
		Loan		2 000
		Creditors		600
	R11 883			R11 883

The net income earned by the enterprise during January and added to the balance sheet under owner's equity is generally described as **retained income**. It simply represents the return received by the owner on his investment (capital) in the enterprise and which he has not yet withdrawn.

The balance sheet above is presented in the horizontal or so-called T-form, in other words, the assets and equity are on opposite sides of each another.

Earlier on in this chapter it was noted that the basic accounting equation (assets = owner's equity + liabilities) can be adapted to the form: assets − liabilities = owner's equity.

This means that the balance sheet can also be set out in a **vertical form**, as shown in the following example:

EXCELSIOR SERVICES BALANCE SHEET AT 31 JANUARY 19.2		Section
OWNER'S EQUITY	9 283	OWNER'S EQUITY SECTION
Opening balance	9 000	
Add: Net income	283	
	R9 283	
ASSETS	11 883	ASSET SECTION
Equipment	6 883	
Cost	7 000	
Less: Depreciation	(117)	
Debtors	2 600	
Cash in bank	2 400	
Less: LIABILITIES	(2 600)	LIABILITIES SECTION
Loans	2 000	
Creditors	600	
Net assets	R9 283	

(The heading EXCELSIOR SERVICES / BALANCE SHEET AT 31 JANUARY 19.2 is marked HEADING.)

From the retained income element of owner's equity it can be seen that the enterprise earned a net income of R283 during January. The balance sheet does not, however, provide details about the composition of this net income.

Details of the net income – or loss – that arose between one balance sheet date and the next are given in the **income statement**. An income statement is simply a summary of the income and expenses of the entity for a specific period – in other words, a summary of those income and expense items which influenced owner's equity during the period concerned.

In the following example the different sections comprising the income statement should be noted:

EXCELSIOR SERVICES INCOME STATEMENT FOR THE MONTH ENDED 31 JANUARY 19.2		Section 1 Heading
INCOME		Section 2 Income
Services rendered	1 000	
EXPENSES	717	
Salaries	500	Section 3 Expenses
Repair costs: Equipment	100	
Depreciation: Equipment	117	
Net income for the month	R283	Section 4 Net income (loss)

Owners and managers are interested in a periodic summary of the results of all transactions concluded during a specific period rather than in the results of each individual transaction. Accordingly, regular reports on the information arising from transactions are furnished by means of the financial reports, namely the income statement and the balance sheet.

The period covered by an income statement is known as the **financial period**, and the date on which the balance sheet is drawn up is called the **balance sheet date**.

A balance sheet may be viewed as a snapshot of the financial position at a particular moment in time, while an income statement may be compared to a film covering the events during a specific period.

6

THE ACCOUNTING SYSTEM

The **AIM** of this chapter is to introduce the **general ledger**, one of the most important aids in the accounting system, to illustrate its use in the double-entry system of accounting and to introduce the **trial balance**.

6.1 THE ACCOUNT

The previous chapter explained how the financial position of an entity could be recorded in terms of the basic accounting equation. Each financial transaction produces a change in one or more elements of the equation. The duality principle, on the other hand, requires that the accounting equation should always be in balance. The need to comply with this requirement when recording transactions actually serves as a control for the accuracy of the records. **However, it would be impractical to compile a new equation after each transaction.**

Furthermore, although it is possible it would be equally impractical to compile an amended balance sheet after every transaction. An alternative procedure for accumulating and storing all transaction data until it is needed, is required. One of the primary functions of the management of an enterprise is to exercise control over its assets and operating activities. Therefore management will be interested in changes occurring in individual items. The **account** is used as a means of recording the effect of transactions on individual items. An account is simply a record of all the transactions relating to a specific item. The form of the account employed depends on the particular accounting system used. In its simplest form, the account is a page or card allotted to each item for which a detailed record of transactions is deemed necessary. In more sophisticated systems (for example those using computers), such records are kept in the form of magnetic tapes and/or discs.

We shall again review the transactions of Excelsior Services for January 19.2 as recorded within the framework of the basic accounting equation in the previous chapter.

EXCELSIOR SERVICES
TRANSACTIONS DURING JANUARY 19.2

	ASSETS			= OWNER'S EQUITY		+ LIABILITIES	
January 19.2	Equipment	Debtors	Cash in bank	Capital	Income and expenses	Creditors	Loans
1	+6 000	+3 000	+1 000	+7 000		+3 000	
3			+2 000	+2 000			
5	+1 000					+1 000	
10			−1 500			−1 500	
15		−800	+800				
18						−2 000	+2 000
20			+600		+600		
22		+400			+400		
26			−500		−500		
28					−100	+100	
31	−117				−117		
	+R6 883	+R2 600	+R2 400	+R9 000	+R283	+R600	+R2 000

ACCOUNTS

The individual records in which all transactions relating to a specific item are recorded are called **accounts**. In the above example there are separate accounts for equipment, debtors, cash, capital, retained income, creditors and loans. **An account can be defined as the formal record of an enterprise's transactions in respect of a specific item**.

In practice, transactions are not recorded directly in the form of the basic accounting equation, as above, but rather in formal accounts. Such accounts consist of a **heading**, a **positive side for recording increases in a specific item** and a **negative side for recording decreases in the item**.

6.2 CLASSIFICATION OF ACCOUNTS INTO BASIC GROUPS

The question that arises is, what accounts are necessary? The type and number of accounts necessary for a specific system will be determined by the nature of the enterprise concerned and the scope of its activities. In each case it will be necessary to determine at the outset what accounts will be needed in the accounting system and, consequently, for compiling a ledger.

We have already seen that the basic elements of accounting are **assets** and **equity**, the latter being subdivided into owner's equity and liabilities. In the previous chapter these elements were outlined and developed within the context of basic accounting equation. Furthermore, it was decided that owner's equity should be subdivided because it is affected by income and expenses. Consequently, we may conclude that at least the following groups of accounts should be opened:

- ☐ Assets
- ☐ Liabilities
- ☐ Owner's equity
  - — Initial investment (or capital)
  - — Income accounts
  - — Expense accounts.

The classification of accounts into these basic groups is of considerable importance, since this classification is also used to group items in accounting records and in the accounting reports. It also **provides a basis for the logical development of the method used to record the effect of transactions on accounts**.

6.3 FORM OF AN ACCOUNT AND THE CONCEPTS DEBIT, CREDIT, DEBITING AND CREDITING

The conventional account is presented in T-form, with the heading written above the horizontal line and the transactions entered on either the left or right-hand side of the vertical line, depending on whether they represent increases or decreases in the item concerned. The left-hand side of an account is called the **debit side** and the right-hand side the **credit side**, thus:

BANK	
Debit side	Credit side

An entry on the debit side of an account is called a **debit**, and an entry on the credit side is called a **credit**.

The process of **debiting** an account entails making an entry on the debit side; while **crediting** an account entails making an entry on the credit side. The abbreviation **dr** is used for **debit**, and **cr** for **credit**.

The standard form of a formal general ledger account is as follows:

Dr			NAME OF ACCOUNT				Cr
Date	Details	Folio	Debit amount	Date	Details	Folio	Credit amount

Another common form for the general ledger account found especially in mechanised systems, is the so-called three-column ledger account:

Date	Details	Folio	Dr	Cr	Balance

The terms 'debiting' and 'crediting' must **not** be associated with 'increase' and 'decrease' respectively. As has already been stated, 'debiting' an account simply means that an entry is made on the left-hand side of the account; similarly, 'crediting' an account entails an entry on the right-hand side of the account. The terms debiting and crediting therefore enable us to distinguish between items which are recorded on opposite sides of an account.

The balance of an account is the difference between the total monetary values of the debit and credit entries on an account.

The balances of certain accounts increase when debited, while the balances of other accounts increase when credited. The reason for this apparently contradictory behaviour can be found in the basic accounting equation:

ASSETS = OWNER'S EQUITY + LIABILITIES

- ☐ The **balance** of an account generally appears on the **same** side as that on which the item appears in the accounting equation.
- ☐ The balance of an account is **increased** by an entry on the same side as that on which the item appears in the accounting equation.
- ☐ The balance of an account is accordingly **decreased** when an amount is entered on the opposite side from the side on which the item appears in the accounting equation.

The following conclusions can be made from these propositions:

Asset accounts appear on the left-hand side (debit side) of the equation. The balance of an asset account is therefore usually a debit balance, which is increased by entries on the debit side and decreased by entries on the credit side.

Liability accounts appear on the right-hand side (credit side) of the equation. The balance of a liability account is therefore usually a credit balance, which is increased by entries on the credit side and decreased by entries on the debit side.

Owner's equity appears on the right-hand side (credit side) of the equation and is therefore increased by additional entries on the credit side and decreased by additional entries on the debit side. From the analysis of the entries in the previous chapter, we already know that **income** items increase owner's equity and **expense** items decrease owner's equity. It follows, therefore, that income accounts should have credit balances and be increased by entries on the credit side and decreased by entries on the debit side. Conversely, expense items usually have a debit balance which is increased by additional entries on the debit side and decreased by additional entries on the credit side.

These propositions can be illustrated schematically as follows:

ASSETS = OWNER'S EQUITY + LIABILITIES

ASSETS

Dr ASSET ACCOUNTS	Cr
+	−
Increase on debit side *Balance* = debit balance	*Decrease* on credit side

OWNER'S EQUITY

Dr CAPITAL	Cr
−	+
Decrease on debit side	*Increase* on credit side *Balance* = credit balance

INCOME ACCOUNTS	
−	+
Decrease on debit side	*Increase* on credit side *Balance* = credit balance

EXPENSE ACCOUNTS	
+	−
Increase on debit side *Balance* = debit balance	*Decrease* on credit side

LIABILITIES

Dr LIABILITY ACCOUNTS	Cr
−	+
Decrease on debit side	*Increase* on credit side *Balance* = credit balance

Note especially the situation with regard to owner's equity accounts, which can be summarised as follows:

Dr −	Cr +
	Capital
	Income
Expenses	

By making a few changes, the accounting equation may be illustrated in the following block format:

CATEGORY 1: ASSETS

Dr	Cr
Increase	Decrease

CATEGORY 2: EQUITY

Dr	Cr
Decrease	Increase

CATEGORY 3:
EXPENSES AND LOSSES

Dr	Cr
Increase	Decrease

CATEGORY 4:
INCOME AND PROFITS

Dr	Cr
Decrease	Increase

Category 1 (asset accounts) and category 3 (expense and loss accounts) will thus be debited each time the balance of the account is to be increased and credited if the balance must decrease as a result of a particular transaction. On the other hand, accounts in category 2 (equity accounts) and category 4 (income and profit accounts) will be credited if the balance of the account must be increased and debited if the balance should be decreased.

6.4 HOW ACCOUNTS ARE SET OUT IN THE GENERAL LEDGER

A separate account is opened for every asset, liability, owner's equity, income and expense item.

The collective term for all these accounts is the **general ledger**. This term originated from the custom of keeping all accounts, each on a separate page, in a special book called the general ledger. Although modern accounting practice favours alternative recording media such as magnetic tapes or discs rather than books, the term general ledger is still used to denote a collection of accounts.

We have already established that there is a direct relationship between accounts and the accounting equation. Accounts for items on the left-hand side of the equation have debit balances, while accounts for items on the right-hand side of the equation have credit balances.

Because the entries for transactions which have occurred during the month are made in accordance with the **duality principle**, the total of the debit balances must equal that of the credit balances in the general ledger. The equality of the accounting equation is therefore maintained in the general ledger.

We now look again at the basic accounting equation of Excelsior Services as it appeared at the end of January 19.2:

Example 6.1

ASSETS					=	EQUITY						
						Owner's equity				Liabilities		
Equipment		Debtors		Cash		Capital		Retained income		Creditors		Loan
R6 883	+	R2 600	+	R2 400	=	R9 000	+	R283	+	R600	+	R2 000

Remember that this equation was also presented in the form of a balance sheet:

EXCELSIOR SERVICES
BALANCE SHEET AT 31 JANUARY 19.2

ASSETS		EQUITY		
Equipment	6 883	Owner's equity		9 283
Debtors	2 600	Capital: J Smith	9 000	
Cash in bank	2 400	*Add*: Retained income	283	
		Loan		2 000
		Creditors		600
	R11 883			R11 883

Bearing in mind what was said in the previous paragraph, we can base the structure of the accounts in the books of Excelsior Services upon either the accounting equation or the balance sheet.

LEDGER OF EXCELSIOR SERVICES

Dr	EQUIPMENT		Cr
19.2 Jan 31	Balance	6 883	

Dr	DEBTORS		Cr
19.2 Jan 31	Balance	2 600	

Dr	CASH IN BANK		Cr
19.2 Jan 31	Balance	2 400	

Dr	CAPITAL: J SMITH		Cr
	19.2 Jan 31	Balance	9 000

Dr	RETAINED INCOME		Cr
	19.2 Jan 31	Balance	283

Dr	LOAN		Cr
	19.2 Jan 31	Balance	2 000

Dr	CREDITORS		Cr
	19.2 Jan 31	Balance	600

Total of debit balances (R11 883) = Total of credit balances (R11 883)

6.5 RECORDING TRANSACTIONS IN THE GENERAL LEDGER: APPLICATION OF THE DOUBLE-ENTRY SYSTEM

Earlier it was stated that a transaction is a pre-arranged transfer of value from one party to another. For the sake of completeness, all transactions must be recorded in accounts. The accounting system used to show the effect of transactions on the accounts is based on the three important premises introduced in the previous chapter:

- ☐ Every transaction affects at least two items in the accounting equation (or in the accounts).
- ☐ The effect of all transactions must be stated in terms of money.
- ☐ The accounting equation must balance after the effect of each (and therefore every) transaction has been brought into account.

These three premises jointly constitute what is known as the **duality principle** and, as already discussed, form the basis of the **double-entry system**, according to which the total of the debit entries must be equal to the total of the credit entries.

Before a transaction can be recorded, it must be analysed. This process entails:

- ☐ ascertaining what asset or equity items are affected
- ☐ applying the debit and credit principle.

Example 6.2

The following transactions of H Jones, a public accountant, will be used to illustrate the application of the debit/credit analysis procedure and the recording of the transactions in ledger accounts:

March 19.4

1 H Jones opens a bank account for his public accounting practice, H Jones and Co, and deposits R3 000 of his private resources into the account. (Therefore the entity which is to be reported on is H Jones and Co.)

2 The company pays R400 rental for March for offices serving as business premises for the practice.

3 Office equipment purchased for R1 500 cash.

4 Roux Printers supply printing and stationery amounting to R200 to the firm on credit.

15 On completion of an assignment, H Jones and Co received a fee of R500.

20 The firm does accounting work for Marx Dealers and debits their account with R800. The client undertakes to pay the account in four instalments of R200 each.

25 Pays the typist's salary for the month, R350.

28 H Jones withdraws R400 from the firm's bank account for his own use.

29 Pays the monthly telephone bill, R40.

30 Pays R100 on account to Roux Printers.

31 Receives the first payment from Marx Dealers.

The annual depreciation on equipment is 20%, one-twelfth of which must be written off in March.

It must be emphasised that, on analysing and recording the above transactions, for every debit entry made in an account in the general ledger there must be a corresponding credit entry. This is the logical application of the double-entry system.

☐ March 1: H Jones invests R3 000 in the firm H Jones and Co:

Date	Analysis of the transaction	Accounting procedure	Entry
19.4 Mar 1	The asset **bank*** 'increases' by R3 000 **Owner's equity** is created ('increases') by R3 000	To increase an asset, debit the asset account To increase equity, credit the equity account	Debit: Bank Credit: Capital: H Jones

Dr	BANK	Cr	Dr	CAPITAL: H JONES	Cr
19.4 Mar 1 Capital: H Jones	3 000			19.4 Mar 1 Bank	3 000

*As was stated in the previous chapter, it is assumed that, in the case of 'cash transactions', all cash received will be deposited in the enterprise's bank account, and all payments will be made from that account. The title of the account is reduced, from now on, simply to **'Bank'**.

Note that in the debit entry of the bank account there is a **reference** to the account in which the opposite portion of the double-entry can be found. Similarly, in the capital account there is a corresponding **cross-reference** to the account in which the 'other leg' of the double-entry has been entered. The date of the transaction is also recorded in the account.

☐ March 2: Pays rental, R400:

Date	Analysis of the transaction	Accounting procedure	Entry
19.4 Mar 2	An expense item **rental paid** of R400 arises. This item represents a decrease in the owner's equity The asset **bank** decreases by R400 as a result of the payment	To increase an expense item (i e to decrease the owner's equity), debit the account To decrease an asset, credit the equity account	Debit: Rental paid Credit: Bank

Dr	BANK	Cr	Dr	RENTAL PAID	Cr
19.4 Mar 1 Capital: H Jones 3 000	19.4 Mar 2 Rental	400	19.4 Mar 2 Bank	400	

☐ March 3: Buys office equipment for R1 500 cash:

Date	Analysis of the transaction	Accounting procedure	Entry
19.4 Mar 3	The asset **office equipment** increases by R1 500 The asset **bank** decreases by R1 500	To increase an asset, debit the account To decrease an asset, credit the account	Debit: Office equipment Credit: Bank

Dr BANK Cr

Dr			Cr		
19.4			19.4		
Mar 1	Capital: H Jones	3 000	Mar 2	Rental	400
			3	Office equipment	1 500

Dr OFFICE EQUIPMENT Cr

Dr			Cr		
19.4					
Mar 3	Bank	1 500			

☐ March 4: Roux Printers supplies stationery on credit, R200:

Date	Analysis of the transaction	Accounting procedure	Entry
19.4 Mar 4	Expenses decrease **owner's equity** by R200 **Creditors** increase by R200	To decrease owner's equity, debit the relevant expense account To increase creditors, credit the account concerned	Debit: Printing and stationery Credit: Roux Printers (a creditor)

Dr PRINTING AND STATIONERY Cr

Dr			Cr		
19.4					
Mar 4	Roux Printers	200			

Dr ROUX PRINTERS Cr

Dr			Cr		
			19.4		
			Mar 4	Printing and stationery	200

Note that (as opposed to the direct recording of expenses in the accounting equation) in the accounting system they are debited to the different expense accounts concerned first and not directly to owner's equity.

☐ March 15: The firm renders services for cash, R500:

Date	Analysis of the transaction	Accounting procedure	Entry
19.4 Mar 15	The asset **bank** increases by R500 Owner's equity **(fees)** increases by R500	To increase an asset, debit the asset account To increase owner's equity, credit the account concerned	Debit: Bank Credit: Fees

Dr BANK Cr

Dr			Cr		
19.4			19.4		
Mar 1	Capital: H Jones	3 000	Mar 2	Rental	400
15	Fees	500	3	Office equipment	1 500

Dr FEES Cr

Dr			Cr		
			19.4		
			Mar 15	Bank	500

☐ March 20: Services rendered on account, R800:

Date	Analysis of the transaction	Accounting procedure	Entry
19.4 Mar 20	The asset **Marx Dealers** (a debtor) increases by R800 Owner's equity (**fees**) increases by R800	To increase an asset, debit the account To increase owner's equity, credit the relevant account	Debit: Marx Dealers (a debtor) Credit: Fees

MARX DEALERS

Dr			Cr		
19.4					
Mar 20	Fees	800			

FEES

Dr			Cr		
			19.4		
			Mar 15	Bank	500
			20	Marx Dealers	800

As in the case of expenses, income is not credited directly to owner's equity; it is credited to the relevant income account first.

☐ March 25: Pays salaries, R350:

Date	Analysis of the transaction	Accounting procedure	Entry
19.4 Mar 25	Expenses decrease the owner's equity by R350 The asset **bank** decreases by R350	To decrease owner's equity, debit the relevant expense account To decrease an asset, credit the asset account	Debit: Salaries Credit: Bank

SALARIES

Dr			Cr		
19.4					
Mar 25	Bank	350			

BANK

Dr			Cr		
19.4			19.4		
Mar 1	Capital: H Jones	3 000	Mar 2	Rental	400
15	Fees	500	3	Office equipment	1 500
			25	Salaries	350

☐ **March 28: Drawings by the owner, R400:**

Date	Analysis of the transaction	Accounting procedure	Entry
19.4 Mar 28	**Drawings** by the owner decrease his investment in the enterprise by R400 The asset **bank** decreases by R400	To decrease owner's equity, debit the account concerned To decrease an asset, credit the account concerned	Debit: Drawings: H Jones Credit: Bank

Dr BANK Cr

19.4			19.4		
Mar 1	Capital: H Jones	3 000	Mar 2	Rental	400
15	Fees	500	3	Office equipment	1 500
			25	Salaries	350
			28	Drawings: H Jones	400

Dr DRAWINGS: H JONES Cr

19.4					
Mar 28	Bank	400			

☐ **March 29: Pays telephone bill, R40:**

Date	Analysis of the transaction	Accounting procedure	Entry
19.4 Mar 29	Expenses decrease owner's equity The asset **bank** decreases	To decrease owner's equity, debit the account concerned To decrease an asset account, credit the account concerned	Debit: Telephone Credit: Bank

Dr BANK Cr

19.4			19.4		
Mar 1	Capital: H Jones	3 000	Mar 2	Rental	400
15	Fees	500	3	Office equipment	1 500
			25	Salaries	350
			28	Drawings: H Jones	400
			29	Telephone	40

Dr TELEPHONE Cr

19.4					
Mar 29	Bank	40			

☐ **March 30: Pays creditor on account, R100:**

Date	Analysis of the transaction	Accounting procedure	Entry
19.4 Mar 30	A liability (**creditor**) decreases An asset **bank** decreases	To decrease a liability, debit the account concerned To decrease an asset, credit the account concerned	Debit: Roux Printers Credit: Bank

BANK

Dr				Cr	
19.4			19.4		
Mar 1	Capital: H Jones	3 000	Mar 2	Rental	400
15	Fees	500	3	Office equipment	1 500
			25	Salaries	350
			28	Drawings: H Jones	400
			29	Telephone	40
			30	Roux Printers	100

ROUX PRINTERS

Dr				Cr	
19.4			19.4		
Mar 30	Bank	100	Mar 4	Printing and stationery	200

☐ **March 31: Payment received from debtor, R200:**

Date	Analysis of the transaction	Accounting procedure	Entry
19.4 Mar 31	An asset **bank** increases An asset **debtors** decreases	To increase an asset, debit the account concerned To decrease an asset, credit the account concerned	Debit: Bank Credit: Marx Dealers

BANK

Dr				Cr	
19.4			19.4		
Mar 1	Capital: H Jones	3 000	Mar 2	Rental	400
15	Fees	500	3	Office equipment	1 500
31	Marx Dealers	200	25	Salaries	350
			28	Drawings: H Jones	400
			29	Telephone	40
			30	Roux Printers	100

MARX DEALERS

Dr				Cr	
19.4			19.4		
Mar 20	Fees	800	Mar 31	Bank	200

☐ **March 31: Provide for depreciation on equipment for the month, at the annual rate of 20%:**

Date	Analysis of the transaction	Accounting procedure	Entry
19.4 Mar 31	**Depreciation** is an expense item and therefore decreases owner's equity The asset **office equipment** decreases in value through use	To decrease owner's equity, debit the expense item concerned To decrease an asset, credit the account concerned	Debit: Depreciation Credit: Office equipment

Dr	OFFICE EQUIPMENT		Cr
19.4 Mar 31 Cash	1 500	19.4 Mar 31 Depreciation	*25

Dr	DEPRECIATION		Cr
19.4 Mar 31 Office equipment	25		

*The amount allowed for depreciation for the month, at an annual rate of 20%, is calculated as follows: R1 500 × 20% × $\frac{1}{12}$ = R25.

This last transaction is an example of an expense which has arisen from the use of an asset. The asset, equipment, is decreased by the amount of the depreciation – in this case R25 – for the month in question. The depreciation cost is recorded in an **expense account** as **depreciation**.

An analysis of the equipment account shows that the equipment was originally acquired for R1 500 and that R25 of this has been consumed to date.

In **practice**, depreciation is not recorded directly in the equipment account (as in the example above), since it would later become difficult to determine from the account the original cost price of the equipment. Instead, a special account, called **accumulated depreciation**, is opened. This is a contra-account to the asset account, equipment. The purpose of the contra-account is that when read simultaneously with the asset account, it decreases the balance of the asset account by the amount of the balance of the contra-account. The asset account and the contra-account, therefore, form a unit.

OFFICE EQUIPMENT

19.4 Mar 3 Bank	1 500		

ACCUMULATED DEPRECIATION: OFFICE EQUIPMENT

		19.4 Mar 31 Depreciation	25

DEPRECIATION

19.4 Mar 31 Accumulated depreciation	25		

The end result is the same as when the accumulated depreciation is recorded directly in the asset account. From now on the contra-account method will be used exclusively.

The complete set of accounts in the general ledger of H Jones and Co for March 19.4 would be as follows:

Dr — BANK — Cr

19.4			19.4		
Mar 1	Capital: H Jones	3 000	Mar 2	Rental	400
15	Fees	500	3	Office equipment	1 500
31	Marx Dealers	200	25	Salaries	350
			28	Drawings: H Jones	400
			29	Telephone	40
			30	Roux Printers	100

Dr — OFFICE EQUIPMENT — Cr

19.4					
Mar 3	Bank	1 500			

Dr — ACCUMULATED DEPRECIATION: OFFICE EQUIPMENT — Cr

			19.4		
			Mar 31	Depreciation	25

Dr — CAPITAL: H JONES — Cr

			19.4		
			Mar 1	Bank	3 000

Dr — DRAWINGS: H JONES — Cr

19.4					
Mar 28	Bank	400			

Dr — ROUX PRINTERS — Cr

19.4			19.4		
Mar 30	Bank	100	Mar 4	Printing and stationery	200

Dr — MARX DEALERS — Cr

19.4			19.4		
Mar 20	Fees	800	Mar 31	Bank	200

Dr — FEES — Cr

			19.4		
			Mar 15	Bank	500
			20	Marx Dealers	800

Dr — RENTAL — Cr

19.4					
Mar 1	Bank	400			

Dr		PRINTING AND STATIONERY		Cr
19.4				
Mar 3	Roux Printers	200		

Dr		TELEPHONE		Cr
19.4				
Mar 29	Bank	40		

Dr		SALARIES		Cr
19.4				
Mar 25	Bank	350		

Dr		DEPRECIATION: OFFICE EQUIPMENT		Cr
19.4				
Mar 31	Accumulated depreciation: Office equipment	25		

6.6 BALANCING AN ACCOUNT

In the recording process both the debit and the credit sides of an account are used. All amounts entered on one side of an account are increases, which must be added together; all amounts entered on the opposite side are decreases which must be deducted. For example, if the bank balance increases, the amount is recorded on the debit side (left-hand side) of the bank account, while any decrease in the bank balance is recorded on the credit side (right-hand side).

Thus the bank account of H Jones and Co would appear as follows:

Dr			BANK		Cr
19.4			19.4		
Mar 1	Capital: H Jones	3 000	Mar 2	Rental	400
15	Fees	500	3	Office equipment	1 500
31	Marx Dealers	200	25	Salaries	350
			28	Drawings: H Jones	400
			29	Telephone	40
			30	Roux Printers	100

Because this is an asset account, the items appearing on the debit side will increase the amount of cash available, while payments on the credit side will decrease the amount (ie cash in bank) available.

The difference between the total debit and the total credit of an account is known as the **balance** of the account. When the total debits of an account exceed the total credits, the balance constitutes a **debit balance**, and conversely, when the credits exceed the debits, there is a **credit balance**.

The balance of an account is calculated as follows:

(1) Add up the debit side of the account and enter the total in pencil.
(2) Add up the credit side of the account and enter the total in pencil.

(3) Subtract the smaller total from the larger. The 'difference' determined in this way constitutes the balance of the account concerned. This balance is entered onto that side of the account with the smallest total.

(4) The totals are now entered. After entering the balance discussed in (3) above, the totals of the debit and credit sides will obviously be the same.

(5) Finally, the balance entered above the totals in (4) is now carried over to the opposite side and entered below that side's total, and constitutes the opening balance at the beginning of the new month's transactions.

The balance of the bank account above would be calculated as follows:

Dr			BANK				Cr
19.4				19.4			
Mar 1	Capital: H Jones		3 000	Mar 2	Rental		400
15	Fees		500	3	Office equipment		1 500
31	Marx Dealers		200	25	Salaries		350
				28	Drawings: H Jones		400
				29	Telephone		40
				30	Roux Printers		100
	(1) Determine total of debit side (pencil total) →		3 700				
					(2) Determine total of credit side (pencil total) →		2 790
				31	Balance	c/d	910 ← (3) Enter balance as calculated
			R3 700				R3 700
	(4) Enter totals of debit and credit sides to balance account						
Apr 1	Balance	b/d	910				
	(5) Bring down balance from opposite side where it was entered in step (3)						

After balancing, the bank account has a debit balance. This method has summarised all the transactions in the account into a single amount which can be read directly from the account.

6.7 THE TRIAL BALANCE

As stated above, the balance on an account is the difference between the total debits and total credits. If the total debits exceed the total credits, the result is a **debit balance**, and if the total credits exceed the total debits, the result is a **credit balance**.

From time to time, after all the transactions up to and including a certain date have been recorded in the general ledger and before the financial statements are prepared, it is both good practice and desirable to test the accuracy of the accounting procedures for recording transactions in the general ledger.

Since all transactions have been recorded in compliance with the double-entry system (whereby each debit entry must have a corresponding credit entry), it follows that the **total of all the debit balances** must be equal to the **total of all the credit balances** in the general ledger.

In order to confirm this, all the debit and credit balances in the general ledger are determined and then recorded in a statement known as a **trial balance**.

A trial balance is a list of all accounts in the general ledger which have balances at a specific date. The names and balances are recorded in the trial balance in the order in which they appear in the general ledger.

H JONES AND CO	Dr	Cr
Bank	910	
Office equipment	1 500	
Accumulated depreciation: Equipment		25
Capital: H Jones		3 000
Drawings: H Jones	400	
Roux Printers		100
Marx Dealers	600	
Fees		1 300
Rental	400	
Printing and stationery	200	
Telephone	40	
Salaries	350	
Depreciation: Office equipment	25	
	R4 425	R4 425

If the debit and credit sides of the trial balance agree, the accounting aspect of the records can be taken as correct, although mistakes could have been made in recording the transactions. This matter is discussed in the next chapter.

6.8 COMPILING FINANCIAL STATEMENTS FROM THE TRIAL BALANCE

The trial balance is a useful aid in drawing up financial statements since, being a reproduction of the balances in the ledger, it contains all the items required for the financial statements.

For example, the financial statements of H Jones and Co, based on information contained in the trial balance above, would appear thus:

H JONES AND CO INCOME STATEMENT FOR THE MONTH ENDING 31 MARCH 19.4		
Fees		1 300
Less: Expenses		1 015
Rental	400	
Printing and stationery*	200	
Telephone	40	
Salaries	350	
Depreciation: Office equipment	25	
Net income		R285

*Assuming that on 31 March 19.4, the stock of stationery and printing was nil.

Before the balance sheet of H Jones and Co is illustrated, the classification of assets and liabilities is discussed in more detail.

6.8.1 Classification of assets

Assets are classified, according to their nature, as either **fixed** or **current** assets. **Fixed assets are assets which have a lifespan longer than the normal operating cycle of the undertaking, or, where the operating cycle is less than a year, which have a lifespan of longer than a year**. The operating cycle of an enterprise is the cycle from the start of normal business activities until the conclusion thereof. For example, in the case of a normal trading entity, the cycle commences with the purchase of trading stock and continues while the goods are held in stock until they have been sold, perhaps on credit, and until the cash is received from the customer and is again applied for the purchase of trading stock. We defined fixed assets as those assets which have a lifespan longer than the operating cycle: fixed assets do not, therefore, form part of the cycle. Fixed assets are those possessions of the entity which provide the facilities which enable it to operate – the land and buildings, machinery and equipment, office equipment and vehicles to mention the most important facilities.

Current assets, on the other hand, consist of cash and all other assets which can reasonably be expected to be realised in cash or sold or consumed within the normal business cycle of the entity, or, if the cycle is less than a year, then within a year. Therefore they are the assets which revolve in the cycle and consist mainly of:

- cash, which is converted through purchases into
- trading stock, which is converted through cash sales to cash or through credit sales into
- debtors' balances, that is the amounts owing to the undertaking and which on collection are again converted into cash, so completing the cycle.

6.8.2 Classification of liabilities

Liabilities are divided, according to their terms, into long-term and short-term or current liabilities. Long-term liabilities are those which are payable after more than a year. Current liabilities are short-term liabilities, payable within a year, mainly from current assets.

The above classification is applied in the following balance sheet.

6.8.3 Net current assets

The net current assets of an undertaking represent the difference between the current assets and the current liabilities.

H JONES AND CO BALANCE SHEET AT 31 MARCH 19.4		
OWNER'S EQUITY:		
Capital: H Jones		
Initial investment 1/3/19.4	3 000	
Add: Net income	285	
	3 285	
Less: Drawings	400	
		R2 885
NET ASSETS:		
Fixed assets		1 475
Office equipment		
Cost price	1 500	
Less: Accumulated depreciation	25	
Net current assets		1 410
Current assets	1 510	
Debtors	600	
Bank	910	
Less: Current liabilities		
Creditors	100	
		R2 885

7

PROCESSING ACCOUNTING DATA

The **AIM** of this chapter is to explain the following:

- ☐ the concept of the accounting cycle
- ☐ the function of books of prime entry (journals)
- ☐ posting from the journals to the general ledger
- ☐ limitations of the trial balance
- ☐ tracing errors.

7.1 INTRODUCTION

The preceding chapters have introduced the basic accounting elements, namely assets, liabilities, owner's equity, income and expenses, as well as the accounting equation. Different types of transactions were analysed to determine their effect upon the basic accounting equation. Then the accounting equation and the analysis of transactions were extended to introduce the accounting system contained in a ledger. The fact that every transaction has a dual effect was emphasised constantly, the recording of this dual effect being the most important aspect of the double-entry system.

Thus the previous sections have provided a framework within which to study the processing of accounting data. Thus far little attention has been focused on the formal recording procedures of accounting, since our aim has been to ensure a thorough understanding of the basic elements of accounting and their relationship within the double-entry system.

In this chapter we introduce some of the procedures used to record the wide range of transactions which arise in the course of the business activities of an enterprise.

7.2 THE ACCOUNTING CYCLE

The formal recording procedures occur within a specific framework, known as the **accounting cycle**.

7.2.1. Source documents

We already know that the economic activities of an enterprise occur via **transactions**. In the examples used in the preceding chapters, the various business transactions were presented as cut-and-dried data. In practice, the details of each transaction must be determined from documentation known as **source documents**. A wide variety of source documents exists, for example receipts, invoices, cash slips and cheque counterfoils.

Source documents usually contain the following information:

- the **nature** of the transaction (eg a credit sale or a cash payment)
- the **amount** of the transaction
- the **date** of the transaction
- the **parties** to the transaction.

The completion of a source document is the **first step** in the **accounting cycle**, and provides the information needed later for recording the transaction in the accounting records.

7.2.2 Recording

An undertaking normally has a wide variety of transactions which have to be entered in the accounting records. The recording of these transactions is the **second step** in the accounting cycle. To facilitate the recording process the transactions must be arranged into groups having common characteristics.

Recording takes place, as will be explained later, by the **journalising** and **posting** of transaction data and, where necessary, also includes **adjustments** to the recorded data.

7.2.3 Reporting

The processing of recorded data, which includes **closing off the ledger**, leads to the next step in the accounting cycle, namely reporting. **Reporting** the undertaking's business result and its financial position takes place, as we have already seen, via the financial statements.

Therefore reporting is a communication function.

7.2.4 Analysis and interpretation

The reporting function ensures that accounting information is conveyed to interested users of the information who will **analyse** and **interpret** it. This is the **fourth step** in the accounting cycle.

Furthermore, the owner(s) of the undertaking can measure the profitability and the short and long-term financial stability of the enterprise against empirical norms. If the analysed results are not in line with these norms, the causes for the deviations or shortcomings must be determined or **interpreted**.

7.2.5 Decision making

Analysis and interpretation of financial information enables interested persons to make **decisions** regarding an undertaking (eg whether the sale of a particular product must be continued or not).

Such decisions taken by the management of an undertaking influence its future transactions. This is the last step in the accounting cycle and also completes the cycle, as shown in the diagram below:

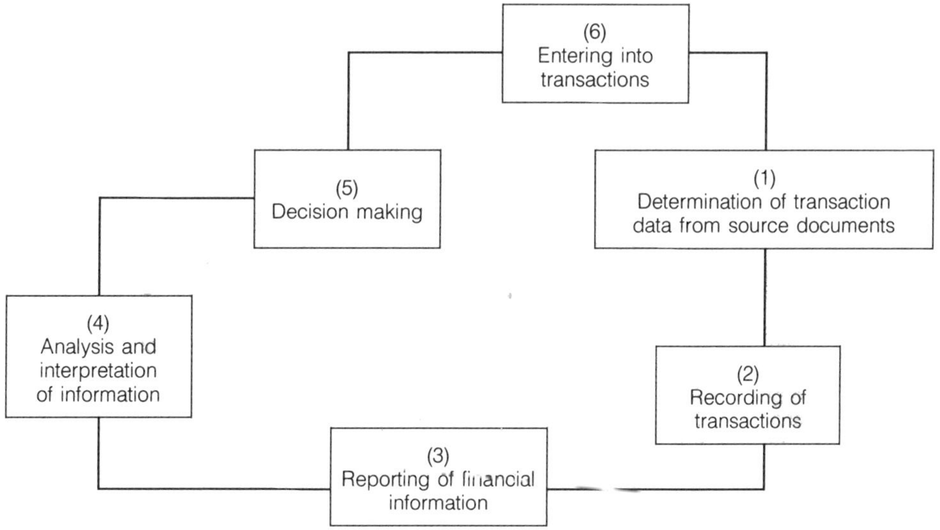

7.3 BOOKS OF PRIME ENTRY: JOURNALS

Although ledger accounts, as discussed in chapter 6, to a large extent constitute a condensation of transaction data, their principal function is classification and storage. What with the rapid pace of modern business, entering each transaction individually in a ledger account is just as impractical as adjusting the accounting equation (or the balance sheet) after each transaction. Since the extent of the transactions undertaken by a business is almost unlimited, the transactions must be analysed and recorded before being entered into the ledger. **Analysis and initial recording is the second step in the accounting cycle**.

Transaction data from source documents is recorded in the books of prime entry initially and thereafter posted to the ledger accounts.

This step is known as **journalising**. The initial records of transactions are referred to as **journals or books of prime entry**.

The journal is a chronological record of the transactions undertaken by a business and, as a book of prime entry, serves as a link between the source documents and the ledger accounts.

In practice different types of journals or books of prime entry are used. This facilitates the allocation of duties, in that different people can work on separate books of prime entry. The use of journals also provides more information about the transactions, since ledger accounts provide only limited information.

In this chapter only three types of journals are discussed:

- ☐ the general journal
- ☐ the cash receipts journal
- ☐ the cash payments journal.

Other types of journals are discussed in later chapters.

It must be emphasised that the journal does not replace the ledger (in fact the use of the journal does not change the most important function of the ledger, viz collection and classification) and second, that no transaction can be entered in the ledger before it has been recorded in a book of prime entry.

As indicated, the recording of the various elements of a transaction in a book of prime entry is known as journalising, and a journalised transaction is known as a **journal entry**.

Journal entries can take various forms, as we will see later; nevertheless each journal entry should contain the following information:

- ☐ Date of the transaction.
- ☐ Description of the accounts which must be debited and credited.
- ☐ The amount (or amounts) which are debited and credited.
- ☐ A short description of the transaction, usually known as the narration.

7.4 THE GENERAL JOURNAL

The basic book of prime entry is known as the **general journal**. Shown below is a general journal page (the headings of the various columns are shown here purely for the sake of clarity and will not be repeated in subsequent examples):

GENERAL JOURNAL				
Date	Details	Folio	Debit	Credit

This journal is also known as a two-column journal.

The **folio column** is used to indicate the ledger account to which a specific item is posted. Each ledger account also has a folio column indicating the page of the journal from which the amount has been posted, so that complete cross-referencing exists. Another function of the folio column is that the reference entered in the folio column serves to confirm the posting of the amount.

Example 7.1

The transaction below illustrates the basic journalising and posting process:

H Botha commences business as an estate agent, known as HB Agency, on 1 February, and transfers office equipment, which he owns and which is valued at R1 000, to the business.

This transaction will be journalised as follows:

Explanatory notes

HB AGENCY GENERAL JOURNAL				J1 ← (7)
(1) → 19.4				
(2) → Feb 1	Office equipment		1 000	
	(3) → Capital: H Botha			1 000
	(4) → Equipment brought in by owner			
			↑ (5)	↑ (6)

Explanatory notes

(1) The year, month and day on which the transaction was concluded are entered at the top of the page in the date column. As will be seen below, several transactions can be entered on one journal page. The year and month are re-entered on that page only in the case of a change. The day's date is usually entered for each transaction.

(2) The title of the account to be debited is entered in the details column, next to the date column.

(3) The title of the account to be credited is also entered in the details column, but slightly indented.

(4) The narration (a brief explanation) of the transaction is entered below the entry in the details column. Often, as in the example, the narration includes a reference to the source documents concerned.

(5) The amount to be debited is entered in the debit column.
(6) The amount to be credited is entered in the credit column.
(7) For ease of reference, all journal pages are numbered consecutively.

7.5 POSTING TO THE GENERAL LEDGER

After a transaction has been journalised, the next step in the accounting cycle is the transfer of the essential information regarding each journal entry to the ledger. This procedure is known as posting.

HB AGENCY

GENERAL JOURNAL				J1
19.4 Feb 1	Office equipment Capital: H Botha Office equipment brought in by owner	L1 L8	1 000	 1 000

(1) (2) (4) (3)

GENERAL LEDGER

OFFICE EQUIPMENT							L1
19.4 Feb 1	Capital: H Botha	J1	1 000				

CAPITAL: H BOTHA							L8
				19.4 Feb 1	Office equipment	J1	1 000

Explanatory notes

(1) The debit amount and journal reference, as well as the date of the transaction, are transferred to the debit side of the relevant ledger account.
(2) To complete the cross-reference of the debit posting, the number (code) of the relevant ledger account is entered in the folio column of the journal.
(3) The credit amount and journal reference, as well as the date of the transaction, are transferred to the credit side of the relevant ledger account.
(4) To complete the cross-reference of the credit posting, the number (code) of the relevant ledger account is entered in the folio column of the journal (L = ledger and J = journal).

Note that ledger accounts do not usually provide comprehensive explanations of transactions. Generally, the description of an item in a ledger account consists of the title of the other ledger account involved in the transaction. The explanation as given in the journal can be traced by means of the journal reference in the ledger.

7.6 SPECIFIC JOURNALS OR BOOKS OF PRIME ENTRY

If all transactions are recorded in a general journal, each transaction will have to be posted individually to the relevant ledger account. This is impractical and therefore transactions are recorded in specific and individual (usually columnar) journals. Transactions are classified into groups which are similar in nature. Each repetitive type of transaction is recorded in a specific columnar journal or book of prime entry. Specific journals reduce the work load involved in repeating individual journal entries for similar transactions and posting these transactions to the general ledger.

7.6.1 The cash receipts journal[1]

All transactions in respect of cash receipts that will result in an increase in the bank balance of the undertaking are recorded in this journal (or book of prime entry), and from here are posted to the general ledger.

7.6.2 The cash payments journal[1]

All transactions in respect of cheque payments by the undertaking which will result in a decrease in the bank balance are recorded in this journal.

Example 7.2 illustrates the basic journalising and posting procedures in respect of the above journals. In this example frequent reference is made to the relevant source documents:

Example 7.2

H Botha commences business on 1 February 19.4 as an estate agent, known as HB Agency, and concludes the following transactions during February:

19.4

February
- 1 Botha transfers office equipment, which he owns and which is valued at R1 000, to the business.
- 2 Botha opens a bank account for the agency by depositing R5 000 into the account (as per receipt 001 of the agency).[1] On the same day the agency invests R1 200 on fixed deposit with X Bank (cheque no A001).
- 3 The agency pays R1 200 rent, by cheque no A002, for the office premises for the three months ended 30 April 19.4.
- 4 The business buys additional office furniture for R2 000 and pays by cheque no A003.
- 5 Stationery is purchased on credit from Durban Printers for R700 (invoice no DD799).
- 6 Completes a transaction for a client and receives commission of R500 for services rendered (receipt no 002).
- 7 Pays wages for the week: R150 by cheque no A004.
- 14 Pays wages for the week: R150 by cheque no A005.
- 15 Completes a transaction for Azed Builders and invoices them for commission of R800 (debit note no HB001).
- 20 H Botha withdraws R300 for his own use by cheque no A006.
- 21 Pays wages for the week: R150 by cheque no A007.
- 25 Azed Builders pay R400 on account (receipt no 003).
- 27 Pays R300 on account to Durban Printers by cheque no A008.
- 28 Enters into a transaction with Durban Building Society to render services to them for a fixed remuneration of R300 by month. On the same day the building society pays R300 commission in respect of March (receipt no 004).
- 29 Pays the telephone account for the month: R50 by cheque no A009.

1 As explained previously, the examples in this book assume that all monies are deposited in the undertaking's bank account, and that all cheque payments are made from the undertaking's bank account (unless otherwise stated).

The transactions will be recorded as follows:

☐ **Cash receipts**

HB AGENCY						
CASH RECEIPTS JOURNAL – FEBRUARY 19.4						(CRJ1)
Date	Details	Folio	Receipt no	Bank (Dr)	Commission received (Cr)	Sundries (Cr)
19.4						
Feb 2	H Botha: Capital	L5	001	5 000		5 000
6	Commission received	—	002	500	500	
25	Azed Builders	L4	003	400		400
28	Commission	—	004	300	300	
				R6 200	R800	R5 400
				(L2)	(L8)	
				Debit the total to the bank account	Credit the total to the commission account	Entries in the sundries column are credited individually to the relevant accounts in the general ledger

Explanatory notes

(1) The above is an example of a simple columnar cash receipts journal. Such a journal may comprise as many columns as are required.

(2) When posting from the cash receipts journal to the ledger the dual entry is maintained in the following manner:

	Dr	Cr
Bank account	6 200	
Capital		5 000
Azed Builders		400
Commission		800
	R6 200	R6 200

(3) Note that cash receipts which are similar in nature (in the above example, commission received) are recorded in the same column in the cash receipts journal. At the end of the month only the **total of the commission received column** is posted to the relevant account in the ledger. Note where the folio references are placed.

(4) Items which cannot be grouped together in this way because they are very different in nature are recorded in the sundries column and are posted individually to the relevant ledger accounts.

(5) All cash receipts are recorded both:

☐ in an analysis column (eg the sundries or commission received column) **and**

☐ in the bank column.

Therefore the totals of the analysis columns will always tally with the total of the bank column (in the example above R5 400 + R800 = R6 200). This is known as the **cross-casting** of a subsidiary journal.

(6) Note the folio reference (CRJ1) of the cash receipts journal which is, as has already been explained, used in the posting procedure.

☐ Payments by cheque

HB AGENCY

CASH PAYMENTS JOURNAL – FEBRUARY 19.4 (CPJ1)

Date	Details	Folio	Cheque no	Sundries (Dr)	Wages (Dr)	Bank (Cr)
19.4						
Feb 2	Fixed deposit: X Bank	L3	A001	1 200		1 200
3	Rental	L10	A002	1 200		1 200
4	Office equipment	L1	A003	2 000		2 000
7	Wages	—	A004		150	150
14	Wages	—	A005		150	150
20	Drawings	L6	A006	300		300
21	Wages	—	A007		150	150
27	Durban Printers	L7	A008	300		300
29	Telephone	L12	A009	50		50
				R5 050	R450	R5 500
					(L11)	(L2)

Entries in the sundries column are **debited invividually** to the relevant accounts in the general ledger

Debit total of wages column to wages account

Credit total to bank account

Explanatory notes

(1) The above is an example of a simple columnar cash payments journal. Such a journal may comprise as many columns as are required.

(2) When posting from the cash payments journal to the ledger the dual entry is maintained in the following manner (see the general ledger below):

Savings account	Dr	1 200	
Rent	Dr	1 200	
Office equipment	Dr	2 000	
Drawings	Dr	300	
Durban Printers	Dr	300	
Telephone	Dr	50	
Wages	Dr	450	
Bank account	Cr		5 500

(3) Note that cash payments which are similar in nature (in the above example, wages) are recorded in the same column in the cash payments journal. At the end of the month only the total of the wages column is debited to the wages account.

(4) Items which cannot be grouped together in this way because they are very different in nature are recorded in the sundries column and are posted individually to the relevant ledger accounts.

(5) All payments are recorded both:

☐ in an analysis column (eg the sundries or wages column) **and**

☐ in the bank column.

The totals of the analysis columns will therefore always tally (cross-cast) with the total of the bank column (ie R5 050 + R450 = R5 500).

(6) Note the folio reference (CPJ1) of the cash payments journal which, as has already been explained, is used in the posting procedure.

The remaining transactions which occurred during the month do not consist of cash receipts or payments and therefore cannot be recorded in one of these two subsidiary journals. They are recorded in the general journal.

☐ **General journal**

HB AGENCY GENERAL JOURNAL – FEBRUARY 19.4		J1		
		Folio	Dr	Cr
19.4 Feb 1	Office equipment Capital: H Botha *Office equipment brought in by owner*	L1 L5	1 000	 1 000
Feb 5	Stationery Durban Printers *Stationery bought on credit from Durban Printers per invoice no DD799*	L9 L7	700	 700
Feb 15	Azed Builders Commission *Client invoiced per invoice no HB001 for services rendered*	L4 L8	800	 800

☐ **Posting to the general ledger**

The entries in the subsidiary journals are now posted to the general ledger and the relevant folio references are recorded in the journals and the ledger (in this example the ledger accounts have been allocated consecutive numbers for the sake of simplicity). As will be explained later, systematically codified account systems and folio references are often used.

HB AGENCY GENERAL LEDGER							
Dr			OFFICE EQUIPMENT		(Account L1)		Cr
19.4 Feb 1 4	 Capital: H Botha Bank	 J1 CPJ1	 1 000 2 000				
Dr			BANK		(Account L2)		Cr
19.4 Feb 18	Receipts	CRJ1	6 200	19.4 Feb 28	Payments	CPJ1	5 500
Dr			FIXED DEPOSIT		(Account L3)		Cr
19.4 Feb 2	Bank	CPJ1	1 200				

Dr		AZED BUILDERS				(Account L4)	Cr
19.4 Feb 15	Commission	J1	800	19.4 Feb 25	Bank	CRJ1	400

Dr		CAPITAL: H BOTHA				(Account L5)	Cr
				19.4 Feb 1 2	Office equipment Bank	J1 CRJ1	1 000 5 000

Dr		DRAWINGS: H BOTHA				(Account L6)	Cr
19.4 Feb 20	Bank	CPJ1	300				

Dr		DURBAN PRINTERS				(Account L7)	Cr
19.4 Feb 27	Bank	CPJ1	300	19.4 Feb 5	Stationery	J1	700

Dr		COMMISSION				(Account L8)	Cr
				19.4 Feb 15 28	Azed Builders Bank	J1 CRJ1	800 800

Dr		STATIONERY				(Account L9)	Cr
19.4 Feb 5	Durban Printers	J1	700				

Dr		RENTAL				(Account L10)	Cr
19.4 Feb 3	Bank	CPJ1	1 200				

Dr		WAGES				(Account L11)	Cr
19.4 Feb 18	Bank	CPJ1	450				

Dr		TELEPHONE				(Account L12)	Cr
19.4 Feb 28	Bank	CPJ1	50				

☐ Extraction of a trial balance

As explained in the previous chapter, the accounts in the general ledger are now balanced (provisionally with pencil totals) and a trial balance is extracted as follows:

HB AGENCY
TRIAL BALANCE – 28 FEBRUARY 19.4

Office equipment	L1	3 000	
Bank	L2	700	
Fixed deposit	L3	1 200	
Azed Builders	L4	400	
Capital: H Botha	L5		6 000
Drawings: H Botha	L6	300	
Durban Printers	L7		400
Commission	L8		1 600
Stationery	L9	700	
Rental	L10	1 200	
Wages	L11	450	
Telephone	L12	50	
		R8 000	R8 000

7.7 LIMITATIONS OF THE TRIAL BALANCE

The fact that the debit and credit balances of a trial balance agree is *prima facie* evidence of the accuracy of the accounting records; it is not indisputable evidence that there are no errors in the records.

7.7.1 Errors not revealed by a trial balance

☐ Errors of omission

The **complete omission** of an entry – in other words neither the debit nor the credit portion of the transaction is recorded.

☐ Posting to the wrong account

An item is posted to the **correct side** of the ledger, but to the **wrong account**, for example stationery to the value of R150 is bought for cash from J Erwee.

BANK

	150

STATIONERY

J ERWEE

150	

In this example the amount has been incorrectly debited to Erwee's account instead of to stationery, but the trial balance will still balance.

☐ **Compensating errors**

Incorrect addition, balancing or posting on one side of the ledger is coincidentally compensated for by an identical error made on the other side of the ledger.

☐ **Errors of principle**

In this case the principle underlying the recording of the transaction is faulty, for example debiting repairs to a motor vehicle to the motor vehicle account instead of to the repairs account.

7.7.2 Errors which are revealed by a trial balance

The failure of a trial balance to balance can be attributed to one or more of the following errors:

(a) The trial balance has been incorrectly cast.

(b) An error has been made in transferring the ledger balances to the trial balance:
- (i) an incorrect amount has been transferred to the correct side of the trial balance
- (ii) debit balances in the ledger have been transferred to the credit side of the trial balance, or *vice versa*
- (iii) a ledger balance has been entirely omitted from the trial balance
- (iv) a ledger balance has been entered twice in the trial balance.

(c) Balances of the ledger accounts have been incorrectly calculated:
- (i) either the debit or the credit side, or both, have been incorrectly added and therefore the balance of the account is incorrect
- (ii) the debit and credit sides have been correctly added, but the balance has been incorrectly calculated.

(d) Postings to the ledger from a journal may be incorrect:
- (i) a debit item in the journal may have been posted as a credit item, or *vice versa*
- (ii) an incorrect amount has been posted
- (iii) the posting of a debit or a credit has been entirely omitted
- (iv) a debit or a credit has been posted twice.

(e) The debit and credit balances in one or more journal entries may be incorrect.

7.7.3 Tracing errors in the trial balance

Discrepancies in the trial balance can be traced more easily when trial balances are drawn up monthly. If the trial balance of the previous month balanced, the error must have occurred in the current month.

To trace a discrepancy in a trial balance, the following steps should be carried out in the order listed. The general aim of this method is to 'work back' – in other words, the last step completed before the trial balance was extracted is the first one to be scrutinised, and so on until the error is traced. If the debit and credit balances on the trial balance differ, the procedure is as follows:

(a) Cast each column in the trial balance again.

(b) Check the transfer of ledger balances to the trial balance and ensure that:
- (i) the amounts have been transferred correctly
- (ii) the amounts have been transferred to the correct side.

(c) Recalculate the balances of the ledger accounts to ensure that they are correct.

(d) Check the transfers from the journals to the ledger.

(e) Check the accuracy of the amounts in the journal entries. The following should be noted:

(i) Where two columns of figures differ by 1, for example 1 000; 100; 10;1; 0,1; 0,01, the difference is likely to be a casting error in the trial balance, ledger or journal.

(ii) A difference between the two columns of the trial balance which can be divided by 2 may indicate that a debit balance equal to half the difference has been entered as a credit balance, or *vice versa*. Should a debit balance be transferred as a credit to the trial balance, the debit side will reflect a shortfall of that amount and the credit side will be overstated by the same amount.

Therefore the difference will be twice the actual amount involved in the error.

In this case an error involving an amount equal to half of the difference between the two sides may have been made. If such an error is traced the amount must be correctly transferred and recorded.

(iii) If the difference between the two columns is divisible by 9, the error may be due to a transposition of numbers: in other words the digits are not in the correct order, for example, 34 written as 43, or 360 as 630. If the difference is divided by 9, the resulting quotient will represent the difference between the digits which have been reversed.

For example, if R36 has been written as R63, the difference in the trial balance will be R27 and the quotient will be 3 (27 ÷ 9) – that is the difference between 6 and 3 in the transposed amount. If the quotient is a single digit, the transposition occurred in the tens and the units columns. If the quotient has two digits the transposition took place in the tens and hundreds columns, for example R360 written as R630. The difference between these two amounts is R270 and the quotient is 30 (270 ÷ 9), that is the transposition between 6 and 3 in the hundreds and tens columns. In this instance discrepancies must be looked for on both sides of the trial balance where the difference between the figures in the columns is equal to the specific quotient, for example if R321 184 is written R312 184, the difference will be R9 000. The quotient is therefore 1 000. This indicates a discrepancy in the thousands and ten-thousands columns, the 21 being written as 12.

(iv) Alternatively, if the difference in the trial balance is divisible by 9, the discrepancy may also be due to a one-column shift: in other words a digit may have been moved either one place to the right or to the left, without changing the order of the digits as in (iii) above. For example, R48,60 is written as R4,86. The difference on the trial balance in this case will be R43,74 (48,60 – 4,86) and if this is divided by 9, the quotient will be R4,86. The trial balance must be checked for an amount in which the figures 486 occur in that order and if such an amount does occur, further investigation should be made into the accuracy of this entry.

Similarly, if the difference on the trial balance is divisible by 99, a two-column shift could have occurred, for example if R48,60 was written as R4 860, etc.

8

THE ADJUSTMENT PROCESS

The **AIM** of this chapter is to discuss typical adjustments that must be made to ledger accounts before financial statements can be prepared.

8.1 THE PRE-ADJUSTMENT TRIAL BALANCE

In paragraph 7.6 the following trial balance was extracted from the general ledger of HB Agencies at 28 February 19.4:

HB AGENCIES
TRIAL BALANCE AT 28 FEBRUARY 19.4

Office equipment	L1	3 000	
Bank	L2	700	
Fixed deposit	L3	1 200	
Azed Builders	L4	400	
Capital: H Botha	L5		6 000
Drawings: H Botha	L6	300	
Durban Printers	L7		400
Commission	L8		1 600
Stationery	L9	700	
Rental	L10	1 200	
Wages	L11	450	
Telephone	L12	50	
		R8 000	R8 000

The trial balance shown above is referred to as a **pre-adjustment** trial balance. Before the income statement and balance sheet of the undertaking at 28 February 19.4 can be prepared, it is important to determine whether all income, expenses and the attendant assets and liabilities relating to February have been taken into account.

8.2 THE FINANCIAL PERIOD

It has already been pointed out that an enterprise usually conducts its business without interruption and on a permanent basis. Since managers and owners and also the State (especially for the purpose of annual taxation) require regular information regarding the enterprise's financial result and financial position, it is customary to determine the profit or loss **periodically**. Therefore the life of an enterprise is divided into equal intervals of time which vary in length according to managerial requirements. However, at least annually, reports are issued to both the owners and the State. These intervals of time are referred to as (monthly/yearly) **financial periods**.

8.3 ADJUSTMENT OF ACCOUNTS

The **accrual principle**, which arises as a result of the accounting period concept, is dealt with in chapter 4. This principle determines that only income realised during a specific period, and only those expenses incurred during that same period, should be brought into account in determining the profit for that period.

It was explained further that an enterprise could receive cash representing income in a period other than that in which it was received. Similarly, the enterprise could incur expenses related to a period other than that in which they are incurred.

To determine the profit and financial position correctly, it is necessary to apportion income and expenditure to the period to which they pertain.

The **matching principle**, also dealt with in chapter 4, similarly requires that income and expenses incurred to generate that income be accounted for in the **same financial period**.

To give effect to the accrual and matching principles, it is necessary to examine all income and expense accounts and the facts pertaining to all income and expense items. Where necessary, appropriate **adjustments** must be made to these accounts before the financial statements can be prepared.

8.4 TYPICAL ADJUSTMENTS

Adjustments fall into two categories according to the length of the term relating to the adjustment, namely **short-term** and **long-term adjustments**.

Short-term adjustments apply where income or expenditure is apportioned to successive periods falling within the space of a year, for example income or expenses received or incurred during a specific period, but which pertain to the previous or following period. Long-term adjustments apply to income received or expenses incurred during a period, but which pertain to a whole series of future periods.

In the case of short-term adjustments, the period to which the specific income or expenditure relates is usually definite. Long-term adjustments, on the other hand, generally require a judgemental estimation of the total duration of the periods to which the item must be apportioned.

8.5 SHORT-TERM ADJUSTMENTS

Short-term adjustments can be classified into the following categories:

- ☐ Prepaid expenses
- ☐ Inventory adjustments
- ☐ Accrued expenses
- ☐ Provision for accrued expenses
- ☐ Income received in advance
- ☐ Accrued income.

8.5.1 Prepaid expenses

A prepaid expense is an expense which, although paid during a specific financial period, also pertains to subsequent periods. Only that part of the expense relevant to any particular period or consumed within that period may be brought into account as an expense for that period; the rest of the prepaid expense is by nature an asset, since the entity will only consume or utilise it in subsequent periods.

The short-term apportionment of an expense involves three steps:

(i) Ascertain which accounts must be adjusted and determine the balance of these accounts
(ii) Apportion the balance to its appropriate expense and asset elements
(iii) Record the adjustment.

Example 8.1

Step (i) Identifying the appropriate account

On 3 February 19.4, HB Agencies pays R1 200 **in advance** for three months' rental.

Step (ii) Apportion the item to its asset and expense elements

The monthly rental is therefore R1 200 ÷ 3 = R400 per month. By the end of February only R400 of the total amount paid has actually been used as rental. This means that only R400 can be taken into account as a rental expense for February. The remaining R800 represents an amount which will only be used in the future (i e the asset element).

This can be represented as follows:

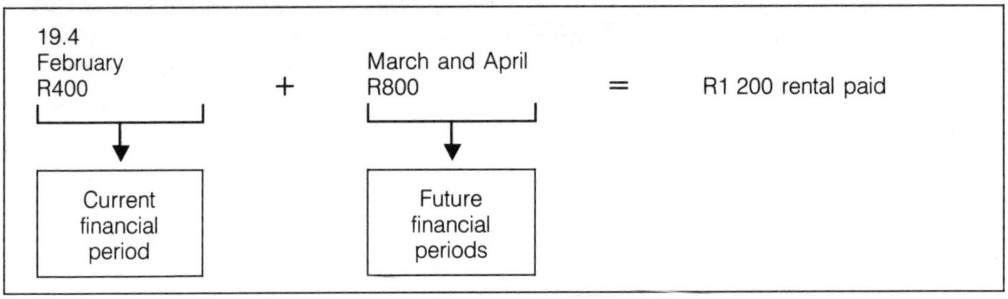

The account 'rental' therefore consists of an expense as well as an asset element:

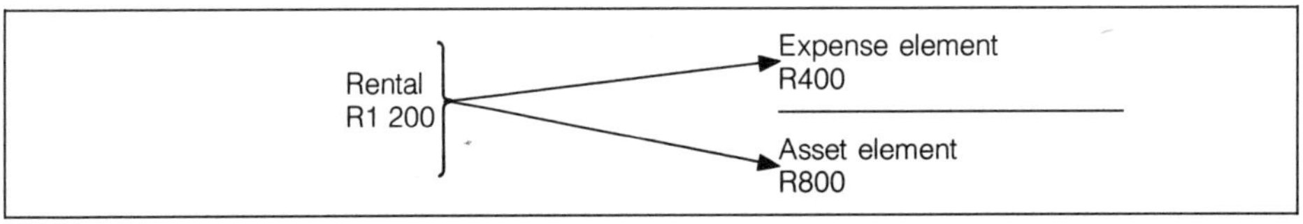

Step (iii) Recording the adjustment

The asset element must be transferred from the rental account (an expense account) to an asset account, rental prepaid. This step can be represented schematically as follows:

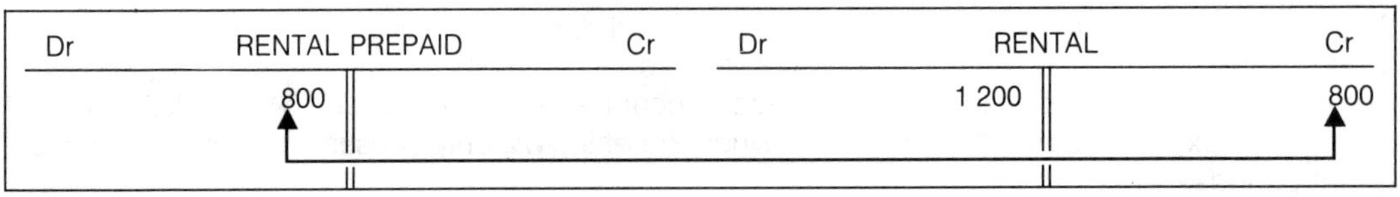

This transfer is an adjustment transaction which is recorded by means of a journal entry (known as an adjustment journal entry) and posted to the relevant ledger accounts:

GENERAL JOURNAL				J2
19.4 Feb 28	Rental prepaid Rental *Recording of prepaid rental*	L13 L10	800	 800

Dr			GENERAL LEDGER				Cr
			RENTAL			Account no L10	
19.4 Feb 10	Bank	CPJ1	1 200	19.4 Feb 28	Rental prepaid	J2	800
			RENTAL PREPAID			Account no L13	
19.4 Feb 28	Rental	J2	800				

The balance on the rental prepaid account (R800), which is equivalent to a 'debtor', will be shown under **current assets** on the balance sheet. The balance of the rental account, R400 (R1 200 – R800), will appear in the income statement for February as an **expense**.

8.5.2 Inventory adjustments

The need for inventory adjustments arises when, during a financial period, an enterprise has purchased goods which have not been completely consumed by the end of that period. Expenditure on goods becomes an expense only when those goods are consumed.

Example 8.2

HB Agencies buys stationery on 5 February at a cost of R700. The expenditure is debited to the stationery account. On 28 February (the closing or accounting date of the financial period in question, ie the month of February) there is still stationery inventory of R500, at cost, on hand.

The stationery account on 28 February therefore has an asset as well as an expense element:

Stationery account (total cost price = R700) →	Expense element = stock consumed during February = R200 (R700 – R500)
	Asset element = stock on hand = R500 (total stock available – stock consumed (R700 – R200))

The situation is recorded as follows:

GENERAL JOURNAL				J2
19.4 Feb 28	Stationery stock Stationery *Recording of stock on hand at 28 February 19.4*	L14 L9	500	 500

Dr			GENERAL LEDGER				Cr
			STATIONERY STOCK		Account no L14		
19.4 Feb 28	Stationery	J2	500				
			STATIONERY		Account no L9		
19.4 Feb 28	Durban Printers	J1	700	19.4 Feb 28	Stationery stock	J2	500

The debit on the stationery account is an **expense** item which will appear in the income statement for February, while the stationery on hand (that is, the balance of R500 on the stationery inventory account) will be entered as a **current asset** in the balance sheet.

8.5.3 Arrear or accrued expenses

These are expenses incurred during a specific financial period but which have not yet been paid:

- ☐ To determine the profit correctly for the period, the expense must be brought into account.
- ☐ If the balance sheet is to give a fair reflection of the financial position, the corresponding liability must be shown.

Recording this type of adjustment also involves three separate steps:

(i) Identify the account concerned.
(ii) Determine the amount still owed.
(iii) Record the adjustment by debiting the specific account with the amount still owing and crediting the corresponding liability.

Example 8.3

Step (i) Identify the account concerned

A trial balance for the agency shows that wages of R450 were paid during February. Analysis of the wages account shows that wages of R150 are paid weekly; it also shows that wages paid to date cover only the period to 21 February (3 × R150 = R450).

Step (ii) Determine the amount still owed

Thus on 28 February, one week's wages (R150) still have to be paid to employees for services rendered during February.

Step (iii) Record the adjustment

Dr	WAGES	Cr
Bank	450	
Wages accrued	150	

Dr	WAGES ACCRUED	Cr
	Wages	150

GENERAL JOURNAL				Page 2
19.4 Feb 28	Wages Wages accrued *Recording of wages due for the week 21 – 28 February 19.4*	L11 L15	150	 150

Dr		GENERAL LEDGER					Cr
			WAGES			Account no L11	
19.4 Feb 28 28	 Bank Wages accrued	 CPJ1 J2	 450 150 600				
			WAGES ACCRUED			Account no L15	
				19.4 Feb 28	 Wages	 J2	 150

The balance of the wages account is reflected on the income statement as an expense for the specific period under consideration. 'Wages accrued' is equivalent to creditors and is shown under **current liabilities** in the balance sheet.

8.5.4 Provision for accrued expenses

It frequently happens that a specific expense item cannot be determined with complete accuracy at the end of a financial period. Often, too, it is known that an expense has been incurred by an enterprise with respect to a specific period, but at the end of that period no enforceable liability yet exists.

In cases where, at the end of a period, an expense has not yet become an enforceable liability, or where the amount has not been finally determined, the following three steps are required to bring the transaction into account:

(i) Identify the account concerned.
(ii) Determine the amount.
(iii) Record the transaction by debiting the expense account concerned and crediting a provision account.

Example 8.4

Assume that on 26 February the enterprise sends one of its typewriters for a service which has not yet been completed by 28 February. The cost of servicing the typewriter is estimated at R20.

GENERAL JOURNAL				J2
19.4 Feb 28	Repairs: Office equipment Provision for repairs: Office equipment *Provision for expected expenses pertaining to repair of typewriter*	L16 L17	20	 20

Dr		GENERAL LEDGER					Cr
		REPAIRS: OFFICE EQUIPMENT				Account no L16	
19.4 Feb 28	Provision for repairs	J2	20				
		PROVISION FOR REPAIRS: OFFICE EQUIPMENT				Account no L17	
				19.4 Feb 28	Repairs	J2	20

Provision for repairs is a short-term liability (a 'creditor') and will appear as a current liability in the balance sheet, while 'repairs' is an expense for the period under consideration and therefore will be shown in the income statement.

8.5.5 Income received in advance

Income received may have to be allocated to at least two accounting periods. The same three steps mentioned previously must be followed:

(i) Identify the account to be adjusted and determine the balance on the account.

(ii) Apportion the balance on the account between the income element (that portion earned during the current period) and the liability element (that portion of the amount already received but for which services still have to be rendered during a future period).

(iii) Record the adjustment by crediting the liability element of the total income received to an income received in advance account, and debiting income received.

Example 8.5

Step (i) Identify the appropriate account

On 28 February 19.4, HB Agencies concludes a contract to supply professional services to Durban Building Society for a fixed fee of R300 per month. The first payment is received on 28 February, being an advance payment of the fee for March. This amount is included in the commission account (R1 600) on the pre-adjustment trial balance at 28 February.

Step (ii) Apportion the balance to the accounts concerned

The balance of the commission account will be apportioned as follows:

	CURRENT PERIOD	FUTURE PERIOD
Balance on commission at 28/2/19.4 (R1 600) =	February 19.4 R1 300 ↓ Income element	March 19.4 R300 ↓ Liability element

Dr	COMMISSION		Cr
Commission received in advance	300	Balance	1 600

Dr	COMMISSION RECEIVED IN ADVANCE		Cr
		Commission	300

Step (iii) Record the adjustment

GENERAL JOURNAL				J2
19.4 Feb 28	Commission Commission received in advance *Commission due in March, but received in February*	L8 L18	300	 300

Dr			GENERAL LEDGER				Cr
			COMMISSION			Account no L8	
19.4 Feb 28	Commission received in advance	J2	300	19.4 Feb 15 28	Azed Builders Bank	J1 CRJ1	800 800
			COMMISSION RECEIVED IN ADVANCE			Account no L18	
				19.4 Feb 28	Commission	J2	300

The credit balance (R300) on the commission received in advance account appears in the balance sheet as a **current liability**. The balance on the commission account after adjustment (R1 300), being income earned, is shown in the income statement.

8.5.6 Accrued income

This is income earned during a specific period but which has not yet been received. Again the income and the related asset will have to be recorded in the financial period under consideration so that the financial result and the financial position are reflected correctly and so that there is compliance with the realisation and matching principles.

The same adjustment procedure as before is followed.

Example 8.6

On 2 February 19.4, HB Agencies invests R1 200 on fixed deposit at 10% interest per annum. The interest earned during February, although not received, must nevertheless be calculated and recorded. The formula to calculate the interest is:

$$\text{Capital} \times \text{Interest rate} \times \text{Time} = \text{Interest}$$

Accordingly, on 28 February Botha's practice will calculate the interest accrued and due to it for February 19.4 as R10 (1 200 × 10% × 1 month).

The adjustment is recorded as follows:

GENERAL JOURNAL				J2
19.4 Feb 28	Interest receivable Interest earned *Interest at 10% on savings account due for February*	L19 L20	10	 10

Dr			GENERAL LEDGER				Cr
			INTEREST RECEIVABLE			Account no L19	
19.4 Feb 28	Interest earned	J2	10				
			INTEREST EARNED			Account no L20	
				19.4 Feb 28	Interest receivable	J2	10

The R10 interest accrued constitutes the asset element in the adjustment and will appear in the balance sheet as a **current asset**. The credit balance of R10 on the interest received account constitutes the **income element** and will eventually be reflected in the income statement for February.

8.6 LONG-TERM ADJUSTMENTS

When an enterprise incurs expenditure from which it expects to derive a long-term benefit, the expense is fairly apportioned over the entire period for which the asset is utilised. The most common example of this is the acquisition of fixed assets which have a relatively long but nevertheless limited lifespan. Long lifespan denotes any period exceeding 12 months. In accounting practice, assets with a long but limited lifespan are considered to become valueless eventually, since part of the asset is used each year until it is completely consumed.

Machinery provides a good example. If an enterprise spends a large amount on the acquisition of machinery, the total amount will not be brought into account as an expense in the period in which the machinery was acquired; rather, it will be apportioned over the estimated lifespan of the machinery. The lifespan of a fixed asset cannot be determined with certainty at the time of its acquisition, and it requires technical knowledge and judgement to estimate its lifespan. This contrasts with short-term adjustments, where there is usually certainty about the periods to which the adjustments relate.

The cost of a fixed asset is usually apportioned by writing off depreciation.

The same three steps listed before are followed in the adjustment procedure:

(i) Identify the account and the amount concerned.
(ii) Apportion the asset/expense elements according to the information available.
(iii) Record the adjustment.

Example 8.7

Step (i) Identify the accounts concerned

Early in February 19.4 HB Agencies purchases office equipment to the value of R3 000. The assets are used by the enterprise during February, therefore an appropriate portion of the cost must be apportioned to the period under consideration.

Step (ii) Apportion the amount

Assume that the enterprise has estimated that the lifespan of the equipment is 10 years, and that it must be written off in full over this period. The depreciation for one month will be:

$$R3\ 000 \times \frac{1}{120}\ \text{(months)}$$

$$= R25 \text{ per month}$$

(Note that depreciation can also be calculated on a percentage basis: a lifespan of 10 years means that $^1/_{10}$ of the cost (=10%) can be allocated annually to the cost item 'depreciation', eg R3 000 × 10% × 1 month = R25).

Step (iii) Record the adjustment

GENERAL JOURNAL				J2
19.4 Feb 28	Depreciation Accumulated depreciation: Office equipment *Provision at 10% per annum on cost price for furniture and equipment for February*	L21 L22	25	 25

Dr			GENERAL LEDGER				Cr
			DEPRECIATION			Account no L21	
19.4 Feb 28	Accumulated depre-ciation: Office equipment	J2	25				
			OFFICE EQUIPMENT			Account no L1	
19.4 Feb 1	Capital: H Botha Bank	J1 CPJ1	1 000 2 000				
			ACCUMULATED DEPRECIATION: OFFICE EQUIPMENT			Account no L22	
				19.4 Feb 28	Depreciation: Office equipment	J2	25

The latter is a new account. It is known as an asset contra account, because the credit balance of this account must be subtracted from the debit balance (or cost) of the asset account concerned in order to determine the book value of the asset. The accumulated depreciation can also be credited directly to the asset account, but this procedure is not recommended, since depreciation is purely an estimate of that part of the cost of an asset which is apportioned as an expense during a specific financial period.

The cost of the asset should preferably be shown separately from the estimated depreciation in the records, otherwise useful information may be lost.

In modern business practice detailed asset registers are kept, giving accurate details and descriptions of each specific asset.

The debit balance on the depreciation account is shown as an expense in the income statement, while the asset and accumulated depreciation accounts appear as follows in the balance sheet:

HB AGENCIES BALANCE SHEET AT 28 FEBRUARY 19.4		
Fixed assets		
Office equipment		1 983
At cost price	2 000	
Less: Accumulated depreciation	17	

In practice, where an undertaking has more than one type of fixed asset, the following layout is usually followed:

BALANCE SHEET AT . . .			
Fixed assets	Cost price	Accumulated depreciation	Net value
Land and buildings	50 000	—	50 000
Machinery and plant	100 000	30 000	70 000
Motor vehicles	90 000	40 000	50 000
Office equipment	10 000	2 000	8 000
	R250 000	72 000	178 000
Current assets			

8.7 THE POST-ADJUSTMENT TRIAL BALANCE

In this chapter a number of typical adjustments have been discussed. It is now possible to draw up an adjusted trial balance which reflects the adjusted balances of the accounts. This adjusted trial balance forms the basis for the preparation of the financial statements and is discussed further in chapter 9.

9

THE CLOSING PROCEDURE AND PREPARATION OF FINANCIAL STATEMENTS

The **AIM** of this chapter is to explain, first, the closing off of the relevant ledger accounts to final accounts and, second, the preparation of financial statements from a post-adjustment trial balance.

9.1 THE USE OF A WORKSHEET

In the previous chapter we described how, once all transactions had been recorded in the ledger, adjustment entries were made in the journal and posted to the general ledger, and an adjusted trial balance was extracted. In practice a **columnar worksheet** is often used as an aid to facilitate the adjustment process, the closing off of the general ledger and the eventual preparation of financial statements. The steps below are usually followed in drawing up a worksheet:

- ☐ The pre-adjustment trial balance is transferred to a 10-column worksheet (columns 1 and 2).
- ☐ Any required adjustments are debited or credited to the relevant items in the **adjustment columns** (columns 3 and 4) and noted for later reference. The adjustment entries may necessitate that additional items (accounts) are included in the worksheet in order that a double-entry may be completed for each item in the adjustment columns. Once the adjustments have been completed the debit and credit sides of the adjustment columns must balance.
- ☐ When the adjustments are complete, the post-adjustment trial balance is entered in the next two columns (columns 5 and 6).
- ☐ The items from the post-adjustment trial balance are allocated to the income statement and balance sheet columns; income and expense items to the income statement columns (columns 7 and 8) and assets, owner's equity and liability items to the balance sheet columns (columns 9 and 10).
- ☐ The debit and credit columns of the income statement are cast to determine the difference between the total debits and total credits. The difference constitutes the net profit or loss, depending whether the credit (income) or the debit (expense) amount is larger.
- ☐ The net profit (or loss) is entered in the balance sheet columns of the worksheet. A profit (as in the example below) will increase owner's equity and therefore must be credited. After the profit (or loss) has been recorded, the balance sheet columns must agree.

The completed worksheet can now be used as a basis from which to record the adjustment journal entries and the closing entries for the ledger and to prepare the financial statements. However it must be emphasised that the worksheet is only a 'working paper', and does not form part of the formal recording process.

Once again it is emphasised that the income statement and balance sheet **columns** in the following worksheet **are not** the **financial statements** of the undertaking. The worksheet is only a 'working paper' which is used to facilitate the adjustment and closing processes. Later in the chapter it will be explained that 'formal' financial statements still have to be prepared.

Example 9.1

The procedure for drawing up a worksheet is illustrated in the trial balance and adjustments of HB Agencies in chapter 8.

HB AGENCIES
WORKSHEET FOR THE MONTH ENDED 28 FEBRUARY 19.4

	Pre-adjustment trial balance (1)		Adjustments (2)		Post-adjustment trial balance		Income statement		Balance sheet	
	1	2	3	4	5	6	7	8	9	10
Account no	Dr	Cr	Dr	Cr	Dr	Cr	Dr	Cr	Dr	Cr
L1 Office equipment	3 000				3 000				3 000	
L2 Bank	700				700				700	
L3 Fixed deposit	1 200				1 200				1 200	
L4 Azed Builders	400				400				400	
L5 Capital: H Botha		6 000				6 000				6 000
L6 Drawings: H Botha	300				300				300	
L7 Durban Printers		400				400				400
L8 Commission		1 600	(5) 300			1 300		1 300		
L9 Stationery	700			(2) 500	200		200			
L10 Rental	1 200			(1) 800	400		400			
L11 Wages	450		(3) 150		600		600			
L12 Telephone	50				50		50			
	R8 000	R8 000								
L13 Rental prepaid			(1) 800		800				800	
L14 Stationery inventory			(2) 500		500				500	
L15 Wages accrued				(3) 150		150				150
L16 Repairs: Equipment			(4) 20		20		20			
L17 Provision for repairs: Equipment				(4) 20		20				20
L18 Commission received in advance				300		300				300
L19 Interest receivable			(6) 10		10				10	
L20 Interest earned				(6) 10		10		10		
L21 Depreciation: Office equipment			(7) 25		25		25			
L22 Accumulated depreciation: Office equipment				(7) 25		25				25
			R1 805	R1 805	R8 205	R8 205	1 295	1 310	6 910	6 895
Net income (R1 310 – R1 295)							15			15
							R1 310	R1 310	R6 910	R6 910

(1) Refer to paragraph 8.1.
(2) Refer to examples 8.1 to 8.7 in chapter 8.
(3) Note that because columns 7 – 10 are only an allocation of the balances in the post-adjustment trial balance (columns 5 and 6), they are equal to the total of the latter **two columns**: (ie Column 7 + Column 9 [R1 295 + R6 910 = R8 205] = Column 8 + Column 10 [R1 310 + R6 895 = R8 205]).

9.2 FINAL ACCOUNTS OF A SERVICE ENTERPRISE

We referred earlier to the basic groups into which accounts can be classified:

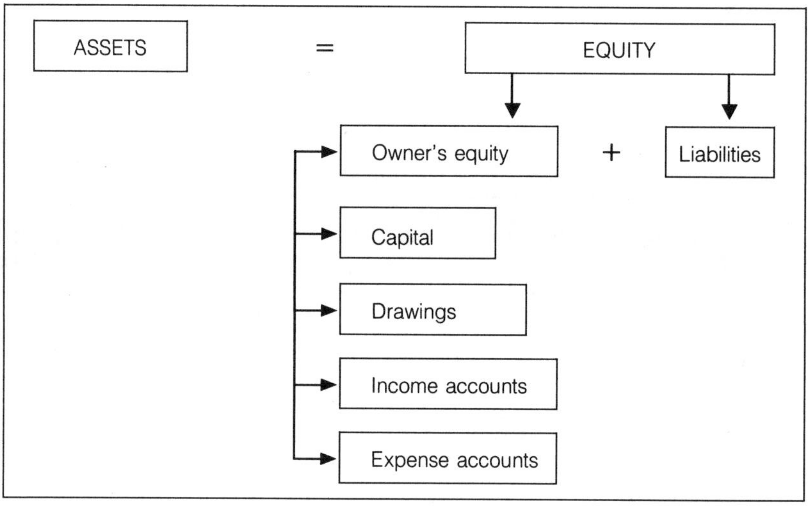

The income and expense accounts are **nominal accounts** in which income and expense items are entered temporarily, before being summarised periodically, the net result being transferred to the owner's equity account.

Those accounts to which the balances of the various income and expense accounts are transferred for the purpose of determining the eventual net income or net loss are called **final accounts**. The final accounts are designed to meet the specific requirements of an enterprise. A non-trading enterprise will use a single **income account** to record all income and expense items and from which to determine its net income. In contrast, a trading concern generally uses two accounts for determining profits; a **trading account** to determine **gross profit** and an **income account** to determine **net profit**. Gross profit is the difference between the proceeds from sales and the cost of the goods sold; net profit is the amount that remains once all other operating costs have been deducted from gross profit. A manufacturing concern will also use a **manufacturing account** to determine the cost of goods manufactured before these costs are transferred to the trading account.

A more detailed discussion of these accounts follows in later chapters.

9.2.1 Income account

The example below illustrates the transfer of items from the various nominal accounts to the final account to determine net income at the end of a period and the eventual transfer of net income to the owner's equity account.

As usual these transfers are done according to the double-entry system.

Any debit to an account must be accompanied by a corresponding credit to another account.

The following is a diagrammatic representation of the closing process:

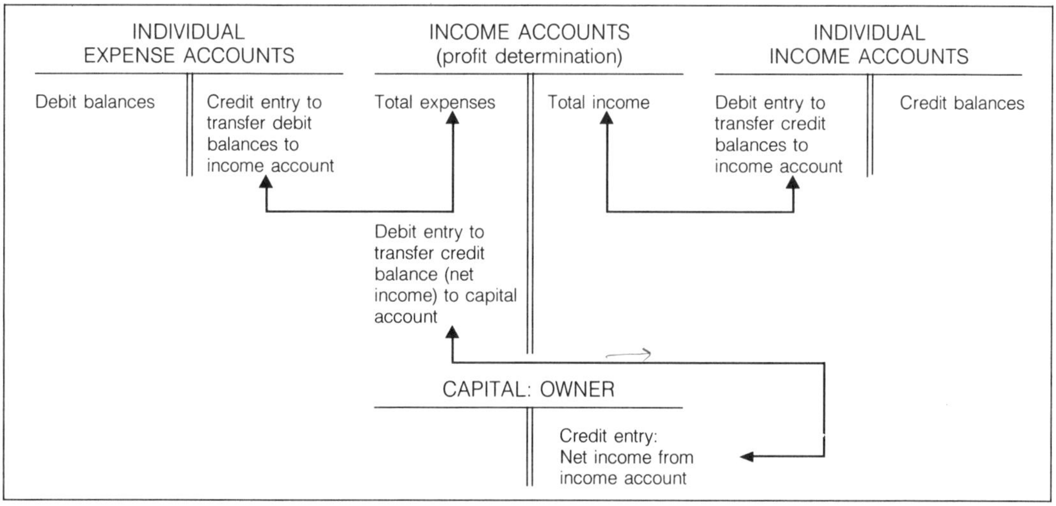

The income and expense accounts are closed off at the end of every financial period by transferring them to a single (or final) account in the ledger, that is the income account. These transfers from the nominal accounts are the first phase of the process of closing the ledger. The worksheet is a useful aid in the closing process, since all nominal accounts are reflected in the income statement columns of the worksheet.

Example 9.2

The closing entries of HB Agencies will appear as follows:

HB AGENCIES
GENERAL LEDGER[1]

INCOME ACCOUNT — Account no L23

Dr		Cr	
Expenses	1 295	Income	1 310

STATIONERY (L9)

Balance	200	Income account	200

RENTAL (L10)

Balance	400	Income account	400

WAGES (L11)

Balance	600	Income account	600

TELEPHONE (L12)

Balance	50	Income account	50

REPAIRS: OFFICE EQUIPMENT (L16)

Balance	20	Income account	20

DEPRECIATION (L21)

Balance	25	Income account	25

COMMISSION (L8)

Income account	1 300	Balance[2]	1 300

INTEREST EARNED (L20)

Income account	10	Balance	10

(1) Only the nominal income and expense accounts are shown.
(2) The balances shown are those determined after the necessary adjustments have been made. (Refer to the post-adjustment trial balance on the worksheet.)

These transfers to the final account are recorded by means of journal entries (known as **closing entries**) and posted to the ledger:

GENERAL JOURNAL				
19.4				
Feb 28	Commission	L8	1 300	
	Interest earned	L20	10	
	Income account	L23		1 310
	Closing transfers of income items to final account for February 19.4			
Feb 28	Income account	L23	1 295	
	Stationery	L9		200
	Rental	L10		400
	Wages	L11		600
	Telephone	L12		50
	Repairs: Office equipment	L16		20
	Depreciation	L21		25
	Closing transfers of expense items to final account for February 19.4			

9.2.2 Current account

After the income and expense items have been transferred to the income account, the balance on this account is determined in the usual way. A **credit balance** (ie income exceeds expenses) **represents a profit, while a debit balance** (ie expenses exceed income) **represents a loss**. The income account is now closed off by transferring the profit or loss to the owner's equity account. This transfer can be made directly to the capital account, but usually the owner's investment in the business is kept separately in a **current account**, showing net profit (or loss) and drawings.

Example 9.3

INCOME ACCOUNT			
Expenses	1 295	Income	1 310
Net profit to current account: H Botha	15		
	R1 310		R1 310

CAPITAL: H BOTHA			
		19.4	
		Feb 28 Balance	6 000

CURRENT ACCOUNT: H BOTHA			
19.4		19.4	
Feb 28 Drawings	300	Feb 28 Net profit	15

DRAWINGS: H BOTHA			
19.4		19.4	
Feb 20 Bank	R300	Feb 28 Current account	R300

The transfer of the profit (or loss) and the drawings to the current account of the owner are the final entries in the closing process. These entries are also made by means of closing entries in the journal, which are then posted to the ledger.

Income account Current account: H Botha *Transfer of net profit*	15	 15
Current account Drawings: H Botha *Transfer of drawings to current account*	300	 300

9.3 PREPARATION OF FINANCIAL STATEMENTS

In chapter 1 accounting is shown as encompassing identification, measurement, recording, processing, interpretation and communication of the financial result of an enterprise's activities. This chapter and the preceding one have covered the identification, measurement, recording and processing functions, which are carried out by means of the various steps in the accounting cycle. We have noted, further, that the result of an enterprise's operations is determined by using certain accounts in the ledger.

Financial statements are drawn up separately from the ledger accounts in order to aid the **interpretation** and **communication** functions. The nature of financial statements or reports is discussed in chapter 1. The most important financial reports are the income statement and balance sheet.*

9.3.1 Income statement

The income statement of HB Agencies for February 19.4 will be reflected as follows:

HB AGENCIES INCOME STATEMENT FOR THE MONTH ENDED 28 FEBRUARY 19.4		
Income		1 310
Commission	1 300	
Interest earned	10	
Expenses		1 295
Repairs: Office equipment	20	
Rental	400	
Wages	600	
Stationery	200	
Telephone	50	
Depreciation: Office equipment	25	
Net income		R15

*It must be emphasised that the income statement and balance sheet are not ledger accounts, but are prepared separately from the ledger.

9.3.2 Balance sheet

☐ **Conventional form**

HB AGENCIES BALANCE SHEET AT 28 FEBRUARY 19.4		
ASSETS		2 975
Fixed assets		
Office equipment		
At cost price	3 000	
Less: Accumulated depreciation	25	
Investments		
Fixed deposit		1 200
Current assets		2 410
Cash in bank	700	
Debtors	400	
Stationery on hand	500	
Rental prepaid	800	
Interest accrued	10	
Total assets		R6 585
EQUITY		
Owner's equity		5 715
Capital: H Botha	6 000	
Current account	(285)	
Net income	15	
Less: Drawings	(300)	
Current liabilities		870
Commission received in advance	300	
Creditors	400	
Wages accrued	150	
Provision for repairs: Office equipment	20	
Total equity		R6 585

☐ **Modern form**

The above balance sheet can also be set out in the modern format currently used in practice. This layout divides the balance sheet into two main sections, viz:

— Capital employed
  This section represents all equity items with the exception of creditors and other current liabilities. Therefore it incorporates owner's equity and long-term liabilities.

— Employment of capital
  This section represents all asset items. **Net current assets**, being the difference between total current assets and total current liabilities, appears in this section. The net current asset figure plays an important role in the analysis of the liquidity of an undertaking (i e the ability of an undertaking to meet its short-term liabilities).

When the modern format is used, the balance sheet above will appear as follows:

HB AGENCIES BALANCE SHEET AT 28 FEBRUARY 19.4					
CAPITAL EMPLOYED					
Owner's equity			5 715		
Capital: H Botha				6 000	
Current account: H Botha				(285)	
Net income for February					15
Less: Drawings					(300)
			R5 715		
EMPLOYMENT OF CAPITAL					
	Cost price	Accumulated depreciation	Net value		
Fixed Assets					
Office equipment	3 000	25	2 975		
Investments					
Fixed deposit			1 200		
Net current assets			1 540		
Current assets				2 410	
Cash in bank					700
Debtors					400
Stationery on hand					500
Rental prepaid					800
Interest accrued					10
Current liabilities				(870)	
Commission received in advance					300
Creditors					400
Wages accrued					150
Provision for repairs: Office equipment					20
			R5 715		

9.4 THE ACCOUNTING CYCLE

The discussion in previous chapters shows very clearly that the life of an enterprise is divided into accounting periods and that each period constitutes a repetitive accounting cycle. We have now discussed all the steps in that cycle. It is important that you understand each step fully and grasp the relationship between the various steps of the cycle.

In previous chapters we used accounting periods of only one month to explain the complete accounting cycle. It was assumed that the enterprise closed its accounts monthly, beginning a new business cycle at the start of each month.

Although it is common practice to provide monthly internal reports, most concerns only report once a year to outside interest groups such as shareholders.

The annual accounting period of an enterprise may coincide with the calendar year or, alternatively, may coincide with the natural business year of the undertaking which usually starts and ends when its activities are at an ebb.

The different steps in the accounting cycle can be represented diagrammatically as follows:

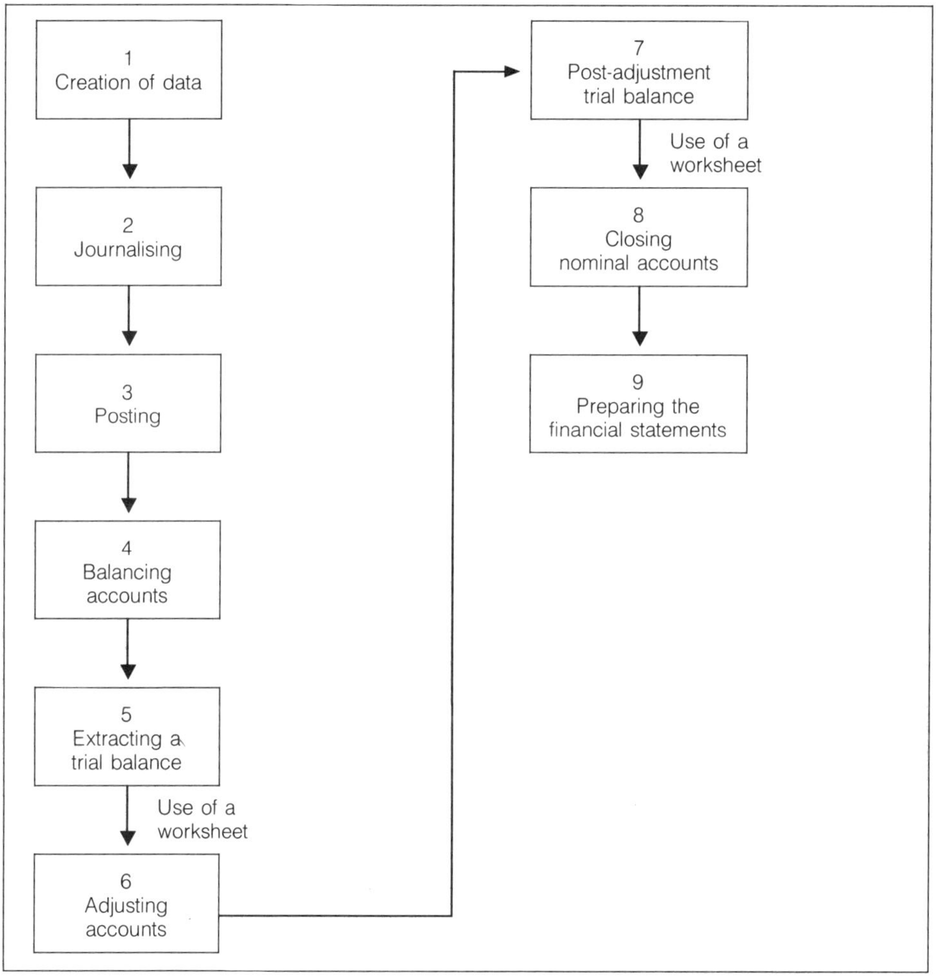

10

DETERMINATION OF PROFITS IN A TRADING CONCERN

In previous chapters the importance of profit determination and the processing of accounting data for providing the figures for profit determination has been emphasised. The **AIM** of this chapter is to explain how, using the financial statements, the gross profit and net profit of a trading concern are calculated. In a trading concern both inventory and inventory determination are very important factors in ascertaining profit.

10.1 DETERMINATION OF COST OF SALES AND GROSS AND NET PROFIT

In order to establish the basic principles our discussions thus far have dealt, for the sake of simplicity, with the accounting records and financial reports of service undertakings only.

Service undertakings offer some or other kind of service and usually do not have physically saleable products. Examples of such undertakings are professional firms of architects, accountants, lawyers and medical practitioners; transport services such as airlines, bus services and shipping lines; certain utility undertakings such as electricity suppliers; and personal service concerns such as hairdressers, clubs and church associations. In these types of enterprise income is realised as services are rendered during the financial period, and to calculate their profit all costs incurred during that same period are brought into account, in total, against income. Thus the procedure for determining profit in a service undertaking can be represented as follows:

Income	–	Expenses	=	Profit

A trading concern, on the other hand, earns its profit by purchasing merchandise which is then sold at a profit. The difference between the proceeds from sales and the cost price of the goods sold is the **gross profit**. All operating costs, that is marketing, administration and financing costs, are written off against the gross profit and any amount remaining is the net income (or net profit).

The gross profit is determined by means of a trading account from where it is transferred to an income account which, in turn, is used to determine the net income (or net profit).

In order to meet the demand for their merchandise, trading concerns must ensure that they have on hand a supply of merchandise which is available for sale. The expenses incurred during any specific period on the acquisition of stock are therefore not necessarily equal to the cost of the goods sold during the same period. One of the most important elements in determining profit in a trading concern is the determination of the **cost of sales**.

The procedure for determining profit in a trading concern is represented as follows:

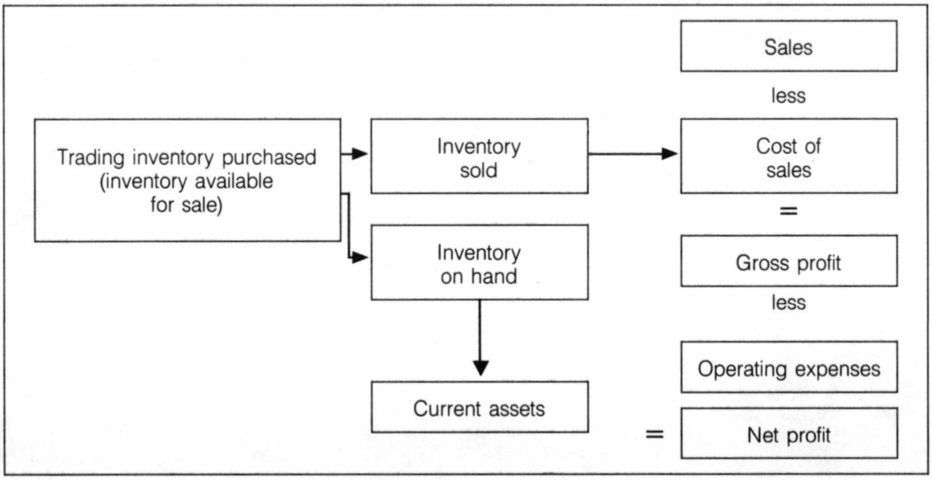

In principle, the procedure followed to determine the cost of sales is the same as that used before to determine the cost of goods consumed.

When goods are bought they are first of all debited to an inventory account, that is an asset account.

Example 10.1

Assume that, during May 19.7, AZ Motors buys 10 vehicles at a cash price of R6 000 each.

Recording of inventory available at cost price in the asset account

BANK

		Inventory: Vehicles (10 × R6 000)	60 000

INVENTORY: VEHICLES

Bank (10 × R6 000)	60 000		

As this inventory is sold, the purchase price of the units sold is transferred from the inventory account to a cost of sales account.

Assume that, during May 19.7, AZ Motors sells seven of the vehicles at a cash price of R7 000 each.

This transaction comprises two steps:

- ☐ the receipt of cash for the sales; and
- ☐ the transfer of the cost price of the units sold to an expense account.

☐ Recording sales

BANK

Sales: Vehicles (7 × R7 000)	49 000		

SALES: VEHICLES

		Bank	49 000

☐ Transferring cost of goods sold from asset (inventory) account

INVENTORY: VEHICLES

Bank (10 × R6 000)	60 000	Cost of sales: Vehicles (7 × R6 000)	42 000

COST OF SALES: VEHICLES

Inventory: Vehicles	42 000		

The gross profit on the vehicles is therefore:

Sales less cost of sales	=	Gross profit
R49 000 – R42 000	=	R7 000

Proof:	One unit is sold for	7 000
	One unit costs	6 000
	∴ Gross profit per unit	R1 000

Sales during the month: 7 units
∴ Gross profit: $7 \times$ R1 000 = R7 000

Similar to the determination of cost of goods consumed, the cost of sales can be determined by either the direct or the indirect method.

For a dealer trading in large inventory items (such as motor cars), it is relatively easy to identify which units have been sold. It is a simple process, when a particular unit is sold, to transfer the cost of that unit directly from the inventory account to the cost of sales account. The advantage of this direct method is that the relevant inventory and cost accounts are constantly up to date; and hence this is referred to as the **perpetual inventory system**.

A prerequisite for the application of this method, however, is that every item in the inventory should be identifiable and measurable. This is obviously not possible in retail undertakings such as grocery stores because of the impossibility of keeping a unit cost record for every item. Therefore most enterprises dealing in large volumes of 'lower priced' merchandise make no attempt to determine the cost of sales simultaneously with each sales transaction. Instead they wait until the end of the financial period to take a physical check of all the goods still on hand and then determine the cost of these goods from their records and use this figure (inventory on hand) to determine the cost of the goods sold. This method is known as the **periodic stocktaking method**.

Recording can be done by one of two methods:

- ☐ recording of purchases in an inventory account
- ☐ recording of purchases in a purchases account.

Example 10.2 Recording of purchases in an inventory account

This method corresponds with the method used in the case of the perpetual stock-taking method.

On 1 June X Wholesalers had goods on hand with a cost price of R10 000. During June the enterprise purchased additional goods at a cost of R15 000. Its sales for the period totalled R16 000.

Inventory taken on 30 June showed that goods on hand, at cost, amounted to R14 000.

The gross profit of X Wholesalers for the month is:

Opening inventory at cost price		Additions at cost price		Total inventory available		Closing inventory at cost price		Cost of sales
R10 000	+	R15 000	=	R25 000	−	R14 000	=	R11 000

Sales	=	16 000
Cost of sales	=	11 000
∴ Gross profit	=	R5 000

BANK

(1) Sales	16 000	(2) Inventory	15 000

INVENTORY

Balance (opening inventory)	10 000	(3) Cost of sales	11 000
Bank	15 000	Balance (closing inventory)	14 000
Balance	14 000		

COST OF SALES

(3) Inventory	11 000	(4) Trading account	11 000

SALES

(5) Trading account	16 000	(1) Bank	16 000

TRADING ACCOUNT

(4) Cost of sales	11 000	(5) Sales	16 000
Gross profit	5 000		

Example 10.3 Recording of purchases in a purchases account: Periodic method

This method is frequently used in smaller undertakings.

The following illustration assumes the same particulars as used in example 10.2.

BANK

(1) Sales	16 000	(2) Purchases	15 000

PURCHASES

(2) Bank	15 000	(4) Trading account	15 000

TRADING ACCOUNT

(3) Opening inventory	10 000	(5) Sales	16 000
Purchases	15 000	(6) Closing inventory	14 000
	25 000		
Gross profit	5 000		
	30 000		30 000

SALES

(5) Trading account	16 000	(1) Bank	16 000

INVENTORY

Balance (opening inventory)	10 000	(3) Trading account	10 000
(6) Trading account (closing inventory)	14 000		

This method does not use a cost of sales account. When the financial statements are prepared the trading account is also drawn up, as follows:

TRADING ACCOUNT		
Sales		16 000
Opening inventory	10 000	
Purchases	15 000	
	25 000	
Less: Closing inventory	14 000	
Cost of sales		11 000
Gross profit		R5 000

10.1.1 Trading inventory

The merchandise on hand at the start of an accounting period is called the opening (or initial) inventory, and the merchandise on hand at the end of the period is called the closing (or final) inventory. Since accounting periods are consecutive, the closing inventory of one period always constitutes the opening inventory of the subsequent period.

10.1.2 Income from sales, returns and discounts

Income from sales (both cash and credit) consists of the gross proceeds from the sale of merchandise, less returns and trade discounts. Returns occur when customers return the goods purchased for some reason. It is important for management to know the extent of returns in relation to the business' turnover. If this ratio is disproportionately large, it could be a sign of inefficiency in either the buying or the sales department of the enterprise. Returns obviously reduce the gross turnover and therefore are recorded separately before being brought into account against sales.

Different types of discount are allowed in practice, the most important being:

(a) Discount allowed at the time of sale
- ☐ cash discount on cash sales – this type of discount usually varies between 2½% and 10%
- ☐ trade discount to trade buyers – this type of discount varies according to the type of enterprise, but is generally between 10% and 50%.

(b) Discount allowed for the prompt settlement of accounts. A discount of 2½% is usually allowed for payment within 10 to 30 days, the discount being allowed at the time of settlement of the account.

Discount allowed at the time of sale, that is as in (a), is usually deducted from the selling price, only the net selling price being brought into account as income. Therefore this type of discount has a direct influence on gross profit.

Discount allowed for prompt settlement of accounts, that is as in (b), is taken into account only once the full amount of the original sale has been brought into account as income. This discount is regarded as a separate financing cost item and is not shown in the trading account, but in the income account. Therefore it has no influence on gross profit.

10.1.3 Cost of inventory purchased

The cost of merchandise purchased comprises:

- □ the price charged by the supplier, and
- □ all other costs incurred in transporting the goods to the place where the merchandise is available for sale.

The price charged by the supplier is the net invoice price after trade discount has been allowed. For example, a supplier may have an item on his price list costing R100 less 20%. The 20% discount allowed to dealers is known as trade discount and the net invoice (or purchase) price of the item is R80. To determine the total cost price the additional expenses, such as freight to the dealer's premises, customs charges and import duty, must be added. These additional items are usually recorded separately at first, and transferred to the inventory account during the closing process.

If goods are returned to the supplier (known as a purchases return), or if the supplier reduces his selling price, the total cost price will be reduced. Purchases returns are generally recorded separately at first, and later transferred to the inventory account.

10.2 EXAMPLE EXPLAINING THE CLOSING-OFF PROCEDURE IN A TRADING CONCERN

Example 10.4

The example below illustrates the profit-determining process and the eventual preparation of financial statements of a commercial enterprise using the alternative method explained in example 10.3.

ELS TRADERS
PRE-ADJUSTMENT TRIAL BALANCE AT 31 DECEMBER 19.1

Acc no		Dr	Cr
11	Shop fittings	5 000	
12	Accumulated depreciation:		
	Shop fittings (balance 31/12/19.0)		500
21	Inventory (opening)	20 000	
22	Debtors	20 000	
23	Bank	16 300	
31	Capital: G Els		15 000
32	Drawings: G Els	1 500	
41	Trade creditors		25 000
51	Sales		71 000
52	Sales returns	1 000	
55	Discount received		800
60	Purchases	40 000	
61	Purchases returns		1 500
63	Freight in	1 500	
67	Discount allowed	500	
71	Salaries	6 000	
72	Rental	2 000	
		R113 800	R113 800

Additional information:

(1) The cost of the closing stock at 31/12/19.1 amounts to R15 000.
(2) Depreciation, at 20% per annum, on the cost of the shop fittings must be provided.

The following two **adjustment journal entries** must be made first:

Journal J1

19.1 Dec 31	Inventory Trading account *Cost price of inventory on hand brought into account*	21 80	15 000	 15 000
Dec 31	Depreciation: Shop fittings Accumulated depreciation *Provision of depreciation at 20% on cost price of fittings*	73 12	1 000	 1 000

After the above adjustments have been posted to the general ledger, the following **closing journal entries** are made to close the nominal accounts in the general ledger:

Journal J2

19.1 Dec 31	Trading account Inventory *Closing transfer*	L80 L21	20 000	 20 000
	Sales Trading account *Closing transfer*	L51 L80	71 000	 71 000
19.1 Dec 31	Trading account Sales returns *Closing transfer*	L80 L52	1 000	 1 000
	Trading account Purchases *Closing transfer*	L80 L60	40 000	 40 000
19.1 Dec 31	Purchases returns Trading account *Closing transfer*	L61 L80	1 500	 1 500
	Trading account Freight in *Closing transfer*	L80 L63	1 500	 1 500

Alternatively, all the transfers to the trading account can be made via a combined journal entry, as follows:

Journal J2

Sales	L51	71 000	
Purchases returns	L61	1 500	
Inventory	L21		20 000
Sales returns	L52		1 000
Purchases	L62		40 000
Freight in	L63		1 500
Trading account	L80		10 000
Closing transfers			

Journal J3

Discount received	L55	800	
Profit and loss account	L81		800
Closing transfer			
Profit and loss account	L81	9 500	
Discount allowed	L67		500
Salaries	L71		6 000
Rental	L72		2 000
Depreciation	L73		1 000
Closing transfers			
Capital: G Els	L31	1 500	
Drawings: G Els	L32		1 500
Transfer of balance on drawings account			

After the adjustments and closing entries have been posted, the general ledger of Els Traders will appear as follows:

ELS TRADERS
GENERAL LEDGER

SHOP FITTINGS — L11

19.1 Dec 31	Balance	b/d	5 000				

ACCUMULATED DEPRECIATION: SHOP FITTINGS — L12

				19.1 Dec 31	Balance	b/d	500
					Depreciation	J1	1 000

INVENTORY — L21

19.1 Dec 31	Balance (opening inventory)	b/d	20 000	19.1 Dec 31	Trading account	J2	20 000
	Trading account (closing inventory)	J1	15 000				

			DEBTORS				L22
19.1 Dec 31	Balance	b/d	20 000				
			BANK				L23
19.1 Dec 31	Balance	b/d	16 300				
			CAPITAL: G ELS				L31
19.1 Dec 31	Drawings	J3	1 500	19.1 Dec 31	Balance	b/d	15 000
			DRAWINGS: G ELS				L32
19.1 Dec 31	Balance	b/d	1 500	19.1 Dec 31	Capital: G Els	J3	1 500
			TRADE CREDITORS				L41
				19.1 Dec 31	Balance	b/d	25 000
			SALES				L51
19.1 Dec 31	Trading account	J2	71 000	19.1 Dec 31	Balance	b/d	71 000
			SALES RETURNS				L52
19.1 Dec 31	Balance	b/d	1 000	19.1 Dec 31	Trading account	J2	1 000
			DISCOUNT RECEIVED				L55
19.1 Dec 31	Profit and loss account	J3	800	19.1 Dec 31	Balance	b/d	800
			PURCHASES				L60
19.1 Dec 31	Balance	b/d	40 000	19.1 Dec 31	Trading account	J2	40 000
			PURCHASES RETURNS				L61
19.1 Dec 31	Trading account	J1	1 500	19.1 Dec 31	Balance	b/d	1 500

FREIGHT IN							L63
19.1 Dec 31	Balance	b/d	1 500	19.1 Dec 31	Trading account	J2	1 500

DISCOUNT ALLOWED							L67
19.1 Dec 31	Balance	b/d	500	19.1 Dec 31	Profit and loss account	J3	500

SALARIES							L71
19.1 Dec 31	Balance	b/d	6 000	19.1 Dec 31	Profit and loss account	J3	6 000

RENTAL							L72
19.1 Dec 31	Balance	b/d	2 000	19.1 Dec 31	Profit and loss account	J3	2 000

DEPRECIATION							L73
19.1 Dec 31	Accumulated depreciation: Shop fittings	J2	1 000	19.1 Dec 31	Profit and loss account	J3	1 000

The next step is to determine the **gross profit** for the year. This is done by **balancing** the trading account. The gross profit is then transferred to the profit and loss account via the following journal entry:

19.1 Dec 31	Trading account Profit and loss account *Transfer of gross profit*		25 000	25 000

The last step in closing off the general ledger of a trading concern is to transfer the **net profit** (or loss, if applicable) to the owner's capital account, as follows:

Profit and loss account Capital: G Els *Transfer of net profit to owner*		16 300	16 300

This process can be illustrated as follows:

			TRADING ACCOUNT				L80
19.1 Dec 31	Inventory (opening)	J2	20 000	19.1 Dec 31	Inventory (closing)	J1	15 000
	Sales returns	J2	1 000		Sales	J2	71 000
	Purchases	J2	40 000		Purchases returns	J2	1 500
	Freight in	J2	1 500				87 500
			62 500				
	Profit and loss account (gross profit)	J3	25 000				
			87 500				87 500
			PROFIT AND LOSS ACCOUNT				L81
19.1 Dec 31	Discount allowed	J3	500	19.1 Dec 31	Discount received	J3	800
	Salaries	J3	6 000		Trading account (gross profit)	J3	25 000
	Rental	J3	2 000				25 800
	Depreciation	J3	1 000				
			9 500				
	Capital: G Els (net profit)	J3	16 300				
			25 800				25 800
			CAPITAL ACCOUNT: G ELS				L31
19.1 Dec 31	Drawings	J3	1 500	19.1 Dec 31	Balance	b/d	15 000
					Profit and loss account (net profit)	J3	16 300

Looking at the general ledger of Els Traders you will notice that all the accounts except the following asset or equity accounts have been closed off: shop fittings, accumulated depreciation on shop fittings, stock, debtors, bank, capital and creditors.

These are the accounts which form the balance sheet of the undertaking.

10.3 FORMAL FINANCIAL STATEMENTS OF A TRADING CONCERN

The formal financial statements can now be prepared from the information contained in the trading account, the profit and loss account and the asset and equity accounts.

ELS TRADERS
INCOME STATEMENT FOR THE YEAR ENDED 31 DECEMBER 19.1

Net sales		70 000
Gross sales		71 000
Less: Sales returns		1 000
Less: Cost of sales		45 000
Inventory 1 December 19.1		20 000
Add: Purchases	40 000	
Freight on purchases	1 500	
	41 500	
Less: Purchases returns	1 500	40 000
		60 000
Less: Closing inventory		15 000
Gross profit on sales		25 000
Add: Discount received		800
		25 800
Less: Operating expenses		9 500
Salaries		2 000
Rent		6 000
Discount allowed		500
Depreciation		1 000
Net profit		R16 300

Trading account section (Net sales to Gross profit on sales)

Profit and loss account section (Gross profit on sales to Net profit)

ELS TRADERS
BALANCE SHEET AT 31 DECEMBER 19.1

OWNER'S EQUITY:	
Capital: G Els	29 800
Balance 31 December 19.0	15 000
Add: Net income	16 300
	31 300
Less: Drawings	1 500
	R29 800
REPRESENTED BY:	
Fixed assets	
Shop fittings	3 500
At cost price	5 000
Less: Accumulated depreciation	1 500
Net current assets:	26 300
Current assets	51 300
Inventory	15 000
Debtors	20 000
Bank	16 300
Less: Current liabilities	25 000
	R29 800

10.4 GROSS PROFIT PERCENTAGE

Gross profit is the difference between the proceeds from sales and the cost of the goods sold. Assume that an article bought for R80 is sold for R120 after administrative and marketing costs of R20 have been incurred. The gross profit is thus R40, that is the difference between the selling price of R120 and the cost of R80. In calculating the gross profit, operating costs such as administrative, marketing and financing expenses are not taken into account.

Gross profit is calculated as a separate amount because it gives a clear indication of any commercial enterprise's achievement in its most important activity, viz the sale of goods at a profit, irrespective of any other activities it must perform to support its primary activity.

The gross profit is usually expressed as a percentage of either the selling price or the cost price.

In the example above gross profit percentage on selling price would be calculated as follows:

$$\frac{\text{Gross profit} \times 100}{\text{Selling price}} = \frac{40 \times 100}{120} = 33^1/3\%$$

The gross profit percentage on cost is calculated as follows:

$$\frac{\text{Gross profit} \times 100}{\text{Cost price}} = \frac{40 \times 100}{80} = 50\%$$

A commercial enterprise usually has a pricing policy which aims at earning a specific gross profit percentage. Selling prices are determined in accordance with the pricing policy by adding the desired gross profit percentage to the cost price of the merchandise.

If the enterprise desires a gross profit of 20% on cost price (or, alternatively, 16,67% on selling price), then an article with a cost price of R40 will have to be priced at R48. Theoretically, the total gross profit earned during any specific period should equal 20% of the cost price of goods sold, or 16,67% of the total sales. The actual gross profit percentage is generally calculated periodically in order to determine the correlation between actual performance and planned performance.

11

INTRODUCTION TO ACCOUNTING SYSTEMS

The **AIM** of this chapter is to discuss certain fundamental aspects of systems, systems design and systems procedure.

11.1 INTRODUCTION

In chapter 1 we explained that the function of accounting was to create the financial information required for making decisions regarding the management of an undertaking. The design and implementation of accounting systems is therefore one of the most important functions of an accountant. Consequently, it is important for an accountant to develop expertise in the design and implementation of systems so that he can apply his theoretical knowledge on a practical level.

11.2 THE NATURE OF ACCOUNTING SYSTEMS

A system is a process whereby a specific output is produced by a given input. In an **information system**, data is processed to provide **information**. **Data** is a collection of unprocessed facts, while **information** is data or facts which have been processed into a meaningful form.

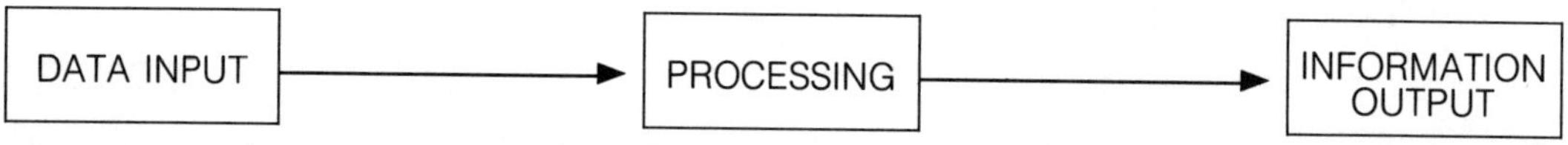

In the normal course of events a business undertaking will enter into a large variety of transactions. The details of a particular transaction are referred to as **transaction data**. The term **transaction data** therefore refers to the facts which completely describe a specific transaction.

The aim of an accounting system is to record the transaction data and then to process this data to provide information which is ultimately collected in the financial and management reports of the enterprise.

There are two stages in the development of an accounting system, namely **systems analysis** and **systems design**.

11.3 SYSTEMS ANALYSIS

A good accounting system must comply with at least the following fundamental requirements:

- ☐ The system must provide decision makers with timeous and accurate information relevant to their responsibilities and requirements.
- ☐ The internal control measures must be adequate to ensure the protection of assets and the provision of reliable information.
- ☐ The system must be sufficiently flexible to accommodate changes in the volume of activities and in the operating procedures without requiring drastic modifications.

A thorough knowledge of the activities of the undertaking and its information and control requirements is an essential prerequisite for the development of an effective system which meets the necessary criteria.

The procedure of surveying the undertaking's activities and information and control requirements, is known as **systems analysis**.

Systems analysis comprises the following five steps:

- ☐ Identification of the activities of an undertaking.
- ☐ Analysis of the organisational structure.
- ☐ Determination of information needs.
- ☐ Determination of the availability of data.
- ☐ Determination of internal control requirements.

11.3.1 Identification of activities

The **first step in systems analysis** is to study the operating process in order to identify all the activities and the accounts which are affected by these activities.

The activities in an operating process and the accounts influenced can, for the sake of simplicity, be depicted in a matrix, as in figure 11.1.

Figure 11.1 Sub-systems in a trading concern

ACTIVITIES	INCOME	EXPENSES	CASH	DEBTORS	CREDITORS
Cash purchases		Purchases	0		
Credit purchases		Purchases			0
Cash sales	Sales		0		
Credit sales	Sales			0	
Settlement Creditors			0		0
Settlement Debtors			0	0	
Current expenses		Expense	0		0

The use of a matrix gives the systems analyst an indication of the different sub-systems in the total accounting system

For example, the matrix shows that the cash system must provide for cash purchases, cash sales, payments to creditors, payments by debtors and the payment of current expenses.

11.3.2 Organisational structure

The second step in the process of systems analysis is to analyse the organisational structure.

The organisational structure reflects how an enterprise is divided into departments, sections and posts. The organisational structure is usually shown in an **organigram**.

The organisation of a typical manufacturing concern is shown in figure 11.2.

Figure 11.2 Organisational structure of a manufacturing concern

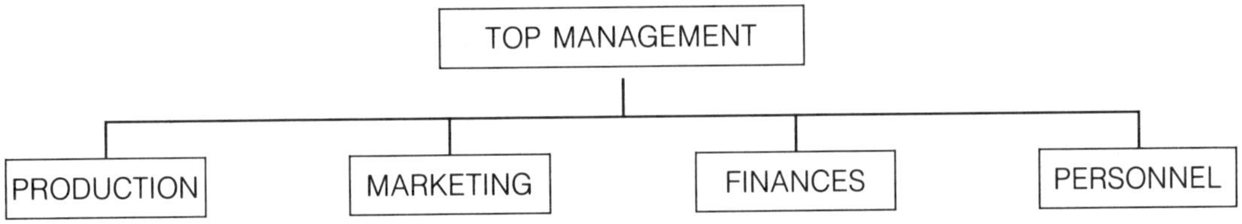

The purpose of analysing the organisational structure is to assess the responsibilities and activities of each department, division or post. This will give an indication of the information needs of each entity.

Depending on the nature and scope of the duties which must be performed in order that a particular departmental function may be carried out, departments can be divided into sections and subsections, which in turn can be subdivided into individual posts.

The financial department, for example, can be subdivided into four sections, namely financial records, budgeting, credit control and data processing. These subsections may again be divided into specific functions and then into the individual posts of the various clerks and operators.

Figure 11.3

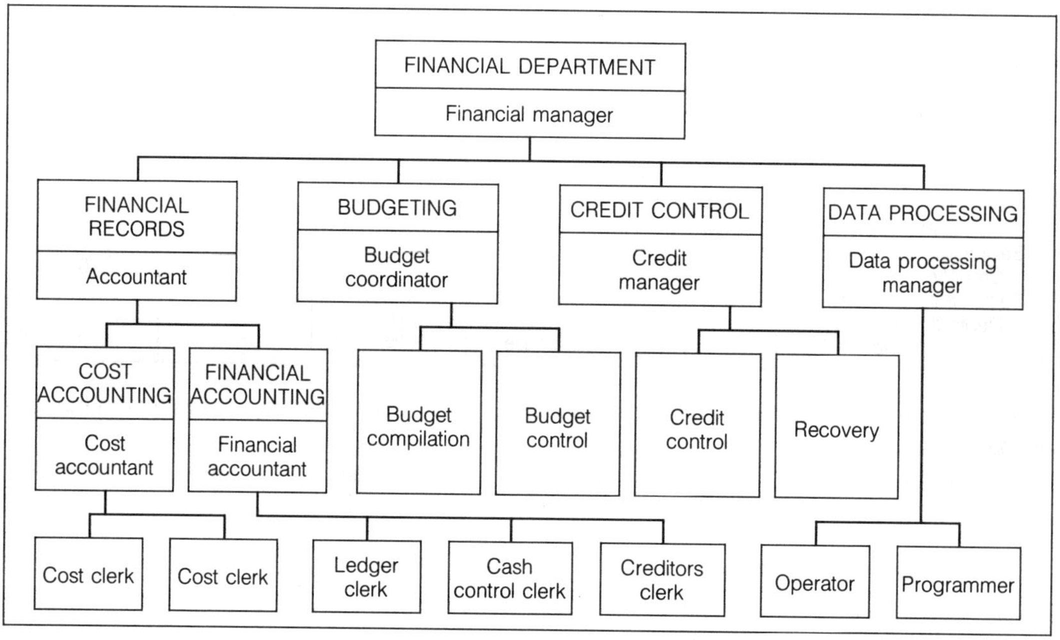

11.3.3 Information needs

The third step in systems analysis is to assess the information needs of each information user.

Information needs include the following:

- ☐ Information reflecting the financial position and results of the enterprise.
- ☐ Management information, needed internally for the effective administration of operations.

The information needs of each user are determined by specifying in detail the information they require in order to perform their duties.

It is the function of the systems analyst to determine the nature, form, frequency and timing of reporting required by each internal user.

Top management, for example, will specify the form, detail and frequency of financial reports. The systems analyst will also take cognisance of statutory and professional regulations and standards pertaining to the information.

In computerised systems it is frequently necessary to specify the scope and format of the information as well, for example the length of the field and whether alpha, numeric or alphanumeric. This information, which is necessary for programming, will be determined by the requirements of the specific software.

A complete specification of information needs serves as a guideline for the design of reports and gives an indication of the data that will be required and the journals, accounts and processing which will make up the system.

11.3.4 Availability of data

The next step in the analysis process is to identify the specific data emanating from the transactions and other activities of the undertaking.

Either a **forward-looking** or a **retrospective** approach can be used in analysing data.

In a **forward-looking** analysis all the data which has already been generated by the transactions is identified.

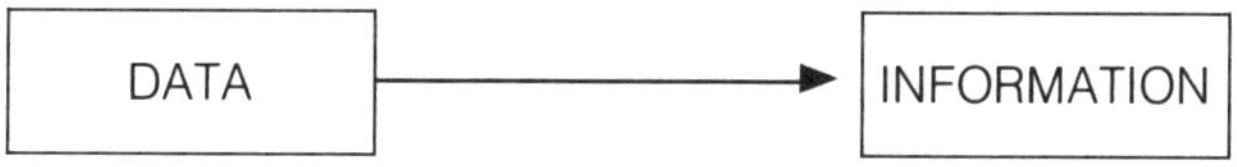

Then it is decided which information must be processed from the available data.

For example, if sales invoices include the addresses of clients, consideration can be given to recording sales according to geographical area.

In a **retrospective approach, the information desired is analysed to determine whether or not the data is available**.

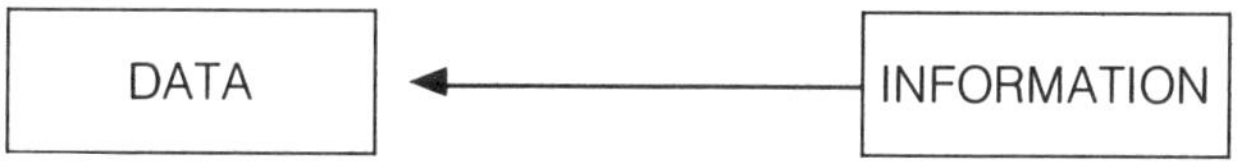

As a result of this analysis, a decision may be made to create and **capture** data that is not yet available.

The content, source, volume, frequency and time of input of all data in the system must be fully specified, as must the responsibility for the accuracy, timeliness and capture of the data. In computerised systems the volume and format of the data must also be specified.

Volume of data is an important factor in the decision as to which type of system should be used. A manual system may be satisfactory if volumes are low, whereas a large volume of data may justify a computerised system.

The analysis of the availability of data provides a guideline for the design of source documents, journals and accounts and for processing methods and procedures.

11.3.5 Internal control measures

Control is action which ensures that predetermined standards are maintained.

The control function consists of three elements:

- ☐ The determination of standards.
- ☐ A comparison of the actual situation with these standards.
- ☐ Corrective action.

Control may be exercised before or after an event. Where control is exercised after the event, corrective action takes place once the deviation becomes known; while if control is exercised before the event, corrective action is taken timeously to prevent possible deviations.

Internal control is the control incorporated into the undertaking's **accounting** and **operating systems** to ensure that the financial information provided by the accounting system is complete, accurate and reliable; that the undertaking's assets are protected against loss or fraud; that managerial policy is adhered to; and that operations are executed effectively.

The internal control measures applicable to accounting or operating systems can be either **accounting** or **organisational** controls.

Accounting controls use the data and information of the different systems as control measures.

Organisational controls refer to rules for the performance and division of duties.

It is the responsibility of the systems analyst to determine which controls should be incorporated in the system and the accounting and organisational measures required in the system.

11.3.5.1 Organisational internal control

Internal controls which are incorporated in the organisational structure are based on the following principles:

- ☐ The undertaking must have an adequate organisational structure.
- ☐ Each person's responsibilities, authority and duties in the organisation, together with the policy, methods and procedures according to which they must be performed, should be communicated in a clearly defined manner to the incumbents of each post.
- ☐ Personnel must have the training, experience and personal attributes to perform their duties competently.
- ☐ The responsibility and authority for any one function should be delegated to only one person.
- ☐ Duties should be divided in such a way that no single person has overall control over a complete procedure in an accounting cycle.
- ☐ Provision should be made for one person to control the work of another.
- ☐ Persons responsible for keeping asset records should not also have control over those assets. This prevents misappropriation of assets which can be concealed by falsification of the records.
- ☐ The undertaking must operate an effective accounting system, together with the necessary support systems which are adapted to the nature and scope of the work.
- ☐ Staff performing any particular task should be rotated regularly on any particular task and annual leave should be compulsory for all staff.
- ☐ Assets should be adequately insured against loss as a result of fire or storm damage, theft, etc.
- ☐ In large enterprises the internal audit function is the salient feature of the internal control system. It is the responsibility of the internal audit department to evaluate the financial and operating activities of the undertaking.

11.3.5.2 Accounting control

Accounting control relies on the principle that the data or information serves as the basis for controlling the accuracy of further handling of those transactions. The effectiveness of accounting control is independent of organisational control.

Accounting control is maintained by means of:

- ☐ control totals
- ☐ guideline amounts.

Control totals are used in three principal ways:

(a) The accounting records of assets serve as a control to confirm the physical existence of those assets.
- ☐ Cash on hand must agree with cash register totals.
- ☐ Equipment and other assets on hand are checked annually against the applicable asset accounts.

(b) Successive steps in the accounting process are compared with the initial entries.
- ☐ Before a batch of invoices is entered in a computerised system, the batch total is determined. Once the invoices have been posted the input total is compared with the total calculated manually.

(c) The total of a number of entries to various accounts is determined independently in a control account and it must be ensured that the total of all the entries to the individual accounts agrees with the control total.
- ☐ The totals of all the debits and credits made in a series of individual debtors' accounts are also debited and credited to a debtors control account. The total of all the balances on the debtors' accounts must agree with the total on the control account.

Guideline amounts are standards or limits against which actual expenses or income are measured.

11.4 SYSTEMS DESIGN

In the systems design process the system is designed to comply with the specifications determined by systems analysis.

In chapter 7 it was pointed out that initially transactions are recorded in **source documents** and then in **journals**, and finally they are classified and stored in **ledger accounts**. The processed information is extracted from the ledger accounts for drawing up the **financial reports**. The various steps in this process may be represented as follows:

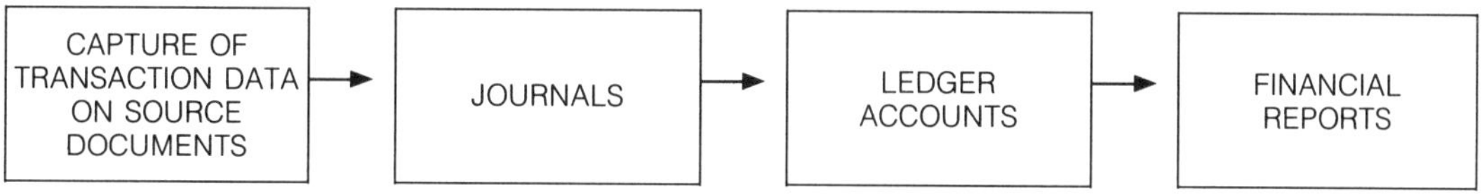

The design of any accounting system within this framework comprises the following stages:

- ☐ Planning the **procedures** according to which the system will function
- ☐ The design of the (i) **source documents**, (ii) **journals**, (iii) **ledger accounts** and (iv) **final reports**
- ☐ The design of the necessary **internal control measures**.

11.5 SYSTEMS PROCEDURE

There are two steps in the development of a systems procedure:

- □ Planning document flow.
- □ Description of procedures.

Data flows through various processes in an information system from the point of origination to the final report in which the information is eventually contained.

SALES DEPARTMENT	DEBTORS SECTION	ACCOUNTANT	CONSUMER
SOURCE DOCUMENT	RECORDED IN DEBTOR'S ACCOUNT	PROCESSING	REPORT

The flow of data through the entire process must be planned before the complete procedure can be described. The **document flow diagram** is a useful tool for representing the flow of information in a system schematically.

11.5.1 Planning document flow

The information flow chart of an undertaking has a separate column for each division in which activities occur. The chart indicates in which division source documents originate, the flow of documents between divisions, and where permanent records such as journals and ledger accounts are maintained.

Frequently special symbols such as those depicted in figure 11.4 are used to describe a system in terms of a document flow chart.

Figure 11.4 Information flow chart symbols

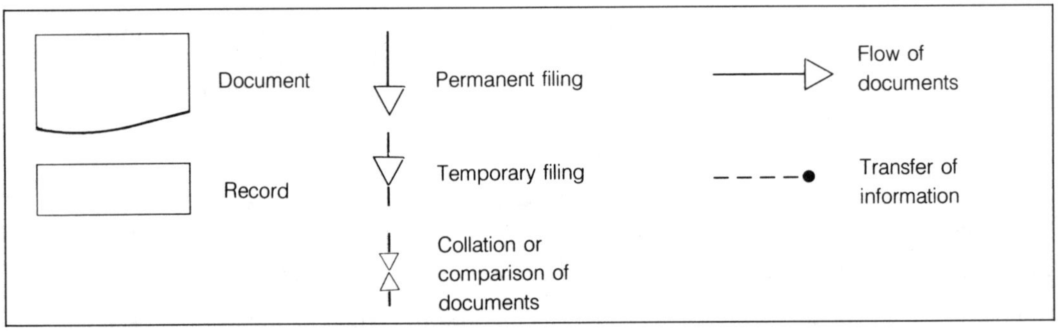

A document flow chart for a small enterprise which purchases and sells goods for cash and uses a micro-computer to maintain its cash book, is illustrated in figure 11.5.

Figure 11.5

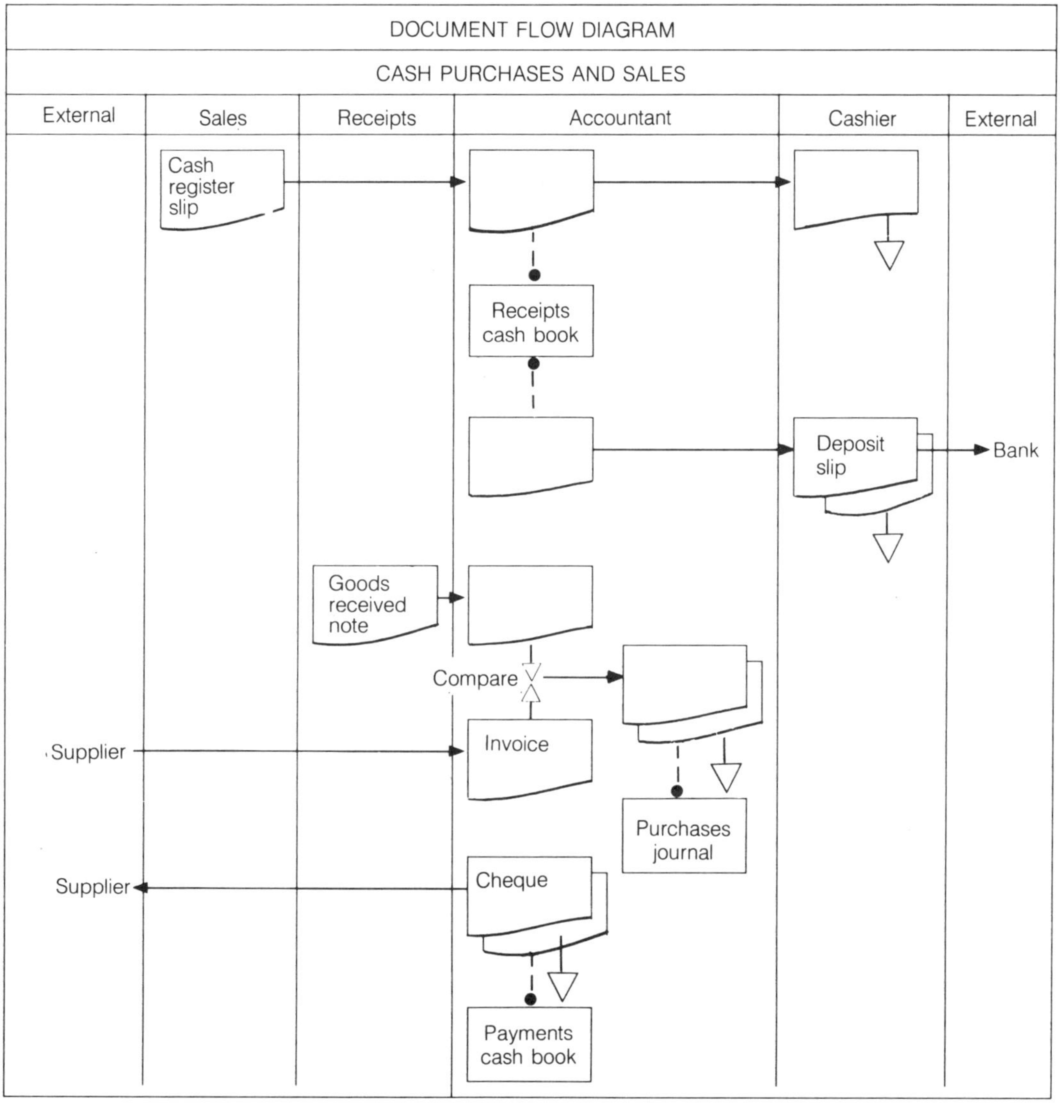

11.5.2 Description of procedures

Once the document flow has been planned, the full procedures and methods of the system are described. A comprehensive description of a procedure will contain at least the following elements:

- □ a **description** of every step in the procedure
- □ the **sequence** and **timing** of the different steps
- □ the **method** for executing each step
- □ who is **responsible** for each step
- □ which **source documents**, **records and equipment** are to be used in each step.

The **procedure** for recording payments in a cash book, for example, can be described as follows:

PROCEDURE	METHOD
1 Record payment in cash book.	1 **Accountant** receives **cheque book counterfoils** and **supporting documents** daily from **treasurer** and records the following information in the cash book: ☐ Date of cheque ☐ Number of cheque ☐ Payee ☐ Amount ☐ Analyses amount in analysis columns. 2 **Accountant** obtains **bank statements**, **paid cheques** and **bank debit notes** from the **bank** weekly. 3 **Accountant** controls entries in cash book against paid cheques. 4 **Accountant** records **date**, **description and amount** of **bank debits** in **cash book** weekly. 5 **Accountant** calculates **bank charges** weekly and records in cash book.
2 Record deposits in cash book.	
3 Reconcile cash book.	

11.6 DESIGN OF SOURCE DOCUMENTS

SOURCE DOCUMENTS → JOURNALS → LEDGER ACCOUNTS → FINANCIAL REPORTS

A source document is the document in which 'transaction data' is recorded when the transaction occurs.

Suppose that on 15 January 19.8 Boumaat Limited sells 10 bags of cement, which cost R3 each, for R40 on account to Peter Smith of 12 Dwars Street, Pretoria. The following would be the transaction data:

Type of transaction: credit sale
Date: 15 January 19.8
Item sold: 10 bags cement
Selling price: R40
Purchaser: Peter Smith
Address: 12 Dwars Street, Pretoria
Cost price: R30

Listed below are the most common transactions in a trading concern and the source documents on which the transactions are recorded:

TRANSACTION	SOURCE DOCUMENTS
Cash sales	Cash register slips
Credit sales	Sales invoices
Credit purchases	Suppliers' invoices
Transaction	Source documents
Payments	Cheque book counterfoils
Cash receipts	Receipts or other proof of receipt
Bank deposits	Bank deposit slips
Salaries and wages	Salary and wages register

The relationship between source documents and the various transactions in the business cycle is represented schematically in figure 11.6:

Figure 11.6

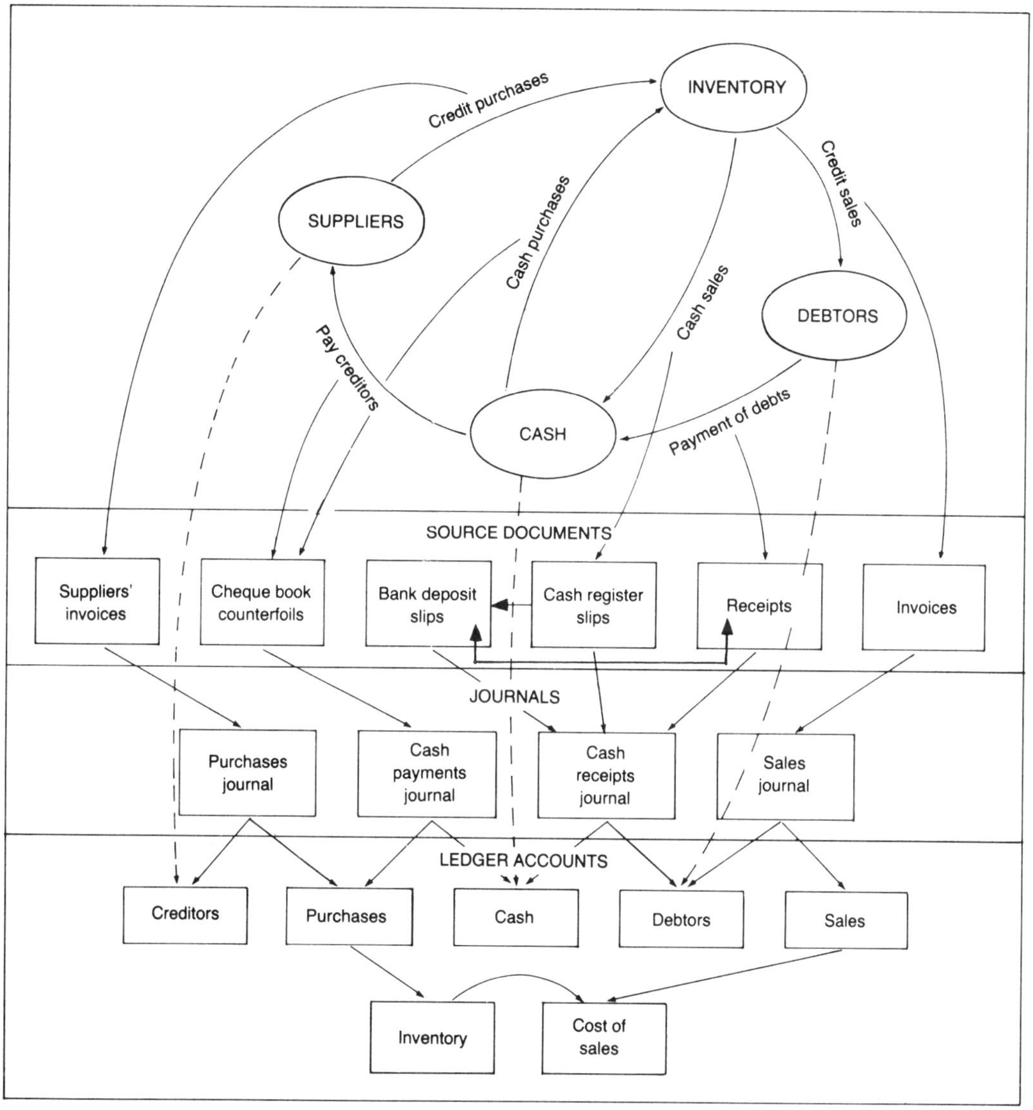

A separate source document is designed for each type of transaction to suit the information requirements and data processing procedures of the specific transaction.

Once data has been fed into a system it can be used for different purposes. A source document should contain as much as possible of the data necessary for processing all the information needed by any user.

A source document should contain at least the following:

- ☐ The serial number of the source document.
- ☐ The nature of the transaction.
- ☐ The amount of the transaction.
- ☐ The date of the transaction.
- ☐ The identities of the persons involved in the transaction.

Source documents should be numbered sequentially. The sequential number constitutes a reference to a specific document for audit purposes and ensures proper internal control over source documents. If documents were not numbered sequentially it would be difficult, for example, to ensure that all documents in a set were accounted for. To ensure control over source documents a register should be maintained in which all the source documents that have been printed or are being used are recorded. The used and unused inventory of documents should be checked against the register regularly.

Each source document should be signed by the person responsible for its completion. If further authority for a specific transaction is required, the person who grants that authority should also sign the document.

The design of the document flow in a system also determines how many copies of each source document should be prepared. At least one copy of a source document should be filed permanently for future reference and for audit purposes.

In computerised systems the layout of source documents should facilitate keyboard input of the data. For example, the sequence of information on the source document and the sequence in which it is keyed in should be the same.

11.7 DESIGN OF JOURNALS

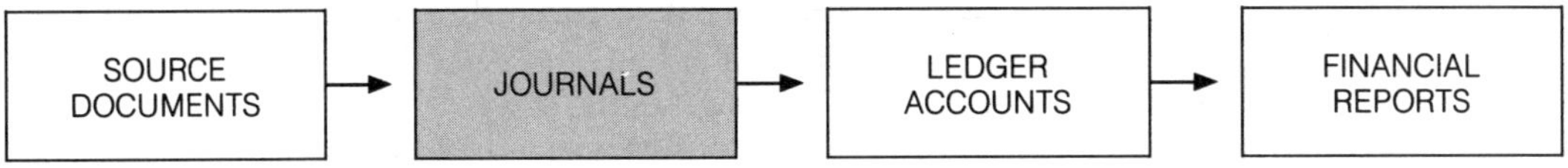

The next step in systems design is designing the journals in which the information from the source documents is recorded. Once again the schematic representation of the operating cycle can be used to illustrate how journals within the system are designed (refer to figure 11.6).

The principal purpose of a journal is to record transactions chronologically and to analyse them according to the ledger accounts affected.

The simplest form of journal is the **general journal**, which was discussed in chapter 7. The general journal makes provision only for the analysis of individual transactions by balancing the debit and credit elements of each transaction.

In cases where numerous transactions all influence a specific account a special journal only for that account can be used, for example for cash receipts, cash payments, credit purchases and credit sales.

In its simplest form a special journal is designed with only a single amount column. All amounts which are posted individually to separate accounts but in total to a single account are entered into this column.

A sales journal could appear as follows:

Figure 11.7

SALES JOURNAL JANUARY 19.4				
Date	Debtors	Invoice no	Folio	Amount
19.4	Debit			
Jan 2	J Smit	41378	S14	360,00
16	A de Wit	41379	D12	80,40
18	M van Wyk	41380	V26	120,77
24	K van der Merwe	41381	V13	470,32
30	PL Smal	41382	S6	32,40
31	W de Lange	41383	D20	516,20
	Credit: Credit sales		S23	R1 580,09

The individual sales are debited to the accounts of the individual debtors and the total credit sales are credited to the credit sales account.

A fairly common occurrence is that more than one account is repeatedly influenced by a series of similar transactions. In the special journal in the example above, only the credit sales account is credited. However, suppose that a store is divided into several different departments and that the credit purchases for each department have to be identified separately. In this case an **analysis journal** would be used.

In an analysis journal there is a separate amount column for each ledger account which is repeatedly influenced by a series of transactions.

Figure 11.8

ANALYSIS JOURNAL JANUARY 19.4										
Date	Creditors	Folio	Total	Groceries	Hardware	Textiles	Advertising	Sundry		
								Item	Folio	Amount
19.4										
Jan 4	Adlam	C1	400,10	200,10	100,00	100,00				
16	Johnsons	C2	880,40	680,40				Cleaning		200,00
18	Pinto	C3	1 040,78	400,70	640,08					
19	Rollpress	C4	160,72				160,72			
22	Textilia	C5	390,40			390,40				
24	Tee Vee	C6	560,00				560,00			
26	Trio Motors	C7	360,40					Petrol		360,40
			R3 792,80	R1 281,20	R740,08	R490,40	R720,72			R560,40

11.8 DESIGN OF GENERAL LEDGER ACCOUNTS

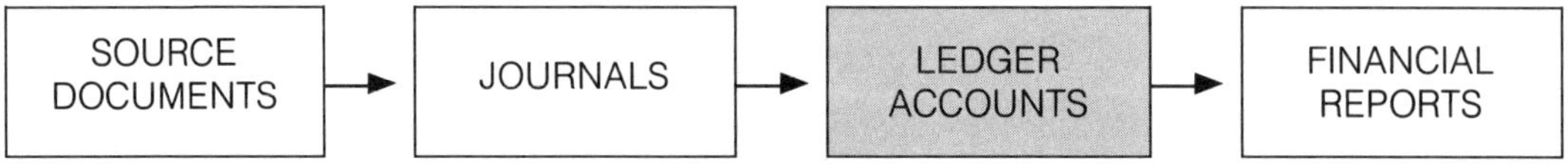

The third step in the accounting process is the transfer of information from the journals to the **ledger accounts**. The relationship between source documents, journals and accounts is reflected in figure 11.6.

In chapter 6 we stated that information is classified and stored in ledger accounts. The information for each item requiring a separate record, is kept in a separate account. The information that must be provided by the accounting system determines which accounts are needed.

The composition of a set of accounts in the ledger constitutes the basis for the design of an accounting system; therefore the decision as to which accounts to use and which information to store in each account is probably the most important step in the design of an accounting system.

The design of the ledger encompasses decisions about:

- ☐ the form and content of an account
- ☐ the accounts which will make up the ledger
- ☐ the coding of accounts.

11.8.1 The form and content of accounts

The basic design of accounts was discussed in chapter 6. When a system is designed the information desired will also determine the nature and form of the data recorded in an account. If the information is not recorded in an account it cannot be reproduced in a report. Therefore to satisfy information needs an account must be designed so that it contains more than the minimum information as discussed in chapter 6.

Frequently in manual systems only the journal from which a specific transaction has been posted is referred to in the details column of the account, for example:

			STATIONERY				S4
Jan 11 Feb 6	Bank Bank	C1 C2	300,60 50,10				

It is more meaningful to specify the other person involved in the transaction in the details column – then enquiries can be made without referring to the original journal, for example:

			STATIONERY				S4
Jan 11 Feb 6	Penkor Wen T	C1 C2	300,60 50,10				

An account can also be designed to make provision for recording quantities, for example:

				PETROL					P12
Mar 1 Apr 2	A Garage B Garage	60ℓ 40ℓ	P1 P4	35,00 25,00					

When additional information is included in an account provision should be made for that information in the relevant journal and source documents.

The date of a transaction is useful for management purposes. For example, in credit control over debtors it is necessary to know for how long an amount has been outstanding. In computerised systems the ageing of outstanding amounts is done by the system. Therefore it is important that the correct date of the transaction is recorded and not, for example, the date on which the amount was posted. In such a case it is also important that the date is recorded in the correct format.

Often it is also desirable to record the reference number of the relevant source document in the account in place of or in addition to the folio reference number of the journal. This is especially useful in debtors' accounts, because it facilitates enquiries by the undertaking or the debtor.

			JOHN SMITH				
Jun 11 14	Invoice 412 Invoice 635	S1 S3	412,60 120,40	Feb 2	Credit note 318 Receipt 217	CN4 C3	60,00 400,00

In debtors' and creditors' accounts, in particular, full addresses, credit limits and other information is recorded for the purpose of credit control, marketing and purchasing.

11.8.2 Design of ledgers

The accounts that satisfy the information needs of an undertaking are described and codified in a **chart of accounts**. The chart of accounts is a list of accounts which is used in the undertaking's accounting system and includes a description and number for each account. Although the description of an account gives an indication of the recorded transactions, the accounting system frequently provides specific instructions regarding the use of each account.

In an accounting system accounts are classified into different categories, depending on their nature, and coded accordingly. The categories correspond with the classifications in the financial reports which are prepared from the information in the accounts. For example, accounts can be categorised as fixed assets, liquid assets, other assets, owner's equity, long-term liabilities, short-term liabilities, income and expenses.

A typical chart of accounts for a trading concern is illustrated in figure 11.9. This chart of accounts provides a framework which can be extended and adapted by any particular undertaking.

Figure 11.9

THEORETICAL CHART OF ACCOUNTS FOR A TRADING CONCERN

CATEGORY 1: ASSETS

10 FIXED ASSETS
1000: Land
1010: Buildings
1011: Accumulated depreciation: Buildings
1030: Furniture and fittings
1031: Accumulated depreciation: Furniture and fittings
1040: Vehicles
1041: Accumulated depreciation: Vehicles

11 INTANGIBLE ASSETS
1100: Goodwill

12 INVESTMENTS AND LOANS

15 CURRENT ASSETS
1500: Trading inventory
1509: Consumable inventory
1510: Payments in advance
1540: Debtors
1541: Provision for doubtful debts
1560: Bills receivable
1580: Bank
1590: Cash

CATEGORY 2: EQUITIES

20 OWNER'S EQUITIES
2000: Capital
2001: Current account
2002: Drawings

23 FINAL ACCOUNTS
2300: Trading account
2330: Income account

25 LONG-TERM LIABILITIES
2500: Bond on fixed property
2540: Loan

29 CURRENT LIABILITIES
2900: Short-term loans
2910: Creditors
2920: Bills payable
2940: Overdue accounts

CATEGORY 3: EXPENSES AND LOSSES

31 COST OF SALES
3100: Cost of sales
3110: Purchases
3111: Purchases returns
3130: Import expenses
3140: Freight on purchases

33 ADMINISTRATIVE AND SALES EXPENSES
3300: Salaries and wages
3305: Rent
3310: Repairs and maintenance
3315: Rates and taxes
3320: Advertisements
3325: Licences
3330: Insurance
3335: Bank charges
3355: Printing and stationery
3390: Depreciation

38 LOSSES
3800: Inventory losses
3801: Cash shortages
3802: Loss on sale of fixed assets

39 FINANCING EXPENSES
3900: Interest on bank overdraft
3901: Interest on loans

CATEGORY 4: INCOME AND PROFITS

40 TRADING INCOME
4000: Sales
4001: Sales returns

41 INCOME FROM SERVICES
4100: Commission
4110: Fees received

42 INCOME FROM INVESTMENTS
4200: Dividends
4210: Interest
4220: Rent

49 PROFITS AND EXTRAORDINARY INCOME
4900: Profit on sale of fixed assets
4920: Extraordinary income

11.8.3 Subsidiary ledgers and control accounts

Where a large number of similar accounts occurs in an accounting system, these accounts can be transferred from the general ledger to subsidiary ledgers. A single control account is maintained in the general ledger for each subsidiary ledger and the balance on the control account must agree with the sum of the balances on all the individual accounts in the subsidiary ledger, as reflected in figure 11.10.

Figure 11.10

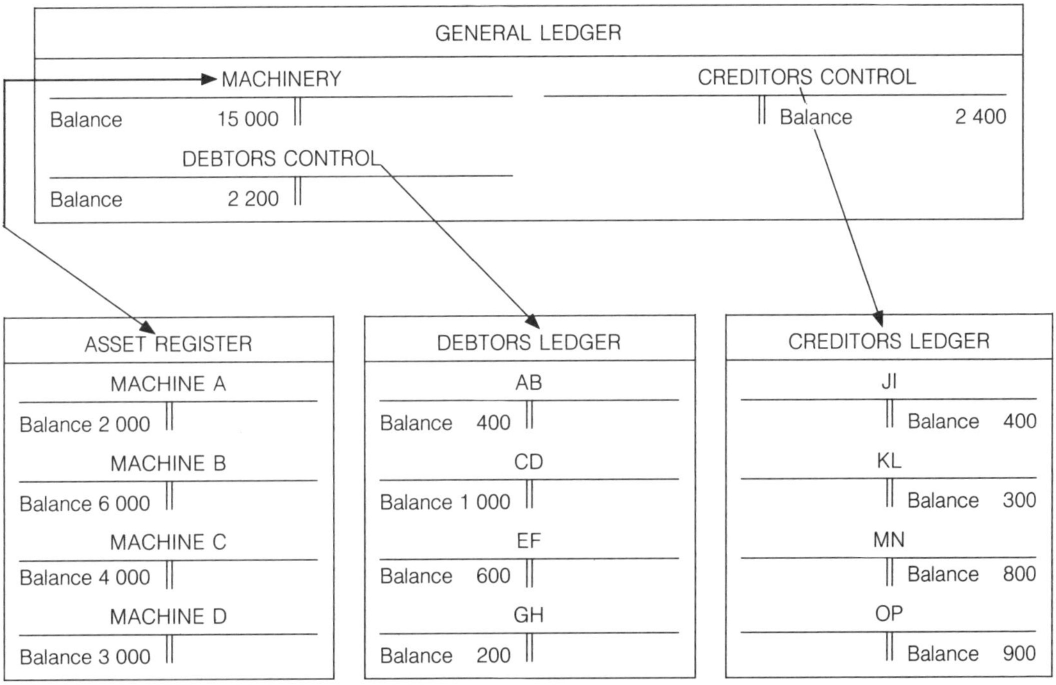

Note that the subsidiary ledger for machinery is known as the **asset register**.

Subsidiary ledgers are usually used in practice for:

- ☐ debtors
- ☐ creditors
- ☐ fixed assets
- ☐ inventory.

The use of subsidiary ledgers in an accounting system has important **advantages**.

First, the number of accounts in the general ledger is reduced significantly. **Second**, it is possible to operate a separate chart of personal accounts in a system designed specifically for that purpose. This simplifies the administrative function and ensures more effective control.

The principle underlying subsidiary ledgers is that the **total** of all individual entries in the separate accounts in the subsidiary ledger is recorded in the relevant control account in the general ledger. Therefore the single balance on the control account should at any stage be equal to the sum of the balances on the individual accounts in the subsidiary ledger.

The transactions in the subsidiary ledgers are posted from special journals designed so that amounts posted to subsidiary ledgers are recorded and summarised in one column. Each individual transaction is posted to the relevant account in the subsidiary journal, while the total of all the transactions is posted as one amount to the control account. This procedure is illustrated in more detail in the next chapter.

11.9 REPORTS

The form, layout and quality requirements of financial statements will be discussed fully in other chapters.

From a management information point of view it is important that the information needs of a user are determined and that the report meets these needs.

Each user of information needs this information in order to execute responsibilities. A report ought to be designed to meet these needs in the most effective and efficient manner. A report should provide the relevant information clearly, accurately and timeously. Superfluous information can often be confusing. Inaccurate or insufficient information is of little or no value and often the time spent preparing the report is a waste.

Information should be provided so that action can be initiated timeously. Information should be the key that leads to timeous action. It is the duty of the systems designer to design the report in such a way that it meets this requirement.

11.10 ELECTRONIC DATA PROCESSING (EDP)

Rapid development in the field of computers has led to increased computerisation of business systems.

The effectiveness of an accounting system is increased when it is able to furnish information which is more usable, more accurate and more timeous and when it provides better internal control. Efficiency increases as the value of the system increases in relation to the cost thereof.

Computerised systems are more effective than manual systems because of their tremendous speed in processing data, their large data storage capacity and their accuracy. On the other hand, as a result of the relatively high cost of equipment, software and specialised personnel, computerised systems are much more expensive than manual systems. Therefore the effectiveness and efficiency of alternative systems should be considered thoroughly.

It is also important that the accountant has sufficient knowledge of electronic data processing (EDP) to use computerised accounting systems.

EDP, however, is a broad discipline which should be studied in detail in specialised courses. The purpose of this discussion of the subject is merely to make the student aware of the different facets of EDP and to indicate the areas to which an accountant should pay special attention.

It is necessary to discuss the most important technical aspects of computers briefly in order to point out their impact on accounting systems.

11.10.1 Types of computers

A computer system consists of the following components, as reflected in figure 11.11:

- ☐ A central processing unit (CPU).
- ☐ Input units.
- ☐ Output units.
- ☐ Data storage units.
- ☐ Software.

Figure 11.11 A computer system

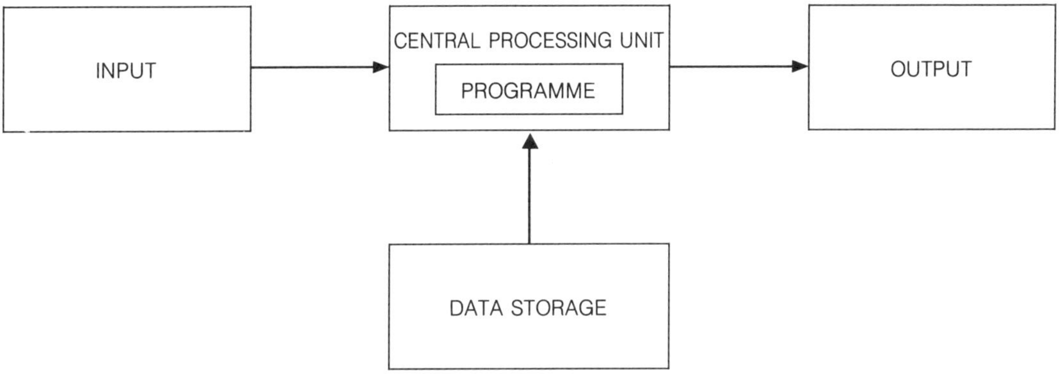

The core of a computer system is the **central processing unit (CPU)**, in which the processing of data takes place electronically according to defined **programmes**. Data is fed to the CPU through an **input unit** and processed information is made available to the user via an **output unit**. The computer equipment is referred to as **hardware**. The programmes are referred to as **software**.

Computers are classified according to their size as micro-computers, mini-computers or mainframe computers.

Micro-computers or personal computers are table models used mainly by one person for a single application at a time. A micro-computer consists typically of the following configuration: a processing unit with 64 K to 640 K[1] internal memory, a keyboard, a single or dual disc drive, a screen and a printer. Although the scope and complexity of the work which can be done on micro-computers is relatively limited, they are used to an increasing extent in stand-alone accounting systems.

A mini-computer typically has a processor with a memory of 2 to 8 megabytes and a processing speed of 0,6 to 11 MIPs[2], which is much faster than that of micro-computers. The fixed disc drive of a mini-computer has a much greater capacity than that of a micro-computer.

As opposed to the single work station of a micro-computer, mini-computers usually have 6 – 8 work stations and can also support multiple output units. The setting-up cost of a typical mini-computer configuration is about 10 times more than that of a micro-computer.

1 K = 1 000 characters.
2 Million instructions per second.

A mainframe computer typically has a processor with an internal memory of 4 to 256 megabytes and a processing speed of 1 to 100 MIPs. A mainframe computer has multi-work stations and multi-processing capabilities and can operate a large number of peripherals simultaneously. A mainframe computer has external storage capacity of approximately 1 gigabyte and additional capacity on permanent magnetic discs on real-time disc drives.

The operation of installing a mainframe computer requires a team of specialised supporting personnel and the computer must be in specially equipped, air-conditioned housing. The setting-up and operating costs of a mainframe computer are substantially higher than those of a mini-computer.

For the purpose of discussing simple accounting systems, we will deal only with the micro computer.

11.10.2 The micro-computer system

The operation of a micro-computer system is discussed briefly to point out its impact on accounting systems.

In a micro-computer system the most important input units are the **keyboard** and the **disc drive**. Data is entered into the central processing unit manually via the keyboard. As an input unit the disc drive reads data in its magnetic form from the disc.

A disc drive may handle floppy discs which are inserted and then removed and stored separately, or it may be a fixed disc which resides permanently in the drive. A micro-computer typically has a single or dual disc drive which has either two floppy disc drives or one floppy disc drive and a fixed disc drive. The storage capacity of a fixed disc is 10 to 40 megabytes compared with the 360 K of a floppy disc. The diskettes are stored separately outside the system until the data they contain is needed.

The most important output units in a micro-computer system are the screen, the printer and the disc drive.

The screen or visual display unit (VDU) displays the data which has been entered via the keyboard as well as the results of any processing. Any output can also be printed in a format suitable for the user via the printer.

When data is written onto discs via the processor, the disc drive functions as an output medium. The discs (floppy or fixed) are therefore the medium on which data is stored permanently in a micro-computer system.

The central processing unit of a micro-computer consists of:

☐ the processing unit
☐ an internal memory
☐ a control unit.

The **processing unit**, which is the heart of the computer, does arithmetical calculations and logical processing of data according to a programme of coded instructions which it receives from the control unit.

The **internal memory** stores the programme and the data being processed at any particular moment.

A **programme** is a set of instructions given to the computer. The programme is written in a **programming language** by a programmer and then loaded into the internal memory via the input unit.

There are usually two types of programmes in the internal memory at any time, namely:

☐ an operating systems programme
☐ an applications programme.

The operating system is a set of instructions which regulates the operations of the different components of the system, for example the operation of the input and output units, the transfer of data between units, etc. The operating system resides in the internal memory, either permanently or is loaded each time the computer is switched on.

The applications programme is a set of instructions which determines the steps in the data processing procedure. For example, the applications programme defines the various steps in an accounting system. An applications programme is loaded into the internal memory only when it is required for a specific application.

The **control unit** receives instructions from a programme in the internal memory, which in turn issues machine-coded instructions to all the components of the system.

To be able to write instructions in machine code requires a high level knowledge of computers. It would be impractical to expect every computer user to be a technical expert, therefore different **programme languages** have been developed which allow the instructions to be written in words or mathematical symbols. The programming language can be converted to coded instructions in the control unit by means of a **compiler**.

In the programming language BASIC, **PRINT A * B** is an instruction to the computer to calculate the product of A and B and to display the answer on the screen.

Data that has to be processed must be loaded via the input medium into the internal memory, where the processing unit manipulates the data according to the instructions of the applications programme.

The processed results are reloaded into the internal memory, from where they are transferred to an output unit such as a screen, printer or data storage unit, according to instructions.

To be able to operate a specific programme on a specific computer configuration:

- ☐ the programme must be compatible with the operating system of the computer concerned
- ☐ the programming language must be compatible with the compiler
- ☐ the internal memory must be large enough to accommodate the programme and the data being processed
- ☐ the external storage capacity must be sufficient to accommodate all data.

11.10.3 Applications programmes

A programme for a specific application, such as an accounting system, can be obtained in two ways. The user may write his own programme or buy a programming package which has been written for a specific application.

There are two levels of programming language – high level programming languages and fourth generation languages.

In order to write a special applications programme in a high level programming language, the logic of each step in the data processing procedure must be defined and codified according to the syntax rules of that particular programming language. In order to be able to write a good programme, a thorough knowledge of a programming language is essential.

Generally it is not necessary for an accountant to be fluent in a high level programming language.

In fourth generation programming languages the data processing procedures are contained in a single powerful instruction. As a result these languages are easier to use and also more effective than the high level languages.

Accountants should preferably have a knowledge of the fourth generation languages which have been developed for micro-computers. These languages are especially useful for financial modelling, such as budgets. Usually an accountant does not need in-depth knowledge of the fourth generation languages applicable to mainframe computers.

A wide variety of commercial software packages covering the spectrum of accounting systems – general ledger, debtors, creditors, stock, salaries and wages, etc – is available. These programmes are usually available in separate modules for each application and are available for micro, mini and mainframe computers. The packages for micro-computers are available on floppy discs together with comprehensive manuals.

In order to use a software package for a specific application it is usually necessary to define only the characteristics of the application. For example, the user will define which ledger accounts are to be used and the codes for each.

The question often arises whether an undertaking should develop its own software for specific applications, or buy a software package. The efficiency and effectiveness of each alternative should be considered before this question is answered.

By developing programmes, it may be possible to satisfy certain specific needs of the undertaking more effectively. On the other hand, programming is an expensive process which requires personnel who have the relevant qualifications and experience. If the quality of customised programming is suspect, this could cost the undertaking dearly.

The cost of programming can be reduced considerably by the use of fourth generation languages.

Off-the-shelf software packages are usually much cheaper than customised packages, but because these packages have been written for general use they do not always satisfy all the needs of a particular undertaking. Generally, within limits, these packages can be adapted.

11.10.4 Guidelines

The following guidelines should be taken into account in a computerised accounting system:

- ☐ The characteristics of the system are determined by the information and control needs of the undertaking and not *vice versa*.
- ☐ The effectiveness of the accounting system must be weighed against its efficiency.
- ☐ The capacity of the computer system must suit the nature and volume of the work.
- ☐ The effectiveness and efficiency of customised programmes must be weighed against off-the-shelf packages.
- ☐ The technical characteristics of the applications software must be compatible with that of the hardware, for example in respect of the operating system and the compiler.
- ☐ The personnel operating the system must have the relevant training and competency.

12

ACCOUNTING SYSTEMS: APPLICATIONS (Purchases, Inventory, Sales and Cash)

The **AIM** of this chapter is to explain the systems specifically applicable to trading concerns.

12.1 INTRODUCTION

In the previous chapter we saw that the transactions arising from the business activities of an undertaking are recorded within the framework of an accounting system.

Purchases, **storage** and **sales** of trading goods are the vital elements in the operating cycle of a trading concern. The transactions arising from the purchasing and sales activities are the basis for the design of the relevant journals.

In this chapter the emphasis is on:

- ☐ purchasing systems and procedures, the purchases journal and the creditors ledger
- ☐ inventory records
- ☐ sales systems and procedures, the sales journal and the debtors ledger
- ☐ recording cash receipts and payments.

12.2 PURCHASES

12.2.1 Objectives of a purchasing system

The **primary aim** of a purchasing system is the timeous and accurate recording of purchase transactions; **first**, to ensure that at any given time the accounting records correctly reflect the financial position and result, and **second**, to provide timeous management information necessary for running the business.

The **secondary aim** of the system is to facilitate control over purchase transactions by ensuring that each transaction is authorised, that goods ordered are received on time and in good condition, that the correct price has been charged, that all obligations to suppliers are recorded, and that accounts are settled on time.

12.2.2 Systems applicable to credit purchases

Every undertaking that buys goods or services on credit should have a system which meets at least the following requirements:

- ☐ All credit transactions must be recorded fully at the time of the transaction.
- ☐ The relevant expense or asset account must be debited with the correct amount.
- ☐ The relevant creditor's account and the control account must be credited with the correct amount.
- ☐ All payments to creditors and credits received from them must be debited to the correct creditor's and control accounts when the transactions occur.
- ☐ The outstanding balances on the creditor's accounts must be kept up to date continuously.

The most effective system for an undertaking will be determined by its particular circumstances, but a system for credit purchases will usually contain the following elements:

- ☐ control over ordering and receipt of goods and services purchased
- ☐ the recording of source documents in relevant journals and accounts

- ☐ maintenance of creditors' accounts and control account
- ☐ payments to creditors.

12.2.3 Purchasing procedure: Control over ordering and receipt of goods and services

The purchasing procedure commences when the need for certain goods arises in the stores or a sales department, or in any other department where goods are traded or consumed.

The first control measure applied in the purchasing procedure is that all purchases should be properly authorised. This implies that there must be a responsible person who has the authority to decide which goods may be purchased, in what quantities and at what prices. The first step of the purchasing procedure, then, is a properly authorised request to the purchasing department to purchase the relevant goods or services. In the flow chart below this request is represented by a **requisition** sent from an inventory control department to the purchasing department. In practice this procedure can be implemented in several different ways. In a small enterprise, for example, it will probably be the same person who determines the need and places the order.

The purchasing department checks the authorisation of the requisition. If this is in order the buyer will locate a supply of the goods needed, negotiate the conditions of sale with the supplier, and place an order. In the system depicted in the flow chart, two copies of the order are sent to the receiving department. These two copies are called **goods received notes (GRN)**. One copy of the order is kept by the ordering department to serve as a basis for follow-up action if the order is not delivered on time.

The **goods received note** is a key document in the creditors system because it confirms that the goods or services for which the undertaking has been invoiced, were actually received. An invoice from a supplier is not *prima facie* evidence that goods or services were supplied. Invoices from suppliers should be accepted only if there is proof of delivery.

Below is a typical **order form**. On the copy which serves as a goods received note provision is made for the signature of the person receiving the goods.

Figure 12.1

	Order	No 4168
PO Box 4168 Pretoria 0001	EKOMARK 72 14th Street Pretoria	Tel (012) 47-6680 Telex 'Ekom'

To: Abel & Co PO Box 2160 Germiston	Date: 24 April 19.7

Please deliver the following			
Item			Price
1 doz APX shirts 3 doz WPK suits			
Delivery address	Method of delivery	Delivery date	Terms
72 14th Street Pretoria	Road	5 May 19.7	30 d.d.
Order form		W Nel	

K Roos

Received by

Goods received note

On receipt the goods are checked against the particulars of the order, as detailed in the GRN. If they agree, the receiving clerk signs both GRNs. One GRN is filed with the copy of the original order as proof that the order has been executed and the other is forwarded to the accounts department. If there is an error in the consignment – for example, a discrepancy in quantity or a problem with the quality – the receiving clerk records this on the GRN.

Information flow diagrams are useful tools for developing and describing accounting systems and procedures. An information flow diagram is a schematic representation of the flow of information from different documents and records through the various departments in an undertaking.

For example, the procedure for credit purchases can be represented as follows in an information flow diagram:

In the flow diagram the symbol ↓ indicates that the copies of the documents in question are filed in the department where they originated.

Figure 12.2

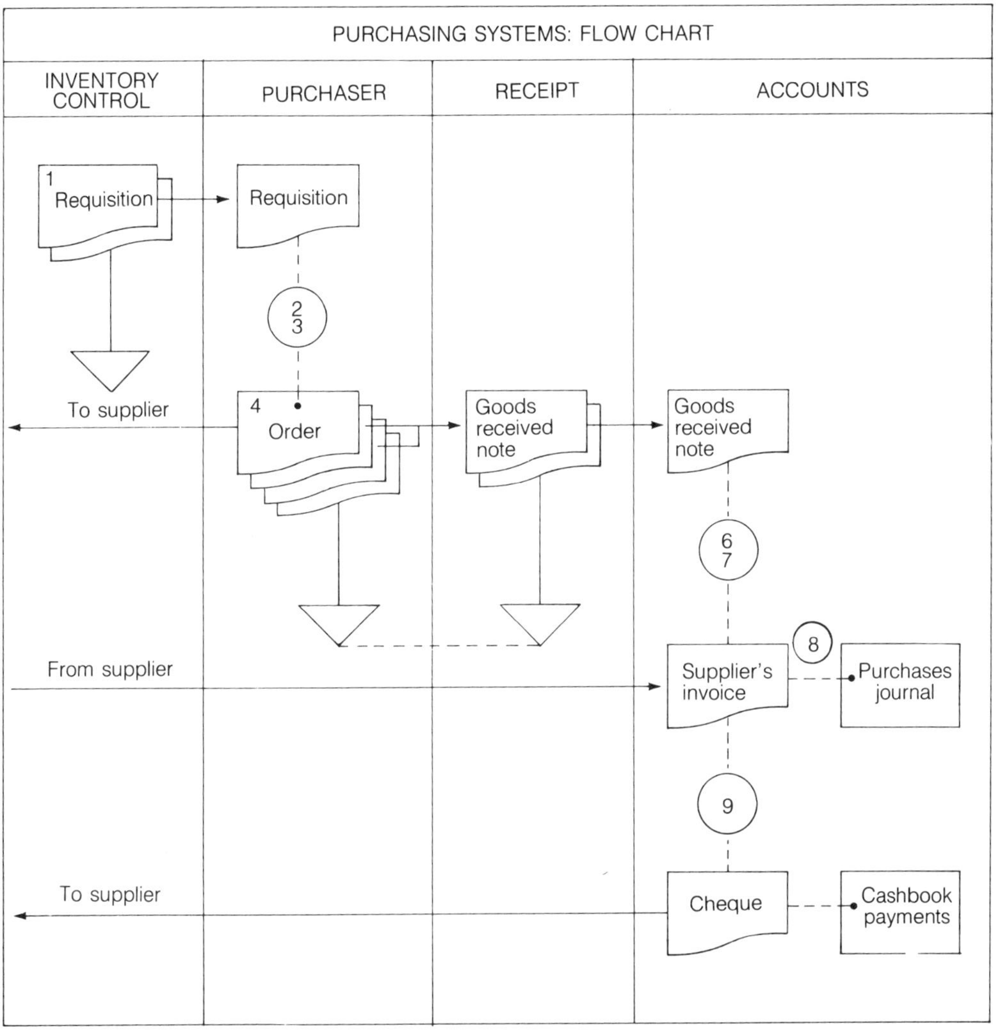

Explanatory notes

(1) The inventory control department sends a requisition to the buyer and files one copy.
(2) The buyer checks the authorisation for purchases.
(3) The buyer negotiates conditions of purchase with the supplier.
(4) The order is made out in quadruplicate; one copy is sent to the supplier, the second and third copies are sent to the receiving department, and the fourth is filed.
(5) Upon receipt the goods are checked against the details on the order. The goods received note is forwarded to the accounts department. The third copy of the order can now be filed.
(6) When the invoice is received it is checked against the order and the fact that the goods have been received in good condition is confirmed.
(7) The invoice and consequently the payment are now approved.
(8) The invoice is recorded in the purchases journal.
(9) A cheque is made out and forwarded to the supplier.

12.2.4 Recording of credit purchases: The purchases journal, creditors ledger and creditors control account

Generally the supplier's **invoice** and a **goods received note** (GRN) constitute the source documents for a credit purchase transaction. As an internal control measure, goods should be processed only if they are supported by the relevant goods received note.

The purchases journal is used specifically for recording credit purchases, and is designed to meet the particular circumstances of an undertaking.

The information from the source documents is used to record credit purchases in the **purchases journal**. From there the entries are posted to the creditors ledger. (In mechanised and computerised systems, recording in the journal and in the relevant **ledgers** takes place simultaneously.)

□ Maintenance of creditors' accounts

A creditor's account is basically the same as any other general ledger account. In addition it usually contains full details of the creditor, for example his name and address, and often also details regarding credit terms and conditions of payment. As is the case with debtors' accounts, in manual or mechanised systems creditors' accounts are usually kept on separate pages or cards. In computerised systems they are stored on magnetic media.

□ Maintenance of a creditors control account

The principles underlying the maintenance of control accounts have already been discussed in the previous chapter.

If individual and control accounts are kept it is important that the creditors control account (or accounts if more than one is kept, e g as a result of alphabetical splitting: creditors control account A – F, creditors control account G – K) is kept up to date and that it is compared regularly with the total of the individual accounts. This ensures that all transactions relating to creditors have been recorded.

The use of an analysis purchases journal together with a creditors ledger and a creditors control account is illustrated in example 12.1.

In the example the purchases journal has been designed, *inter alia*, to provide for two specific trading departments in the undertaking.

The comprehensive description of each transaction in the purchases journal facilitates later reference. The minimum information necessary to identify a transaction is the creditor's name, the invoice number, the date of the transaction and the amount on the invoice.

Sometimes, if source documents are also numbered consecutively, this number will be recorded in the purchases journal. The complete set of source documents, comprising at least the invoice and relevant GRN, is filed either in the order in which they were recorded in the purchases journal, or according to creditor.

The invoice amounts are posted individually to the appropriate creditor's account in the creditors ledger. The particulars of each transaction, especially the date, invoice number and amount, are recorded in detail in the creditor's account.

The total of the creditors column is credited to the creditors control account at the end of the applicable accounting period (usually a month). Similarly, the total purchases of each purchasing department for the period are debited to the relevant purchases accounts in the general ledger. Consequently, the double entry is maintained.

Example 12.1

PURCHASES JOURNAL
MAY 19.7 — Page 1

Date	Creditor	Invoice number	Folio	Creditors	Men's clothing	Ladies' clothing	Sundries Item	Sundries Folio	Sundries Amount
19.7 May 8	Abel & Co	320	A3	400,00	100,00	300,00			
14	R Outfitters	X537	R6	50,00	50,00				
20	S Evert & Co	9807	E9	300,00					
22	Abel & Co	510	A3	750,00	400,00	350,00			
26	Johns Brothers	LB803	J7	80,00		80,00			
28	R Outfitters	X802	R6	60,00	60,00				
31	Paperman	413	P4	20,00			Packing material	860	20,00
	XY Garage	416	X2	40,00			Petrol	810	40,00
				R1 700,00	R910,00	R730,00			R60,00
				(250)	(501)	(502)			

GENERAL LEDGER

PURCHASES: MEN'S CLOTHING — 501

19.7 May31	Creditors	PJ1	910				

PURCHASES: LADIES' CLOTHING — 502

19.7 May31	Creditors	PJ1	730				

CREDITORS CONTROL — 250

				19.7 May31	Balance		950
					Purchases	PJ1	1 700

PETROL AND OIL — 810

19.7 May 31	Creditors	PJ1	40				

PACKAGING MATERIAL — 860

19.7 May31	Creditors	PJ1	20				

CREDITORS LEDGER

Date	Details	Folio	Dr	Cr	Bal
ABEL & CO — A3					
19.7 May 1	Balance			460	460
8	Invoice 320	PJ1		400	860
22	Invoice 510	PJ1		750	1 610
S EVERT & CO — E9					
19.7 May 1	Balance			280	280
20	Invoice 9807	PJ1		300	580
JOHNS BROTHERS — J7					
19.7 May 1	Balance			100	100
26	Invoice LB803	PJ1		80	80
PAPERMAN — P4					
19.7 May 1	Invoice 413	PJ1		20	20
R OUTFITTERS — R6					
19.7 May 1	Balance			60	60
14	Invoice X537	PJ1		50	110
28	Invoice X802	PJ1		60	170
XY GARAGE — X2					
19.7 May 1	Balance			50	50
31	Invoice 416	PJ1		40	90

In the example the alternative 3-column account format is used in the creditors ledger. This format has the advantage that the balance on the account can be determined after each transaction. Therefore the account is always up to date, unlike the conventional T-format where the balance is usually determined only at the end of the month. Compare the account of Abel & Co above with the following conventional layout:

Dr				ABEL & CO			Cr
19.7 May 31	Balance	b/d	1 610	19.7 May 1 8 22	Balance Invoice 320 Invoice 510	b/d PJ1 PJ1	460 400 750
			R1 610				R1 610
				19.7 May31	Balance	c/d	1 610

□ **Comparison of the balance of the control account with the total of the balances of the individual creditors accounts**

The importance of this procedure has already been emphasised. In the above example the balance on the creditors control account is R2 650 (Cr) (R950 + R1 700). In order to make the comparison, a list of the balances in the creditors ledger is drawn up as follows:

Creditors balances 31 May 19.7

Abel & Co	R1 610
S Evert & Co	580
Johns Brothers	180
Paperman	20
R Outfitters	170
XY Garage	90
	R2 650

□ **Settlement of creditors' accounts**

It is important for the creditors' system to make provision for a procedure that ensures the prompt settlement of creditors' accounts, so that discounts allowed for timeous settlement are not lost, or legal action is not taken against the concern for failure to pay creditors.

Usually invoices are stamped as being approved for payment. A typical stamp of approval may appear as follows:

Figure 12.3

APPROVAL OF INVOICE

Date: 8 May 19.7

Supplier's number		A3
Allocation	Account number	
Men's clothing Ladies' clothing	501 502	100 300 R400

Price checked	BW
Calculations checked	AN
Approved for payment	JK
Cheque number	4176623

It is also important that the balances on the individual creditors' accounts are compared regularly (at least monthly) to the statements received from creditors. This procedure ensures that all transactions with a specific creditor are reflected correctly.

12.3 INVENTORY

12.3.1 Objectives of inventory systems

In earlier paragraphs we discussed purchasing systems. The next phase in the business cycle is **inventory control**.

In the determination of the financial result and the financial position the primary objective of inventory systems is to calculate the cost of inventory used or sold and to estabish the value of inventory on hand.

However, inventory systems also have secondary objectives of:

- ☐ exercising physical control over stock
- ☐ supporting management information for the planning and control of the enterprise's activities.

12.3.2 Physical control

The principle underlying physical control over inventory is that if a record is kept of the movement of inventory, it should be possible to determine how much inventory is on hand. For control purposes the actual physical inventory on hand can be checked against this theoretical figure.

12.3.3 Management information

It is essential that an enterprise always maintains sufficient inventory to meet demand. This is especially applicable with regard to trading inventory, raw materials, consumable stock or any other goods which are sold or consumed continuously. The need for availability demands high inventory levels, while the need for maximum yield on investment requires low inventory levels. Management must be constantly aware of the amount invested in inventory so that the purchasing programme can be regulated to keep inventory at optimum levels. Inventory systems are designed to provide information on inventory levels.

12.3.4 Procedure for inventory management

Inventory levels are regulated by two basic aspects of managerial policy, namely the decisions regarding:

- ☐ when to purchase
- ☐ what quantity to purchase.

The **re-order point method** is used to decide when additional stock must be acquired. According to this method inventory must be augmented when stock on hand reaches a certain re-order point. The re-order point is equal to the amount sold or consumed during the **purchases lead time**, plus a safety or buffer stock.

The purchases lead time is the period which elapses between the placing of an order with a supplier and receipt of the goods. The example below helps to illustrate the re-order point and the lead time:

Assume that an enterprise consumes inventory at the rate of 350 units per week and that the purchase lead time is four weeks. The re-order point is $4 \times 350 = 1\ 400$ units. If there is uncertainty regarding the purchases lead time, provision must be made for a buffer or safety stock. If the lead time could vary from four to six weeks, provision for buffer stock of at least two weeks (i e 700 units) must be allowed. Then the re-order point will be set at $1\ 400 + 700 = 2\ 100$ units.

Figure 12.4 Determining re-order point for inventory

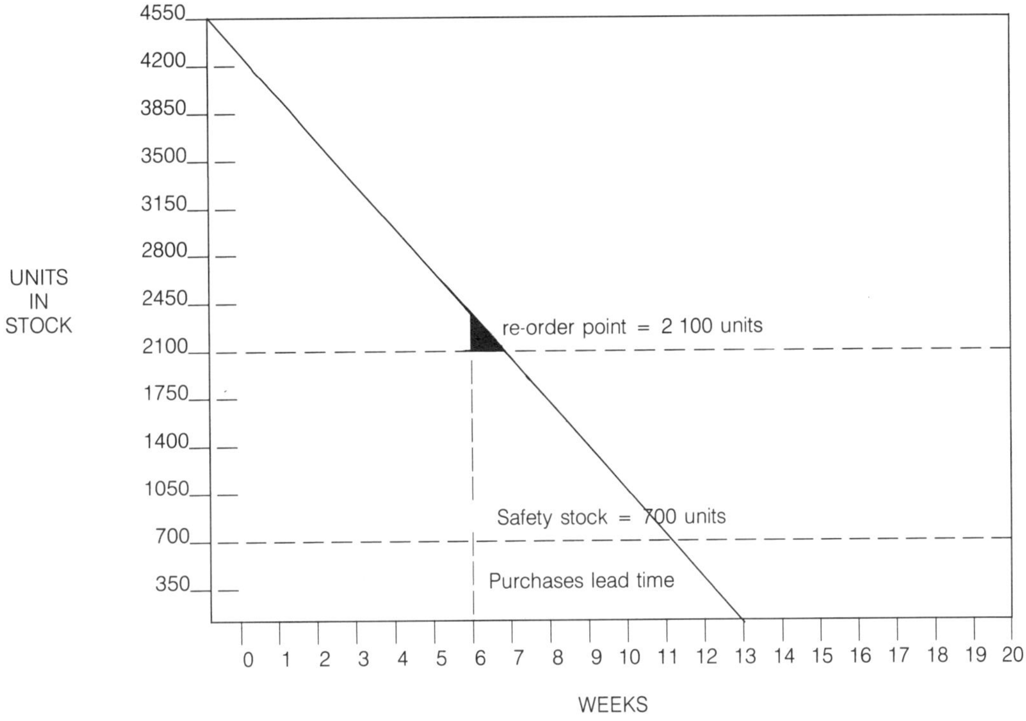

It is evident that management must be constantly aware of inventory levels so that it knows when a re-order point has been reached.

Quantities to be purchased are determined by taking into account future demand, which is often deduced from past demand.

12.3.5 Keeping inventory records

There are two different systems of keeping a record of the quantity of goods in stock, viz the **perpetual inventory system** and the **periodic inventory system**.

The **periodic inventory system** involves physical stocktaking in order to determine the cost price of goods sold (consumed). The cost of goods consumed during a specific period (and between two stock takings) is determined at the end of each period as follows:

Opening inventory at cost	+	Purchases at cost	−	Closing inventory at cost	=	Cost price of goods used

Practical considerations, such as the relative simplicity and low cost of implementing the periodic inventory system, have resulted in the system being used extensively by small businesses. Its disadvantage, however, is that physical stock losses are not identified.

The **perpetual inventory system** is a method of recording whereby a continuous record of the movement of specific items in and out of stock is kept. The inventory records are continuously updated with the sales or purchases of each item so that the number of items in stock is reflected accurately. Physical stock taking can be combined with the perpetual inventory system: most concerns using this system take physical stock periodically or count stock continuously and systematically during the course of a financial year so that all items are counted at least once a year. The physical count serves as a control over the perpetual inventory records, and any discrepancies are investigated and adjusted.

An inventory record consists of a separate **inventory card** for each item, that is a loose-leaf system of one page per inventory item. The inventory records actually comprise part of a subsidiary ledger and the values in the records must agree with the balances on the control account.

The following is an example of a typical inventory card:

Figure 12.5

Item ....
Storage location ....
Code no ....

Date	Reference	Received			Issued			Balance		
		Units	Unit price	Total	Units	Unit price	Total	Units	Unit price	Total

The procedure followed in a perpetual inventory system is illustrated in the flow chart below:

Figure 12.6

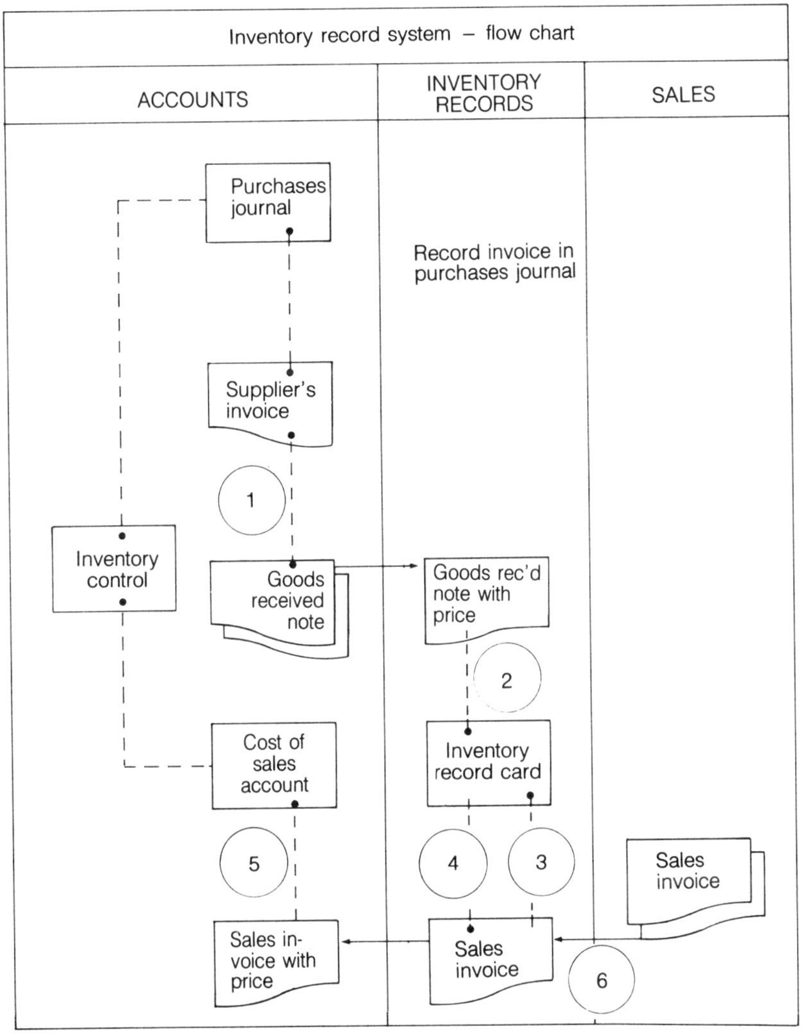

Explanatory notes

Accounts department:
(1) calculates the cost price of goods and records this on the copy of the GRN, which is forwarded to inventory records.
Inventory records department:
(2) records the quantities and prices of goods received on the stock card;
(3) records the quantities sold from the invoice onto the stock card;
(4) records the cost price of goods sold on the invoice and sends it to the accounts department.
Accounts department:
(5) records the invoice in the cost of sales account.
Sales department:
(6) sends one copy of the sales invoice to the inventory records department.

The procedure for recording inventory in the perpetual inventory records is adjusted to suit the particular requirements in each case.

The recording procedure is initiated when the accounts department receives an invoice, with an accompanying goods received note, for goods purchased. The unit cost of the goods is calculated from the invoice and recorded. This copy of the GRN is sent to the inventory records department, where it is entered on the stock card as a receipt. At the same time, the accounts department records the invoice total in the inventory control account via the purchases journal. Therefore the total purchases in the inventory control account should agree with the total purchases on the individual inventory cards.

The inventory records department also receives copies of all sales invoices. From the sales invoices the quantities of each item sold are recorded on the inventory record card. The cost of the goods sold is entered from the inventory cards onto the copy of the invoice which is forwarded to the accounts department, where the quantities and cost prices of goods sold are recorded in the inventory control account via the sales journal.

12.4 SALES

12.4.1 Objectives of sales systems

As far as the financial records are concerned, the **primary aim** of sales systems is to record correctly the income from sales, on the one hand, and obligations of debtors, on the other.

The **secondary objectives** of sales systems are to maintain internal control over sales transactions and debt collection and to provide information for planning purposes. For example, a sales manager will want to monitor the performance of the sales staff and the sales trends of different product lines continuously. This will be accomplished only if the system provides an uninterrupted flow of necessary information.

12.4.2 Systems for granting credit

Each undertaking that grants goods or services on credit needs a system which meets the following minimum requirements:

- ☐ Credit transactions must be recorded fully at the time they take place.
- ☐ The relevant income account must be credited with the correct amount.
- ☐ The relevant debtor's and control accounts must be debited with the correct amount.
- ☐ All payments by debtors or any other authorised credits must, when received or authorised, be credited to the correct debtor's and control accounts.
- ☐ The outstanding balances on debtors' accounts must be kept up to date continuously.
- ☐ Statements must be prepared and sent to debtors regularly.

A system for credit transactions usually consists of:

- ☐ recording details of the transactions on source documents
- ☐ recording the source documents in journals
- ☐ maintenance of debtors' accounts
- ☐ rendering of accounts
- ☐ credit control.

12.4.3 Source documents

Two types of information should be contained in source documents, viz:

- ☐ financial information – to record the transaction completely
- ☐ other information needed by management and which does not affect the accounting records.

For example, in the design of a sales invoice, the transaction data that must be contained in the source document will be determined as follows:

TRANSACTION DATA IN A SOURCE DOCUMENT*	
INFORMATION REQUIRED	TRANSACTION DATA THAT MUST BE CONTAINED IN A SOURCE DOCUMENT
(a) For recording in accounting records:	
(1) Debit to debtor's account: For each customer, the amount and date of each transaction	(1) Name and address of customer (2) Amount of transaction (3) Date of transaction
(2) Credit to credit sales account: Total credit sales per month	(2) Amount of transaction (3) Date of transaction
(b) For management decision making:	
(1) Control over sales personnel: Sales per salesman per period Discount allowed	(4) Name of salesman (2) Amount of transaction (7) Discount allowed
(2) Planning the marketing in different geographical areas	(1) Address of customer
(c) For operating activities:	
(1) Delivery of goods	(5) How and where customer desires delivery to be made
(2) Recovery of debtors	(1) Name and address of customer (5) Description of transaction (2) Amount of transaction
(3) Payment conditions	(6) Full address where customer must effect settlement (7) Terms of settlement
(4) Calculation of sales tax	(8) Sales tax

*The numbers refer to the example of the sales invoice at the beginning of the chapter.

A sales invoice which is designed and completed according to the outline above will appear as follows:

Figure 12.7

INVOICE
GNK LIMITED
BUILDING MATERIALS
141 Gordon Road
Pretoria

Phone (012) 47-6138
Telex 'Genka'

(6) PO Box 4160
Alkant Ridge 0081

SOLD TO	DELIVERY				DATE 14/3/19.1 (3)
(1) ALMA BUILDERS PO BOX 431 PRETORIA 0001	(5) ALMA BUILDERS 413 NYALA ROAD MONTANA				SALESMAN
ORDER NO 743	PER	ROAD	RAIL	COLLECTED	(4) J SMITH

ITEM	Quantity	Unit price	Total	
(5) Rotsvas Paint 20ℓ	10	R8,30	83,00	(2)
(7) *Less:* 5% Discount			4,15	
			78,85	
(8) *Plus:* General sales tax			9,46	
			R88,31	

(7) TERMS: 2,5% 10 days, net 30 days

The non-financial information in the invoice (e g address, credit terms) appears on the debtor's account, but is not recorded again in the sales journal, for example.

12.4.4 Recording credit sales: The sales journal, debtors ledger and the debtors control account

A journal for recording sales transactions, known as a **sales journal**, is used to transfer the financial information from the source documents to the accounting system. In a manual system the sales invoices are recorded individually in the sales journal. Then each transaction is posted individually to the relevant debtor's account in the debtors ledger. At the end of the financial period (usually monthly) the total credit sales is debited to the debtors control account and credited to the sales account in the general ledger. This procedure is illustrated in example 12.2.

The sales journal will also be designed to suit the information needs of the particular undertaking. Example 12.2 illustrates a sales journal which makes provision for two sales departments.

In computerised systems, information is recorded simultaneously in the debtors' accounts and in the general ledger.

☐ **Sales tax**

In terms of sales tax legislation, every business is legally obliged to pay to the State, on a monthly basis, the prescribed general sales tax (GST) which it collected on the sale of goods and services.

The sales journal will be designed to make provision for recording sales tax from the sales invoices, as illustrated in example 12.2.

☐ **Debtors control account**

A debtors control account should always be kept for each set (e g alphabetically A – F, G – K) of debtors' accounts. The debtors control account is an important control instrument which ensures that all transactions relating to a particular debtor's account have been recorded in the system. Therefore it is important that the total of balances on the individual debtors' accounts is agreed periodically (at least monthly) with the balance on the debtors control account.

The procedure is illustrated in example 12.2.

Example 12.2

SALES JOURNAL – MAY 19.8							Page 10
Date	Account debited	Invoice number	Folio	Debtors	Men's clothing	Ladies' clothing	Sales tax
19.8							
May 2	H Fourie	120	F8	100,00	89,00		11,00
6	J Wright	121	W5	150,00		134,00	16,00
12	P Stone	122	S7	130,00	116,00		14,00
14	E Willis	123	W4	80,00		71,00	9,00
20	H Fourie	124	F8	200,00	178,00		22,00
28	E Willis	125	W4	240,00		216,00	24,00
				R900,00	383,00	421,00	96,00
				(301)	(501)	(502)	(407)

Individual amounts are posted daily to the debtors ledger

Totals are posted to the general ledger at the end of the month

DEBTORS LEDGER

Date	Details	Folio	Dr	Cr	Bal
H FOURIE					**F8**
19.8					
May 2	Invoice 120	SJ10	100		100
20	Invoice 124	SJ10	200		300
P STONE					**S7**
19.8					
May 12	Invoice 122	SJ10	130		130
E WILLIS					**W4**
19.8					
May 14	Invoice 123	SJ10	80		80
28	Invoice 125	SJ10	240		320
J WRIGHT					**W5**
19.8					
May 6	Invoice 121	SJ10	150		150

GENERAL LEDGER

DEBTORS CONTROL ACCOUNT							**301**
19.8 May 31	Sales	SJ10	900				
SALES: MEN'S CLOTHING							**501**
				19.8 May 31	Debtors	SJ10	383
SALES: LADIES' CLOTHING							**502**
				19.8 May 31	Debtors	SJ10	421
GENERAL SALES TAX							**407**
				19.8 May 31	Debtors	SJ10	96

Note that the total of the debtors column is debited to the debtors control account in the general ledger, and that the double entry is maintained by crediting the totals of the sales columns and the sales tax column to the relevant accounts.

As in the case of creditors, the accuracy of the balance of the debtors control account (R900) can be checked by drawing up a list of balances from the debtors ledger:

FOLIO	LIST OF DEBTORS' BALANCES	
F8	H Fourie	R300
S7	P Stone	130
W4	E Willis	320
W5	J Wright	150
		R900

The **sales tax account** is similar in nature to a creditor's account: the tax on sales transactions is collected on behalf of the State and must be paid over within a specified time. The procedure is illustrated in a later chapter.

12.4.5 Returns and other credits

At the same time that goods are despatched to a customer, they are invoiced to him at the selling price. However, the goods may be unacceptable to the client, for example they may have been damaged in transit, or the wrong goods may have been delivered. In this case the buyer will either send the goods back (known as **returns**) or may be compensated by being given an **allowance**, for example a reduction in the selling price. In both instances the buyer will be issued with a **credit note** informing him that his account has been reduced by the amount indicated on the credit note. In the case of sales, the terms used are **sales returns** and/or **allowances** and in the case of purchases, **purchases returns** and/or **allowances**.

These transactions are analysed in the normal manner and can be recorded in the general journal. Where these types of transactions occur frequently two additional books of first entry, namely the **sales returns journal** and the **purchases returns journal**, can be used.

Example 12.3

SALES RETURNS JOURNAL
AUGUST 19.9

Date	Account credited and description	Credit note number	Folio	Amount
19.9				
Aug 3	R Marais: damaged goods	207		15,00
13	J Walker: defective materials	208		18,00
20	M Jones: not ordered	209		20,00
25	F Roux: damaged goods	210		3,00
31	Debit: Sales returns		404	
	Credit: Debtors control		121	R56,00

The individual journal entries are credited daily to the relevant debtors' accounts. At the end of the month the total of the returns is debited to the sales returns account and credited to the debtors control account. When the general ledger is closed off, the debit balance on the sales returns account is transferred to the debit side of the sales account in order to calculate net sales.

12.4.6 Debtors' accounts

Debtors' accounts can be kept in various ways.

In manual systems the debtors' accounts are kept in bound or loose-leaf books. In mechanised systems they are kept on loose cards, and in computerised systems they are kept on magnetic tapes or discs.

The basic form of a debtors' account is the same as that of a general ledger account. The essential financial information appearing in a debtor's account is:

- ☐ the name and reference number of the debtor
- ☐ the date of each transaction
- ☐ the source document reference number of each transaction
- ☐ the outstanding balance.

In the design of a debtor's account, provision is also made for recording the details needed for collection of the debt, such as the debtor's full address, telephone and telex numbers, credit limit and credit terms, and arrangement with regard to discount.

In mechanised and computerised systems the outstanding balance is automatically analysed according to age. This age analysis is extremely useful for credit control purposes.

Figure 12.8 A debtor's account

PO Box 816
EVATON 0012
Credit terms: 30 days — 436 Church Street, EVATON — TELEX 31X42
Credit rating: AA

		Dr	Cr	Balance
19.9				
Jan 1	Balance	436,00		436,00
20	Invoice 413	80,00		516,00
31	Credit note 26		20,00	496,00
6	Receipt 211		400,00	96,00

AGE ANALYSIS:

CURRENT	30 days	60 days	90 days	Total
60,00	36,00	—	—	96,00

12.4.7 Rendering of accounts

To effectuate the collection of outstanding amounts, **statements** must be rendered to debtors regularly (at least monthly). In essence a statement is a document reflecting the debtor's account in the books of the undertaking. It serves as notice to the debtor that he must settle the amount owing on the statement.

Statements can take various forms and contain different types of information. Often they contain only the outstanding balance at the end of the previous period for which a statement was rendered, the transactions which took place during the current period and the outstanding balance at the end of the current period. Alternatively, however, all the transactions comprising the outstanding balance can be shown.

In manual systems, statements are usually prepared from the information in the debtors' accounts. In loose-leaf systems photostats of debtors' accounts are often made to serve as statements which are sent to debtors. In mechanised systems the statement is usually a loose duplicate of the account which is always kept up to date. These duplicate statements are drawn periodically and sent to debtors. In computerised systems the programme usually makes provision for statements to be printed from the debtors' accounts stored on the magnetic tape.

Whichever system is used, it is important to ensure that the total of the balances on the statements agree with the total of the balances on the debtors' accounts. This ensures that a statement has been prepared for every account.

12.4.8 Design of a sales system

In the previous few paragraphs the various elements of and the transaction data involved in a credit sales system were discussed. To ensure an effective sales/debtors system, the methods and procedures of the system should be put into writing.

The procedure for processing a credit sale transaction can be explained, for example, as follows:

- ☐ The salesman completes an invoice in four-fold at the finalisation of each credit sale transaction. The original invoice is handed to the client and the other three copies are sent to the invoice clerk.
- ☐ The invoice clerk records the first copy in the sales journal and then files it. He sends the second and third copies to the debtors' clerk.
- ☐ The debtors' clerk records the transaction in the debtor's account from the second copy and files the second copy permanently and the third copy temporarily. The latter copy is sent later, together with the statement, to the debtor.
- ☐ The invoice clerk totals the amounts of all the recorded invoices for each month in the sales journal.
- ☐ The invoice clerk debits the debtors' control account and credits the credit sales account in the general ledger with the total credit sales from the sales journal.
- ☐ The debtors' clerk prepares a monthly statement for each debtor from the individual debtors' accounts and attaches copies of the invoices which appear on the statement before sending the statement to the debtor.

The efficacy of information flow diagrams was referred to in the discussion on purchases systems. The procedure for credit sales, as described above, would be reflected in an information flow diagram as follows:

Figure 12.9

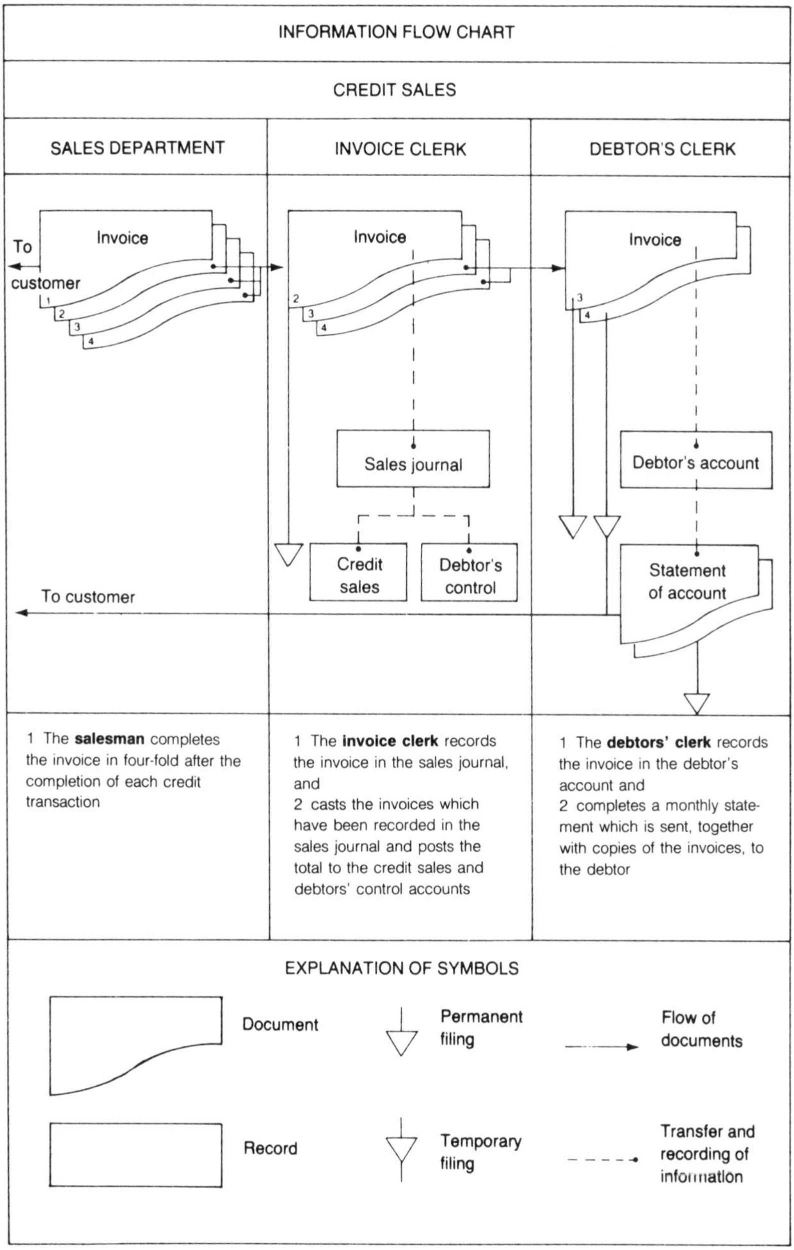

12.5 CASH

12.5.1 Cash receipts

The procedure for recording cash receipts will be determined by the nature of the receipt as well as the information required about the transaction.

Four main sources of cash can be distinguished.

- ☐ **Cash received on conclusion of a sales transaction**

Certain sales transactions such as goods sold in a department store, or tickets sold at a theatre box-office, do not require the identity of the purchaser to be recorded.

A ticket, cash register slip or cash sales invoice serves as record of the sale. These are totalled daily and serve as proof of the total cash which should be on hand.

Sometimes cash sales have to be analysed for managerial purposes, for example cash receipts according to departments, groups of products, or regions.

- ☐ **Cash received from trade debtors**

These monies may be received either personally or through the post; in either case a proof of receipt must be prepared with the following particulars: date, debtor's name, amount paid, and discount allowed (if any). The receipts must be officially prenumbered and strict control must be exercised over their use and the availability of blank forms. Mail must be opened in the presence of two officials, and postal receipts recorded before the cash is handed to the cashier.

- ☐ **Cash received from other sources**

Cash may also be received from transactions of a capital nature, such as the sale of assets, capital input by owners, loans received, repayments of loans granted, and deposits reclaimed. Complete information about these transactions is needed and it is important that the details of the transaction, as in the case of debtors, are properly documented.

- ☐ **Cash recovered by the bank**

The bank, acting on a client's instruction, may recover certain monies on his behalf, or agents and branches may deposit cash directly into the enterprise's bank account. In such cases the bank will issue the business with a receipt which serves as a source document for the transaction.

The following diagram illustrates the cash receipts procedure:

Figure 12.10

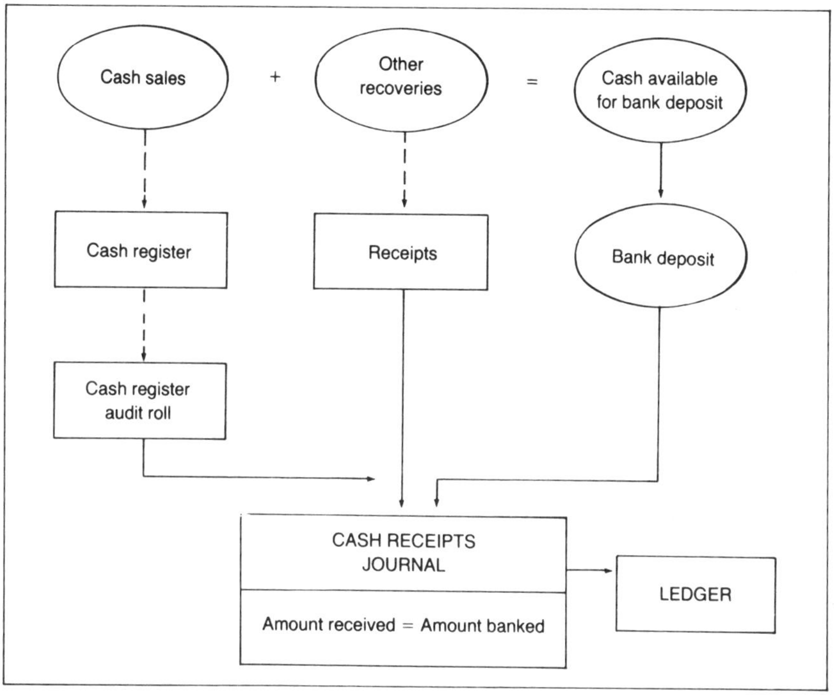

12.5.2 The cash receipts journal

All cash received is recorded in the cash receipts journal. This journal is compiled from source documents such as cash register totals and slips, cash sales invoices and receipts.

The most important advantage of keeping a special journal is that similar transactions can be grouped together and recorded and the total of a large number of transactions can be posted to the ledger accounts as a single amount.

The purpose is to determine the total cash received from a given source in a given period. The format and design will differ from one enterprise to another. The following example illustrates the posting of entries to the debtors ledger and the general ledger.

Example 12.4

CASH RECEIPTS JOURNAL
MAY 19.8 — Page 5

Date	Details	Folio	Bank Dr	Sundries Cr	Cash sales Cr	Debtors Cr
19.8						
May 7	Cash sales for the week		180,00		180,00	
14	Cash sales for the week		210,00		210,00	
16	Interest on investment	612	80,00	80,00		
20	H Fourie: Payment on account	F8				100,00
	Cash sales for the week		260,00		160,00	
27	E Willis: Payment on account	W4	80,00			80,00
28	Cash sales for the week		320,00		320,00	
			R1 130,00	R80,00	R870,00	R180,00
			(201) (dr)		(501) (cr)	(212) (cr)

Totals are posted at end of month

Individual amounts in the debtors column are posted to the debtors accounts in the debtors ledger

(a) Individual amounts in the sundries column are posted to the general ledger
(b) Therefore the total is not posted at the end of the month

DEBTORS LEDGER

Date	Details	Folio	Dr	Cr	Bal
H FOURIE					**F8**
19.8					
May 2	Invoice 120	SJ10	100		100
20	Invoice 124	SJ10	200		300
	Bank	CRJ5		100	200
P STONE					**S7**
19.8					
May 12	Invoice 122	SJ10	130		130
E WILLIS					**W4**
19.8					
May 14	Invoice 123	SJ10	80		80
28	Invoice 125	SJ10	240		320
	Bank	CRJ5		80	240
J WRIGHT					**W5**
19.8					
May 6	Invoice 121	SJ10	150		150

GENERAL LEDGER

Date	Details	Folio	Dr	Cr	Bal
BANK					**211**
19.8					
May 31	Total receipts	CRJ5	1 130		1 130
DEBTORS CONTROL					**212**
19.8					
May 31	Sales	SJ10	900		900
	Bank	CRJ5		180	720
SALES					**501**
19.8					
May 31	Debtors	SJ10		900	(900)
31	Bank	CRJ5		870	(1 770)
INTEREST ON INVESTMENT					**612**
19.8					
May 16	Bank	CRJ5		80	(80)

The posting is as follows:

- ☐ The total of the debtors column is **credited** to the debtors control account in the ledger. Each entry is posted to the credit side of the relevant debtor's account in the debtors ledger. The total credit on the debtors control account must agree with the individual amounts credited to the debtors' accounts.
- ☐ The total of the cash sales column is **credited** to the sales account. (Credit sales are recorded in the sales journal.)
- ☐ The **total** of the '**sundries**' column is **not** posted since the amounts are credited **individually** to the account concerned. Therefore the folio number will be recorded opposite each **individual sundries amount**. However, only one amount is posted from the other columns, with a single folio reference opposite the total.
- ☐ The total of the bank column is **debited** to the bank account in the ledger. This total must agree with the total sum of the analysis columns.
- ☐ There is no 'balance' on the cash receipts journal; it merely serves as a book of first entry.

Appropriate analysis columns may be used according to the frequency with which certain items occur. However, a 'sundries' column must always be provided for items not occurring regularly. The principal function of analysis columns is to eliminate repetitive postings.

12.5.3 The cash payments journal

All cash payments are recorded in the cash payments journal. This journal is compiled from source documents such as cheque book counterfoils and corroborative documentation such as invoices and authorisations for payment.

The most important control measure is that all payments (except petty cash payments) must be made by cheque and that these payments must be controlled and authorised.

The following example illustrates the functioning of the cash payments journal in conjunction with the creditors ledger, control accounts and the general ledger.

Example 12.5

CASH PAYMENTS JOURNAL
MAY 19.8 — Page 8

Date	Details	Chq no	Folio	Bank	Sundries	Purchases	Creditors
19.7							
May 3	SAR&H: Freight on purchases	0124	511	30,00	30,00		
5	Rent for May	0125	512	300,00	300,00		
7	Goods bought for cash	0126		400,00		400,00	
18	Abel & Co	0127	A3	400,00			400,00
24	Goods bought for cash	0128		280,00		280,00	
25	R Outfitters	0129	R6	50,00			50,00
31	Salaries	0131	513	604,00	604,00		
31	Receiver of Revenue: GST	0131	407	96,00	96,00		
				R2 160	R1 030	R680	R450
				(110)		(501)	(301)

Amounts are posted individually from sundries column to general ledger

Payments to creditors are posted individually during the month, to the creditor's account in the creditors ledger

Totals are posted to the general ledger at the end of the month

CREDITORS LEDGER

Date	Details	Folio	Dr	Cr	Bal
	ABEL & CO	A3			
19.7					
May 8	Invoice 320	PJ1		400	400
22	Invoice 510	PJ1		750	1 150
28	Bank	CPJ8	400		750
	R OUTFITTERS	R6			
19.7					
May 14	Invoice X537	PJ1		50	50
28	Invoice X802	PJ1		60	110
25	Bank	CPJ8	50		60
	S EVERT & CO	E9			
19.7					
May 20	Invoice 9807	PJ1		300	300
	JOHNS BROTHERS	J7			
19.7					
May 26	Invoice JB803	PJ1		80	80

GENERAL LEDGER

BANK — 110

Date	Details	Folio	Amount	Date	Details	Folio	Amount
				19.7 May 31	Total payments	CPJ8	2 160

CREDITORS CONTROL — 301

Date	Details	Folio	Amount	Date	Details	Folio	Amount
19.7 May 31	Bank	CPJ8	450	19.7 May 31	Purchases	PJ1	1 640

PURCHASES — 501

Date	Details	Folio	Amount	Date	Details	Folio	Amount
19.7 May 31	Bank	CPJ8	680				

FREIGHT ON PURCHASES — 511

Date	Details	Folio	Amount	Date	Details	Folio	Amount
19.7 May 31	Bank	PJ1	30				

RENT — 512

Date	Details	Folio	Amount	Date	Details	Folio	Amount
19.7 May 5	Bank	CPJ8	300				

SALARIES — 513

Date	Details	Folio	Amount	Date	Details	Folio	Amount
19.7 May 31	Bank	CPJ8	604				

SALES TAX — 407

Date	Details	Folio	Amount	Date	Details	Folio	Amount
19.7 May 31	Bank	CPJ8	96	19.7 May 31	Sales	SJ10	96

12.5.4 The bank account in the general ledger

Items appearing in the 'sundries' column are again debited individually to the appropriate accounts. At the end of the month the total payments are credited to the bank account as a single item. Folio references are recorded in the usual manner.

Notice again that the balance in the ledger is maintained by the use of the double-entry system. In other words, the sum of those items debited individually to the ledger is equal to the total of the single credit posted to the bank account in the ledger and vice versa.

The cash receipts journal and the cash payments journal, being books of prime entry, are typical columnar journals from which the debit and credit are posted to the general ledger at the end of each month. Therefore the cash receipts and cash payments journals do not have balances. The use of these two journals can be represented diagrammatically as follows:

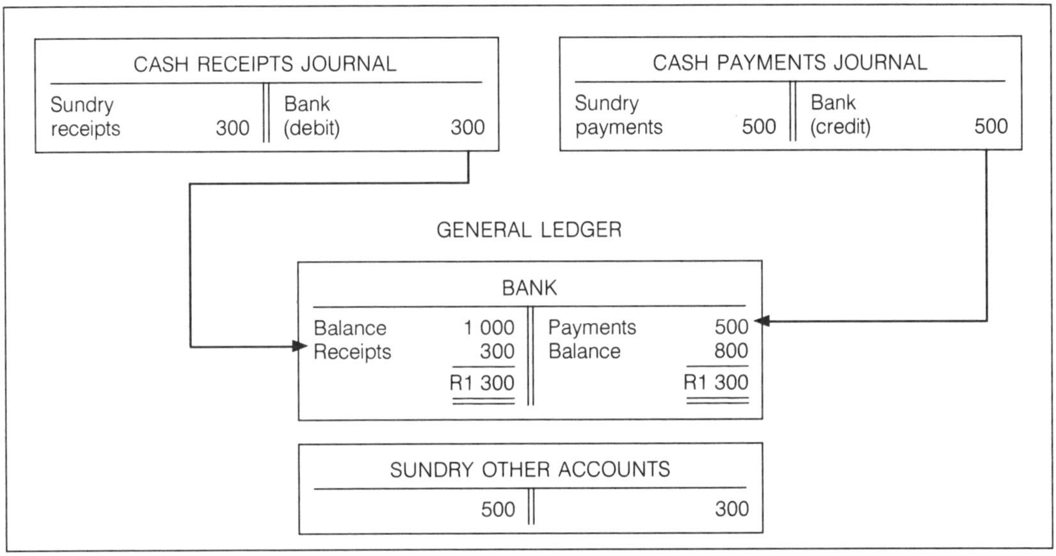

13

CASH

The **AIM** of this chapter is to emphasise the importance of internal control, to explain the reconciliation of the undertaking's records with those of the bank, and to discuss the function of the petty cash book.

13.1 THE NATURE AND IMPORTANCE OF CASH

Money is a medium of exchange and an indicator of value. Cash, as an indicator of value, is the means used to quantify all transactions, assets and obligations.

Cash is the most liquid form of money and therefore an enterprise's most active asset. It is the beginning and end of the business cycle (cash – inventory – sales – cash) and the life-blood of the business organism. It is the function of management to ensure that sufficient cash is available to meet the needs of the enterprise. A sound cash flow is the basis for a financially healthy enterprise. Nearly all the transactions which are recorded involve a flow of cash either **to** the enterprise (a receipt) or **from** the enterprise (a payment). The cash flow generated by some transactions is not immediate, but will take place at a later stage, for example stock bought on credit.

Cash may be defined as any legal medium of exchange which is immediately negotiable and free of restrictions. It includes coins, notes, cheques, postal orders, savings deposits and bank deposits. An essential requirement is that it must be immediately available as legal tender; therefore loans to employees, postage stamps and fixed period deposits cannot be regarded as 'cash' for balance sheet purposes since they are subject to conversion before they are available as cash.

13.2 INTERNAL CONTROL OVER CASH

Because cash is the most liquid asset, it is the most easily misused. Therefore every enterprise must have an effective internal control system for cash.

In smaller enterprises the owner or manager usually exercises personal control over all cash transactions. In larger enterprises, however, it is impossible for one person to exercise individual control; therefore the accounting system of the enterprise must be designed to include adequate control measures over cash flow. The design of this system should include control totals at various points against which the accuracy of a series of items can be tested.

A sound cash control system should meet at least the following requirements:

- ☐ Employees' duties and functions must be separated to ensure that those persons who receive, pay out or handle cash in any way are not involved in the recording function. This prevents a person from misappropriating funds and concealing the fact by forging entries in the books. The functions of employees must be divided in such a way that an error by one employee will be revealed, in the normal course of his duties, by another employee. This means that the collusion of at least two employees is necessary if funds are to be embezzled.
- ☐ Cash receipts must be recorded in such a way that the actual cash received can be checked against an independent daily record. Therefore a source document must be prepared as soon as cash is received. The source document should show the amount, the date of receipt, the reason for the receipt, and, where applicable, the person who made the payment. Examples of this type of source document are receipts, cash sales slips, invoices and control and audit rolls used in cash registers.
- ☐ All cash received must be banked daily and no payments should be made from the receipts. This ensures that cash is safe overnight and the bank deposit slips serve as a control total for cash received.
- ☐ All payments except petty cash payments (see par 13.5) must be made by cheque. Cheques must be countersigned and supported by a properly controlled and authorised source document which serves as proof of payment. The functions of the employees handling cheques must be separated from those of the employees recording the transactions.

- ☐ Cash must be verified, that is the actual amount of cash on hand must be compared with the source documents. The cash received should be checked daily by an official who is not responsible for the receipt and handling of cash. This person will unlock the cash register, replace the daily audit roll with a new roll, count the cash in the drawer in the presence of the cashier or counter assistant, and replace the cash float. The amount of cash received must agree with the total of the transactions registered on the audit roll.
- ☐ The cash records must be compared with the bank statement; this is known as bank verification. Also, the bank balance according to the records is reconciled with the balance on the bank statement. The daily cash deposits, cheque payments and bank verification ensure that the internal records can be compared with an external bank statement. The bank statement is forwarded by the bank to its clients regularly, together with cashed cheques and other debit notes. This statement shows the opening balance, all deposits credited, cheques and other items debited, and the closing balance.

13.3 RECORDING THE CASH FLOW

Cash is received from various sources and used for different purposes. The recording of cash receipts and payments in the cash receipts and cash payments journals, and the posting of these entries to the general ledger, the debtors ledger and the creditors ledger, is discussed in detail in a previous chapter.

13.4 RECONCILIATION OF THE BANK STATEMENT BALANCE WITH THE BANK ACCOUNT BALANCE

Periodically (usually monthly) the bank supplies its clients with a statement showing the opening balance, all deposits credited, all cheques debited (paid out), various debits and credits supported by documentation, and the closing balance. Cancelled (paid out) cheques and other debit notes are enclosed with the bank statement. Different banks may use different formats and symbols in their statements. Example 13.1 is an illustration of a typical bank statement.

The following abbreviations are used in example 13.1:

SO	– Stop order:	Orders signed by a client in favour of, for instance, an insurance company for monthly premiums paid by the bank on behalf of the client.
LF	– Ledger fees:	Charges for handling the bank account; related to the volume of transactions on the account.
CO	– Commission:	Commission levied on cheques exchanged (usually country cheques). This may include a levy for collection of cheques.
I	– Interest:	Interest levied on an overdrawn balance.
CB	– Cheque book:	Charges for cheque books issued to the client (including the stamp duty on each cheque).
UC	– Unpaid cheque:	Debit for cheque(s) deposited and for which payment was refused by the drawer's bank owing for example, to insufficient funds.
B	– Bill:	Bills recovered or paid on behalf of the client.
EC	– Error corrected:	Code used to correct errors on the bank statement.

Example 13.1

L M Jones
77 King Street
JOHANNESBURG 2001

Acc no/Rek no
01-27734-3691

Date Datum	Chq no Tjekno	Cheques/Tjeks	Deposits/Deposito's	Balance/Saldo
				3 248,85 OD
Feb 23'77			633,13	2 615,72 OD
Feb 23'77	280	26,00–		2 641,72 OD
Feb 24'77		15,60–CO	7 771,16	5 113,84 *
Feb 24'77	284	230,00–		4 883,84 *
Feb 26'77	285	10,14–		4 873,70 *
Mar 2'77	272	1,00–		4 872,70 *
Mar 3'77	286	44,50–		
Mar 3'77	287	50,00–		4 778,20 *
Mar 4'77	288	26,00–		
Mar 4'77	290	500,00–		
Mar 4'77	291	3 716,00–		
Mar 4'77	292	20,00–		
Mar 4'77	293	13,63–	20,03	522,60 *
Mar 7'77	294	21,00–		501,60 *
Mar 9'77	269	25,00–		
Mar 9'77	289	93,17–		
Mar 9'77	295	34,30–		349,13 *
Mar 10'77	278	19,23–		
Mar 10'77	296	40,00–		
Mar 10'77		1,75–CB		288,15 *
Mar 16'77	298	20,00–		268,15 *
Mar 17'77	297	60,10–		
Mar 17'77	51	40,00–		168,05 *
Mar 18'77	52	44,00–		124,05 *
Mar 21'77		3,08–LF		
		6,07–I		114,90 *
Mar 22'77	299	547,00–		432,10 OD
Mar 25'77			647,88	215,78 *
Mar 28'77	53	34,42–		181,36 *
Mar 29'77			1 000,00	1 181,36 *
Mar 29'77	54	250,00–		931,36 *
Mar 31'77	55	1 008,43–		
Mar 31'77	56	15,98–		93,05 OD
Apr 1'77			779,55	686,50 *
Apr 1'77	57	14,50–		
Apr 1'77	61	50,00–		622,00 *

THE SA BANK — DIE SA BANK

For your attention:
The bank will assume that the statement as rendered is correct unless notice of any discrepancies in connection with entries is received within 14 days of delivery hereof

Vir u aandag:
Die bank sal aanneem dat die staat soos gelewer juis is tensy kennis van enige verskille insake inskrywings binne 14 dae vanaf datum van lewering hiervan ontvang word

NB:
Kindly advise the bank of any change of address

LW:
Stel asseblief die bank in kennis van enige verandering van adres

Explanation of abbreviations/
Verklaring van afkortings:
SO – Stop order/aftrekorder
LF – Ledger fees/Boekgelde
SU – Sundries/Diverse
EC – Error corrected/ Fout gekorrigeer
CO – Commission/Kommissie
I – Interest/Rente
CB – Cheque book/Tjekboek
UC – Cheque unpaid/ Tjek onbetaald
B – Bill/Wissel
DO – Debit order/Debietnota
SR – Statement rendered/ Staat gelewer

Usually the balance on the bank statement does not agree with the balance on the bank account in the enterprise's nominal ledger, or with the balance appearing on the counterfoils of its cheque books. This discrepancy is not necessarily due to an error; rather, the difference can be accounted for or, in other words, **reconciled**.

The following are the most common causes of differences between the balance shown in the records of the enterprise and those of the bank:

(a) Items appear in the enterprise's books but are not yet reflected in the bank's records, for example:
- ☐ Outstanding cheques. These are cheques which have been drawn by the enterprise, but have not yet been presented for payment.
- ☐ Deposits not yet credited by the bank.

(b) Similarly, the bank's books may show various items not yet recorded by the enterprise, for example:
- ☐ Charges for services rendered by the bank (ledger fees).
- ☐ Commission on cheques.
- ☐ Unpaid cheques.
- ☐ Bills recovered or paid by the bank on behalf of the enterprise. Although the bank notifies the enterprise immediately of unpaid cheques and of bills paid or recovered via debit or credit notes, the enterprise usually records these items only when the bank reconciliation statement is prepared.

(c) Errors made by either the enterprise or the bank.

Whatever the nature of these differences, a reconciliation statement can be prepared to account for and clarify the differences. The reconciliation statement therefore reconciles the balance according to the enterprise's books (for convenience, hereafter referred to as the bank account balance) with the balance shown in the bank's books (hereafter referred to as the bank balance).

The following bank statement and cash journals are used to explain the procedure followed in reconciling the bank balance:

Example 13.2

XY BANK LIMITED

Mr M Ras
PO Box 12078
JOHANNESBURG

BANK STATEMENT

Date and code		Cheque no	Cheques and other debits	Deposits	Balance
Jun 30					√4 000,68
Jul 1	CO		,20	√500,40	4 500,88
3		591	√70,00		4 430,88
4				√300,80	4 731,68
7		592	√300,00		4 431,68
	CB		5,00		4 426,68
9		590	√600,00	√700,13	4 526,81
12		589	√150,23		4 376,58
14				√115,27	4 491,85
18		593	√700,11		3 791,74
20	CO		,80	√480,34	4 271,28
24				√80,92	4 352,20
25		597	√310,47		4 041,73
26	CU (J Wiese)		20,92	√2 000,37	6 021,18
27				√300,00	6 321,18
28	B			300,00	6 621,18
29		598	√500,00		6 121,18
	LF		10,00		6 111,18
30				√117,00	6 228,18
31		600	√400,00	√300,00	6 128,18
	SO		25,00		6 103,18
					The last amount in this column is thc balance

M RAS CASH RECEIPTS JOURNAL							Page 17
Date	Details	Folio	Sundry ledger accounts (Cr)	Sales (Cr)	Discount allowed (Dr)	Debtors (Cr)	Bank (Dr)
19.2							
Jul 1	Cash sales: slips 1 – 50			200,40			
	Debtors: receipts 1 – 10					300,00	√500,40
4	Cash sales: slips 51 – 58			200,00			
	Debtors: receipts 11 – 17				30,00	130,80	√300,80
9	Cash sales: slips 59 – 70			300,13			
	Debtors: receipts 18 – 30				40,00	440,00	√700,13
14	Cash sales: slips 71 – 77			115,27			√115,27
20	Cash sales: slips 78 – 85			80,34			
	Debtors: receipts 31 – 40					400,00	√480,34
24	Debtors: receipts 41 – 45					80,92	√80,92
26	Capital deposited: receipt 46	301	1 800,00				
	Debtors: receipts 47 – 50				10,00	210,37	√2 000,37
27	Cash sales: slips 86 – 90			300,00			√300,00
28	Cash sales: slips 91 – 100			117,00			√117,00
30	Cash sales: slips 101 – 105			300,00			√300,00
31	Cash sales: slips 106 – 108			500,00			500,00
			R1 800,00	R2 113,14	(R80,00)	R1 562,09	R5 395,23
				(401)	(520)	(201)	(202)

CASH PAYMENTS JOURNAL – July 19.2									Page 16
Date	Details	Chq no	Folio	Sundry ledger accounts (Dr)	Purchases (Dr)	Discount received (Cr)	Creditors (Dr)	Bank (Cr)	
19.2									
Jul 1	J Wilmans: On account	589					150,23	✓150,23	
2	S Stols: Rent	590	620	600,00				✓600,00	
	Perskor: Advertising	591	625	70,00				✓70,00	
10	T Roux: On account	592				30,00	330,00	✓300,00	
11	Fourie & Co: Cash purchases	593			700,11			✓700,11	
12	AB Ltd: Truck	594	110	2 000,00				2 000,00	
15	XY Printers: Stationery	595	630	40,00				40,00	
18	G Nel: On account	596				20,00	340,00	320,00	
20	Mooi River Traders: On account	597					310,47	✓310,47	
21	M Ras: Drawings	598	301	500,00				✓500,00	
25	Krost & Co: Furniture	599	115	200,00				200,00	
31	J Johns: Salary	600	640	400,00				✓400,00	
	F du Preez: Salary	601	640	300,00				300,00	
				R4 110,00	R700,11	(R50,00)	R1 130,70	R5 890,81	
					(600)	(530)	(310)	(202)	

Explanatory notes:

(1) Cross-cast of receipts:
R1 800,00 + R2 113,14 + R1 562,09 – R80,00 = R5 395,23

(2) Cross-cast of payments:
R4 110,00 + R700,11 + R1 130,70 – R50,00 = R5 890,81

It is explained in the previous chapter that the cash receipts and cash payments journals are posted to the general ledger at the end of the month. The items in the sundries columns are posted individually, while the **totals** of the other columns (including the two bank columns), are posted at the end of the month.

The **bank account** in the general ledger will contain, *inter alia*, the balance at the end of the previous month. In this example it is assumed, for the sake of simplicity, that the opening balances on the bank statement (R4 000,68) and the bank account are the same. The bank account at the end of July 19.2 will contain the following information:

BANK ACCOUNT							202
19.2				19.2			
Jul 1	Balance		✓4 000,68	Jul 31	Payments	CPJ16	5 890,81
	Receipts	CRJ17	5 395,23				

At the end of the month when the bank account is balanced it will be seen that there is a favourable or **debit balance** of R4 000,68 + R5 395,23 – R5 890,81 = **R3 505,10**. Therefore, according to the enterprise's records there is R3 505,10 in the bank. This balance is recorded as a preliminary balance on the debit side of the bank account. The record of the enterprise's bankers, that is the **bank statement**, shows a credit or favourable balance of **R6 103,18**. Before the books of the enterprise can be closed off, these two balances must be **compared** and **reconciled**.

In order to reconcile the two balances, each reconcilable item must be traced. This is done by comparing the bank statement with the bank account and the cash receipts and payments journals and ticking (✓) the items which agree. Obviously the items will appear on opposite sides in the records of the enterprise and the bank.

A cheque drawn by the enterprise is eventually posted to the **credit side** of the bank account from the cash payments journal. When this same cheque is paid by the bank, the bank credits its own cash account and **debits** the undertaking's account with the amount of the cheque.

Compare the given bank statement and cash receipts and payments journals after the corresponding items have been checked and ticked off:

☐ **As regards the cash receipts and payments journals**

(i) The deposit on 31 July in the cash receipts journal has not been ticked off. The deposit was recorded by the bank on 1 August and therefore will appear on the following month's bank statement.

(ii) The following cheques were not ticked off in the cash payments journal:

Number	594	R2 000
	595	R40
	596	R320
	599	R200
	601	R300

These are the outstanding cheques which have not yet been presented for payment.

☐ **As regards the bank statement**

(iii) The receipts or credit side of the bank statement shows a bill for R300 on 28 July which has not been ticked off. This is a bill recovered by the bank on behalf of the enterprise, which has not yet been recorded by the enterprise.

(iv) The debit side of the bank statement (i e in the cheques and other debits column) shows various items not yet ticked off, viz:

☐ Jul	1	Commission	0,20
	7	Cheque book	5,00
	20	Commission	0,80
	29	Ledger fees	10,00
			R16,00

These items are usually grouped together under the description '**bank charges**'.

☐ An unpaid cheque for R20,92, apparently included with the deposit of R80,92 made on 24 July.

☐ A stop order for R25 on 31 July (it is assumed that this was for the owner's insurance).

> Those items which have not been ticked off are therefore the **reconcilable** items.

The reconcilable items consist of:

(a) Items **not ticked off in the cash receipts and payments journals**

(b) Items **not ticked off on the bank statement**.

These items are treated as follows:

- ☐ The items under (a) already appear in the enterprise's records and therefore are not recorded again. They are recorded in a special statement, the **bank reconciliation statement**, which is prepared at least monthly.
- ☐ The items which have not been ticked off on the bank statement are items which still have to be recorded in the enterprise's books.

☐ Recording items which appear on the bank statement, but not in the records of the enterprise (items (iii) and (iv) above)

No further transactions can be recorded in the cash receipts and cash payments journals, since they have already been closed off for the month and posted to the general ledger. In fact, items that are entered in the accounting system to rectify the balance on a ledger account are merely **adjustments** and therefore are recorded by means of an adjustment journal. Item (iii) is a receipt which has not yet been recorded, while the other items are mainly payments in respect of bank charges and insurances, but include an unpaid cheque which must be debited to the relevant debtor's account.

The relevant adjustment journal entry is as follows:

GENERAL JOURNAL			Page 19
Bank charges		16,00	
Debtors control account: Unpaid cheque J Wiese		20,92	
Drawings		25,00	
Bills receivable			300,00
Bank account		238,08	
Recording of items appearing on July 19.2 bank statement			

This journal entry is posted in the usual way to the general ledger, and in the case of the unpaid cheque, also to the relevant debtor's account in the debtors ledger. Therefore, as far as the general ledger is concerned:

BANK CHARGES

19.2							
Jul 31	Bank	J19	16,00				

DRAWINGS

19.2							
Jul 31	Bank	J19	25,00				

DEBTORS CONTROL

19.2							
Jul 31	Bank	J19	20,92				

BILLS RECEIVABLE

				19.2			
				Jul 31	Bank		300,00

BANK ACCOUNT

19.2				19.2			
Jul 1	Balance	b/d	4 000,68	Jul 31	Payments	CP16	5 890,81
Jul 31	Receipts	CR17	5 395,23				
	Bank statement adjustments	J19	238,08				

The '**adjusted**' balance on the bank account is now a favourable balance of R3 743,18, viz:

BANK ACCOUNT

	4 000,68		5 890,81
	5 395,23	Balance b/d	3 743,18
	238,08		
	9 633,99		9 633,99
Balance c/d	3 743,18		

> This adjusted bank account balance is the amount which must agree with the bank statement balance.

The final step in the reconciliation of the bank account and bank statement balances is the preparation of the **bank reconciliation statement**. This statement contains the items which already appear in the enterprise's records but have not yet appeared in the bank's records. It must be emphasised that unlike the adjustment journal entry above, the bank reconciliation statement is **not** part of the double-entry process.

Different methods may be used to prepare the bank reconciliation statement. For example, it can start with the bank statement balance, which is reconciled to the bank account balance, or *vice versa*. The first method is used below:

BANK RECONCILIATION STATEMENT
31 JULY 19.2

Credit balance according to bank statement			6 103,18
Less: Outstanding cheque nos:	594	2 000,00	
	595	40,00	
	596	320,00	
	599	200,00	
	601	300,00	2 860,00
			3 243,18
Add: Deposit not yet credited			500,00
Balance according to bank account			R3 743,18

In the reconciliation statement above, the bank statement balance is the starting point and is reconciled **to the bank account balance**. The outstanding cheques are deducted from the bank statement balance, because they have already been recorded in the cash payments journal and are therefore already accounted for in the bank account balance. Similarly, the deposit which has already been accounted for in the bank account is added, because it has not yet been included in the bank statement balance.

The following alternative approach (which also starts with the bank statement balance and reconciles to the bank account balance) confirms the accuracy of the above procedure.

Alternative presentation:

	Dr	Cr
Credit balance according to bank statement		6 103,18
Cheques not yet debited by bank: per list	2 860,00	
Deposit not yet credited by the bank		500,00
	2 860,00	6 603,18
∴ Debit (favourable) balance (according to bank account)	3 743,18	
	R6 603,18	R6 603,18

The preparation of the following month's reconciliation statement can best be explained by means of an example.

Example 13.3

Below is a summary of the information appearing in the records of M Ras for August 19.2, and on his bank statement for August 19.2.

BANK ACCOUNT		
Debit side:		
Opening balance (as adjusted in the July bank account)		3 743,18
Deposits: Aug 4	500,00	
11	300,00	
15	700,00	
22	2 000,00	
31	200,00	3 700,00
		7 443,18
Credit side:		
Cheques issued: nos 602	150,00	
603	200,00	
604	100,00	
605	800,00	
606	3 000,00	
607	400,00	
608	350,00	5 000,00
'Provisional' balance of bank account		R2 443,18

BANK STATEMENT					
			Cheques and other debits	Deposits	Balance
Aug 1					6 103,18
2				500,00	6 603,18
3		594	2 000,00		4 603,18
	CO		3,18		4 600,00
5				500,00	5 100,00
7		595	40,00		5 060,00
		601	300,00		4 760,00
	LF		5,00		4 755,00
12				300,00	5 055,00
14		602	150,00		4 905,00
		605	800,00		4 105,00
16		606	3 000,00		1 105,00
				700,00	1 805,00
18		596	320,00		1 485,00
21		603	200,00		1 285,00
	CO		2,00		1 283,00
		604	100,00		1 183,00
				2 000,00	3 183,00
31		607	400,00		2 783,00

In contrast to the previous month, the opening balances on the bank account and the bank statement differ. The reconciliation statement at 31 July accounted for this difference. When compiling the reconciliation statement at 31 August those items appearing in the July reconciliation statement must be checked first to ascertain which of the items are reflected in the August bank statement.

Corresponding items will be ticked off as before. From this it will be seen that cheque no 599 is still outstanding. Thereafter the usual comparison of the August bank account and bank statement is carried out.

The following items cannot be ticked off on the bank statement:

CO	3,18
LF	5,00
CO	2,00
Thus: Bank charges	R10,18

The August bank charges will again be entered in the bank account, thereby reducing the provisional balance of R2 443,18 to R2 433,00. The reconciliation statement is compiled as follows:

			Dr	Cr
Credit balance according to bank statement				2 783,00
Cheques not debited by bank: nos	599	R200		
	608	R350	550,00	
Deposits not credited by bank				200,00
				2 983,00
Debit (favourable) balance (according to bank account)			2 433,00	
			R2 983,00	R2 983,00

Regular reconciliation of the bank account is an important cash control function in an enterprise. Errors and items requiring adjustment are revealed timeously by the process of regular reconciliation. If the reconciliation statement is compiled by a responsible official whose function does not include the handling and recording of receipts and payments, it can provide an effective control measure against certain types of cash theft.

13.5 THE PETTY CASH JOURNAL

In an earlier paragraph the use of cheques was recommended as a means of payment because it reduces the handling of cash, thereby serving as an additional control measure. Nevertheless, an enterprise may need to pay cash for certain smaller items such as postage, telegrams, etc. Therefore most enterprises keep a **petty cash float**.

A cheque for a specific amount known as the **petty cash float** is drawn and cashed for this purpose. The float is kept entirely separate from the monies received by the enterprise in the normal course of its business. These receipts, as stated earlier, must be banked in full.

A separate journal, known as the **petty cash book**, is used to record all payments made from the petty cash float. Payments are confirmed by sequentially numbered petty cash slips, usually signed by the persons authorising and receiving the payment. Alternatively, petty cash slips may be countersigned by two officials. Periodically a responsible official compares the total payments with the supporting documentation and the cash on hand is counted and compared with the book balance. Then the petty cash float is restored to its original balance by drawing a cheque for the precise amount paid out during the period. This system of restoring the petty cash fund to the original balance is known as the **imprest system**. The amount of the float will be determined by the needs of the enterprise.

It is important that the official responsible for keeping and administering the petty cash fund should not handle other cash funds as well, and if the size of enterprise allows, the petty cash book should preferably be written up by someone other than the cashier in charge of petty cash. The initial cheque drawn for the petty cash fund should be entered in the cash payments journal. The example below illustrates the function of the imprest system in the petty cash book system.

Example 13.4

		CASH PAYMENTS JOURNAL		Folio CPJ3
Date	Details	Sundries	Other analysis columns	Bank
19.7 Oct 1	Petty cash – initial advance	50,00		50,00

The amount appearing in the sundries column is posted to the debit side of a **petty cash control account** in the general ledger. The receipt of the float is also recorded in the special subsidiary journal, the petty cash book. The petty cash book is generally columnar to allow for the allocation of repetitive transactions, as shown below:

PETTY CASH JOURNAL – OCTOBER 19.7											Folio 1
Receipts			Payments								
Date	Folio	Amount	Date	Details	P/cash voucher	Folio	Sundries	Postages	Wages	Stationery	Total
19.7			19.7								
Oct 1	CB3	50,00	Oct 3	Wages	1				10,00		10,00
20	CB4	47,00	10	Stamps	2			8,00			8,00
				Wages	3				10,00		10,00
			15	Telegrams	4			4,00			4,00
			18	Paper and ink	5					7,00	7,00
			20	Advertising		(71)	8,00				8,00
						(70)	8,00	12,00	20,00	7,00	47,00
				Balance			50,00				50,00
		R97,00					R58,00	R12,00	R20,00	R7,00	R97,00
Nov 1	Bal	50,00						(72)	(73)	(74)	

The cash on hand and the payments, which amounted to R47, were checked on 20 October. On the same date a cheque was drawn to restore the float, bringing the balance on hand to R50 once again.

13.5.1 Posting from the petty cash book

(a) The receipts side of the petty cash book serves purely as a memorandum column. As was explained above, petty cash cheques are posted from the cash payments journal to the debit side of the petty cash control account in the general ledger.

(b) Payments are posted as follows:

- ☐ All items in the 'sundries' column are posted individually to the debit side of the separate accounts.
- ☐ The **totals** of all the other payments analysis columns are posted to the debit side of the account concerned.
- ☐ The total of the payments (R47,00) is posted to the **credit side** of the petty cash control account.

Example 13.5

GENERAL LEDGER					
PETTY CASH CONTROL ACCOUNT					Folio 70
19.7 Oct 1 20	 Bank Bank	 50,00 47,00 R97,00	19.7 Oct 31	 Petty cash payments Balance	 47,00 50,00 R97,00
Nov 1	Balance	50,00			
ADVERTISING					Folio 71
Oct 20	Petty cash	8,00			
POSTAGE					Folio 72
Oct 31	Petty cash	12,00			
WAGES					Folio 73
Oct 31	Petty cash	20,00			
STATIONERY					Folio 74
Oct 31	Petty cash	7,00			

13.6 THE CASH BUDGET

In the foregoing discussion of the nature and recording of cash transactions, the control to be exercised over cash was emphasised repeatedly. Effective control and effective management control do not, however, result simply from accurate recording and control of completed transactions; an effective system of advance planning is also necessary. Cash can be put to its best use only if the enterprise's future needs have been accurately determined and evaluated.

In the managerial process the **cash budget** forms an integral part of a network of budgets ranging from expected sales, expected production, inventory, expenses, capital expenditure and estimated income to the budgeted balance sheet.

The considerations affecting the cash budget and its function and application are discussed comprehensively in chapter 23, together with other aspects of financing.

13.7 VALUATION AND PRESENTATION OF CASH IN THE FINANCIAL STATEMENTS

There is no problem with valuing cash, as its cash value is also its realisable value. Since cash is a current asset, it is customary to group the favourable bank balance, petty cash balance and other immediately available cash items, for example amounts held as deposits, as a single total in the balance sheet under the heading **bank and cash balances**.

This implies that all cash, in whatever form, is immediately available to the enterprise. Where amounts held as deposits are material they are frequently shown as a separate item. Suitable headings in this regard would be: **bank balances and cash**, **immediately available deposits**, and **short-term deposits**.

A bank overdraft is shown as a current liability; in the balance sheet it is never deducted from a favourable balance in cases where the enterprise might, for instance, have an overdraft with one banking institution and a favourable balance with another.

14

CREDIT GRANTED: DEBTORS AND BILLS

The **AIM** of this chapter is to explain specific aspects affecting debtors and bills. The valuation of debtors is discussed, taking into account doubtful and irrecoverable debts.

14.1 INTRODUCTION

A credit transaction arises when a debt resulting from the purchase or sale of something, or the lending or borrowing of money, is payable at a **later** date. According to the **matching principle**, income **earned** during a specific period should be brought into account during that same period, irrespective of when it is **received**. Similarly, value sacrificed during a certain period will be brought into account as an expense during that period, irrespective of when **payment** is made.

In the case of credit transactions, the matching principle requires that transactions must be recorded in the period in which they occur. This gives rise to debts (assets) which are receivable and obligations (liabilities) which are payable.

Any individual or undertaking who is in debt to another enterprise is called a **trade debtor** (in the case of credit sales) or a **loan debtor** (in the case of loans).

The recording of credit sales and the origin of and payment by debtors has already been discussed. This chapter concerns credit terms, discount allowed, irrecoverable debts, the valuation of debtors, bills receivable, various loans granted and the internal control applicable to the granting of credit.

14.2 CREDIT TERMS

An enterprise usually has a specific credit policy governing the amount of credit that may be granted to a client and the time he will be allowed to meet his obligations. These requirements may vary from client to client; some clients may be required to pay immediately, while others may be granted 30 or 60 days (the credit term) to pay a particular invoice. These conditions are usually specified on the invoice. If the seller requires immediate payment upon delivery of the goods, the conditions specified on the invoice will be 'cash' or 'net cash'.

If the client has been granted credit, the invoice will indicate the credit terms. The credit term normally commences as from the date of invoice, but may also commence from the date of the monthly statement which is forwarded to the client.

If an invoice is payable within a specific number of days, for example 30 days from date of invoice, the terms are known as '30 days net', which can be abbreviated to 'n/30'.

14.3 DISCOUNT ALLOWED

To encourage prompt payment of credit purchases, many enterprises offer their customers a settlement discount. Settlement discount allows the client to deduct a certain amount from an invoice which is settled within a prescribed time, that is the discount period. Thus the notation '1/20 n/30' means that although the credit term is 30 days, the buyer may deduct 1% of the invoice amount if payment is made within 20 days of the date of the invoice.

Example 14.1

A client purchases goods to the value of R1 000 per invoice 833. His credit term is 30 days. He is allowed a 1% discount on the invoice amount, provided the invoice is settled within 20 days.

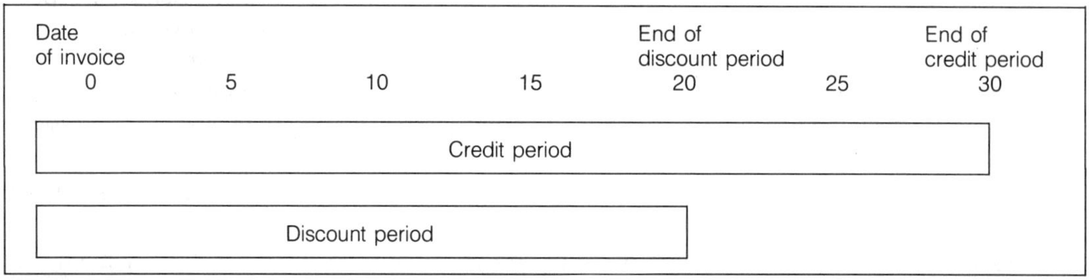

Thus, provided that he settles the account within the first 20 days, he may deduct R10 cash discount and pay only R990.

The settlement discount allowed on credit sales is known as sales discount or **discount allowed**. Settlement discount on credit purchases is known as purchases discount or **discount received**.

Settlement discount is not deducted from sales but is treated as a separate item in the income statement, because the granting of settlement discount is a financing transaction which is independent of the marketing and sales activities of the enterprise. In practice, however, such discounts are often deducted from sales or purchases (whichever is the case) and only the net sales or purchases figure, after discount, is shown in the income statement.

It should always be borne in mind, however, that the principal objective of accounting is to provide decision makers with meaningful information. Information on settlement discount gives rise to decisions relating to the enterprise's financing activities, in other words to the flow of funds. An enterprise's sole objective in granting discount is to recover its debts as soon as possible in order to have the cash available. For this reason it is important for the decision maker to know the total amount of the settlement discount which may then be evaluated, for instance, by comparing it with the interest saved on available cash.

On the other hand, the performance of the sales department is judged in terms of total sales, regardless of how or when the client settles his account. Because of financing considerations an enterprise may change its policy regarding settlement discount; this change of policy should not, however, affect the activities of the sales department.

Example 14.2

On 3 May 19.7, J Smith buys goods to the value of R100 from Supermarket, which grants him credit terms of 30 days. However, if he pays the amount within 15 days, 5% discount will be allowed. Smith pays the invoice on 10 May, thus settling the amount within the prescribed time. Therefore Supermarket will receive only R100 – 5% = R95 in full settlement of the invoice.

The sales and settlement transactions will be reflected as follows in the books of Supermarket:

GENERAL LEDGER

DEBTORS CONTROL

Sales	100	Bank	95

SALES

		Debtors control	100

BANK

Debtors control	95		

DEBTORS LEDGER

J SMITH

Sales	100	Bank	95

Smith's account (and the control account) must be credited with an additional R5, since his account was paid in full. This missing credit is the sales discount or discount allowed, and can be recorded by means of the following journal entry:

19.7 May 10	Discount allowed Debtors control (J Smith) *Discount of 5% allowed to debtor on sales of R100*	5	 5

GENERAL LEDGER

DEBTORS CONTROL

Sales	100	Bank	95
		Discount	5

SALES

		Debtors control	100

BANK

Debtors control	95		

DISCOUNT ALLOWED

Debtors control	5		

DEBTORS LEDGER

J SMITH

Sales	100	Bank	95
		Discount	5

Since there is a direct relationship between the discount deducted by a debtor and his payment, the **cash receipts journal** is generally extended to allow for journalising the discount. The following example illustrates the procedure clearly.

Example 14.3

CASH RECEIPTS JOURNAL
MAY 19.8 — Page 5

Date	Details	Folio	Sundries	Cash sales	Debtors	Discount allowed	Bank
19.8							
May 7	Cash sales for the week			180			180
14	Cash sales for the week			210			210
16	Interest on investment	612	80				80
20	H Fourie: Payment on account	(F8)			100	5	95
	Cash sales for the week			160			~~255~~ 160
27	E Willis: Payment on account	(W4)			80	3	77
28	Cash sales for the week			320			320
			R80	R870	R180	R8	R1 122
				(501) (Cr)	(212) (Cr)	(611) (Dr)	(211) (Dr)

Totals are posted at the end of the month

Individual amounts in the debtors column are posted to the debtor's account in the debtors ledger

(a) Individual amounts in the sundries column are posted to the general ledger, and
(b) therefore the total is not posted at the end of the month

DEBTORS LEDGER

			Dr	Cr	Bal
H FOURIE					**F8**
19.8					
May 2	Invoice 120	SJ10	100		100
20	Invoice 124	SJ10	200		300
	Bank and discount	CRJ5		100	200
P STONE					**S7**
19.8					
May 12	Invoice 122	SJ10	130		130
E WILLIS					**W4**
19.8					
May 14	Invoice 123	SJ10	80		80
28	Invoice 125	SJ10	240		320
	Bank and discount	CRJ5		80	240
J WRIGHT					**W5**
19.8					
May 6	Invoice 121	SJ10	150		150

GENERAL LEDGER

			Dr	Cr	Bal
BANK					**211**
19.8					
May 31	Total receipts	CRJ5	1 122		1 122
DEBTORS CONTROL					**212**
19.8					
May 31	Sales	SJ10	900		900
	Bank	CRJ5		180	720
SALES					**501**
19.8					
May 31	Debtors	SJ10		900	(900)
31	Bank	CRJ5		870	(1 770)
DISCOUNT ALLOWED					**611**
19.8					
May 31	Debtors	CRJ5	8		8
INTEREST ON INVESTMENT					**612**
19.8					
May 16	Bank	CRJ5		80	(80)

The totals of the various analysis columns of the cash receipts journals remain in balance (as can be seen below), because the debits of any journal entry must be equal to the corresponding credits.

Sundries		Cash sales		Debtors	Discount allowed		Bank
(Cr) 80	+	(Cr) 870	+	(Cr) 180	(Dr) 8	+	(Dr) 1 122
		R1 130				R1 130	

The number and types of columns used in the cash receipts journal will be determined by the nature and requirements of the enterprise concerned.

14.4 DOUBTFUL AND IRRECOVERABLE DEBTS

When goods and services are sold on credit there is always the danger of some clients not paying their debt. If it seems unlikely that a debt will be paid, payment is termed **doubtful**; when there is no hope of recovering the debt it is termed **irrecoverable** (sometimes also known as a bad debt).

While being aware of the danger of doubtful debts, an enterprise is nevertheless prepared to sell on credit provided that doubtful debts can be kept within reasonable limits. Credit sales increase total sales and therefore also profit, while irrecoverable debts are a loss emanating from granting credit.

According to the matching principle a doubtful debt arises at the time when the credit is granted, although it is not immediately recognised as such. A doubtful debt is the result of an error of judgement; an error in granting credit and the fact that the customer does not pay. Although the irrecoverability of the debt only becomes apparent later, the doubtful debt is nevertheless a loss for that period in which the sales and credit transaction took place. This principle is not always applied assiduously in practice.

The danger of doubtful debts, the fact that irrecoverability becomes known only at a later stage and that a bad debt represents a loss for the period in which the sale took place, means that an estimate of doubtful debts must be made for each specific financial period. This estimate must be brought into account as a loss for the period, by means of a provision for doubtful debts. There are two advantages of creating a provision for doubtful debts:

- ☐ The estimated loss is provided for during the period in which the corresponding income was earned.
- ☐ The debtors balance is shown in the balance sheet at net realisable value, since the provision is deducted from the gross amount of debtors.

In larger companies, estimating and providing for doubtful debts is usually done monthly, while in smaller concerns it is calculated and brought into account at the end of the financial period.

14.4.1 Estimating doubtful debts

There are two methods of calculating doubtful debts:

- ☐ On the basis of credit sales.
- ☐ On the basis of outstanding debtors.

In the latter method one of the following criteria may be used:

- ☐ A percentage of the total debtors.
- ☐ Age analysis.

Example 14.4

(a) Estimation based on credit sales

The premise underlying this method is that history repeats itself. If, over the last five years, the average percentage of bad debts to credit sales was, say, 2%, then the estimate for this period may also be taken as 2% of credit sales for the period.

The chief advantage of this method is that it is simple to calculate and to apply. Its disadvantage, however, is that it bears no relationship to the amount owing by debtors.

(b) Estimation based on the amount of outstanding debtors

Two approaches can be applied; bad debts can be calculated as a percentage of debtors, or, using a more scientific method, according to the age of the outstanding debtors.

☐ As a percentage of total outstanding debtors

This method, like the previous one, relies on past experience. The example below illustrates the calculation:

Year	Debtors at 31 December R	Amounts written off R	%
1	115 000	6 000	5,2
2	110 000	5 400	4,9
3	135 000	7 150	5,3
4	120 000	5 575	4,7

Based on past experience, the provision for doubtful debts in Year 5 can reasonably be estimated at 5% of the amount of debtors outstanding at the end of that year.

☐ According to the age analysis of the debtors

An age analysis consists of a schedule classifying all outstanding amounts according to the length of time for which they have been outstanding. Each amount is considered individually to determine its recoverability. The following is an example:

Example 14.5

AB ENTERPRISES LTD
DEBTORS AGE ANALYSIS SCHEDULE AT DECEMBER 19.5

Customer	Total due	Current debts	Period overdue (months) 1	2	3	longer than 3
K Janse	1 000	500	300	150	50	—
J Smith	1 800	200	100	400	500	600
P Roos	1 500	300	1 200	—	—	—
G de Wet	700	—	—	—	—	700
Others	95 000	14 000	29 400	12 450	22 450	16 700
Total	R100 000	R15 000	R31 000	R13 000	R23 000	R18 000
% of total	100	15	31	13	23	18

Competent staff will consider each debt individually, and on the basis of past experience will decide whether or not it is doubtful. Those balances overdue the longest will obviously be given most attention, and based on this evaluation a list of doubtful debts will be compiled. The total of the list will be the provision for the year.

The age classification can also be used to apply a sliding scale of percentages (based on previous experience) as follows:

Example 14.6

	Amount	Estimated percentage irrecoverable	Provision for doubtful debts
Not yet payable	15 000	1	150
Overdue for:			
1 month	31 000	2	620
2 months	13 000	3	390
3 months	23 000	5	1 150
Longer than 3 months	18 000	10	1 800
	R100 000		R4 110

Estimates based on credit sales and an age analysis (providing debts have been outstanding for less than one year) are practical applications of the matching principle, since losses are brought into account in the period during which the corresponding income was earned. On the other hand, an estimate based on the amount of outstanding debtors relies on a valuation of the particular balance sheet item.

14.4.2 Provision for irrecoverable debts

There are various methods of providing for irrecoverable debts. In this section the so-called 'direct method' is discussed.

14.4.2.1 Creating a provision for irrecoverable debts

Once the amount of **debts** that are **estimated as irrecoverable** has been determined according to one of the above methods, the amount is recorded as follows by means of an adjustment journal entry.

Irrecoverable debts Provision for irrecoverable debts *Provision for the year*		

The debit balance on the irrecoverable debts account is transferred to the profit and loss account at the end of the period and written off as a loss. The credit balance on the provision account is a contra item to an asset account. As with accumulated depreciation in the case of fixed assets, it will reduce the value of the asset, debtors.

Example 14.7

On 28 February 19.6, the end of the first financial year of Zerbo Traders Ltd, the company's trade debtors amounted to R400 000.

They decided to create a provision of 5% of outstanding debtors as irrecoverable debts.

The presentation below shows how the entry is recorded in the journal and general ledger and how it is disclosed in the balance sheet:

☐ **General journal: Creating the provision**

			Page 9
19.6 Feb 28	Irrecoverable debts Provision for irrecoverable debts *Creating a provision for irrecoverable debts @ 5% of outstanding debtors R400 000*	20 000	20 000

☐ **General ledger**

DEBTORS CONTROL

19.6 Feb 28	Balance		400 000				

PROVISION FOR IRRECOVERABLE DEBTS

				19.6 Feb 28	Irrecoverable debts	J9	20 000

IRRECOVERABLE DEBTS

19.6 Feb 28	Provision for irrecoverable debts	J9	R20 000	19.6 Feb 28	Income account	J9	R20 000

□ Closing entries

In the closing process the balance on the irrecoverable debts account is transferred to the profit and loss account by means of a closing journal entry.

Profit and loss account	20 000	
Irrecoverable debts		20 000
Transfer of estimated loss in respect of irrecoverable debts		

□ Presentation in balance sheet

Current assets		380 000
Debtors	400 000	
Less: Provision for irrecoverable debts	20 000	

Some aspects must be clarified at this point:

1 Although the above presentation in the balance sheet is technically correct, in practice it is often shown only as a 'net' amount.

2 Although no income tax implications have been discussed up to now, it should be pointed out that a 'provision' for irrecoverable debts is not an allowable expense in the determination of the undertaking's taxable income. The Receiver of Revenue allows only actual irrecoverable debts which have been written off. The fact that certain items are not allowed as deductions for income tax purposes does not mean that, in determining its income, an undertaking should only take into account expenses and losses that are allowable. The financial statements of an undertaking are not prepared primarily for the Receiver of Revenue; they are prepared for the use of the management and owners of the undertaking. The debtors must be valued accurately even though the Receiver of Revenue does not allow the provision.

3 It follows, too, from the consistent application of the accrual and matching principles (refer again to para 14.1 and 14.4) that (a) an asset must be properly valued and (b) provision must be made for all expenses/losses (such as irrecoverable debts) which must be brought into account against the income (sales/debtors) that is generated in the same period. The asset (debtors) which arises from the sale of merchandise will be over-valued if an undertaking knows, from experience, that a certain percentage of debtors will not be recovered and this contingency is not provided for. Therefore a provision is created to reflect debtors at a realistic (recoverable) value in the balance sheet. The writing off of the irrecoverable amount which arises from the creation of the provision as a loss against sales (from whence debtors originated) is therefore pursuant to the matching principle.

4 No entry is made in the debtors control account or the debtors ledger at the point when the provision is created.

14.4.2.2 Increase in the provision for irrecoverable debts

Example 14.8

Assume that the outstanding debtors of Zerbo Traders have increased to R500 000 a year later (28 February 19.7), but that the same percentage is maintained in the provision for irrecoverable debts. The entry will be recorded as follows (assuming, of course, that all debts have actually been recovered in the meantime):

□ **Journal**

Irrecoverable debts	5 000	
Provision for irrecoverable debts		5 000
Increase in provision to 5% of outstanding debtors (R500 000) = R25 000		
Existing provision 20 000		
∴ Amount required R5 000		

□ **General ledger**

DEBTORS CONTROL ACCOUNT

19.7							
Feb 28	Balance		500 000				

PROVISION FOR IRRECOVERABLE DEBTS

				19.6			
				Feb 28	Balance		20 000
				19.7			
				Feb 28	Irrecoverable debts		5 000
							25 000

IRRECOVERABLE DEBTS

19.6				19.6			
Feb 28	Provision for irrecoverable debts		R20 000	Feb 28	Income account		R20 000
19.7							
Feb 28	Provision for irrecoverable debts		5 000				

The balance of R5 000 on the irrecoverable debts account is again transferred to the profit and loss account, while the debtors are shown at R475 000 (i e R500 000 less the provision for irrecoverable debts of R25 000).

14.4.2.3 Decrease in the provision for irrecoverable debts

A decrease in the provision for irrecoverable debts can result in a credit entry in the profit and loss account.

Example 14.9

On 28 February 19.8 the debtors of Zerbo Traders Ltd amount to R425 000. The percentage applied to irrecoverable debts remains unchanged:

☐ **Journal**

Provision for irrecoverable debts		3 750	
Irrecoverable debts			3 750
Decrease in provision as follows:			
Existing balance	*= R25 000*		
Needed 5% × 425 000	*= 21 250*		
∴ Written back	*R3 750*		

☐ **General ledger**

DEBTORS CONTROL

19.8					
Feb 28	Balance	425 000			

PROVISION FOR IRRECOVERABLE DEBTS

19.7			19.6		
Feb 28	Balance	25 000	Feb 28	Irrecoverable debts	20 000
			19.7		
			Mar 1	Irrecoverable debts	5 000
		R25 000			R25 000
19.8			19.7		
Feb 28	Irrecoverable debts	3 750	Feb 28	Balance	25 000
	Balance	21 250			
		R25 000			R25 000
			19.8		
			Mar 1	Balance	21 250

IRRECOVERABLE DEBTS

19.6			19.6		
Feb 28	Provision	R20 000	Feb 28	Income account	R20 000
19.7			19.7		
Feb 28	Provision	R5 000	Feb 28	Income account	R5 000
19.8			19.8		
Feb 28	Income account	R3 750	Feb 28	Provision	R3 750

The credit balance on the irrecoverable debts account will be transferred to the credit side of the profit and loss account, while the debtors will be disclosed in the balance sheet as follows:

Current assets	
Debtors	425 000
Less: Provision for irrecoverable debts	21 250
	R403 750

14.4.3 Writing off actual irrecoverable debts

In the previous paragraph the creation and adjustment of a **provision for possible irrecoverable debts** was discussed. From this discussion it is obvious, and this must be emphasised, that the creation or adjustment of a provision for irrecoverable debts requires no entry in the debtors control account or the individual debtors' accounts in the debtors ledger. The reason for this is that the provision is merely an estimate of the bad debts which may materialise. The creation of a provision does not provide for an allocation to individual debtors.

However, once the provision has been established **all actual bad debts must be written off (debited) against the provision**.

Example 14.10

1 The balance on the provision for irrecoverable debts account of Zerbo Traders Ltd amounted to R21 250 on 28 February 19.8 (refer to previous example). During the year ended 28 February 19.9 the following debtors went insolvent and no dividend is expected from the insolvent estates.

	Amount	Debt originated in
Akon	6 000	Year ended 28/2/19.8
Band	1 500	Year ended 28/2/19.8
Dicks	8 300	Year ended 28/2/19.8
Williams	1 200	Year ended 28/2/19.9
	R17 000	

2 The total debtors on 28/2/19.8 was R425 000. During the year credit sales amounted to R900 000 and R708 000 was collected from debtors.

3 The provision for irrecoverable debts must be maintained at 5% of outstanding debtors. The following entries are necessary in order to record the above information:

☐ **Journal entries**

– **For writing off actual bad debts**

Provision for irrecoverable debts			17 000	
Debtors control account				17 000
Writing off of amounts due by the following insolvent debtors:				
	Debtors ledger folio			
Akon	*A10*	*6 000*		
Band	*B27*	*1 500*		
Dicks	*D7*	*8 300*		
Williams	*W7*	*1 200*		
		R17 000		

The total credit of R17 000 transferred to the debtors control account is also posted from the above journal entry to the individual debtors' accounts in the debtors ledger.

– **For the adjustment of the provision on 28/2/19.9**

After the above journal entry has been posted to the general ledger, the balance on the debtors control account will be R600 000 (see control account below). The following entry is now required to maintain a provision for irrecoverable debts of 5% of total debtors.

Irrecoverable debts	25 750	
Provision for irrecoverable debts		25 750
Adjustment of provision to 5% of debtors (R600 000) = 30 000		
Current balance of provision 4 250		
Opening balance 21 250		
***Less:** Bad debts written off 17 000*		
∴ Amount needed R25 750		

GENERAL LEDGER

DEBTORS CONTROL

19.8				19.9			
Feb 28	Balance	425 000		Feb 28	Bank (collections)	708 000	
19.9					Provision for irrecoverable debts (bad debts written off)	17 000	
Feb 28	Sales	900 000			Balance	600 000	
		R1 325 000				R1 325 000	
19.9							
Mar 1	Balance	600 000					

PROVISION FOR IRRECOVERABLE DEBTS

19.9			19.8		
Feb 28	Debtors control account (bad debts)	17 000	Mar 1	Balance	21 250
	Balance	30 000	19.9		
			Feb 28	Irrecoverable debts	25 750
		R47 000			R47 000
			19.9		
			Mar 1	Balance (5% × R600 000)	30 000

IRRECOVERABLE DEBTS

19.9			19.9		
Feb 28	Provision for irrecoverable debts	R25 750	Feb 28	Income account	R25 750

The balance of the irrecoverable debts account is again transferred to the profit and loss account on closing off the ledger for the year ended 28 February 19.9.

☐ The matching principle is upheld by writing off actual bad debts against the provision. From the particulars above it can be seen that R15 800 of the debtors originated in the previous financial year and therefore it would be inappropriate to write this off against the income of the current year. Therefore the entry is made **against the provision which is based on the previous year's outstanding debts**.

- The amount of R1 200 (Williams) which arose in the current year is also debited against this provision. This is not a contravention of the matching principle; if the amount which arose in 19.9 (R1 200) had been debited directly to irrecoverable debts (according to the so-called 'direct method'), the amount whereby the provision for irrecoverable debts was adjusted to 5% of outstanding debtors would have been reduced by R1 200, viz:

5% × R600 000	= 30 000
Balance of provision (R21 250 – 15 800)	5 450
∴ Amount required	R24 550

DEBTORS CONTROL ACCOUNT

19.9					
Feb 28	Balance	600 000			

PROVISION FOR IRRECOVERABLE DEBTS

19.9			19.6		
Feb 28	Debtors (written off 19.8)	15 800	Feb 28	Balance	21 250
				Irrecoverable debts	
	Balance	30 000		(adjustment of provision)	24 550
		R45 800			R45 800
			19.9		
			Mar 1	Balance	30 000

IRRECOVERABLE DEBTS

19.9			19.9		
Feb 28	Debtors (written off 29.9)	1 200	Feb 28	Income account	25 750
	Provision (adjustment)	24 550			
		R25 750			R25 750

Thus the actual and possible losses pertaining to irrecoverable debts which are written off against income for the year remain unchanged at R25 750 (compare the previous method).

Since the first method requires fewer calculations, it is the method recommended.

14.4.4 Bad debts

Example 14.11

If an amount which was previously written off as bad is partially or totally recovered, the following entry is made: (Assume that R500 in respect of J Swart was written off on 31/12/19.8 and recovered on 30/4/19.9.)

19.9 Apr 30	Debtors control account (J Swart) Bad debt recovered *Reversal of amount previously written off as bad*	500	 500
Apr 30	Cash Debtors control account *Cash received in settlement of an amount due*	500	 500

The following direct entry is also frequently made:

Cash received Bad debts recovered *Cash received in respect of amount previously written off*	500	 500

The advantage of the first method is that because the entry is made in the individual debtor's account, a complete record of the original write-off and the subsequent recovery will be detailed in his account for future reference.

14.4.5 Irrecoverable debts in the income statement

The item irrecoverable debts is treated separately in the income statement. It is not deducted from sales, since it relates specifically to the function of credit control and has no bearing on sales performance.

It is the function of the credit control department, after ascertaining the creditworthiness of clients, to approve credit transactions and after the sale to accept responsibility for recovering the debt. The effectiveness of the credit control department has a considerable effect on the recoverability or otherwise of debts. The sales department, in contrast, has no influence in this sphere.

To provide the various decision makers with meaningful information, irrecoverable debts should be treated as a separate item.

14.5 TRADE DEBTORS

14.5.1 Valuation and disclosure in the financial statements

The purpose of a provision for irrecoverable debts is two-fold: it provides for losses in the year concerned and brings the total amount owed by debtors into agreement with the amount it is expected will be received. Therefore the debtors item in the balance sheet is shown at net realisable value, as follows:

Current assets		
Trade debtors	50 000	
Less: Provision for irrecoverable debts	2 000	48 000

It has become customary not to show the provision separately in the balance sheet. Therefore the following item is usually seen in published financial statements:

Current assets	
Trade debtors after provision for irrecoverable debts	48 000

If the debtors have been pledged or used as surety for a debt incurred by the enterprise, this fact must be disclosed by way of a note to the financial statements.

If some debtors' accounts, for one reason or another, show a credit balance, and the total of these balances is **substantial**, the amount should be shown together with trade creditors, since it constitutes a liability. It should not be shown as a reduction of the debit balance.

In the case of instalment sale (hire-purchase) transactions, the **instalment sale (hire-purchase) debtors** must be shown separately from the trade debtors. The reason for this is that amounts owed by instalment sale (hire-purchase) debtors are not immediately realisable. Theoretically speaking, such debtors should be shown as a medium-term and not a current asset, since in most cases repayments are over a period of longer than one year. In practice, however, they are treated as a current asset.

14.5.2 Analysis and interpretation of financial statements

Trade debtors form part of an enterprise's operating capital and liquidity and represent an important link in the operating cycle (viz cash – inventory – debtors – cash). Therefore their recoverability is essential.

An enterprise's credit policy is used as a criterion against which the actual position is measured. Management must monitor those debtors' accounts which are overdue constantly in order to guard against possible losses. Every debtor's account should be analysed regularly by means of **ageing schedules**.

Two other analyses which give an indication of the general condition of debtors and the application of an enterprise's credit policy are the average **settlement period** and the annual **debtors turnover rate**.

If a company's policy is to allow 30 days credit and the age analysis of debtors shows that the average settlement period is longer, management should pay attention to the situation.

When the average settlement period and the annual debtors turnover rate is determined, debts arising from **extraordinary transactions** should not be taken into account. In future the debtors figure used will be that arrived at after the provision for irrecoverable debts has been brought into account.

Example 14.12

Using the following particulars, calculate the average settlement period and the annual debtors turnover rate of Bryanston Traders for 19.4 and 19.5:

	19.3	19.4	19.5
Net credit sales	80 000	82 800	91 800
Debtors	7 500	8 600	7 210

The debtors settlement period is calculated by dividing the average debtors for a specific year by average daily credit sales for the same year:

	19.4	19.5
1 Credit sales	R82 800	R91 800
2 Days per annum	365	365
3 Credit sales per day (1 ÷ 2)	R227	R251
4 Average debtors (7 500 + 8 600)		
$\frac{(7\,500 + 8\,600)}{2}$	R8 050	
$\frac{(8\,600 + 7\,210)}{2}$		R7 905
Average settlement period = (4 ÷ 3)	35 days	31 days

Thus, during 19.4 debtors were allowed an average of 35 days to settle their accounts. During 19.5 the settlement period was 31 days, which implies an improvement in both credit control and recovery, since in 19.5 credit sales increased by R9 000, or more than 10%, compared with 19.4.

The **formula** for the calculation is:

$$\frac{\text{Average debtors}}{\text{Credit sales} \div 365}$$

∴ for 19.4

$$\frac{8\,050}{82\,800 \div 365} = 35 \text{ days}$$

$$\frac{\text{Average debtors} \times 365}{\text{Credit sales}}$$

∴ for 19.5

$$\frac{7\,905 \times 365}{91\,800} = 31 \text{ days}$$

In practice, the period used is frequently taken as 360 days instead of 365 days.

The annual **debtors turnover rate** (i e the ratio of credit sales to debtors) is calculated by dividing net credit sales by the average debtors.

Example 14.13

19.4

$$\frac{82\,800}{8\,050} = 10{,}3 \text{ times}$$

19.5

$$\frac{91\,800}{7\,905} = 11{,}6 \text{ times}$$

In 19.5 debtors were recovered approximately 11,6 times. This may be compared with previous years' figures or with the standard for the industry concerned. An increased debtors turnover rate indicates an improvement in the recovery and control of debtors and reflects a relative decrease in investment in debtors and, consequently, a better utilisation of the enterprise's operating capital.

The management of an enterprise should also determine the ideal ratio of cash to credit sales for its particular type of business, and should try to achieve and maintain that ratio.

Outsiders will have difficulty calculating these two ratios, since they have to rely on published financial statements which usually do not show credit sales as a separate figure. Where accurate figures are not available, total sales may be used (these are also sometimes not published), but any change in the pattern of cash sales to credit sales will invalidate these calculations.

14.5.3 Internal control

The following internal control measures should be applied if adequate control is to be maintained over debtors:

- ☐ The concern should have a properly formulated credit policy which takes into account its ability to grant credit, the nature and practices of the business sector within which it operates, and the general economic conditions.
- ☐ Clients' creditworthiness must be ascertained before credit is granted. Larger enterprises have a separate credit control department which carries out this function and follows up cases of non-payment.
- ☐ Regular statements of account must be sent to clients to keep them informed about amounts owing and the terms of settlement.
- ☐ The functions of approving credit, recording transactions, compiling statements of account and handling cash must be kept separate.
- ☐ Similar transactions must be recorded in subsidiary journals and a control account must be kept in the ledger.
- ☐ Only authorised persons may approve the provision for doubtful debts and the writing off of irrecoverable debts.
- ☐ Loose-leaf debtors accounts or debtors cards make it possible for the accounting work related to debtors to be allocated to various employees.
- ☐ Circulars must be sent to debtors periodically to ascertain whether they agree that the balances on their accounts are correct.

These internal control measures also apply to bills receivable and sundry accounts, discussed below.

14.6 CREDIT CARD SALES AND CHARGES

Nowadays, sales via credit cards such as Master or Visa cards issued by banks are common in most retail organisations. The banks bear the costs of processing the information and collecting outstanding amounts. They also absorb the losses arising from irrecoverable debts.

For these services the banks charge the retailer a fee of between 0,5% and 5% of the total credit card sales. The retailer deposits the debit notes resulting from credit card sales with the relevant bank and the bank credits the retailer's bank account with the amount of the debit notes deposited, less the credit card fee.

The retailer records the transactions as follows:

XY Bank Credit sales *Credit card debit notes deposited*	30 000	 30 000
Credit card charges XY Bank *Fees charged by bank*	300	 300

Credit card sales are also made to customers who present credit cards which are not issued by a bank, for example American Express and Diner's Club cards. In these cases the retailer sends the debit notes to the credit card company concerned and in turn receives a cheque from the company for the net amount (i e sales less credit card fee). The credit card company is treated as an ordinary debtor in the books of the retailer:

Credit card company Credit sales *Sales per credit cards*	20 000	 20 000
Bank Credit card charges Credit card company *Receipt of amount owing less fees levied*	19 800 200	 20 000

14.7 TREATMENT OF BILLS RECEIVABLE IN THE ACCOUNTING RECORDS

14.7.1 Negotiable documents

As has already been indicated, the modern business world makes extensive use of credit, most sales of goods or services being on credit. Most credit sales are on the 'open account' basis; in other words there is merely an agreement between seller and buyer that the seller's conditions regarding the payment of the outstanding amount owed will be adhered to by the buyer. Usually settlement must be made within 30 days. In recent years the tremendous increase in the use of **credit cards**, issued by financial institutions to their customers, has done much to simplify these transactions.

Bills, although no longer widely used, are still important in the wholesale trade and in foreign transactions. Bills also have certain characteristics which make them **negotiable documents**. A financial document is negotiable if it can be transferred from one person to another. This is achieved by the holder **endorsing** the document and **delivering** it to the other party. Bearer documents are transferred by delivery alone. To be negotiable, a financial document or bill must have the characteristic that, under given circumstances, the new owner's rights are unalienable, even though his predecessor's rights were defective or invalid.

14.7.2 Bills

☐ **Definition**

A bill is a negotiable document. It is an unconditional, written instruction issued by one person to another whereby the latter is instructed to pay on demand, at a specified or specifiable future date, a certain sum of money, either to the order of the person specified, or to the bearer.

☐ **Parties to the bill**

There are at least three parties to a bill, namely the drawer, the drawee and the payee or bearer. The three parties need not be different persons; the same person can be a party to the bill in more than one capacity. For example, the drawer can specify that the money must be paid to himself; therefore he is both drawer and payee simultaneously.

Figure 14.1

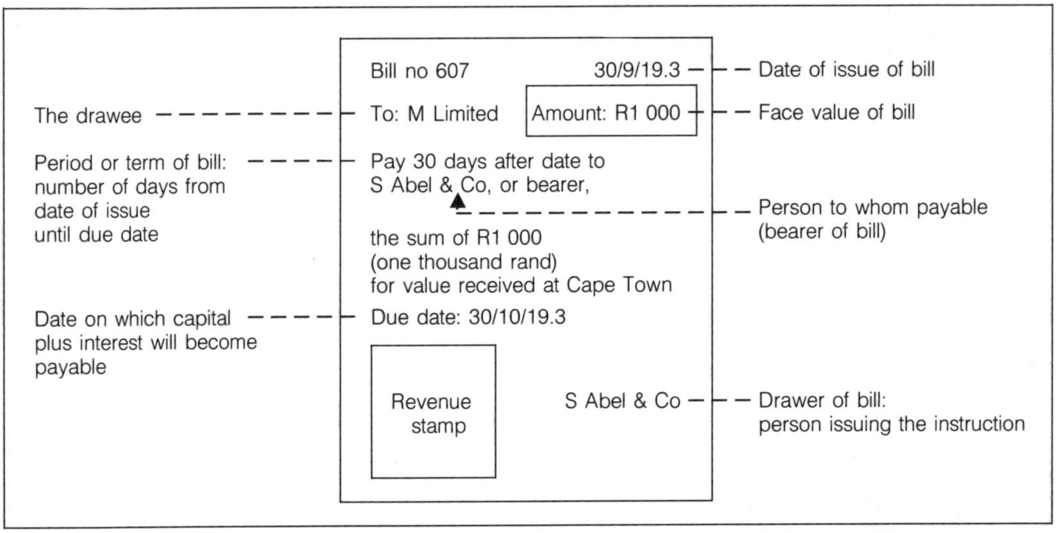

Note the following in respect of the above bill: it fulfils all the requirements of a negotiable document and the drawer and payee are the same person. Bear in mind that the bill represents a **bill receivable** for S Abel & Co and a **bill payable** for M Limited.

☐ **Obligations of parties to the bill, and procedures to be followed**

The drawer (S Abel & Co) will draft and sign the bill and forward it to the drawee (M Limited) for formal **acceptance**. The drawee indicates his acceptance of the bill by means of his signature and noting the date of acceptance across the face of the bill. After acceptance, the bill is returned to the payee (in the example, the drawer, S Abel & Co) who will safeguard it until the due date. The payee usually places the bill with his bankers for safekeeping and collection. On the due date the bill is presented to the drawee for payment; he then redeems or honours the bill.

□ Bearer and order bills

Our definition of a bill stated that it could be made out to 'bearer', in which case any person in possession of the bill on the due date could claim payment from the drawee. This means that the right to receive payment of a bill can be transferred to another person merely by handing it to him or her.

If the word 'bearer' is crossed out and replaced by 'order' (pertaining to the possible negotiability of the document) it means that the drawee is instructed to pay the amount concerned to the payee, or to any other person specified by him in writing, or to any holder subsequently specified. Such written specification must appear on the bill itself (usually on the back) and is known as an **endorsement**. The negotiation of an 'order' bill is completed when the payee delivers the document to the subsequent title-holder of the bill (the endorsee). Thus a bill is a negotiable document, since all rights and obligations of the payee can be transferred by him to another party. The latter, in turn, is entitled to transfer the bill to another holder.

□ Non-payment or dishonouring of a bill

This occurs when the drawee refuses or is unable to pay or honour a bill. If a bill has already been transferred by the payee to another party, the latter has right of recourse against the payee or any former holders of the bill, except where the words 'not negotiable' have been included in the endorsement.

However, before a claim can be instituted the person who presented the bill must give verbal or written notice, 'without delay', of the dishonouring of the bill to the party or parties against whom he wishes to institute his claim. This is known as 'noting a bill'. The holder must then issue a **formal protest** against the non-payment through a notary. This protest serves as proof of the dishonouring and as such is used to institute legal proceedings against the drawee. All expenses incurred in connection with a dishonoured bill, together with the amount of the bill plus interest, can be recovered from the drawee.

□ Discounting a bill

The holder can convert a bill into cash before the due date, by negotiating its sale to a financial institution. Then the buyer is entitled to claim payment of the bill on the due date. It is standard practice for the financial institution concerned to charge interest on the bill for the period until the due date.

This type of transaction is known as **discounting** a bill.

14.7.3 Interest and proceeds from bills

□ Determining the due date

A bill can be payable on presentation or on a specific date (e g 30 June 19.3) or on a determinable future date. The determinable date is usually a specific period after the date of the bill, for example three months after date or 60 days after date.

No problems arise where the due date is **specifically** determined. If the due date is given as a certain number of months after the date of the bill, the applicable month is simply determined and the due date is then the same date as that of the bill. A bill dated 25 April, payable three months after date, for example, is payable on 25 July. However, an exact calculation is necessary where the due date is a certain number of days after the date of the bill. For example, a bill dated 15 April and payable '90 days after date' is payable on 14 July, viz:

Remaining days in April (30 – 15)	15	
May	31	
June	30	76
Days needed in July		14
		90

Note that calculations automatically exclude the date of issue of the bill, but the due date is included.

☐ Calculating interest

It is not necessary to charge interest on bills, but it is done frequently. The calculation of interest is based on three factors, namely the capital amount, the interest rate and the relevant period. The following formula is used for calculating the interest:

	Capital	×	Rate	×	Time	=	Interest
or	C	×	R	×	T	=	I

It is common business practice to calculate interest on a basis of 360 days per year. Thus the interest on a bill of R1 000 for 90 days at 8% will be:

$$\text{R1 000} \times 0{,}08 \times \frac{90}{360} = \text{R20}$$

There are several short-cut methods of calculating interest, but these are not discussed here. Financial institutions rely mainly on published interest tables to determine the interest due on specific amounts for any particular period.

☐ The value of a bill on due date

If the bill is interest-free the value on the due date is the same as its face value. However, if the bill does bear interest, the value on the due date is the face value plus interest. Thus the value on the due date of a R1 000, 8%, 90 day bill is:

$$\begin{aligned} \text{DDV} &= \text{C} + \text{I} \\ &= 1\,000 + (1\,000 \times ,08 \times \frac{90}{360}) \\ &= 1\,000 + 20 \\ &= \text{R1 020} \end{aligned}$$

☐ Determining discount

If a bill is discounted before its due date, the purchaser will expect a discount. This discount will be based on three factors, namely the value on the due date, the discount rate and the time, that is:

$$\text{Discount} = \text{DDV} \times \text{R} \times \text{T}$$

On a R1 000, 60 day bill which does not bear interest, the discount at a rate of 6% will be:

$$R1\ 000 \times 0{,}06 \times \frac{60}{360} = R10$$

☐ Proceeds of the bill

This same bill will realise R990 (R1 000 – R10), that is (DDV – discount) or

$$R1\ 000 - (1\ 000 \times 0{,}06 \times \frac{60}{360}) = R990$$

Due care must be taken in calculating the proceeds of an interest-bearing bill. The formula (DDV – discount) remains the same, but it must be remembered that the value on due date comprises the **capital sum + interest**.

Example 14.14

Assume that a R1 000, 90 day bill, bearing interest of 8%, is discounted at a bank 60 days before the due date, at a discount rate of 6%. The proceeds of the bill are calculated as follows:

$$\begin{aligned}
\text{Return} &= \text{DDV} - \text{discount}\\
&= (\text{Capital} + \text{Interest}) - (\text{DDV} \times \text{R} \times \text{T})\\
&\quad (1\ 000 \times 0{,}08 \times \frac{90}{360})^{*} - (1\ 020 \times 0{,}06 \times \frac{60}{360})^{\dagger}\\
&= 1\ 020 - 10{,}20\\
&= \text{R}1\ 009{,}80
\end{aligned}$$

*Interest is calculated on the capital sum.
†Discount is calculated on the value on due date.

14.7.4 Recording of bills receivable

☐ Receipt of a bill in settlement of a debtor's account

Assume that on 31 March 19.3, AB Limited sells goods worth R2 000 to K Smuts. This transaction is entered in the sales journal and the general ledger as follows:

Example 14.15

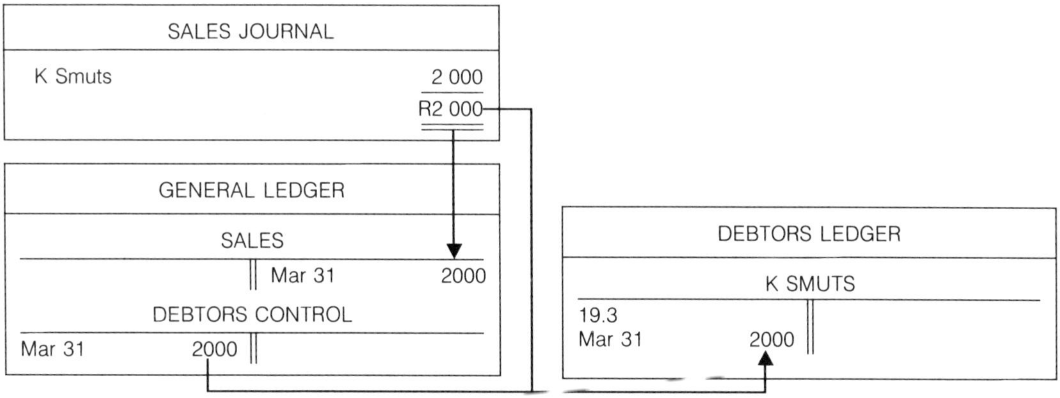

On 1 April, a three month bill is drawn on K Smuts at a rate of 8% and he accepts the bill. Where bill transactions take place infrequently, the acceptance of a bill may simply be journalised as follows:

Bills receivable	2 040	
Debtors		2 000
Interest receivable		40
Bill no 3 for three months at 8% accepted by K Smuts in settlement of his account		

Once the journal entry has been posted to the ledger, the position is as follows:

GENERAL LEDGER

SALES

			Mar 31	Debtors	2 000

DEBTORS CONTROL

		2 000	Apr 1	Bills	2 000

BILLS RECEIVABLE

Apr 1	Debtors and interest	2 040			

INTEREST RECEIVABLE

			Apr 1	Bills	40

DEBTORS LEDGER

K SMUTS

Mar 31	Sales	2 000	Apr 1	Bills	2 000

Thus one asset (debtors) is replaced by another asset (bills receivable).

☐ Payment of a bill on due date

If the above bill is paid on due date the amount received will be entered in the cash receipts journal and credited to the bills receivable account, Thus, as a journal entry:

Example 14.16

19.3 Jul 1	Bank	2 040	
	Bills receivable		2 040
	Settlement of bill no 3 received on due date		

The entry in the general ledger will be as follows:

BILLS RECEIVABLE

Apr 1	Debtors and interest	2 040	Jul 1	Cash	2 040

□ Discounting a bill

Assume that on 1 May the bill accepted by K Smuts on 1 April is discounted by AB Limited with their bankers, at a discount rate of 6%. The discount on the bill is:

DDV × R × T
= R2 040 × 0,06 × 2 months
= R20,40

The proceeds from discounting the bill are therefore R2 040 – R20,40 = R2 019,60. The transaction can be journalised as follows:

Example 14.17

19.3 May 1	Bank Discount on discounting Bills receivable *Discounting of bill no 3 at bank at a discount rate of 6%*	2 019,60 20,40	 2 040,00

The bank credits the discounter's account with the full amount of the bill and simultaneously debits him with the interest. Therefore the discounter should make the opposite entries in his cash book, namely:

- □ debit the full amount of the bill, and
- □ debit the amount of the discount.

When this journal entry is posted to the ledger, the total amount of R2 040 will be credited to the bills receivable account.

The bank, being the holder of the bill, will present it to K Smuts on due date. Since AB Limited no longer owns the bill, settlement thereof (by K Smuts to the bank) does not entail an entry in the books of the previous holders (AB Limited).

When AB Limited surrender the bill to the bank on discounting they endorse the bill, in effect guaranteeing payment by K Smuts on due date. If K Smuts defaults, the bank has a right of recourse against AB Limited. AB Limited therefore has a **contingent liability** in respect of the bill until its due date, when K Smuts must settle the bill; thereafter its liability lapses. Should K Smuts default, the liability reverts to AB Limited. When a balance sheet is drawn up it is essential to determine the total amount of all discounted bills which have not expired by the date of the balance sheet and disclose the contingent liability in a note to the balance sheet.

□ Dishonouring a bill

The method used to record a dishonoured bill depends on whether or not the bill was discounted.

(a) If still in possession of the drawer

Refer to the above example. Should K Smuts dishonour the bill which he has previously accepted when it is presented to him on due date by AB Limited, the following journal entry will be required:

Example 14.18

19.3 Jul 1	K Smuts Bills receivable *Reversal of dishonoured bill no 3*	2 040	 2 040

GENERAL LEDGER

DEBTORS CONTROL

Mar 31 Sales	R2 000	Apr 1 Bills receivable	R2 000
Jul 1 Bills	2 040		

BILLS RECEIVABLE

Apr 1 Debtors	R2 040	Jul 1 Debtors	R2 040

INTEREST RECEIVABLE

		Apr 1 Bills	40

DEBTORS LEDGER

K SMUTS

Mar 31	Sales	R2 000	Apr 1	Bills	R2 000
Jul 1	Bills	R2 040			

The original entry of the bill is cancelled when the face value plus interest for the period of the bill is debited to K Smuts' account. Noting and other charges incurred in connection with the dishonouring will also be debited to his account, for example:

Noting charges Bank *Settlement of noting charges arising from bill no 3 being dishonoured by K Smuts*	2,00	 2,00
K Smuts Noting charges *Recovery of noting charges*	2,00	 2,00

If K Smuts requests a renewal of the bill after having dishonoured it and this is granted, the old bill is cancelled and a new bill issued for the amount owing plus interest, for example:

K Smuts Interest receivable *Interest at 8% on 60 days: being interest on extended credit period allowed to debtor**	27,20	 27,20

*That is 8% × R2 040 × 60 days.

Smuts now owes R2 040 + R2 + R27,20, so the new bill will be drawn for R2 069,20.

Bills receivable K Smuts *Acceptance of bill no 4 by debtor*	2 069,20	 2 069,20

(b) If discounted at the bank

In this case the bank will simply debit AB Limited's current account with the amount of the dishonoured bill, plus costs, and forward the relevant debit note to the business. This debit note is the source document for the following entry in the cash payments journal of AB Limited:

CASH PAYMENTS JOURNAL		
19.3 Jul 1	 K Smuts: Dishonoured bill plus noting charges via bank debit note 6792	 R2 042

Accordingly, K Smuts' account (Note: not the bills receivable account) will be debited from the cash payments journal with the outstanding amount.

☐ The bills receivable book

Where an enterprise enters into a large number of bill transactions, it is impractical to make a separate journal entry for each transaction. In such cases a separate journal with the necessary columns is used as a subsidiary journal.

Example 14.19

During July 19.3, the following bill transactions occurred in an enterprise:

July 3	Receive acceptance by A of our 2 m/d (months after date) bill no 113 vir R500, drawn on him on 1 July.
7	Draw bill no 114, R400 for 60 d/d (days after date) on B. Receive his acceptance of 8 July on 9 July.
11	Receive a 3 m/d promissory note for R200, dated 6 July.
14	Bill no 112, 30 d/d, for R100, drawn on D on 1 July was returned. It was formally accepted on 6 July.
20	Forward a R800 bill (no 115) of 1 m/s (month after sight) to E and receive his acceptance dated 23 July, on 25 July.
26	F returned his 2 m/d bill for R90 (dated 22 July).
31	Send a 90 d/d bill for R300 to G for acceptance (see remark 5).

These transactions are recorded in the bills book as follows:

BILLS RECEIVABLE BOOK
JULY 19.3

Bill no	Date of receipt	Drawer	Acceptor	Date of bill	Date of acceptance	Period	Due date Jan	Feb	Mar	Apr	May	Jun	Jul	Aug	Sep	Oct	Nov	Dec	Folio	Amount	Remarks
112	Jul 1	Self	D	1/7	6/7	30 d/d							1						D6	100	Paid 31/7 CB16
113	3	Self	A	1/7	3/7	2 m/d									1				A10	500	
114	9	Self	B	7/7	8/7	60 d/d									5				B3	400	
P	11	C	C	6/7	—	3 m/d										6			C2	200	
115	25	Self	E	20/7	23/7	1 m/s								23					E12	800	Discounted 28/7 J10
P	26	F	F	22/7	—	2 m/d									22				F6	90	
																				R2 090	
							4												2	1	3

Explanatory notes

(1) The total of the bills accepted during the month is debited to the bills receivable control account and credited to the debtors control account in the general ledger.
(2) The bills are also posted to the individual acceptor's accounts (indicated by folio numbers) in the debtors ledger.
(3) The remarks column is used for additional information, as indicated.
(4) The due date columns give the expiry dates for easy reference.
(5) A bill can be regarded as 'received' only once it has been accepted. Therefore, the bill drawn on G has not been entered into the bills book as yet. A signed promissory note, however, is immediately binding on the signatory and can therefore be entered into the bills receivable book upon receipt.

Where bill payments are received frequently, it is usual to provide a separate **bills received** column in the cash receipts book.

Accepted bills are valuable documents and, as in the case of cash, must be controlled properly. They must be safely stored immediately upon receipt. The balance on the bills receivable control account must be compared regularly with the items in the bills book and with the bills on hand.

14.7.5 The valuation and disclosure of bills receivable in the financial statements

Bills receivable are current assets and are shown as such in the balance sheet, together with other current assets. They are shown at face value, less any possible provision for doubtful recovery. Bills receivable are often combined with debtors as a single amount, shown as **debtors and bills**.

Where bills which are not yet due have been discounted, a note including the amount of the bills discounted must be made to this effect in the financial statements, since they represent a contingent liability. If any bills receivable have been mortgaged or otherwise encumbered as security for an obligation, this fact must also be disclosed in the financial statements.

As in the case of debtors, proper provision should be made for any bills that could possibly be irrecoverable.

15

INVENTORY

The **AIM** of this chapter is to emphasise the importance of the inventory figure, explain stock taking procedures and discuss the valuation and disclosure of stock in the financial statements with reference to Statement AC 108 (the valuation and disclosure of stock within the framework of the historical cost system).

15.1 INTRODUCTION

Preceding chapters have referred to use of the inventory figure in determining profits and the presentation of inventory in the financial statements.

The recording and control of purchases, the storage and sale of inventory and payments for purchases were also emphasised.

In this chapter special attention is given to the valuation and disclosure of inventory (including work-in-progress) in financial statements which have been prepared on the historical cost basis. This discussion is based on Statement AC 108,[1] which is referred to frequently.

In many organisations inventory represents a considerable portion of the assets; the **valuation** and **disclosure** of inventory has a material influence on the determination and presentation of an undertaking's financial position and operating results.[2]

Thus far it has been asssumed that the 'cost' of inventory is given, but this chapter devotes attention specifically to:

- ☐ the nature of inventory
- ☐ how the figure for inventory on hand is determined
- ☐ different methods of inventory valuation
- ☐ the disclosure of inventory in the financial statements.

15.2 DESCRIPTION OF INVENTORY

Inventory is tangible property:

- ☐ held for sale in the normal course of business
- ☐ in the process of production, with a view to sale
- ☐ to be consumed during the production of saleable goods or services.[3]

The inventory of **retailers** and wholesalers comprises finished goods which are ready for sale.

The **manufacturer** usually has four different categories of inventory:

- ☐ Finished goods which are for sale.
- ☐ Uncompleted goods still in the process of being manufactured.
- ☐ Raw and other materials used in manufacturing the product.
- ☐ Consumable inventory, consumed in the manufacturing process. Examples are: packaging material, fuel, maintenance material and machine parts. Normally consumable inventory is regarded as an asset only if it is a material amount, otherwise it is written off when purchased.

NB

The purpose for which goods are purchased or manufactured is an important criterion in determining whether or not the item forms part of inventory. Motor vehicles purchased would constitute stock for a motor dealer, but fixed assets for an individual.

1 AC 108: Valuation and presentation of inventory in the context of the historical cost system issued by the Accounting Practices Board, April 1983.
2 AC 108 par .02.
3 AC 108 par .03.

The manufacturing process and the calculation of the cost of manufactured goods is discussed in detail in a separate chapter. In the present chapter the discussion is restricted to finished products which are purchased for the purpose of resale.

The accounting responsibility for inventory is related to two aspects:

- □ determining the **physical quantities** which should be on hand
- □ the **valuation** of the physical inventory.

15.3 PHYSICAL STOCK TAKING

A stock count entails the systematic and physical counting of all items forming part of the inventory. Although some enterprises have a stock count several times during the course of a financial year and others make use of continuous inventory systems, it is generally deemed necessary that a stock count is carried out at least annually – usually at the end of the financial year.

The periodic, physical counting of inventory is an indispensable requirement for inventory control; **it serves as a check on perpetual inventory records**. In cases where inventory records are not kept a physical count is absolutely essential for determining profits. Physical stock taking also provides an opportunity for checking on the condition of the goods, and may help to reveal flaws in the system of recording, storing and handling inventory.

Stock taking requires proper planning insofar as the timing of the stock count and drawing up instructions and procedures governing the count are concerned.

Various methods are used to determine the physical quantities of items in stock. Basically teams are used, the first member counting, weighing, measuring or estimating and calling out the description and quantity to the second member, who records the particulars on a prepared (and usually prenumbered) inventory sheet.

The following general rules may serve as guidelines for a stock count:

- □ Inventory must be arranged in such a way that it is easy to count.
- □ Purchases and sales immediately before the closing date must be counted correctly to ensure that goods are not counted twice or omitted altogether.

Only goods which are the **property of the enterprise** should be included in the count.

The decision as to which items to include in the inventory is often a difficult one. For example, the enterprise may have purchased goods which are not yet on the premises at the time of counting, or goods may have been sold but not yet despatched and therefore are still on the premises. The deciding factor is the legal ownership over the goods; all goods over which the enterprise has right of ownership and for which it has paid or has an obligation to pay, irrespective of whether they are on the premises, must be included in the stock count.

Legally, right of ownership over goods passes from the seller to the buyer on delivery. In the case of goods in transit, delivery is determined by the conditions of the transaction. For example, if goods are despatched 'free on board' by the seller, the goods belong to the purchaser as soon as they have been delivered by the seller to the point of despatch and must be included in the purchaser's inventory.

The same distinction applies to goods sold. At the time of the stock count there may still be goods on the premises the right of ownership of which has been transferred to the customer, that is he has paid or undertaken to pay for the goods, but requested delivery at a later stage. These goods will not be included in the enterprise's inventory.

- ☐ A numbered identification label is attached to each type of item. Once the item has been counted the total is written on the label to serve as a means of checking whether all items have been counted.
- ☐ Prenumbered inventory lists giving a description of all inventory items must be used. The total on the identification label must be recorded on the relevant inventory list.
- ☐ To complete the inventory lists, the unit price of each item is entered on the relevant list and the total value of each item is calculated.
- ☐ Random test checks must be performed at all stages of the count, from counting to the final inventory total.
- ☐ The stock count may take weeks and can cause disruption; therefore careful planning and supervision by an official who does not normally have any duties connected with the storage is essential.
- ☐ The actual inventory on hand must be reconciled with the records (inventory cards) and the necessary adjustments made.

15.4 THE IMPORTANCE OF CORRECT INVENTORY VALUATION

Correct valuation of inventory is extremely important, since it affects both the income statement and the balance sheet and also because the investment in inventory usually constitutes a considerable percentage of total assets. An incorrect valuation of inventory will affect various other items in the financial statements; namely the cost of sales, the gross and net profit for the period in which the mistake appears, and the current assets and owner's equity at the end of the financial year. Moreover, since the closing inventory of one financial year forms the opening inventory of the following period, any incorrect valuation of closing inventory in a specific year will also influence the cost of sales and the gross and net profit in the following period.

Example 15.1

The following are the income statements of a trading concern for 19.2 and 19.3:

	19.2		19.3	
Sales		400 000		500 000
Cost of goods sold:		150 000		270 000
Opening inventory	100 000		150 000	
Purchases	200 000		300 000	
	300 000		450 000	
Less: Closing inventory	150 000		180 000	
Gross profit		250 000		230 000
Less: Operating expenses		130 000		150 000
Net profit		R120 000		R80 000

If the closing inventory for 19.2 was incorrectly valued and should have been R100 000 instead of R150 000, the effect of the mistake will be as shown in the table below:

	19.2			19.3		
	With incorrect inventory end 19.2	With correct inventory end 19.2	Influence of incorrect inventory	With incorrect inventory end 19.3	With correct inventory end 19.3	Influence of incorrect inventory
Cost of sales	150 000	200 000	Too low	270 000	220 000	Too high
Gross profit	250 000	200 000	Too high	230 000	280 000	Too low
Net profit	120 000	70 000	Too high	80 000	130 000	Too low

	Profit 19.2		Profit 19.3		
Incorrect inventory:	R120 000	+	R 80 000	=	R200 000
Correct inventory:	R 70 000	+	R130 000	=	R200 000

Since the incorrect and correct inventory figures (being the closing inventory for 19.2 and the opening inventory for 19.3) cancel each other out over the two-year period, the **total net profit** for the two years is the same in each case. This does not minimise the seriousness of a mistake in the inventory figure, which could result in the incorrect interpretation and analysis of the income statement of each financial year, as well as adversely influencing managerial decisions. The gross profit percentage on turnover for 19.2 based on the correct inventory would be 62,5% $\frac{(250\,000 \times 100)}{(40\,000)}$, while in fact it should be only 50%, $\frac{(200\,000 \times 100)}{(40\,000)}$.

15.5 VALUATION OF INVENTORY AT HISTORICAL COST

The generally accepted standard in accounting practice is that inventory should be valued at the lower of historical cost and net realisable value.[4]

15.5.1 Factors in determining historical cost

The primary accounting basis for recording inventory is **historical cost**. The historical cost of inventory comprises the **total**:

- purchase costs
- processing costs
- other costs incurred to bring the inventory to its present location and condition.[5]

Purchase costs comprise the purchase price, including import duties and other purchase levies, transport and handling costs, and all other costs directly related to acquisition, taking into account discount, rebates and subsidies on purchases.[6]

Conversion costs are the costs incurred to bring the inventory to its present location and condition.[7] These are costs which can be allocated specifically to manufactured units, such as direct

4 AC 108 par .25.
5 AC 108 par .04.
6 AC 108 par .05.
7 AC 108 par .06.

labour, direct material and production overheads incurred in normal production activities, as well as other overheads which have to be incurred in the particular circumstances to bring the inventory to its present location and position.

The matching of historical costs with the related income in the financial statements requires that inventory should be valued at historical cost. In practice, there are diverse interpretations as to how production and other overheads should be treated in the **determination of historical costs**.[8]

Production overheads are costs (excluding direct material and labour) incurred in the production process, for example indirect material and labour, depreciation, maintenance of factory buildings and equipment and the cost of factory management and administration.[9]

Production overheads must be analysed in order to determine what portion thereof has been applied to bring the inventory to its present location and condition, so that this portion can be included in processing costs when the historical costs of the inventory are determined.[10]

Other overheads (i e overheads which are not production carrying costs) are sometimes incurred to bring inventory to its present location and condition (e g designing goods to customers' specifications).

Usually, other overheads such as sales and general administration carrying costs are not considered to be costs related to bringing the inventory to its present location and condition.

15.5.2 Methods of determining cost price

When an enterprise has paid different prices for different lots of an inventory item and only a portion of the goods is left at the end of the financial period, it must be determined which of the various prices paid must be regarded as the purchase price of those items still on hand.

The method used to allocate costs to inventory and thereby to determine the cost price of goods sold should be the method that results in the most realistic determination of profit for that specific enterprise.

The following methods are those generally used to determine cost price:

- ☐ The specific identification method: The actual cost of a specific item is allocated to that item.
- ☐ Average cost price method: The total cost price of the goods available for sale is divided by the total number of units to obtain an average cost price per unit (also called the weighted average method).
- ☐ First-in-first-out method (FIFO): This method assumes that those items purchased first will be sold first. The items still in stock are thus considered part of the most recent purchases.
- ☐ Last-in-first-out method (LIFO): This method assumes that the items most recently purchased will be sold first. Inventory on hand is thus considered part of the earliest purchases.
- ☐ Base stock method.
- ☐ Standard cost method.

8 AC 108 par .07.
9 AC 108 par .09.
10 AC 108 par .10.

Any of these methods **can** be used to determine the cost of goods still on hand, as well as the **cost of goods sold**.

The FIFO, LIFO, weighted average and specific identification methods all use **costs** which have been incurred by the enterprise at some stage.[11]

Example 15.2

The following data for March 19.6 will be used to illustrate the various methods:

INVENTORY DATA: ITEM X
MARCH 19.6

(a) Purchases:			R		Total
1 March 19.6: purchase	100 units	@	1,00	=	100
8 March 19.6: purchase	300 units	@	1,10	=	330
15 March 19.6: purchase	200 units	@	1,20	=	240
22 March 19.6: purchase	300 units	@	1,30	=	390
29 March 19.6: purchase	100 units	@	1,40	=	140
	1 000				R1 200
(b) Sales: 1-31 March: 600 units					
(c) On hand: 31 March 19.6: 400 units					

(1) The specific identification method

The basis of this method is that specific costs are identified and allocated to specific inventory items. The method is suitable where goods are purchased or manufactured for a specific project, in other words the inventory items are not interchangeable.[12]

Therefore this method will be used especially in the case of items having a high unit cost and where relatively few items are kept in stock, for example valuable jewellery pieces.

Example 15.2 (1)

In this case the exact purchase date of each of the 400 units in stock on 31 March must be determined.

Assume that the information is compiled as follows:

20 units purchased on 1 March
80 units purchased on 8 March
100 units purchased on 15 March
100 units purchased on 22 March
100 units purchased on 29 March

11 AC 108 par .16.
12 AC 108 par .17 and .30.

The cost price of the inventory on hand on 31 March is thus:

	R
20 units @ 1,00 =	20
80 units @ 1,10 =	88
100 units @ 1,20 =	120
100 units @ 1,30 =	130
100 units @ 1,40 =	140
Cost of goods on hand:	R498

The cost price of goods sold is thus:

Total cost price =	1 200
Cost of inventory on hand =	498
	R702

The following is a complete record of inventory movement:

Date	Units			Unit price	Cost of sales	Cost of goods on hand
	Purchases	On hand	Sales			
				R		
1/3	100	20	80	@ 1,00	80	20
8/3	300	80	220	@ 1,10	242	88
15/3	200	100	100	@ 1,20	120	120
22/3	300	100	200	@ 1,30	260	130
29/3	100	100	—	@ 1,40	—	140
					R702	R498
Therefore: cost of goods sold				=	702	
cost of goods on hand				=	498	
					R1 200	

Where the inventory consists of a large number of items, each with a relatively low individual value, this method is obviously not practical.

(2) The weighted average method

This method is suitable in cases where a large number of homogeneous inventory items is kept in stock.

There are two possible approaches to the calculation of average cost price:

Example 15.2 (2)

(a) Pure accounting average

The pure accounting average cost price per item of the March purchases would be determined as follows:

$$\frac{\text{Total cost}}{\text{Total number of items}} = \frac{\text{R1 200}}{\text{R1 000}}$$

$$= \text{R1,20}$$

Since 600 units have been sold, the cost price of sales is 600 x R1,20 = 720
and the cost price of stock on hand, 400 x R1,20 = 480

R1 200

(b) Weighted average

A new average cost price is calculated after each purchase, as follows:

Purchases		Unit cost per lot	Cost price		Weighted average cost*
Per lot	Total units		Per lot	Total	
100	100	R1,00	R100	R 100	R1,00 (R100 ÷ 100)
300	400	R1,10	R330	R 430	R1,075 (R430 ÷ 400)
200	600	R1,20	R240	R 670	R1,117 (R670 ÷ 600)
300	900	R1,30	R390	R1 060	R1,178 (R1 060 ÷ 900)
100	1 000	R1,40	R140	R1 200	R1,20 (R1 200 ÷ 1 000)

*Calculated after purchase of each new lot.

From this it can be seen that after each lot has been purchased, the average cost price must be re-calculated.

The average cost price method tends to reduce the influence of fluctuating costs on net income. Generally it is used by undertakings which hold stock for a relatively long period, or which purchase large quantities of goods with a relatively low unit value for different prices at different times. The costs that would be incurred to determine the specific value of each of these items would be out of proportion to the benefit derived.

Criticism levelled at this method is that it does not result in the pure application of current costs and current income and therefore the balance sheet value of inventory is not in line with the most recent replacement costs. For example, according to the calculations above, inventory on the balance sheet will be valued at R1,20 per unit, whereas the most recent replacement cost is actually R1,40 per unit.

(3) The first-in-first-out method (FIFO)

This method is especially suitable where a large number of homogeneous items is on hand, and it is immaterial whether the older or more recent items are sold. It is based on the approach that it is better to sell the older inventory first.

According to this method, and using the same data as in previous examples, the cost of goods on hand and the cost of goods sold will be calculated as follows:

Example 15.2 (3)

Date	Purchases	Unit price	Sales	On hand	Cost of goods sold	Cost of goods on hand
		R				
1/3	100	1,00	100		100	
8/3	300	1,10	300		330	
15/3	200	1,20	200		240	
20/3	300	1,30		300		390
29/3	100	1,40		100		140
					R670	R530

The FIFO method of valuation is widely used, since it tends to value inventory at current prices. In the income statement, however, older prices are brought into account against current selling prices.

Statement AC 108 stipulates that (with the exception of the LIFO basis of valuation explained below) inventory should be accounted for at historical cost on the FIFO basis or on the basis of weighted average cost.[13]

(4) The last-in-first-out method (LIFO)

According to this method, the cost of goods sold and the value of inventory on hand for the example above will be calculated as follows:

Example 15.2 (4)

Date	Purchases	Unit price	Sales	On hand	Cost of goods sold	Cost of goods on hand
		R				
1/3	100	1,00		100		100
8/3	300	1,10		300		330
15/3	200	1,20	200		240	
20/3	300	1,30	300		390	
29/3	100	1,40	100		140	
					R770	R430

According to the last-in-first-out method, the cost of goods most recently received is debited first against income as cost of goods sold.

Therefore, in times of rising prices the LIFO method will result in a lower net income than in instances where FIFO is applied.

The 'older' costs are used for inventory valuation (as may be seen from the example above). Thus this method emphasises the importance of current prices for ascertaining the cost of goods sold rather than for valuing goods still on hand.

According to Statement AC 108 (par .31), the LIFO basis can be applied in the RSA provided that the **difference between the inventory amount on the balance sheet** and one of the following is disclosed, viz:

- ☐ either the lower of inventory as determined by applying the FIFO basis or the basis of weighted average cost or the net realisable value (refer to the following paragraph).
- ☐ the lowest of the current replacement value at balance sheet date or net realisable value.

The additional disclosure requirements in terms of AC 108 paragraph .31 give due recognition to the fact that the balance sheet value of inventory on the LIFO basis can be unrealistically low in times of rising prices (compare also para (5) below).

☐ Advantages and disadvantages of the LIFO method

Proponents of the LIFO method maintain that it results in a more accurate matching of cost and income in that the most recent costs are brought into account against current selling prices. Furthermore,

13 AC 108 par .29.

they point out that for the duration of a business cycle the LIFO method will tend to show a more reasonable income under deflationary conditions than any other method. This helps to minimise the fluctuations of the business cycle, thereby promoting economic stability. It also has certain tax benefits.

Opponents of the method maintain that the use of this method tends to reduce the benefit of the balance sheet, since inventory valuation is based on older price levels which may bear no relationship to current prices. Thus the LIFO method only partly solves the problem of price levels.

(5) A comparison of the different cost methods and their different suppositions concerning the flow of costs

While the specific identification method is based on actual costs, the average price method, the FIFO and the LIFO cost price methods are each based on a specific supposition concerning the **flow of costs**. Each of these suppositions produces a different result, as may be seen from the example below:

	Average cost price	FIFO	LIFO
Sales (e g 400 @ R4,00)	1 600	1 600	1 600
Cost of goods sold	720	670	770
Gross profit	R 880	R 930	R 830

In a period of rising prices (as in the case of March in example 15.2), FIFO produced the highest and LIFO the lowest gross profit, while the average cost price method tended to minimise the effect of changing prices. In a period of falling prices FIFO and LIFO will produce exactly the opposite result.

The consequences of using the different methods to determine the **value** of **closing inventory** must also be compared:

	Specific identification			
Cost of goods sold	702	720	670	770
Value of closing inventory	498	480	530	430
Total cost of purchases	R1 200	R1 200	R1 200	R1 200

Note that the cost of goods sold plus the value of the closing inventory must equal the total cost of purchases, regardless of the method used. During a period of rising prices the value of closing inventory according to the FIFO method will be higher than that according to the LIFO method, since the most recent (and therefore highest) prices are allocated to goods on hand. In a period of falling prices the FIFO method will attach a lower value to goods on hand than the LIFO method.

Standard costs

In undertakings which make use of budgets and budget control systems, standard costs are allocated to each inventory item.

The standard cost is determined in advance and serves as a standard for that price at which inventory **should** be purchased, as well as a basis on which budgets are prepared. Statement AC 108 allows the use of this method, provided that the results so obtained are a reliable approximation of the lower of historical cost and net realisable value.[14]

According to the standard cost system, all purchases are recorded at standard price and the difference between the standard and the actual prices is journalised as a **variance**:

Example 15.3

An enterprise's standard cost for article A is R5 per unit. During March 19.3, 400 units are purchased for R2 130. The journal entry for the purchases will be recorded as follows:

Inventory (standard cost)	xx	
Purchase price – variation	x	
Creditors		xx
Purchase of inventory for the month		

A variance may be favourable (credit) or unfavourable (debit). It gives an indication of the effectiveness of the purchasing policy.

All inventory is valued at standard cost, but in the preparation of the financial statements a decision must be taken regarding the treatment of variances. If the standard costs are reasonable and realistic the variances will be small and therefore can be written off against income, so that inventory will be valued purely on standard cost for the purpose of the financial statements.

However, if the variances are relatively large, for example due to price fluctuations, a conservative policy must be followed whereby the variances are debited proportionately to stock on hand and cost of sales. This means that the standard variance account will be closed off and that the inventory and the cost of sales will be 'revalued' at cost price.

(7) The base stock method

This method is comparable to the LIFO method, the difference being that in this case the premise is that an undertaking must maintain a certain level of inventory in order to trade effectively.

The base inventory of various items identified by the undertaking corresponds to fixed assets, although it is not accounted for as such. Inventory over and above the minimum (base) inventory is accounted for by one or other of the recognised methods. Although this method results in a reasonable matching of current costs and current income, it is not a satisfactory method because the determination of base stock is extremely arbitrary.

15.6 VALUATION OF INVENTORY BELOW HISTORICAL COST

15.6.1 Introduction: The concept 'net realisable value'

Paragraph 15.5 discussed the valuation of inventory at historical cost.

If the selling price of inventory declines or if the inventory is damaged or is partially or totally obsolete, the **historical cost thereof will no longer be realisable**.[15]

14 AC 108 par .32.
15 AC 108 par .21.

In this instance the most suitable value will be net realisable value (NRV).

> Net realisable value is the selling price it is estimated will be realised in the normal course of business, less the costs that will have to be incurred to accomplish the sales.[16]

The practice of writing off inventory at **below** historical cost conforms with the **basic principle of prudence**, which determines that current assets should not be valued in excess of their expected realisable value.[17]

The policy underlying this rule is that if the value of inventory decreases during a specific year, then this decrease must be reflected in the **income statement for that year**.

15.6.2 Application of the NRV principle

The lowest of cost or NRV principle can be applied to:

- ☐ each individual item in the inventory;
- ☐ the main groups or categories of inventory; or
- ☐ the inventory as a whole.

Example 15.4

Using the different methods of applying the NRV principle to determine inventory value								
				Calculations		Value applied		
Stock item	Quantity	Unit price	NRV	Total cost	Total NRV	Individual items	Inventory groups	Inventory in total
Group 1:								
Item 1.1	10	5,00	4,00	50,00	40,00	40,00		
Item 1.2	20	4,00	5,00	80,00	100,00	80,00		
Item 1.3	15	3,00	2,00	45,00	30,00	30,00		
Total Group 1:				175,00	170,00		170,00	
Group 2:								
Item 2.1	100	1,00	0,90	100,00	90,00	90,00		
Item 2.2	150	0,70	0,60	105,00	90,00	90,00		
Item 2.3	200	0,50	0,60	100,00	120,00	100,00		
Total Group 2:				305,00	300,00		300,00	
TOTAL INVENTORY:				480,00	470,00			470,00
						R430,00	R470,00	R470,00

16 AC 108 par .07.
17 AC 108 par .22.

When writing off the decline in value of individual items, main groups or categories of inventory, or inventory as a whole, realised losses may not be off-set against unrealised increases in value.[18]

15.6.3 Evaluating the NRV principle

The NRV principle is applied to make provision for anticipated losses and arises from the policy of conservatism. It is based on the premise that a decrease in the purchase price of goods will result in a decrease in the selling price of the goods, and consequently the normal profit margin will be eliminated or reduced.

However, there is a lack of theoretical support for the NRV principle.

The following arguments are raised against the NRV principle:

- It constitutes a deviation from the cost principle.
- It represents an exaggerated application of the policy of conservatism, whereby provision is made for possible losses as soon as these become known.
- If the losses do not materialise, future profits will be adversely affected.

The NRV principle is therefore somewhat arbitrary and is based on doubtful supposition regarding the normal profit margin. However, this does not imply that any substantial decrease in the value of unsold inventory should not be accounted for.

15.7 RETAIL INVENTORY SYSTEMS AND ESTIMATION OF INVENTORY

Retailers sometimes use a variety of inventory systems (besides the periodic and perpetual inventory systems), depending on the nature and distinctive character of the undertaking as well as practical considerations and the cost factor.

The following are some examples:

- Where inventory consists of a few large and easily identifiable items such as motor vehicles, pianos, washing machines or caravans, a variety or combination of the following records can be used:
  - Full details of the item are recorded in the stock book when the item is purchased. When the item is sold this is noted against the relevant description. The unsold inventory, as reflected in the stock book, will be confirmed periodically by a physical stock taking.
  - The goods are labelled, especially in the case of machinery, which is identifiable by serial number. A record is kept of receipts and issues according to description and serial number.
- Goods can be labelled with the selling price and the cost price, in code. As goods are sold, the details are recorded so that sales and cost of sales are always noted.
- For certain purposes it may be desirable or necessary to estimate the value of the inventory without stock taking or determining the value of the inventory by one of the above methods. In this case, and where the inventory has been damaged or destroyed, for example by fire, the **gross profit method** is frequently used in the preparation of interim financial statements.

18 AC 108 par .22.

Example 15.6

Assume that the trading accounts of Excelsior Enterprises for the previous three years were as follows:

	Previous years			Total
	1	2	3	
Sales	100 000	200 000	300 000	600 000
Cost of goods sold	76 000	152 000	222 000	450 000
Gross profit	R 24 000	R 48 000	R 78 000	R150 000
Gross profit % on turnover	24%	24%	26%	25%

The average gross profit percentage over the preceding three years was 25%.

The following information is available for Year 4:

	R
Inventory 1 January	50 000
Purchases during Year 4	500 000
Sales during Year 4	400 000

Using the average gross profit percentage for the preceding three years, the closing inventory can be estimated as follows:

INCOMPLETE WORKSHEET			Percentage of sales
Sales		400 000	100
Cost of goods sold:			
Opening inventory	50 000		
Purchases	500 000		
	550 000		
Estimated closing stock	? (d)	? (c)	? (a)
		R ? (b)	25

COMPLETED WORKSHEET			Percentage of sales
Sales		400 000	100
Cost of goods sold:			
Opening inventory	50 000		
Purchases	500 000		
	550 000		
Estimated closing stock	250 000 (d)	300 000 (c)	75 (a)
		R100 000	25

- ☐ If the gross profit percentage is 25%, the percentage of the cost of goods sold must be 75%.
- ☐ If the gross profit percentage is 25%, the gross profit must be 25% × 400 000 = R100 000.
- ☐ If the gross profit is R100 000, the cost of sales must be R300 000.
- ☐ If the cost of sales is R300 000, the estimated closing inventory must be:

Total costs	=	550 000
Cost of goods sold	=	300 000
		R250 000

This method is based on the assumption that the gross profit percentage on sales will remain essentially the same for each financial year; which makes it suitable for application in concerns which have a reasonably stable ratio between cost of sales and sales.

In determining the estimated inventory, due consideration must be given to factors which could result in a material deviation of the average percentage. The figure calculated is an estimated value for the inventory; it makes no provision for inventory losses, so a physical count is also necessary.

- ☐ Large retailers such as supermarkets, which have a huge range of items and a rapid turnover rate, have difficulty in applying the perpetual inventory system. Periodic physical stock taking to determine profits is also not always feasible.

This problem is eliminated by using the **retail method**, which relies on the supposition that the ratio between cost price and selling price can be determined if the mark-up is known.[19]

The price at which goods are to be sold is determined by adding a mark-up to the cost price to cover operating costs plus profit. The mark-up on cost price can be expressed either as a percentage of the selling price, or as a percentage of the cost price.

Example 15.7

Assume that a mark-up of R25 is added onto the cost price of an item (R100) to make the selling price R125. The percentage mark-up can be expressed as follows:

Selling price	125
Cost price	100
	R25

(i) Percentage profit on cost price $\frac{25}{100} = 25\%$

(ii) Percentage profit on selling price $\frac{25}{125} = 20\%$

If only the selling price of an item and the gross profit percentage on cost price are known, the cost price can be calculated as follows:

Gross profit = 25% on cost price = 20% on selling price

If selling price is 100, cost price is R80

If selling price is 125, cost price is $\frac{80}{100} \times 125 = \text{R}100$

The retail method serves two purposes, namely to calculate an inventory figure without a physical stock taking and to facilitate centralised inventory control over several branches or departments. Goods

19 Refer also AC 108 par .18.

are invoiced at selling price to the departments or branches, while the head office records show the inventory at cost and selling prices. Sales are recorded in the usual manner. The difference between the goods invoiced and the actual sales should indicate the sales value of the goods still on hand (at selling price).

Example 15.8

	Cost price	Retail selling price
Opening inventory	60 000	90 000
Purchases	540 000	810 000
Total goods available	R600 000	900 000
Sales for the period		774 000
Estimated inventory at retail selling price		R126 000
Cost percentage (ratio of cost to retail selling price)		
$\frac{600\ 000}{900\ 000} = 66\frac{2}{3}\%$		
Estimated inventory @ cost ($66\frac{2}{3}\% \times$ R126 000) = R84 000		

An enterprise may find it necessary to change the fixed retail selling price in the course of the financial period; in other words the inventory may be marked either up or down, for example because of end-of-season sales. Such adjustments to the previously fixed selling price will obviously affect the gross profit – and consequently also the value of the inventory.

When inventory is calculated according to the retail method, price increases are included in the calculation of the total value of goods available for sale. Decreases in price, on the other hand, are excluded when the cost percentage is calculated, but are added back in sales. Consequently, when the cost percentage is applied to the retail selling price, a lower cost percentage and a lower inventory figure result.

Example 15.9

	Cost price	Retail selling price
Opening inventory	60 000	90 000
Purchases during period	540 000	810 000
Price increases (for example)		30 000
	R600 000	R930 000

In our previous example the relevant ratios were:

Gross profit %	Cost %
$\frac{300\ 000}{900\ 000}$	$\frac{600\ 000}{900\ 000}$
$= 33\frac{1}{3}\%$	$= 66\frac{2}{3}\%$

The price increase of R30 000 has the following effect:

Gross profit %	Cost %
$\frac{330\ 000}{930\ 000}$	$\frac{600\ 000}{930\ 000}$
= 35,484%	= 64,516%

Sales during the period	774 000	
Add: Price reductions (e g during end-of-season sale)	24 000	798 000
Estimated inventory at selling price	R132 000	(930 000 – 798 000)
∴ Estimated inventory at cost price (64,516% × R132 000) =	R85 161	

When the retail price method is used, the ratio of cost price to retail price is assumed to be relatively uniform for all goods sold in a specific department or at a specific branch. In practice, large departmental stores determine separate percentages for each department.

For proper inventory control physical stock taking must be done periodically, irrespective of whether the gross profit or retail price method is used.

This method also implies that inventory can be classified into groups having identical mark-ups, that opening inventory and purchases can be expressed in terms of selling prices, and that changes in prices and mark-ups will be recorded and brought into account during that period.

15.8 CONSISTENCY IN THE APPLICATION OF PROCEDURES

From the above discussion it is obvious that the valuation of inventory, as with other aspects of accounting, can be made by applying one of various alternative methods. **Consistency in the application of the method selected** is, however, of prime importance. This applies to every field of accounting, but especially to inventory. Inconsistency in inventory valuation, cost allocation and presentation in the financial statements will render comparison of the operating results and the financial position of the enterprise meaningless. The concept consistency does exclude changes in methods of valuation or the classification of inventory items; it merely requires that this information should be fully disclosed. A change in the basis of inventory valuation must be disclosed by means of a note to the financial statements explaining the nature and effect of the change.

15.9 DISCLOSURE OF INVENTORY IN THE FINANCIAL STATEMENTS

The total inventory sold or consumed (unless allocated to other asset accounts) and any amount written off to net realisable value for the period should be taken into account against operating income.[20]

Inventory is a current asset and includes items purchased, manufactured, processed or developed by the company which are intended for sale in the normal course of its business. Inventory must be shown as a separate item, and if necessary must be classified under appropriate sub-headings which could include the following:

- ☐ Raw materials.
- ☐ Finished products.
- ☐ Merchandise.
- ☐ Consumable stores and maintenance parts.
- ☐ Work in progress.
- ☐ Contracts in progress.

The basis of valuation of inventory must be specified in a suitable description for example:

- ☐ At cost price.
- ☐ At the lower of cost or net realisable value.
- ☐ At the lowest of cost, net realisable value or replacement value.
- ☐ At any other explicitly expressed value.

If cost price is used, the basis of determining cost must be indicated and it must be stated whether the method of valuation is the same as that used in the previous year.

A change in the accounting policy in respect of inventory which will have a material effect on the financial statements should be disclosed and quantified.[21]

If the inventory is encumbered to secure an obligation of either the enterprise or a third party, details of the encumbrance, including the amount secured, must be disclosed by way of a note.

15.10 ANALYSIS AND INTERPRETATION OF INVENTORY IN THE FINANCIAL STATEMENTS

We have already noted, in the discussion of cash and debtors, that there is an optimum level of investment in any asset which, together with an optimum investment in other assets, should contribute to the most profitable result. Consequently, in any enterprise the main aim of inventory control is to determine and maintain the optimum level of investment in inventory. Two aspects of inventory control are especially important: on the one hand, insufficient inventory could result in a drop in sales or a delay in production; and on the other, excessive investment in inventory could result in unnecessary costs and the possible risk of obsolescence. The optimum level for every enterprise lies between

20 AC 108 par .38.
21 AC 108 par .42.

these two points, but can be determined only if all related factors such as the nature and size of the enterprise, the type of goods traded, etc are taken into account.

In order to keep inventory at an optimum level, investment in inventory should be monitored constantly against predetermined criteria. The most widely used of these criteria are **inventory turnover rate** and **number of days' inventory on hand**.

15.10.1 Inventory turnover rate

The **inventory turnover rate** represents the ratio between inventory and the cost of sales.

Example 15.11

Cost of goods sold during the year		R100 000	1
Inventory on hand at cost price:			
1 January	R15 000		
31 December	R25 000		
∴ Average inventory		$\frac{15\,000 + 25\,000}{2}$ = R20 000	2
Inventory turnover rate (1 – 2)		= $\frac{100\,000}{20\,000}$ = 5 times per year	

The enterprise in the above example sold and replaced its inventory fives times during the year, in other words the cost of goods sold was five times the average cost of the goods on hand.

Although a high turnover rate usually denotes effective management, the ratio can vary greatly from one enterprise to another. An enterprise which has a policy of high volume sales and low profit margin will naturally have a greater inventory turnover than an enterprise which has a policy of low volume and high profit margin.

15.10.2 Number of days' inventory on hand

As in the case of debtors, the inventory turnover figure can also be considered from a different angle. From the above example we can calculate that on average inventory is on hand for 365 ÷ 5 = 73 days.

A low inventory turnover rate (or the fact that inventory is too long in stock) can be attributed to or result in one or more of the following factors:

- ☐ Overinvestment in inventory.
- ☐ Excessive purchases of inventory.
- ☐ Superfluous slow-moving inventory.
- ☐ An increased risk of obsolescence.
- ☐ Excess storage facilities being necessary.
- ☐ An increased risk of loss as a result of fire or storm damage, as well as higher insurance costs.

15.11 PROBLEMS ENCOUNTERED WHEN USING HISTORICAL COST AS A BASIS FOR INVENTORY VALUATION

It is an important accounting principle that costs must be matched with the income generated as a result of incurring those costs. In other words, value sacrificed must be off-set against value received in order to measure the increase (profit) in owner's worth.

While the cost price of an item is equal to its value, no problem arises. However, in a period of rising prices (inflation) historical costs are no longer a measure of value. For example, an inventory item was purchased for R10 and sold for R20, yielding a profit of R10, but the replacement cost of that item is R12. The R10 can no longer be regarded as distributable profit; a portion must be retained to provide for uninterrupted replacement of inventory so that the enterprise's activities can continue.

The matching of value sacrificed with value received has resulted in the modern tendency to regard current costs, and not the cost price, as the cost incurred. The use of the LIFO method of inventory valuation is a step in this direction.

Although historical cost price accounting (and profit determination) will never become redundant, it must be borne in mind that the value of historical cost price as a means of determining costs is decreasing.

Various accounting bodies have already recommended that in addition to using cost price, the profit and valuation of assets and current cost information should be disclosed. It is suggested that the operating profit or loss should be shown after debiting the value (at the date of consumption) of the stock sold during the period.

16

FIXED ASSETS AND INVESTMENTS

The **AIM** of this chapter is to explain the recording, scrapping and disclosure of tangible and intangible fixed assets and investments.

16.1 NATURE OF ASSETS

In an accounting sense the term '**asset**' is used first, to refer to something which has **value, since value can be derived from it**, and second, to refer to any **right to value**. The concept asset therefore refers to something which can be used or consumed in the future to generate value. **Legal ownership** is **not** the only criterion for classifying something as an asset; for instance, someone who buys an item on hire-purchase does not become the owner of that item until the full purchase price has been paid. Nevertheless, the item is still recorded as an asset together with the corresponding obligation. Similarly, although a lessee never becomes the owner of the item leased, he may record that item as an asset providing that the corresponding obligation is also shown.

In an accounting sense 'ownership' usually implies 'legal ownership', but there are exceptions; an interest in a tangible or intangible object, or a **right to value**, combined with **right of possession** and **right of use** also constitutes an asset for the interested party.

If a person is the owner of the value or economic benefit arising from a specific source, then that source is an asset for the person concerned and he is the economic owner, although he may not be the legal owner. In such a case accounting substance should take precedence over legal form in ascertaining the most suitable accounting procedure.

The chief function of accounting is to determine profits. The generation of income, however, requires capital investment in order to provide the facilities needed by an enterprise to operate continuously and indefinitely.

Historically, expenses which are incurred but not allocated as a cost during a period are **deferred costs**. From an accounting point of view, they represent an asset. If these costs can be recovered within a year they are current assets, and if they are recoverable over a longer period they are fixed assets.

This classification of assets is essential for determining profits and also to show the enterprise's position at a specific time, in other words, the composition of its assets and the nature of its obligations.

The purpose of acquiring fixed assets is to **use** them to generate income. They are **not** acquired for the purpose of **resale**. The fixed assets must produce goods which generate income, or in other words they must be used in the business' operations.

The largest category of fixed assets is **tangible**, such as land, buildings, machinery and vehicles. There are also **intangible** fixed assets such as patents, copyrights, trade marks and goodwill. Another group is external assets, known as **investments**.

16.2 CLASSIFICATION OF ASSETS

Fixed assets and investments can be classified as follows:

(1) Tangible fixed assets

- Land which is not subject to depreciation or depletion through use, since it is never 'consumed'.
- Manufactured assets such as buildings, machinery and vehicles, the value of which decreases in the course of time as a result of the use thereof. These assets are subject to depreciation which must be apportioned annually as a cost.

- ☐ Natural resources which, through use, are subject to depletion; for example mines, oil and gas wells, and plantations.

(2) Intangible fixed assets

- ☐ Rights such as copyrights, patents, trade marks and goodwill.
- ☐ Deferred expenses and debits such as the preliminary expenses of a company.

(3) Investments

- ☐ Fixed period investments earning a fixed income.
- ☐ Investments in ordinary shares of other companies (interest in other enterprises).
- ☐ Sundry investments such as pension funds, housing schemes and insurance policies.
- ☐ Investment properties.

16.3 THE HISTORICAL COST OF FIXED ASSETS

The cost price of a fixed asset is calculated in terms of the cash (or equivalent money value) necessary to purchase the asset, as well as all the additional expenses which may be necessary to get the asset into a condition and location so that it is ready for use. For this reason, all expenses relating to the acquisition of the asset and its preparation for productive use are considered part of the cost price of the asset and are capitalised by debiting the asset account.

These expenses include the purchase price, legal costs, transport costs, installation costs and sales tax. (However, financing costs on loans raised to acquire the asset are not included.)

16.3.1. Land

All expenses incurred in acquiring land and getting it to a condition suited to its intended use, must be regarded as the cost of the land. Therefore all costs incurred from the date of purchase until such time as the land is ready for use are part of the cost of the land.

The cost of the land may include option costs, the purchase price, legal costs and transfer duty, the cost of the registration of servitudes, the settlement of outstanding costs related to the land, for example municipal rates, clearance and levelling costs, and any costs involved in demolishing existing structures. In brief, it includes all costs incurred in acquiring possession, access and right of disposal, and in ensuring that the land is in a useable condition.

If the land is purchased for the purpose of erecting a building, all costs incurred up to the commencement of excavations will be regarded as costs related to the land. Income generated by the sale of material obtained from demolitions will constitute a reduction in the cost price.

Example 16.1

Assume that an enterprise acquires premises, with an existing building, at a cost of R150 000, with the intention of erecting a factory on the site. According to the agreement of sale, the agent's commission of R5 000 is payable by the purchaser. Transfer and other legal costs pertaining to the transaction amount to R10 000. The cost of demolishing the old building is R2 000, while material from the demolished building is sold for R500. The cost of excavating the site for erection of a new building is R25 000. The enterprise raised a mortgage bond of R100 000 to purchase the land; bond charges of R4 000 are payable.

The cost price of the site was R166 500, determined as follows:

Net purchase price	150 000
Add: Agent's commission	5 000
Transfer and other legal costs	10 000
Net demolition costs (R2 000 – R500)	1 500
Total cost price	R166 500

The excavation costs form part of the cost price of the building still to be erected, and not of the site. Bond charges are a financing cost which are also not included in the cost price of the land. NB

If land is purchased with the intention of using it for a specific purpose at a later date, all costs incurred while the land is not in use form part of the cost price and must be capitalised. If, however, these costs are not to be recovered, they should be written off.

Costs involved in landscaping the property, for instance the cost of laying out gardens and paths, are capital costs and form part of the cost of the land. The initial outlay must be distinguished from maintenance, which will be written off as an expense.

Several properties may be bought for a single lump sum. In this case the reasonable market value of each property is generally used as a basis for the proportionate allocation of the purchase price, so that the cost of each property can be determined.

Land may be acquired other than for cash, for example it may be exchanged for another asset, it may be purchased by issuing shares in a company, or it may be inherited. In these cases the reasonable market value of the other asset is considered as the purchase price of the land. Inherited land must be recorded at a reasonable market price, the credit being taken to a non-distributable reserve account.

16.3.2 Manufactured assets

The cost price of fixed assets constructed by the enterprise itself or purchased complete, such as buildings, machinery, equipment and vehicles, also includes all costs involved in getting the asset into a condition suited to its intended purpose.

The cost price of a building is influenced by the manner in which it is acquired. If an existing building is purchased, the cost price will include the purchase price and all repair costs incurred initially to get the building into a useable condition.

If a building must still be erected, the enterprise may either engage a building contractor or undertake the construction itself. Where the work is done by a contractor, the cost price of the building will include the contract price plus all additional expenses incurred to make the building suitable for the enterprise's needs. If the enterprise erects the building itself, the cost price of the building will include expenses such as labour, material, professional fees payable to architects and quantity surveyors, for example, and insurance payable during the construction period.

The cost price of machinery, equipment and vehicles includes all expenses related to the acquisition and preparation of these assets for use. These expenses include the following items:

- ☐ Invoice price (less discount).
- ☐ Sales tax.
- ☐ Transport and clearance charges.
- ☐ Installation costs.

Example 16.2

Assume that an enterprise acquires a truck for a cash price of R5 000 less 10% discount, and then installs an air conditioner at a cost of R300. The total cost price of the truck will be calculated as follows:

Net purchase price (R5 000 – 10%)	4 500
Add: General sales tax	540
Air conditioner	300
Total purchase price	R5 340

16.3.3 Natural resources

Natural resources can be classified into three categories:

- ☐ Mineral resources which may be exploited through mining.
- ☐ Liquid resources such as oil and gas which may be exploited through boreholes.
- ☐ Harvested products such as food crops, orchards, fisheries and plantations. This category has more of an agricultural nature and therefore differs from exploitable resources in that the resources do not exist until they have been planted by man.

Exploiting natural resources involves three steps:

- ☐ Prospecting for, finding and acquiring an exploitable property. Prospecting costs and the cost of testing samples form part of the cost price of the natural resource. If the property is purchased, then the purchase price of the property is also part of the cost of the natural resource. If the property is leased, the periodic lease payments usually form part of the operating costs, but they can be discounted at current value and capitalised.
- ☐ Development of the property. Once deposits of the natural resource have been found and the right of use has been obtained, the property must be developed to make exploitation possible. This development may entail the sinking of boreholes, shafts and tunnels and all these development costs form part of the cost of the natural resource. Development costs also include the cost of the machinery and equipment that must be installed.
- ☐ The actual exploitation costs are regarded as **operating costs** and therefore do **not** form part of the capital costs.

16.3.4 Intangible assets

As has already been indicated, this type of asset is not of a physical nature; rather, it is classified as an asset because of the rights or advantages it has for the 'owner'. The value of this type of asset is often determined by general business factors as the asset may have an uncertain existence. Examples are patents, copyrights, research costs on uncompleted projects, trade marks and trade names.

If the asset is purchased, the purchase price and all costs relating to the purchase, such as legal costs and taxation, constitute the cost of the asset.

Sometimes the asset is not purchased from an outsider, but the enterprise itself undertakes development of the project. In this case the cost is more difficult to determine and all costs incurred during development must be recorded accurately. If the project eventually appears useless and unlikely to produce any asset, the costs must be written off as a loss.

The cost of an intangible asset may even be indeterminable. In this case the procedure recommended is either to record the asset at a nominal value of R1, or to have the asset valued, or to quantify the advantages arising from the asset and capitalise them.

16.3.5 Investments

Investments, like any other fixed asset, are recorded in the enterprise's books at cost. The cost price is generally the cash paid and comprises all costs incurred to acquire the asset, such as the purchase price of the investment, broker's fees, stamp duty, taxation and any other cost involved in the purchase transaction.

An investment may be acquired in exchange for another asset; in such a case the market value or a reasonable valuation of the asset received in exchange must be regarded as the purchase price of the investment.

16.4 TREATMENT OF COSTS INCURRED AFTER THE INITIAL ACQUISITION OF ASSETS

As has already been stated, the process whereby an expense is debited to an asset account is described as **capitalisation** of the expense, which is then known as a capital expense. It has also been stated that all expenses related to the **acquisition** of an asset must be capitalised. However, this is not necessarily the case with expenses incurred **after** the initial acquisition of an asset; some of these expenses can rightly be treated as operating costs.

The following are examples of expenses incurred in respect of an asset after its initial acquisition:

- ☐ Continuous maintenance costs incurred in keeping an asset functioning and ensuring its productive capacity.
- ☐ Costs related to periodic, large-scale repairs to an asset.

The benefit derived from some of these expenses may also extend to future financial periods and therefore should be capitalised. Other expenses, on the other hand, will benefit only that period in which they are incurred, and therefore should be treated as operating costs for that specific financial period.

If related income and expenses are to be matched accurately – an essential prerequisite for effective profit determination – then it is important to distinguish between capital and operating expenses. If capital expenses are erroneously treated as operating expenses, both the enterprise's assets and its net income for the current year will be too low, and in future financial periods the same error will result in the net income being too high, while the assets will still be too low. Conversely, erroneous capitalisation of operating expenses will have the opposite effect.

Therefore it is essential that an enterprise establishes a realistic policy for differentiating between capital expenses and operating costs, and that it applies this policy consistently. The following factors must be taken into consideration in the formulation of such a policy:

- ☐ **Probable lifespan of the item purchased in relation to the normal financial period of the enterprise**

If the item is expected to have a lifespan longer than the current financial period, then future periods will also derive benefit from the use of this asset. Such an item must be capitalised and brought into account as a cost on an acceptable and appropriate basis for each financial period during which it is used (refer to depreciation procedures in par 16.6).

- ☐ **Materiality and repetitive nature of the expense**

Items with a relatively short lifespan and a relatively low value may be treated as operating costs without having a material influence on the enterprise's profits. This applies especially if such items are purchased regularly.

- ☐ **Influence of the expense on the asset's estimated lifespan**

If an expense prolongs the useful lifespan of an asset beyond initial expectations, it should be capitalised; if not, it should be treated as an operating cost.

One of the factors determining the estimated lifespan of an asset is the maintenance policy in respect of the asset during its lifespan. Therefore maintenance costs incurred by the enterprise during the normal course of business are regarded as operating costs, while the cost of large-scale repairs to prolong the lifespan of the asset are capitalised.

16.5 RECORDING THE PURCHASE OF A FIXED ASSET

When an asset is purchased the appropriate asset account is debited with the cost price. In a previous discussion it has already been said that general ledger accounts are kept for each type of asset such as land, buildings, machinery, etc. These accounts serve as **control accounts**, which should be backed up by **asset registers*** containing full particulars of all the items in each asset account kept in the general ledger.

16.6 DEPRECIATION OF FIXED ASSETS[1]

16.6.1 Definitions

It has already been stated at the beginning of this book that most fixed assets used in an undertaking are subject to depreciation.

Depreciation is the allocation of the **depreciable amount** of a **depreciable asset** over its estimated **useful life**.

*Refer to the internal control over fixed assets in paragraph 16.9.

1 The major portion of this paragraph is taken from Statement AC 106 (GAAP).

A **depreciable asset** is an asset that:

- ☐ is expected to be used during more than one financial period
- ☐ has a limited **useful life** (the period over which a depreciable asset is expected to be used by an undertaking)
- ☐ is held by an undertaking for its own use.

The **depreciable amount** of a depreciable asset is:

- ☐ the historical cost price
- ☐ another amount which has replaced the historical cost in the financial statements, **less**
- ☐ the estimated **scrap value** (i e the value which the asset may still have at the end of its useful life).

16.6.2 The necessity for depreciation

A characteristic of any depreciable asset is that it is held for the purpose of earning income and not for the purpose of being sold in the normal course of business. The amount at which it is shown in the balance sheet is normally the historical cost **less amounts provided for depreciation**.

Depreciation is a measure of wear and tear, consumption or other loss of value of a fixed asset which arises as a result of use, the lapsing of time, or obsolescence due to technological advancement or changes in the market.

> Depreciation is **allocated to accounting periods** in such a manner that a reasonable amount is set off in each financial period during the expected useful life of the asset.

In many undertakings depreciable assets constitute a considerable portion of the total assets. Therefore depreciation can have a meaningful effect on the presentation of the financial position and the determination of the operational result. It is sometimes contended that it is unnecessary to provide for depreciation if the market value of an asset exceeds its book value. Depreciation should, however, be set off against the depreciable amount in every accounting period, irrespective of the higher market value.

16.6.3 Recording depreciation

That portion of the depreciable amount of an asset which is apportioned as a cost during a specific period is debited to a **depreciation expense account**. Accordingly, to balance the double entry the assets account should be credited with the same amount. In practice, however, it is not the asset account, but a separate account, the **accumulated depreciation account**, which is credited with the periodic depreciation. Thus there are two relevant accounts* in the general ledger, namely the asset account, in which the cost of the asset remains unchanged as long as the asset is in the enterprise's possession, and the accumulated depreciation account, which at any given time shows the total depreciation written off.

---

*The depreciation expense account, being an expense, is closed off at the end of the financial period by being transferred to the income account.

The difference between the debit balance on the asset account and the credit balance on the accumulated depreciation account is the **net book value** of the fixed asset, which represents that portion of the depreciable amount of the fixed asset which has not yet elapsed and therefore has not been apportioned as a cost to a specific period.

16.6.4 Determination of depreciation

(1) Introduction

The recording of fixed assets and the related, periodic writing off of depreciation is based on the concept of the accounting entity as a going concern with an indefinite lifespan. Depreciation is the systematic distribution of the cost of a fixed asset over its useful life so that the cost of using the asset is appropriately matched or apportioned to the income generated by that use. Therefore the going concern and financial period principles underly the depreciation process. Fixed assets, in other words, merely represent deferred expenses, and the depreciation process is simply a means of allocating the deferred expenses to the correct financial period. Thus, with depreciation the emphasis is on the systematic and realistic apportionment of the expenses involved in using the fixed assets. Accordingly, the balance sheet does not show the current market value of fixed assets, nor does the depreciation provided measure the decrease in value over a period.

The concept depreciation as used in accounting does not imply the physical ageing of an asset. **Depreciation is simply a process of apportionment and not a process of valuation.** The depreciation provided for a specific period is that portion of the total cost price of an asset allocated by this process to the period concerned.

(2) Factors affecting the determination of depreciation

It is not always easy to determine what portion of the depreciable amount of a fixed asset must be allocated to any specific period, since a variety of factors have to be taken into consideration. The following are significant factors:

- ☐ **Cost price**: As stated in an earlier section of this chapter, cost is the purchase price plus any additional expenses necessary to prepare an asset for use.

- ☐ **Lifespan of an asset**: The lifespan of an asset cannot be determined in advance and must therefore be estimated. This requires judgement, which is usually based on experience with similar assets. The present condition of the asset and the company's policy regarding the replacement of assets will also be determining factors. The lifespan of an asset can be measured in terms of **time** (duration of the asset's estimated use), **production** (the total number of units an asset is expected to produce), or **service** (e g the distance it will travel), or some similar criterion.

  It is usual to distinguish between the technical lifespan of a fixed asset and its economic lifespan. The technical lifespan is determined by factors relevant to the particular asset concerned. The technical lifespan of an asset terminates when it can no longer provide the service for which it was acquired, or maintenance costs become prohibitive. The economic lifespan is determined by external factors such as technological advancements (e g modernised production methods, and changing fashions) and terminates, for example, when the asset's production capability becomes uneconomical because of such technological advancements.

Due to rapid technological development, the economic lifespan of an asset is often shorter than its technical lifespan. However, an asset whose economic lifespan has expired may be used for other purposes. The shorter of either the economic or the technical lifespan of an asset is regarded as its lifespan.

For our purposes, hereafter lifespan is referred to as a comprehensive concept, and no distinction will be made between technical and economic lifespan. Therefore the useful lifespan of a depreciable asset should be estimated taking the following factors into account:

- ☐ expected physical wear and tear
- ☐ obsolescence
- ☐ legal, contractual or other restrictions on the use of the asset, such as applicable lease contracts.

The useful lifespan of important depreciable assets should be **reviewed** periodically. Depreciation rates for current and future periods should be adjusted if the revised expected useful lifespan differs materially from the previous estimation. If necessary the effect of such a change should be disclosed in the accounting period in which the change takes place.[2]

☐ **Estimated scrap value**: The scrap value is the **net realisable value**[3] that will be obtained for the asset at the end of its useful lifespan.

As explained in paragraph 16.6.1, the depreciable amount of an asset is its historical cost (or another value which has replaced historical cost) less the scrap value of the asset.

The scrap value of an asset is often indeterminable; in such a case it should be ignored in the determination of the depreciable amount. However, if the scrap value is material, it should be estimated either at the date of acquisition of the asset **or** at the date of any future revaluations of the asset.

Cost price is the only factor that can be determined with certainty. All other factors must be estimated by means of careful judgement and experience, so that the depreciation determined is realistic.

16.6.5 Methods of calculating depreciation

Various methods can be used to calculate the periodic depreciation, and each method may differ significantly from the others. All factors must be prudently evaluated before any specific method is selected. The most important factor is to obtain a proper match of the cost of the service capacity consumed with the income generated by the use of the asset.

To ensure the comparability of the results of the operations of the undertaking from one period to another, the method of depreciation used must be applied **consistently**, unless a change in circumstances justifies a change in method. If there is a change in method during any accounting period, the effect of this change, if material, should be disclosed and the reason for the change should be given.[4]

---

2 GAAP Statement AC 106 par .31.
3 The estimated gross scrap value less the expected selling price.
4 GAAP Statement AC 106 par .2.

The most generally used methods are the following:

(1) The fixed instalment method

According to this method (also known as the straight-line method), depreciation is regarded as a function of time. An equal portion of the amount subject to depreciation is allocated to each accounting period over the total lifespan of the asset. This method may be illustrated as follows:

Example 16.3

Assume that the cost price of a specific machine on 1/1/19.1 is R16 700 and that the lifespan of the asset is estimated to be four years. The estimated trade-in value at the end of the fourth year is R700. The annual depreciation is therefore:

$$\frac{16\,700 - 700}{4} = \text{R4 000 per annum}$$

From this data, the following asset and depreciation table may be drawn up for the four years:

ASSET AND DEPRECIATION SCHEDULE: FIXED INSTALMENT METHOD				
Date	Cost price	Annual depreciation	Accumulated depreciation	Net book value
Date of purchase	16 700	—	—	16 700
End of year 1	16 700	4 000	4 000	12 700
End of year 2	16 700	4 000	8 000	8 700
End of year 3	16 700	4 000	12 000	4 700
End of year 4	16 700	4 000	16 000	700
TOTAL DEPRECIATION:		R16 000		

As shown in the table above, when the fixed instalment method is used:

- ☐ the annual provision for depreciation remains the same
- ☐ the accumulated depreciation is increased annually by an equal amount
- ☐ the net book value is decreased annually by the same amount until the estimated trade-in value is reached at the end of the last year of the asset's lifespan.

(2) Diminishing amount methods

These methods are also known as **accelerated methods** of calculating depreciation and are based on the premise that the decrease in an asset's value is greater in the first years of use than in later years. These methods usually result in depreciation which decreases constantly from year to year and are therefore known as diminishing amount methods. Two of these methods are described:

☐ The fixed-percentage-on-reducing-balance method

When this method is used a **fixed percentage** of the **net book value** (i e cost less accumulated depreciation) is written off in each accounting period. The fixed percentage is selected so that the cost of the asset is virtually totally written off during its lifespan. The percentage chosen is often twice the percentage used in the fixed instalment method. Looking at example 16.3 it can be seen that a percentage (rate) of 25% was used automatically, since the estimated lifespan of the asset was four years. If the fixed instalment method is applied to the same data, a constant percentage of 50%

must be applied at the end of each year to the reducing balance at the beginning of the year. The asset and depreciation schedule will appear as follows:

Example 16.4

ASSET AND DEPRECIATION SCHEDULE: FIXED PERCENTAGE METHOD					
Date	Cost price	Calculation of depreciation	Annual depreciation	Accumulated depreciation	Net book value
Date of purchase	16 700	—	—	—	16 700
End of year 1	16 700	50% × 16 700	8 350	8 350	8 350
End of year 2	16 700	50% × 8 350	4 175	12 525	4 175
End of year 3	16 700	50% × 4 175	2 088	14 613	2 087
End of year 4	16 700	50% × 2 087	1 043	15 656	1 044
TOTAL DEPRECIATION: R15 656					

The net book value at the end of the fourth year is deemed to be the scrap value of the asset.

The journal and ledger entries for the four years will be as follows:

19.1 Dec 31	Depreciation: Machinery Accumulated depreciation: Machinery *Provision for depreciation for the year ended 31/12/19.1*	8 350	8 350
	Income account Depreciation: Machinery *Closing entry*	8 350	8 350
19.2 Dec 31	Depreciation: Machinery Accumulated depreciation: Machinery *Provision for depreciation for the year ended 31/12/19.2*	4 175	4 175
	Income account Depreciation: Machinery *Closing entry*	4 175	4 175
19.3 Dec 31	Depreciation: Machinery Accumulated depreciation: Machinery *Provision for depreciation for the year ended 31/12/19.3*	2 088	2 088
	Income account Depreciation: Machinery *Closing entry*	2 088	2 088
19.4 Dec 31	Depreciation: Machinery Accumulated depreciation: Machinery *Provision for depreciation for the year ended 31/12/19.4*	1 043	1 043
	Income account Depreciation: Machinery *Closing entry*	1 043	1 043

MACHINERY ACCOUNT

19.1					
Jan 1	Cost price	16 700			

ACCUMULATED DEPRECIATION: MACHINERY

19.1			19.1		
Dec 31	Balance	R8 350	Dec 31	Depreciation 19.1	R8 350
			19.2		
19.2			Jan 1	Balance	8 350
Dec 31	Balance	12 525	Dec 31	Depreciation 19.2	4 175
		R12 525			R12 525
			19.3		
19.3			Jan 1	Balance	12 525
Dec 31	Balance	14 613	Dec 31	Depreciation 19.3	2 088
		R14 613			R14 613
			19.4		
19.4			Jan 1	Balance	14 613
Dec 31	Balance	15 656	Dec 31	Depreciation 19.4	1 043
		R15 656			R15 656
			19.5		
			Jan 1	Balance	15 656

DEPRECIATION: MACHINERY

19.1			19.1		
Dec 31	Accumulated depreciation	R8 350	Dec 31	Income account	R8 350
19.2			19.2		
Dec 31	Accumulated depreciation	R4 175	Dec 31	Income account	R4 175
19.3			19.3		
Dec 31	Accumulated depreciation	R2 088	Dec 31	Income account	R2 088
19.4			19.4		
Dec 31	Accumulated depreciation	R1 043	Dec 31	Income account	R1 043

□ Sum-of-the-years-digits method

This method determines depreciation for any period by multiplying the cost (less scrap value) of an asset by a fraction. The denominator is the sum of the total number of periods constituting the estimated lifespan of the asset, while the numerator is the estimated remaining lifespan at the beginning of the period concerned.

Example 16.5

If the lifespan of an asset is estimated to be four years, the denominator of the fraction will be ten (i e 1+2+3+4). A different numerator will be used each year, for example 4/10 at the end of the first year. Using the same data as before, the asset and depreciation schedule may be presented as follows:

ASSET AND DEPRECIATION SCHEDULE: SUM-OF-THE-YEARS-DIGITS METHOD						
		Calculation of depreciation				
Date	Cost price	Year digit	Fraction	Annual depreciation	Accumulated depreciation	Net book value
Date of purchase	16 700	—	—	—	—	16 700
End of year 1	16 700	4	$4/10 \times$ R16 000	6 400	6 400	10 300
End of year 2	16 700	3	$3/10 \times$ R16 000	4 800	11 200	5 500
End of year 3	16 700	2	$2/10 \times$ R16 000	3 200	14 400	2 300
End of year 4	16 700	1	$1/10 \times$ R16 000	1 600	16 000	700
		10				
		TOTAL DEPRECIATION:		R16 000		

Where the calculation is more complex, the following formula may be used to find the year digit or denominator:

$$J = \frac{N(1+N)}{2}$$

Where: N = Estimated lifespan
J = Total of the series

If this formula is applied to the above data, the calculation is as follows:

$$J = N\frac{(1+N)}{2}$$
$$= 4\frac{(1+4)}{2}$$
$$= 4 \times 2{,}5$$
$$\therefore J = 10$$

(3) Production methods

☐ Production unit method

This method is based on the premise that depreciation should be linked to the use of the asset. Unlike the methods discussed above, time is not a determining factor. The illustration below uses the same data as the previous examples; however, the lifespan of the asset is expressed not in years, but in terms of the estimated number of **units** it will produce, say 40 000.

Example 16.6

$$\frac{\text{Cost price less scrap value}}{\text{Estimated number of units to be produced during lifespan}} = \text{Depreciation per unit}$$

$$= \frac{16\,700 - 700}{40\,000} = \text{R0,40 per unit}$$

ASSET AND DEPRECIATION SCHEDULE: PRODUCTION UNIT METHOD						
Date	Cost price	Units produced annually	Depreciation per unit	Annual depreciation	Accumulated depreciation	Net book value
Date of purchase	16 700	—	—	—	—	16 700
End of year 1	16 700	15 000	0,40	6 000	6 000	10 700
End of year 2	16 700	10 000	0,40	4 000	10 000	6 700
End of year 3	16 700	10 000	0,40	4 000	14 000	2 700
End of year 4	16 700	5 000	0,40	2 000	16 000	700
TOTAL DEPRECIATION:				R16 000		

The schedule shows that:

- ☐ the annual provision for depreciation is directly linked to the number of units produced during that year
- ☐ accumulated depreciation increases in direct proportion to the number of units produced during a specific year
- ☐ the net book value decreases correspondingly, in direct proportion to the number of units produced in a specific year.

☐ Variations of the production method

Variations of the production method include 'hours worked', 'distance covered', etc. The basic premise, however, remains the same: the asset is written off proportionally according to the hours it has worked or the distance it has covered, etc. Once again time is not a determining factor. The depreciation rate will be calculated and expressed in terms of 'cents per hour' or 'cents per kilometre'.

16.6.6 Revision of depreciation rates

The depreciation rate applied to an asset which has been in use for some time may have been either too high or too low, owing to, for example, an incorrect initial estimate of the lifespan or scrap value of the asset. If a correction based on new information involves a material change to the annual provision for depreciation, the rate must be revised. Generally the revision is done according to one of the following two methods:

- ☐ Adjustment to future financial periods only.
- ☐ Correction of past records, together with adjustments to future periods.

In the first method the **remaining net book value** is apportioned to **the remaining lifespan** of the asset. In the second method the **accumulated profit carried forward from previous periods**

is corrected by applying the rate which should have been used. This rate will also be applied to all future periods.

16.6.7 Depreciation on assets acquired during the course of a financial period

There are several methods which can be used to calculate depreciation on assets bought during the course of a financial period. The most commonly used method, however, bases the calculation on the number of months for which the asset has been in use during the period concerned. This can be illustrated by means of the following example.

Example 16.7

Assume that an enterprise whose financial year ends on 31 December purchases an asset for R5 500 on 1 October. The asset's scrap value is estimated at R500, and its lifespan at 10 years. The annual depreciation, to be written off in the next financial year, is R500. In the year of purchase, however, it is $500 \times 1/4$ (i e for the three months from 1 October to 31 December) = R125.

16.6.8 Treatment of natural resources (diminishing assets)

Natural resources such as ore deposits must be treated as fixed assets in the same way as other assets which are subject to depreciation. Accordingly, initially they are recorded at cost. The value of the resource decreases as the ore is mined. This decrease in the value of a natural resource is known as **depletion**, and such assets are generally described as diminishing assets. Relevant factors to be taken into consideration are:

- ☐ determining the amount of the periodic depletion
- ☐ apportioning the depleted part of the asset's cost against income
- ☐ transferring the undepleted portion of the asset to future periods.

The periodic depletion is generally calculated according to a **production basis** similar to the production unit method applied to depreciation:

$$\frac{\text{Total costs of diminishing asset}}{\text{Estimated tonnage to be mined}} = \text{Depletion rate per unit}$$

The actual units produced annually multiplied by the relevant rate represents the depletion for the period concerned.

Example 16.8

Assume that a mining concern pays R500 000 for the purchase of a property having an estimated ore deposit of 1 million kg.

$$\text{Depletion per unit} = \frac{\text{R500 000}}{\text{1 000 000}}\ \text{kg}$$
$$= \text{50 cents per kg}$$

If 20 000 kg is mined during a specific period, the depletion for that period is 20 000 × 50c = R10 000.

This is recorded as follows:

Depletion costs: Mine	10 000	
Accumulated depletion		10 000
Depletion costs written off		

Depletion costs form part of the costs of mining the ore; that is, they form part of the costs incurred in obtaining an asset (ore, which is trading inventory). While the ore remains unsold the depletion costs, together with other mining expenses such as wages, form part of the costs pertaining to a current asset (trading inventory) on hand.

Assume that 5 000 kg of the 20 000 kg of ore mined this year was still in stock at the end of the year:

MINING COSTS				COST OF SALES	
Depletion costs	10 000	Transfer to cost of sales ($\frac{3}{4}$ × 50 000)	37 500 →	37 500	
Other	40 000	Closing inventory ($\frac{1}{4}$ × 50 000)	12 500		
	R50 000		R50 000		

As in the case of depreciation a later adjustment in the rate may become necessary, for instance after revaluation of the available ore. The accounting procedure used is the same as that described for the adjustment of depreciation rates.

16.6.9 Treatment of 'intangible' fixed assets

Intangible fixed assets such as patents, copyrights, trade marks, goodwill and leasehold rights are non-physical assets that have value for an enterprise. Ownership of intangible assets is sometimes embodied in contracts, certificates or other documentary evidence, while in other cases such as goodwill there is no such definitive evidence of ownership.

Intangible assets, like other fixed assets, are also initially recorded at cost price. This includes registration, purchase or development expenses, as well as all other expenses related to the acquisition of the asset. The **value** of an intangible asset may far exceed its cost price, as in the case of a patent protecting the manufacture and sale of a highly profitable product. Certain intangible assets have a limited lifespan and therefore must be written off. The periodic allocation of the cost of an intangible asset over its lifespan is known as **amortisation**.

□ Patents and trade marks

Patents and trade marks represent exclusive rights registered with the Registrar of Patents and Trade marks. Patents grant the exclusive right of production, use or sale of a discovery or process for a specific period.

The cost of registering the patent and other related costs are capitalised as the cost price of that patent, and generally are amortised over the lifespan of the patent. The same procedure applies to trade marks and copyrights.

□ Leasehold property

The 'asset' part of a leased asset comprises the acquisition of the right to use the property or goods. If a lump sum is paid in advance, this must be written off over the period of the agreement.

However if the lease is paid periodically (monthly or annually), one of the following two methods may be applied:

- The periodic amount may be summarily written off as a lease expense.
- The present value of future payments may be capitalised as an asset with a corresponding liability. The asset is then depreciated normally, while the payments serve to settle the liability.

□ Goodwill

Goodwill is a general term embracing various intangible factors all closely related to an enterprise's reputation and its ability to realise above-average profits. Factors such as the possession of valuable patents and copyrights, high-quality and lucrative products, effective management, favourable location, and so forth all play a role in the existence of goodwill.

Goodwill is recorded only if it is bought. Therefore it often represents the difference between the amount paid for the purchase of an existing enterprise and the value of the net assets obtained. Generally goodwill is written off according to a suitable method.

□ Amortisation of intangible assets

The amortisation of intangible assets is very similar to the writing off of depreciation, but the way in which it is recorded is different. Instead of a there being a separate account for accumulated depreciation, the periodic amortisation is credited directly to the asset account.

Example 16.9

Assume that a patent is purchased for a total of R5 000. The remaining lifespan of the patent is 10 years.

The annual amortisation is:

Amortisation of patent Patent account *Annual amortisation of patent*	500	500

PATENT

At cost price	5 000	Amortisation of patent	500

AMORTISATION OF PATENT

Patent account	500		

The balance on the latter account is transferred to the income account, while the asset is shown as follows in the balance sheet:

Patent: At cost price less amounts amortised	4 500

The annual amortisation of intangible assets will also sometimes require adjustment. If, due to the development of a new and improved process, the patent in the example above has no further value six years after it was purchased, the balance of the cost of the patent is written off as a loss resulting from obsolesence.

16.6.10 Treatment of investments

Investments are not usually subject to depreciation arising from use or depletion. In contrast, investments frequently increase in value.

Economic and political conditions may also cause the value of investments to fluctuate, but depreciation on investments is not written off unless it is obvious that the value of that investment has decreased permanently and is unlikely to recover.

16.6.11 The treatment of land and buildings [5]

Depreciation is not normally provided for on **real estate**, unless it is subject to depletion (refer to para 16.6.8).

However, if the value of the **freehold land** has been affected by adverse circumstances it may be necessary to write down the recorded amount to recognise the decrease in value.

Buildings have a limited lifespan that may be materially affected by technological and area changes, which will necessitate reducing their value.

16.6.12 Investment properties [6]

These properties are classified as such by the management of an undertaking on the basis of their intention and the particular circumstances. Investment properties are held mainly by undertakings whose activities consist mainly of investments such as insurance companies and property investment companies. Nevertheless, any other undertaking can hold investment property even though the holding of investments is not its main activity.

---

5 AC 106 par .17.
6 AC 106 par .20.

Property can normally be classified as being of either a **specialised** or a **non-specialised** nature. **Specialised property** is the type of property that is seldom, if ever sold, unless, because of the specialised nature of the buildings, their construction, arrangement, size, location, etc, they are sold as part of the undertaking which owns the building. **Non-specialised property** is the type of property for which there is a general demand, which does not require alteration to be suitable for a variety of undertakings and activities, and which can usually be bought and sold on the open market for immediate occupation or rental.

A specialised property will not normally be classified as an investment property. However, property such as a hotel or cinema, which can be bought, sold or leased on the open market and which can be valued according to its commercial potential, can be classified as a non-specialised property and consequently be treated as an investment property.

The management of an undertaking is responsible for deciding which properties should be classified as investment properties, on the basis of their intention and the particular circumstances. This classification is not changed unless there is a change of intention in the particular circumstances.

It is acknowledged that there are two acceptable, but different, approaches to the accounting treatment of investment property. According to one method buildings are considered to be depreciable assets, whereas according to the other, the property is considered to be an investment and the most recent **open market value** is disclosed in the financial statements and provision is made for any permanent decline in value. **Open market value** is the price at which the investment property can reasonably be expected to be sold, provided that it is an 'arm's length' transaction between a willing, able and informed buyer and a willing, able and informed seller.

The open market value can be determined by an independent or an internal valuation by persons who, in management's opinion are considered to be capable. Where all or some of the shareholders or owners are not involved in the management of the undertaking, it may be advisable for internal valuations to be supported by an occasional independent valuation. In the intervening years the valuations will have to be reviewed by management, first, to ensure that no factors have arisen which will make the disclosure misleading, and second, to determine whether there has been any permanent decline in value.

16.7 SCRAPPING OR ALIENATION OF ASSETS

If an enterprise wishes to dispose of an asset it may scrap the asset, sell it outright, or trade it in as partial payment on the purchase of a new asset.

Whichever way the asset is disposed of, the relevant entries must be recorded properly. Proper recording includes:

- ☐ Recording the sale of the asset.
- ☐ Removing the cost of the asset and the accumulated depreciation (i e the net book value) from the books.
- ☐ Recording any profit or loss on scrapping or alienation of the asset.

16.7.1 Scrapping an asset without sale

In the case of an asset which is no longer economically serviceable and which can be neither sold nor traded in, but must simply be dismantled or disposed of as scrap, the recording procedure depends on whether the asset was, at that time, entirely written off. If it was entirely written off no loss will be incurred when the asset is scrapped, if it was not written off a loss may possibly arise.

☐ **If an asset has been written off entirely**

Example 16.10

An asset purchased a considerable time ago for R6 000, and which has been entirely written off, is dismantled and disposed of as scrap. The scrapping is recorded via the following journal entry:

Accumulated depreciation Asset account *Scrapped asset written off*	6 000	 6 000

ASSET ACCOUNT

Cost price	R6 000	Transfer: Accumulated depreciation on scrapping of asset	R6 000

ACCUMULATED DEPRECIATION

Asset account: Balance transferred on scrapping of asset	R6 000	Total depreciation provided	R6 000

Thus the cost and accumulated depreciation pertaining to the asset are removed from the books entirely.

☐ **If an asset has not been written off entirely**

Example 16.11

The same particulars as in example 16.10 are applicable, except that only R5 000 has been provided for depreciation to date. The scrapping of the asset therefore causes a loss of R1 000, the position being as follows:

Original cost price of asset	6 000
Total depreciation allowance	5 000
Book value written off as loss	R1 000

The journal entry on scrapping the asset is:

Accumulated depreciation Loss on scrapping of asset Asset account *Scrapped asset written off*	5 000 1 000	 6 000

The ledger accounts will appear as follows:

ASSET ACCOUNT

Cost price	R6 000	Accumulated depreciation	R5 000
		Loss on scrapping	1 000

ACCUMULATED DEPRECIATION

Asset account: Balance transferred on scrapping of asset	R5 000	Total depreciation provided to date	R5 000

LOSS ON SCRAPPING OF ASSET

Asset account	R1 000	Transfer to income account	R1 000

16.7.2 Sale of an asset

The procedure for recording the sale of an asset subject to depreciation is similar to that described above, except that the receipt of cash or another asset at the time of sale must be recorded. The asset can be sold at a profit or a loss, or without making either. If an asset is sold for **more than its net book value** this represents a profit, if it is sold for **less than its net book value** a loss occurs.

☐ **Sale of an asset for more than its net book value**

Example 16.12

A motor vehicle purchased by an enterprise several years ago for R6 000 is sold on 31 December 19.6 for a cash price of R1 200. On that date the accumulated depreciation amounted to R5 000.

The profit or loss on the sale of an asset is the difference between the net book value of the asset and its selling price:

Cost of asset	6 000
Accumulated depreciation on date of sale	5 000
∴ Net book value	1 000
Selling price	1 200
∴ Profit on sale of asset	R200

The entries in respect of the sale of the asset (including the cash transaction) are journalised as follows:

Cash Motor vehicle realisation account *Receipt of selling price*	1 200	 1 200
Motor vehicle realisation account Motor vehicle account *Transfer of original cost price of vehicle sold to realisation account*	6 000	 6 000
Accumulated depreciation: Motor vehicles Motor vehicle realisation account *Transfer of accumulated depreciation on vehicle sold to realisation account*	5 000	 5 000
Motor vehicle realisation account Profit on sale of fixed asset *Transfer of profit on vehicle sold*	200	 200*

*This amount will ultimately be transferred to the income account.

After the above journal entries have been posted, the relevant ledger accounts appear as follows:

MOTOR VEHICLE ACCOUNT

Cost price	R6 000	Transfer: Motor vehicle realisation account	R6 000

ACCUMULATED DEPRECIATION: MOTOR VEHICLES

Transfer: Motor vehicle realisation account	R5 000	Balance	R5 000

MOTOR VEHICLE REALISATION ACCOUNT

Motor vehicle account:		Cash: Selling price	1 200
Transfer of cost	6 000	Accumulated depreciation	
Profit on sale of assets	200	transferred	5 000
	R6 200		R6 200

☐ Sale of an asset for less than its net book value

Example 16.13

An enterprise owns 10 delivery vehicles, all bought on 1 March 19.2 for R8 000 each. The annual depreciation provided is 20% on the original cost price. On 28 February 19.5, one of these vehicles is sold for R2 500.

The following journal entries are made:

Cash Motor vehicle realisation account *Receipt of selling price*	2 500	2 500
Motor vehicle realisation account Delivery vehicles account *Transfer of cost price of delivery vehicle sold on 28/2/19.5*	8 000	8 000
Accumulated depreciation: Delivery vehicles Motor vehicle realisation account *Transfer of accumulated depreciation to 28/2/19.5 on vehicle sold (see calculation no 2)*	4 800	4 800
Loss on sale of fixed asset Motor vehicle realisation account *Transfer of loss on vehicle sold (see calculation no 3)*	700	700

Calculations

1 Total accumulated depreciation on 10 delivery vehicles on 28/2/19.5 is calculated as follows:
20% per year for three years on R80 000 (cost price) = R48 000

2 Accumulated depreciation on one vehicle ($^1/_{10}$ × R48 000) = R4 800

3 Loss on sale

Cost price of vehicle	8 000
Accumulated depreciation to date of sale	4 800
∴ Net book value	3 200
Selling price	2 500
∴ Loss on sale	R700

The relevant ledger accounts will appear as follows:

DELIVERY VEHICLES

Cost price: 10 vehicles @ R8 000 each	80 000	Transfer: Motor vehicle realisation account (1 × R8 000)	8 000
		Balance (9 × R8 000)	72 000
	R80 000		R80 000
Balance	72 000		

ACCUMULATED DEPRECIATION: DELIVERY VEHICLES

Transfer: Motor vehicle realisation account (1 × R4 800)	4 800	Balance (per asset account no 1)	48 000
Balance (9 × R4 800)	43 200		
	R48 000		R48 000
		Balance	43 200

MOTOR VEHICLE REALISATION ACCOUNT

Motor vehicle account: Transfer of cost price	8 000	Selling price	2 500
		Accumulated depreciation	4 800
		Loss on sale of asset	700
	R8 000		R8 000

16.7.3 Trading in of assets

It is common practice to trade in an old asset when acquiring a new one (usually of the same type). The trade-in value allowed by the seller is deducted from the selling price of the new asset and the purchaser pays, or undertakes to pay, the balance owing. As with the sale of an asset, trading in an old asset can give rise to either a profit or a loss, depending on whether the trade-in value is higher or lower than the net book value.

Example 16.14

☐ **Trading in an asset for more than its net book value**

A new machine, X, is purchased for R10 000. An old machine, the cost of which was R6 000 and on which depreciation of R5 000 had been provided, is traded in. R1 400 is received as a trade-in, the balance of the purchase price being paid in cash.

These transactions are recorded via the following journal entries:*

Machinery	10 000	
Seller		10 000
New asset purchased		
Seller	10 000	
Machinery		1 400
Cash		8 600
Settlement of purchase price by trading in machine Y and cash payment		
Accumulated depreciation	5 000	
Machinery		5 000
Transfer of accumulated depreciation on machine Y on trade-in		
Machinery	400	
Income account		400
Recording of profit on trading in machine Y		

*It is possible to replace these journal entries, as before, with one comprehensive journal entry. Note, too, that the method used here is an alternative generally used in practice; the realisation account is omitted and all entries pertaining to the trade-in are made to the asset account. The use of a realisation account is always recommended in such cases.

The asset account of machine Y and the accumulated depreciation account will thus appear as follows:

MACHINE Y

Cost price	6 000	Accumulated depreciation	5 000
Profit on trade-in	400	Seller: Trade-in value received	1 400
	R6 400		R6 400

ACCUMULATED DEPRECIATION

Transfer: Machine Y	R5 000	Balance: Total provision to date	R5 000

When an asset is traded in for less than its net book value, basically the same entries are made. The only difference is that a loss, and not a profit, occurs.

16.8 DEPRECIATION: MANAGERIAL AND OTHER CONSIDERATIONS RELATING TO DEPRECIATION

16.8.1 Choice of depreciation method

The decision as to which method of depreciation an enterprise should adopt is important, since the provision for depreciation exercises a significant influence on the determination of realistic profit figures.

The **fixed instalment method** is simple to apply and is satisfactory when the assets are used consistently. However, the following objections are raised against this method:

- A fixed amount is debited against income as depreciation, regardless of fluctuations in the volume of production.
- As the asset ages repair costs generally increase, and the amount debited against income for repairs plus depreciation becomes steadily larger.

The production methods, which provide for depreciation in direct proportion to production, are preferable in cases where the decrease in the value of the asset is principally due to usage.

The **diminishing amount methods** are based on the assumption that an asset provides greater service during the first few years of its lifespan, and that the depreciation provided according to this method results in a more equitable matching of income and expenditure. An additional reason for using this method is to counteract the second disadvantage of the fixed instalment method listed above, namely that of rising repair costs in later years. Rising maintenance costs are partially counteracted because the annual depreciation is calculated on a decreasing balance, thereby resulting in a more proportional debit in respect of expenses.

An enterprise should select the method that suits its own particular circumstances best.

16.8.2 Depreciation and replacement of assets

Provision for depreciation reserves funds for the replacement of assets, although these funds may not be used for such replacement. The funds are reserved by virtue of the fact that the writing off of depreciation results in profit, being the difference between the total cash inflow and the depreciation written off.

Consequently, that portion of the total cash inflow which is equal to the depreciation is not regarded as profit, but is retained within the enterprise. Theoretically these funds are retained for the replacement of assets. The total funds reserved in this way over the lifespan of the asset will, in effect, equal the original cost price of that asset. In practice, however, the funds retained as a result of depreciation written off are not necessarily applied specifically for replacing specific assets.

Rather, these funds form part of a general pool, available to the enterprise for investment as and when required.

16.8.3 Depreciation and changes in price levels

When prices are stable no problems are encountered in recording fixed assets on a cost basis and calculating depreciation in terms of this cost. In the aforegoing discussion of the role played by depreciation in determining net income, the existence of stable prices was implicitly assumed.

However, the dramatic increase in price levels during the past few years has given rise to the opinion that net income would be determined more realistically if depreciation was based on the estimated **replacement cost** rather than on the original cost. An alternative suggestion is to adjust the annual provision for depreciation in accordance with a **price index** which measures changes in the purchasing power of money. This would mean that depreciation, like other operating expenses such as wages, would be expressed in terms of the current value of the rand.

Providing for depreciation on the basis of increased replacement costs sometimes also necessitates the **revaluation** of the asset in the balance sheet. This is done to present more realistic figures (consider, for example, land purchased many years previously), and to relate depreciation to the values on which they are calculated. Assets shown at historical cost are frequently undervalued in relation to current prices. Revaluations are especially important in take-overs of enterprises, since low valuations may result in too low a take-over price.

The revaluation of fixed assets is a complex procedure in which values must be based on the current replacement cost of the asset's remaining useful lifespan.

16.8.4 Depreciation and income tax

In recent years the State has granted notable special tax allowances in respect of investment in production facilities. Thus, when calculating taxable income, entrepreneurs have the opportunity of writing off a large portion of their expenditure on production facilities during the first year of an asset's use as wear and tear. This serves as an incentive for investments of this nature.

From an accounting point of view, however, the principles outlined in this chapter regarding the determination of profit must still be applied, regardless of how taxable income is determined. As stated, the enterprise must choose a fair and reasonable depreciation method which is suited to its own particular circumstances, and should not adapt the method to accommodate specific tax considerations.

16.9 INTERNAL CONTROL OVER FIXED ASSETS

The basic components of an effective system of control over current assets have already been mentioned and, by and large, can be applied to fixed assets. The most important features are outlined below:

- Proper control must be exercised over the acquisition and sale of fixed assets wherever necessary. Control over fixed assets begins when the acquisition of a particular asset is considered. First, a proper **system of authorisation** must exist and management must give written approval for the proposed investment in a specific asset. Also, a specific amount must be budgeted for each asset.

  Since the decision to purchase a new asset or to replace an existing one will have a long-term effect on the adaptability and earning capacity of an enterprise, careful consideration must be given to the income which investment in the asset may produce, as well as to the related costs. These decisions are usually known as **capital budgeting decisions**. Capital budgeting includes, *inter alia*, a consideration of the project's return on capital. If the investment can provide a satisfactory net income, the project will probably be approved.

Management's written approval must also be obtained for the sale of any asset.

- Person(s) who **order** an asset must have full authority. All orders must be carefully controlled and all goods received should be carefully checked against the relevant orders. Similarly, the sale of any asset must be handled by a properly authorised official, who should carry out the decision to dispose of the asset according to instructions.
- The relevant **legal documents**, for example deeds, investment certificates, sales contracts and other proof of ownership, must be kept safe.
- All assets must be properly accounted for by means of control accounts, supported by appropriate **asset registers**.* In other words, the general ledger will have a control account for each type of asset, while particulars of each asset are shown in the asset register. For example, separate control accounts will be kept in the ledger for machinery and equipment, furniture, motor vehicles, etc, together with separate accounts showing the accumulated depreciation on each of these accounts. An asset register will also be kept for each type of asset.

  The asset register should contain particulars about the purchase price, maintenance, repairs and depreciation, as well as a complete description of the asset.

Example 16.15

Assume that an enterprise has only two machines, namely a machine of type X and a machine of type Y. The following particulars apply to the machines:

Date		Type X	Type Y
19.3 Mar 1	Purchased	4 000	—
19.4 Mar 1	Purchased	—	6 000
19.4 Feb 28	Provision for depreciation	400	—
19.5 Feb 28	Provision for depreciation	400	600
19.6 Feb 28	Provision for depreciation	400	600

*In the case of investments, the register is referred to as an investment register.

The relevant ledger accounts will be as follows on 1 March 19.6:

MACHINERY — 50

Date		Details	Amount	Date		Details	Amount
19.3				19.6			
Mar	1	Bank	4 000	Feb	28	Balance	10 000
19.4							
Mar	1	Bank	6 000				
			R10 000				R10 000
19.6							
Mar	1	Balance	10 000				

ACCUMULATED DEPRECIATION: MACHINERY

Date		Details	Amount	Date		Details	Amount
19.6				19.4			
Feb	28	Balance	2 400	Feb	28	Depreciation	400
				19.5			
				Feb	28	Depreciation	1 000
				19.6			
				Feb	28	Depreciation	1 000
			R2 400				R2 400
				19.6			
				Mar	1	Balance	2 400

The asset register must contain the following information:

ASSET REGISTER AND DEPRECIATION REPORT

Folio 1

Item: Machine type X
Identification number: X70943
Estimated lifespan: 10 years
Annual depreciation: R400

General ledger account: Machinery – account no 50
Purchased from: X Manufacturers Ltd
Estimated scrap value: R50

Date	Details	Folio	Asset record			Depreciation record		
			Dr	Cr	Balance	Dr	Cr	Balance
19.3 Mar 1	Purchase, paid per cheque no 709	C30	4 000		4 000			
19.4 Feb 28	Provision for depreciation: 19.3/4	J10					400	400
19.5 Feb 28	Provision for depreciation: 19.4/5	J20					400	800
19.6 Feb 28	Provision for depreciation: 19.5/6	J28					400	1 200

Final writing off/sale of asset:

ASSET REGISTER AND DEPRECIATION REPORT								
Item: Machine type Y Identification number: Y8024 Estimated lifespan: 10 years Annual depreciation: R600			General ledger account: Machinery – account no 50 Purchased from: R Engineering Ltd Estimated scrap value: R50					Folio 2
Date	Details	Folio	Asset record			Depreciation record		
			Dr	Cr	Balance	Dr	Cr	Balance
19.4 Mar 1	Purchase, paid per cheque no 940	C45	6 000		6 000			
19.5 Feb 28	Provision for depreciation: 19.4/5	J20					600	600
19.6 Feb 28	Provision for depreciation: 19.5/6	J28					600	1 200
Final writing off/sale of asset:								

- ☐ Assets must be comprehensively **insured** and the insurance policy should be reviewed regularly.
- ☐ A continual inventory count must be carried out on fixed assets. The physical count must be compared with and checked against the records.
- ☐ Where possible, fixed assets should have an **identification mark**, such as an asset number, and must be properly supervised, stored and maintained.

16.10 DISCLOSURE OF FIXED ASSETS AND INVESTMENTS IN THE FINANCIAL STATEMENTS

16.10.1 Fixed assets

All fixed assets, appropriately described, are grouped in the balance sheet under the heading **fixed assets**.

☐ **Land and buildings**

Land is generally grouped with buildings, without showing separate values. Often it is simply described as fixed property. In the case of companies, however, it is compulsory to disclose additional information such as the location and description of the fixed property.

☐ **Plant, machinery, equipment, loose tools, fittings**

These fixed assets are normally shown under condensed headings which give an adequate description, for example: plant and machinery; or plant, machinery and equipment; or plant, machinery and vehicles.

☐ **Goodwill, patents and trade marks**

These assets must be described according to their nature.

☐ Depreciation and write-offs

The **basis of depreciation** used to determine the amounts written off depreciable assets should be included in the disclosure of accounting policy.

The expression **accumulated depreciation** should be used to describe the total amount provided for depreciation, unless other terms such as **redemption** describe the nature of the provision more precisely.

The total cost as well as the total accumulated depreciation of all tangible assets must be shown either in the balance sheet or in an addendum thereto.

In the case of intangible fixed assets, the **valuation method** used must be clearly indicated, for example at cost, or at cost less amounts written off. If fixed assets are revalued they must be described accordingly, and all applicable information should be disclosed, for instance at sworn valuation (June 19.6), etc. In addition to the assets which are the property of the enterprise it has become customary to disclose details of leased assets as well as the total obligations in respect of future lease payments.

Details of any **encumbrance** of the enterprise's assets in guarantee of the obligations of a third party or those of the enterprise itself, must be disclosed.

Where feasible, the total or estimated amount of any material **contracts for capital expenditure** which have not otherwise been provided for, must be disclosed. Similarly, if material, the total capital expenditure authorised by the enterprise's management but not yet contracted for must be disclosed and, where possible, the source of funds from which this expenditure will be made should be given.

Example 16.16

Fixed assets	Cost price/ valuation	Accumulated depreciation	Net
Land and buildings on erf 586, Randburg, valued at R40 000 by P Nel, sworn valuator, on 1 June 19.4 at market value (1)	40 000	—	40 000
Plant, machinery and equipment	20 000	8 000	12 000
	R60 000	R 8000	R52 000
Goodwill, patents and trade marks at cost less amounts written off			5 000
			R57 000

Notes

1 The land and buildings are encumbered by a first bond as surety for a loan (shown under long-term obligations).
2 Total contracts for capital expenditure in respect of erection of buildings not provided for in financial statements amount to R20 000.
3 The management has authorised the purchase of additional machinery costing an estimated R10 000; these contracts have not yet been concluded.
4 These capital commitments will be financed from the enterprise's own funds.

16.10.2 Investments

Investments may be shown as fixed assets, current assets or assets which are neither fixed nor current, depending on their nature.*

It is customary to show long and medium-term investments under a separate heading, **investments**. The basis of valuation must also be stated, for example at cost, at cost less amounts written off, or at the lower of cost and net realisable value.

In the case of shares, the financial statements should disclose whether or not the shares are quoted on a recognised stock exchange. Short-term investments or investments which are traded (e g in the case of an investment company or a stockbroker) are classified as current assets.

More permanent investments are shown in the balance sheet as follows:

Example 16.17

Investments		
Listed at cost (market value: R5 500)	6 000	
Unlisted at cost (directors' valuation: R16 000)	12 000	
Fixed deposit	30 000	48 000

16.11 EVALUATING THE EFFECTIVENESS OF THE UTILISATION OF FIXED ASSETS

The investment of funds in fixed assets is governed by the nature of the enterprise and therefore will vary considerably from one enterprise to another. A manufacturing enterprise will have a far greater investment in plant and machinery, for example, than a trading concern. However, the ratio of the investment in fixed assets and total assets, as well as sales, must be in line with the general ratios for that particular type of business.

Over-investment in fixed assets must be guarded against, since funds are unproductively committed over a long period, thereby prejudicing the profitability of the enterprise in the long term. Fixed assets also produce fixed costs such as depreciation, maintenance, insurance and interest; therefore over-investment also renders the enterprise liable to long-term fixed costs, which are in fact wasted costs.

For this reason the utilisation of fixed assets must be monitored constantly. The **turnover rate of fixed assets**, which measures the relationship between investment in fixed assets and turnover, is often used as a criterion for judging the utilisation of fixed assets. The following abbreviated financial statement is used to illustrate the calculation and interpretation of this ratio.

*See schedule A for the separate disclosure of investments in subsidiary companies, holding companies and fellow subsidiaries.

Example 16.18

X MANUFACTURERS BALANCE SHEETS AT 31 DECEMBER	19.3	19.4
Assets		
Fixed assets (net)	8 500	21 000
Current assets	24 000	30 000
	R32 500	R51 000
Owner's equity and liabilities		
Owner's equity	15 500	20 000
Long-term liabilities	5 000	14 000
Current liabilities	12 000	17 000
	R32 500	R51 000
Net sales	R25 500	R42 000

The ratio is calculated by dividing the net sales by the book value of fixed assets:

	19.3	19.4
$\frac{\text{Net sales}}{\text{Fixed assets}}$	$\frac{25\ 500}{8\ 500} = 3{,}00$ or 300%	$\frac{42\ 000}{21\ 000} = 2{,}00$ or 200%

In 19.3 sales constituted 300% of the book value of fixed assets. In other words, each R1 invested in fixed assets produced R3 in sales. In 19.4 the ratio dropped to 2:1. This might indicate a possible over-investment in fixed assets. Although sales increased considerably from 19.3 to 19.4 (65%), the investment in fixed assets increased by 147%.

17

CURRENT LIABILITIES AND LONG-TERM LIABILITIES

The **AIM** of this chapter is to provide a more detailed discussion of aspects relating to current and long-term liabilities.

17.1 THE NATURE OF LIABILITIES

Liabilities arise from past transactions of the undertaking and are legal obligations which must be settled in the future by the sacrificing of economic benefit.

In most cases the amount payable and the date on which the obligation must be settled are fixed or can be forecast with reasonable certainty.

The problems regarding the recognition, valuation and classification of assets are also applicable to liabilities.

☐ Recognition of liabilities

The time factor is important in the recognition of liabilities. Often if a liability has been omitted from a particular financial period, the relevant expense for that period is also not recorded. Thus the operating result for the period is calculated incorrectly.

Liabilities should be recorded when obligations arise, but this rule may be difficult to implement. If a transaction which will result in the undertaking making future payments is entered into, for example when goods are bought on credit, then a liability arises and is recognised as such. However, some obligations are not the result of direct transactions. One of the most important reasons for adjustments at the end of an accounting period is to recognise obligations which have not yet been recorded (such as wages and interest accrued). The general criterion is that the obligation must arise from a **past** transaction.

An undertaking can also enter into an agreement in respect of **future** transactions, for example a company may agree to pay one of its officials a certain salary for the ensuing year. This agreement may entail a certain commitment, but it is not an obligation; it concerns a future transaction and at this point is merely a **contingent liability**.

☐ Valuation of liabilities

Liabilities are usually valued at their monetary value or at a reasonable market value of the goods or services that must be delivered to settle the liability. Generally the amount is determined and known, but in some cases it may have to be estimated, for example a dealer who offers a service warranty with the vehicles he sells. The obligation is definite, but the amount has to be estimated.

□ Classification of liabilities

The correct classification of liabilities is just as important as that of assets. It is essential for the proper disclosure of liabilities in the financial statements, and it also has an important impact on the analysis and interpretation of the financial result and position of the undertaking.

Liabilities are classified into two main groups:

- **Current liabilities**: These are liabilities which must be settled within the next 12 months or within the normal business cycle of the undertaking.
- **Long-term liabilities**: These are liabilities which need not be settled within the normal business cycle of the undertaking.

17.2 CURRENT LIABILITIES

This section discusses the most common current liabilities.

17.2.1 Trade creditors

The purchase of goods and services on credit, the consequent obligations to be met at a later date and the settlement of the debt have already been discussed in a previous chapter. The recording of credit purchase transactions in the purchases journal, the creditors ledger and the creditors control account have also been discussed.

□ Discount received

As in the case of debtors, where credit is granted for prompt settlement of debts **discounts** may also be granted when payment is made to creditors within a specific period.

Example 17.1 illustrates the accounting procedures pertaining to discount received.

Example 17.1

CASH PAYMENTS JOURNAL
May 19.7 — Page 8

Date	Details	Folio	Sundries	Purchases	Creditors	Discount received	Bank
19.7							
May 3	SAR & H: Freight on purchases	511	30				30
5	Rent for May	512	300				300
7	Goods purchased for cash			400			400
18	Abel & Co	A3			400	10	390
14	Goods purchased for cash			280			280
25	R Outfitters	R6			50	2	48
31	Salaries	513	700				700
			R1 030	R680	R450	R(12)	R2 148
				(501)	(301)	(406)	(110)

Amounts are posted individually from the sundries column to the general ledger

Payments to creditors are posted individually to creditors' accounts in the creditors ledger during the month

Totals are posted to the general ledger at the end of the month

CREDITORS LEDGER

Date	Details	Folio	Dr	Cr	Bal
ABEL & CO					**A3**
19.7					
May 8	Invoice 320	PJ1		400	400
22	Invoice 510	PJ1		750	1 150
18	Bank and discount	CP8	400		750
R OUTFITTERS					**R6**
19.7					
May 14	Invoice X537	PJ1		50	50
28	Invoice X802	PJ1		60	110
25	Bank & discount	CP8	50		60
S EVERT & CO					**E9**
19.7					
May 20	Invoice 9807	PJ1		300	300
JOHNS BROTHERS					**J7**
19.7					
May 26	Invoice JB803	PJ1		80	80

GENERAL LEDGER

Date	Details	Folio	Dr	Cr	Bal
BANK					**110**
19.7					
May 31	Total payments	CP8		2 148	(2 148)
CREDITORS CONTROL					**301**
19.7					
May 31	Purchases	PJ1		1 640	(1 640)
	Bank and discount	CP8	450		(1 190)
DISCOUNT RECEIVED					**406**
19.7					
May 31	Creditors	CP8		12	(12)
PURCHASES					**501**
19.7					
May 31	Bank	CP8	680		680
FREIGHT ON PURCHASES					**511**
19.7					
May 31	Bank	CP8	30		30
RENTAL					**512**
19.7					
May 5	Bank	CP8	300		300
SALARIES					**513**
19.7					
May 31	Bank	CP8	700		700

The credit balance on the creditors control account (R1 640 – R450) = R1 190 agrees with the total of the creditors' balances:

Abel & Co	750
R Outfitters	60
S Evert & Co	300
Johns Brothers	80
	R1 190

The cash payments journal cross-balances as follows:

Sundries Dr		Purchases Dr		Creditors Dr	=	Discount received Cr	Bank Cr
1 030	+	680	+	450		12	2 148
		R2 160				R2 160	

☐ Valuation and presentation of trade creditors in the financial statements

Trade creditors represent a short-term obligation of the enterprise and must be shown at the amount payable under the heading **current liabilities** as **trade creditors**.

Any material creditors which are not trade creditors must be disclosed separately.

☐ Analysis and interpretation of trade creditors

If the credit purchases or the cost of sales are known, the following formula can be used to determine **the length of time taken by the enterprise to pay its creditors**. = Settlement period

$$\frac{\text{Average creditors}}{\frac{\text{Cost of sales}}{365}} \quad \text{or} \quad \frac{\text{Average creditors} \times 365}{\text{Cost of sales}}$$

(Assume that cost of sales ÷ 365 = average purchases per day.)

Knowledge of the settlement period gives an indication of the creditworthiness and liquidity of the enterprise.

17.2.2 Bills payable

Similar to credit sales and bills receivable, credit purchases can be made by means of bills payable, or an amount owing on a creditor's open account can be converted to a bill. This corresponds to the function of bills receivable on credit sales. Bills payable, like bills receivable, can be either interest-bearing or interest-free, and this will influence the recording of the bill.

Example 17.2

Assume that goods to the value of R1 000 are bought from Carson Limited, who has drawn a 90 d/d bill at 8% interest on the enterprise concerned. After formal acceptance of the bill the following entry is made in the enterprise's journal:

Creditors control account Interest payable Bills payable *Acceptance of bill no 709 by Carson Limited, drawn at 90 d/d plus interest at 8%, in settlement of amount owing*	1 000 20	 1 020

On payment of the bill, the following entry will be made:

Bills payable account Bank *Honouring of bill no 709*	1 020	 1 020

Where justified by the volume of transactions, a special bills payable book similar to the bills receivable book may be kept.

If a bill payable is renewed on or before the due date, or is dishonoured on the due date, the original recording of the bill must be reversed, any noting charges recorded, and the credit balance on the creditor's account reinstated (as in the case of bills receivable).

Example 17.3

Assume that the previous bill is dishonoured on the due date and that Carson Limited debits the enterprise with R3 noting charges:

Bills payable Noting charges Creditors control *Cancellation of bill payable in favour of Carson Limited on the due date and recording of noting charges payable*	1 020 3	 1 023

The amount payable in the form of bills payable is shown in the financial statements as a current liability. It can also be shown together with trade creditors as **trade creditors and bills payable**.

17.2.3 Sales tax payable

The levying of general sales tax (GST) has already been discussed in a previous chapter. An undertaking which sells goods and which is subject to GST must collect the tax and pay it over to the Receiver of Revenue periodically.

Due to the continuous nature of an undertaking's activities, a current liability in respect of sales tax still to be paid over will exist at the end of every financial period.

17.2.4 Current portion of long-term liabilities

If any portion of a long-term liability must be settled out of current assets within the next 12 months, it is classified as a current liability. Assume, for example, that an undertaking has a loan of R300 000 which must be paid annually in three equal instalments. The first payment of R100 000 will be classified as a current liability and the balance as a long-term liability.

17.2.5 Arrear or accrued liabilities

These obligations arise from transactions which have already been concluded and are usually due for payment in the near future; therefore they are classified as current liabilities.

17.2.6 Provisions (estimated obligations)

Provisions are actual obligations of an undertaking, the exact amount of which will be known only at some later date. The only accounting problem is to estimate and record the amount of the obligation.

A good example of such an estimated obligation is that of a trader who guarantees his product for a specified period. An obligation therefore exists for the duration of the guarantee. The amount, however, is uncertain and must be estimated on the basis of past experience. At the conclusion of the sale the amount is debited to an expense account (e g product warranty costs). The corresponding credit will be taken to a 'provision for product warranty' account. Most guarantees are for a period of 12 months or less, and therefore the provision is a current liability.

There is no specific order in which current liabilities should be shown in the balance sheet.

There are two alternative methods, viz in order of due date, the first item being the liability payable first, or in order of size, the first item being the largest. The first method tends to cause problems because the date of payment is frequently decided by the enterprise itself; furthermore, trade creditors consist of different amounts owing to different creditors, each payable at a different time. The second method seems rather pointless, since the largest debt in one year could be the smallest debt in the following year.

According to South African practice, short-term liabilities are shown as follows:

Current liabilities		
Trade creditors and bills payable	xx	
Bank overdraft	xx	
Tax payable	xx	
Dividends and interest payable	xx	
Sundry expenses accrued	xx	xxx

17.3 LONG-TERM LIABILITIES

Long-term liabilities differ from short-term liabilities in that they exist in the enterprise for a period longer than a year, they are payable over a period longer than a year, and usually the enterprise must provide **security** for this type of obligation.

Different types of long-term liabilities are found in practice, the most important being long-term loans, mortgage bonds, debentures, hire-purchase creditors and lease obligations.

The financial statements of an undertaking usually show long-term liabilities at the amount which must be repaid, together with details of their general nature. The liabilities are classified under appropriate headings and sub-headings, with an indication as to whether any of the company's obligations are secured by a specific asset(s). Both the liability and the encumbered asset must be described. Where there are numerous long-term liabilities, they are listed in order of increasing liquidity, that is the liability payable last is listed first and the liability payable first is shown last.

17.3.1 Loans and mortgages

Loans made to an enterprise are regarded as long-term loans if repayment extends over a period longer than one year. These loans are usually raised for the purpose of obtaining assets and therefore are usually secured. Where the loan is raised to purchase fixed property, a bond is registered over the property concerned and the loan is known as a mortgage bond.

The following minimum particulars must be given in the financial statements in respect of loans and mortgage bonds:

- ☐ The relevant interest rates.
- ☐ The relevant dates of repayment.
- ☐ The amounts of the repayments, where applicable.

If desired, only the amount of the debt may be shown on the balance sheet, while further particulars are disclosed by way of a note to the financial statements.

Theoretically, accounting practice requires that any payments and interest due within a year should be shown as a current liability, since they are payable within the next accounting period. We feel, however, that it is more meaningful to show the total debt (capital plus interest) as a single amount under long-term liabilities and to disclose by means of a note that a certain capital amount plus interest is payable in the next accounting period.

17.3.2 Debentures

Debentures, like shares and other long-term loans, constitute a means of obtaining long-term capital for investment in the enterprise. Debentures are subject to contractual conditions and are usually secured. Interest is paid on debentures periodically, but **generally** the capital amount is paid back only after the due date.

Debentures differ from ordinary loans in that the lender offers the debentures for sale to the public according to a debenture trust deed and a trustee protects the interests of the debenture holders. Debentures also differ from share capital in that they do not carry any voting rights, are subject to a fixed interest rate, and are repayable on a specific date, for a specific amount, in a specific manner. In legal terms, therefore, a debenture is a debt owed by the company to the debenture holder and is subject to the conditions specified in the debenture trust deed.

The financial statements must disclose full details concerning the type of debenture, the date of repayment, the amount to be repaid, and the security provided.

The following example illustrates the disclosure of debentures in the balance sheet:

Long-term liabilities 8% R100 debentures redeemable at par on 30 June 19.3	R2 000

(Security for the debentures, if applicable, should be indicated.)

17.3.3 Suspensive sale creditors

Assets may sometimes be bought on suspensive sale, in which case the purchase price is repayable over a specified period. If this period is longer than one year, the debt must be recorded as a long-term liability. The seller remains the legal owner of the asset until the full purchase price has been paid – the asset serves as security for the debt.

When as asset is purchased on suspensive sale, the following entry will be made:

Asset	xx	
Suspensive sale creditor		xx
Purchase of asset on suspensive sale, repayable over three years in equal instalments of Rx monthly		

The asset is classified in the balance sheet according to its nature and a note is made to the effect that it has been secured.

Strictly speaking, the amount owing to the creditor must be separated into amounts payable within the next 12 months and amounts payable thereafter, and these must be shown under current and long-term liabilities respectively. Once again, an indication must be given as to whether the debt is secured over any asset.

17.4 LEASE CONTRACTS

In recent years there has been considerable growth in the leasing of assets and virtually any asset can be leased, notable examples being land, buildings, vehicles and equipment.

Leasing is a form of financing which is particularly useful in cases where the lessee does not have the necessary funds available, or where the cost of leasing is lower than the cost of other forms of financing.

In conventional accounting no entry is made in the books when a lease agreement is entered into, because the lessee is not the owner of the asset. This differs from a suspensive sale transaction, where the 'lessee' will eventually become the owner. Many regard this as one of the advantages of leasing, since the liability (which may be substantial and extend over several years) need not be shown in the financial statements. Only the annual leasing costs are shown in the income statement.

Nevertheless it is sound accounting practice to disclose in a note to the financial statements the particulars of the leased assets in use and the obligations arising therefrom.

More recent trends in accounting practice prefer that the leased asset is recorded (and properly described) and that the corresponding liability is capitalised at the present value of future payments. This method allows proper disclosure of both the assets being used by the enterprise and the source of financing (the liability).

17.5 INTER-COMPANY LOANS

Long or short-term loans made to or by companies within a group are shown separately in the financial statements. In other words, they are not classified as long-term or short-term liabilities, since when consolidated group statements are prepared, inter-company liabilities are eliminated.

The following particulars must be shown separately:

- ☐ The total amount owed by the holding company to its subsidiaries (asset).
- ☐ The total amount owed by the subsidiary company to its holding company and fellow subsidiaries within the group.
- ☐ A distinction must also be made between debentures and other debts.

17.6 OTHER LIABILITIES

17.6.1 Contingent liabilities

A contingent liability is not a liability and cannot therefore be treated as such. In accounting terms, a contingent liability refers to a possible obligation, the amount of which may or may not be determinable, which has arisen from past transactions and which may possibly (but not necessarily) become a legal debt in the future. The distinction between a contingent liability and a liability is the uncertainty as to whether the former entails any enforceable obligation. Examples are bills receivable and debtors which have been discounted, guarantees given to or on behalf of other enterprises and third parties, and legal actions which may be instituted against the enterprise.

For an item to be classified as a contingent liability, there must be **uncertainty** regarding both the **contingency** and the **amount** of the liability. Where the contingency, but not the amount, is known, the amount should be estimated, provision should be made for it, and it should be disclosed in the financial statements. Provision should also be made in cases where contingent liabilities may possibly result in a loss to the enterprise.

Contingent liabilities are disclosed in those notes to the financial statements which are more directly concerned with the balance sheet. Details must include the general nature of any encumbrance of the enterprise's assets as security for obligations to any person and, where possible, the amount concerned. This applies to any contingencies for which provision has **not** been made in the financial statements.

17.6.2 Contracts relating to capital expenditure

Obligations arising from contracts for capital expenditure differ from contingent liabilities in that the former are a positive action to incur an obligation. Examples are capital expenditure authorised and approved by the undertaking, but not yet contracted; contracts for capital expenditure for which provision has not been made; and amounts owing on contracts, which will be paid only on completion of the work concerned.

The notes to the financial statements must disclose full details of capital contracts, and must specify the source from which the funds to meet the total or estimated amounts of capital expenditure will be obtained.

17.6.3 Income accrued and monies received in advance

Deferred income refers to an obligation arising from advance payment for goods or services. The duration of deferred income is generally relatively short, since the services are provided either during the same financial year, or in the following year. In some cases, however, payments may be made to cover several years; these payments must then be credited **pro rata** to income over the period.

Outstanding balances should be shown as a liability, with, if possible, particulars of the nature and the duration thereof. Examples of deferred income are insurance premiums received in advance (by the insurer) and lease payments and lease premiums received in advance.

The opposite situation occurs in cases where income has already been generated, but is only received (i e realised) over several years. This includes, for example, profit on the sale of goods on instalment and financing income on loan transactions. The income must be credited to the income account periodically, but the outstanding balance is usually regarded as a reserve and deducted from the total amount of the debt (debtor). The nature of the deduction must be described appropriately.

17.7 INTERNAL CONTROL

- The most important aspects of internal control over creditors are, first, that transactions must be approved, and second, that prompt payment must be made to the correct creditor. (Prompt payment ensures that discounts are received and that the reputation of the enterprise is enhanced.)
- Staff members whose duties entail the recording of credit transactions must not be involved in the actual payment of accounts. In other words, there must be a separation of duties. The use of loose-leaf creditors accounts or creditors cards makes it possible for the accounting duties relating to creditors to be allocated to more than one employee.
- Where there is a large number of credit transactions, subsidiary books should be used, together with a ledger control account.
- Regular checks must be carried out to compare and reconcile individual creditors' balances with their statements of account.

18

FINANCIAL REPORTING: CHARACTERISTICS AND REQUIREMENTS

The **AIM** of this chapter is to explain the nature and characteristics of financial reporting and compliance with the requirements thereof.

18.1 INTRODUCTION: THE COMMUNICATION PROCESS

It is obvious that the purpose of the financial reports of any type of enterprise is to transfer or communicate financial information.

Communication is important in any undertaking; with the flow of information being co-ordinated by means of a communication system. There is a specific relationship between organisation, communication and decision making. The communicator takes an **occurrence** (e g a transaction), **processes** (codifies and classifies) it, and **records** and then transmits the **information** (message) to the **receiver**, who **receives**, **interprets** and **reacts to** the information.

The communication process can be represented schematically as follows:

Figure 18.1

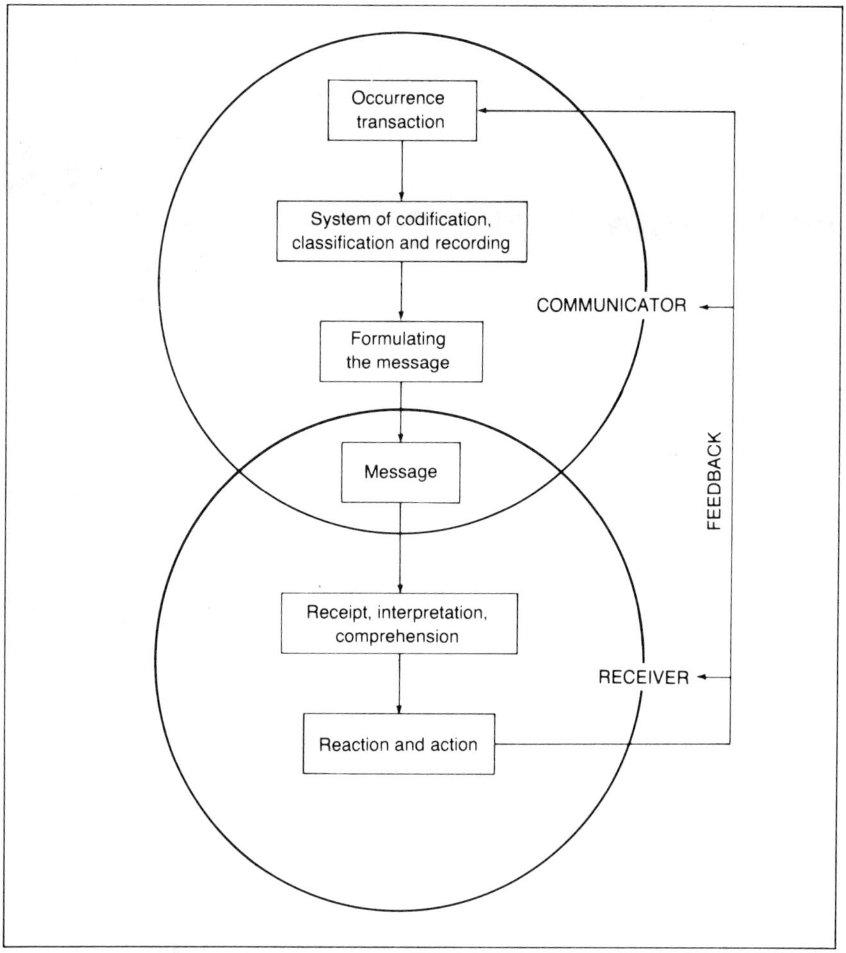

If the message is formulated in such a way that is is **not understood** by the receiver, **no communication** has in fact taken place. However, if the receiver understands the message but is **unable to use the information** for his purposes, then the communication process has been **futile**.

Therefore the information that is communicated must be:

- ☐ understandable
- ☐ useful.

Financial statements are the vehicle for communicating financial information (the message) to users of financial statements and other interested parties. In this instance the communication process is known as **reporting**.

18.2 TYPES OF REPORTING

Since the information contained in financial reports must serve as a basis for decision making, the compiler must know who is going to use the particular report, and for what purpose.

Financial reports may be classified into two broad categories according to their use, namely:

- ☐ Responsibility reports.
- ☐ Information reports.

18.2.1 Responsibility reports

The purpose of responsibility reports is to determine the performance of specific, responsible people within their sphere of responsibility and to communicate this information: first, to the person concerned, and subsequently, to the party to whom he is accountable.

☐ External reporting

The annual financial statements constitute the basis for external responsibility reports concerning management's responsibility towards the owners of the enterprise.

The information required by the owners in order to judge the account given by management will determine the amount of detail contained in the annual financial statements. The owners, not being directly involved in managing the enterprise, are chiefly concerned about how the capital they provide is transformed into assets, the financial position, the earnings, and how the earnings have been utilised for reinvestment and distribution.

However, the financial information contained in the annual statements can never provide a complete picture of an enterprise's position; it simply describes the historic implications of those economic occurrences which can be recorded in monetary terms. To complete the picture it is necessary to take into account all the other factors influencing the enterprise's affairs.

☐ Internal reporting

Internal responsibility reporting generally requires far greater detail than that required of external reporting.

Each manager in an enterprise has a specific responsibility and financial reports for internal responsibility reporting will be geared to show the performance in each specific sphere of responsibility.

The general manager will require summarising financial reports which will enable him to judge the performance in each sphere of responsibility. Reports for any specific divisional manager, on the other hand, will deal with the performance of that particular division only, but in greater detail than that presented to the general manager.

The principle of responsibility reporting on the basis of spheres of responsibility is illustrated in example 18.1 with reference to the income statement.

Example 18.1

RESPONSIBILITY REPORTING

Owners

Sales	62 578
Profit before taxation	7 628
Taxation	558
Profit after taxation	7 070
Less: Dividends	4 930
	2 140
Retained income at beginning of year	1 370
Retained income at end of year	R3 510

General manager

Sales:		62 578
Product A	30 408	
Product B	32 170	
Less: Cost of sales		42 316
Opening inventory	3 400	
Production costs	48 630	
	52 030	
Closing inventory	9 714	
Gross profit		20 262
Sales costs	5 604	
Administrative costs	6 430	
Financing costs	600	12 634
Net profit		R7 628

Production manager

Material consumed:	
Product A	8 460
Product B	10 230
Direct labour	14 460
Electricity	6 000
Maintenance	3 480
Factory rental	4 000
Depreciation	2 000
Production costs	R48 630

In the report to owners, sales and profit before taxation are shown as two single amounts. The report presented to the general manager shows the various income and expense items comprising the net profit, in summarised form. The report presented to the production manager sets out the production costs of R48 630, shown as a single amount in the general manager's report, in detail.

18.2.2 Information reports

The purpose of information reports is to provide a decision maker with the information necessary for making a specific decision. Therefore the nature and content of this type of report is based on the information needs of the user.

When an information report is to be compiled the purpose for which the report will be used must be identified. Then the report is compiled so that the particular information required for a specific purpose is disclosed clearly and accurately.

Frequently information reporting makes use of **reporting by exception**. In other words, reporting includes only those items requiring attention.

For example, a report to a credit manager responsible for collecting outstanding debts will not contain information regarding all debts, but only those in arrear.

18.3 QUALITATIVE CHARACTERISTICS OF REPORTING

From the preceding discussion it follows that, in essence, reporting relates to the **information needs** of the different groups of users of financial statements. What with the diversity of the requirements of the various interested parties, external statements can be seen merely as **generalised financial statements**, in other words, the same set of statements must satisfy the needs of all the different users. Therefore objective determination and communication of financial information is extremely important. Generalised external financial statements are the most important means of communicating financial accounting information periodically to investors, creditors and outsiders. The financial statements are 'generalised' because of their potential use by a wide variety of interested parties, and 'external' because the users are not part of the undertaking.

In practice, accounting information is neither perfect nor simple. The information provided by the financial reporting process is often the result of estimations, classifications and allocations, as well as subjective judgement. The results of economic activity in a dynamic economy are uncertain and due to a combination of many factors. Thus, despite the impression of accuracy given by financial reporting in general and financial statements in particular, estimations and approximations (which are based on certain rules and conventions) play an important role.

Therefore a number of **fundamental characteristics** with which accounting information must comply, have been developed. Compliance with these characteristics enhances the **usefulness** of financial statements.

The characteristics are known as **qualitative characteristics** (or standards whereby financial information is judged) and are linked to the requirements for good information. There are two basic qualitative characteristics:

- ☐ Relevance.
- ☐ Reliability.

18.3.1 Relevance

Accounting information is used as an aid in decision making. **Relevant** information is information which influences the behaviour of the decision maker. If a decision has to be made as to which of two machines which can be applied for the same purpose should be purchased; the purchase price, production capacity and estimated useful lifespan of each machine will be relevant information, since these factors will influence the decision. Information regarding the colour of the machine is totally irrelevant.

To be relevant the information must also have **predictive value** and **feedback value**. This reduces the uncertainty regarding past, present and future occurrences and makes it possible to confirm previous estimations. Thus the information for the current quarter can be used to prepare estimations for the full year. In this case the information is relevant because it reduces the uncertainty regarding the annual figures. The annual statements can be used as feedback for controlling the estimations.

In order to be relevant the information must also be **timeous**. It must be available while it still has the capacity to influence a decision. If the information contained in the periodic quarterly statements is received only at the end of the year, it is no longer relevant.

18.3.2 Reliability

Reliability is the quality characteristic which ensures that financial information is reasonably free of errors and subjective judgements. This characteristic ensures that the information presented is what it purports to be.

To be reliable, accounting information must be:

- ☐ Verifiable.
- ☐ Objective (or neutral).
- ☐ Fully disclosed.

☐ **Verifiability**

Information is verifiable if different persons using the information in different ways arrive at the same conclusion.

It is important that accounting information should be verifiable because of the potential conflict of interests between those preparing and those using it. Information is usually prepared by the management of the undertaking, who will want to reflect it as optimistically and favourably as possible in the financial statements. The requirement that it should be verifiable protects users from over-optimistic management information.

Not all accounting information is equally verifiable: cash on hand can easily be ascertained and is highly verifiable, whereas depreciation is less verifiable. The various methods of depreciation and estimation of the possible useful lifespan and the different scrap values that can be decided upon, make it possible for depreciation to have more than one acceptable value.

Generally accepted accounting practice attempts to limit the lack of verification to a reasonable level.

☐ **Objectivity**

Verification is enhanced by the characteristic of **objectivity**, which implies that financial information must be free from prejudice and bias. The information must be **neutral**, in other words the accounting procedures and principles used should not be chosen with a view to influencing users in a predetermined manner.

☐ **Complete disclosure**

Financial statements should disclose all the material information necessary for a proper understanding of the statements. This information may relate to the most recent financial period, as well as to future periods. The **accounting policy** followed should also be disclosed. Both the above aspects and many others which promote complete disclosure are dealt with in **statements of generally accepted accounting practice** (GAAP). These aspects are discussed more fully in the next chapter.

18.4 CONCEPTS WHICH AID THE INTERPRETATION OF FINANCIAL INFORMATION

Persons using the information contained in financial statements must know how to interpret it. To assist users in their interpretation, the following concepts are used in accounting:

- ☐ Comparability and consistency.
- ☐ Quantitative limitations
  - – cost benefit
  - – materiality.
- ☐ Prudence.

18.4.1 Comparability

Comparability enhances the characteristics of relevancy and reliability and contributes to improving the usefulness of accounting information.

Accounting information is more useful if it can be compared with similar information relating to the undertaking's previous financial period and similar information from other undertakings.

In order for accounting information to be comparable:

- ☐ common accounting methods should be applied to similar economic occurrences, and
- ☐ different accounting methods should be applied to dissimilar economic occurrences.

Comparability includes the concept **consistency**.

18.4.2 Consistency

Generally accepted accounting practice frequently allows undertakings to record and disclose the same type of transaction in different ways. However, GAAP also requires that once an undertaking has **decided upon a method of disclosure, it must be applied consistently**.

Accounting information reflects the economic activities of an undertaking. If the accounting methods are allowed to be changed haphazardly, the reflection of the economic activities may be distorted. The characteristic consistency is applied to prevent such distortion. Consistency requires that the method selected in respect of a particular item is applied consistently from year to year, and that the same criteria should be applied to all related transactions.

Since financial statements are based on the principle of consistency, users of statements can assume that no **arbitrary** changes in accounting methods or disclosure procedures have occurred.

Consistency does not imply that changes in methods or procedures cannot be made. If changes are considered necessary, the justification for such changes and the nature and financial effect thereof must be fully disclosed.

18.5 QUANTITATIVE RESTRICTIONS ON ACCOUNTING INFORMATION

It may not be viable to disclose even the most useful accounting information unless:

- ☐ the benefit of providing the information exceeds the cost thereof
- ☐ the information is significantly material.

These two aspects, viz the cost benefit and the materiality considerations, are quantitative limitations on the application of the qualitative characteristics already discussed.

18.5.1 Cost benefit consideration

It costs money to provide accounting information, just as it costs money to provide any other commodity. The costs of providing accounting information include those incurred in the compiling, processing, editing and analysing of the information. Unless the value of the information exceeds the cost of obtaining and using it, it may not be desirable to provide certain information.

18.5.2 Materiality

Relevant information may or may not be material. Information is material if, all the circumstances taken into account, the size (scope) of a specific item is such that it would influence the judgement of a reasonable person.

Materiality is a function of size as well as circumstance. Assume, for example, that a large undertaking with branches throughout the country treated an asset bought for R100 as an expense instead of capitalising it. It may be relevant to know that the asset was not capitalised, but in this case the information is not material.

The extent of the error (R100) and the circumstances (a large enterprise) will not influence the decisions of any user of the financial statements. In other words, relevant information is not always material. Therefore materiality imposes limitations on the application of each of the qualitative characteristics discussed.

18.6 PRUDENCE

Accountants tend to base their decisions on logic and information which will result in the most reasonable outcome. When making judgements or estimations they are often faced with uncertainties. In such cases they always apply the principle of prudence. In other words, where material uncertainty exists as to what accounting procedure to use, the accountants will generally choose the procedure which is least likely to inflate assets or income.

Although prudence is a useful tool when uncertainty exists, the misuse thereof can result in inaccurate and misleading financial statements. Prudence often conflicts with proper disclosure and consistency.

The discussion in this chapter can be represented diagrammatically as follows:

Diagram 18.3

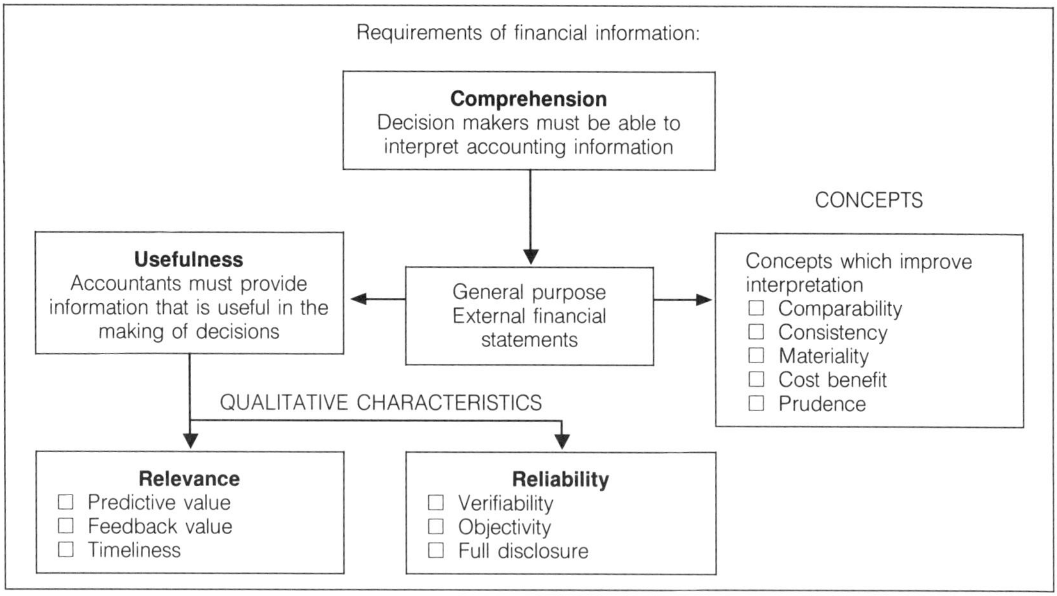

19

GENERALLY ACCEPTED ACCOUNTING PRACTICE

The **AIM** of this chapter is to explain the nature and meaning of GAAP.

19.1 INTRODUCTION: ACCOUNTING PRACTICE AND THEORY

In this chapter we give consideration to certain basic assumptions specific to accounting which have already been mentioned in previous chapters. The knowledge that you have acquired through studying the preceding sections of this book should enable you to understand a more comprehensive discussion of these and other aspects related to the fundamental bases of financial accounting.

The function of man as a whole is based on certain underlying assumptions. We assume, for example, that it is safe to cross a street when the traffic light shows green. This and many other assumptions dictate our daily behaviour. In the same way, a set of **basic assumptions or concepts serve as guidelines for the accounting discipline**.

These guidelines influence the manner in which accounting information is reported. Consequently the practical application of accounting is more comprehensible if the underlying theoretical bases of accounting are studied.

This chapter attempts to provide such understanding, in contrast to the previous chapters, which concentrated on specific practices and the procedures necessary to record transactions and disclose financial information.

19.2 DEFINITION OF GAAP

If each undertaking reported its own financial information as it saw fit, the result would be chaos. To bring order into the accounting and reporting processes, over the years the accounting profession has developed an underlying basis for measuring and disclosing the results of business transactions and events. This consists of a set of **assumptions, concepts and procedures which together are known as generally accepted accounting practice** (GAAP).

The existence of GAAP does not imply that all undertakings should measure and report on all financial activities in the same manner. No two undertakings are alike, therefore it would be impractical to have an inflexible system of measurement and reporting. The accounting profession developed GAAP as a framework which embraces the fundamental principles of measurement and reporting, but within which a certain amount of diversity is possible.

19.3 THE NATURE OF ACCOUNTING PRINCIPLES

Accounting principles are entirely different from scientific principles. The latter principles are substantiated by extensive experimentation and observation. For example, detailed research and experimentation has ascertained that the speed of light is 300 000 km per second, and that every molecule of water is made up of two atoms of hydrogen and one atom of oxygen.

In contrast to the laws of nature, accounting principles are not **discovered**; they are **formulated** to meet the objectives of financial reporting. In other words a balance sheet is prepared to reflect the financial position of an enterprise at a particular time. This type of disclosure cannot be proved to be correct or incorrect.

It is, however, the generally accepted method of reporting on the financial position of an enterprise.

19.4 THE DEVELOPMENT OF GAAP

Over the past few years the development of accounting standards has enjoyed attention, not only in the USA, but also internationally.

In South Africa, the South African Institute of Chartered Accountants (SAICA) has taken the initiative by establishing an Accounting Practices Committee. After preparing statements of GAAP, the latter body makes them available to interested parties for their comment and eventually presents an Exposure Draft to the Accounting Practices Board (APB) for approval.

The Accounting Practices Board was established in 1973 with the following principal objective: the establishment and acceptance of what the Board (APB) considers is or should be generally accepted accounting practice.

19.5 APPROACH TO SETTING ACCOUNTING STANDARDS

The approach adopted in respect of the setting of standards is to **identify the accounting practices that are desirable** and thereby to **limit differences in and the variety of accounting practices without introducing rigid uniformity or laying down an inflexible set of rules for all circumstances**. The objective is to **produce standards with as general as possible an application, but which eliminate undesirable alternatives**. This process may well go further than codifying existing practice. However, not all situations can be catered for. It must be recognised, therefore, that it will be necessary to exercise **judgement** in applying statements of GAAP.

Section 286(3) of the Companies Act requires that 'the financial statements of a company shall in conformity with generally accepted accounting practice, fairly present the state of affairs . . . and the profit or loss. . . .'

The overriding requirement of the Companies Act is **fair presentation**. The existence of a standard is an aid to both comparability and fair presentation; however, compliance with a standard is no guarantee that fair presentation will be achieved in the financial statements. Even though compliance with accounting standards is not necessarily sufficient for fair presentation, the standards are nevertheless highly influential and persuasive in that respect. Accordingly it is necessary for **deviations to be disclosed in an explanatory note to the financial statements**.

It is recognised that there may be **exceptional circumstances** in which a statement of GAAP is not strictly applicable because, all the circumstances taken into consideration, fair presentation will not be achieved, that is compliance with GAAP would be misleading.

Such circumstances are encountered in certain specialised undertakings which cannot be catered for fully by a general standard. Other exceptions are unusual transactions, where compliance with one or other of the fundamental accounting concepts cannot be achieved by also complying with a statement of GAAP.

19.6 APPLICATION OF STATEMENTS OF GAAP

From the preceding it follows that practical problems will arise in the application of statements of GAAP. Many of these problems will be solved if the **spirit** rather than the letter of GAAP statements is applied. The overriding requirement of fair presentation should always be borne in mind.

There are two considerations in particular which affect the application of GAAP.[1]

☐ **Substance over form**

Transactions and other events should be accounted for and presented in accordance with their substance and financial reality, and not merely in accordance with their legal form.

☐ **Materiality**

Financial statements should disclose all items which are material enough to affect evaluations or decisions.

Statements of GAAP are important in the preparation of all financial statements (not only those of a company) which profess to be prepared in accordance with generally accepted accounting practice.

The premise of statements of generally accepted accounting practice is that in order for the users of financial statements to have a proper understanding and interpretation of financial statements, it is important that they are aware of the main assumptions upon which such statements are based.

Statement AC 101[2] distinguishes between:

- ☐ accounting concepts
- ☐ accounting bases
- ☐ accounting policies.

19.7 CONCEPTS UNDERLYING GAAP

Generally accepted accounting practice is based on various assumptions or fundamental concepts.

Accounting concepts can be defined as broad basic assumptions which underlie the periodic financial statements of business entities. The following concepts are distinguished:

- ☐ the accounting entity concept
- ☐ the going concern concept
- ☐ the consistency concept
- ☐ the prudence concept
- ☐ the monetary standard
- ☐ historical cost
- ☐ the matching concept

☐ **Accounting entity concept**

An accounting entity is a specific entity which is reported on. An accounting entity can be an individual, a business undertaking, a body in the public sector, etc.

---

1 AC 100 Preface to Statements of Generally Accepted Accounting Practice; The South African Institute of Chartered Accountants; Johannesburg, April 1983.

2 AC 101 Disclosure of Accounting Policies; SAICA Johannesburg, 1974: Par .04.

In accounting an entity is considered to be independent of its owners, creditors, management or employees. The financial reports have no bearing on the economic activities of the individuals who may have an interest in the entity.

□ Going concern concept[3]

The going concern concept assumes that the entity will continue in operational existence for the foreseeable future. This means that the income statement and balance sheet assume no intention or necessity to liquidate or significantly curtail the scale of operation.

□ The consistency concept[4]

The consistency concept requires consistency in the accounting treatment of like items within each accounting period, and from one period to the next.

□ The prudence concept[5]

The prudence concept entails that revenue and profits are not anticipated, but are recognised by inclusion in the income statement only when realised in the form of cash or of other assets, the ultimate cash realisation of which can be assessed with reasonable certainty. Provision is made for all known liabilities (expenses and losses) regardless of whether the amount of these is known with certainty or is the best estimate in the light of the information available.

□ The monetary standard

This concept assumes that economic information must be measured in terms of a monetary unit (e g the rand in South Africa), and makes possible the summarising and analysis of accounting information through the processing of figures. A desk and a vehicle cannot be added together, but their cost prices, expressed in a common accounting unit (the monetary value), can be added together.

The monetary standard does not imply that the relevant information is quantifiable (e g the quality of the employees in an undertaking is not quantifiable).

The monetary standard rests on the assumption that the value of the monetary unit of measurement remains stable and unchanged. This implies, for example, that the purchasing power of the rand in 19.6 has the same value that it had in 19.1. In times of inflation or recession this assumption is obviously not valid. For example, during inflationary periods the general purchasing power of the monetary unit will decline. This aspect is discussed in more detail in a later chapter.

□ Historical cost

The application of this concept results in assets and liabilities being recorded in the accounting records at the time of their acquisition at their historical cost or fair market value. In the course of time the fair market value may change, but the recorded value remains unchanged in the accounting records.

Historical costs can be verified and are presently still being used in the preparation of financial statements, although there is a strong belief that, in times of inflation, historical costs become irrelevant.

---

3 Ibid, par .04.
4 Ibid, par .06.
5 Ibid, par .07.

☐ **The matching concept**[6]

The matching concept assumes that revenue and costs are accrued (i e recognised as they are earned or incurred, and not as money is received or paid), matched with one another insofar as their relationship can be established or justifiably assumed, and dealt with in the income statement for the period to which they relate; provided that where the matching concept is inconsistent with the prudence concept, the latter prevails. Revenue and profits dealt with in the income statements are matched with associated costs and expenses by including the costs incurred in earning them (so far as these are material and identifiable) in the same account.

If financial statements are prepared on the basis of assumptions which **differ** in **material** respects from any of the generally accepted fundamental accounting concepts, these facts should be disclosed in the financial statements.[7]

19.8 ACCOUNTING BASES[8]

Accounting bases are methods developed for applying fundamental accounting concepts to financial transactions for the purpose of financial statements, and in particular for:

- ☐ determining in which accounting periods the revenue and costs should be recognised
- ☐ determining the amounts at which items should be stated in the balance sheet.

As is explained in chapter 2, there is more than one acceptable method of treating a specific transaction under different circumstances.

Accounting bases are more diverse and numerous than fundamental accounting concepts, since they have evolved in response to the variety and complexity of types of business and business transactions, and for this reason there may justifiably be more than one recognised accounting basis for dealing with a particular item.

Over time a variety of accounting practices have been developed. These are designed to provide consistent, fair and, as far as possible, objective solutions to accounting problems in particular circumstances. For example, bases have been developed for calculating depreciation and the amount at which stock should be stated.

Accounting bases provide an orderly framework for periodic reporting, but sound judgement must be exercised in the preparation of financial statements.

Where a choice of acceptable accounting bases is available, judgement must be exercised in choosing the bases appropriate in the circumstances and which are best suited to fair presentation of the concern's result and financial position. The bases thus adopted become the concern's **accounting policies**.

---

6 Ibid, par .05.
7 Ibid, par .21.
8 Ibid, par .08.

19.9 ACCOUNTING POLICIES[9]

Accounting policies are the specific accounting bases judged by a business enterprise to be the most appropriate to its circumstances and adopted for the purpose of preparing its financial statements.

In circumstances where more than one accounting basis is acceptable, the accounting policy followed can significantly affect a concern's reported results and financial position. The financial **statements can be evaluated properly only if the policies followed in dealing with significant items are disclosed**. For this reason adequate disclosure of accounting policies is essential to the fair presentation of financial statements.

The accounting policy followed in dealing with material or key items should be **disclosed** by means of clear, reasonable and concise notes in the determining of the result for a period and presenting the financial position.[10]

Aspects in respect of which different accounting bases are recognised and the accounting policy should be disclosed include, *inter alia*, the following:

- ☐ Depreciation of fixed assets.
- ☐ Treatment and amortisation of intangible assets such as research and development costs, goodwill, patents and trade marks.
- ☐ Stock and work-in-progress.
- ☐ Long-term contracts.
- ☐ Deferred taxation.
- ☐ Instalment transactions.
- ☐ Lease and lessor transactions.
- ☐ Conversion of foreign currencies.
- ☐ Consolidation policies.
- ☐ Property development transactions.
- ☐ Warranties for products or services.

Disclosure is discussed in more detail in chapter 23.

9 Ibid, par .10.
10 Ibid, par .22.

20

OWNER'S EQUITY AND THE FORM OF ENTERPRISE

The **AIM** of this chapter is to explain the specific characteristics of partnerships, close corporations and companies.

20.1 INTRODUCTION

Accounting principles and procedures are relevant to all business activities, regardless of the type of entity or the form of enterprise within which the activity is conducted. However, principles and procedures are applied in different ways, because of different approaches and viewpoints and because legal requirements and practice affect the **distribution of profit** and the **owner's equity** in each type of enterprise.

The basic types of enterprise are:

- the sold proprietorship
- the partnership
- the close corporation
- the company.

Two further forms, which are not discussed here, are trusts and co-operatives.

An individual (the entrepreneur) can establish a **sole proprietorship** easily and practically without having to satisfy any statutory requirements. He can arrange it into departments, trade through agents and establish branches.

In conjunction with other entrepreneurs he may form a temporary or permanent **partnership**, which can have the same departmental, branch and agent structure. Larger groups of owners may also form **close corporations** or **companies**, which can also have the same trading structure as sole proprietorships and partnerships.

Companies can also be in association with other companies, referred to as associated or affiliated companies. If they hold the controlling interest in another company, that company is known as a subsidiary of the holding company.

20.2 THE SOLE PROPRIETORSHIP

The individual wishing to start a business does not encounter too many obstacles – usually only a trading licence is required. Anyone rendering professional services must also comply with the admission requirements set by the professional body concerned.

All the decisions are made by the individual, to whom all the profits (losses) accrue. The individual is personally responsible for all the enterprise's liabilities and is the sole owner of the assets.

The **owner's equity** of a sole proprietor consists of the capital introduced plus profits earned, less any losses suffered and any amounts withdrawn from the enterprise.

The composition and presentation of owner's equity have already been discussed in previous chapters.

20.3 THE PARTNERSHIP

20.3.1 Introduction

A partnership is a legal relationship created by an agreement between two or more, **but not more than** 20, persons. According to this agreement each person contributes to a lawful enterprise for the purpose of making a profit, which is to be divided among the partners. An analysis of this description will reveal that the essential requirements for the formation of a partnership are the following:

- ☐ there must be a valid agreement
- ☐ according to which each partner contributes something
- ☐ with the purpose of making a profit
- ☐ which will be to the mutual advantage of all the partners.

The formation of a partnership requires no formalities – for instance no written agreement is required – but it is customary and preferable for the agreement to be in writing. Thus the agreement can be written, oral or tacit, that is by conduct.

20.3.2 Legal position of partnerships

South Africa has no legislation pertaining specifically to partnerships, therefore common law principles apply. A partnership is not a legal person and has no independent legal existence separate from that of its constituent members. The partners are jointly and severally responsible for the rights and obligations of the partnership – in other words they have mutual rights to all the assets and are jointly responsible for all the obligations.

According to South African company law a partnership, with a few exceptions, may not consist of more than 20 members. If the number of members exceeds 20 the partnership becomes invalid and ceases to have any legal existence.

20.3.3 The partnership agreement

As has already been stated, the agreement should preferably be in writing. The contents of such an agreement will depend on individual circumstances. Where an agreement is silent on any specific aspect, common law principles will apply. For example, according to common law, partners have equal rights in the management of the enterprise and their ownership in the enterprise is in the same ratio as that governing the distribution of profits. If, for example, the agreement does not specify the ratio according to which profits should be distributed, then partners will share profits and losses in proportion to their contributions to the partnership (capital), and where such contributions are not specified, the assumption is that partners will share equally in the profits.

It is important that the partnership agreement should be studied before partnership accounts are drawn up in order that the specifications laid down in the agreement are complied with.

A partnership agreement should specify the following essential aspects:

- ☐ The names of the parties forming the partnership.
- ☐ The purpose, nature and scope of the partnership.
- ☐ Name of the partnership.
- ☐ Location of the business.
- ☐ Date of formation and expected duration of the partnership.
- ☐ Contribution made by each partner.
- ☐ Rights, powers and duties of each partner, as well as any restriction thereon.
- ☐ Decisions concerning the financial year, books and records.

- ☐ The ratio of profit and loss distribution, including any special provisions for recognising differences in capital contributions (interest on capital) and services rendered by partners (salaries).
- ☐ Specifications covering withdrawals by partners.
- ☐ Specifications in respect of life insurance for partners, treatment of insurance premiums and proceeds of policies.
- ☐ Specifications relating to the retirement, admission or death of partners and dissolution of the partnership.
- ☐ Procedures for settling any disputes between partners.

20.3.4 Partners' contributions

Each partner is expected to contribute something to the partnership. These contributions need not necessarily be of the same nature; they may consist of cash, labour, skills or knowledge. The amount, whatever its form, that a partner contributes to the enterprise is his **capital** invested in the enterprise.

On dissolution of the partnership a partner may recover his capital only after all claims on the enterprise's assets have been settled. In contrast a partner may advance money to the enterprise, thereby becoming a creditor of the partnership with regard to these loans. On dissolution of the partnership these loans take precedence over repayment of capital, but if not secured have the same priority as claims by other creditors.

20.3.5 Relationships between partners as such and with third parties

Unless otherwise specified by the agreement, a partner has no **right** to a salary or compensation for his services or to interest on his capital. However, the partners may determine by mutual agreement any relationship they consider necessary, for example that one or more partner should be denied the right of management or granted only restricted powers, or that on dissolution the assets should be distributed in a specified ratio, or that a specific profit-sharing ratio should apply. The agreement may even specify that losses are to be shared in a ratio different from that governing the distribution of profit. A partner may also be guaranteed a minimum profit.

Partners must show the highest degree of good faith towards each other and must manage the interests of their mutual business as if it were their own. No partner has the right to enrich himself at the expense of the partnership, or to allow his own interests to take precedence over those of the partnership.

Because a partnership is not a legal entity, any action against a partnership must be instituted against all the partners personally. The partners are jointly responsible and therefore must be sued as such. Similarly, partners must institute any action against a third party jointly.

If a partner commits a crime in promoting the interests of the partnership, all the partners will be deemed to be guilty unless they can prove that they had no part in and were unable to prevent the crime.

The relationship between the partnership and the individual partners is very similar to that between a principal and his representatives. Unless a partner's representative powers are restricted by mutual agreement, he has the authority to act on behalf of the partnership in any business relevant to the partnership's scope of activity and the partnership is bound by the arrangements he makes. Where a partner's actions are beyond the power and scope of the partnership's activities, the partnership will not be bound by the arrangements. If a partner exceeds the limits of his powers and concludes a contract with a third party who is unaware of the restrictions binding that partner, the partnership is bound by the arrangement unless the partner has acted *ultra vires* with respect to the partnership. In this case the other partners must either approve the transaction, thereby binding themselves to the arrangements, or repudiate it.

A partnership does not constitute a tax entity. There is no such thing as partnership tax – the individual partners are taxed in their personal capacities on the profits of the partnership.

20.3.6 Dissolving a partnership

Partnerships may be dissolved for one of the following reasons:

- ☐ Voluntary action by the partners (mutual agreement, change in the membership of the partnership by agreement).
- ☐ The unilateral action of one partner (a partner may unilaterally declare the partnership dissolved, but this may render him liable to breach of contract, depending on the circumstances).
- ☐ Legal process (death of a partner, insolvency of the partnership or of a partner, or when a partnership has more than 20 members).

When a partner retires, for whatever reason, the partnership ceases to exist. The remaining partners may continue their enterprise, but must form a new partnership. The admission of a new partner, even where the previous membership remains intact, also entails the dissolution of the earlier partnership and the formation of a new one.

20.3.7 Insolvency of a partnership

The court may sequestrate a partnership's estate either at the request of the partners, that is voluntary sequestration, or at the request of a creditor, that is compulsory sequestration. In both cases the private estates of each partner must also be sequestrated.

The partnership is then dissolved, but creditors can claim against the estate of the partnership only, and not against the estates of the individual partners. To prevent sequestration of his private estate a partner may undertake to pay the partnership's debts, or may offer security, satisfactory to the court, for payment of the debts.

A partner's equity consists of the capital he has contributed plus any profit (or loss) apportioned to him, less any withdrawals he may have made. The accounting aspects of owner's equity are discussed in greater detail in a later chapter.

20.3.8 Extraordinary partnerships

Most partnerships are 'general partnerships' in which the partners bear unrestricted responsibility for their firm's debts. There are, however, certain exceptions.

In a **limited partnership*** the partners' liability for the partnership's debts is limited to the amount of the capital they have undertaken to contribute to the partnership. Further, a **sleeping partner** is excluded from the management of the partnership by agreement. A **commandate** partner is both a sleeping partner and a limited partner.

---

*This type of partnership exists only in the Cape Province and Natal, in accordance with legislation promulgated in 1861 and 1865.

These extraordinary partnerships have one characteristic in common: the extraordinary partner is a partner only in the eyes of the other partners. An extraordinary partner may not act in the capacity of a partner, nor present himself as such to third parties. This type of partnership is seldom encountered today.

20.3.9 Characteristics of the partnership as a type of enterprise

- ☐ **Ease of formation and dissolution:** As has already been noted, a partnership is formed by mutual agreement between two or more parties. Dissolution is effected by either oral or written notice given by a partner to his fellow partners.
- ☐ **Relative flexibility:** Changes in the capital structure of a partnership or important policy changes within the firm are readily effected by mutual agreement of the partners.
- ☐ **Personal nature of a partnership:** Especially in the case of professional practices, a partnership presents a more personal image. To the public this implies a closer link between ownership and management, and consequently a high degree of responsibility.
- ☐ **Personal responsibility:** As has already been mentioned, partners are jointly and severally responsible for all the debts of the partnership. An ordinary partner may be obliged to contribute considerably more than his original capital should the partnership be sequestrated.
- ☐ **Lack of continuity:** The dissolution of a partnership each time a change in its membership occurs may cause third parties to feel less secure than when dealing with a company, for example. In practice a partnership frequently continues without disruption, despite changes in membership.
- ☐ **Limited transfer of ownership:** A partner may not transfer his rights in a partnership without permission from all the other partners.
- ☐ **Restrictions on the raising of loan capital:** A partnership may experience greater difficulty in obtaining finance than a public company, but there is little difference between a partnership and a private company in this respect. Partners are required to assume personal responsibility for loans. In practice banks and financial institutions also require the directors and shareholders of a private company to stand surety for such a loan, and therefore to forfeit the advantage of limited liability.
- ☐ **Income tax:** Since a partnership is not a legal entity, it is not liable for income tax. The profit of a partnership is taxed in the hands of the partners. Thus each partner is taxed on his portion of the partnership's profit according to the progressive sliding scale pertaining to individuals.

20.4 CLOSE CORPORATIONS

20.4.1 Introduction

Since 1 January 1985 it has been possible to incorporate close corporations in terms of the Close Corporations Act, 1984 (Act 69 of 1984) (hereafter the CC Act). Regulations issued in November 1984 and relating to certain administrative and other matters affecting close corporations (hereafter referred to as CCs) must be read in conjunction with the Act.

The CC Act is intended to provide a less complex and more easily administered alternative to a private company as a means of conducting business as a separate legal entity and is aimed specifically at smaller business enterprises.

The administration of corporations falls under the control of the Registrar of Close Corporations, and on payment of the prescribed fee all documents in his possession are available for public inspection.

Prescribed documents that must be submitted to the Registrar have been pre-prepared, minimised and are relatively inexpensive to register. Currently these forms are the following:

- CK1 Founding Statement.
- CK2 Amended Founding Statement.
- CK3 Application for Restoration of Registration.
- CK4 Application for Conversion.
- CK5 Court Alteration to, Replacement of, Addition to Founding Statement.
- CK6 Voluntary Liquidation.

20.4.2 Characteristics of a close corporation

As is the case with companies limited by share capital, a CC makes it possible for smaller enterprises to obtain **legal status**, with a legal identity independent of its members and with **limited liability** and **unlimited existence**. However, because the CC Act avoids much of the administrative complexity associated with companies with limited liability, a CC is simpler and less expensive to operate. A characteristic of the CC Act is that it is intended to be largely self-regulatory and members may lose their limited liability and be jointly and severally responsible for the debts of the CC if they violate certain provisions of the CC Act.

The main requirement of the CC Act is that a corporation should comply with specific **solvency and liquidity requirements** whenever certain payments are made. The corporation can satisfy these solvency and liquidity requirements provided that:

- if, after such payment is made, the corporation's assets, fairly valued, exceed all its liabilities
- the corporation is able to pay its debts as they become due in the ordinary course of its business
- in the particular circumstances, such payment will not in fact render the corporation unable to pay its debts as they become due in the ordinary course of its business.

A CC is suitable for an undertaking which is owned by a few people who are all actively involved in the operation of the business. In terms of the CC Act, the members are all entitled to participate in the management of the business and to act on behalf of the corporation. In contrast with companies, no distinction is made between the owners and management of a corporation.

A close corporation:

- becomes a juristic person on formation and has the capacity and powers of a natural person of full capacity in so far as a juristic person is capable of having such powers or of exercising such powers
- exists indefinitely and remains a juristic person irrespective of any changes in its membership
- provides members with limited liability.

20.4.3 Formation

A CC is formed as soon as a 'Founding Statement' is registered with the Registrar. The Founding Statement must contain the following:

- ☐ the full name of the corporation
- ☐ the principal business to be carried on by the corporation
- ☐ the postal and physical address of the registered office of the corporation
- ☐ the full name of each member and his identity number
- ☐ the size, expressed as a percentage, of each member's interest in the corporation
- ☐ particulars of the contribution of each member
- ☐ the name and postal address of the accounting officer (person or firm)
- ☐ the date of the financial year end of the corporation.

The Founding Statement replaces the Memorandum of Articles of Association and the large number of registers which are applicable to a company. If there is any change to the particulars contained in the Founding Statement, an Amended Founding Statement plus two copies, signed by all members, must be lodged with the Registrar within 28 days of such a change. On registration of the Founding Statement, the Registrar allocates a registration number to the corporation. Corporations must display their full registered names with the addition of CC (or BK), as well as their registration number, on the outside of their business premises and on all:

- ☐ notices and other official publications, including advertisements
- ☐ bills of exchange, promissory notes, endorsements, cheques and orders for money, goods or services purporting to be signed by or on behalf of the corporation
- ☐ letters, delivery notes, invoices, receipts and letters of credit of the corporation.

Every business letter sent by the corporation to any person must contain the names (or initials) and surnames of each member of the corporation.

20.4.4 Liquidation and winding up

The requirements for liquidation and winding up are similar to those laid down by the Companies Act and the Insolvency Act and generally are similar to the requirements applied in company law.

20.4.5 Members of a close corporation

20.4.5.1 Membership

A CC may have a minimum of one and a maximum of 10 members. The general principle is that only **natural** persons may be members of a CC. **Juristic persons** may also be members in the following circumstances:

- ☐ A juristic person who is trustee of a testamentary trust is entitled to a member's interest, provided that such juristic person is not directly or indirectly controlled by any beneficiary of the trust.
- ☐ A juristic person who, in the case of a member who is insolvent, deceased, mentally deranged or otherwise incapable or incompetent to manage his affairs, is a trustee of his insolvent estate or an administrator, executor or curator in respect of such member or is otherwise a person who is his duly appointed legal representative.

20.4.5.2 Contribution and interest of a member

Every person who is to become a member of a corporation, must make an initial contribution, particulars of which must be stated in the Founding Statement. This contribution can be money or other assets or services rendered in connection with and for the purpose of the formation of the corporation. It may not be in the form of future services (for example, future value of free accommodation, interest-free loans, future consultations or management services).

The interest of any member in a corporation is a single interest expressed as a percentage. The term 'single interest' means that two or more persons may not be joint holders of a member's interest in a corporation. There is no requirement that the member's percentage interest must be in relation to his share of total members' contributions. A member's interest generally represents his right to share in the income of the corporation. This right may, however, be varied in accordance with the terms of an association agreement.

A new member may obtain his member's interest by:

- buying it from one or more of the existing members
- making a contribution to the corporation, in which case the percentage of his member's interest is determined by agreement with the existing members. The contribution may consist of an amount of money or any property at a value agreed upon by the new and existing members.

A corporation may give financial assistance to any person for the purpose of acquiring his member's interest. The opposite applies to a company which, by virtue of the 'maintenance of capital' concept, is not allowed to offer such assistance. However, the assistance offered to a new member is controlled in that the corporation:

- must obtain prior written approval from all existing members
- must satisfy the solvency and liquidity requirements of the Act.

The close relationship between members is recognised by the CC Act. If any member wishes to dispose of his interest or part thereof, he may do so only with the consent of all the other members or in terms of the conditions of the association agreement.

If a member should be declared insolvent, the trustee of his insovlent estate may sell his member's interest to the corporation, the other members or a third party (in the latter case, subject to certain conditions).

Subject to any other arrangement in the association agreement, the executor of the estate of a deceased member may transfer the deceased member's interest to his legatee or heir only if all remaining members of the corporation agree to the transfer. If this consent is not given within 28 days, the executor must sell the interest to the corporation, the remaining members or a third party.

The corporation can buy a member's interest, provided that it complies with the written consent and solvency and liquidity requirements of the CC Act, and although it may buy a member's interest, it may not keep such an interest. Any interest purchased in this way must immediately be added to the interest of the remaining members, either proportionally or as per agreement.

20.4.5.3 Limited liability of members

According to the CC Act, members are not liable for the obligations of the corporation simply on account of their membership. Certain transgressions may result in their losing their limited liability and becoming jointly and severally responsible for the debts of the corporation. The circumstances under which members may lose the protection of limited liability are:

- where transactions are concluded in the corporation's name without the use of the abbreviation CC (or BK)
- where the contributions specified in the Founding Statement are not made

- ☐ where the number of members exceeds 10 for a period of six months
- ☐ where the office of accounting officer of the corporation is vacant for six months
- ☐ where they participate in the management of the company while being incapacitated in this respect
- ☐ where the business of the corporation is carried on recklessly, with gross negligence or with the intent to defraud
- ☐ where certain payments are made to members although the corporation does not satisfy the solvency and liquidity requirements of the Act
- ☐ where a corporation is deregistered while having outstanding liabilities. All members and previous members will be jointly and severally liable for any debts incurred by the corporation while they were members
- ☐ where a juristic person holds a member's interest to which he is not entitled. Such juristic person and any nominee will be liable for every debt of the corporation incurred during the time of such contravention.

The loss of limited liability under the above conditions affords creditors some protection and is an alternative to the 'maintenance of capital' concept which forms the basis of company law. It also provides a form of self-regulation in that members who disregard the rules of the system lose their protection by becoming personally and jointly liable for the obligations of the CC. These provisions have made it possible, to a large extent, to remove any criminal provisions from the CC Act.

20.4.5.4 Internal relations

Each member stands in a fiduciary relationship to the corporation and must:

- ☐ act honestly and in good faith and in particular shall exercise the powers which he has in the interests and for the benefit of the corporation, and not exceed these powers
- ☐ avoid any material conflict between his own interests and those of the corporation and notify all members of the nature and extent of any material interest which he may have in any contract of the corporation.

A member of a corporation whose acts or omissions breach this fiduciary relationship shall be liable to the corporation for any loss suffered or any economic benefit derived by the member by reason thereof. Except as regards his duty to exercise the powers that he has in the interests and for the benefit of the corporation, any other conduct of a member shall not constitute a breach of fiduciary duty if such conduct was preceded or followed by the written approval of all the members, who were aware of all the material facts. Any member of a corporation shall be liable to the corporation for loss caused by his failure to act with the degree of care and skill that may reasonably be expected of him. If the relevant conduct was preceded or followed by the written approval of all the members, who were aware of all the material facts, no liability for negligence will arise.

The members of a corporation may enter into a written association agreement which regulates any matter, including the internal relationship between members, provided that this is not inconsistent with the provisions of the Act. New members of the corporation will be bound by an existing association agreement as if they had signed as party thereto. According to the CC Act, the following rules will apply to internal relations, unless the association agreement provides otherwise:

- ☐ Every member is entitled to participate in the carrying on of the business.
- ☐ Every member has equal rights with regard to the management of the corporation.

- ☐ Written consent of 75% of members is required for any change in the principal business of the corporation; the disposal of the whole, or substantially the whole undertaking of the corporation; the disposal of all, or the greater portion of the assets of the corporation; and any acquisition or disposal of immovable property by the corporation.
- ☐ Differences between members regarding matters relating to the corporation are resolved by majority vote.
- ☐ Each member's number of votes corresponds with his percentage interest in the corporation.
- ☐ A corporation must reimburse any member for expenses incurred by him in the ordinary and proper conduct of the business of the corporation and anything done with regard to maintenance of the business or property of the corporation.
- ☐ Payments to members by reason only of their membership must be those amounts agreed upon and effected at such times as the members from time to time agree upon, providing that the corporation meets the solvency and liquidity requirements of the Act. Such payments must be in proportion to their respective interests in the corporation and include payments to members in the ordinary course of business, for example salaries, interest, rent or repayments of loans.

A corporation should not, without the prior written consent of all the members, make a direct or indirect loan to provide security for:

- ☐ any of its members
- ☐ any corporation in which one or more of its members jointly holds more than a 50% interest
- ☐ any company controlled by one or more members of the corporation.

20.4.5.5 External relations

Any pre-incorporation contract entered into by an agent or trustee of the corporation can be ratified by the corporation:

- ☐ by the written consent of all the members, and
- ☐ within the time specified in the contract, or if no time is specified, within a reasonable time after incorporation.

A corporation has no equivalent to the directors of a company. Each member is responsible for the operations of the corporation and has an equal right to participate in its management. Each member is an agent of the company in respect of business transacted with third parties in the normal course of business and has the power to bind the corporation. Any act of a member not connected with the ordinary course of the business of the corporation shall not bind the corporation unless it has been authorised or ratified. Where an association agreement restricts the power of any member to represent the corporation or where a member is disqualified from participating in the management of the business of the corporation no act of that member in contravention thereof is binding on the corporation with respect to any person who had, or ought reasonably to have had, knowledge of such restriction or disqualification. Persons who are not members of the corporation, are not entitled to insight into the association agreement, and therefore are considered not to have any knowledge of the conditions therein.

20.5 THE COMPANY

20.5.1 General

The property of an enterprise not having a legal personality, also referred to as a non-incorporated enterprise, belongs to the owner of that enterprise. The owner is personally responsible for the business's obligations and enters into all the legal transactions. Sole proprietorships and partnerships are the usual forms of enterprise without legal personality. With certain exceptions, most small and medium-sized business undertakings, as well as professional persons such as doctors, engineers, architects, accountants and lawyers, function as sole proprietorships or partnerships.

An enterprise which has a **legal personality**, that is an incorporated enterprise, on the other hand, has legal capacity and may own property, incur debts and enter into legal transactions in its **own right**, as if it were a person. Companies and CCs fall into this category.

A company may be described as a group of people (as in the case of a partnership) co-operating to make a profit. A company, however, is a **legal person**; it is incorporated according to legislation, and is an entity independent from its owners, who are called **members**. Therefore the company has an existence independent of the existence of its members, and has its own rights and obligations. In South Africa all matters pertaining to companies are governed by the Companies Act, 1973 (Act 61 of 1973).

Companies, as a form of enterprise, came into being to meet the need for:

- ☐ a means of acquiring more capital than is possible for a sole proprietor or a partnership
- ☐ a means of ensuring the continuity and permanence of the enterprise
- ☐ a convenient method of exchanging ownership
- ☐ a procedure to limit the financial responsibility of owners.

20.5.2 Shares and shareholders

In order to raise capital, a company issues shares to investors in the company. By purchasing shares an investor becomes a **shareholder**, or member of the company, and thus acquires owner's equity in the company.

Any person with contractual capacity, including other legal persons, may become a member of a company; this means that one company may be a shareholder or member of another company.

However, a company may not buy its own shares in order to become a member of itself, neither may a partnership become a member of a company, since it lacks legal personality and has no independent existence.

20.5.3 Rights and duties of shareholders

- ☐ **Change in ownership:** A member's interest in a company depends on the number of shares he holds in that company. Since shares are negotiable documents, each member has the power to sell his shares or a portion thereof to other persons with contractual capacity, or to buy additional shares from such persons.

  In the case of a public company, trading in shares is done on a stock exchange, with a stockbroker acting on the instructions of the shareholder.

- ☐ **Right to vote:** A shareholder has a right to vote on policy matters at annual general meetings. His voting rights are proportional to the number of shares he holds. Shareholders also appoint directors to manage the company on their behalf.

- ☐ **Distribution of profits:** Unless otherwise specified, the shareholder is entitled to a proportional share of only those profits which have been declared as dividends.
- ☐ **Right to assets:** Unless otherwise specified, a shareholder has the right, upon liquidation of the company, to share proportionally in the distribution of assets after all creditors' claims have been met.

20.5.4 Formation and management of a company

☐ Formation

One or more persons must take the initiative to form a company. They are known as the **founders** of the company. In order to form a company they must comply with the prescribed procedure for registration as laid down by the Companies Act. Briefly, this procedure is the following:

- ☐ The **memorandum** and articles of association are drawn up, usually with the aid of an attorney.
- ☐ Then the **articles of association** and memorandum are submitted, together with other prescribed forms, declarations and fees, to the Registrar of Companies.
- ☐ The company is formed when the Registrar certifies on the memorandum and the articles of association that the company has been incorporated.
- ☐ The Registrar then issues the company a certificate to commence business.

The most important aspects set out in the memorandum are:

- ☐ the purpose of forming the company, as well as its principal business activity
- ☐ the name of the company
- ☐ particulars of the share capital with which the company is registered.

In addition, the company's registered offices and postal address, and the name of its auditors must be indicated in the prescribed manner.

A company's external characteristics are largely determined by the memorandum, while its internal affairs and management are regulated by the articles of association. The rules laid down control matters pertaining to shares, the transfer of shares, authority to borrow, meetings, voting rights, powers and duties of directors, etc.

☐ Management

The management of a company is vested in the **board of directors** appointed by the shareholders in accordance with the Companies Act and the statutes.

The board of directors is the co-ordinating force of the company and its policy maker. The directors are not usually involved in the routine, daily activities of the company; they delegate these responsibilities to management and its staff.

The relationship between owners and management can be represented schematically as follows:

Figure 20.1

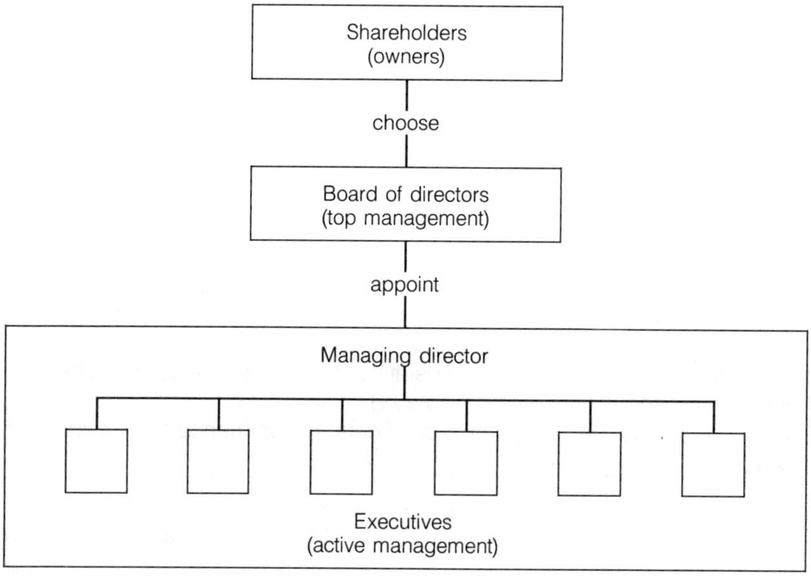

20.5.5 Types of companies

Two types of companies exist in South Africa, viz:

☐ Companies having share capital. ☐ Companies limited by guarantee.

The latter type of company seldom occurs, therefore only companies having share capital are discussed below.

Companies with share capital can be one of two types:

☐ Public companies. ☐ Private companies.

The name of a public company ends in 'Limited', while that of a private company ends in '(Proprietary) Limited'. The minimum number of members for a public company is seven, while a private company may have only one member.

When a small group of entrepreneurs who are able to provide the capital for an undertaking themselves form a company, they usually form a private company. The general public cannot become members of a private company; therefore the latter enjoys certain privileges not accorded to public companies in terms of the provisions of the Companies Act.

A private company can be considered to be a partnership in the form of a company. The statutes of a private company impose the following limitations:

- ☐ The transfer of shares is restricted.
- ☐ The number of members is limited to 50.
- ☐ The public cannot be invited to subscribe for shares or debentures.

A public company is not subject to these limitations.

20.6 THE DIFFERENCE BETWEEN COMPANIES, PARTNERSHIPS AND CLOSE CORPORATIONS

The following table shows the basic differences between the three forms of enterprise discussed in this chapter:

Characteristic	Sole proprietor	Partnership	Company	Close corporation
1 Number of members	One – the owner	Two or more, but not more than 20	Public company: Seven or more – no limit Private company: One or more – limited to 50	One or more, with a maximum of 10
2 Formation	Simple, only permits/licences depending on the type of business/occupation	Simple. Preferable to have a partnership agreement	Strict requirements in terms of Companies Act. Certificate to commence business required	Specific requirements, but uncomplicated. Founding statement and registration certificate required
3 Legal entity	Not a separate legal entity. Owner liable for obligations of the undertaking	Not a separate legal entity. Partners are jointly and severally liable for debts	A legal entity. Liability of shareholders in both types of company limited to amount invested in shares	Legal entity. Limited liability provided prescribed solvency and liquidity requirements are met
4 Management	Management by the owner. Responsibility and control rests with the same person	Management by owners. Joint responsibility and control	Public company: Must have two or more directors Private company: Must have at least one director	All members participate in management unless association agreement stipulates otherwise
5 Name of undertaking	No legal requirements	No legal requirements	Public company: Name ends with 'Limited' Private company: Name ends with '(Proprietary) Limited'	Name ends with CC (English) and BK (Afrikaans)
6 Policy changes	Unlimited within the constraints of the undertaking	With common consent	Limited – approval of directors and shareholders required	By mutual agreement
7 Provision of capital	Limited to capital contribution of one person – the owner	Limited to the number of partners and their personal contributions	Public company: Obtains capital through the issue of shares to members Private company: Obtains capital through the issue of shares to founders	Limited to members' contributions in terms of members' interest in the corporation
8 Income tax	Profit of the undertaking regarded as personal income of the owner and taxed accordingly	Each partner pays individually on his share of the profits	Company pays tax on profits. Shareholders taxed on dividends received from company	Close corporations are taxed at company rates. Members are not taxed on profits distributed

Characteristic	Sole proprietor	Partnership	Company	Close corporation
9 Transfer of rights	Not transferable	Not freely transferable – consent of partners a prerequisite	Public company: Freely traded and transferred Private company: Consent of fellow shareholders required for a transfer	Members may transfer their interest with the consent of all the other members. An amended founding statement is required
10 Continued existence	Theoretically the undertaking ceases to exist when the owner dies, although this is not always the case in practice	If a partner withdraws, the partnership is dissolved and a new partnership must be formed	Unlimited existence except for liquidation	Unlimited existence except for deregistration or liquidation

The owner's equity of the shareholders consists of the share capital plus the reserves, including the retained income, of the company. The accounting aspects hereof are discussed in more detail in a later chapter.

Profit distribution and allocation will be determined by the form of enterprise and the decision of the owner(s). In the case of a company, this decision rests with the management of the company, subject to the approval of the members.

21

ACCOUNTING ASPECTS OF THE PARTNERSHIP

The **AIM** of this chapter is to discuss various aspects of accounting specific to partnerships.

21.1 INTRODUCTION

The nature and characteristics of partnerships are discussed in chapter 20.

21.1.1 The temporary partnership

Entrepreneurs sometimes find it necessary to form a temporary partnership in order to conclude a series of transactions or to carry out a specific project, and share the resulting profit or loss according to a predetermined ratio.

This temporary partnership is automatically dissolved once the specific series of transactions or the project has been completed. In order that the affairs of the temporary partnership may be planned properly, it is essential that a partnership agreement is drawn up.

Temporary partnerships are also referred to as **joint ventures** or **consortiums**. The intended activities may range from straightforward business transactions to mammoth projects lasting several years and involving large-scale capital investment.

The only difference between a temporary and a permanent partnership is that the former terminates at a specific time or after a specific occurrence. Since the accounting treatment of both types is the same, they will simply be discussed as permanent partnerships.

The formation of a partnership – whether temporary or permanent – gives rise to both an economic entity and an accounting entity, and as an entity it must be accounted for by means of its own set of accounting records.

21.1.2 The permanent partnership

The accounting procedures and practices for recording the transactions and compiling the financial reports of a partnership are generally the same as those for any other form of enterprise geared to profit making. The nature of the partnership as a form of enterprise requires that attention be paid to certain accounting aspects, especially owner's equity accounts, at the time when:

- ☐ a partnership is established
- ☐ profit (or loss) is shared
- ☐ financial statements are compiled
- ☐ a new partner is admitted or an existing partner retires
- ☐ the partnership is dissolved.

This chapter deals mainly with the establishment of a partnership, the distribution of profit (or loss) and the compilation of financial statements.

21.2 RECORDING OWNER'S EQUITY IN PARTNERSHIPS

21.2.1 The difference between capital and profit

Owner's equity in a partnership, as in any other type of enterprise, is represented by the net assets of an enterprise. However, it is essential that each partner's equity is recorded separately.

Generally, a distinction is made between each partner's **capital contribution** and **retained profit**.

When owner's equity in partnerships is recorded, the two accounts below are usually used for each partner.

- Capital account

This account is used to record the relatively **permanent** contribution made by a partner to the firm.

- Current account

In addition to the capital account, it is customary to open a current account for each partner in the books of the partnership to record all the **current transactions** which influence a partner's equity, for example his share of the profit or loss, interest on capital, drawings, interest on drawings, and goods taken for personal use.

Frequently a separate account is used to record each partner's withdrawals. At the end of the financial year the balance on the drawings account is transferred to the partner's current account.

21.2.2 Valuation of contributions made by partners

It is apparent from the description of a partnership that on entering a partnership, each partner is expected to make a contribution. The nature of each partner's contribution need not be the same; a contribution may consist of **cash** or **other assets**, or even specialised **knowledge** or skill. The **amount** or the **value** (if in a non-monetary form) placed on a partner's contribution to the firm represents capital invested in the enterprise.

A problem which may arise when a partnership is established is difficulty in placing a value on assets other than cash contributed by a partner to the firm. All partners must agree that the value placed on such assets is fair and reasonable.

Sometimes a partner may contribute his own existing business to a new partnership. If the business is taken over for an amount greater than its net book value, the difference is regarded as **goodwill** and is recorded as such in the books of the newly formed enterprise.

A partner may contribute certain rights and contracts, or even expertise in the field in which the firm intends to operate. The value of such contributions must be **capitalised** and shown as an asset in the books of the partnership in order to determine the partnership's capital investment.

Example 21.1

The following are the abbreviated balance sheets of A and B on 28 February 19.8. In terms of a lease agreement, A has been conducting his business on premises belonging to B. On 1 March 19.8 they decide to form a partnership.

A
BALANCE SHEET AT 28/2/19.8

ASSETS	Cost price	Depreciation	Book value	EQUITIES	
				Capital	47 000
Fixed assets				Current liabilities	
Machinery	20 000	9 000	11 000	Creditors	4 000
Vehicles	8 000	3 000	5 000		
	R28 000	R12 000	16 000		
Current assets			35 000		
Inventory			20 000		
Debtors			14 000		
Cash			1 000		
			R51 000		R51 000

B
BALANCE SHEET AT 28/2/19.8

ASSETS		EQUITIES	
Fixed property at cost	70 000	Capital	40 000
		Bond on fixed property	30 000
	R70 000		R70 000

The partnership agreement stipulates that all existing assets and liabilities will be taken over at the following valuations:

A:	Machinery at book value	11 000
	Vehicles at market value	4 000
	Inventory at book value	20 000
	Debtors less provision for doubtful debts	12 000
	Goodwill	10 000
		57 000
	Less: Creditors	4 000
		R53 000
B:	Buildings at market value	80 000
	Less: Bond	30 000
		R50 000

In order to improve the liquidity of the concern, B will contribute an additional R5 000 in cash.

The opening journal entries in the partnership's books will appear as follows:

			Remarks
Machinery	11 000		1
Vehicles	4 000		1
Inventory	20 000		1
Debtors	14 000		2
Goodwill	10 000		3
Provision for doubtful debts		2 000	2
Creditors		4 000	
Capital A		53 000	
Recording A's contributions to partnership at agreed values			
Fixed property	80 000		1
Cash	5 000		
Bond		30 000	
Capital B		55 000	
Recording B's contributions to partnership			

Remarks:

(1) **Fixed assets:** Fixed assets are shown in the partnership's books at the values at which they were taken over, regardless of their original cost price and any provision for depreciation. Depreciation will be calculated on the new values and the expected economic life of the asset.

(2) **Debtors:** Debtors are usually shown in the partnership's books at book value, since at the time of valuation it may be difficult to determine which debtors will not settle their accounts. The net result of the revaluation is obtained by creating a provision for doubtful debts which is equal to the difference between the original book value and the revalued amount.

(3) **Goodwill:** The value of the goodwill pertaining to A's present enterprise may be based on one or more different factors, such as quality of products or services provided, effectiveness of management, the possession of valuable patent rights and agencies, favourable location or expert knowledge. Generally 'goodwill' is reflected in an enterprise's books only if it is actually purchased. Where, for example, a specific value is placed on goodwill on the purchase or take-over of a business (i e a 'price' was paid for it, as in this example), the goodwill is shown as such in the firm's balance sheet.

21.2.3 Loans and advances

Over and above his original capital contribution, a partner may make a **loan** or advance to the partnership (as a separate accounting entity) in his **personal capacity**. In the case of such loans the partner is regarded as a creditor of the partnership, and the loan does not form part of his 'permanent' investment (capital) in the partnership. Loans of this type usually bear **interest** at a specified rate, the interest being an expense incurred in the normal course of the partnership's affairs and not part of the profit distribution. These loans, unlike the partners' capital contributions, are usually repayable after a certain period.

21.3 DETERMINATION AND DISTRIBUTION OF PARTNERSHIP PROFIT

21.3.1 Determination of profit

The partnership agreement should stipulate the manner in which profit (or loss) should be divided. The partnership profit is calculated periodically in the income statement, in the same way as for any other type of enterprise. However, since there are several owners sharing the profit (or loss) on a predetermined basis, there must be an allocation of the profit.

21.3.2 Distribution of profit

Partnership profit (or loss) may be divided in any way agreed upon by the partners. Although the ratio in which profit is allocated may be linked to the capital contributed, this need not necessarily be the case, since a partner's value to the firm may also be affected by other factors such as his business acumen, qualifications, expertise and the amount of time he gives to the enterprise.

If profit (or loss) is to be allocated fairly, at least two factors, namely capital invested and services provided, should be taken into consideration.

A partner who has invested more capital or who provides more services than other partners should, generally speaking, receive a larger portion of the profit. Similarly, if the partnership suffers a loss such partner should bear a greater proportion of that loss.

Generally the following methods are used to divide profit:

- ☐ specified (fixed) ratios
- ☐ partners' relative capital investments
- ☐ services contributed by partners.

The following data is used to illustrate the different methods of profit allocation (and some variations thereof):

- ☐ A and B have been in partnership since 1 January 19.2.
- ☐ A made an initial investment of R80 000 on 1 January 19.2 and a further investment of R20 000 on 1 April 19.2.
- ☐ On 1 January 19.2 B invested R160 000, R10 000 of which he withdrew on 1 October 19.2.
- ☐ The partnership agreement stipulates that at the end of each month each partner may draw R1 000 as an advance on expected profit. (Note: These withdrawals in no way affect the distribution of the net profit – they are simply debited against the partners' current or drawings accounts.)
- ☐ The profit earned by the firm for the year ended 31 December 19.2 amounted to R60 000.

☐ Specified or fixed ratio

If no profit-sharing ratio is agreed upon or stipulated by the partners, the profit is divided equally according to common law principles. Partners may, however, specify any ratio which they deem appropriate.

Example 21.2

Assume that the agreement between A and B stipulates that A, by virtue of wider experience in the partnership's sphere of activity, should receive 3/5 of the profit, while B receives the remaining 2/5. Then the profit will be allocated as follows:

Net profit to be allocated	A (3/5 or 60%)	B (2/5 or 40%)
R60 000	R36 000	R24 000

☐ **Relative capital ratio of partners**

Since capital invested is an income-generating factor, the relative capital contributed by each partner must be considered when the profit-sharing ratio is determined. Since balances on capital accounts change, the intended capital ratio must be stipulated clearly, for example:

- ☐ the capital ratio as at the **beginning** of the period
- ☐ the capital ratio as at the **end** of the period
- ☐ the **average ratio during** the period.

Example 21.3 Division according to initial capital ratio

Net profit to be allocated	A	B
R60 000	Capital: R80 000 Ratio: 1/3 (1) Share: R20 000	Capital: R160 000 Ratio: 2/3 (2) Share: R40 000
(1) A: $R\frac{80\ 000}{240\ 000} = 1/3$ (2) B: $R\frac{160\ 000}{240\ 000} = 2/3$		

Example 21.4 Division according to closing balances on capital accounts

Net profit to be allocated	A	B
R60 000	Closing balance: R100 000 (1) Ratio: 2/5 Share: R24 000	Closing balance: R150 000 (2) Ratio: 3/5 Share: R36 000
(1) A: R80 000 + R20 000 = 100 000 $\therefore \frac{100\ 000}{250\ 000} = 2/5$ of 40% (2) B: R160 000 − R10 000 = 150 000 $\therefore \frac{150\ 000}{250\ 000} = 3/5$ of 60%		

Example 21.5 Division according to average capital ratio

Since the amount of capital invested by each partner may change considerably during the course of any financial period, it is preferable to use the average capital as the basis for profit division, because this represents the funds actually available for use by the firm during that year. The **average figure** may be calculated in various ways, for example daily and quarterly. In the example below the calculations are based on monthly figures:

Partner	Date	Contribution	Total	Weight factor (months unchanged)	Weighted product
A:	1 Jan	+ 80 000	80 000	3	240 000
	1 Apr	+ 20 000	100 000	9	900 000
				12	R1 140 000
		∴ Average capital:		$\frac{R1\ 140\ 000}{12}$	= R95 000
B:	1 Jan	+ 160 000	160 000	9	1 440 000
	1 Oct	− 10 000	150 000	3	450 000
				12	R1 890 000
		∴ Average capital:		$\frac{R1\ 890\ 000}{12}$	= R157 500

Net profit to be allocated	A	B
R60 000	R22 574 (1)	R37 426 (2)

(1) A: 95 000 ∴ $\frac{95\ 000}{252\ 500}$ = 22 574

(2) B: 157 500 ∴ $\frac{157\ 500}{252\ 000}$ = 37 426

Totals: R252 500 and R60 000

21.3.3 Service contributions by partners

As compensation for services rendered by partners to the partnership (e g a partner serving as full-time manager to the partnership), the partnership agreement usually provides for payment of a salary to such partners over and above their share of the profit, allocated in the normal profit-sharing ratio.

This practice gives rise to two contradictory points of view:

- Legally, the salary paid to a partner is an **integral part of the procedure of allocating profit (or loss)**. Partners cannot, as members of the partnership, enter into a contractual relationship of employer/employee with themselves. Like the owners of sole proprietorships, partners cannot legally employ themselves, nor pay themselves salaries. Legally, therefore, the 'salary allowance' awarded to partners is regarded as a portion of their share of the profit.

☐ Despite the legal point of view above, salaries paid to partners are frequently treated as **salary expenses** in the income statements of partnerships. This procedure arises from the **entity concept**; the partnership, as an accounting entity, is deemed to be an economic unit. In order to determine the return on capital* of the unit, the cost of all resources applied in generating income must be brought into account. The work performed by a partner on behalf of the partnership represents the use of a resource, and as such it must be treated as a cost in determining the profit of the enterprise.

☐ **Remuneration for services**

Example 21.6

Assume that, according to the agreement, B receives a salary of R10 000 per annum, after which the profit is divided equally. The profit will be allocated as follows:

	Net profit	A	B
Net profit before salary	60 000		
Less: Salary awarded	(10 000)		10 000
Net profit after salary	50 000		
Profit divided equally	(50 000)	25 000	25 000
		R25 000	R35 000
		= R60 000	

☐ **Loss and remuneration for services**

Where an agreement stipulates that a partner should receive a salary, this must be paid to him irrespective of whether there is sufficient profit.

*It is important to the owner of an enterprise to know whether the concern (as a separate entity) is profitable and whether it is worthwhile continuing the business. If not, it may be financially more rewarding to employ his talents in an alternative manner.

Example 21.7

Assume that the firm made a profit of only R8 000, and that R10 000 is due to B as his salary, after which the profit (or loss) is to be divided equally:

	Net profit	A	B
Net profit before salary	8 000		
Less: Salary awarded	(10 000)	—	10 000
Net profit after salary	(2 000)		
Loss divided equally	(2 000)	(1 000)	(1 000)
		(R1 000)	R9 000
		= R8 000	

21.3.4 Bonus payable to managing partner

Partnership agreements often stipulate that a managing partner should receive a **bonus** based on a percentage of the net income.

Example 21.8

Assume that the partnership agreement between A and B allows for a bonus of 10% of net income payable to managing partner B, and for the remaining profit to be divided equally. If the net income is R66 000, the allocation will be as follows:

	Net profit	A	B
Net profit before bonus	66 000		
Less: Bonus to B (10%)	(6 600)		6 600
Profit after bonus	59 400		
Profit divided equally	(59 400)	29 700	29 700
		R29 700	R36 300
		= R66 000	

21.3.5 Interest on capital

In order to compensate a partner **who has made a larger capital contribution than another partner**, it is customary for interest on capital to be brought into account before the remaining profit (or loss) is allocated in a specified ratio. If the agreement stipulates that 10% interest on capital should be brought into account first, this means that a **limited** portion of the profit is divided according to the ratio of the partners' capital, and the balance probably according to a different ratio.

Should the partners agree to bring interest on capital into account, they must stipulate the **interest rate** as well as the basis for the calculation (average, opening or closing capital balances).

☐ Allocation of interest on capital on making a profit

Example 21.9

Assume that the partnership agreement stipulates that interest of 10% per annum on the partners' average capital should be paid and the remaining profit divided equally.

	Net profit	A	B
Net profit before interest on capital	60 000		
Less: Interest on average capital			
A: 10% x R95 000	(9 500)	9 500	
B: 10% x R157 500	(15 750)		15 750
Net profit after interest on capital	34 750		
Profit divided equally	(34 750)	17 375	17 375
		R26 875	R33 125
		= R60 000	

Interest on capital paid for unequal capital contributions automatically represents remuneration for capital invested; therefore it is a division of available profit and not an operating cost.

If, on the other hand, a partner were to **lend** the partnership money, the interest on the **loan** would be regarded as an **operating cost**.

☐ Allocation of interest on capital on making a loss

Example 21.10

Assume that the partnership suffers a loss of R40 000, and that the stipulations concerning interest on capital and division of profit are the same as in example 21.9. The interest stipulation must be given effect despite the loss suffered, unless the partners decide otherwise.

	Net loss	A	B
Net loss before interest on capital	(40 000)		
Less: Interest on average capital			
(calculated as in example 17.9)	(25 250)	9 500	15 750
	(65 250)		
Loss divided equally	(65 250)	(32 625)	(32 625)
		(R23 125)	(R16 875)
		= (R40 000)	

An analysis of the above calculation reveals that B's capital shows a net increase in relation to A's capital, in spite of the loss suffered.

	A	B	Difference
Capital originally provided	80 000	160 000	80 000 in B's favour
Division of loss after taking into account interest on capital	−23 125	−16 875	
Balance	R56 875	R143 125	86 250 in B's favour
			+R6 250

An increase in one partner's capital in relation to that of another when the firm has suffered a loss seems illogical. However, the loss is not attributable to capital investment. B, having contributed considerably more capital than A, is compensated for this contribution in the form of interest on capital.

21.3.6 Adjustments and corrections in respect of previous financial periods

It is not uncommon for a concern to find that mistakes were made in the determination of profit in an earlier financial period, for example errors in the calculation of depreciation and the valuation of inventory and omissions of income and/or expenses. In a partnership there is the additional possibility that there may have been non-compliance with the stipulations of the partnership agreement concerning, for example, the allocation of profit.

The essence of these errors is whether:

- the correction should be treated as part of the current year's profit determination; or
- it should be treated as an adjustment to the partners' equity at the beginning of the current year.

Each case must be treated on its own merit. The materiality of the error will usually be the deciding factor in the choice of the method of adjustment.

21.4 FINANCIAL STATEMENTS OF PARTNERSHIPS

Details of the allocation of net income to partners are usually disclosed in the appropriation section of the income statement. Particulars of partners' equity can be included in the partnership's balance sheet, or may be disclosed in an explanatory note to the balance sheet.

The following abbreviated example illustrates the characteristic form of the financial statements of a partnership:

Example 21.11

AB DEALERS
INCOME STATEMENT FOR THE YEAR ENDED 31 DECEMBER 19.2

Sales			500 000
Less: Cost of sales			300 000
Gross profit on sales			200 000
Less: Operating costs			180 000
Profit available for division			R20 000
Divided as follows:	A	B	
Salary B	—	10 000	10 000
Interest on capital	4 000	2 000	6 000
Profit divided equally	2 000	2 000	4 000
	R6 000	R14 000	R20 000

BALANCE SHEET AT 31 DECEMBER 19.2

			A	B	
ASSETS		EQUITIES			
Sundry assets (details)	100 000	Owner's equity			83 000
		Capital	40 000	38 000	
		Current accounts (note)	1 000	4 000	
			R41 000	R42 000	
		Sundry liabilities			17 000
	R100 000				R100 000

Note: Partners' current accounts

	A	B
Credit balance 31 December 19.1	2 000	2 000
Add: Salary	—	10 000
Interest on capital	4 000	2 000
Net profit	2 000	2 000
	8 000	16 000
Less: Drawings	7 000	12 000
	R1 000	R4 000

21.5 GOODWILL

It is the aim of any trading concern to build up a sound reputation. This reputation may be based on the quality of the services or goods supplied, the efficiency of good management, the ownership of valuable patents and agencies, or the fact that the business premises are located in a central and convenient place.

Since no price was paid for it, this 'value' or intangible asset which a concern builds up is usually not reflected in the financial statements. In accounting terms it is known as **goodwill**. When a concern is purchased and a value is placed on the goodwill (i e a price is paid) it will be reflected as such in the statements.

In the case of companies this value is reflected by the market price of the shares. However, in the case of sole proprietorships, partnerships and close corporations, it is necessary to make a subjective valuation thereof.

Therefore, on the purchase or sale of a concern, or on the dissolving of a partnership, it is common practice to value the assets, including goodwill.

21.6 ADMISSION OF A NEW PARTNER

Providing the existing partners approve, a new partner can be admitted to a partnership in one of two ways, namely:

- ☐ by purchasing an interest directly from one or more of the existing partners; or
- ☐ by contributing cash and/or assets to the partnership in order to obtain an interest.

As soon as a new partner is admitted the old partnership ceases to exist. However, it is not necessary to close off the books of the partnership, since the partnership as a form of enterprise still exists. All that is required is to make the necessary entries to give effect to the admission of the new partner. (NB)

The ways in which an interest can be obtained are presented schematically in figure 21.1.

Figure 21.1

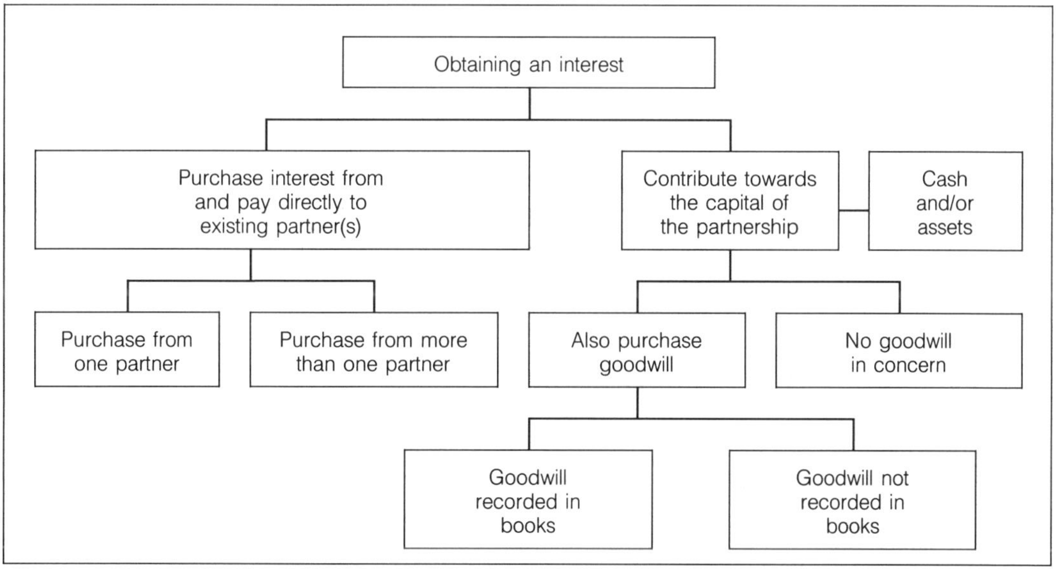

21.6.1 Admission by way of direct purchase of a partner's interest

When a partner is admitted in this way, no entries are necessary in the asset or liability accounts of the partnership. However, an adjustment must be made to the capital accounts.

Example 21.12

Case 1

On 31 December 19.3, A and B, who share profits in the ratio 2:3, decide to admit C to the partnership from 1 January 19.4. At 31 December 19.3 the balance on A's capital account is R21 000 and on B's R30 000. C is admitted on condition that he purchases one half of B's share for R25 000 cash, which he has to pay directly to B and not into the partnership.

One half of B's share = R15 000 ($\frac{1}{2}$ × R30 000), and the journal entry is as follows:

Capital B Capital C *Admission of C as new partner*	15 000	 15 000

No entry is made in respect of the R25 000, since this is a private transaction between B and C. Although C purchases one half of B's **interest**, this does not necessarily mean that this portion of the profit (or loss) will be allocated to him. The profit-sharing ratio is a matter which must be agreed upon specifically.

Assume that it is also agreed that B will relinquish one half of his share of the profit to C. The new profit-sharing ratio will be as follows:

A:	$\frac{2}{5}$
B: ($\frac{3}{5} - (\frac{1}{2} \times \frac{3}{5})$)	$\frac{3}{10}$
C: $\frac{1}{2} \times \frac{3}{5}$	$\frac{3}{10}$

Note that although the book value of B's interest was R30 000, C was prepared to pay R25 000 for half of the interest. This indicates that goodwill existed and that B brought this into account in calculating the value of his interest.

After the admission of C the capital will appear in the balance sheet as follows:

Capital	A:	21 000
	B:	15 000 (30 000 – 15 000)
	C:	15 000

Note that the total capital (R51 000) is the same as it was before C's admission, since C made no cash contribution to the assets of the partnership.

Case 2

The circumstances are the same as in case 1, but C pays R25 000 for one third of A's interest plus one third of B's interest. (In other words, C purchases a one-third interest in the partnership from A and B.)

The journal entry will be as follows:

Capital A: ($\frac{1}{3}$ × R21 000) Capital B: ($\frac{1}{3}$ × R30 000) Capital C *Admission of C as new partner*	7 000 10 000	 17 000

In this case A and B must decide how much of the R25 000 should be paid to each of them.

If it is accepted that C will also receive a one-third share of the profit, the new profit-sharing ratio will be as follows:

A: $(2/5 - (1/3 \times 2/5))$	$4/15$
B: $(3/5 - (1/3 \times 3/5))$	$6/15$
C: $((1/3 \times 2/5) + (1/3 \times 3/5))$	$5/15$

After the admission of C the capital will appear as follows:

Capital A:	14 000 (21 000 – 7 000)
B:	20 000 (30 000 – 10 000)
C:	17 000

Note once again that the total capital remains the same.

21.6.2 Obtaining an interest by contributing to the capital

Where a new partner brings cash and/or assets (hereinafter referred to as sundry assets) into the partnership, the journal entry is simple: debit sundry assets and credit the new partner's capital account. However, where goodwill is involved this must be determined and credited to the 'old' partners in their 'old' profit-sharing ratio first, since this intangible asset forms part of their capital in the concern.

Before the various cases which may be encountered are explained, a procedure to be followed when admitting a new partner under these circumstances is recommended:

- ☐ Determine the amount of capital which must be credited to the new partner.
- ☐ Determine the total capital of the partnership.
- ☐ Determine whether goodwill is involved.
- ☐ Determine whether and to what extent the old partners must bring in or withdraw capital to bring the various capital balances into an agreed ratio (if applicable in terms of the agreement).
- ☐ Journalise goodwill (if any).
- ☐ Journalise the new partner's capital.
- ☐ Journalise adjustments in respect of old partners' capital (where applicable).

Example 21.13

A and B are partners in AB Traders, sharing profit (or loss) in the ratio 2:3. They decide to admit C as a partner with a one-third share in the partnership and a one-third share in the profit (or loss).

Before the admission of C the balance sheet of AB Traders was as follows:

AB TRADERS
BALANCE SHEET

Sundry assets	100 000	Capital A	20 000
		Capital B	30 000
		Sundry liabilities	50 000
	R100 000		R100 000

The profit-sharing ratio between A and B remains the same as before, in other words:

A: $2/5 - (1/3 \times 2/5) = 4/15$
B: $3/5 - (1/3 \times 3/5) = 6/15$
(or 4:6 or 2:3)
C's share of the profit is $1/3$ or $5/15$
The new profit-sharing ratio is therefore A:B:C = 4:6:5

□ Admission without goodwill

Assume that C pays R25 000 for his one-third share in the partnership.

(a) Total capital of the partnership is therefore 3 × R25 000 = R75 000

(b)

Capital	A	20 000
	B	30 000
	C	25 000
Total capital		R75 000

(Thus there is no goodwill involved.)

(c) The journal entry will be as follows:

Sundry assets	25 000	
Capital C		25 000
Admission of C as partner		

The balance sheet of the partnership after the admission of C will be as follows:

ABC TRADERS
BALANCE SHEET

Sundry assets	125 000	Capital A	20 000
		Capital B	30 000
		Capital C	25 000
		Sundry liabilities	50 000
	R125 000		R125 000

□ Admission with goodwill

Example 21.14

Assume that C pays R30 000 for his one-third share in the partnership.

(a) Total capital is therefore 3 × R30 000 = R90 000

(b)

Capital	A	20 000
	B	30 000
	C	30 000
		80 000
∴ Total capital		90 000
Goodwill		R10 000

In other words, the current capital of A and B = R50 000. However, their capital is valued at $2/3 \times$ R90 000 = R60 000, thus goodwill = R10 000.

The asset goodwill has been built up by the old partners. For purposes of admission of the new partner, this asset, which does not yet appear in the books of the partnership, is allocated to the old partners in their profit-sharing ratio.

(c) The following journal entries will be made:

Goodwill	10 000	
Capital A: (2/5)		4 000
Capital B: (3/5)		6 000
Goodwill on admission of C		
Sundry assets	30 000	
Capital C		30 000
Admission of C as partner		

The balance sheet will be as follows after the admission of C:

ABC TRADERS
BALANCE SHEET

Sundry assets		Capital A	24 000
(100 000 + 30 000)	130 000	Capital B	36 000
Goodwill	10 000	Capital C	30 000
		Sundry liabilities	50 000
	R140 000		R140 000

However, it may also happen that the new partner brings goodwill into the partnership. In this case an agreement will be reached as to its value and it will be debited, together with all the other assets brought in, with a credit to the new partner's capital account.

☐ Admission with goodwill but without it being shown in the books

Because the partnership does not pay for goodwill (unless, of course, it has purchased it), and because its determination and value involves such a strong subjective element, partners are often hesitant to show it in the books. They then agree that goodwill will be determined for purposes of admission of a new partner, but that it will not be shown in the books.

In this case, the goodwill is still credited to the old partners in the old profit-sharing ratio, but then is written back to **all** the partners in the **new profit-sharing ratio**.

Example 21.15

Goodwill is R10 000, as in the previous example, and the journal entries are as follows:

Goodwill
  Capital A: (2/5)
  Capital B: (3/5)
Goodwill on admission of C
	10 000	
		4 000
		6 000

Sundry assets Capital C *Admission of C as partner*	30 000	 30 000
Capital A: (4/15) Capital B: (6/15) Capital C: (5/15) Goodwill *Goodwill in new profit-sharing ratio written back*	2 666 4 000 3 334	 10 000

The balance sheet will appear as follows after the admission of C:

ABC TRADERS BALANCE SHEET			
Sundry assets	130 000	Capital A: (20 000 + 4 000 − 2 666)	21 334
		Capital B: (30 000 + 6 000 − 4 000)	32 000
		Capital C: (30 000 − 3 334)	26 666
		Sundry liabilities	50 000
	R130 000		R130 000

21.7 RETIREMENT OF A PARTNER

On the retirement of a partner the accounting procedure is basically the same as on the admission of a new partner.

The partner's interest in the concern is valued and, if goodwill exists, it is credited to the partners' capital accounts.

The retiring partner must be reimbursed for his share on some or other agreed basis. If the reimbursement is not paid in cash, it will be transferred to a loan account and paid as agreed.

Example 21.16

Case 1

On 31 December 19.4, A decides to retire from the partnership. Goodwill is valued at R15 000. It is agreed that the amount owing to A will be credited to a loan account and repaid to him in five annual instalments at 10% interest per annum. In future the remaining partners will share profit (or loss) in their old profit-sharing ratio.

On 31 December 19.4 the capital balances are as follows:

A: R25 000
B: R35 000
C: R30 000

The following journal entries will be made:

Goodwill
  Capital A: (4/15)
  Capital B: (6/15)
  Capital C: (5/15)
Goodwill on A's retirement
	15 000	
		4 000
		6 000
		5 000

Capital A: (25 000 + 4 000) Loan account A *Transfer to loan account of amount owing to A*	29 000	 29 000

In future B and C will share profit (or loss) in the ratio 6:5, as previously they shared profit in the ratio 6/15 and 5/15.

Case 2

The same circumstances as in the previous case apply, but the remaining partners decide that goodwill should not be shown in the books.

The journal entries to be made are the same, but the following additional entry must also be made:

Capital B: (6/11) Capital C: (5/11) Goodwill *Goodwill written back*	8 182 6 818	 15 000

21.8 SIMULTANEOUS RETIREMENT AND ADMISSION OF PARTNERS

The accounting procedure for simultaneous retirement and admission is the same as for an independent retirement and an independent admission, but it is preferable to finalise the transactions for the old partnership, namely the retirement, before making the entries for the admission, that is the new partnership.

22

CLOSE CORPORATIONS

The nature and characteristics of close corporations are discussed in chapter 18. The **AIM** of this chapter is to explain the accounting, reporting and financial aspects of close corporations.

22.1 ACCOUNTING AND REPORTING REQUIREMENTS

22.1.1 Keeping accounting records

A corporation must keep such accounting records as are necessary to fairly present the state of affairs and business of the corporation and to explain the transactions and financial position of the corporation. These requirements correspond with the requirements of section 284 of the Companies Act. The requirements, although similar, differ in some respects. The most important requirements are the following.

Companies and close corporations (CCs) must keep the following records:

- records showing assets and liabilities
- a register of fixed assets
- records containing daily entries of all cash received and disbursed
- records of all credit purchases or sales and services received or rendered on credit, in sufficient detail to identify the nature of the transactions and the parties concerned
- statements of annual stock taking
- records enabling the value of stock at the end of the year to be determined
- vouchers supporting entries in the accounting records.

A corporation must also keep the following:

- records of members' contributions, undrawn profits, revaluations of fixed assets and amounts of loans to and from members, in sufficient detail to identify the nature and purpose of the individual transactions clearly.

These records must be kept in such a manner as to provide adequate precautions against falsification and to facilitate the discovery of any such falsification. A corporation which fails to keep such records, and every member who fails to take all reasonable steps to prevent falsification, is guilty of an offence. However, if the members entrusted the duty of keeping the accounting records or maintaining a system of internal control to a 'competent and reliable person', this would be sufficient defence.

22.1.2 Financial year

The financial year of a CC is its annual accounting period. A CC must specify the date of the end of its financial year in its founding statement. As is the case with other information in the founding statement, the date of the end of the financial year may be changed by registering an amended founding statement.

22.1.3 Annual financial statements

The members of a corporation must, within a maximum of nine months after the end of every financial year, have financial statements prepared. The financial statements must be approved and signed by or on behalf of every member of the corporation and must consist of:

- a balance sheet and notes thereto
- an income statement or any similar financial statement, where such form is appropriate, and any notes thereto.

The financial statements must disclose separately the aggregate amounts at the end of the financial year and any changes in these amounts during the year of the following items:

- ☐ contributions by members
- ☐ undrawn profits
- ☐ revaluations of fixed assets
- ☐ amounts of loans to members
- ☐ amounts of loans from members.

The Close Corporations Act does not require a directors' report or an auditor's report and also does not contain a schedule comparable to schedule 4 of the Companies Act, which lays down specific requirements for the preparation of annual financial statements.

22.1.4 Generally accepted accounting practice and the financial statements of close corporations

The financial statements of a CC must, in conformity with generally accepted accounting practice appropriate to the business of the corporation, fairly present the state of affairs of the corporation at the end of the financial year concerned and the result of its operations for the year. Fair presentation is the main requirement in the preparation of the financial statements of a CC. The Close Corporations Act does not contain any specific disclosure requirements, and this places the onus on members to ensure that the detail disclosed in the financial statements is pertinent and sufficient to provide a fair presentation.

The requirement that the financial statements must be prepared in accordance with generally accepted accounting practice implies that the four basic accounting concepts (going concern, matching, prudence and consistency) serve as the basis for the financial statements of a CC.

These four concepts are the basis of the periodic financial statements of all business concerns and are so generally accepted that they require no explanation in published financial statements. Due to the diverse and complex nature of different enterprises and business transactions, over the years many methods have been developed for applying these concepts to individual financial transactions. When financial statements are prepared, bases applicable to these concepts and suitable to the specific circumstances of the enterprise must be used. In determining applicable bases, attention should be paid to substance over legal form and to materiality.

As with other forms of enterprise, the basis of presentation, usually called the accounting policy, should be disclosed in the financial statements of a corporation. The concept materiality implies that the accounting policy should be disclosed for all those items which are considered material or critical to the fair presentation of the result of operations for the period and the financial position at the end of the period.

In determining what constitutes generally acceptable accounting policy for the business of a particular corporation, the needs of the members and the primary users of the financial statements should be taken into account.

Over the years, accounting practices in the various economic and industrial environments have developed in such a manner as to record and fairly present transactions and occurrences specific to these environments. In deciding what is 'suitable for the business', consideration should also be given to the commercial and management activities of the corporation and the accepted accounting practice in the working environment of the corporation. A company which is converted to a corporation does not change its economic and industrial nature. The previous accounting practices of the company converted to a corporation are therefore still relevant and applicable to its new legal form. Some of the disclosures required by the Companies Act which are not considered to be material or which are unnecessary for fair presentation can, however, be ignored.

It is the responsibility of the members to ensure that the financial statements fairly present the affairs of the corporation and that they have been prepared in accordance with generally accepted accounting practice suitable to the business of the corporation. If the members fail to comply with this responsibility, they can be guilty of mismanagement.

22.2 THE ACCOUNTING OFFICER

22.2.1 Appointment

The Act requires every corporation to appoint an accounting officer. No person qualifies for appointment unless he is a member of a recognised profession which:

- ☐ as a condition of membership requires its members to pass an examination in accounting and related fields of study
- ☐ has the power to exclude from membership those persons found guilty of negligence in the performance of their duties or of conduct which is discreditable to their profession.

The Minister may from time to time publish the names of those professions whose members are qualified to act as accounting officers.

If the office of accounting officer is vacant for six months, those members who are aware thereof become jointly and severally liable for all the debts of the corporation incurred while the post is vacant.

The Close Corporations Act does not lay down any requirements regarding the remuneration of the accounting officer; this must be mutually agreed upon by the accounting officer and the members.

22.2.2 Duties

The duties of the accounting officer are detailed in the Close Corporations Act. The accounting officer is required to:

- ☐ determine whether the financial statements are in accordance with the accounting records
- ☐ determine the accounting policies applied in the preparation of the financial statements
- ☐ report to the members on the above matters.

Where the accounting officer is a member or employee of a corporation, he must state this fact in his report. In performing his duties the accounting officer has, in accordance with the Close Corporations Act, right of access to the accounting records and other information of the corporation and is entitled to obtain any necessary explanations from members. If, during the performance of his duties, an accounting officer becomes aware of any contravention of a provision of the Close Corporations Act, he must describe the nature of the contravention in his report, irrespective of whether the contravention is material.

If the accounting officer becomes aware during the performance of his duties that any change in the particulars of the founding statement have not been registered, or that the financial statements indicate that as at the end of the financial year concerned the corporation's liabilities exceed its assets, he must report forthwith, by registered post, to the Registrar. If the accounting officer at any time knows, or has reason to believe, that the corporation is not carrying on business and has no intention of resuming operations in the foreseeable future, he must immediately report same to the Registrar.

22.2.3 Resignation or removal

An accounting officer who resigns or who is removed from office must immediately inform every member of the corporation thereof in writing and must send a copy of his letter to the registered office of the corporation. An accounting officer who is removed from office must consider the reasons for his removal. If he considers that he was removed for invalid reasons, he must immediately inform the Registrar and send a copy of his letter to every member of the corporation.

22.3 THE TAXATION SITUATION OF THE CLOSE CORPORATION AND ITS MEMBERS

A corporation is defined as a company in the Income Tax Act and will be considered to be a private company for purposes of taxation. A member of a corporation is included in the definition of 'shareholder' as it appears in the Income Tax Act. A member of a corporation is considered to be an officer of the corporation, and, since he is actively involved in its affairs, the employee fringe benefit provisions of the Income Tax Act will normally be applicable to him. Such a member will, for example, be entitled to any retirement gratuities. A member of a corporation who is usually a resident of the Republic of South Africa will, unless the Commissioner for Inland Revenue decides otherwise, be a provisional taxpayer.

The taxable income of a corporation is subject to normal income tax at the same rate as a company (currently 50%).

The dividend income of a CC is subject to normal taxation, but a one-third deduction is allowed. Generally, distributions of income to members are not subject to tax in the hands of members. The 'deemed' income provisions in respect of advances, loans and distribution of assets by private companies are not applicable to a corporation. A CC is not *per se* liable for undistributed profits tax, but is not exempt from donations tax. In particular, it should be noted that if there is a change in a member's interest without sufficient compensation, liability for donations tax may arise.

22.4 CONVERSION OF A COMPANY TO A CLOSE CORPORATION

An existing company comprising 10 or less members who are all natural persons or who otherwise qualify for membership may be converted to a corporation. The requirements are that:

- every member of the company becomes a member of the corporation
- an application form signed by all the members, containing a statement that upon conversion the assets of the corporation, fairly valued, will exceed its liabilities and that the corporation will be able to pay its debts as they become due in the ordinary course of its business, must be lodged with the Registrar

- ☐ a written statement by the auditor of the company that there is no reason to believe that a material irregularity has taken place or is taking place in the company, must be lodged with the Registrar
- ☐ a founding statement must be submitted.

The requirements in respect of cancellation of the registration of a company which is converted into a corporation are detailed in section 29B of the Companies Act, 1973 as amended.

The total members' contributions arising from the conversion must not be greater than the excess of the fair value of assets over liabilities which are to be transferred. Any portion of such excess which is not reflected as members' contributions can be divided among the members after conversion, but due consideration should be given to the tax implications arising from such action. Members' contributions in a corporation need not necessarily be in relation to the number of shares they held in the company before conversion.

On registration of a corporation which is converted from a company, all the assets, rights, liabilities and obligations of the company are vested in the corporation. The conversion will have no influence on any legal proceedings instituted by or against the company, or any liability of an officer or director of the company against the company, or any liability of the company towards a third party as surety. On conversion of the company the corporation must immediately, in writing, inform all creditors and all other parties to contracts or legal proceedings in which the company was involved at the time of the conversion.

22.5 EXAMPLE OF FINANCIAL STATEMENTS

The following example of the financial statements of a CC contain more information than is required by the Act. The most important additions are:

- ☐ the inclusion of a cash flow statement
- ☐ the inclusion of a statement of net investments of members analysed separately for each member
- ☐ a description of transactions with members which were taken into consideration in the determination of net income.

A cash flow statement is not specifically required by the Close Corporations Act, but is included in the proposed statements because it will assist members in determining the source and application of liquid funds.

A statement of net investments of members provides the following in total and in respect of individual members: the balances and movements in members' contributions, net income earned but not distributed by the corporation, surpluses arising from revaluation of fixed assets and loans to and from members.

According to the Close Corporations Act, the financial statements of a corporation need show only the total amounts at the end of the financial year and the movements in these amounts separately. In any case the total amounts at the end of the year will be disclosed separately on the balance sheet, but it is recommended that a separate summary showing net investment of members and movements in this investment, be included. This statement is considered to be of benefit to members in that it provides an overview of their total investment in the corporation and also of amounts owing to or by individual members. If this statement is not prepared it will be necessary to disclose the movements in these amounts as a note to the financial statements.

Financial statements of a corporation are prepared for the benefit of the members and should assist them in the management and control of the business of the corporation. For this reason transactions with individual members, which are included in net income, should be disclosed. This disclosure will facilitate proper decision making and any judgement of future prospects.

Although the following example is intended only as a guide as to the format of the financial statements of a CC, the overriding requirement is that the financial statements must satisfy the needs of members. Therefore the amount and nature of the information provided in the financial statements of a specific corporation must be adapted to suit the individual circumstances and requirements of members.

Page 1

KYNOS CC (85/000847)
(Previously trading as Kynos (Pty) Limited)

FINANCIAL STATEMENTS FOR THE 11 MONTHS ENDED
28 FEBRUARY 19.6

CONTENTS

Approval

The financial statements as set out on pages 2 to 6 have been approved by all the members and are signed on their behalf on 31 March 19.6 by:

____

Members

____

ACCOUNTING OFFICER'S REPORT

I have performed the duties of accounting officer of Kynos CC for the year ended 28 February 19.6 in accordance with the requirements of the Close Corporations Act, 1984. No audit has been conducted and no opinion is expressed on the fair presentation of the financial statements.

Based on the performance of our duties we report that the financial statements as set out on pages 1 to 5 are in agreement with the accounting records and have been prepared in accordance with generally accepted accounting practice as details in note 1 to the financial statements.

Johannesburg
30/04/19.6

____

(Name)

(If the accounting officer is a member of the corporation, this fact must be indicated in his report, as must the fact that all the members of the corporation agreed, in writing, to his appointment.)

The report will also contain the applicable qualifications, for example:

> We also report in accordance with the terms of section 62(2)(a) of the Close Corporations Act, 1984, that section 46(a)(iv) of the above Act was contravened in that fixed property was purchased on 28 November without the written consent of all members.

Page 2

KYNOS CC (85/000847)
(Previously trading as KYNOS (Pty) Limited)

INCOME STATEMENT FOR THE 11 MONTHS ENDED 28 FEBRUARY 19.6

	11 months to 28/02/19.6		Year to 31/03/19.5	
	R		R	
TURNOVER (Note 1.2)		280 699		264 637
COST OF SALES		180 544		188 078
GROSS TRADING PROFIT		100 155		76 561
OTHER INCOME		1 602		1 675
Profit on sale of equipment	—		294	
Interest received	1 602		1 381	
		101 757		78 236
ADMINISTRATIVE, SALES AND GENERAL OPERATING EXPENSES		76 219		65 009
Accounting officer's remuneration (19.5 Auditor's fees)	2 700		2 880	
Advertising	4 100		2 983	
Commission	4 107		3 911	
Depreciation	1 080		1 180	
Equipment	530		580	
Vehicles	550		600	
Doubtful debts	1 516		800	
Insurance	2 140		1 660	
Lease (vehicles)	8 268		7 176	
Members' salaries (19.5 Directors' remuneration)	36 000		32 000	
Office salaries	6 209		5 300	
Rental (property)	5 800		5 000	
Travelling costs	4 299		3 100	
OPERATING INCOME BEFORE INTEREST		25 538		12 246
Interest paid		1 393		945
INCOME BEFORE TAXATION		24 145		11 301
Taxation		12 072		5 650
INCOME AFTER TAXATION		12 073		5 651
Distribution to members		9 000		—
Retained income: For the year (19.5 Retained income)		3 073		5 651
Retained income: Beginning of year		—		4 443
Retained income: End of year (19.5 Retained income transferred to members' contributions)		R3 073		R10 094

The accounting officer's report and the notes to the financial statements should be read in conjunction with the income statement:

Page 3

KYNOS CC (85/000847)
(Previously trading as Kynos (Pty) Limited)

BALANCE SHEET AT 28 FEBRUARY 19.6

	Notes	28/02/19.6	31/03/19.5
		R	R
FUNDS APPLIED			
Members' interests (19.5 Share capital and reserves)	2	30 003	25 094
Loans from members (19.5 Shareholders' loans)	2	16 500	23 414
		R46 503	R58 508
APPLICATION OF FUNDS			
Fixed assets	1.3, 4	6 700	6 822
Net current assets		39 803	41 686
Current assets		56 601	63 240
Inventory	1.4, 3	21 777	18 814
Debtors		27 321	40 802
Loans to members		3 000	—
Short-term deposits		4 000	3 000
Cash and bank balances		503	624
Current liabilities		16 798	21 554
Creditors		16 798	19 502
Taxation		—	2 052
		R46 503	R48 508

The accounting officer's report and the notes to the financial statements should also be read in conjunction with the balance sheet.

Page 4

KYNOS CC (85/000847)
(Previously trading as Kynos (Pty) Limited)

NOTES TO THE FINANCIAL STATEMENTS AT 28 FEBRUARY 19.6

1 Accounting policy
The financial statements have been prepared in accordance with generally accepted accounting practice appropriate to the corporation and are consistent with the previous year. The main accounting policies of the corporation are:

1.1 Basis of preparation
The financial statements have been prepared on the historical cost basis, except for certain properties which have been revalued.

1.2 Turnover
Turnover, which excludes general sales tax, comprises amounts invoiced for goods supplied and services rendered.

1.3 Fixed assets
(Describe depreciation policy.)

1.4 Inventory
(Describe valuation policy.)

2 Transactions with members
Net income has been determined after the following transactions with members:

	Mr A	Mr B	Total
	R	R	R
Interest paid	1 173	—	1 173
Rental	—	5 800	5 800
Salaries	20 000	16 000	36 000
	21 173	21 800	42 973
Interest received	—	250	250
	21 173	21 550	42 723

3 Inventory
(Details of inventory composition.)

4 Fixed assets
(Details of cost, accumulated depreciation and book value.)

Page 6

KYNOS CC (85/000847)
(Previously trading as Kynos (Pty) Limited)

CASH FLOW STATEMENT FOR THE YEAR ENDED 28 FEBRUARY 19.6

	11 months to 28/02/19.6	Year to 31/03/19.5
	R	R
Operating income	25 588	12 246
Add back: Depreciation and other items not influencing cash flow	1 080	886
Funds from business operations	26 618	13 132
Changes in operating capital	5 762	(3 644)
Inventory	(2 963)	(13 025)
Debtors	13 481	(4 656)
Creditors	(2 704)	13 823
Taxation	(2 052)	214
Funds generated from operations	32 380	9 488
Less:	(23 474)	(6 595)
Interest paid	(1 393)	(945)
Taxation paid	(13 081)	(5 650)
Distributions to members	(9 000)	—
Net cash generated from business operations	8 906	2 893
Other cash flow	(8 027)	3 483
Loan to member	(3 000)	—
Loan repaid to member	(6 914)	2 696
Contributions by members	1 887	—
Purchase of fixed assets	—	(953)
Proceeds on sale of fixed assets	—	1 740
Net increase in liquid funds	R879	R6 376

Page 7

STATEMENT OF MEMBERS' NET INVESTMENT

Members' interests	Mr A 60%	Mr B 40%	Total 100%
Contributions introduced at beginning of year			
Equity of Kynos (Pty) Limited at 1/3/19.5	15 056	10 038	25 094
Add: Surplus on revaluation of property	575	383	958
Balance at beginning of year	15 631	10 421	26 052
Movements during the year			
Special taxation i.r.o. conversion	(605)	(404)	(1 009)
Contributions introduced	3 532	2 355	5 887
Contributions repaid	(2 400)	(1 600)	(4 000)
Net income	7 244	4 829	12 073
Distributions	(5 400)	(3 600)	(9 000)
Balance at end of year	R18 002	R12 001	R30 003
Members' loans			
Shareholder's loan ex Kynos (Pty) Limited	23 414	—	23 414
Repayments to members during year	(6 914)	(3 000)	(9 914)
	16 500	(3 000)	13 500
Total	R34 502	R9 001	R43 503

23

ACCOUNTING ASPECTS OF A COMPANY

The general nature of a company was dealt with in chapter 20. The **AIM** of this chapter is chiefly to introduce the disclosure requirements in respect of certain items in the financial statements of companies. These requirements, which are contained mainly in schedule 4 of the Companies Act, 1973, are not discussed in detail (refer to appendix A). The share capital and the reserves and profit of a company are also discussed.

23.1 INTRODUCTION

In South Africa all matters pertaining to companies are governed by the Companies Act, 1973 (Act 61 of 1973).The Registrar of Companies, based in Pretoria, administers the Act. The Act comprises 17 chapters, with a total of 443 sections and a further five schedules.

Schedule 4, consisting of 72 paragraphs, is of special interest to the accounting profession. It lists stipulations additional to those given in the Act in respect of the annual financial statements and interim reports.

23.2 GENERAL ASPECTS OF COMPANIES

23.2.1 The prospectus

A public company usually obtains the greater part of its capital (share capital) by inviting the general public to subscribe for one or more shares and so to become members of the company.

The document used for this purpose is known as the prospectus, and can be advertised in the press or may be available from banks or other financial institutions or from stockbrokers. The information to be contained in the prospectus is prescribed by the Companies Act. A prospectus is a document which serves to introduce the company to the public and should contain information which will enable the prospective investor to decide on the value of the investment and whether or not the investment is attractive.

Because it has limited private ownership, a private company may not issue a prospectus inviting the public to buy shares and become members.

23.2.2 Share capital

The capital which shareholders invest in a company is known as share capital. As proof of his investment a shareholder receives a share certificate noting the number of shares he holds.

☐ Authorised share capital

The share capital with which a company is incorporated according to its memorandum and articles is known as the **authorised share capital**. This is the maximum share capital that the company may issue; any change in the amount of authorised share capital may be made only in a manner prescribed by the Act.

☐ Issued share capital

It is not necessary that the entire number of authorised shares is offered to prospective investors. For various reasons the company may decide to keep a number of shares in reserve. The shares issued are known as **issued share capital** and the difference between the authorised and issued share capital is known as the **unissued or reserve share capital**.

☐ Value of shares

A company may be authorised to issue shares either **with or without a par value**.

The par value, or nominal value, is supposed to be an indication of the shares' 'value'. However, since the value of the shares changes, their par value may be misleading. Even when the shares are issued the price paid for them is often higher than their par value.

There is no material difference between par value and no par value shares; no par value shares were created to eliminate the effect of the misleading indicator of value.

A company's shares must be either with or without par value; a combination of the two is not permitted. However, if different classes of shares are issued (see below) it is permissible to issue ordinary shares without par value and preference shares with par value, or *vice versa*.

☐ Share premium

If the company sells a share at a price higher than its par value the difference is known as a **share premium**. If a share with a nominal value of R1 is issued at R1,50, the share premium is 50 cents.

The share premium is recorded in a separate account in the books and may be handled only in the manner prescribed by the Act. The share premium is regarded as part of the share capital.

In the case of no value shares, there is obviously no share premium.

☐ Classes of shares

The two classes of shares most commonly encountered are **ordinary shares** and **preference shares**.

— Preference shares

Preference shares are distinguished from other shares in that they have preferential rights to dividends and bear a fixed dividend percentage, for example 100 8% preference shares of R1 each.

Preference shareholders are entitled to their dividends only when profit is available for distribution and the dividend has been declared in accordance with the stipulations of the articles.

An investor wanting a fixed income and a reasonable degree of security will generally be interested in preference shares.

Preference shares may also be **cumulative**, that is have a fixed dividend which if not declared or paid in any specific year results in a contingent liability to the company in the form of **arrear preference dividends**.

We have already mentioned that a company may not purchase its own shares. The exception is **redeemable preference shares**, a special category of preference shares which may be repurchased and redeemed by the company in a manner and at a price determined beforehand.

— Ordinary shares

Ordinary shares qualify for payment of dividends only after provision has been made for payment of dividends on preference shares. Ordinary shares, unlike preference shares, are not entitled to a fixed dividend; thus they have an unlimited participation in the profit, depending upon the availability of such profit and the dividends which are recommended and approved.

☐ Recording of share capital

In the recording of share capital a distinction must be made between par value and no par value shares.

— **Shares with par value**

Example 23.1

Assume that AB Company issues 1 000 ordinary shares of R1 each at R1,50 per share. The journal entry will be as follows:

Cash Ordinary share capital account Share premium account *Issue of ordinary shares nos 1 – 1 000 at a premium of 50 cents each, according to directors' resolution*	1 500	 1 000 500

If the company invites the public to subscribe for shares (which is usually the case), the use of an interim account may be necessary. Popular shares, especially, may be over-subscribed. The directors must decide on a basis of allocation and the balance of monies received must be repaid.

Example 23.2

AB Company invites the public to subscribe to 1 000 ordinary shares of R1 at R1,50 each. Applications are received for 2 000 shares and the directors decide to issue one share for every two subscribed.

The journal entries will be as follows:

Cash Application account *Applications for 2 000 ordinary shares at a premium of 50 cents per share*	3 000	 3 000
Application account Ordinary share capital account Share premium account *Allocation of 1 000 ordinary shares of R1 each, at a 50 cent premium according to directors' resolution*	1 500	 1 000 500
Application account Cash *Repayment of application monies on 1 000 ordinary shares*	1 500	 1 500

— **No par value shares**

Where no par value shares are issued a **stated capital account** is used. This is a term created by the Act.

Example 23.3

AB Company issues 1 000 no par value shares at R1,50 each. The journal entry is as follows:

Cash Ordinary shares: Stated capital account *Issue of 1 000 ordinary no par value shares, nos 1 – 1 000, at R1,50 each, per directors' resolution*	1 500	 1 500

When investors trade shares between themselves no entries are made in the company's books. The entries above were made only when the shares were originally issued to the public. Any change in ownership of the company's shares must, however, be recorded in its **share register**.

23.2.3 Reserves, profits and dividends

☐ General

The principles and methodology for determining and calculating profit are the same for all forms of enterprise. Unlike the sole proprietorship and the partnership, however, shareholders in a company have no implicit claim on the profit. In other words, the total profit need not necessarily be divided among the shareholders.

Because the company is a legal person, the profit belongs to it and is distributed to the shareholders only when paid out in the form of dividends. This does not imply that shareholders have no say over the profit. Usually the directors make an annual recommendation as to the manner in which the profit should be applied, and their recommendation, with the required motivation, is laid before the shareholders for approval at the **annual general meeting**. If the shareholders do not approve the recommendation, then the manner in which the profit should be applied will have to be decided upon at the meeting.

☐ Reserves

Profit which is not distributed is retained as a **reserve** and shown as such in the balance sheet.

Before providing for dividends the directors can decide to retain a portion of available profit for a specific purpose, for example as a reserve for increased replacement costs of fixed assets, or as a reserve for redemption of debentures or transfer to a general reserve. These types of reserves, which the company may dispose of and which are available for distribution, are known as **distributable reserves**.

Non-distributable reserves, in contrast, can be either statutory or voluntary. Voluntary non-distributable reserves generally arise as a result of a management decision that profit from an extraordinary transaction should not, according to sound accounting practice, be available for distribution; for example, profit arising from the revaluation of fixed assets is regarded as unrealised and therefore not available for distribution.

If redeemable preference shares are redeemed and the redemption or part thereof is not financed by a new issue of shares, an amount equal to the amount financed from own sources must be transferred to a capital redemption reserve fund. Profit on the sale or revaluation of fixed assets is considered to be unrealised and therefore not available for distribution.

☐ Dividends

In a later chapter the financing aspects of dividends will be considered in greater detail. Generally speaking, the declaration and payment of dividends must comply with the following three requirements:

- ☐ **Profits** must be **legally** available for dividends. A company may not, for example, pay dividends from funds obtained from issuing shares to shareholders. This requirement is imposed to ensure that the company's capital is maintained, thereby protecting the interests of shareholders and creditors. Therefore, if a company does not make a profit it cannot declare a dividend.
- ☐ The intended payment must be financially viable, that is the company's general financial position must be taken into account.
- ☐ The proposed dividend must be officially approved at the annual general meeting.

From an accounting point of view, two dates are important regarding the payment of dividends, namely:

- ☐ the date on which the dividend is declared
- ☐ the date on which the dividend is paid.

As soon as the directors propose or recommend a dividend, provision is made in the books by debiting the dividend account and crediting the provision for dividend account. The dividend account is then closed off to the appropriation section of the income account. Obviously, if the proposed dividend is changed at the annual general meeting, the entry will have to be adjusted.

When the dividend is paid the provision for dividend account is debited.

☐ Journalising profits and dividends

Example 23.4

AB Company Limited made a net operating profit of R500 000 for the year ended 30 June 19.9. The directors decided to appropriate the profit as follows:

- ☐ Provision for a dividend of 10 cents per share on the 100 000 issued shares. The dividend must still be approved by the shareholders at the annual general meeting.
- ☐ Transfer R290 000 to a general reserve.
- ☐ Transfer R100 000 to a reserve for increased replacement cost of assets.

The directors' decision will be journalised in the books as follows:

Income account (dividends)	10 000	
Income account (transfer to general reserve)	290 000	
Income account (transfer to reserve for increased replacement cost of assets)	100 000	
Provision for dividends		10 000
General reserve		290 000
Reserve for increased replacement costs of assets		100 000
Provision for dividends and transfer to reserves, in accordance with directors' resolution		

NOTE: The balance of R100 000 on the income account represents accumulated profit (or retained income) and is shown as a distributable reserve in the balance sheet.

23.3 COMPANY ANNUAL REPORTS

23.3.1 Obligation to report

Every company is obliged, in terms of the Companies Act, to report at least once a year to its shareholders, debenture holders and the State concerning its financial affairs.

In terms of the Companies Act the directors are obliged, for each financial year of the company, to have audited **annual financial statements** compiled in one of the official languages and to present these statements to the **annual general meeting**. The financial statements must be approved by the board of directors and signed on its behalf by two directors.

At least 21 days before the date of the annual general meeting, copies of the financial statements must be sent to the following people:

- every member of the company
- every debenture holder
- all other persons entitled to receive notice of general meetings.

In addition, on the date that the financial statements are despatched to members, a public company must forward a certified copy to the Registrar of Companies. Public companies are also required to supply their members with **interim reports** giving information concerning the first half of the financial year.

23.3.2 Contents of the annual report

According to the Companies Act the annual financial statements must consist of at least the following:

- a balance sheet
- an income statement
- a funds statement
- a directors' report
- an auditor's report.

23.3.3 The principle of disclosure

One of the most important requirements of the Companies Act concerning accounting information is the extent to which financial information **must be disclosed** to the shareholders of a company and to other users of the company's financial statements. Over the years it has become common practice to compel companies by means of legislation to disclose certain information.

The principle of disclosure is fundamental to South African company legislation. In accordance with this principle the Companies Act requires that certain **prescribed minimum information** be disclosed for the information and benefit of **interested parties**.

This disclosure applies from the time of registration of the company, when its constitutional documents (Memorandum and Association Agreement) are registered by the Registrar of Companies and made available for public inspection.

Disclosure requirements apply to the company from the time of its incorporation until its deregistration. The process is as follows:

- ☐ At the date of incorporation the constitutional documents become public property.
- ☐ When capital must be canvassed for, a prospectus must be published.
- ☐ During the company's life **annual financial information which complies with certain minimum requirements must be published in the form of annual reports**.
- ☐ On deregistration, this information is published in the *Government Gazette*.

The compulsory disclosure of information concerning a company plays an important role in protecting shareholders, investors and creditors and satisfying their information requirements. According to Gower in *The Principles of Modern Company Law:**

> On the basis that 'forewarned is forearmed', the fundamental principle underlying the Companies Act has been that of disclosure . . . disclosure still remains the principle safeguard on which the Companies Act pins its faith, and every succeeding Act . . . has added to the extent of the publicity required.

The South African Companies Act of 1973 has continued this tendency: schedule 4, which relates specifically to the contents of the annual financial statements, contains 72 paragraphs compared with the 27 paragraphs of its predecessor, the Eighth Schedule of the Companies Act of 1926.

Proper disclosure of financial matters in financial reports is prescribed in South Africa by more than just company legislation. It embraces mainly the following:

- ☐ Statutory prescriptions for the preparation of annual financial statements of companies as contained in the Companies Act, 1973 (Act 61 of 1973) and in schedule 4 of that Act.
- ☐ Statements of generally accepted accounting practice which are issued by the Accounting Practices Board. These statements contain specifically recommended or alternative accounting practices which are considered to be generally accepted in accounting practice.
- ☐ Guidelines issued by the South African Institute of Chartered Accountants.

23.3.4 Prescribed information

In accordance with article 285(3) of the Companies Act the financial statements should, in conformity with generally accepted accounting practice, fairly present the state of affairs of the company and of its business at the end of the financial year concerned, as well as of the company's **profit or loss** for that financial year. Furthermore, the financial statements must **at least** comply with the particulars prescribed in schedule 4.

The requirement that it should be a **fair presentation** is the overriding objective and companies should supply additional information whenever necessary in order to realise this objective.

---

*Gower, LCB. 1979. *The Principles of Modern Company Law*. 4th ed. p 497.

In the interests of fair presentation of the financial position of the company at its accounting date, the Companies Act, and in particular schedule 4, contain detailed requirements concerning:

- ☐ which **items** of shareholders' equity, assets and liabilities are to be disclosed in the **balance sheet** and what **information** in respect of such items must be disclosed
- ☐ specifically which information must be provided in the income statement in respect of the profit or loss for the period.

Due to the fact that certain minimum information must be disclosed when preparing the balance sheet and income statement of a company, it is necessary to distinguish clearly between:

- ☐ **disclosable** and
- ☐ **non-disclosable** items.

Disclosable items include the compulsory minimum information which **must** be disclosed in the statements. Although it has become common in practice to disclose only those items required to be disclosed by law or according to generally accepted accounting practice, the company may disclose as much additional information as it considers necessary.

The minimum requirements with which annual financial statements should comply constitute a vast topic on their own, and are not discussed in detail in this book. The following broad outline of items which **must** be reported on is considered sufficient.

A summary of the minimum requirements with which the annual financial statements of a company must comply is given in appendix A of this book.

Note, however, that the annual financial reports, which are prepared in accordance with schedule 4 of the Companies Act, serve a specific purpose, namely external reporting by the directors to the shareholders of the company. The minimum information laid down in schedule 4 will usually be insufficient for internal reporting to the management of the enterprise. Often, especially in the case of smaller undertakings, the management and the owners are the same persons, in which case far more than merely the minimum information is necessary.

The minimum information prescribed in schedule 4 for the balance sheet is fairly comprehensive. The minimum prescribed information for the income statement, on the other hand, is merely a very short summary of the information contained in the various reports in which net income and the appropriation thereof appears.

☐ The balance sheet

— Shareholders' equity and liabilities

Liabilities and shareholders' equity must be summarised, together with such particulars as are necessary to disclose their general nature, and classified under headings and subheadings appropriate to the company's business. The following must be distinguished:

- ☐ authorised share capital, with an indication of the classes of shares
- ☐ issued share capital, with an indication of the classes of shares
- ☐ share premium account
- ☐ non-distributable reserves
- ☐ distributable reserves
- ☐ long-term liabilities
- ☐ indebtedness to subsidiary companies
- ☐ current liabilities and provisions.

— **Assets**

Similarly, assets must be summarised, together with such particulars as are necessary to disclose their general nature, and classified under headings and subheadings appropriate to the company's business. Fixed assets, current assets and assets which are neither fixed nor current must be shown separately as follows:

- ☐ fixed assets
- ☐ goodwill, patents and trade marks
- ☐ investments in and loans to subsidiary companies
- ☐ loans to holding companies and fellow subsidiaries
- ☐ investments
- ☐ current assets.

Where a company (H Ltd) is a member of another company (S Ltd), and H Ltd either:

- ☐ controls the composition of the board of directors of S Ltd, or
- ☐ owns more than half the equity share capital of S Ltd,

then H Ltd is the **holding company** of S Ltd and S Ltd, in turn, is a subsidiary of H Ltd.

Together H Ltd and its subsidiary(ies) form a **group** of companies. Since the well-being of the holding company is inevitably linked to that of its subsidiaries, the Companies Act requires that holding companies must present **group annual financial statements** to their shareholders at the annual general meeting. This topic falls outside the scope of this book.

However, legislation still requires that particulars of **interest in subsidiaries** (e g shares in and loans to subsidiaries and fellow subsidiaries) and interest in **associated companies** (i e companies in which between 20% and 50% interest is held), as well as particulars of loans to subsidiaries, holding companies and fellow subsidiaries, must be disclosed in the statements.

☐ The income statement

Various items appear in the income statement, the following, for example, being disclosable:

- ☐ turnover
- ☐ operating income.

The latter concept requires further explanation. Although the disclosure of turnover is a requirement, details of purchases and most operating and administrative expenses need **not** be disclosed. Consequently, the published annual income statement does not include a trading section, nor is the gross profit disclosed.

The first item in a published income statement is usually the following:

Operating income for the year before taking into account items listed below	Rx

This item has two components:

'**Operating income**' comprises gross profit **plus** any other income items **less** any expense items which do not have to be disclosed.

'**Items listed below**' are those items which **must** be disclosed in terms of the Companies Act, viz:

- ☐ profit on share transactions and income from investments, distinguishing between income from listed investments (i e from shares of companies listed on the stock exchange) and income from unlisted investments

- ☐ income from subsidiaries
- ☐ profit/loss on disposal of assets and profit/loss of an extraordinary nature
- ☐ provision for depreciation, interest, directors' remuneration, auditor's remuneration and provision for taxation.

At this point it is necessary to consider some aspects of normal company taxation. Once the **taxation liability** (if any) of the company has been estimated for the financial period concerned, it is recorded by means of the following journal entry:

Income account Receiver of Revenue *Provision for taxation for the year ended 28/2/19.7*	xxx	 xxx

The debit item is shown in the income statement as 'taxation', while the credit item is shown as a current liability in the balance sheet.

If the company has made any provisional payments in respect of any specific financial year in accordance with the provisional taxation system, the Receiver of Revenue's account is debited in the books of the company.

Example 23.5

Assume that the following particulars apply to the year ended 28 February 19.6:

☐ Provision for taxation	R80 000
☐ Provisional payments made:	
31 August 19.5	R30 000
28 February 19.6	R30 000

Treatment in the income statement:

Income before taxation	R xxx
Taxation	80 000
Income after taxation	R xxx

Treatment in the balance sheet:

Current liabilities:	
Receiver of Revenue (R80 000 – (30 000 + 30 000))	R20 000

Periodically the State levies a **loan** on taxpayers (calculated as a percentage of the taxpayer's taxable income). If such an amount is levied on a company, when it is paid it will appear as an asset in the balance sheet until it has been repaid by the State. Since such a loan (known as a **loan levy**) is usually over five years, it is not classified as a fixed or current asset and therefore is disclosed separately between these two asset categories in the balance sheet.

23.3.5 Supplementary information in financial statements

The Act provides for two methods of supplementing the accounting information in the annual financial statements, namely:

- ☐ the directors' report
- ☐ the use of notes to the financial reports.

The **directors' report** must, in accordance with schedule 4 of the Companies Act, review the company's business and operations, and the result thereof, during the accounting period concerned. It must take into account every fact or circumstance material to a clearer understanding of the state of affairs of the company, including a statement of the proportion of profit (or loss) attributable to the various classes of the company's business.

Furthermore, the report must deal with any material fact or circumstance which has arisen in the period between the accounting date and the date of the report. Schedule 4 also prescribes other specific matters which must be covered in the directors' report.

The use of **notes** to provide information which should be contained in the financial statements obviates the necessity of incorporating in the financial reports the **finer details** which tend to obscure the more important facts which should be communicated. In large companies most of the details are disclosed by means of notes. In smaller concerns which have less complicated annual reports, most of the details can be included in the financial reports themselves.

In practice, besides the directors' report, the annual financial reports of a company also include a **chairman's report**. The chairman's report usually reviews the company's activities during the financial period concerned, the prospects for the future and any other matters of interest not discussed elsewhere in the annual report.

Annual reports of companies also frequently contain a **historical review** of the financial result for the previous five or even 10 years, details about management (i e names of top management) and sundry information necessary for the correct interpretation of the reports.

Example 23.6 Framework

AB LIMITED
BALANCE SHEET AT 31 DECEMBER 19.7

	Notes	
CAPITAL EMPLOYED		
Ordinary share capital	2	xxx
Share premium account	3	xxx
Non-distributable reserves	4	xxx
Distributable reserves	4	xxx
Ordinary shareholders' equity		xxx
Preference share capital	2	xxx
		Rxxx
EMPLOYMENT OF CAPITAL		
Fixed assets	6	xxx
Investment in subsidiaries	7	xxx
Other investments	8	xxx
Loan levy		xxx
Net operating capital		xxx
CURRENT ASSETS		xxx
Inventory	9	xxx
Debtors	10	xxx
Bank balances and cash		xxx
CURRENT LIABILITIES		xxx
Loans	5	xxx
Creditors		xxx
Bank overdraft		xxx
Dividends proposed	18	xxx
DEFERRED EXPENSES	11	xxx
		Rxxx

AB LIMITED
INCOME STATEMENT FOR THE YEAR ENDED 31 DECEMBER 19.7

	Notes	
TURNOVER	13	Rxxx
NET OPERATING INCOME	14	xxx
OTHER INCOME		
Income from subsidiaries	15	xxx
Income from investments	16	xxx
		xxx
NET INCOME before taxation	17	xxx
NET INCOME		xxx
PREFERENCE DIVIDEND	18	xxx
NET INCOME ACCRUING TO ORDINARY SHAREHOLDERS		xxx
TRANSFER TO RESERVES		xxx
ORDINARY DIVIDENDS	18	xxx
RETAINED INCOME: For the year		xxx
RETAINED INCOME: Beginning of year		xxx
RETAINED INCOME: End of year		Rxxx

NOTES TO THE FINANCIAL STATEMENTS AT 31 DECEMBER 19.7

1 ACCOUNTING POLICY

The company's main accounting policies are:

1.1 Fixed assets

Land and buildings are not depreciated. Depreciation on equipment and plant is written off on a fixed instalment basis using rates deemed to be suitable for writing off the assets over their expected economic lifespan.

1.2 Inventory

Inventory is valued at the lower of cost or net realisable value on a FIFO basis. Inventory is valued on a basis which is consistent with previous years.

2 SHARE CAPITAL	
Authorised	
xxx Ordinary shares of R1 each	
xxx 8% Preference shares of R1 each	
Issued	
xxx Ordinary shares of R1 each	xxx
xxx 8% Preference shares of R1 each	xxx
	Rxxx
3 SHARE PREMIUM ACCOUNT	
The following amounts were written off against this account during the year:	
Preliminary expenses	xx
Share issue expenses	xx
	Rxx
4 RESERVES	
4.1 Non-distributable	
Capital redemption reserve fund	xxx
Reserve created by revaluation of land and buildings	xxx
	xxx
4.2 Distributable	xxx
General reserve	xxx
Retained income	xxx
	Rxxx
5 LONG-TERM LIABILITIES	
5.1 Secured	
Secured by a first mortgage bond over land and buildings. The interest rate is 9%, the bond is repayable in 10 equal annual instalments from 30 June 19.8	xxx
Less: Payments payable within one year, transferred to current liabilities	xxx
5.2 Unsecured	
10% Redeemable debentures, redeemable on 30 June 19.9 at par	xxx
	Rxxx

	Cost price	Accumulated depreciation	Book value
6 FIXED ASSETS			
Land and buildings (give description, date of acquisition and cost price) (secured – refer note 5)	xxx	—	xx
Machinery and equipment	xxx	xx	xxx
	Rxxx	Rxx	xxx
Goodwill, patents and trade marks at cost *less* amounts written off			xx
			Rxxx

7 INVESTMENTS IN SUBSIDIARIES	
Shares at cost	xxx
Loans	xx
	Rxxx
8 OTHER INVESTMENTS	
8.1 In listed companies, at cost (market value Rxxx)	xxx
8.2 In unlisted companies, at cost (directors' valuation Rxxx)	xxx
	Rxxx

List of names of companies in which investments are held, and extent of the investment

9 INVENTORY	
Inventory consists of:	
Trading inventory	xxx
Consumable inventory	xxx
	Rxxx
10 DEBTORS	
Included under debtors are short-term loans to directors, Rxx	Rxxx
11 DEFERRED EXPENSES	
These include:	
Preliminary expenses	xxx
Share issue expenses	xxx
	Rxxx

12 CONTINGENT LIABILITIES
A contingent liability exists in respect of product guarantees furnished to customers.

13 TURNOVER
Represents net sales.

14 NET OPERATING INCOME

In the calculation of net operating income the following items were taken into account:

Income		
Profit on disposal of fixed asset		Rxx
Expenses		
Loss on disposal of fixed asset		xx
Depreciation on fixed assets		xx
Interest on loans		xx
Lease payments on depreciable moveable property		xx
Directors' remuneration:		
For services as director	xx	
For other services	xx	xxx
Auditor's remuneration:		
Fee for audit	xx	
Fee for other specified services	xx	
Expenses	xx	xxx
		Rxxx

15 INCOME FROM SUBSIDIARIES

Dividends	xx
Interest	xx
Management fees	xx
	Rxxx

16 INCOME FROM INVESTMENTS

Dividends received:	
Listed shares	xx
Unlisted shares	xx
	Rxxx

17 TAXATION

Normal taxation on taxable income for the year	Rxxx

18 DIVIDENDS

Preference dividend: Paid	Rxx
Ordinary dividend: Paid	xx
Proposed	xx
	Rxxx

Example 23.7

Sashwood Limited was incorporated on 1 July 19.3 with an authorised share capital of 300 000 shares of R1 each, comprising 200 000 ordinary shares and 100 000 10% preference shares.

The following trial balance was prepared at 30 June 19.8 from the records of the company:

TRIAL BALANCE AT 30 JUNE 19.8	Dr	Cr
Goodwill at cost	40 000	
Land and buildings at cost	200 000	
Plant and machinery at cost	150 000	
Accumulated depreciation: Plant and machinery 30 June 19.7		70 000
Listed investments at cost	20 000	
Unlisted investments at cost	10 000	
Inventory 1 July 19.7	48 000	
Debtors	40 000	
Provision for doubtful debts		1 000
Cash in bank	2 000	
Loan levy	4 000	
Ordinary shares issued		200 000
10% Preference shares issued		50 000
Share premium account		8 000
Capital redemption reserve fund		15 000
General reserve		30 000
Retained income 30 June 19.7		15 000
Receiver of Revenue (provisional payments)	6 000	
Sundry creditors		32 000
7% R100 Debentures – secured by a mortgage bond over land and buildings		40 000
Sales		234 600
Salaries and wages	26 000	
Rates and taxes	600	
Purchases	125 000	
Sales returns	1 000	
Administrative expenses	18 000	
Interim dividend paid (ordinary shares)	5 000	
	R695 600	R695 600

Additional information:

(1) Provision must be made for:
- ☐ interest on debentures (full year)
- ☐ annual dividend on preference shares
- ☐ a final dividend of 6% on ordinary shares
- ☐ depreciation on plant and machinery at 15% on cost
- ☐ directors' remuneration R2 500
- ☐ auditor's remuneration R3 000
- ☐ transfer of R5 000 to general reserve
- ☐ taxation R20 000.

(2) Inventory at 30 June 19.8 amounted to R60 000.

(3) The provision for doubtful debts must be adjusted to 5% of outstanding debtors at 30 June 19.8.

(4) The market value of the listed investments was R25 000 at 30 June 19.8.

(5) The directors' valuation of unlisted investments was R16 000 at 30 June 19.8.

(6) The following dividends on the above investments for the year ended 30 June 19.8, were received during July 19.8:
- ☐ on listed investments R1 500
- ☐ on unlisted investments R2 000.

(7) Assessment rates, which remained unchanged during the year, were paid only for the period 1 July 19.7 to 31 March 19.8.

Required:

(1) Prepare a detailed income statement for the year ended 30 June 19.8.
(2) Prepare an income statement for the year ended 30 June 19.8 which discloses only the minimum information required by the Companies Act.
(The calculation of operating profit, as disclosed in this income statement, must be given.)
(3) Prepare a balance sheet as at 30 June 19.8.

The financial statements which are prepared in (2) and (3) must also comply with generally accepted accounting practice.

Detailed income statement

SASHWOOD LIMITED
INCOME STATEMENT FOR THE YEAR ENDED 30 JUNE 19.8

Sales		234 600
Less: Returns		1 000
		233 600
Less: Cost of sales		113 000
Opening inventory		48 000
Purchases		125 000
		173 000
Less: Closing inventory		(60 000)
Gross profit for the year		120 600
Add: Dividends on listed investments		1 500
Dividends on unlisted investments		2 000
		124 100
Less: Expenses		76 600
Salaries and wages		26 000
Administrative expenses		18 000
Rates and taxes (600 + 200)		800
Depreciation (15% × R150 000)		22 500
Provision for doubtful debts (5% × R40 000 – 1 000)		1 000
Interest on debentures (6% × R4 000)		2 800
Directors' remuneration		2 500
Auditor's remuneration		3 000
Net income for the year before taxation		47 500
Less: Taxation		20 000
Net income for the year after taxation		27 500
Less: Transfer to general reserve	5 000	
10% Preference dividend	5 000	
Interim dividend on ordinary shares	5 000	
Final dividend on ordinary shares	12 000	27 000
Retained income: For the year		500
Retained income: Beginning of year		15 000
Retained income: End of year		R15 500

Income statement in compliance with minimum requirements

The Companies Act (and in particular schedule 4) does not require disclosure of the following items in this income statement:

- ☐ returns
- ☐ cost of sales (including the elements thereof)
- ☐ gross profit
- ☐ salaries and wages
- ☐ administrative expenses
- ☐ assessment rates
- ☐ provision for doubtful debts.

It has already been mentioned that **operating income** is the critical figure in an income statement which contains only the minimum information. The calculation of this figure takes into account all non-disclosable items. In this instance it is calculated as follows:

Sales	234 600	
Less: Returns	(1 000)	233 600
Less: Cost of sales		113 000
		120 600
Less: Salaries and wages	26 000	
Administrative expenses	18 000	
Assessment rates	800	
Provision for doubtful debts	1 000	(45 800)
OPERATING PROFIT		R74 800

SASHWOOD LIMITED
INCOME STATEMENT FOR THE YEAR ENDED 30 JUNE 19.5

Turnover		R233 600
Operating income for the year before taking into account items disclosed separately below		74 800
Income from investments		3 500
Dividends on listed investments		1 500
Dividends on unlisted investments		2 000
		78 300
Less: Depreciation on fixed assets		22 500
Interest on loans (debentures)		2 800
Directors' remuneration		2 500
Auditor's remuneration		3 000
		30 800
Net income before taxation		47 500*
Less: Taxation		20 000
Net income after taxation		27 500
Less: Transfer to general reserve	5 000	
Dividends paid and proposed	22 000	27 000
Retained income: For the year		500
Retained income: Beginning of year		1 500
Retained income: End of year		R15 500

*Note that net income before taxation is the same in both income statements.

Balance sheet

SASHWOOD LIMITED
BALANCE SHEET AT 30 JUNE 19.8

CAPITAL EMPLOYED			
Share capital			
Authorised:			
200 000 Ordinary shares of R1 each			200 000
100 000 Preference shares of R1 each			100 000
			R300 000
Ordinary shareholders' interest			273 500
Ordinary shares issued: 200 000 Shares of R1 each			200 000
Share premium account			8 000
Capital redemption reserve fund			15 000
Distributable reserves:			50 500
General reserve			35 000
Retained income			15 500
Preference shares issued: 50 000 10% Preference shares of R1 each			50 000
TOTAL SHAREHOLDERS' INTEREST			323 500
LONG-TERM LIABILITIES			
7% R100 Debentures – secured by a mortgage bond over land and buildings			40 000
			R363 500
EMPLOYMENT OF CAPITAL		Accum-ulated	
FIXED ASSETS	Cost price	depre-ciation	Book value
Land and buildings	200 000	—	200 000
Plant and machinery	150 000	92 500	57 500
	R350 000	R92 500	257 500
Goodwill at cost			40 000
			297 500
Investments at cost			30 000
Listed (market value R25 000)			20 000
Unlisted (directors' valuation R26 000)			10 000
Loan levy			4 000
Net current assets			32 000
Current assets			103 500
Inventory			60 000
Debtors (40 000 – 2 000)			38 000
Income accrued (1 500 + 2 000)			3 500
Cash in bank			2 000
Current liabilities			(71 500)
Sundry creditors (R32 000 + 2 800 + 2 500 + 3 000 + 200)			40 500
Receiver of Revenue (R20 000 – 6 000)			14 000
Shareholders for dividends: Ordinary shares (final dividend)			12 000
Preference shares			5 000
			R363 500

24

COST ACCOUNTING AND PRODUCTION COST SYSTEMS

The **AIM** of this chapter is to explain the function of cost accounting, the classification of costs, the two basic production cost systems – job costing and process costing – and the determination of unit costs.

24.1 THE SCOPE OF COST ACCOUNTING

Cost accounting is that sphere of accounting which relates to the determination of the cost of activities and products for the purposes of profit determination and management.

Profit is the difference between income and the cost incurred in generating that income. In every enterprise where expenses are incurred in the production of items which will not be sold during the period in which they are produced, it is necessary, when determining profit, to ascertain the cost price of goods manufactured and to bring into account only the cost of those products sold against the income from sales.

Since all business concerns want to make a profit, constant planning and control of costs (long and short term) is essential and therefore management needs continuous costing data upon which to base its decisions. To be able to use the costing data rationally and meaningfully, whatever the purpose, a thorough knowledge of the **nature of costs** within the dynamic environment of an enterprise's activities is necessary.

24.2 COST CONCEPTS

Before discussing the classification of costs, it is necessary to explain some of the concepts used in cost accounting.

☐ Factors of production

In order to do business, an entrepreneur of a manufacturing concern combines a number of basic factors known as **factors of production**, *inter alia* labour, capital (in the form of buildings, machinery and equipment), natural resources (such as raw materials and other materials) and entrepreneurship.

☐ Expenses

The amounts an entrepreneur pays to obtain the factors of production are known as **expenses**. As soon as these amounts are expended in obtaining these factors, they represent manufacturing costs.

☐ Costs

Costs are the factors of production which an enterprise must sacrifice in order to manufacture a product. This sacrifice of the factors of production is known as **value sacrifice**. Unfortunately, not all value sacrifices are effective, and therefore they are not necessarily costs. If a product has to be scrapped due to poor manufacture, the sacrifice of the factors of production has served no purpose. The application of ineffective value sacrifice is known as **wastage**. Only the application of effective value sacrifice becomes costs.

24.3 CLASSIFICATION OF COSTS

Costs can be classified, *inter alia*, according to the following:

- ☐ the function of which the cost forms a part
- ☐ the elements of manufacturing costs
- ☐ the reaction thereof to changes in production levels
- ☐ the relationship thereof to products, processes, sections or departments
- ☐ the degree to which they can be controlled.

Different categories of costs are used for different applications of costing data. In cost control, for example, costs would be classified according to the degree to which they may be controlled. For the purposes of profit determination, however, these same costs would be classified according to their reaction to changes in production levels. Thus the purpose for which the costing data is used determines the category according to which the costs are classified.

24.3.1 The functional classification of costs

The total costs of a manufacturing concern can be classified functionally as **product costs**, **marketing costs**, **administrative costs** and **financing costs**. The production process transforms material into a product through the use of labour and other production facilities. The costs incurred in executing the production process are the **product costs**, which constitute the **cost of the product**. Product costs therefore consist of three elements, namely **direct material**, **direct labour** and **overheads**.

The marketing costs incurred in exposing the product to the market and selling it, the financing costs, consisting chiefly of the interest cost on borrowed funds, and the administrative costs incurred in managing and administering the business are **period costs** and do not form part of the product costs. Instead, they are written off in total against income in the period in which they were incurred.

The accounting system of a manufacturing concern must make provision for the determination of product costs. First, these product costs are essential to determining the cost of both work in progress and finished products. In order to determine income accurately, the cost of products sold must be properly identified. Second, product costs must be ascertained for the sake of efficiency and profitability. The management of an enterprise uses cost analysis and other aids to determine standards and budgets and thus operate effectively. If actual production costs are known these can be compared with the norms or standards which have been set and corrective action can be taken if necessary. Management also relies on product costs when compiling price lists and tendering for contracts.

However, the distinction between product and period costs is not always clear or easily determined. Manufacturing costs such as direct raw materials, direct labour and general manufacturing costs are usually regarded as product costs, while sales and administrative costs are regarded as period costs. Sometimes it may be difficult to distinguish between product and period costs – for example the cost of maintaining and processing labour records will be regarded by some enterprises as a manufacturing overhead and by others as an administrative cost.

24.3.2 Classification according to the elements of manufacturing costs

The practical allocation of manufacturing costs gives rise to the following classification of costs:

☐ **Direct material**

This is the material which is consumed directly in the manufacture of the product, for example wood for furniture.

☐ **Direct labour**

This is labour directly applied in converting the material into a finished product, for example the wages of the persons operating the manufacturing equipment.

☐ **Manufacturing overheads**

These are manufacturing costs (over and above direct material and direct labour) which are incurred when a product is manufactured, for example power consumption, insurance and depreciation of manufacturing equipment. This cost classification will be referred to again in the next chapter.

24.3.3 Classification according to the behaviour of costs at various production levels

Costs can be classified by the way in which they react to changes in production levels as **fixed**, **variable** or **semi-variable** costs. The production levels are measured by the volume of activity which occurs in a production unit in a specific period. This measurement can be in terms of the number of products produced during a specific period, or the number of direct labour hours or machine hours recorded during that period for the production unit.

☐ **Fixed costs**

Fixed costs are costs which remain constant during a given period for a given potential capacity, irrespective of the degree to which the capacity is utilised during that period.

> Assume, for example, that a factory building of 1 000 m^2 is leased at a cost of R3 000 per annum, and that a maximum of 6 000 products can be produced on the premises each year. The rental remains constant at R3 000, regardless of the number of products actually produced during the year.

Fixed costs usually relate to the relatively long-term facilities which provide the capacity for the enterprise to carry out its activities; for example, *inter alia*, the cost of providing buildings, machinery and equipment, vehicles and permanent staff. Fixed costs arise as a result of management decisions to provide the facilities or capacity and can generally be altered only by management decision. Fixed costs are also referred to as **capacity costs**.

Fixed costs can be represented graphically as follows:

Figure 24.1

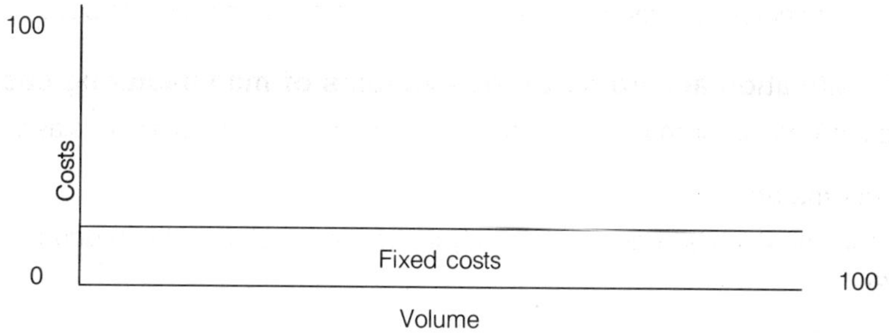

Therefore the **total** fixed costs remain constant, despite changes in production levels. In contrast, the **fixed cost per unit** changes with fluctuations in production levels. Assume, for example, that the total fixed costs are R5 000. Regardless of whether 100 or 1 000 units are manufactured, this figure remains the same. The fixed cost per unit, however, will be:

$$R\frac{5\,000}{100} = \text{R50 per unit in the first case}$$

and

$$R\frac{5\,000}{1\,000} = \text{R5 per unit in the second case.}$$

☐ Variable costs

Unlike fixed costs, variable costs **change with fluctuations in the volume of activity**.

> **Variable costs tend to remain constant per unit, but to change in total**. Usually the extent of the variable cost per unit is determined by management policy, but changes in the number of units or the volume of activity determine the total variable costs.

Variable costs can be represented graphically as follows:

Figure 24.2

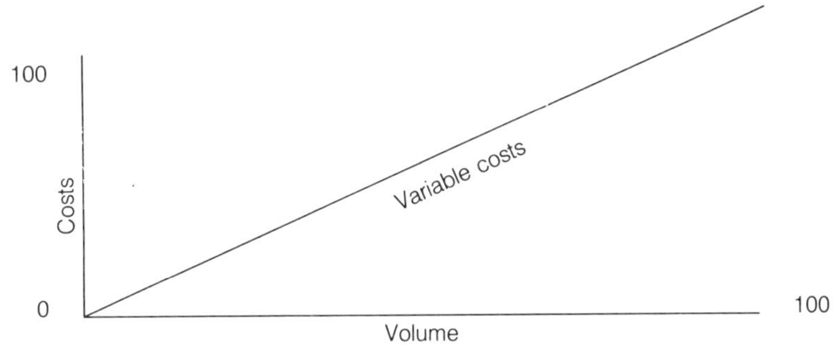

☐ Semi-variable costs

These are costs which consist of fixed as well as variable cost elements, and which therefore do not vary in direct proportion to changes in production levels.

For purposes of control it is important that a suitable method is used to split semi-variable costs into their fixed and variable elements. Maintenance costs of manufacturing equipment is a good example of a semi-variable cost. Some maintenance costs are incurred irrespective of whether the equipment is used; these constitute the fixed cost element. However, if it happens that the more the equipment is used in the operating process, the greater the maintenance costs incurred, this is the variable cost element of maintenance costs.

The following simplified example illustrates the division of a cost into its fixed and variable elements.

Example 24.1

The following information is obtained from the accounting records of X Limited:

Month	Number of units manufactured	Maintenance costs
		R
January	3 000	9 000
February	5 000	12 000

The following information can be determined from the above:

- ☐ variable costs per unit
- ☐ total fixed costs
- ☐ total variable costs per unit
- ☐ fixed costs per unit.

This is accomplished as follows:

1 Determine the difference in units produced and the difference in maintenance costs.

Month	Units	Costs	
January	3 000	9 000	
February	5 000	12 000	
Difference	+~~R~~2 000	+R3 000	or R1,50 per unit $(R\frac{3\,000}{2\,000})$

2 The variable costs per unit remain constant and therefore will be the same for both months.

3 The total fixed costs can now be determined as follows:

Total costs January	9 000
Less: Variable element	
3 000 units × R1,50	4 500
∴ Total fixed costs	R4 500

The total fixed costs remain constant and therefore will be the same for January and February.

4 The total variable costs are therefore:

	Units produced	×	Variable costs per unit	= Total
January	3 000	×	1,50	= R4 500
February	5 000	×	1,50	= R7 500

5 Fixed costs per unit:

January $R\frac{4\,500}{3\,000}$ = R1,50 per unit

February $R\frac{4\,500}{5\,000}$ = R0,90 per unit

This information can be represented graphically as follows:

Figure 24.3

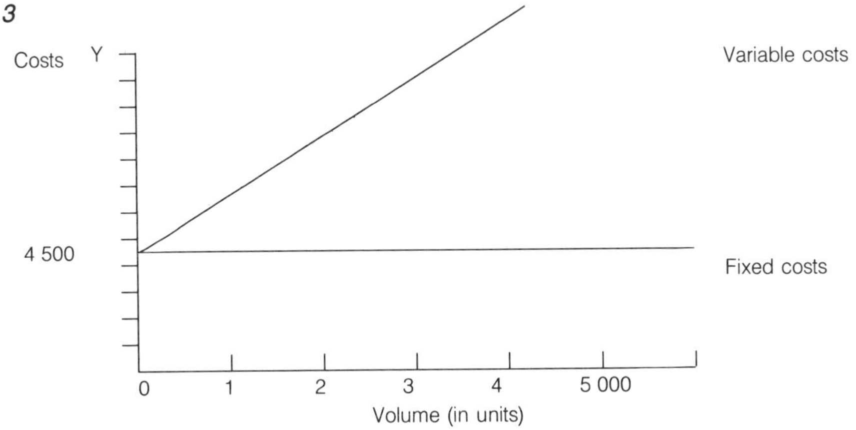

24.3.4 Direct and indirect costs

A **direct cost** is a cost which may be allocated directly to a specific product, process or department. The terms **direct** and **indirect** refer specifically to a product, process or department. An **indirect cost** is a cost which, although related to a specific product, process or department, cannot be allocated directly thereto.

In a manufacturing process the cost of material consumed will be regarded as a direct cost of the product whenever it is possible to measure the cost of material consumed in producing each product. The maintenance cost of machinery will be regarded as an indirect product cost, since it is impossible to determine the exact amount of the total cost relevant to a specific product. However, these same maintenance costs will constitute a direct departmental cost for the department in which they are incurred.

24.3.5 Controllable and uncontrollable costs

The concepts controllable and uncontrollable pertain to the person exercising control. A cost is **controllable** when it can be influenced by the action of the person exercising control. Material consumed, for example, is a cost controllable by the production foreman. However, depreciation on machinery in the same department would **not** be **controllable** by the same foreman, since he has no influence over the writing off of depreciation.

24.4 PRODUCTION COST SYSTEMS

A production cost system is a system whereby production costs are compiled according to cost types and allocated to different production processes, from where they are transferred first to an inventory account as the cost price of completed products and finally to cost of sales.

There are **two** basic types of production cost system, namely **process cost systems** and **job cost systems**.

Process cost systems are used where large runs of homogeneous products are manufactured using the same production facilities, for example in oil refineries, saw mills, shoe factories and canning factories. In a process cost system the total cost incurred in the production process during a specific period is determined and then the cost per product is calculated by dividing the total cost of the process by the number of products manufactured during that period.

Job cost systems are used where heterogeneous products, that is different types of products, are manufactured using the same production facilities. Construction enterprises, shipbuilders and general engineering workshops are examples of enterprises which would use a job cost system. In a job cost system the cost of each different product or job is compiled and ascertained separately.

24.4.1 Job cost systems

In a job cost system each of the three inventory accounts (materials, uncompleted work and finished products) is supported by subsidiary records or subsidiary ledgers, dealt with below:

- **Material inventory book:** Each type of material is recorded in this book on a separate ledger card showing the quantities and unit cost.

Figure 24.4

MATERIAL INVENTORY CARD							
Inventory number: Description: Supplier:				Re-order quantity: Minimum quantity:			
Document reference	Date	Received		Issued		Balance	
		Quantity	Price	Quantity	Price	Quantity	Price

- **Cost ledger:** This contains a **job cost card** for each job in progress. These job cost cards serve as subsidiary records for work-in-progress. As shown in figure 24.5, each of these cards shows the cost of direct material, direct labour and allocated overheads pertaining to the particular job.

  After a job is completed, the total cost of the job is divided by the number of units comprising the job to obtain a **unit cost**.

Figure 24.5

JOB COST CARD								
Customer: Product: Quantity:				Job number: Date commenced: Date completed:				
	Direct material		Direct labour			Production overheads		
Date	Requisition number	Amount	Timesheet number	Hours	Amount	Allocation basis	Rate	Amount
Total job cost								

☐ **Finished goods ledger:** Each card in this ledger is identified by an inventory number and a description of the product, and shows quantities, unit cost and total costs.

Figure 24.6

FINISHED PRODUCTS INVENTORY CARD								
Inventory number: Description:					Minimum quantity:			
	Acquisitions			Sales		Balance		
Date	Job cost card number	Quantity	Unit price	Invoice number	Quantity	Quantity	Unit price	Total cost

In order to illustrate a job cost system, the following example is used throughout: Azed Manufacturers manufactures two products, A and Z, for its own purposes. Two raw materials, B and C, are used in these products, while material D is used generally in the factory rather than being incorporated in the product. This information is analysed below in each subsection.

□ Recording material costs

When purchased material is received this is recorded on the relevant material inventory cards. At the end of the financial period the total material purchased is posted from the purchases journal to the material control account. The balance on the control account must agree with the total of the balances on the various cards in the material ledger account. The issue of material on receipt of an inventory requisition is recorded on the appropriate inventory card and in the control account. Requisitions for direct material are recorded on the relevant job cards and debited to the production account, while indirect material is debited to the production overheads account.

Assume that Azed Manufacturers made the following purchases and issues during the first month of its operation:

	(1) Purchases	(2) Issues
	R	R
Material B	5 000	2 000 (for job 1)
Material C	3 000	1 000 (for job 2)
Material D	1 000	400

The effect of these transactions can be presented schematically as in example 24.2.

□ Recording labour costs

In order to identify the labour costs of specific jobs, **timesheets** are used to ascertain the time spent by employees on each specific job. Then hourly wage tariffs are used to determine the labour costs of the various jobs. Particulars are transferred periodically from the timesheets to the job cards.

Assume that Azed Manufacturers incurred the following labour costs:

	Hours	Cost
		R
(3) Direct labour – job 1	400	1 600
job 2	200	800
(4) Indirect labour for the period		1 000

These transactions can be presented schematically as in example 24.3.

□ Recording overheads

In the discussion of the procedures for recording material and labour, it was said that indirect material and indirect labour are to be recorded in the production overheads account. Periodically other overhead items are transferred to this account from the separate accounts in which they were recorded when the costs were incurred. As was explained earlier, this account is described as the **actual production overheads account**.

Assume that, in addition to indirect material costs and indirect labour costs, Azed Manufacturers incurs the following overheads during the current financial period: power and water consumption R300; maintenance of equipment R200; depreciation on equipment R200. These costs are transferred, via the following journal entry, from the individual cost accounts to the production overheads account.

(5) Production costs	700	
Power and water consumption		300
Maintenance: Equipment		200
Depreciation: Equipment		200
Overheads for the relevant period		

(For the sake of brevity the original transfers from the appropriate subsidiary journals to each of these separate accounts are not shown.)

Example 24.2 Entries for purchases and issues of material

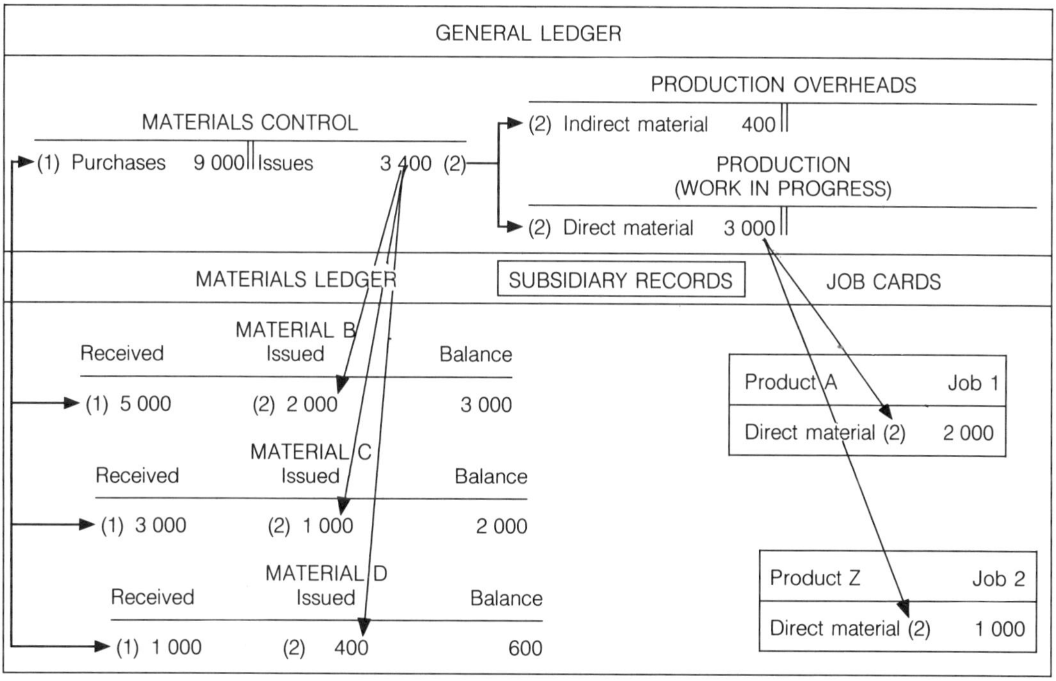

Example 24.3 Entries for labour costs

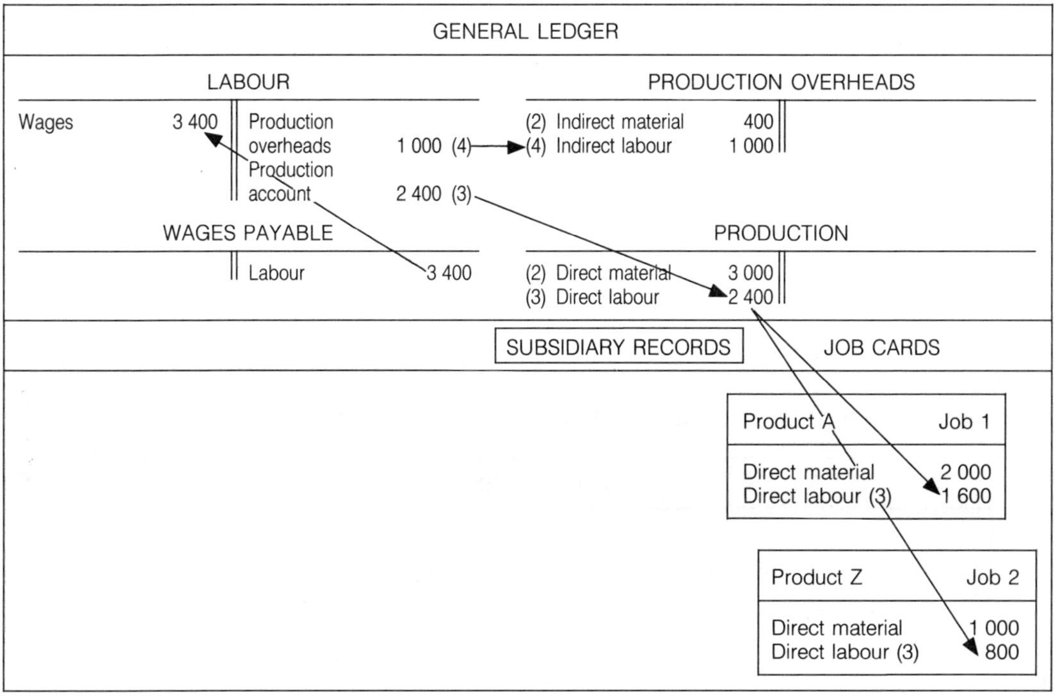

It is relatively easy to identify direct material and labour costs by making use of material requisition forms and timesheets. However, it is impossible to trace general manufacturing costs **directly** to the cost of a specific product: instead, an estimating procedure is used to apply an overhead rate.

□ The overhead rate

The concepts and procedures underlying the determination of overhead rates are comprehensive and sometimes complicated. In this section only the basic outline is discussed. This is sufficient for an understanding of the use of these rates in determining product costs.

Before the start of a financial period the management of an undertaking usually compiles a budget. Sales estimates are traced to production budgets which, in turn, are used to estimate the expected use of equipment and the level of the enterprise's activities. Different criteria may be used to measure these activities, for example direct labour hours and machine hours. Using historical data and predicted activity levels, the total production overheads can be estimated. Then the overhead rate can be calculated by dividing the total estimated production overheads by the selected activity standard.

Assume, for example, that the number of direct labour hours worked has been selected as the most suitable standard of activity in a specific situation, and that the estimated number of direct labour hours is 100 000, while the total production overheads are estimated at R300 000. The overhead rate will be R3 per direct labour hour in this case, calculated as follows:

$$\text{Overhead rate} = \frac{\text{Estimated overheads}}{\text{Estimated direct labour hours}}$$

$$= \frac{\text{R300 000}}{\text{100 000 hours}}$$

$$= \text{R3 per direct labour hour}$$

If a certain production lot during a specific accounting period took 75 hours, overheads of R225 (75 hours × R3) will be allocated thereto.

Using a predetermined overheads rate, the overheads for any job can be calculated at any time during the production process.

As **actual overheads** arise during the period they are debited to an **overheads account**. Overheads allocated to production during the period are **credited** to the overheads account. In theory, the actual overheads should be equal to allocated overheads. In practice, however, this never happens and the difference must be either written off against income or written back to production costs, depending on the circumstances.

This allocation procedure is illustrated in example 24.4 with reference to the example of Azed Manufacturers.

(6) Production costs Overheads *Allocation of overheads of R1 200 to job 1 and R600 to job 2*	1 800	 1 800

Once the overheads have been entered on the job cards they contain particulars of all overheads incurred in respect of each job to date.

Note that the overheads allocated (R1 800) are R300 less than the overheads actually incurred. In practice there are several reasons why the amount apportioned in any specific financial period will not agree exactly with the overheads actually incurred. First, calculation of the overheads rate is based on **estimates** of the total overheads and of the production activity (measured in labour hours) for the year. Furthermore, the production activity may vary from month to month and the overheads can also vary. Therefore, a debit or a credit balance may arise on the overheads account from one month to the next. A debit balance on the overheads account indicates that overheads are **underapplied** or **underabsorbed**, while a credit balance indicates that overheads are

over-applied or **overabsorbed**. A balance on the overheads account at the end of the financial period (year) can be closed off by transfer to the cost of goods sold account, for example:

(7) Cost of goods sold Production overheads *Transfer of underabsorbed overheads*	300	 300

A balance on the overheads account actually relates to unfinished goods, finished goods still in stock and cost of goods sold. If the balance is material it may be apportioned to each of these categories on a reasonable basis (e g the direct labour hours allocated to each category).

Example 24.4 Allocation of overheads

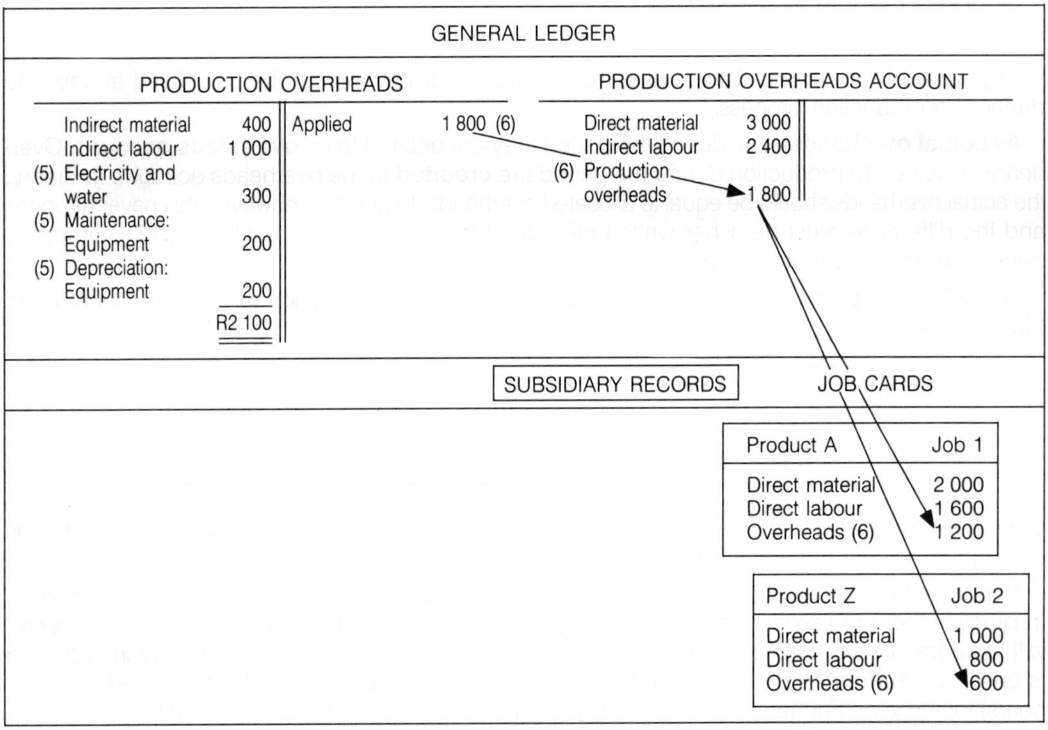

☐ Recording completed goods

On completion of a job the unit cost of each item in that job is obtained by dividing the total cost by the number of units produced. The job card may then be removed from the production ledger for filing. At the same time the necessary entries are made on the appropriate inventory cards in the finished goods ledger, showing quantities, unit costs and total costs. At the end of the period an additional entry is made, debiting the finished goods account and crediting the production cost account.

When the goods are sold the appropriate entry is made on the inventory cards and at the end of the period the finished goods account is credited and the cost of goods sold account is debited.

Assume that Azed Manufacturers completed job 1 during the first month and that 1 000 units were produced. During the month 600 of these units were sold. Job 2 is still in progress.

The records are kept as shown in example 24.5 and the journal entry is as follows:

(7) Finished goods Production *Job 1 (1 000 units) of product A completed at a cost of R4,80 each*	4 800	4 800
(8) Cost of goods sold Finished goods *Cost of 600 units of product A sold at R4,50 per unit*	2 880	2 880
(9) Debtors Sales *Sales of 600 units of product A*	3 200	3 200

Example 24.5 Recording finished goods

GENERAL LEDGER

PRODUCTION ACCOUNT

Direct material	3 000	Job 1	4 800
Direct labour	2 400	Balance	2 400
Overheads	1 800		
	R7 200		R7 200
Balance (job 2)	2 400		

FINISHED GOODS

(7) Production costs	4 800	Cost of goods sold	2 800
		Balance	1 920
	R4 800		R4 800
Balance (400 units at R4,80)	1 920	(8)	

COST OF GOODS SOLD

Finished goods	2 880		

DEBTORS

Sales	3 200		

SALES

		Debtors	3 200

SUBSIDIARY RECORDS

(9)

SUBSIDIARY RECORDS

FINISHED GOODS LEDGER

Cost price R4,80 Product A		
Acquired	Sold	Balance R
1 000		4 800
	600	1 920

JOB CARDS

Product A	Job 1
Direct material	2 000
Direct labour	1 600
Overheads	1 200
1 000 units	R4 800
∴ Cost per unit = R4,80	

Product Z	Job 2
Direct material	1 000
Direct labour	800
Overheads	600
	R2 400

After transactions (7) to (9) have been recorded, the entries in the relevant accounts and subsidiary records will be recorded as shown in figure 24.7. The following points should be noted:

- There is a definite link between the physical flow of goods and the related bookkeeping entries.
- The different subsidiary records give a detailed analysis of the total amounts and balances in the related control accounts in the general ledger.
- The sale of finished goods gives rise to entries for both cost and selling prices of finished goods.

Figure 24.7

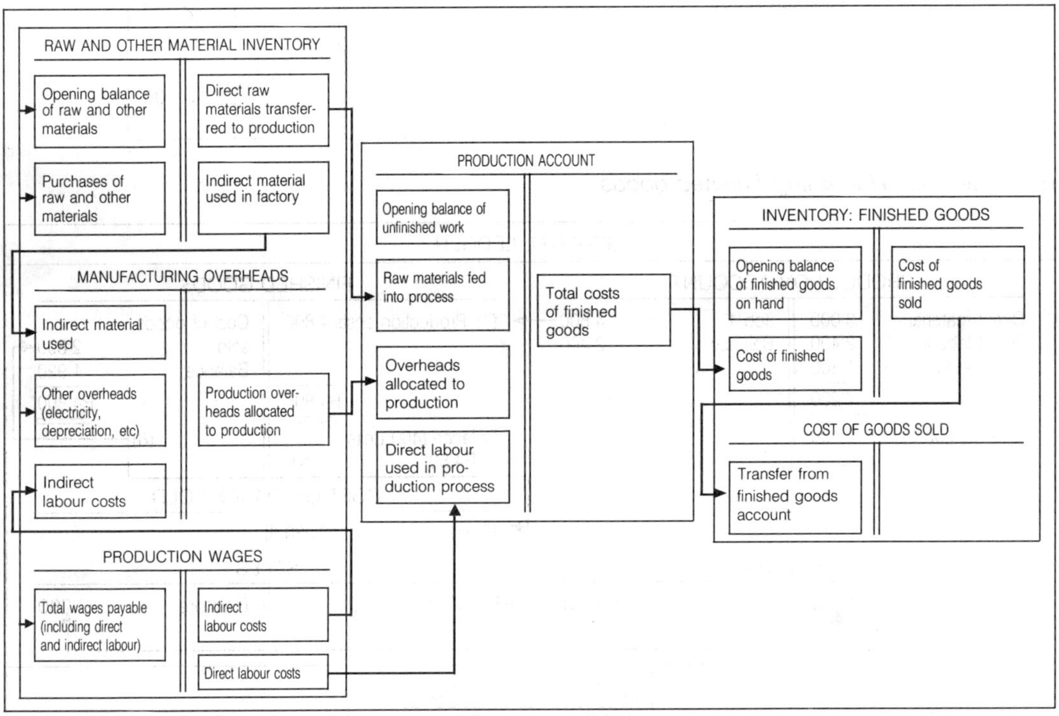

24.4.2 Process costing systems

In the introductory paragraph of this section it was noted that process cost systems are used where large runs of homogeneous products are manufactured using the same production facilities. In job costing systems, costs must be identified with each specific job in order to determine unit costs. In contrast, costs in a process costing system are identified with a **cost centre** (a processing or production department) **for a specific period**, usually a month. A separate production cost account is kept for each production department and the costs for a specific period (e g a month) are compiled in these accounts. At the end of the period the costs for each cost centre are summarised in a production cost statement. This report provides the unit cost information necessary to ascertain the cost of goods transferred from one process to another and eventually to finished goods. Thus, while a job cost system uses only one production cost account supported by a number of job cards, a process cost system comprises various production cost accounts, each supported by a periodic production cost statement.

The following figure illustrates the process cost flow in the manufacture of a liquid which is produced in two consecutive processes.

Figure 24.8

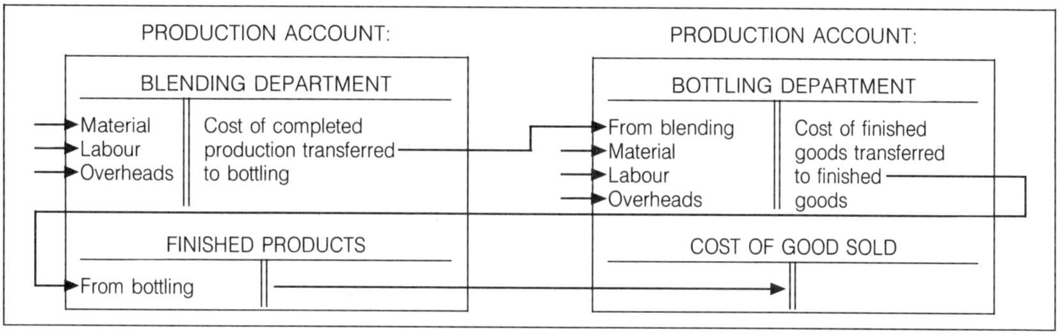

The diagram shows clearly how the completed output from the first department becomes the direct material input for the following processing department. Usually additional raw material, labour and overheads are introduced in the subsequent process. As the products move through each consecutive department appropriate costs are added, and these accumulate to form the total manufacturing cost of completion of the products.

☐ Ascertaining unit costs

In order to trace the cost of products transferred from one department to another and eventually to finished goods, it is necessary to calculate unit costs. Basically this entails the calculation of average costs.* Assume that during June of the current year, the blending department incurred the following costs: direct raw materials R4 200; direct labour R6 000; overheads R2 400. Production amounted to 2 400 litres. The unit cost for each litre is therefore:

$$\frac{\text{Total costs for June}}{\text{Total production}} = \frac{\text{R12 600}}{\text{2 400 litres}}$$

$$= \text{R5,25 per litre}$$

This calculation assumes that the manufacture of the 2 400 litres of liquid was begun and completed during June. If a number of units were unfinished at the beginning and at the end of the month concerned, it would not be correct to calculate the total cost for the month as if the total production of the 2 400 litres had been begun and completed during the month. Assume, for example, that of the 2 400 litres handled in June, 600 litres (lot A) were already 25% complete in May, and 300 litres

*Other methods are also used, but these fall outside the scope of this book.

(lot C) were 50% complete at the end of June. In order to calculate the unit cost for June, the processing of the 2 400 litres must be converted into **equivalent units** of finished product:

	Lot	Units handled in June (litre)	Portion completed during June	Equivalent units
From opening inventory	(lot A)	600	×75%	450
Begun and completed during June	(lot B)	1 500	×100%	1 500
Begun, but not completed during June	(lot C)	300	×50%	150
		2 400		2 100

If it is assumed that the raw materials, labour and overheads are accumulated on a regular basis during the production process, the correct unit cost for the month would be:

$$\frac{\text{Total cost}}{\text{Equivalent units processed}} = \frac{\text{R12 600}}{2\ 100}$$

$$= \text{R6 per litre}$$

An additional factor complicating the calculation of unit cost is the fact that in many manufacturing processes raw materials are added to the process at a different time or rate from labour and overheads (jointly termed **conversion costs**). For example, raw materials may be added at the beginning of the process, while conversion costs are incurred gradually throughout the course of processing. In this case it will be necessary to use different quantities of equivalent units in calculating the unit costs of raw materials and of conversion costs for the same production run (see example 24.6).

☐ **Raw materials**

Since all raw materials are added at the beginning of the process (i e in the previous month when processing commenced with lot A), no equivalent units for material are shown during the current month. The total cost of raw material will, however, be allocated to any run commenced during the month (both B and C).

☐ **Conversion costs**

The 600 units (lot A) commenced during the previous month will be calculated as only 75% × 600 equivalent units, since only 75% of the processing occurred during this month. The units begun and completed during the current month (lot B) will be allocated the full equivalent conversion costs, since all processing was carried out during the month. The closing inventory of 300 units still being processed (lot C) represents 150 equivalent units, since only 50% of the processing on this lot occurred during the current month.

Because the equivalent units for raw material and conversion costs are different, the unit cost of the two components must be calculated separately:

$$\frac{\text{Direct material cost}}{\text{Equivalent units}}$$

$$= \frac{4\,200}{1\,800}$$

$$= \text{R}2{,}333 \text{ per litre}$$

$$\frac{\text{Conversion costs}}{\text{Equivalent units}}$$

$$= \frac{6\,000 + 2\,400}{2\,100}$$

$$= \text{R}4{,}00 \text{ per litre}$$

Total cost of a completed unit manufactured during the period = R6,333.

Example 24.6

Illustration of the calculation of equivalent units*

Production runs	Portion of work carried out in the current month: 0%	25%	50%	75%	100%	Equivalent units material	Equivalent units conversion
(a) Opening inventory: Work in progress 600 units 25% complete							
Material						0	
Conversion costs		—	—	→			450
(b) Begun and completed in this period: 1 500 units							
Material	—	—	—	→		1 500	
Conversion costs	—	—	—	→			1 500
(c) Closing inventory: Work in progress: 300 units 50% complete							
Material	—	—	—	→		300	
Conversion costs	—	→					150
						1 800	2 100

Example 24.7

Illustration of a simple process cost system

For the sake of simplicity the matter of equivalent units, valuation of stock using bases other than average cost, partly completed goods, etc are not brought into account.

Remden Limited commenced production on 1 January 19.6. The company manufactures a patent medicine called 'Remsa'. The manufacturing process is carried out in two separate departments.

*Raw materials are added at the beginning of the period; conversion costs are added regularly throughout processing.

In department 1 the various ingredients of the medicine are ground and mixed. The product is then transferred to department 2 where it is bottled, labelled and packed into cardboard boxes. All costs in both departments are deemed to have been incurred at the start of the process.

The company has decided to use a predetermined overhead rate of 50% of the direct labour cost. The following data is relevant for January 19.6:

(1) Raw and other materials purchased on credit, R60 000
(2) Direct raw material issued per material requisitions to department 1, R39 500
(3) Packaging material purchased on credit, R10 000
(4) Packaging material issued to department 2, R8 000
(5) Indirect material issued, R3 000
(6) Wages paid in cash, R13 000
The timesheets show that wages should be allocated as follows:
(7) Department 1, R7 000
(8) Department 2, R5 000
(9) Indirect wages, R1 000
(10) Sundry production overheads: R2 000 paid in cash
(11) On 31 January overheads were allocated to the production department on the basis of the predetermined overhead rate
(12) During January department 1 commenced manufacture of 20 000 litres of Remsa; by 31 January 15 000 litres had been transferred to department 2
(13) By 31 January, 12 000 litres of the product had been transferred to completed inventory.

REMDEN LIMITED
GENERAL LEDGER

RAW AND OTHER MATERIALS

(1)	Creditors	60 000	(2)	Issued to department 1	39 500
			(5)	Overheads	3 000
				Balance	17 500
		R60 000			R60 000
	Balance	17 500			

CREDITORS

			(1)	Raw materials	60 000
			(3)	Packaging material	10 000

PACKAGING MATERIAL

(3)	Creditors	10 000	(4)	Issued to department 2	8 000
				Balance	2 000
		R10 000			R10 000
	Balance	2 000			

PRODUCTION OVERHEADS ACCOUNT

(5)	Raw and other materials:		(11)	Allocation to:	
	Indirect material	3 000		Department 1 (calculation 1)	3 500
(9)	Wages: Indirect labour	1 000		Department 2 (calculation 2)	2 500
(10)	Bank: Sundries	2 000			
		R6 000			R6 000

REMDEN LIMITED
GENERAL LEDGER

WAGES

(6)	Bank	13 000	(7)	Allocation to department 1	7 000
			(8)	Allocation to department 2	5 000
			(9)	Allocation to overheads	1 000
		R13 000			R13 000

BANK

			(6)	Wages	13 000
			(10)	Overheads	2 000
					R15 000

PRODUCTION ACCOUNT: DEPARTMENT 1

(2)	Raw material issued	39 500	(12)	Transfer to department 2	
(8)	Wages allocated	7 000		(calculation 2)	37 500
(11)	Overheads allocated	3 500		∴ Inventory on hand	12 500
		R50 000			R50 000
	Inventory	12 500			

PRODUCTION ACCOUNT: DEPARTMENT 2

(12)	Transfer from department 1	37 500	(13)	Transferred to finished	
(4)	Packaging material	8 000		goods (calculation 3)	42 400
(9)	Wages allocated	5 000		∴ Inventory on hand	10 600
(11)	Overheads allocated	2 500			
		R53 000			R53 000
	Inventory	10 600			

FINISHED GOODS

(13)	Transfer from department 2	42 400			

Calculations:

1 Allocation of overheads:
Basis: 50% of direct labour costs

Labour costs	Rate	Allocation
Department 1: R7 000	× 50% =	3 500
Department 2: R5 000	× 50% =	2 500
		R6 000

2 Cost of products transferred from department 1 to department 2:

			Costs
Units manufactured	=	20 000 litres (100%)	50 000
Transferred to department 2	=	15 000 litres (75%)	37 500
On hand in department 1	=	5 000 litres	R12 500

Alternative calculation:

Cost per unit department 1 $= R\frac{50\ 000}{20\ 000} \times R2{,}50 = R10\ 600$ per unit

∴ Transferred to department 1 = 15 000 × R2,50 = R37 500

On hand = 5 000 × R2,50 = R12 500

3 Cost of finished products transferred to finished goods:

				Costs
Units received from dept 1	=	15 000	=	53 000
Transferred to finished goods	=	12 000	=	42 400
On hand in department 2		3 000	=	R10 600

Alternative calculation:

Transferred to finished products $= R\frac{53\ 000}{15\ 000} \times R3\ 533 = R53\ 000$ per unit

Transferred to finished products	=	12 000 × R3,533 =	42 000
On hand in department 2	=	3 000 × R3,533 =	10 600
			R53 000

From the above it can be seen that all manufacturing costs are compiled in the respective production accounts first and eventually treated as the product costs of finished goods.

Remden Limited's inventory on 31 January consists of the following:

Raw and other materials:	R17 500 at purchase price
Packaging material:	R2 000 at purchase price
Goods in department 1:	R12 500 at cost of manufacture
Goods in department 2:	R10 600 at cost of manufacture
Finished goods:	R42 400 at cost of manufacture

25

MANUFACTURING ENTERPRISES

The **AIM** of this chapter is to explain the accounting characteristics of manufacturing enterprises.

25.1 THE DIFFERENCE BETWEEN MANUFACTURING AND TRADING CONCERNS

The discussion of accounting systems and procedures in the first section of this book was devoted mainly to trading and service concerns.

A trading enterprise buys and sells manufactured goods. A manufacturing enterprise, in contrast, buys and processes material, and then sells the resulting manufactured products. A motor car manufacturer, for instance, buys steel, rubber, aluminium, plastic, etc, which is used to manufacture motor vehicles which are sold to dealers (the trading concern). These dealers, in turn, sell vehicles to customers.

From an accounting point of view the activities of manufacturing and trading enterprises are very similar, especially their administration, sales and financing activities. Therefore the accounting principles and most of the procedures discussed thus far can be applied by manufacturing enterprises. The main difference between the accounting principles of manufacturing and trading enterprises is their method of **cost accumulation and cost determination** for (i) **inventory valuation** and (ii) the **calculation of the cost of goods sold**. This difference arises from the fact that trading enterprises buy completed goods, while manufacturers **make** the goods sold by dealers. This difference is clearly illustrated in the following comparative calculation of the cost of goods sold by a manufacturing enterprise and a trading enterprise:

Example 25.1

MANUFACTURING ENTERPRISES		TRADING ENTERPRISES	
Opening inventory of finished goods	1 000	Opening inventory of trading merchandise	1 000
Add: Cost of goods manufactured	4 000	*Add*: Cost of goods purchased	4 000
Goods available for sale	5 000	Goods available for sale	5 000
Less: Closing inventory of finished goods	2 000	*Less*: Closing inventory of trading goods	2 000
Cost of goods sold	R3 000	Cost of goods sold	R3 000

The **'cost of goods manufactured'** item in the manufacturing enterprise therefore corresponds to the 'cost of goods purchased' item in the trading enterprise. In both cases these amounts represent the cost of finished goods available for sale. The trading enterprise, having purchased its goods in a 'finished' form, experiences little difficulty in determining their cost. The manufacturing enterprise, on the other hand, has to account for the **cost of converting** the raw materials into finished goods (also known as **manufacturing costs**).

In converting the raw materials into finished products the manufacturer makes use of labour, machinery and equipment, and incurs numerous other manufacturing costs such as power consumption, maintenance of machinery, etc. All these costs must be added to the cost of raw materials to determine the cost of manufactured goods for any period.

Therefore the accounting records of a manufacturing enterprise must be extended to make provision for recording the various additional costs peculiar to manufacturers.

25.2 THE ELEMENTS OF MANUFACTURING COSTS

The three most important elements of manufacturing costs are **material**, **labour** and **manufacturing overheads**. In costing terminology, material and labour costs together are known as **primary costs**, while the term **conversion costs** represents the combination of labour and general manufacturing costs.

25.2.1 Material

The portion of the raw material used in the manufacturing process and readily identifiable and measurable as part of the finished product is termed **direct material**. Direct material is recorded as a separate element of the manufacturing cost.

Indirect material, in contrast, is that portion of the material which either cannot readily be identified as a basic component of the finished product, or is used in such small quantities in the manufacturing process that it does not justify the effort necessary to determine its cost per unit. In the manufacture of a suit of clothing, for example, the cloth used would constitute the direct material, while the thread used, although readily identifiable as part of the finished product, is regarded as **indirect material** and treated as part of the general manufacturing overheads, since its cost is so small in relation to the total cost of the suit.

25.2.2 Labour

The cost of **direct labour** includes the wages of factory personnel directly involved in the manufacture of a product. Therefore it includes the wages of machine operators, fitters and other employees, whether artisans or manual labourers, involved in manufacturing the product. Direct labour is also accounted for as a separate cost element.

Indirect labour, in contrast, includes the wages of those employees not directly involved in the manufacture of products. Indirect labour, like indirect raw materials, forms part of the general manufacturing cost. Examples are the wages of factory cleaners, security staff and supervisors.

The distinction between direct and indirect labour is an important one. Direct labour is used to convert raw materials into finished products. If the production rate has to be increased, it may be necessary to work overtime or to recruit more workers, thus increasing direct labour costs. A decrease in production rate will eliminate overtime, and possibly entail retrenching some of the labour force, resulting in a drop in direct labour costs. Direct labour costs, then, vary in direct proportion to production volume. This enables the management of an undertaking to estimate the direct labour costs when planning the required production volume.

Indirect labour costs, on the other hand, are not directly related to changes in production volume to the same extent. For example, a 10% increase or decrease in the number of units manufactured will be unlikely to affect the number of cleaners and security staff employed, or their wages. However, substantial changes in production volume will affect indirect labour costs.

25.2.3 Manufacturing overheads

That portion of the costs associated with the manufacturing process but not readily identifiable as a direct part of the completed product is known as the **production or manufacturing overheads**.

In addition to indirect material and indirect labour, it includes such items as factory rental, power and water consumption, insurance, maintenance of equipment and depreciation. Selling and general administrative expenses do not form part of the manufacturing overheads, since they are part of the marketing and administrative functions of the enterprise which are not part of the manufacturing function.

25.3 SPECIAL ACCOUNTS IN THE ACCOUNTING SYSTEM OF A MANUFACTURING CONCERN

By virtue of the nature of a manufacturing enterprise's activities, it will always require more ledger accounts than a trading enterprise. The ledger must provide for aspects such as machinery and equipment, inventory, raw materials, work-in-progress, finished goods, etc. It is necessary to devote special attention to the various inventory accounts.

At any given time a manufacturer will have different types of inventory on hand: **material inventory** ready for use in the manufacturing process; **partially completed** products still in the process of being manufactured; and **finished goods** which must be dispatched to dealers. This can be represented as follows:

Figure 25.1

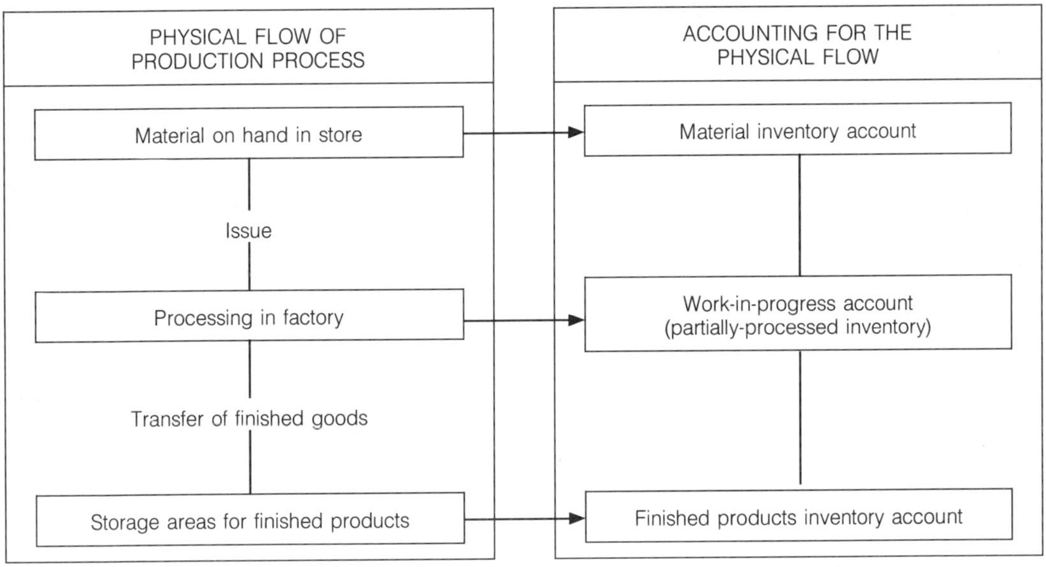

Inventory records and different inventory accounts must be kept in order to determine the cost of **each** type of inventory at the end of a financial period. All three inventory accounts are asset accounts and are usually kept according to a perpetual inventory system. At the same time they are **control accounts** supported by the appropriate subsidiary records (as will be explained later).

25.4 MANUFACTURING ACCOUNTS: A BASIC EXAMPLE

A simple example is used to illustrate the basic concepts of manufacturing accounts. This example emphasises two phases of manufacturing accounts, namely the accumulation of manufacturing costs and tracing these costs as they flow through consecutive stages of (i) work in progress, (ii) finished goods, and (iii) cost of goods sold.

25.4.1 Compilation of manufacturing costs

The interdependence between the accounts shown below is basic to all manufacturing accounting systems. In practice, however, different combinations of accounts may be used. In presenting these basic concepts it has been assumed, for the sake of simplicity, that there was no opening inventory in any of the inventory accounts and, for the sake of convenience, quantities have been omitted and only monetary amounts are shown.

(1) The purchase of material

Material Creditors *Material purchased on credit*	10 000	10 000

CREDITORS			MATERIAL INVENTORY	
	10 000 ←	(1)	→ 10 000	

The procedure for the purchase and control of material has already been discussed in chapter 11. All material purchased (both direct and indirect) is recorded in the inventory account.

(2) Recording of wages payable

Wages Wages payable *Wages for the period*	6 000	6 000

WAGES PAYABLE			WAGES	
	6 000 ←	(2)	→ 6 000	

In this case wages include both direct and indirect wages.

(3) Recording of other factory costs such as manufacturing overheads

Manufacturing overheads	10 000	
Accumulated depreciation		4 000
Power and water bills payable		3 000
Insurance paid in advance		2 000
Property tax payable		1 000
Recording of manufacturing overheads		

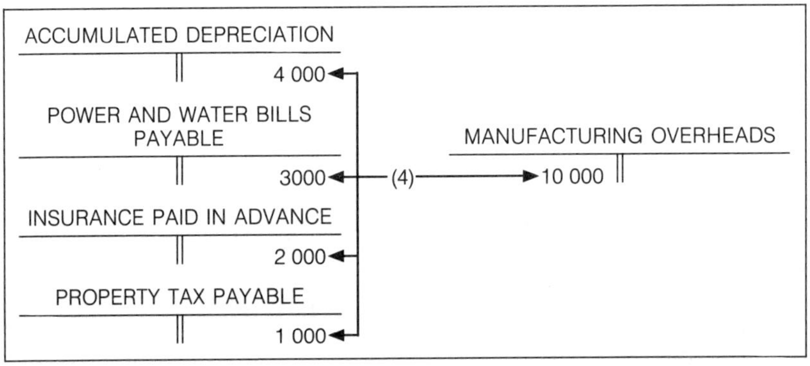

At this stage all manufacturing cost items have been accumulated in the material inventory account, wages account and manufacturing overheads account. The next step is to trace the flow of these cost items to the finished goods and cost of goods sold account.

25.4.2 The flow of costs through the accounts

The descriptions, journal entries and explanations given numerically below for each step link up with the diagram in example 25.2.

It is recommended that after you have studied the transaction you trace each transaction in the example.

(4) Recording the issue of raw materials

Work in progress	6 000	
Manufacturing overheads	2 000	
Material inventory		8 000
Material issued		

This entry reflects the requisition of material inventory for use and consumption in the manufacturing process. Direct material is debited directly to the work-in-progress account, while indirect material forms part of the production overheads. The portion of inventory not used during the financial period under review becomes the material inventory on hand at the end of the period, and is represented by the balance on the material inventory account (see item A in example 25.2).

(5) Recording the allocation of labour costs

Work in progress	5 000	
Manufacturing overheads	1 000	
Wages		6 000
Labour costs allocated		

The wages account for the period is allocated in total; direct labour is debited to the work-in-progress account and indirect labour is debited to the manufacturing overheads account. This allocation of the total wages to direct and indirect labour is based on an analysis of wage records such as timesheets.

(6) Recording the allocation of manufacturing overheads

Work in progress	13 000	
Manufacturing overheads		13 000
Manufacturing overheads allocated		

With this entry, the third and final portion of the manufacturing cost is transferred to the work-in-progress account.

(7) Recording completed production

Finished goods	20 000	
Work in progress		20 000
Finished goods transferred		

This entry reflects the allocation of costs to completed production, and the transfer of these costs from work in progress to finished goods. Chapter 26 explains how the amount in this entry is determined from the production records.

After the above entry has been made, the balance remaining in the work-in-progress account represents the costs allocated to the uncompleted inventory account (see item B in example 25.2).

(8) Recording cost of goods sold

Cost of goods sold	14 000	
Finished goods		14 000
Finished goods sold		

By means of this entry, the cost of goods sold is transferred to the cost of goods sold account. The balance remaining on the finished goods account represents the cost of the closing inventory of finished goods (see item C in example 25.2).

Example 25.2 reflects the results of the previous entries as the various items comprising the total manufacturing costs move through the manufacturing process.

Example 25.2

MATERIAL INVENTORY

(1) Creditors (purchases)	10 000	Work in progress (issue direct material) (4)	6 000
		Production overheads (issue indirect material) (4)	2 000
		Inventory	2 000
	R10 000		R10 000
(A) Inventory on hand	2 000		

WORK IN PROGRESS

(4) Direct material	6 000	Finished goods (7)	20 000
(5) Direct wages	5 000	Inventory unfinished goods	4 000
(6) Production overheads	13 000		
	R24 000		R24 000
Inventory (B)	4 000		

WAGES

(2) Wages payable	6 000	Work in progress (direct wages) (5)	5 000
		Production overheads (indirect wages) (5)	1 000
	R6 000		R6 000

FINISHED GOODS

(7) Work in progress	20 000	Cost of goods sold (8)	14 000
		Inventory	6 000
	R20 000		R20 000
Inventory (C)	6 000		

PRODUCTION OVERHEADS

(3) Depreciation	4 000	Work in progress (6)	13 000
(3) Power consumption	3 000		
(3) Insurance	2 000		
(3) Property tax	1 000		
(5) Indirect wages	1 000		
(4) Indirect material	2 000		
	R13 000		R13 000

COST OF GOODS SOLD

(8) Finished goods	14 000		

- ☐ Entries (1) to (3) classify manufacturing costs according to the three accounts representing the basic cost elements: material, labour and manufacturing overheads.
- ☐ Entry (4) reflects the requisition of both direct and indirect material.
- ☐ The balance on the material account (item A) represents the cost of raw material in stock at the end of the financial period.
- ☐ Entry (5) reflects the allocation of total (direct and indirect) labour costs.
- ☐ The total debits (R13 000) on the manufacturing overheads account represent the general manufacturing costs actually incurred at this time.
- ☐ Entry (6) reflects the appropriation of manufacturing overheads to the work-in-progress account.
- ☐ Once entry (6) has been completed, the work-in-progress account has been debited with all three elements of manufacturing cost.
- ☐ Entry (7) transfers the cost of finished goods to the finished goods account. The balance of R4 000 (item B) represents the cost of the inventory of unfinished goods still on hand at the end of the financial period.
- ☐ Entry (8) reflects the transfer of cost of sales from the finished goods account to the cost of goods sold account. The balance of R6 000 on the finished goods account (item C) represents the cost of finished goods already manufactured but not yet sold.

25.5 THE INCOME STATEMENT OF A MANUFACTURING CONCERN

The income statement of a manufacturing concern follows the same format as that of a trading concern, but must naturally provide for those aspects peculiar to a manufacturing concern.

As in the case of a trading concern, if the manufacturing concern is a company, its published income statement will contain only the minimum prescribed information. The following example, however, illustrates a detailed income statement of a manufacturing concern compiled for internal management purposes.

Example 25.3

The following information is obtained from the financial statements of Dominec Manufacturers for May 19.7:

Inventory	1 May 19.7	31 May 19.7
	R	R
Finished goods	40 000	80 000
Unfinished goods	15 000	25 000
Raw materials	10 000	15 000

	R
Raw material purchases	160 000
Freight on materials purchased	5 000
Direct wages	80 000
Factory rental	3 500
Depreciation on manufacturing equipment	1 500
Power consumption (factory)	2 000
Maintenance of equipment	500
Insurance on manufacturing equipment	500
Indirect labour	1 000
Indirect material	1 000
Sales	300 000
Sales and administrative costs	40 000

Required:

Prepare a detailed income statement for the month ended 31 May 19.7.

Solution:

DOMINEC MANUFACTURERS LIMITED
INCOME STATEMENT FOR THE MONTH ENDED 31 MAY 19.7

	R	R
Manufacturing section		
Material consumed		160 000
Opening inventory	10 000	
Purchases	160 000	
Freight in	5 000	
	175 000	
Closing inventory	15 000	
Direct labour		80 000
Primary costs		240 000
Manufacturing overheads		10 000
Factory rental	3 500	
Depreciation: Equipment	1 500	
Power consumption	2 000	
Maintenance of equipment	500	
Insurance on equipment	500	
Indirect labour	1 000	
Indirect material	1 000	
		250 000
Add: Unfinished goods (opening inventory)		15 000
		265 000
Deduct: Unfinished goods (closing inventory)		25 000
Production costs of finished goods (transferred to trading section)		R240 000
Trading section		
Sales		300 000
Deduct: Cost of sales		200 000
Opening inventory finished goods	40 000	
Add: Production costs of finished goods from manufacturing section	240 000	
	280 000	
Deduct: Closing inventory finished goods	80 000	
Gross profit transferred to profit and loss section		R100 000
Profit and loss section		
Gross profit transferred from trading section		100 000
Deduct: Sales and administrative costs		40 000
Net income		R60 000

For the sake of clarity, in the layout above the income statement is divided into the three applicable subdivisions. The following would be a more appropriate layout:

DOMINEC MANUFACTURERS LIMITED
INCOME STATEMENT FOR THE MONTH ENDED 31 MAY 19.7

Sales		300 000	Sales of finished goods
(1) Cost of material consumed	160 000		
Material			Manufacturing costs section
Opening inventory	10 000		
Purchases: Material	160 000		
Freight on purchases	5 000		Raw material
Material available for use	175 000		
Less: Closing inventory	15 000		
(2) Direct labour	80 000		Labour
(3) Production overheads	10 000		
Indirect labour	1 000		
Indirect material	1 000		
Power consumption	2 000		Overheads
Maintenance of plant	500		
Factory rental	3 500		
Insurance on factory	500		
Depreciation on plant	1 500		
(4) Total manufacturing costs	250 000		
(5) *Add:* Opening inventory Unfinished goods	15 000		Work in progress
Total goods in progress during the year	265 000		
(6) *Less:* Closing inventory Unfinished goods	(25 000)		
(7) Cost of finished goods manufactured	240 000		
(8) *Add:* Opening inventory finished goods	40 000		
(9) Cost of goods available for sale	280 000		Finished goods section
(10) *Less:* Closing inventory finished goods	(80 000)		
(11) Cost of goods sold		200 000	
(12) GROSS PROFIT		100 000	
Less: Sales and administrative costs		40 000	
NET INCOME		R60 000	

26

ASPECTS OF FINANCING

The **AIM** of this chapter is a broad discussion of the basic principles of financing in order to facilitate a meaningful study of the analysis and interpretation of financial statements.

26.1 THE FINANCING FUNCTION

The primary objective of the financing function is to plan and implement the **financial structure** most suitable for an undertaking.

The **financial structure** of a specific undertaking consists of the different sources of finance as depicted on the equity side of the balance sheet.

26.2 CAPITAL REQUIREMENTS

In financing terminology, the total funds invested in an undertaking are known as the **capital** invested.

Capital can be divided into **own capital**, which is represented by owner's equity, and **outside capital**, which is represented by liabilities.

Investment in the assets of an undertaking gives rise to **capital requirements** which must be financed from various sources, as represented in example 26.1:

Example 26.1

FX LIMITED
BALANCE SHEET AT 31 DECEMBER 19.1

				R'000
		Assets		
Investment in assets	Fixed capital	**Fixed assets**		540
		Land and buildings	300	
		Equipment	240	
	Current capital	**Current assets**		420
		Inventory	250	
		Debtors	150	
		Cash	20	
	Total capital requirement			R960

SOURCES OF FINANCING

			R'000
		Shareholders' equity	
Financing structure	Own capital	Share capital	200
		Retained income	280
			480
		Long-term liabilities	
	Borrowed capital	15% Mortgage bond	300
		Current liabilities	
		Trade creditors	180
	Total capital		R960

The capital requirements depend on the nature and extent of the activities of the undertaking, which in turn are determined by management policy and various internal and external operating factors.

Management decides on the nature of the undertaking, the extent of its capacity, the assets needed and the financing which will be utilised.

The investment necessary for financing the fixed assets represents the fixed capital requirements.

Management may, for example, decide to erect a factory which can manufacture 2 million tons of cement a year. The fixed assets, land, buildings, machinery and equipment necessary to create the capacity for 2 million tons per annum requires an investment of, say, R200 million. In other words, there is a fixed capital requirement of R200 million.

The investment in current assets represents the current capital requirements. The investment in current assets is dependent on the turnover that can be achieved during a particular period, costs, selling prices, credit terms and other operating factors. The investment in current assets will change continuously as the factors which influence it change.

Material inventory of R4 million, finished products of R2 million and debtors of R4 million are necessary to operate the cement factory at a capacity utilisation of 1,8 million tons per annum. Current capital requirements are therefore R10 million. If the output is increased to 2 million tons per annum, the current capital requirements will increase proportionately.

Capital requirements which are not subject to short-term fluctuations and which can usually be changed only by long-term investment decisions are known as permanent capital requirements.

The fixed capital requirements plus that portion of the current capital requirements which remains reasonably constant, form the permanent capital requirements.

That portion of the current capital requirements which is continuously subject to fluctuations forms the varying capital requirements.

Therefore a distinction can be made between permanent capital requirements and varying capital requirements, as shown in figure 26.1.

Figure 26.1 Permanent and varying capital requirements

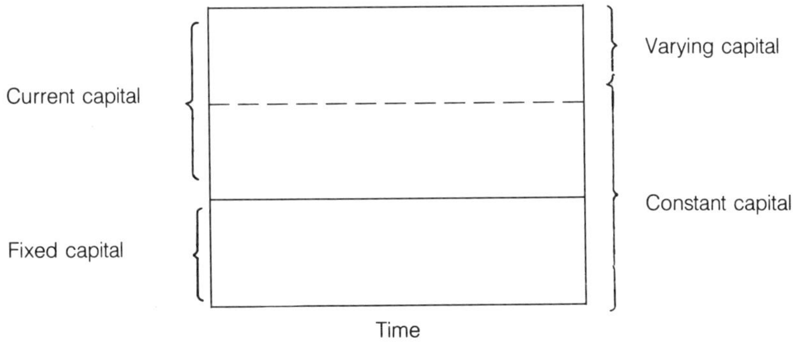

It is the responsibility of the financial planner to determine the permanent and varying capital requirements and to find the most suitable financing sources for these requirements.

26.3 NET CURRENT CAPITAL REQUIREMENTS

Net current capital is the difference between current assets and current liabilities.

Net current capital of FX Limited at 31 December 19.1 is calculated as follows:

Current assets		420 000
Inventory	250 000	
Debtors	150 000	
Cash	20 000	
Less: Current liabilities		180 000
Net current capital		R240 000

Net current capital is determined primarily by the structure of the undertaking's operating cycle.

The **operating cycle** is the cycle which the current capital completes in the normal course of business.

In a trading concern the operating cycle commences when trading inventory is bought on credit and is on hand for a particular period. The goods are then sold on credit terms. At the end of the credit period the debtors pay and the undertaking receives cash. This cash is applied to settle the creditors' accounts.

The operating cycle of a trading concern is shown in figure 26.2.

Figure 26.2 The operating cycle

There is a close relationship between current assets and liabilities in the operating cycle. The acquisition of current assets creates current liabilities which are settled by conversion of the current assets. In other words, the investment in current assets creates a current capital requirement which is financed by current liabilities.

Therefore it is useful to utilise net current capital requirements as a point of departure for financing decisions.

Net current capital requirements are influenced by:

- ☐ the management policies of the undertaking and its suppliers in respect of current assets and liabilities
- ☐ the effectiveness of management
- ☐ cost and price levels
- ☐ the volume of activities.

26.3.1 Influence of management policy on current capital

In order to control net current capital, the management of an undertaking usually lays down policies relating to the following factors which influence current assets:

- ☐ Stock turnover rate.
- ☐ Credit terms granted to debtors.
- ☐ Minimum cash balances.

The policy decision of suppliers regarding credit terms is in turn a factor which influences current liabilities.

Changes in management policy directly influence net current capital requirements, as shown in example 26.2. The example illustrates how the net current capital requirements more than doubled as a result of a change in policy regarding credit terms, without there being any change in sales levels. Consequently, the undertaking will be obliged to find additional financing of R31 890 (viz the difference between R55 589 and R23 699).

26.3.2 Effectiveness of management

Management policy regarding stock turnover rate and credit terms is merely a guideline. In practice the actual stock turnover rate and credit terms will deviate from policies, especially if there is no proper control over current assets and liabilities.

The nature of the effect of changes in turnover rates and credit terms on net current capital requirements will be identical to that caused by changes in policy.

26.3.3 Changes in price and cost levels

Changes in the costs or selling prices of the undertaking's products, for example as a result of inflation, have a direct influence on the net current capital requirements. An increase in costs and prices will increase the net current capital requirements, and *vice versa*. This effect is also illustrated in example 26.2.

26.3.4 Volume of activities

The extent of the investment in net current capital is dependent on the volume of activities. When the level of turnover changes, the investment in inventory, debtors and suppliers' credit usually also changes. Current assets will change proportionately more than current liabilities when the period for which operating capital is tied up in current assets is longer than the suppliers' credit terms. This means that increased turnover results in greater net current capital requirements and *vice versa*. The influence of a change in turnover is illustrated in example 26.2.

Example 26.2 Factors influencing current capital

	BASE CASE	CHANGE IN PERIOD	COSTS AND PRICES CHANGE	QUANTITIES CHANGE
	R / R	R / R	R / R	R / R
Sales per annum	1 000 × 180 = 180 000	1 000 × 180 = 180 000	1 000 × 200 = 200 000	1 500 × 200 = 300 000
Cost of sales	1 000 × 100 = 100 000	1 000 × 100 = 100 000	1 000 × 120 = 120 000	1 500 × 120 = 180 000
Material purchases	1 000 × 72 = 72 000	1 000 × 72 = 72 000	1 000 × 84 = 84 000	1 500 × 84 = 126 000
Average inventory	90 days	120 days	90 days	90 days
Debtors' credit term	30 days	60 days	30 days	30 days
Creditors' credit term	90 days	45 days	90 days	90 days
Current assets				
Inventory	90/365 × 100 000 = 24 658	120/365 × 100 000 = 32 877	90/365 × 120 000 = 29 589	90/365 × 180 000 = 44 384
Debtors	30/365 × 180 000 = 14 795	60/365 × 180 000 = 29 589	30/365 × 200 000 = 16 438	30/365 × 300 000 = 24 658
Cash	2 000	2 000	2 000	2 000
	41 452	64 466	48 027	71 041
Less: Creditors	90/365 × 72 000 = 17 753	45/365 × 72 000 = 8 877	90/365 × 84 000 = 20 712	90/365 × 126 000 = 31 068
Net current capital	R23 699	R55 589	R27 315	R39 973

26.4 SOURCES AND FORMS OF FINANCE

26.4.1 Difference between equity and outside sources of capital

A source of finance refers to the supplier of finance. A form of finance refers to a specific type of finance. For example, trade creditors are a **source** of financing and suppliers' credit, which is provided by trade creditors, is a **form** of financing.

To create an optimum financing structure, the forms of financing must be matched to the capital requirements of the undertaking. Therefore it is necessary to study the characteristics of the different forms of finance.

When the financing decision is being made it is important to distinguish between the characteristics of equity and borrowed capital.

Equity capital is financing provided by the owners at their own risk, or capital generated internally by the undertaking.

Borrowed capital is finance provided to the undertaking by external suppliers of capital in the form of loans or other types of credit.

26.4.2 Long-term sources

☐ Own capital

Own capital as a source of finance can be divided into owner's equity and specific reserves, each of which is uniquely involved in the financing of an undertaking. Equity capital can be divided into contributed equity capital and retained income.

(1) Contributed equity capital

Equity capital is the primary source of financing which the owners contribute to provide the initial permanent capital requirements of the undertaking.

Therefore equity capital is also referred to as controlling capital. Equity capital contributions by owners are usually permanent capital which is not repayable. The share capital of companies and the members' contributions in close corporations, partnerships and sole traders are the most important forms of contributed equity capital. According to the Companies Act and the Close Corporations Act, the share capital in companies and the capital contributions in close corporations are both regarded as permanent capital. In non-incorporated undertakings there are no legal restrictions on the repayment of owners' capital. In practice, however, it is considered to be permanent capital.

The owners' capital carries the full risk of the undertaking. Profit is the reward owners receive for the use of equity capital. Profit is added to the equity capital and, conversely, a loss is absorbed by equity capital.

(2) Retained income

Profit which is not distributed to owners but is retained in the undertaking is an important form of financing and is part of equity capital. This source of financing is under the full control of the owners, who decide what portion of the profit will be distributed and what portion will be retained.

The decision regarding the retention of available profit is influenced by mainly two factors, namely:

> ☐ the expectations of the owners
> ☐ the capital requirements which can be financed by retained income.

First, the owners expect their investment to be maximised from the earnings of the undertaking.

> The profit which the undertaking earns is added to equity capital.

Second, the owners expect at least a portion of the accumulated profit to be paid out in cash.

> The distribution of profit is in the form of drawings by owners of non-incorporated undertakings and dividends to the shareholders of companies.

The owners decide on the distribution of available profit, taking into consideration the rate of return expected on the investment.

The distribution of profit is further limited by the capital requirements which must be financed by equity capital. These capital requirements arise in one of two ways:

First, they can arise as a result of normal business operations. Various factors may contribute to an increase in net current capital requirements. If no external capital is utilised, the requirements will absorb the available equity capital.

Second, the owners may decide in advance on an expansion of capital which must be financed by a retention of income out of equity capital.

(3) Specific reserves

The creation of specific reserves out of income before profit determination, for example provision for depreciation, has the effect that income retained in the undertaking becomes available for internal financing. This is an important form of finance, especially when relatively large amounts are provided in this manner. Because the reserves are created from income before profit determination, they are not distributable and are also considered to be permanent capital.

> Assume that the net income of an undertaking is R100 000 before depreciation is taken into account. This means that R100 000 is available for application. A provision of R20 000 for depreciation reduces the net income to R80 000, but there is still R100 000 available for application. Only R80 000 thereof can be distributed as profit, while the balance of R20 000 is retained in the undertaking as a source of finance.

☐ **Dividend policy**

The dividend policy of a company plays an important role in the financing process. The factors which influence the retention of profit as discussed in the previous paragraph also apply in respect of dividend policy. In addition to these factors, a company must bear in mind that the market for its shares is influenced to a large extent by its dividend policy. Management's dividend policy, which takes into account the financing requirements of the undertaking, may not necessarily please shareholders, who expect a regular, constant or growing dividend. The attitude of the capital market may influence the ability to attract new capital.

□ The role of the stock exchange

The stock exchange plays an important role in the acquisition of capital. The shares and debentures of public companies, also known as stock, are freely transferable and therefore negotiable. A public company can thus attract new capital by issuing shares or stock to the public. The success of a public issue is to a large extent dependent on the negotiability of the relevant shares or debentures.

The Johannesburg Stock Exchange is an institution where the shares and debentures of public companies can be traded at prices which are determined by supply and demand. Any public company which satisfies the requirements of the stock exchange for a listing can have its shares or debentures listed on the exchange.

The supply of and demand for stock is influenced by a number of other factors, for example national and international economic conditions and the financial position and profit expectations of the company concerned. The market price of stock usually differs from the price at which it was originally issued.

The possibility of profit on capital is an important consideration when investing in stock. The negotiability of stock makes it an attractive form of investment for the supplier of capital, who can realise his capital at any time.

□ Long-term outside capital

Financing for a period longer than five years is regarded as long term. Long-term outside capital is mostly in the form of fixed interest loans or debentures. A long-term loan constitutes a single indivisible liability of the debtor to a specific creditor for the period in question. Debentures, on the other hand, are subdivided into transferable units, each of which can be issued to different debtors. Both these forms of financing are usually for a fixed period and are to be redeemed in a predetermined manner. Long-term loans and debentures are often secured by bonds over fixed property (the most common form of security).

Interest rates on long-term forms of finance are determined largely by supply and demand factors on the capital market. Therefore the trend of interest rates is an important consideration in the timing of financing. Usually interest rates on long-term loans and debentures remain constant over the period of the loan or debentures. The reward for the use of borrowed capital is a fixed liability which is in no way linked to the earnings of the undertaking.

26.4.3 Medium-term financing

Medium-term financing is for a period of between one and five years. There is a wide variety of financing forms which can be applied specifically to medium-term capital requirements. Except for strictly period loans, most medium-term forms of financing are linked to specific types of transactions, for example financial leases and instalment sale transactions.

The supplier of finance in a non-redeemable financial lease contract leases an asset to a lessee without the transfer of ownership to him. In some instances the lessee has the option to purchase at the end of the period. Thus, a lease enables an undertaking to use an asset without applying capital for its acquisition.

Instalment credit is a form of finance for the purchase of assets in which the purchaser settles the purchase price in instalments, with or without interest, over the relevant period. The ownership of the financed asset is transferred to the purchaser on purchase, except in the case of instalment sale (hire purchase), when ownership is transferred only after the full liability has been settled.

26.4.4 Short-term sources

The period for short-term financing is less than one year. The most important sources of short-term financing are short-term loans by banking institutions and suppliers' credit in various forms.

☐ **Short-term loans**

A bank overdraft granted by a commercial bank on the current account of a client is a very common type of short-term loan. Often security in some form or other is required for this type of credit. A bank overdraft usually has a maximum limit, called a facility, and a fixed period. During the period of the loan the balance on the current account varies as transactions take place. Interest is charged on the outstanding balance only, and the interest rate is dependent on the creditworthiness of the borrower and the security supplied. The interest rate can change during the period of a loan. Bank overdrafts are especially suitable for providing for fluctuating capital requirements. In practice the facility is often extended at the end of the period, so that by repeated extensions a bank overdraft often assumes the nature of medium-term financing.

☐ **Suppliers' credit**

(1) Open account

Suppliers' credit on open account is a general type of short-term financing for commercial transactions. The supplier opens an account for the customer and debits any purchases he makes to this account. Usually the creditworthiness of the client is established before the account is opened and generally no security is required for the outstanding amount. The period is usually 30, 60 or 90 days, depending on the practice in the specific economic sector.

In undertakings where commercial transactions occur continuously, suppliers' credit on open account forms a reasonably permanent form of financing. The cost of this suppliers' credit is represented by the discount which the undertaking sacrifices by not purchasing for cash.

Assume that an undertaking's monthly purchases of trading goods amount to R10 000, which can be sold for R15 000. Inventory is equivalent to two months' purchases and debtors are equivalent to 1½ months' sales. Suppliers expect payment after 30 days, but allow 2½% discount if goods are purchased for cash. The total discount on annual purchases of R120 000 therefore amounts to R3 000.

The undertaking must decide whether it is an advantage to buy for cash or to make use of suppliers' credit. The alternatives are represented in example 26.3.

Example 26.3 Comparison of cash and credit purchases

DIFFERENCE IN NET CURRENT CAPITAL REQUIREMENTS		
	Credit purchases	Cash purchases
Inventory	20 000	20 000
Debtors	22 500	22 500
	42 500	42 500
Creditors	10 000	—
Net current capital requirements	R32 500	R42 500

DIFFERENCE IN NET INCOME		
Discount on cash purchases	—	3 000
Less: Interest on bank overdraft (12% on R10 000)	—	1 200
Advantage	—	R1 800

In the case of cash purchases, the net current capital requirements are R10 000 higher than in the case of credit purchases. If the R10 000 is financed by a bank overdraft at 12% interest p a, the annual interest will amount to R1 200. The advantage of cash purchases is therefore R1 800 p a, that is the difference between the discount of R3 000 on cash purchases and interest of R1 200 on the bank overdraft.

(2) Factoring

A supplier of credit on open account can discount his debtors to a financier, who will collect the outstanding amounts himself at the end of the credit period. This is known as **factoring** and enables the supplier to give his customers the desired credit and also to collect his money earlier. The discount represents the interest that the financier earns over the period from when the debtors are purchased until they have been settled.

(3) Revolving credit

Revolving credit is a form of suppliers' credit used in commercial transactions. A supplier draws a bill for the outstanding amount of the transaction on a customer, who then accepts the bill. By accepting the bill he accepts liability for settlement of the amount of the bill to the holder thereof. The customer settles the bill on expiry. This type of credit is rarely used in internal transactions, but is still frequently used in import and export transactions.

(4) Acceptance credit

A bill that has been accepted is a negotiable document. The negotiability of bills creates the possibility of acceptance credit for the bearer of the bill. Assume that the supplier sells goods and draws a bill for 90 days on the customer. Because the bill is negotiable, the supplier can discount the bill with a financier before the expiry of the 90 days and so receive his money earlier. The new holder of the bill collects the outstanding amount at the end of 90 days from the debtor who accepted the bill.

The financier discounts the bill at a discount which allows him a return at the ruling acceptance rate for the period of the bill.

26.5 COST OF CAPITAL

It is important for an undertaking to know the cost of capital which it applies, because this gives an indication of the minimum return which must be earned from the assets.

Assets		Capital
Return on assets must be sufficient	to	cover the cost of capital

> Assume that an undertaking lends funds at 15% p a. The cost of capital is therefore 15%. The funds will have to be invested in assets which give a return of at least 15% in order not to show a loss.

The **cost of equity capital** is determined by the rate of return which owners consider to be reasonable. There are various approaches to determining a reasonable rate of return: it can be determined subjectively by those concerned, but more often it is determined scientifically by comparing the risk of the undertaking relative to the rate of return in risk-free investments. The principle is the higher the risk, the higher the expected rate of return.

The cost of borrowed capital is determined by the effective interest rate at which the capital was acquired.

26.5.1 Cost of capital: Non-incorporated enterprises

The **cost of capital** of an enterprise as a whole is often determined as the weighted average cost of the actual combined forms of financing which the undertaking has applied. Depending on how it is used, the cost of capital can be determined before or after tax.

Example 26.4 illustrates the calculation of the weighted average cost of capital of a non-incorporated undertaking. The calculation is shown before and after taxation.

Example 26.4 Weighted average cost of capital

A SMITH – TRADER					
Sources of financing	Capital amount	Cost of capital			
		Before taxation		After taxation	
Equity	100 000	20%[1]	20 000	12%[1]	12 000
Long-term loan (interest rate 12% p a)	50 000	12%	6 000	7,2%[2]	3 600
Bank overdraft (interest rate 15% p a)	10 000	15%	1 500	9%[2]	900
Creditors (no costs)	20 000	—	—		
Total capital	R180 000				
Net earnings			R27 500		R16 500
Cost of capital		$\frac{27\,500}{180\,000}\%$ = 15,278%		$\frac{16\,500}{180\,000}\%$ 9,167%	

1 The owner requires a rate of return of 12% after tax on the equity capital invested in the undertaking. He pays an average 40% tax on net income from the business. Therefore he must earn 20% before tax to earn 12% after tax.

$$\frac{\text{After taxation rate}}{(100-\text{taxation rate})} = \frac{12\%}{(100-40)} = 20\%$$

2 The after taxation interest rate is only 60% of the total interest charge, because the taxable income for taxation purposes is reduced by the total amount of the interest charge. If the total income is considered to be taxable, the interest charges are considered to be reduced by the amount of taxation saved.

The taxation can be tested as follows:

		Before taxation		After taxation
Operating assets		180 000		180 000
Earnings thereon @	15,278% (BT)	27 500	(9,167% AT)	16 500
Less: Interest		7 500		4 500
Net income before taxation		R20 000		R12 000
Earnings on equity of R100 000		20% (BT)		12% (AT)

BT = Before taxation AT = After taxation

Therefore the undertaking must invest the assets of R180 000 at a rate of 15,278% before taxation (which is equivalent to 9,167% after taxation) to cover the cost of capital.

26.5.2 Cost of capital: Companies

In a company the expected return on equity capital is expressed in terms of the return on the market value of the shares. There are different approaches which can be followed. The expected rate of return per share on the market price of the shares is usually considered to be the most realistic basis.

Assume that A Limited has issued share capital of R1 000 000 shares of R1 each. The market price of the shares is 400c each. The shareholders expect a return of 15% after tax on the market price of the shares, that is 15% of 400c = 60c per share. The taxation rate of the company is 42,5%. The cost of capital after taxation can be calculated as in example 26.5.

Example 26.5 Weighted average cost of capital

A LIMITED		
Sources of financing	Amount	Cost of capital
Share capital – 1 000 000 shares @ R1	1 000 000	600 000[1]
Retained income	500 000	
Long-term loan (12%)	200 000	6,9%[2] 13 800
Bank overdraft (15%)	100 000	8,625%[3] 8 625
Creditors	100 000	—
Total capital	R1 900 000	
Total cost of capital		R622 425
Cost of capital after taxation	$\frac{622\ 425}{1\ 900\ 000\%} = 32{,}7\%$	

1 (60c × 1 000 000 shares) 2 12% × (100 – 42,5)% = 6,9% 3 15% × (100 – 42,5)% = 8,625%

The calculation can be tested as follows:

Operating assets	1 900 000
Earnings thereon @ 32,7%	622 425
Less: Interest	22 425
	R600 000
Earnings per share on 1 million shares	60c

26.6 CHOICE OF SOURCES

In selecting the most suitable sources of financing for an undertaking, the following are taken into consideration:

- ☐ return on equity capital
- ☐ liquidity
- ☐ solvency.

26.6.1 Return on equity capital

The undertaking aims to maximise its return on equity capital. The return on equity capital is measured against net income after interest in relation to equity capital. Consider the financial position of FX Limited as illustrated in example 26.6.

Example 26.6

FX LIMITED			
Balance sheet at 31/12/19.1		Income statement for the year 19.1	
	R'000		R'000
Fixed assets	540	Income	192
Current assets	420	*Less:* Interest	66
Total assets	960	Net income before taxation	126
		Taxation (50%)	63
Share capital	200	Net income after taxation	63
Retained income	280		
Shareholders' equity	480		
Long-term liability (@ 16%)	300		
Current liabilities (@ 10%)	180		
	960		

The return on equity capital can be determined as follows:

$$\frac{\text{Net income after interest}}{\text{Equity}} = R\frac{126\ 000}{480\ 000} = 26{,}3\%$$

In order to satisfy specific capital requirements, the undertaking will choose the capital sources that will give the greatest return on equity capital in the long term.

This objective is influenced by:

- ☐ the return on capital
- ☐ the cost of borrowed capital
- ☐ the debt equity ratio
- ☐ the period of the capital requirement.

☐ Return on capital

Return on capital is the return before interest on the total capital invested in the undertaking.

The total capital in FX Limited amounts to R960 000, and the net income before interest amounts to R192 000. Thus the return on capital can be calculated as follows:

$$\frac{\text{Net income before interest}}{\text{Total capital}} = R\frac{192\ 000}{960\ 000} = 20\%$$

Return on capital cannot be altered by financing decisions, because it is calculated on income before interest. Since return on capital is known, it can be used as the starting point for planning return on equity and for planning financing decisions.

☐ Cost of equity capital

The return on equity capital is directly influenced by the cost of borrowed capital.

For any given financing structure (see section 26.1), the return on equity capital will increase as the cost of borrowed capital decreases, and *vice versa*. The undertaking therefore chooses those sources of financing which have the lowest interest charges for the period.

Borrowed capital usually comprises different forms of financing, each having a different cost.

In order to maximise the return on equity capital, a combination of borrowed capital with the lowest average cost, but which still ensures a safe liquidity, should be chosen. Liquidity is discussed in a later paragraph.

☐ Debt equity ratio

The debt equity ratio is the ratio of borrowed capital to own capital.

In the case of FX Limited, the debt equity ratio can be determined as follows:

$$\frac{\text{Borrowed capital}}{\text{Equity capital}} = \text{R}\frac{480\ 000}{960\ 000}$$

$$= 50\%$$

Equity capital is the primary source of finance in an undertaking. Under normal circumstances an external financier will be willing to lend funds to an undertaking only when sufficient equity capital has been introduced in the undertaking to reduce the creditor's risk to an acceptable level. The supplier of borrowed capital therefore expects a sound debt equity ratio in the undertaking. The greater the risks an undertaking is exposed to, the smaller the debt equity ratio. An external financier expects equity capital to be sufficient to absorb any losses before borrowed capital is affected.

If the return on capital is higher than the cost of borrowed capital, the owner will try to apply as much borrowed capital as possible in order to increase the return on equity capital, as illustrated in example 26.7.

Example 26.7

	High equity	Low equity
Total assets	200 000	200 000
Equity	150 000	50 000
Borrowed capital (@ 10% interest)	R50 000	R150 000
Return on assets 20%	40 000	40 000
Interest charges	5 000	15 000
Profit	R35 000	R25 000
Return on equity	23,3%	50%

For any given return on capital, the return on equity capital will increase as the debt equity ratio increases if the interest rate is less than the return on capital. Similarly, the return on capital will decrease with an increase in the debt equity ratio if the average interest rate on debt is higher than the return on capital.

This effect of change in the ratio between equity and borrowed capital is called the **leverage effect**. The leverage effect is **positive** if the cost of capital is higher than the cost of borrowed capital and **negative** if it is lower than the cost of borrowed capital.

If the leverage effect is positive, the undertaking will attempt to finance as much as possible of the total capital requirements from borrowed capital.

Therefore, for a given return on capital and a given interest rate on finance debt, management can adjust the return on owner's equity by adjusting the debt equity ratio; in other words by making use of more or less finance debt. However, the leverage effect cannot be manipulated unrestrainedly by increasing the debt equity ratio to increase the return on equity capital. The greater the debt finance used in an undertaking relative to equity capital, the lower its creditworthiness; in other words the financiers will be less prepared to lend additional finance and the interest on additional loan capital will be higher.

□ The period of the capital requirement

In order to maximise return on equity capital, the period of the capital source should be matched with the period of the capital requirement it must satisfy.

There are two reasons for this:

First, there will be excess financing when the period of the financing is greater than the period of the capital requirement. When the period of the capital requirement is greater than the period of financing, cash flow problems will result.

Second, there is usually a difference in cost between long-term and short-term financing.

Under normal circumstances, therefore, the undertaking should finance more permanent capital requirements by cheaper long-term sources and varying capital requirements by more expensive short-term sources. The total cost of varying short-term sources will be lower during the short periods that they are used than the total cost of the long-term sources which are used continuously, including periods when financing is not required.

Assume that during a year the total capital requirement of an undertaking changes as shown in figure 26.3.

Figure 26.3 Changes in total capital requirement of a specific undertaking

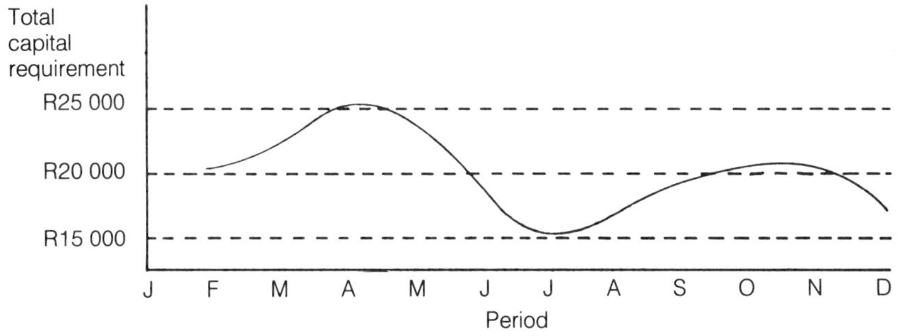

The total capital requirement reaches a maximum of R25 000 during April and a minimum of R15 000 during July.

If the total capital requirement was provided for by long-term sources which bear interest at 12%, the R25 000 capital would have been provided at a cost of R3 000 p a.

Alternatively, only R20 000 could be financed by long-term sources at a cost of R2 400 p a and short-term capital at 15% p a, increasing from the beginning of March to a maximum of R5 000 in April and decreasing to nil at the end of May. Assume that on average R2 500 was borrowed in March, R5 000 in April and R2 500 in May. The interest charges on the short-term capital at 15% p a would therefore amount to R125, and the total cost (i e R125 plus R2 400) of all financing would amount to R2 525, compared with R3 000 in the first alternative.

26.6.2 Liquidity

Liquidity is the ability to meet financial obligations timeously out of funds which are available for immediate application. Liquidity is therefore an extremely important factor in choosing the type of financing.

All forms of borrowed capital entail predetermined obligations in respect of repayment of capital and interest. The undertaking should choose its types of financing and arrange its cash flow in such a way that there are always sufficient funds available to meet its capital repayments and interest obligations.

26.6.3 Solvency

Solvency reflects the excess of assets over liabilities. The greater the excess the lower the risk that losses will absorb owner's equity totally and that creditors will suffer a loss.

If the excess of assets over liabilities is too small, the suppliers of borrowed capital will be reluctant to supply capital to the undertaking or will charge a high interest rate. If the excess of assets over liabilities is too great, the undertaking loses the advantage of the leverage effect.

26.7 SECURITY FOR FINANCING OBLIGATIONS

For any given financial structure the current income of an undertaking should be sufficient to meet its financial obligations, that is interest, capital repayments and dividends.

The ability of an undertaking to meet its obligations can be judged by the extent to which they are covered by income.

26.7.1 Dividend cover

Shareholders expect a satisfactory return on equity capital. In addition, they expect at least a portion of the return to be paid out as dividends.

The dividend cover ratio measures the ability of current income to provide a specific dividend:

$$\text{Dividend cover} = \frac{\text{Income after tax}}{\text{Dividend}}$$

If FX Limited declares a dividend of R20 000, the dividend cover will be calculated as follows:

$$\text{R}\frac{63\ 000}{20\ 000} = 3{,}15 \text{ times}$$

26.7.2 Interest cover

Interest is paid out of income. Therefore it is important to ensure that income is always sufficient to cover the interest charges, especially when income fluctuates from one period to the next.

The interest cover which measures the ratio of interest to available income is useful when the risk that a fixed interest obligation creates when income fluctuates is evaluated. This is illustrated in example 26.8.

Example 26.8 Interest cover

FX LIMITED	
Net income before interest	192
Less: Interest	66
Net profit before taxation	126
Taxation (50%)	63
Net profit after taxation	63

$$\text{Interest cover} = \frac{\text{Net income before interest}}{\text{Interest}} = \frac{192}{66}$$

$$= 2{,}9 \text{ times}$$

26.7.3 Interest and redemption cover

The ability of an undertaking to meet its fixed interest and redemption obligations out of the available cash flow can be evaluated by means of a fixed obligation ratio, as illustrated in example 26.9.

Example 26.9 Fixed obligation cover out of cash flow

Use the information in the income statement in example 25.7. In addition, FX Limited has to repay R2 000 p a on a loan.

Fixed obligation cover

$$\frac{\text{Net income after tax and before interest} + \text{Interest (I} - \text{T)}}{\text{Interest after tax} + \text{Capital repayment}}$$

(where T = taxation rate = 0,42)

$$= \frac{14\ 400\ (\text{I} - \text{T})}{900\ (\text{I} - \text{T}) = 2\ 000}$$

$$= 3{,}3 \text{ times}$$

27

BUDGETS

The **AIM** of this chapter is to explain the principles of financial budgeting and planning as control instruments and to develop skill in preparing and using budgets.

27.1 THE FUNCTION OF A BUDGET

Planning and **control** are the two most important functions of management. **Planning** comprises formulating the objectives of the enterprise and making decisions regarding the activities that must be performed in order to achieve these objectives. **Control** comprises management action to ensure that actual performance complies with the planned objectives. Therefore the planning and control processes are complementary: the objectives set by the planning process constitute the point of departure for the control process.

The planning and control functions in an undertaking are carried out with the aid of a **budget**. In the planning function the budget serves as a financial model in which the expected future activities and results of an undertaking are reflected, and can be compared to an architect's plans for a new building. In the control function the budget serves as a standard against which actual financial performance can be measured, and can be compared to the approved plans which an architect uses to ensure that the building is erected according to plan.

Because budgeting forms an integral part of the planning and control functions in an undertaking, it is important that the accountant responsible for the budget understands the underlying managerial functions. Therefore the planning and control functions in an undertaking are discussed briefly.

27.2 PLANNING

Any planning process usually consists of at least four steps, namely:

- ☐ determining the objectives to be achieved
- ☐ identifying the various alternatives that can be implemented to achieve these objectives
- ☐ deciding which alternative represents the best solution
- ☐ preparing a plan of action to implement the chosen alternative.

In any undertaking three levels of planning can be distinguished, namely **strategic**, **operational** and **financial** planning. Each of these follows the four steps listed above.

Strategic planning is the process whereby an undertaking decides on its objectives and the nature of the business it will conduct to achieve these.

The strategy of a trading concern can be formulated briefly as follows:

ECOMARK STRATEGIC PLANNING
Ecomark operates supermarkets in leased suburban premises and deals only in groceries, hardware and fresh produce. Ecomark's objective is to earn a reasonable return on capital and to maintain a sound financial position.

Operational planning entails planning in detail the activities necessary to achieve the objectives of the undertaking.

Financial planning entails planning the financial implications of the operations, for example planning income, expenses, assets, liabilities and cash flow.

27.3 APPROACH TO BUDGETING

Before a budget can be prepared it is necessary to decide on the various aspects that will form the basis of the budget. First, the **objectives** that must be achieved have to be formulated and the **period** for which the budget must be prepared must be decided upon. Then the **point of departure** must be determined. Last, the **policy factors** or limitations with which the budget must comply should be defined.

27.3.1. Budget objectives

The objectives of an undertaking form the basis for the budget. An **objective** is a specific result which must be strived for and which is specified in terms of certain criteria such as quantity, quality, time, cost, income and profit. Usually one or more main objectives are identified, together with various subsidiary objectives. The budget is prepared to meet these objectives.

The financial objectives of Ecomark, for example, can be formulated as follows:

ECOMARK FINANCIAL OBJECTIVES 19.2	
Gross sales	Increase from R3,8 m 19.1 to R5 m in 19.2
Net profit	R40 000
Return on operating capital	20%

27.3.2 Budget period

Budgets are prepared for a specific period, usually a financial year. Annual budgets are often divided into monthly or even weekly intervals to allow for more accurate planning and control.

27.3.3 Budget starting point

The activities of any enterprise are limited by various factors which must be taken into account in budgeting if the budget is to be realistic. A limiting factor is a situation which cannot be changed during the budget period. For instance, the market for an enterprise's product will determine the quantity of product that can be sold, and the capacity of a factory will determine the level of production possible. Usually the budget is dependent on only one, or maybe two, key limiting factors. Where such a key limiting factor is used as starting point for the budget, it is known as the **budget starting point**. Assume, for example, that an undertaking can sell 30 000 units during a year, but the factory can produce only 25 000 units. In this case production capacity is a key limiting factor and will be used as the budget starting point. Thus the budget will be based on the production and sale of 25 000 units.

It is essential that the correct starting point is chosen for each budget because it influences the validity of the total budget.

27.3.4 Policy factors

Policy can be defined as rules or guidelines set by the management of an undertaking to ensure that sound business practice is maintained. The following example illustrates typical policy formulations in commercial undertakings:

ECOMARK
FINANCIAL POLICY

- ☐ Credit sales may not constitute more than 50% of total sales
- ☐ Debtors are allowed only 30 days credit
- ☐ Inventory of merchandise will be limited to the following ratios to monthly cost of sales:
  - groceries 1,5 ×
  - hardware 2,5 ×
  - fresh produce 0,1 ×

27.4 THE BUDGET STRUCTURE

A budget is compiled from different subsidiary budgets which are determined by the nature and responsibility of the relevant activities.

27.4.1 Functional compilation

The operations of an undertaking generally consist of various functions which are usually allocated to different departments or sections, each of which is the responsibility of a specific manager. Consider, for example, the organisational structure of Ecomark, which is represented diagrammatically in figure 27.1.

Figure 27.1

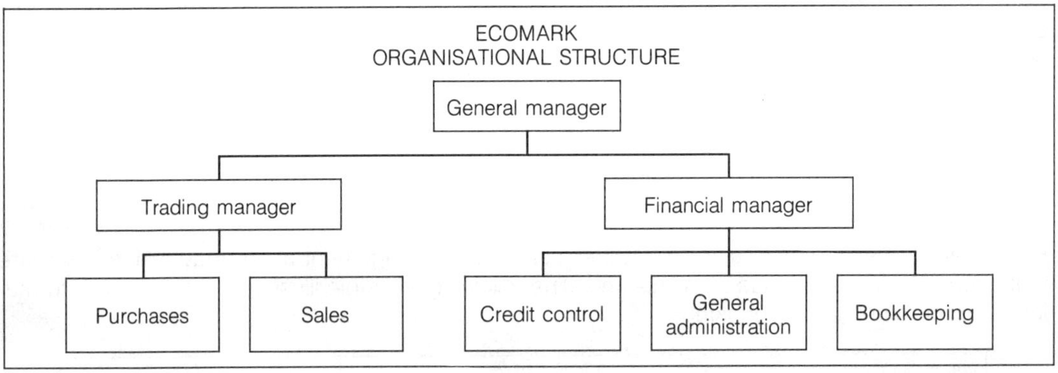

In the budgeting process a separate budget is prepared for each department by the manager concerned in accordance with the objectives and policy set by the executive management of the undertaking. The individual budgets are then combined in a final, coordinated budget.

Ecomark's budget will be subdivided into subsidiary budgets for:

- ☐ trading activities
- ☐ administration.

Each departmental budget is further subdivided according to the different sections within the department.

27.4.2 Operating and financial budgets

The budget for any particular function is subdivided into **operating** and **financial** budgets.

An **operating budget** is a budget for income and expense items, while a **financial budget** is a budget for asset and liability items.

The operating and financial budgets are coordinated by the relationship which exists between income and expense and asset and liability items.

The financial budget for debtors, for example, will be dependent on the operating budget for credit sales and the cash budget for debtors' payments.

The compilation of Ecomark's budget according to responsibility for financial items is reflected in figure 27.2.

Figure 27.2

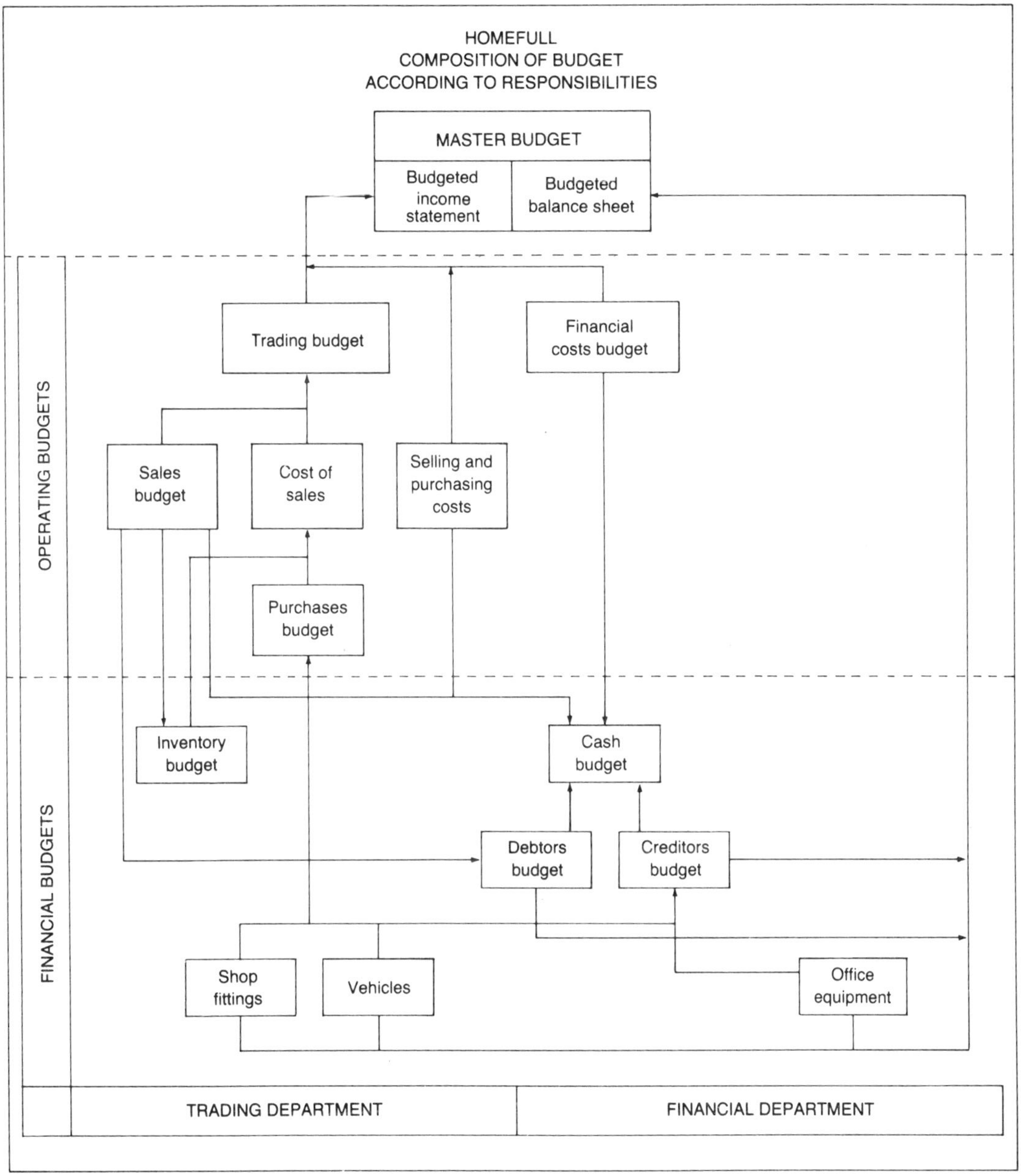

27.5 ELEMENTS OF BUDGETS

A budget consists of a set of elements which can be considered to be its building blocks. The key elements are the budget items, the criteria and norms for each item, and the relationship between the items.

27.5.1 Budget items

Budgeting can be regarded as the compilation of a set of pro forma financial statements for a future period. To prepare a budget the relevant items in the income statement, balance sheet and other supporting statements are identified, and then an amount is budgeted for each item.

The financial reports for the financial period preceding the budget period can be used as a guideline for preparing the budget.

In addition, there are usually various relationships between the budgeted items which must be taken into account in preparing the budget if a realistic result is to be achieved.

27.5.2 Budgeting criteria

The criteria in terms of which each item is budgeted for must be decided upon. A criterion is a unit of measurement. Budget items can be determined in absolute monetary terms, in monetary terms which relate to another item, or in terms of quantities expressed at cost or a certain price.

For example, the following criteria can be used for certain items in the Ecomark budget:

BUDGET ITEM	CRITERIA
Sales	Monetary value of sales
Salaries of sales personnel	Number of sales persons related to turnover and a particular remuneration package
Packaging material	Mass of packaging material related to turnover and cost per mass unit
Debtors	Number of days credit sales outstanding

27.5.3 Budgeting norms

The next step is to allocate values to the criteria for the various budget items. This is done by determining **norms** for the quantities and costs or prices. Budgeting norms are quantitative standards with which budget items must comply if budgeting objectives are to be achieved.

Norms should be considered in relation to the system. In order to achieve a particular output or result, a particular process requiring a specific input must be carried out.

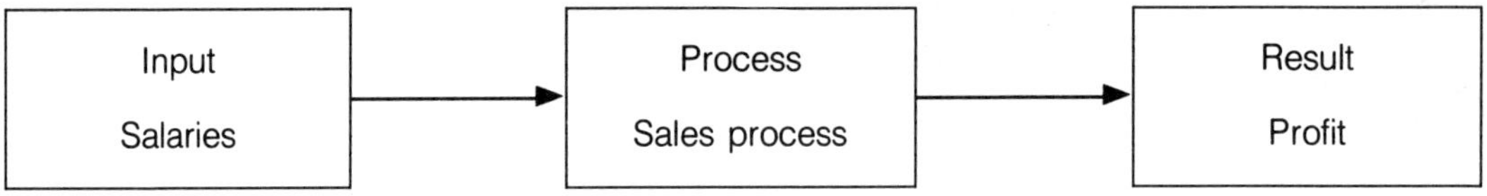

The norms set for the input and process must bear a relation to the results it is hoped will be achieved.

For example, the following norms can be used for certain items in the Ecomark budget:

BUDGET ITEM	NORMS
Sales	R420 000 per month
Salaries of sales personnel	7% of turnover
Packaging material	2% of turnover
Debtors	An average of 30 days credit sales

The managers of the various departments accept responsibility for achieving the norms.

27.5.4 Budget relationships

In order to achieve realistic results the relationships between the various budget items must be identified and taken into account in the preparation of the budget.

There are two types of relationships, namely:

- functional relationships
- value relationships.

Functional relationships are input/output orientated. The independent element in this type of relationship is the designated objective, and the dependent element the input that must be made to achieve the objective.

The approach is to determine the objectives and then to plan the activities that will achieve those objectives in the most effective and efficient manner.

> In order to budget for advertising costs, the sales objectives must be determined. Only then can the nature, extent and cost of advertising be planned and budgeted for.

In **value relationships** the value of the dependent item is dependent on the value of the independent item.

> For example, the amount of outstanding debtors will be determined by the budget for credit sales and debtors' payments.

27.6 BUDGETING PROCEDURE

The first step in preparing a budget is to determine the structure of the budget, that is which subsidiary budgets must be prepared for each department and how they should be coordinated. Next the budget items, criteria and norms must be determined for each subsidiary budget.

Then the budget starting point and its basic budgeted value are chosen and the rest of the budget is developed, taking into consideration any relationships.

Either a single budget or an interval budget approach can be followed in spreading the budget over the budget period.

A single budget for a specific period covers the total period, while an interval budget divides the full budget period into shorter intervals, for example a typical annual budget will be divided into monthly intervals.

Both single budgets and interval budgets are illustrated and discussed.

27.7 THE SINGLE BUDGET

The single budget reflects the budgeted result for a full financial period without indicating the implications of fluctuations or the uneven distribution of activities during that period.

Although the total budgeted result for the full period may appear to be satisfactory, the financial implications of seasonal fluctuations during parts of the full period may be critical for the undertaking. For example, a budget may show a favourable bank balance at the beginning and end of a period, while in fact large bank overdrafts may occur during a low season in that period.

If the financial implications of the fluctuation in activities are not important, then the single budget is a useful financial management tool which is compiled with relative ease.

The compilation of a single budget is illustrated with reference to the data in example 27.1.

Example 27.1

TVREP
TVREP is a private company which specialises in the repair of electronic equipment. The undertaking leases premises in a suburb. Customers who require service telephone the firm, which collects the equipment, repairs it in its workshops and delivers the equipment to the customer. TVREP has five technicians each of whom works 2 000 hours per annum, approximately 90% of their time being productive. The available productive time is used as the budget starting point. Time spent on repairs is charged at a fixed rate, while spares for repairs are charged at cost plus a percentage mark-up. The undertaking's budget for 19.2 is prepared with the aid of a computerised spreadsheet. The budget is prepared in the form of an income statement and a balance sheet. Each item in the budgeted statements is supported by explanatory notes giving details of the applicable criteria, norms and policy. The amounts and other values in the explanatory notes are used in the formulae in order to calculate the particular budget items. All value relationships in the model are also incorporated into the formulae.

The computerised model of a budget is used as a planning tool on a 'what if' basis. The model can be adapted when a change in any one amount in the norms is altered, so that all implications of the change are reflected.

The budgeted income statement of TVREP is shown in example 27.2.

Example 27.2

TVREP (PTY) LIMITED
BUDGETED INCOME STATEMENT

Income				CRITERIA AND NORMS
Services rendered			540 000	Five technicians 2 000 hours/year 90% occupied R60 5x 2000x 90% x R60/h
Profit on spares			200 000	
Sales		400 000		
Less: Cost of sales		200 000		50% gross on sales
Opening inventory	30 000			Given
Purchases	220 000			
	250 000			
Closing inventory	50 000			Given
Total income			740 000	
Less: Expenses			615 357	
Management and administration				
Salaries and benefits		390 000		Salaries budget
Rental		76 800		Rental on 800 m² at R8/m²/month
Auditor's fees		4 000		Estimated
Advertising		18 800		Budgeted on 2% of turnover (940000)
Printing		10 600		Budgeted on 50 sets @ R200 plus R50
Office requirements		960		R80/month
Telephone		2 880		R240/month
Postage		1 200		R100/month
Interest		—		12% on loan
Bad debts		4 700		0,5% turnover
Workshop				
Municipal services		3 600		R300/month
Consumable material		9 000		Five workers @ R150/month
Maintenance: Equipment		12 500		5% of cost price of equipment
Vehicles		4 000		20 c/km for 100 km/50 hours work
Petrol		1 600		80 c/litre/10 litre/100 km
Provision for depreciation		74 717		
Workshop equipment	50 667			20% on cost price
Office equipment	10 050			10% on cost price
Motor vehicles	14 000			20% on cost price
Net profit before taxation			124 643	
Provision for taxation @ 50%			62 322	Prevailing taxation tariff on net profit
Net profit after taxation			R62 321	

For the sake of clarity, the budgeted balance sheet of TVREP is shown in example 27.3 as a computerised six-column worksheet. This worksheet is a convenient manual method which ensures that all transactions are recorded correctly. Of course, in a computerised model the budgeted balance sheet can be calculated directly.

Example 27.3

TVREP (PTY) LIMITED
BUDGETED BALANCE SHEET

	31 December 19.1		Adjustments		31 December 19.2		
	Dr	Cr	Dr	Cr	Dr	Cr	
Fixed assets							
Workshop equipment	250 000		5 000[9]		255 000		New purchases
Office equipment	100 000		1 000[9]		101 000		New purchases
Motor vehicles	70 000				70 000		
Current assets							
Spares inventory	30 000		220 000[6]	200 000[4]	50 000		Spares purchased
Debtors	72 400		846 000[1]		70 108		90% of gross income
				4 700[3]			Bad debts
				843 592[7]			30 days credit allowed
Cash	5 000		94 000[2]		110 663		Cash sales
				6 000[9]			Fixed assets purchased
				62 322[5]			Taxation paid
				535 940[3]			Expenses paid
			843 592[7]				Debtors collected
				227 667[8]			Creditors paid
Share capital		300 000				300 000	
Retained income		51 400		846 000[1]		113 721	90% of gross income
				94 000[2]			Cash sales
			615 357[3]				Expenses
			62 322[5]				Taxation paid
			200 000[6]				Spares used
Current liabilities							
Creditors		26 000		220 000[6]		18 333	Spares purchased
			227 667[8]				30 days credit received
Depreciation							
Workshop equipment		100 000		50 667[3]		150 667	Written off
Office equipment		30 000		10 050[3]		40 050	Written off
Motor vehicles		20 000		14 000[3]		34 000	Written off
	527 400	527 400	3 114 938	3 114 938	656 771	656 771	

The following programme adjustments are made to the worksheet:

1 and 2	The gross income amounts to R940 000 (services rendered R540 000 + sales of spares R400 000). 90% of gross income is on credit and the balance in cash. 1 and 2 credit retained income and debit debtors with R846 000 (services on credit) and cash with R94 000 (cash sales).
3	Total expenses of R615 357 are debited to retained income; the portion paid in cash is credited to cash and non-cash items, viz bad debts of R4 700 and depreciation are credited to debtors and the relevant provisions respectively.
4	The cost of spares sold, R200 000, is credited to spares inventory and debited to retained income.
5	Taxation is deducted from cash and shown as a liability against retained income.
6	Spares to the value of R220 000 purchased on credit are added to inventory and credited to creditors.
7	The assumption is that only 30/360 of credit sales will still be outstanding at the end of the year. The balancing figure of R843 592 represents payments by debtors and is therefore deducted from debtors and debited to cash.
8	The assumption is that only 30/360 of credit purchases are still outstanding. The balancing figure of R227 667 represents payments to creditors and is deducted from creditors and credited to cash.

The accuracy of the budgeted balance sheet in example 27.3 is limited by the accuracy of the assumptions on which it is based. The single budget has inherent limitations which should be noted, viz the closing values of inventory, debtors and creditors are only estimations. If these budgets were prepared on a monthly basis, the closing values would be more accurate.

In addition, there is no indication whether there will be a bank overdraft during the period. This would result in interest charges.

27.8 THE INTERVAL BUDGET

The principles for preparing an interval budget are the same as those for preparing a single budget, the only difference being that the budget period is divided into shorter intervals.

Therefore the structure of an interval budget is more complicated than that of a single budget, and must be planned properly.

The composition of an interval budget is illustrated using the data on Ecomark discussed in previous paragraphs. The structure of Ecomark's budget is shown in figure 27.2.

27.8.1 Operating budgets

☐ **The trading budget**

The trading budget, which is the first element of the budgeted income statement, contains the sales budget and the cost of sales budget and shows the budgeted gross profit.

> Assume that, after thorough market research, the management of Ecomark has reached the conclusion that the enterprise could achieve a turnover of R5 million in 19.2. This turnover is adopted as the sales objective. The starting point of Ecomark's trading budget is, therefore, sales of R5 million. The sales of R5 million are budgeted on the basis of selling prices which will allow a gross profit of R1,8 million.

Example 27.4 shows Ecomark's trading budget.

Example 27.4

ECOMARK
BUDGETED INCOME STATEMENT FOR 19.2

	Note	Jan	Feb	Mar	Apr	May	Jun	Jul	Aug	Sep	Oct	Nov	Dec	Total	Reference
		R	R	R	R	R	R	R	R	R	R	R	R	R	
Trading budget															
Sales budget															
Sales															
Groceries		200 000	180 000	200 000	220 000	210 000	210 000	200 000	220 000	240 000	220 000	260 000	280 000	2 640 000	Estimated
Hardware		108 000	96 000	108 000	112 000	116 000	120 000	118 000	120 000	122 000	130 000	134 000	160 000	1 444 000	Estimated
Fresh produce		72 000	64 000	72 000	74 000	76 000	82 000	78 000	80 000	82 000	84 000	96 000	100 000	960 000	Estimated
Total sales		380 000	340 000	380 000	406 000	402 000	412 000	396 000	420 000	444 000	434 000	490 000	540 000	5 044 000	
Cost of sales															
Groceries	1	150 000	135 000	150 000	165 000	157 500	157 500	150 000	165 000	180 000	165 000	195 000	210 000	1 980 000	Calculated
Hardware	1	59 400	52 800	59 400	61 600	63 800	66 000	64 900	66 000	67 100	71 500	73 700	88 000	794 200	Calculated
Fresh produce	1	36 000	32 000	36 000	37 000	38 000	41 000	39 000	40 000	41 000	42 000	48 000	50 000	480 000	Calculated
Total cost of sales		245 400	219 800	245 400	263 600	259 300	264 500	253 900	271 000	288 100	278 500	316 700	348 000	3 254 200	
Gross profit		134 600	120 200	134 600	142 400	142 700	147 500	142 100	149 000	155 900	155 500	173 300	192 000	1 789 800	
Expenses budget															
Selling expenses		57 367	55 967	57 367	58 277	73 137	58 487	57 927	58 767	61 607	76 257	68 217	98 034	781 411	From 27.6
Administrative expenses		40 600	40 600	40 600	40 600	50 800	42 600	42 600	42 600	42 600	42 600	42 600	42 600	511 400	Estimated
Depreciation		11 250	11 625	12 625	12 625	12 792	12 958	13 458	13 458	13 458	13 542	13 542	13 542	154 875	From 27.10
Bad debts		9 500	8 500	9 500	10 150	10 050	10 300	9 900	10 500	11 100	10 850	12 250	13 500	126 100	From 27.7
Total expenses before interest		118 717	116 692	120 092	121 652	146 779	124 345	123 885	125 325	128 765	143 249	136 609	167 676	1 573 786	
Profit before interest		15 883	3 508	14 508	20 748	– 4 079	23 155	18 215	23 675	27 135	12 251	36 691	24 324	216 014	
Interest		286		213	153	501	391	847	357	40	113			2 900	From 27.11
Profit after interest		15 597	3 508	14 295	20 595	– 4 579	22 764	17 368	23 318	27 094	12 138	36 691	24 324	213 114	
Less: Taxation							40 000						40 000	80 000	Estimated
Net profit after taxation		15 597	3 508	14 295	20 595	– 4 579	– 17 236	17 368	23 318	27 094	12 138	36 691	– 15 676	173 114	
Retained profit: Beginning		415 600	431 197	434 705	449 000	469 596	465 016	447 780	465 148	488 466	515 560	527 699	564 390	498 714	
		431 197	434 705	449 000	469 596	465 016	447 780	465 148	488 466	515 560	527 699	564 390	548 714	671 829	
Less: Dividends													50 000	50 000	Estimated
Retained profit: Closing		431 197	434 705	449 000	469 596	465 016	447 780	465 148	488 466	515 560	527 699	564 390	498 714	621 829	To 27.12

Assumptions and norms:

1 Cost of sales
   - Groceries 75% of sales
   - Hardware 55% of sales
   - Fresh produce 50% of sales

☐ The sales budget

In a trading concern the sales budget usually serves as the starting point for the entire budgeting system. All the other activities and facilities necessary to achieve budgeted sales are planned on the basis of the sales budget and coordinated with each other, due consideration being given to the limiting factors pertaining to each one. The sales budget indicates the quantity of each product that must be sold, as well as the appropriate time and price. The information contained in the sales budget, in turn constitutes the basis for the purchases budget (i e how much of each product should be purchased, taking into consideration the inventory position). Thus sales planning is coordinated with purchases planning. The sales budget also provides information concerning the inflow of cash, while the purchases budget and operating expense budgets provide information about the outflow of cash. These, *inter alia*, serve as the basis for a coordinated cash budget. It is obvious, therefore, that if the starting point is incorrect or defective the entire budget could be incorrect.

The sales budget is based on an advance estimate of sales under expected market conditions, taking into account the marketing strategies being planned by management.

Since a budget actually represents a target for the person responsible to achieve, sales management plays a key role in the drawing up of a sales budget.

The sales manager usually evaluates the sales trends for the period immediately preceding the budget period, and estimates of future sales, which take into consideration the internal and external factors that may influence sales during the budget period, are based on these trends.

At this stage sales estimates are discussed with top management to ensure that they agree with the enterprise's total strategy and overall objectives. Often additional adjustments and supportive planning are carried out at this time. Once agreement between top management and sales management has been reached, the sales estimates are adopted as the sales budget.

A typical sales budget will specify the quantities and sales values of the various product lines according to period (usually per month), and, where applicable, according to geographical area.

Ecomark's sales budget for 19.2 is illustrated in example 27.4.

☐ The cost of sales budget

Cost of sales is budgeted for by applying the budgeted gross profit percentage to budgeted sales, as set out in the trading budget shown in example 27.4.

☐ The purchases budget

The **cost of sales**, which reflects the cost price of the merchandise to be sold, is the starting point for developing the **purchases budget**. The purchases budget shows the amount of goods purchased, taking into account inventory on hand.

Management lays down the policy governing inventory levels. Optimal inventory is influenced by various factors: the frequency of purchases, the lead time between ordering and delivery of an order and the variety of goods to be stocked are all important in determining inventory levels.

> A country dealer purchases goods every quarter and will therefore have to maintain larger inventories of goods than a city dealer, who is able to supplement his inventory daily. The variety of items stocked is another important factor. Consider, for example, the optimum inventory levels for sugar and shoes: a trader who wants to sell R1 000 worth of sugar a week requires no more than R1 000 worth of sugar at the beginning of that week. However, if the same trader wishes to sell R1 000 worth of shoes he may possibly require an inventory of at least R4 000, since he cannot know beforehand what type, colour or size of shoe a purchaser will want. Therefore he will have to stock a wide variety of shoes.

The purchases budget is based on cost of sales as shown in the trading budget in example 27.4. Each month's opening stock is calculated and compared with the norm of its relationship to cost of sales. To calculate budgeted purchases, closing stock is deducted from the difference between opening stock and cost of sales. The purchases budget, which also forms the inventory budget, is illustrated in example 27.5.

☐ Expenses budget

Once the trading budget has been drawn up, the expenses budget is the next step in preparing the budgeted income statement.

A separate expenses budget aimed at the effective and efficient achievement of the department's objective is prepared for each department (see para 27.5.4).

Separate budgets are prepared for the trading and administrative departments of Ecomark. An example of the sales budget for the trading department is shown in example 27.6.

☐ The budgeted income statement

The budgeted income statement is compiled from the various operating budgets as depicted in example 27.4.

Using the budgeted income statement, it is possible to evaluate the combined final result of the various planned activities and to make any necessary adjustments.

27.8.2 Financial budgets

Financial budgets pertain to the asset and liability items comprising the budgeted balance sheet. The balance sheet at the beginning of the period is the basis for all financial budgets. In essence, the financial budgets reflect the budgeted changes in the balance sheet items over the budget period.

Example 27.5

ECOMARK
PURCHASES AND INVENTORY BUDGET 19.2

	Note	Jan	Feb	Mar	Apr	May	Jun	Jul	Aug	Sep	Oct	Nov	Dec	Reference
		R	R	R	R	R	R	R	R	R	R	R	R	
Groceries														
Opening inventory	1	240 000	202 500	225 000	247 500	236 250	236 250	225 000	247 500	270 000	247 500	292 500	315 000	
Less: Cost of sales		150 000	135 000	150 000	165 000	157 500	157 500	150 000	165 000	180 000	165 000	195 000	210 000	From 27.4
Available		90 000	67 500	75 000	82 500	78 750	78 750	75 000	82 500	90 000	82 500	97 500	105 000	
Purchases		112 500	157 500	172 500	153 750	157 500	146 250	172 500	187 500	157 500	210 000	217 500	231 000	Calculated
Closing inventory	2	202 500	225 000	247 500	236 250	236 250	225 000	247 500	270 000	247 500	292 500	315 000	336 000	Calculated
Hardware														
Opening inventory	1	162 000	132 000	148 500	154 000	159 500	165 000	162 250	165 000	167 750	178 750	184 250	220 000	
Less: Cost of sales		59 400	52 800	59 400	61 600	63 800	66 000	64 900	66 000	67 100	71 500	73 700	88 000	From 27.4
Available		102 600	79 200	89 100	92 400	95 700	99 000	97 350	99 000	100 650	107 250	110 550	132 000	
Purchases		29 400	69 300	64 900	67 100	69 300	63 250	67 650	68 750	78 100	77 000	109 450	108 000	Calculated
Closing inventory	2	132 000	148 500	154 000	159 500	165 000	162 250	165 000	167 750	178 750	184 250	220 000	240 000	Calculated
Fresh produce														
Opening inventory	1	3 600	3 200	3 600	3 700	3 800	4 100	3 900	4 000	4 100	4 200	4 800	5 000	
Less: Cost of sales		36 000	32 000	36 000	37 000	38 000	41 000	39 000	40 000	41 000	42 000	48 000	50 000	From 27.4
Available		−32 400	−28 800	−32 400	−33 300	−34 200	−36 900	−35 100	−36 000	−36 900	−37 800	−43 200	−45 000	
Purchases		35 600	32 400	36 100	37 100	38 300	40 800	39 100	40 100	41 100	42 600	48 200	50 000	Calculated
Closing inventory	2	3 200	3 600	3 700	3 800	4 100	3 900	4 000	4 100	4 200	4 800	5 000	5 000	Calculated
Total purchases		177 500	259 200	273 500	257 950	265 100	250 300	279 250	296 350	276 700	329 600	375 150	389 000	To 27.9
Total closing inventory		337 700	377 100	405 200	399 550	405 350	391 150	416 500	441 850	430 450	481 550	540 000	581 000	To 27.12

Assumptions and norms:

1 Opening inventory on 1-1-19.2 per balance sheet at 31-12-19.1 (example 27.12)
Closing inventory on 31-12-19.2 estimated

2 Closing inventory

Groceries	1,5 ×	cost of sales for next month
Hardware	2,5 ×	cost of sales for next month
Fresh produce	0,1 ×	cost of sales for next month

Example 27.6

ECOMARK
SALES EXPENSES BUDGET 19.2

	Jan	Feb	Mar	Apr	May	Jun	Jul	Aug	Sep	Oct	Nov	Dec	Total	Reference
	R	R	R	R	R	R	R	R	R	R	R	R	R	
Salaries and wages	28 067	28 067	28 067	28 067	28 067	28 067	28 067	28 067	28 067	28 067	28 067	56 134	364 871	Estimated
Rental	8 000	8 000	8 000	8 000	8 000	8 000	8 000	8 000	10 000	10 000	10 000	10 000	104 000	Estimated
Advertising	5 000	5 000	5 000	5 000	20 000	5 000	5 000	5 000	5 000	20 000	10 000	10 000	100 000	Estimated
Services:														
To turnover	5 700	5 100	5 700	6 090	6 030	6 180	5 940	6 300	6 660	6 510	7 350	8 100	75 660	Calculated
Maintenance	3 000	3 000	3 000	3 000	3 000	3 000	3 000	3 000	3 000	3 000	3 000	3 000	36 000	Estimated
Packaging:														
To turnover	7 600	6 800	7 600	8 120	8 040	8 240	7 920	8 400	8 880	8 680	9 800	10 800	100 880	Calculated
	57 367	55 967	57 367	58 277	73 137	58 487	57 927	58 767	61 607	76 257	68 217	98 034	781 411	To 27.4

Assumptions and norms:
Services 1,5% of turnover
Packaging 2% of turnover

There are two approaches to compiling financial budgets, namely:

- ☐ the direct result of an operating budget
- ☐ independent planning, usually with the objective of expanding the scope of activities.

The debtors, creditors, inventory and cash budgets are the financial budgets usually directly influenced by the operating budgets. A fixed asset acquisition budget is an example of an independent budget.

☐ Debtors budget

The balance on the debtors account is influenced by credit sales, on the one hand, and the debtors pattern of payment on the other. A debtors budget compiled on the basis of activities directly influencing debtors will be more accurate than a budget compiled on the basis of an indirect factor, for example the average age according to the ageing schedule of debts.

Information regarding credit sales is obtained from the sales budget. Determining the debtors pattern of payment is more difficult. Debtors settlement is determined by (i) credit terms granted to debtors and (ii) the extent to which debtors comply with these terms in making payments. The various practical methods of determining the payment pattern are usually based on the historical recovery pattern of debts in relation to either credit sales or outstanding debts.

(1) Recovery in relation to credit sales

Example 27.7 illustrates the method of determining recovery on the basis of credit sales. According to this method the percentage credit sales recovered during the month of sale, and during every following month, must be determined.

Assume that the management of Ecomark ascertains that 50% of credit sales are settled during the month following that in which sales are made, 25% in the following month, 15% in the third and 5% during the fourth month. The remaining 5% is irrecoverable and is written off. Therefore Ecomark's recovery of debts can be budgeted for as follows:

Example 27.7

ECOMARK
DEBTORS BUDGET 19.2
COLLECTION SCHEDULE

Month	Note	Credit sales	Jan	Feb	Mar	Apr	May	Jun	Jul	Aug	Sep	Oct	Nov	Dec	Bad debts
Balance 1-1-19.2	1	230 000	115 000	103 500	11 500										
January	2	190 000		95 000	47 500	28 500	9 500								9 500
February	2	170 000			85 000	42 500	25 500	8 500							8 500
March	2	190 000				95 000	47 500	28 500	9 500						9 500
April	2	203 000					101 500	50 750	30 450	10 150					10 150
May	2	201 000						100 500	50 250	30 150	10 050				10 050
June	2	206 000							103 000	51 500	30 900	10 300			10 300
July	2	198 000								99 000	49 500	29 700	9 900		9 900
August	2	210 000									105 000	52 500	31 500	10 500	10 500
September	2	222 000										111 000	55 500	33 300	11 100
October	2	217 000											108 500	54 250	10 850
November	2	245 000												122 500	12 250
December	2	270 000													13 500
Budgeted collections			115 000	198 500	144 000	166 000	184 000	188 250	193 200	190 800	195 450	203 500	205 400	220 550	126100

BUDGETED DEBTORS BALANCES

	Note	Jan	Feb	Mar	Apr	May	Jun	Jul	Aug	Sep	Oct	Nov	Dec	Reference
		R	R	R	R	R	R	R	R	R	R	R	R	
Opening balance	3	230 000	295 500	258 500	295 000	321 850	328 800	336 250	331 150	339 850	355 300	357 950	385 300	
Credit sales	4	190 000	170 000	190 000	203 000	201 000	206 000	198 000	210 000	222 000	217 000	245 000	270 000	
		420 000	465 500	448 500	498 000	522 850	534 800	534 250	541 150	561 850	572 300	602 950	655 300	
Less: Collections	5	115 000	198 500	144 000	166 000	184 000	188 250	193 200	190 800	195 450	203 500	205 400	220 550	To 27.11
Bad debts	5	9 500	8 500	9 500	10 150	10 050	10 300	9 900	10 500	11 100	10 850	12 250	13 500	
Closing balance		295 500	258 500	295 000	321 850	328 800	336 250	331 150	339 850	355 300	357 950	385 300	421 250	To 27.12

Assumptions and norms:

1 Outstanding debtors at 1 January, collected as follows
- January 50%
- February 45%
- March 5%

2 Credit sales collected as follows during the year
- During first month after sale 50%
- During second month after sale 25%
- During third month after sale 15%
- During fourth month after sale 5%
- Bad debts 5%

3 Balance on 1-1-19.2 per balance sheet at 31-12-19.1 (example 27.12)

4 Credit sales are 50% of total sales

5 Per collection schedule

(2) Recovery in relation to outstanding debts

According to this method of budgeting, recovery of debts is usually based on the relationship between settlements made during the month and the total debts outstanding at the beginning of the month.

If it is assumed that the average recovery ratio of settlement to outstanding debts during the previous years was 56%, the debtors budget for 19.2 can be compiled as shown in example 27.8.

□ Inventory budget

The inventory budget, like the debtors budget, is compiled from the budgets of those activities which influence inventory. Inventory of merchandise is determined by managerial policy with regard to inventory levels and cost of sales, as reflected in example 27.5.

□ Creditors budget

The trade creditors budget is derived from the purchases budget. The balance on the trade creditors budget is influenced by credit purchases, on the one hand, and by the pattern of credit payments, determined mainly by the credit periods granted by suppliers, on the other.

> The creditors budget for Ecomark in example 27.9 is based on a credit period of 60 days for groceries and hardware. Fresh produce is purchased for cash. It is assumed that 55% of outstanding creditors were paid at the end of the previous financial year in January and 45% were paid in February.

□ Independent financial budgets

Budgets for assets and liabilities not directly influenced by operating activities are a result of management decision, for which independent budgets are prepared. The decisions on these investments are based on management's evaluation of the facilities necessary to support the activities reflected in the operating budgets.

Ecomark is planning to acquire fixed assets during 19.2. A fixed asset budget for 19.2 is shown in example 27.10.

Example 27.8

ECOMARK
ALTERNATIVE DEBTORS BUDGET 19.2
(This alternative is not incorporated in the main budget)

	Note	Jan	Feb	Mar	Apr	May	Jun	Jul	Aug	Sep	Oct	Nov	Dec
		R	R	R	R	R	R	R	R	R	R	R	R
Opening balance	1	230 000	281 700	285 448	306 097	327 533	335 064	343 128	339 076	348 694	364 325	366 453	393 989
Credit sales	2	190 000	170 000	190 000	203 000	201 000	206 000	198 000	210 000	222 000	217 000	245 000	270 000
		420 000	451 700	475 448	509 097	528 533	541 064	541 128	549 076	570 694	581 325	611 453	663 989
Less: Collections	3	128 800	157 752	159 851	171 414	183 418	187 636	192 152	189 883	195 268	204 022	205 214	220 634
Bad debts	4	9 500	8 500	9 500	10 150	10 050	10 300	9 900	10 500	11 100	10 850	12 250	13 500
Closing balance		281 700	285 448	306 097	327 533	335 064	343 128	339 076	348 694	364 325	366 453	393 989	429 855

Assumptions and norms:
1 Balance on 1-1-19.2 per balance sheet at 31-12-19.1 (example 27.13)
2 Credit sales are 50% of total sales
3 Collections represent 56% of balance at end of previous month

Example 27.9

ECOMARK
CREDITORS BUDGET 19.2

	Note	Jan	Feb	Mar	Apr	May	Jun	Jul	Aug	Sep	Oct	Nov	Dec
		R	R	R	R	R	R	R	R	R	R	R	R
Opening balance	1	400 000	321 900	368 700	464 200	458 250	447 650	436 300	449 650	496 400	491 850	522 600	613 950
Purchases	2												
Groceries		112 500	157 500	172 500	153 750	157 500	146 250	172 500	187 500	157 500	210 000	217 500	231 000
Hardware		29 400	69 300	64 900	67 100	69 300	63 250	67 650	68 750	78 100	77 000	109 450	108 000
Fresh produce		35 600	32 400	36 100	37 100	38 300	40 800	39 100	40 100	41 100	42 600	48 200	50 000
		577 500	581 100	642 200	722 150	723 350	697 950	715 550	746 000	773 100	821 450	897 750	1 002 950
Less: Payments	3	255 600	212 400	178 000	263 900	275 700	261 650	265 900	249 600	281 250	298 850	283 800	337 000
Closing balance		321 900	368 700	464 200	458 250	447 650	436 300	449 650	496 400	491 850	522 600	613 950	665 950

Assumptions and norms:

1 Balance on 1-1-19.2 per balance sheet at 31-12-19.1 (example 27.13)
2 From 27.5
3 (a) Creditors on 1-1-19.2 paid as follows
  January 55%
  February 45%
 (b) Groceries and hardware creditors paid as follows
  Month of purchase 0%
  First following month 0%
  Second following month 100%
 (c) Fresh produce is purchased for cash

Example 27.10

ECOMARK
FIXED ASSETS BUDGET 19.2

	Note	Dec	Jan	Feb	Mar	Apr	May	Jun	Jul	Aug	Sep	Oct	Nov	Dec	Reference
		R	R	R	R	R	R	R	R	R	R	R	R	R	
New purchases															
Shop equipment				30 000	80 000										Estimated
Trucks									30 000						Estimated
Office equipment							20 000	20 000				10 000			Estimated
				30 000	80 000		20 000	20 000	30 000			10 000			
Cost price – month end	1														
Shop equipment		620 000	620 000	650 000	730 000	730 000	730 000	730 000	730 000	730 000	730 000	730 000	730 000	730 000	Calculate
Trucks		120 000	120 000	120 000	120 000	120 000	120 000	120 000	150 000	150 000	150 000	150 000	150 000	150 000	Calculate
Office equipment		180 000	180 000	180 000	180 000	180 000	200 000	220 000	220 000	220 000	220 000	230 000	230 000	230 000	Calculate
Depreciation															
This month	2		11 250	11 625	12 625	12 625	12 792	12 958	13 458	13 458	13 458	13 542	13 542	13 542	Calculate
Total provision	3	160 000	171 250	182 875	195 500	208 125	220 917	233 875	247 333	260 792	274 250	287 792	301 333	314 875	Calculate
Net fixed assets		760 000	748 750	767 125	834 500	821 875	829 083	836 125	852 667	839 208	825 750	822 208	808 667	795 125	To 27.12

Assumptions and norms:
1 Balance on 31-12-19.1 per balance sheet; thereafter previous balance plus purchases
2 Depreciation

Shop equipment	15% per annum
Trucks	20% per annum
Office equipment	10% per annum

3 Balance on 31-12-19.1 per balance sheet; thereafter previous balance plus depreciation for month

☐ **The cash budget**

The cash position of a business is a critical element in the operation of its activities. The enterprise needs cash continuously in order to meet its obligations timeously. If the cash available decreases to less than the amount required, the enterprise may experience severe financial difficulties. Therefore it is essential that the enterprise plans its cash flow properly. A cash budget aids timeous determination of the cash position, as well as planning the elimination of problem areas or the application of surplus funds, whatever the case.

☐ **The budgeted balance sheet**

The budgeted balance sheet is compiled from the various financial budgets. Note that the method used here differs from the method used for the single budget. In the example of a single budget, the opening balance sheet is adjusted directly, taking into account the operating budgets. In the interval budget, separate financial budgets are prepared for the balance sheet items and then incorporated into the budgeted balance sheet. Ecomark's budgeted balance sheet for 19.2 can be compiled as follows:

The budgeted balance sheet reflects the expected financial position of the concern if the various operating and financial budgets are executed. At this stage it is possible to evaluate the total budgeted financial performance and to revise planning wherever necessary.

> The budgeted income statement of Ecomark, for example, shows a net income before tax of approximately R213 000 compared with operating capital of R1,8 million at the end of the year, that is, a return on capital of only 11,8% against a target of 20%. In order to improve this return on capital, management, using the budget as a model, can investigate all the different factors and determine which changes will influence the return on capital. Since the budget is a complete model of the enterprise's financial position, it is able to highlight all the implications of changes to any budget item.
>
> The management of Ecomark may, for example, decide to increase sales by lowering selling prices slightly. If this change is made to the budget it will show not only the change in profit, but also changes in debtors, creditors and cash.

27.9 BUDGETARY CONTROL

27.9.1 The budget as a control instrument

Management's control function includes action aimed at ensuring that the enterprise's objectives are achieved.

The principles of control have already been discussed in chapter 11, where it was stated that the control process comprises three elements, namely:

- ☐ the setting of standards
- ☐ the comparison of actual results with the standards
- ☐ corrective action.

Example 27.11

ECOMARK
CASH FLOW BUDGET 19.2

	Note	Jan	Feb	Mar	Apr	May	Jun	Jul	Aug	Sep	Oct	Nov	Dec	Reference
		R	R	R	R	R	R	R	R	R	R	R	R	
Opening balance		20 000	−28 853	680	−21 500	−15 429	−50 567	−79 445	−85 518	−36 042	−4 090	−11 410	44 373	
Receipts														
Cash sales	1	190 000	170 000	190 000	203 000	201 000	206 000	198 000	210 000	222 000	217 000	245 000	270 000	From 27.4
Debtors collected		115 000	198 500	144 000	166 000	184 000	188 250	193 200	190 800	195 450	203 500	205 400	220 550	From 27.7
		325 000	339 647	334 680	347 500	369 571	343 683	311 755	315 282	381 408	416 410	438 990	534 923	
Less: Sales expenses		57 367	55 967	57 367	58 277	73 137	58 487	57 927	58 767	61 607	76 257	68 217	98 034	From 27.4
Administrative expenses		40 600	40 600	40 600	40 600	50 800	42 600	42 600	42 600	42 600	42 600	42 600	42 600	From 27.4
Creditors		255 600	212 400	178 000	263 900	275 700	261 650	265 900	249 600	281 250	298 850	283 800	337 000	From 27.9
Dividend													50 000	From 27.4
Assets purchased			30 000	90 000		20 000	20 000	30 000			10 000			From 27.10
Net before interest		−28 567	680	−21 287	−15 277	−50 066	−39 054	−84 672	−35 685	−4 049	−11 297	44 373	7 289	
Interest on overdraft	2	286		213	153	501	391	847	357	40	113			Calculated
Taxation	3						40 000						40 000	From 27.4
Closing balance		−28 853	680	−21 500	−15 429	−50 567	−79 445	−85 518	−36 042	−4 090	−11 410	44 373	−32 711	

Assumptions and norms:

1 Cash sales are 50% of total sales
2 Interest rate is 12%
3 Taxation is paid at the end of the month

Example 27.12

ECOMARK
BUDGETED BALANCE SHEETS DURING 19.2

	31 Dec	Jan	Feb	Mar	Apr	May	Jun	Jul	Aug	Sep	Oct	Nov	Dec	Reference
	R	R	R	R	R	R	R	R	R	R	R	R	R	
ASSETS														
Net fixed assets	760 000	748 750	767 125	834 500	821 875	829 083	836 125	852 667	839 208	825 750	822 208	808 667	795 125	From 27.10
Current assets														
Inventory	405 600	337 700	377 100	405 200	399 550	405 350	391 150	416 500	441 850	430 450	481 550	540 000	581 000	From 27.5
Debtors	230 000	295 500	258 500	295 000	321 850	328 000	336 250	331 150	339 850	355 300	357 950	385 300	421 250	From 27.7
Bank balance	20 000		680									44 373		From 27.11
Total current assets	655 600	633 200	636 280	700 200	721 400	734 150	727 400	747 650	781 700	785 750	839 500	969 673	1 002 250	
TOTAL ASSETS	1 415 600	1 381 950	1 403 405	1 534 700	1 543 275	1 563 233	1 563 525	1 600 317	1 620 908	1 611 500	1 661 708	1 778 340	1 797 375	
EQUITIES														
Share capital	600 000	600 000	600 000	600 000	600 000	600 000	600 000	600 000	600 000	600 000	600 000	600 000	600 000	
Retained profit	415 600	431 197	434 705	449 000	469 596	465 016	447 780	465 148	488 466	515 560	527 699	564 390	498 714	From 27.4
Shareholders' equity	1 015 600	1 031 197	1 034 705	1 049 000	1 069 596	1 065 016	1 047 780	1 065 148	1 088 466	1 115 560	1 127 699	1 164 390	1 098 714	
Current liabilities														
Creditors	400 000	321 900	368 700	464 200	458 250	447 650	436 300	449 650	496 400	491 850	522 600	613 950	665 950	From 27.9
Bank overdraft		28 853		21 500	15 429	50 567	79 445	85 518	36 024	4 090	11 410		32 711	From 27.11
Total current liabilities	400 000	350 753	368 700	485 700	473 679	498 224	515 745	535 168	532 442	495 940	534 010	613 950	698 661	
TOTAL EQUITIES	1 415 600	1 381 950	1 403 405	1 534 700	1 543 275	1 563 233	1 563 525	1 600 317	1 620 908	1 611 500	1 661 708	1 778 340	1 797 375	

R 1,8m

In paragraph 27.1 it was stated that a budget establishes the objectives that an undertaking wishes to achieve.

In order to exercise control through budgets, it is necessary to measure and evaluate the actual performance of the undertaking against the budget.

One of the important tasks of an accountant is to design the accounting system and the subsequent reports in such a way that budgetary control is possible.

Consider, for example, the financial reports of Ecomark at the end of March 19.2.

Example 27.13

ECOMARK
BUDGETARY CONTROL REPORT MARCH 19.2
INCOME STATEMENT

	March 19.2			Year to date		
	Actual	Budget	Variance	Actual	Budget	Variance
Sales						
Groceries	194 000	200 000	–6 000	562 000	580 000	–18 000
Hardware	101 000	108 000	–7 000	290 000	312 000	–22 000
Fresh produce	70 000	72 000	–2 000	200 000	208 000	–8 000
Total sales	365 000	380 000	–15 000	1 052 000	1 100 000	–48 000
Cost of sales						
Groceries	140 000	150 000	10 000	409 000	435 000	26 000
Hardware	53 000	59 400	6 400	154 000	171 600	17 600
Fresh produce	36 000	36 000		101 000	104 000	3 000
Total cost of sales	229 000	245 400	16 400	664 000	710 600	46 600
Gross profit	136 000	134 600	1 400	388 000	389 400	–1 400
Less: Expenses						
Selling expenses	58 000	57 367	–633	172 250	170 701	–1 549
Administrative expenses	39 600	40 600	1 000	122 000	121 800	–200
Depreciation	12 625	12 625		37 875	35 500	–2 375
Bad debts	10 000	9 500	–500	27 000	27 500	500
Total expenses before interest	120 225	120 092	–133	359 125	355 501	–3 624
Profit before interest	15 775	14 508	1 267	28 875	33 899	–5 024
Interest		213	213	627	499	–128
Profit after interest	R15 775	R14 295	R1 480	R28 248	R33 400	–R5 152

The income statement illustrated in example 27.13 comprises two sections, the first dealing only with the relevant month and the second covering the three months of the previous financial period.

It is essential that the management of the enterprise is aware of the performance for the particular month as well as of the cumulative performance to date. This allows management to review the performance for each specific month on a month-to-month basis, while simultaneously being aware of long-term trends.

Example 27.14 shows the budgeted balance sheet for the year ended 31 March 19.2, as well as the actual balance sheet at 31 March 19.2.

Example 27.14

ECOMARK
BUDGETARY CONTROL REPORT
BALANCE SHEET AT 31 MARCH 19.2

	Actual	Budget	Variance
Assets			
Net fixed assets	722 125	834 500	– 112 375
Current assets			
Inventory	374 100	405 200	– 31 100
Debtors	310 000	295 000	15 000
Bank	45 623		45 623
Total current assets	729 723	700 200	29 523
Total assets	R1 451 848	R1 534 700	– R82 852
Equities			
Share capital	600 000	600 000	
Retained profit	441 848	449 000	– 7 152
Shareholders' equity	1 041 848	1 049 000	– 7 152
Current liabilities			
Creditors	410 000	464 200	– 54 200
Bank overdraft	—	21 500	– 21 500
Total current liabilities	410 000	485 700	– 75 700
Total equities	R1 451 848	R1 534 700	– R82 852

27.9.2 Variable budgets

The budgets discussed thus far are **fixed** budgets. A fixed budget shows a fixed amount for a particular period. The actual amount of an **independent** budget item, such as sales for a particular period, may differ from the budgeted item. However, the fixed budget will still reflect those **dependent** budgeted items for the period which have a bearing on the **independent** budgeted items. For example, the fixed budget will show **material consumption** for budgeted **production** and not for **actual** consumption. Therefore for control purposes it will not be meaningful to compare actual material consumption with budgeted material consumption.

In such circumstances variable budgets are used to exercise meaningful budgetary control. A variable budget reflects the different values that dependent items will have for different values of independent items in a particular period.

The use of a variable budget is shown in example 27.15.

Example 27.15

ECOMARK
VARIABLE BUDGET MARCH 19.2
SELLING EXPENSES

	March 19.2			Year to date		
Selling expenses	Actual	Variable budget	Fixed budget	Actual	Variable budget	Fixed budget
Salaries and wages	28 100	28 067	28 067	83 220	84 201	84 201
Rental	8 000	8 000	8 000	24 000	24 000	24 000
Advertising	5 000	5 000	5 000	15 380	15 000	15 000
Services: To turnover	5 700	5 475	5 700	16 950	15 780	16 500
Maintenance	3 600	3 000	3 000	10 500	9 000	9 000
Packaging: To turnover	7 600	7 300	7 600	22 200	21 040	22 000
	R58 000	R56 842	R57 367	R172 250	R169 021	R170 701

Assumptions and norms:

1 Services 1,5% of turnover
Packaging 2% of turnover

2 Variable budget is based on actual sales for March and
Fixed budget is based on budgeted sales for March.

28

SOURCE AND APPLICATION OF FUNDS STATEMENTS AND CASH FLOW STATEMENTS

The **AIM** of this chapter is to explain the function and preparation of source and application of funds statements and cash flow statements.

28.1 FLOW OF FUNDS

28.1.1 Introduction

The normal business activities of an undertaking result in a flow of goods, services and funds via the undertaking's capital items such as land, buildings and equipment and its operating items such as materials and merchandise. Services are obtained from external sources and applied in a process which in turn provides goods or services to outsiders.

At the same time the undertaking receives funds from business activities, capital injections, loans, credit facilities, the sale of assets and the collection of debts. These funds are applied to pay for goods and services acquired, to repay loans, to pay interest and dividends, and for investment.

The flow of funds is determined largely by the flow of goods and services. Management has a responsibility to regulate the flow of goods and services and the resultant flow of funds in such a manner that the inflow of funds is continuously sufficient to cover the outflow of funds.

The undertaking also has a responsibility to report on the flow of funds to interested parties. Shareholders, owners, suppliers of capital and trade creditors require information regarding the types of funds acquired by the undertaking and how these have been applied. Schedule 4 of the Companies Act, 1973 (as amended) requires that a statement reflecting the source and application of funds during the financial year is attached to the balance sheet of a company.

28.1.2 The flow of funds cycle

Business activities generate funds which are eventually distributed to suppliers of capital as dividends, interest or other profit-sharing forms.

Funds from business activities can either be absorbed as working capital or be released from working capital for discretionary application. Discretionary applications of funds are those applications for which management can decide the purpose, amount and timing in advance, and include the distribution of profit, the acquisition of assets and the repayment of loans.

Funds from business activities are absorbed as working capital when net working capital increases and are released when it decreases. The influence of business activities on changes in working capital depends on numerous internal and external factors, for example the extent of activities, market conditions, price tendencies, credit and inventory policies, and operating effectiveness and efficiency.

Figure 28.1 Flow of funds cycle

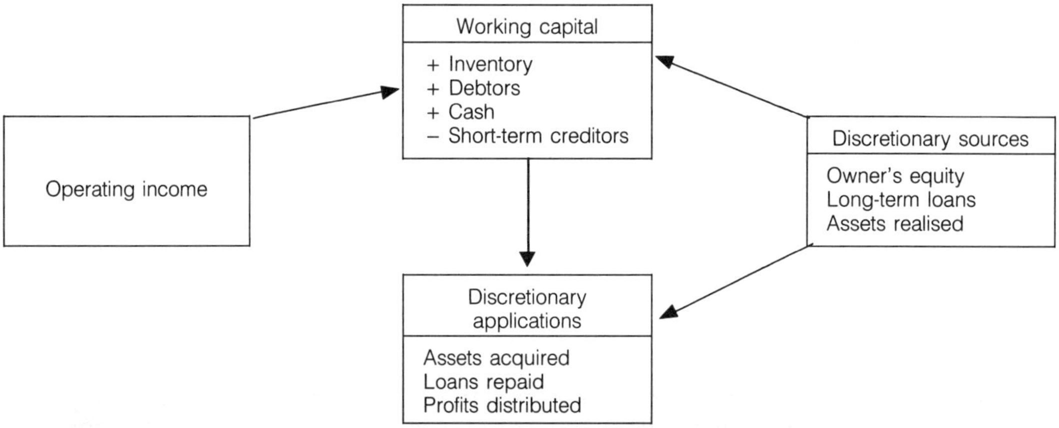

When the financing requirements are greater than the funds generated from business activities, then discretionary sources other than operating income must be utilised. All sources of funds of which management can determine the form, amount and timing, are considered to be discretionary sources. These include capital from owners, long-term loans and the realisation of fixed assets and investments.

The flow of funds cycle is shown in figure 28.1.

Because the balance sheet is a static document which reflects the financial position at a specific date, it cannot reflect the flow of funds during a given period. The income statement, on the other hand, reflects only the income from business activities and not the movement of funds in assets, owner's equity and liabilities.

Therefore, in order to reflect the flow of funds in an undertaking a special report must be compiled. There are two approaches to reporting on the flow of funds. First, funds can be considered as financial means: the statement of source and application of funds prepared in this case will show the flow of all financial means and the corresponding application thereof. Second, only cash funds can be considered: then a cash flow statement will reflect the influence of the cash flow on the cash position and the debt finance.

28.2 STATEMENT OF SOURCE AND APPLICATION OF FUNDS

28.2.1 Nature and application of the funds statement

Funds are defined as all the financial means that can be applied for financing. It is the total of:

- ☐ net inflow from business activities
- ☐ proceeds from the realisation of assets
- ☐ owner's equity introduced
- ☐ debt financing.

The statement of source and application of funds shows the **inflow** of funds from different sources and the corresponding **application** thereof.

Any movement of funds results in a change in the financial position. Therefore a statement of source and application of funds is based on changes in the financial position during a specific period which are caused by the flow of funds. It is also referred to as a statement of variations in the financial position.

Inflow of funds from various different sources	⟹	All applications of funds

The sources and applications of funds are usually classified into various categories, as shown in example 28.1:

Example 28.1 Categories of source and application of funds

SOURCE	APPLICATION

Increase in owner's equity
  Share capital issued
    or
  Capital contributed
	Decrease in owner's equity
	  Capital withdrawn

Increase in retained income
  Funds from business operations
	Decrease in retained income
	  Losses suffered
	  Dividends paid

Increase in liabilities Loans received	

Decrease in fixed assets and investments
  Fixed assets sold
  Investments realised
	Increase in fixed assets and investments
	  Fixed assets acquired
	  Investments made

The changes in current assets and liabilities are usually grouped together and treated as a change in net working capital:

Decrease in operating capital	Increase in operating capital
Decrease in current assets	Increase in current assets
Decrease in debtors	Increase in debtors
Decrease in inventory	Increase in inventory
Decrease in cash and liquid assets	Increase in cash and liquid assets
Increase in current liabilities	Decrease in current liabilities
Increase in trade creditors	Decrease in trade creditors
Increase in bank overdraft	Decrease in bank overdraft
Increase in other short-term financing	Decrease in other short-term financing

The flow of funds in a specific period is calculated by:

- ☐ determining the changes in balance sheet items during the relevant period
- ☐ eliminating the changes which do not represent a flow of funds
- ☐ analysing the remaining changes into their constituent elements and identifying those items which must be disclosed separately
- ☐ preparing the statement of source and application of funds.

28.2.2 Changes in balance sheet items

The first step in determining the flow of funds is to calculate all balance sheet changes during the specific period.

The determination of the changes in the balance sheet items is illustrated in example 28.2:

Example 28.2

ALTA LIMITED
SCHEDULE OF BALANCE SHEET CHANGES

	19.1	19.2	Change
Application:			
Fixed assets	540 000	650 000	+110 000
Investments	100 000	90 000	−10 000
Current assets	80 000	100 000	+20 000
	R720 000	R840 000	
Source:			
Share capital	200 000	300 000	+100 000
Retained profit	100 000	150 000	+50 000
Long-term loans	120 000	110 000	−10 000
Provision – depreciation	240 000	210 000	−30 000
Current liabilities	60 000	70 000	+10 000
	R720 000	R840 000	

The increase in fixed assets indicates that funds were applied for the acquisition of new assets; the decrease in investments indicates a realisation of investments and therefore represents a source of funds; the increase in current assets indicates an application of funds; the increase in share capital, arising from the issue of new shares, is a source of funds; the increase in retained profit derived from operating profit represents a source of funds; the decrease in the long-term loan indicates a repayment of the loan and therefore constitutes an application of funds; the increase in current liabilities represents a source of funds derived from extended credit facilities; the change in the provision for depreciation does not represent a flow of funds and must be eliminated.

28.2.3 Adjustment in respect of entries which do not affect the flow of funds

Not all changes in balance sheet items are caused by a flow of funds, for example provision for depreciation.

The influence of entries which do not represent a flow of funds should therefore be eliminated from the changes in balance sheet items in order that the actual flow of funds may be determined. Note that these entries are not eliminated from the books; they are merely eliminated from the schedule of changes in balance sheet items. Usually transactions with outsiders cause a flow of funds, while internal transactions do not. The following are examples of typical internal transactions which do not affect the flow of funds to or from outsiders:

- ☐ depreciation write offs
- ☐ profits and losses on the sale of assets
- ☐ fully depreciated assets written off
- ☐ revaluation of assets
- ☐ transfers between reserves.

Consider, for example, the following situations:

The movement in the net fixed assets of Alta Limited during 19.2 is illustrated in example 28.3.

Example 28.3

ALTA LIMITED
MOVEMENT IN FIXED ASSETS 19.2

	Cost price	Accumulated depreciation	Net assets
Balance 1/1/19.2	540 000	240 000	300 000
Purchases	+187 000	—	+187 000
Assets	727 000	240 000	487 000
Depreciation	—	30 000	30 000
	727 000	270 000	457 000
Assets sold*	−37 000	20 000	17 000
Assets	−40 000	−40 000	—
Balance 31/12/19.2	R650 000	R210 000	R440 000

*The asset is sold for R7 000, resulting in a loss of R10 000 (book value R17 000 − selling price R7 000).

However, the schedule of changes in balance sheet items in example 28.2 shows a change of only R110 000 for the year. From a schedule of movements in fixed assets it is obvious that the actual flow of funds was as follows:

Funds expended on new assets	187 000
Funds provided from sale of assets	7 000
Net outflow	R180 000

The income statement of Alta Limited in example 28.4 shows a transfer of R50 000 to retained income, and this is also shown in the schedule of balance sheet changes.

The actual cash flow, however, was R90 000.

Example 28.4

ALTA LIMITED	Income statement 19.2	Cash flow
Operating income before adjustments	162 000	+162 000
Add: Investment income	8 000	+8 000
	170 000	
Less: Depreciation	30 000	
Interest	5 000	−5 000
	35 000	
Operating profit before extraordinary items	135 000	
Less: Loss on sale of asset	10 000	
Net profit before taxation	125 000	
Less: Taxation	60 000	−60 000
Net profit after taxation	65 000	
Less: Dividends	15 000	−15 000
Transferred to retained profit	R50 000	+R90 000

The depreciation of R30 000 written off does not represent a cash flow and the loss of R10 000 on the sale of the asset does not completely reflect the cash flow caused by the sale. Therefore these items must be adjusted in the schedule of balance sheet changes in order to show the correct cash flow information.

□ Depreciation write offs

When a fixed asset is acquired an outflow of cash occurs. The purpose of depreciation is to write off the original acquisition cost against income over the lifespan of the asset. Depreciation is the internal entry, that is it does not represent a transaction with an outsider. No cash flow results from writing off depreciation. The change caused by the provision for depreciation must therefore be eliminated in order that the actual flow of funds may be determined.

Depreciation is a debit against income and reduces profit, and consequently retained income. To eliminate the influence of depreciation the following adjustment must be made in the schedule of balance sheet changes:

Provision for depreciation	30 000	
Retained income		30 000

The effect of this adjustment on retained income and other relevant accounts is shown as adjustment 1 in example 28.5. The changes in the relevant balance sheet items of Alta Limited will therefore be adjusted as follows:

	19.1	19.2	Changes
Source:			
Retained income	100 000	180 000 ~~150 000~~	+80 000
Provision for depreciation	240 000	180 000 ~~210 000~~	−60 000

There is a change of R60 000 in the provision for depreciation which must be eliminated.

Example 28.5

ALTA LIMITED
ELIMINATION OF WRITE OFFS ON ASSET

			RETAINED PROFIT		
			Balance 1/1/19.1	100 000	
			Profit before adjustment	162 000	
			Investment income	8 000	
	Depreciation	30 000	Eliminate depreciation	30 000	(1)
	Interest	5 000			
	Loss on asset	10 000	Eliminate loss on asset	10 000	(2)
	Taxation	60 000			
	Dividend	15 000			
		~~190 000~~			
	Balance 31/12/19.2	150 000			
		R310 000		R310 000	
		~~R270 000~~		~~R270 000~~	
			PROVISION FOR DEPRECIATION		
			Balance 1/1/19.2	240 000	
(1)	Eliminate depreciation	30 000	Depreciation written off	30 000	
	Depreciation written off on asset sold	20 000	Eliminate depreciation on asset sold	20 000	(2)
	Accumulated depreciation on		Eliminate accumulated depreciation		
	asset written off	40 000	on asset written off	40 000	(3)
		240 000			
	Balance 31/12/19.2	~~210 000~~			
		R330 000		R330 000	
		~~R270 000~~		~~R270 000~~	
			CASH FLOW FROM SALE OF ASSET		
			Proceeds from sale of asset	7 000	(2)
			ASSETS		
	Balance 1/1/19.2	540 000			
	Purchases	187 000			
(2)	Eliminate cost price of asset sold	37 000	Cost price of asset sold	37 000	
(3)	Eliminate cost price of asset		Cost price of asset		
	written off	40 000	written off	40 000	
				727 000	
			Balance 31/12/19.2	~~650 000~~	
		R804 000		R804 000	
		~~R727 000~~		~~R727 000~~	

☐ Profit or loss on sale of fixed assets

When a fixed asset is sold at a profit or a loss the cash flow is equivalent to the selling price of the asset. If depreciation has been written off on the asset, the profit or loss on the sale is equal to the difference between the book value and the selling price.

The schedule of changes in balance sheet items, however, reflects only the actual cost price in the asset account, the total accumulated depreciation in the accumulated provision for depreciation account, and the profit or loss on the sale in the retained income or reserve account. The actual cash flow will not be clear from the change in the balance sheet item before the necessary adjustments have been made.

Assume that an asset on which R20 000 depreciation has been written off was originally purchased for R37 000 and is now sold for R7 000. The book value of the asset is R17 000. The profit or loss is calculated as the difference between the book value and the selling price, in this case a loss of R10 000 (R17 000 – R7 000).

The sale would have been recorded as follows:

	MACHINERY		
19.1 Original cost price	37 000	19.2 Asset sold	37 000
	PROVISION FOR DEPRECIATION		
19.2 Asset sold	20 000	19.1 Balance	20 000
	ASSET REALISATION ACCOUNT		
19.2 Machinery	37 000	19.2 Depreciation Cash Loss	20 000 7 000 10 000
	R37 000		R37 000
	CASH		
19.2 Asset sold	7 000		
	INCOME ACCOUNT		
19.2 Loss on sale of asset	10 000		

The following elimination must be made to the closing balance sheet items in the schedule of balance sheet changes to determine the flow of funds:

Asset	37 000	
Provision for depreciation		20 000
Retained profit		10 000
Source of funds – sale of fixed assets		7000

The following changes in the relevant balance sheet items of Alta Limited will result:

	19.1	19.2	Changes
Application:			
Fixed assets	540 000	687 000 ~~650 000~~	+147 000
Source:			
Retained profit	100 000	190 000 ~~180 000~~	+90 000
Provision for depreciation	240 000	200 000 ~~210 000~~	−40 000
Sale of fixed asset	—	7 000	+7 000

After this adjustment the change in retained income for the period reflects the actual net cash flow of R90 000, as shown in example 28.4. Note that the item 'sale of fixed assets' is brought into the schedule of balance sheet changes as an additional source. However, this is another change of R40 000 which must be eliminated from the accumulated provision for depreciation.

☐ Scrapping of fully depreciated assets

When an asset has been fully depreciated, it is scrapped by crediting the accumulated depreciation against the cost of the asset. This scrapping must be eliminated because it does not represent a flow of funds.

The following adjustment will have to be made to the closing balance sheet in the schedule of balance sheet changes in order to determine the flow of funds:

Assets	40 000	
Provision for depreciation		40 000

The effect of this adjustment on the relevant accounts is shown as adjustment 3 in example 28.5.

The balance sheet changes of Alta Limited will be adjusted as follows:

	19.1	19.2	Changes
Source:			
Fixed assets	540 000	727 000 ~~687 000~~	+187 000
Provision for depreciation	240 000	240 000 ~~200 000~~	—

The total change in the accumulated provision for depreciation has now been eliminated.

□ Revaluation of assets

A revaluation of assets occurs when the amount at which the asset is recorded in the books changes due to an increase or a decrease in value. This differs from depreciation, which refers specifically to the allocation of the original acquisition costs over the economic lifespan of the asset.

Neither an upward nor a downward revaluation of assets, resulting from an increase or a decrease in value, represents a flow of funds, and like depreciation, should be eliminated.

Upward revaluations of assets are often transferred to a reserve because they are not considered to constitute operating income. The following entry would be made on revaluation of an asset:

Asset	xxx	
Reserve for revaluation of assets		xxx

A downward revaluation of assets can be made against an existing reserve, retained income, or even against income, viz:

Reserve (or retained profit, or income)	xxx	
Asset		xxx

The influence of revaluations on the closing balance sheet items, like depreciation, will have to be eliminated from the relevant items in the schedule of balance sheet changes.

□ Scrapping of current assets

Current assets written off are considered to be operating expenses which reduce operating income, and are not usually eliminated from the closing balance sheet figures.

□ Transfers between reserves

Transfers between reserves, for example a transfer from retained income to a general reserve, do not represent a flow of funds and therefore must be eliminated from the schedule of balance sheet changes.

28.2.4 Items to be disclosed separately

The elimination of those items which do not result in a flow of funds does not always ensure that the actual flow of funds will be reflected accurately. Balance sheet changes often show only the net result of different transactions, which, because of their importance, should be disclosed separately.

The substance rather than the form of transactions should be reflected, therefore the net balance sheet changes should be analysed in order to determine their individual elements, which should then be disclosed separately.

☐ Cash flow from business operations

Business operations are the main source of funds for an enterprise. They should be shown separately and in sufficient detail to indicate the constituent sources of finance.

The Fourth Schedule of the Companies Act also specifically requires that 'net income before deducting taxation, dividends paid and proposed, and any internal provisions and reserves' must be disclosed separately as a source of finance.

Finance charges, investment income and extraordinary items should also be disclosed separately if the amounts are material.

Because the schedule of balance sheet changes reflects only the net changes to retained earnings, adjustments to retained income are necessary to reflect the flow of funds from business activities before those items which must be disclosed separately.

The following adjustments will have to be made to the schedule of balance sheet changes in order to show the inflow of funds from business activities for Alta Limited before interest, investment income, taxation and dividends:

Employment of funds:			
Dividends	15 000		(4)
Taxation	60 000		(5)
Interest	5 000		(6)
Retained income		80 000	
Retained income	8 000		
Source of funds:			
Investment income		8 000	(7)

The effect of these adjustments on retained income is shown in example 28.6.

Example 28.6

ALTA LIMITED
ADJUSTMENTS FOR SEPARATELY DISCLOSED ITEMS

	RETAINED INCOME				
			Balance 1/1/19.1	100 000	
			Profit before adjustment	162 000	
(7)	Transfer investment income	8 000	Transfer income	8 000	
	Depreciation	30 000	Eliminate depreciation	30 000	(1)
	Interest	5 000	Transfer interest	5 000	(6)
	Loss on asset	10 000	Eliminate loss on asset	10 000	(2)
	Taxation	60 000	Transfer taxation	60 000	(5)
	Dividend	15 000	Transfer dividend	15 000	(4)
		262 000			
	Balance 31/12/19.2	~~150 000~~			
		R390 000		R390 000	
		~~R270 000~~		~~R270 000~~	
	APPLICATION OF FUNDS				
(4)	Transfer dividend	15 000			
(5)	Transfer taxation	60 000			
(6)	Transfer interest	5 000			
	SOURCES OF FUNDS				
			Transfer investment income	8 000	(7)

The adjustments in the relevant balance sheet items of Alta Limited will be made as follows:

	19.1	19.2	Changes
Application:			
Interest		5 000	+5 000
Taxation		60 000	+10 000
Dividend		15 000	+15 000
Source:		262 000	
Retained profit	100 000	~~190 000~~	+162 000
Investment income		8 000	+8 000

Retained income now reflects a change of R162 000, which corresponds with the gross operating profit shown in the income statement for 19.2 in example 28.4.

Note that the application of funds on interest, taxation and dividends and the source of funds from investment income are brought in as new, separate items in the 19.2 column in the schedule of balance sheet changes.

☐ Dividends

Dividends are the form in which income is distributed to shareholders. Dividends do not reduce income – they are a distribution of income. The total dividends provided must be shown as an application of funds. Those dividends which have not yet been paid out will be shown as a short-term liability and therefore as a source of funds, since in effect the shareholders to whom the dividends are due are providing the company with short-term credit. Therefore dividends due to shareholders at the end of the financial period will not be reversed to the provision for dividends.

The adjustment showing the dividends paid and proposed separately as an application of funds is illustrated as adjustment (4) above.

☐ Taxation

The total amount provided for taxation must be shown separately in the source and application of funds statement. It can be shown as a deduction from income or as a separate application.

Taxation still due at the end of the financial period will be treated as a short-term liability and therefore as a source of funds. Thus taxation due must not be reversed to the provision for taxation.

The adjustment showing the taxation provided separately is illustrated as adjustment (5) above.

☐ Finance charges and investment income

Finance charges and investment income should be disclosed separately if the amounts are material. Finance charges can be shown separately as an application of funds or as a deduction from operating income.

Investment income can be disclosed separately as a source of funds or can be shown as an addition to operating income.

The adjustments to disclose finance charges and investment income separately are shown as adjustments (6) and (7) above.

☐ Extraordinary items

Extraordinary income or expense items should be shown separately if the amounts are material. However, the manner in which they are disclosed will depend on the nature of the items.

☐ Fixed and other non-current assets

The influence of various types of transactions relating to fixed assets and investments should be disclosed fully. For example, if fixed assets are sold and acquired, the balance sheet changes will show only the net amount.

The total cost of acquisition of fixed and non-current assets should be shown as an **application of funds**, while the total proceeds from the sale of fixed and non-current assets should be shown as a **source of funds**.

These rules also apply when assets are exchanged or traded in.

The effect of the adjustments in the paragraph 'Profit or loss on sale of fixed assets' is that the acquisition costs of new assets and the proceeds from the sale of old assets are shown separately.

☐ Loans received and granted

The total loans received must be shown as a **source** and the total amount repaid as an **application**. It is incorrect to show only the difference between receipts and repayments.

Similarly, the total loans granted or advances made by the undertaking should be shown as an **application**, and repayments of these loans or advances as a **source**.

These criteria do not apply to current assets and liabilities such as trade debtors and creditors, since the changes in these items have already been absorbed by the changes in net working capital.

☐ Owner's equity

The details of all changes to the share capital of companies or the capital introduced into non-incorporated undertakings should be shown in the source and application of funds statements.

☐ Working capital

The net change in working capital is calculated as the difference between the increase and decrease in the various working capital items.

A net decrease in working capital is shown as a source of funds, because it represents a release of funds from working capital.

A net increase in working capital is shown as an application of funds, because it represents an absorption of funds by working capital.

☐ Adjusted schedule of balance sheet changes

After all the items which do not influence the flow of funds have been adjusted in the closing balance sheet and accounted for in the schedule of balance sheet changes, the changes in the actual flow of funds during the period will be reflected as in example 28.7.

Example 28.7

ALTA LIMITED
ADJUSTED SCHEDULE OF BALANCE SHEET CHANGES

	19.1	19.2	Changes
Application:			
Fixed assets	540 000	727 000	+187 000
Investments	100 000	980 000	−10 000
Current assets	80 000	100 000	+20 000
Dividends		15 000	+15 000
Interest		5 000	+5 000
Taxation		60 000	+60 000
	R720 000	R997 000	
Source:			
Share capital	200 000	300 000	+100 000
Retained income	100 000	262 000	+162 000
Long-term loans	120 000	110 000	−10 000
Provision − depreciation	240 000	240 000	—
Current liabilities	60 000	70 000	+10 000
Sale of fixed assets		7 000	+7 000
Investment income		8 000	+8 000
	R720 000	R997 000	

The statement of source and application of funds can now be prepared from the adjusted schedule of balance sheet changes, according to the categories identified in example 28.1. The form of this statement is discussed in paragraph 28.2.6.

28.2.5 Ten-column worksheet

The ten-column worksheet is used when a large number of adjustments have to be made to the schedule of balance sheet changes. The worksheet is an extension of the latter, with additional columns for adjustments, working capital changes and sources and applications of funds.

The use of the ten-column worksheet is illustrated in example 28.10 for BNA Limited. The income statement and fixed asset and depreciation schedule of BNA Limited are given in examples 28.8 and 28.9 respectively.

Example 28.8

BNA LIMITED			
	Income statement 19.1 (R'000)	19.2	Adjustment funds
Sales	4 800	6 200	
Less: Cost of sales	2 784	3 720	
Gross profit	2 016	2 480	
Less: Expenses			
Current expenses	988	1 444	
Interest	78	66	
Depreciation	480	540	(5)
Total expenses	1 546	2 050	
Operating income before taxation	470	430	
Profit on sale of fixed asset		60	(6)
Net income before taxation	470	490	(1)
Provision for taxation	235	245	(2)
Net income after taxation	235	245	
Retained income – 1 January	1 500	1 485	
Available for distribution	1 735	1 730	
Less: Goodwill written off	50	50	(4)
Dividends declared	200	200	(3)
Retained income – 31 December	1 485	1 480	

Example 28.9

BNA LIMITED SCHEDULE OF FIXED ASSETS AND DEPRECIATION				
	19.1		19.2	
	Fixed assets (R'000)	Depreciation	Fixed assets (R'000)	Depreciation
Balance at beginning of year	3 200	1 680	3 000	1 960
Additions during year		480	1 200	540
	3 200	2 160	4 200	2 500
Less: Fully depreciated assets scrapped	200	200	500	500
Assets sold			300	100
Balance at end of year	3 000	1 960	3 400	1 900

Example 28.10

BNA LIMITED SOURCE AND APPLICATION OF FUNDS WORKSHEET 19.1 – 19.2										
	Balance sheets 31 Dec 19.1	31 Dec 19.2	Balance sheet changes		Adjustments		Changes in operating capital Increase	Decrease	Funds Applied	Provided
ASSETS										
Fixed assets										
Land and buildings	2 350	3 053	703						703	
Equipment (cost price)	3 000	3 400	400		500 (7)				1 200	
					300 (6)					
Investments	400	300		100		100 (8)				200
Goodwill	150	100		50	50 (4)					
Current assets										
Inventory	458	978	520				520			
Debtors	789	1 325	536				536			
Cash	877			877				877		
	8 024	9 156								
EQUITIES										
Share capital	3 000	3 800		800						800
Retained profit	1 485	1 480	5		490 (1)	245 (2)				
						200 (3)				
						50 (4)				
Capital reserve		100		100	100 (8)					
Long-term loan	600	500	100						100	
Current liabilities										
Creditors	686	938		252				252		
Bank overdraft		115		115				115		
Unclaimed dividends	210	200	10				10			
Taxation owing	83	123		40				40		
Provision – depreciation	1 960	1 900	60		540 (5)	500 (7)				
						100 (6)				
	8 024	9 156	2 334	2 334						
Funds provided from activities										
Net income before taxation					60 (6)	490 (1)				430
Depreciation written back						540 (5)				540
Funds from sale of fixed assets						260 (6)				260
Funds applied										
Taxation provided					245 (2)				245	
Dividend declared					200 (3)				200	
Net change in working capital							218			218
					2 485	2 485	1 284	1 284	2 448	2 448

The procedure for preparing the ten-column worksheet is as follows:

- ☐ The balance sheets at the beginning and the end of the period are recorded in the first two columns respectively. Usually assets and then the source of finance are recorded.
- ☐ The net changes between the two balance sheet dates are calculated and recorded either in column 3 (applications) or in column 4 (sources), and then balanced.

  A handy rule is that if the item in the opening balance sheet must be debited to obtain the amount on the closing balance sheet, the difference is recorded in the debit column (column 3). Conversely, if the item in the opening balance sheet must be credited, the difference is recorded in the credit column (column 4). This rule is illustrated in figure 28.2:

  Figure 28.2 Guidelines for recording balance sheet changes

BALANCE SHEET CHANGES COLUMNS	
Application Dr	Source Cr
Increase in assets Decrease in equities	Decrease in assets Increase in equities

- ☐ The adjustments that must be made to the balance sheet changes to reflect the actual flow of funds are the following:

  (a) The change in retained income is analysed and the items which should be disclosed separately are transferred to the applicable headings.

  (1) The net income before taxation of R490 000 is debited to retained income and credited to a separate new item under 'funds from business activities'.

  (2) In the books, taxation is debited to income and therefore to retained income, to which income is eventually transferred. The R245 000 taxation for which provision has been made is credited to retained income and debited to a separate new item 'provision for taxation' under the heading 'application of funds'.

  (3) Dividends have been debited to retained income in the books, therefore the dividends of R200 000 declared are credited to retained income and debited to a separate new item 'dividends declared' under the heading 'application of funds'.

  Adjustments (1) to (3) transfer the items included in the net change in retained income, and which should be shown separately, to the appropriate headings.

  (b) Items included in the change in retained income but which do not involve a flow of funds are eliminated from the change.

  (4) Goodwill of R50 000 has been written off by debiting retained income. Since this entry does not represent a flow of funds, it is eliminated by debiting retained income again.

  (5) Depreciation of R540 000 written off on fixed assets during 19.2 does not represent a flow of funds and must therefore be reversed. Depreciation was originally debited to income and hence to retained income (to which income is eventually transferred). The entry for

depreciation is eliminated by crediting retained income and debiting the accumulated provision for depreciation with R540 000.

(6) The profit of R60 000 on the sale of a fixed asset is the difference between the selling price and the book value of the asset and does not represent the cash flow from the transaction. The actual cash flow is equivalent to the price at which the asset was sold. To show the actual cash flow the original entry must be reconstructed and reversed.

From the schedule of fixed assets and depreciation (example 28.9) it can be deduced that the cost of the asset sold was R30 000, against which accumulated depreciation of R100 000 had been written off. Therefore it had a book value of R200 000. The profit of R60 000 is the excess of the selling price over the book value – the book value of R200 000 plus the profit of R60 000 is equal to a selling price of R260 000.

The original entry was:

Cash	R260 000	
Provision for depreciation	100 000	
Profit on sale of asset		R60 000
Fixed assets		300 000

The profit on the sale of the asset was credited to the income account and, in turn, to retained income. The original entry is reversed in the balance sheet changes as follows:

Fixed assets	R300 000	
Retained income	60 000	
Provision for depreciation		R100 000
Source of funds: From sale of fixed asset		260 000

Adjustments (4) to (6) eliminate all the entries made to retained income which did not result in a flow of funds. All the changes in retained income have now been eliminated.

(c) The change in the accumulated provision for depreciation is analysed and all the constituent elements eliminated so that it reflects no change.

(5) The depreciation entry for 19.2 has already been eliminated.

(6) The profit on the sale of fixed assets has already been eliminated.

(7) The schedule of fixed assets and depreciation shows that fully depreciated fixed assets of R500 000 were written off during 19.2. This entry does not represent a flow of funds and consequently must be written back to the balance sheet changes:

Fixed assets	R500 000	
Provision for depreciation		R500 000

Adjustments (5), (6) and (7) eliminate all amounts which constitute the change in retained income.

(d) All changes in reserves which do not represent a flow of funds must be eliminated.

(8) Investments were revalued and the increase in value was credited to a capital reserve fund. Since no cash flow resulted, the entry must be eliminated from the balance sheet changes as follows:

Capital reserve	R100 000	
Investments		R100 000

The balance sheet change in investments now shows the actual purchase of investments which does constitute a flow of funds.

- The amounts in the 'change' column must be adjusted by the amounts in the adjustment columns and the result is transferred to the applicable working capital or funds column.
- The change in the working capital column is balanced and the balancing figure of R218 000 in example 28.8 is transferred to the application of funds in the funds column.

  A net decrease in working capital represents a source of funds, in other words, funds are released from working capital and used for other applications.

  A net increase in working capital represents an application of funds, in other words, long-term funds are utilised to provide working capital.
- The information in the worksheet is now used to prepare the statement of source and application of funds.

28.2.6 Form of the statement of source and application of funds

In the discussion of the flow of funds cycle in paragraph 28.1.1 the influence of working capital requirements on the flow of funds was emphasised. The form of the statement of source and application of funds is designed to emphasise this influence of the net change in working capital on the flow of funds. Therefore the statement of source and application of funds is prepared in two parts:

- the **funds section**, which reflects the funds from business operations and the allocation thereof, all long-term sources and applications, and the net change in net working capital
- the **working capital section**, which shows the changes in the various current assets and liabilities from which the net change in operating capital is calculated and then transferred to the funds section.

The net difference between long-term sources and applications therefore agrees with the net change in net operating capital.

- **The funds statement**

The basic form of the funds statement, as illustrated in example 28.11, uses the different categories of source and application of funds (as identified in paragraph 28.2.1).

Example 28.11 Form of the source and application of funds statement

NAME OF UNDERTAKING
SOURCE AND APPLICATION OF FUNDS FOR THE PERIOD xxx

		Notes
Source of funds:		
From operating activities before items which must be disclosed separately (1)	xxx	Net operating profit before depreciation, other items which are not cash flow, current items which must be disclosed separately such as interest and taxation, and investment income if the amount is material
Add: Income which must be disclosed separately, such as investment income	xxx	
Less: Expenses which must be disclosed separately, such as interest and taxation	(xxx)	The various items are each disclosed separately
Total from operating activities	xxx	
Increase in invested owner's equity		New share capital issued in companies, or capital investments in other undertakings
Increase in long-term liabilities	xxx	Long-term loans concluded or increased
Fixed and other non-current assets realised	xxx	Proceeds from sale of fixed assets, investments realised or repaid loans
Decrease in net working capital	xxx	Excess of increases over decreases in working capital
	xxx	
Funds applied:		
Owner's equity refunded	xxx	For example redeemable preference shares in companies or capital withdrawn from other undertakings
Increase in fixed and other non-current assets	xxx	New assets acquired, investments made, loans granted
Decrease in long-term liabilities	xxx	Long-term loans repaid
Dividend declared	xxx	
Increase in net working capital	xxx	Excess of increases over decreases in working capital
	xxx	

(1) The operating profit after depreciation can also be disclosed by means of an appropriate adjustment for depreciation, for example

Net operating profit	xxx
Add: Depreciation written back	xxx
Funds from operating activities	xxx

In practice, the form of the statement can be adapted to suit the particular circumstances.

The statement is usually more understandable when the various material items are shown separately and the exact nature of each item is described.

Often the composition of the statement is altered to show the result of the difference between source and application of funds, for example:

Source of funds
−
Application of funds
=
Net change in working capital

The statement of source and application of funds of BNA Limited is shown in example 28.12.

Example 28.12

BNA LIMITED SOURCE AND APPLICATION OF FUNDS 19.2		
Source of funds		
From operating activities		
Net income before taxation		430
Depreciation written back		540
		970
Less: Taxation		245
Net income from operating activities		725
New share issue		800
Assets realised		
Fixed assets sold		260
Investments realised		200
Net decrease in working capital		218
		R2 203
Funds applied		
Fixed assets acquired		
Land and buildings		703
Equipment		1 200
Long-term loan repaid		100
Dividend declared		200
		R2 203
Change in net working capital		
Decrease in current assets		
Cash		877
Increase in current liabilities		
Creditors		252
Bank overdraft		115
Taxation owing		40
Funds available from decreases		1 284
Less: Increases in working capital		1 066
Increases in current assets		
Inventory	520	
Debtors	536	
Decrease in current liabilities		
Unclaimed dividend	10	
Net decrease in working capital		R218

☐ Working capital variation statement

The working capital variation statement starts with the categories of changes as identified in paragraph 28.2.1. A typical working capital variation statement is illustrated in example 28.13.

Example 28.13

WORKING CAPITAL VARIATION STATEMENT			
Increase in working capital			xxx
Increase in current assets		xxx	
(Only those items which have increased are	xxx		
separately disclosed)	xxx		
	xxx		
Decrease in current liabilities		xxx	
(Only those items which have decreased are	xxx		
separately disclosed)	xxx		
	xxx		
Less: Decrease in working capital			xxx
Increase in current assets		xxx	
(Only those items which have increased are	xxx		
separately disclosed)	xxx		
	xxx		
Decrease in current liabilities		xxx	
(Only those items which have decreased are	xxx		
separately disclosed)	xxx		
Net increase in current assets			xxx

The order of the sections can be altered to suit the circumstances so that the information is presented in the most meaningful way. If, for example, there had been a net decrease in working capital, the order could have been reversed.

28.2.7 Use of the statement of source and application of funds

The information in the statement of source and application of funds is used to evaluate the investment and financing which occurred during the relevant period. The justification for the investments is examined and the sources which were actually used are evaluated against sound financing principles.

Changes in current assets and liabilities, for example, are compared to policy, changes in price levels and volume of activities, and the period, cost and risk of the form of financing used for working capital are investigated.

Investment in fixed and other long-term assets is judged in relation to the effect that it will have on long-term earning capacity. The period, cost and risk of long-term financing are also investigated.

28.3 CASH FLOW STATEMENTS

In contrast to the concept funds, which includes all sources, cash is defined as cash in bank and on hand and cash equivalents such as liquid investments. Therefore the cash flow statement reflects only the flow of actual cash and the influence this has on loans. A cash flow statement should show the following items separately:

- ☐ Cash flow from normal business activities, but showing finance charges, investment income, taxation and extraordinary items separately.
- ☐ Cash flow arising from transactions with members, such as capital introduced or capital withdrawals and dividends.
- ☐ Cash flow from investments in and the realisation of fixed assets and investments.
- ☐ Movements in loans.
- ☐ Movements in cash.

The net cash flow from business activities is the difference between cash received from business activities and cash paid for goods and services. It is calculated by adjusting operating profit to eliminate entries which do not represent a cash flow and entries which represent changes in working capital items other than cash.

In the case of BNA Limited, for example, the cash flow from business activities would be calculated as follows:

Operating profit		430 000
Depreciation written back		540 000
Changes in working capital items		(804 000)
Increase in inventory	(R520 000)	
Increase in debtors	(536 000)	
Increase in creditors	252 000	
Cash flow from current business activities		R166 000

The increase in inventory and debtors is deducted from operating income because it represents additional capital which is invested in current assets. Similarly, the increase in creditors is added to operating income because it represents cash which has not been paid out.

The cash flow from business activities of R166 000 is calculated after interest. If interest is shown separately, the cash flow from business activities before interest will amount to R232 000. A similar adjustment would have been made for interest on investments. BNA Limited's income statement also shows the provision for taxation of R245 000 and dividends of R200 000. It will be necessary to calculate the actual cash flow in respect of these two items because the balance sheets show outstanding amounts on these items at the beginning and end of the year. The cash flow can be calculated as follows:

	Taxation	Dividends
Amount outstanding at beginning of year	83 000	210 000
Provided during year	245 000	200 000
	328 000	410 000
Amount outstanding at end of year	123 000	200 000
Cash flow during year	R205 000	R210 000

The cash flow statement is prepared in two parts. The first part shows the net cash flow and the second part the influence of the net cash flow on loans and cash balances.

The cash flow of BNA Limited is shown in example 28.14.

Example 28.14

BNA LIMITED CASH FLOW STATEMENT 19.2	
Cash from operating activities	
Operating income before interest and taxation	232
Provided from working capital	
Interest paid	(66)
Taxation paid	(205)
Cash from operating activities	(39)
Transactions with owners	
Share capital issued	800
Dividends paid	(210)
Investment activities	
Sale of fixed assets	260
Investments realised	200
Land and buildings acquired	(703)
Equipment acquired	(1 200)
Increase in net loans	R892
Decrease in cash	877
Increase in net loans	
Increase in bank overdraft	115
Decrease in long-term loan	(100)
	R892

29

ANALYSIS AND INTERPRETATION OF FINANCIAL REPORTS – RATIO ANALYSIS

The analysis and interpretation of the financial information reflected in an enterprise's financial reports represents the last phase in the accounting process. Analysis and interpretation provides the information which supports the decisions taken in running the enterprise. The **AIM** of this chapter is to explain the most important aspects of ratio analysis.

29.1 OBJECTIVES AND USE OF FINANCIAL REPORTS

The financial reports describe the financial result of an enterprise for a specific period and its financial position at the end of that period. The **financial achievement** is not evaluated in these reports, in other words they give no indication whether the enterprise's achievement was satisfactory.

The responsibility for **analysing**, **interpreting** and **evaluating** the information in the reports for a **particular purpose** rests with the **user** of the financial reports. This process of analysis, interpretation and evaluation is discussed in detail in this chapter.

29.2 USERS OF FINANCIAL REPORTS

The information contained in financial reports is used mainly by two groups of people, namely:

- ☐ external users
- ☐ internal users.

The terms 'external user' and 'internal user' are relative to the individual enterprise. **External users** include all persons and institutions who, although they may have a financial interest, nevertheless exist outside the enterprise and are not directly involved in its management. **Internal users**, on the other hand, are generally employed by the enterprise and responsible for its management.

29.2.1 External users and their information requirements

External users comprise, first, those persons and institutions who either have, or are considering the acquisition of, an interest in the enterprise; and second, persons or institutions who, although they have no direct financial interest in the enterprise, for various other reasons such as taxation purposes also require financial information pertaining to the enterprise.

The following are the main external users with a financial interest in the enterprise:

- ☐ **Investors** who, by virtue of a shareholding or otherwise, have an interest in the undertaking and whose primary concern is the profitability or rate of return of the enterprise, as well as its financial position and stability.
- ☐ **Short-term suppliers of credit** who are concerned with the enterprise's liquidity, that is its ability to meet its current liabilities on time.
- ☐ **Long-term suppliers of credit** whose interest lies in the solvency of the enterprise, in other words in whether it is financially sound, whether their investment is fully covered and secured, and whether the enterprise will be able to meet its long-term capital redemption and interest liabilities regularly.

Apart from the owners, creditors and potential owners and creditors, there are numerous other institutions which are interested in financial information about a specific enterprise. The most important external users of financial reports who have no direct interest in the enterprise are government departments such as the Department of Internal Revenue, which is responsible for the levying of income tax, the Central Statistical Services and the Department of Trade and Industries. Other external users include the South African Reserve Bank and various research and employee and employer organisations, which use the information to compile reports on national trends in economic and business conditions in the country. These reports are used by the private and public sectors for policy determination, planning and control.

29.2.2 Internal users and their information requirements

The enterprise's own **personnel**, whose task it is to manage the enterprise in such a way as to achieve the objectives set by the owner's equity group, are the internal users of accounting information. This group of personnel is known as **management**, and is accountable to the owner's equity group.

The nature of an enterprise's activities must be scrutinised in order to accurately describe the use of accounting information within the enterprise itself. For the sake of clarity, these activities can be divided into **management or leadership activities** and **operating activities**.

Management is, above all, a process of planning and control. **Planning** comprises the organisation of internal, controllable circumstances in order to achieve the greatest possible measure of success in attaining the enterprise's objectives under largely uncontrollable external circumstances. **Control** entails action to ensure that the enterprise's activities and results are according to plan. Control implies establishing criteria or standards, evaluating the actual situation and comparing it with the relevant criteria and standards, and taking any necessary corrective action.

Where the extent, diversity and complexity of an enterprise's activities are of such a nature that they cannot be managed by a single person, top management is obliged to delegate certain functions and the resulting activities to subordinates. **Delegating** means instructing someone to perform a specific task, giving him the necessary authority to do the task, holding him responsible for executing the instruction and consequently holding him accountable for the execution of his responsibilities.

Enterprises are usually divided into departments, each of which has a specific function and cooperates with all the other departments to achieve the enterprise's objectives. In a typical large business enterprise, a general manager is responsible to the owner's equity group for the management of the enterprise as a whole. The general manager, however, delegates the various tasks which have to be performed to different departmental managers who, in turn, are accountable to the general manager for carrying out those tasks. Departmental managers, in turn, delegate tasks to subordinates in their departments.

Therefore, every person in a department is responsible for carrying out specific tasks. All the activities within a department form part of that department's function, and by coordinating their functions the different departments strive for the achievement of the enterprise's principal objectives.

29.3 INFORMATION FOR THE PURPOSES OF PLANNING AND CONTROL

The financial reports constitute one of the most important sources of information underlying decision making by managers at different levels within the enterprise. For planning purposes this information gives an indication of the achievement of which the concern is capable and which may be expected in the future. For control purposes the information in the financial reports reflects actual achievement, which may be compared with planned or expected achievement to provide a basis for corrective action.

Before the information contained in the financial reports can be used meaningfully, it must be **analysed** and **interpreted** properly. Two factors are important in the process of analysis and interpretation: first, the **interdependence** of the enterprise's different activities, and second, **trends** which develop with time.

All the activities of an enterprise are related to a greater or lesser degree. This is apparent from the explanation above of the subdivision and coordination of functions within an enterprise. Thus, for example, cost of sales is related to sales, which in turn is related to inventory and debtors. At the same time the nature and extent of the fixed assets determine the capacity of the enterprise, which plays an important role in determining potential sales.

Therefore it is essential that financial reports are interpreted within the framework of the relationships between the different activities of an enterprise.

The results of an enterprise's activities seldom remain static; rather, they are subject to constant fluctuation. The financial information pertaining to a single period cannot reflect these fluctuations. Therefore the meaningful analysis and interpretation of an enterprise's financial performance requires the identification of **trends** rather than a single value.

29.3.1 Analysis and interpretation

It is necessary to distinguish between the two concepts **analysis** and **interpretation**.

The **analysis** of financial information entails additional investigation and processing of that information in order to obtain the specific information required by a specific decision maker for a specific purpose. Periodically the credit manager, who exercises control over the credit department, will have on hand the total amount outstanding. However, to judge the effectiveness of his department he requires more information than merely the total amount owing. For example, by further investigation and processing he can try to establish a trend in the collection pattern – whether relatively more or less debts are being collected.

The **interpretation** of financial information entails determining the causes and implications of situations revealed by the information. A decision maker must be aware of which factors can influence a specific situation and of the possible consequences before he is equipped to decide on further action. If the credit manager notices a drop in the rate of debt collection, he will want to know the cause of this, as well as its possible effect on the enterprise's future cash position.

29.3.2 Shortcomings and limitations of conventional financial statements

The information contained in financial statements cannot be analysed or interpreted meaningfully unless a clear understanding of both the **usefulness** and the **reliability** of the information is obtained. The most important limitation on the usefulness and reliability of information in the financial statements arises from the following two aspects.

☐ Accounting principles and practices

Financial statements reflect information prepared on the basis of accounting systems in which economic transactions are recorded according to accounting practice and specific personal judgements and views. First, there is not complete agreement as to what comprises generally accepted accounting practice. Furthermore, for many aspects of accounting there is a variety of alternative methods and procedures and the choice of any specific method or procedure for a specific set of circumstances is determined by personal conviction and judgement. The reliability of decisions based on personal judgement necessarily depends on the ability and personal integrity of the person making the decision, as well as on the extent to which generally accepted accounting practice has been observed.

The most important areas in which different approaches may be applied and which produce different results under the same circumstances are the policies adopted towards changes in monetary value and the application of the matching principle.

☐ Money as a universal accounting unit

Accounting information is necessarily monetary by nature and is limited to information which can be expressed in terms of monetary units. However, many factors which cannot be expressed or are not practical to express in monetary terms can exert a definite influence on the value of an enterprise, for example the value of an enterprise's management and other employees, or the attitude and opinion of the public towards the enterprise.

Anyone analysing and interpreting financial statements must be aware of the possible limitations of these statements and conversant with the specific accounting system, assumptions, managerial policy, etc in terms of which they have been prepared. Where generally accepted classification systems, principles, uses and judgements are consistently and objectively applied by the accounting system, the analyst of financial statements may assume with a fair degree of certainty that the information contained in the consecutive financial statements of the same enterprise is comparable.

29.4 THE IMPORTANCE OF JUDGEMENTAL CRITERIA

In order to judge whether the financial performance is satisfactory, it must be compared with a standard. There are basically four types of criteria which may be used in such comparisons:

- ☐ An objective, predetermined standard or budget.
- ☐ Historical data particular to the enterprise:
  - — comparable figures for preceding periods, such as the current profit compared with the previous year's profit
  - — related figures, such as profit as a percentage of total capital invested.
- ☐ Data from outside the enterprise:
  - — comparative data for other similar enterprises
  - — comparative data for other enterprises in the same industry.
- ☐ Empirically accepted standards, including the experience and background of the analyst. For example, he will know instinctively what constitutes an acceptable profit percentage for a certain type of enterprise.

29.5 RATIO ANALYSIS

Ratio analysis entails the identification, measurement and evaluation of financial relationships or ratios of the financial position and result.

The ratios used for analysing financial statements can be grouped as follows.

- ☐ Profitability or rate of return.
- ☐ Liquidity.
- ☐ Solvency.
- ☐ Financing structure (see chapters 25 and 27).

Figure 29.1 Rate of return ratios

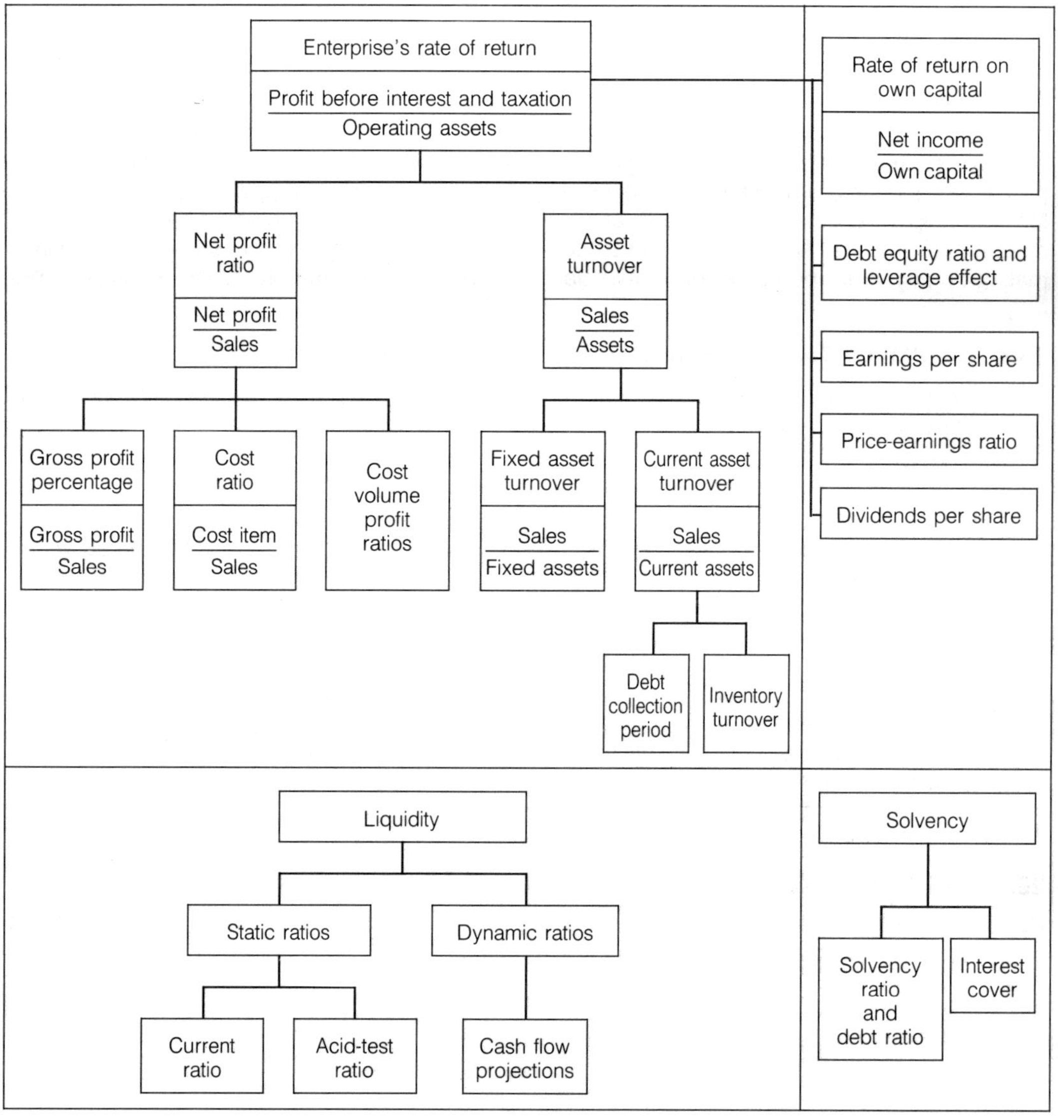

Example 29.1

Ratio analysis is discussed below with reference to the following financial reports prepared for ZA Limited:

ZA LIMITED
COMPARATIVE BALANCE SHEETS AT 31 DECEMBER 19.0, 19.1 AND 19.2

	19.0 (R'000)	19.1 (R'000)	19.2 (R'000)
Fixed assets	120	120	128
At cost price	160	170	188
Less: Depreciation	40	50	60
Investments	10	10	10
Current assets	170	186	212
Inventory	90	106	114
Debtors	70	68	88
Cash	10	12	10
	300	316	350
Share capital			
Ordinary shares of R1 each	70	70	140
Reserves and retained income	10	30	48
Shareholders' equity	80	100	188
Long-term loans	60	60	56
Current liabilities	160	156	106
Creditors	153	149	92
Dividends payable	7	7	14
	300	316	350

ZA LIMITED COMPARATIVE INCOME STATEMENTS FOR THE YEARS ENDED 31 DECEMBER 19.1 AND 19.2				
	19.1 (R'000)		19.2 (R'000)	
Sales				
Credit	360		440	
Cash	50	410	40	480
Cost of sales		(300)		(360)
Gross profit		110		120
Operating costs	68		64	
Depreciation on fixed assets	8		10	
Interest on long-term loan	3	(79)	2	(76)
Net operating profit for the year		31		44
Dividends received on investments		1		1
Net profit for the year before taxation		32		45
Taxation		(10)		(13)
Net income for the year after taxation		22		32
Retained income: Beginning of year		15		30
		37		62
Dividends declared		(7)		(14)
Retained income: End of year		30		48

29.6 RETURN ON CAPITAL

29.6.1 Return on capital of the enterprise

☐ Introduction

The primary objective of a business enterprise is to earn a reasonable yield on the capital invested in that enterprise. Consider, for example, the balance sheet of ZA Limited at 31 December 19.2. Total investment in assets amounts to R350 000. By applying these assets in the operating process the enterprise earns its profit before interest and taxation. In the case of ZA Limited this amounts to R47 000 for 19.2 (net profit before taxation of R45 000 plus interest added back of R2 000).

The profit before interest and taxation gives an indication of the **earning capacity** of the **assets**.

Figure 29.2

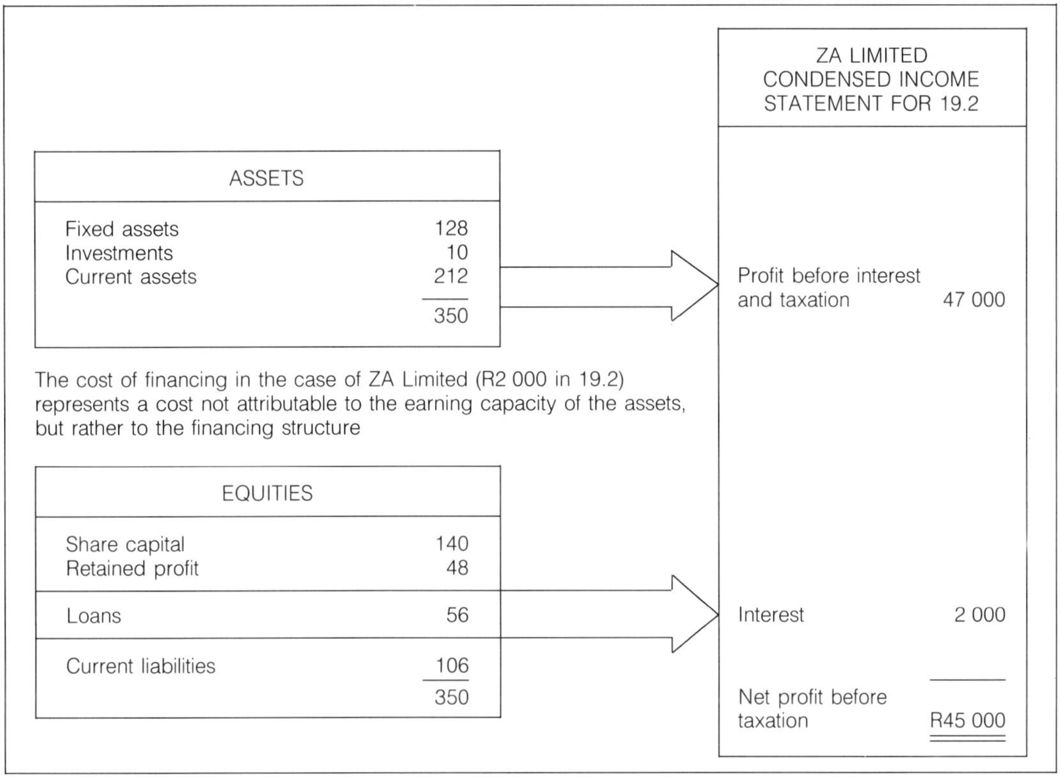

The earning capacity of the assets is called **return on the capital of the enterprise** and is measured by the following ratio:

$$\frac{\text{Profit before interest and taxation}}{\text{Total average assets in operation}}$$

Average assets in operation during the particular period are used to determine the enterprise's return on capital since the profit is earned over the whole year, while the balance sheet shows only the assets at the end of the year. The average of the assets at the beginning and end of the year therefore represents a more realistic basis for calculation.

According to the financial reports for ZA Limited shown in example 29.1, the enterprise's **return on capital** for 19.1 and 19.2 is calculated as follows:

RATIO	19.2	19.1
$\frac{\text{Net profit}}{\text{Average operating assets}}$	$\frac{(45\,000+2\,000)^*}{(350\,000+316\,000)\div 2}$ $=\frac{47\,000}{333\,000}\times 100$ $=14{,}11\%$	$\frac{(32\,000+3\,000)^*}{(316\,000+300\,000)\div 2}$ $=\frac{35\,000}{308\,000}\times 100$ $=11{,}35\%$

*Interest on loan capital added back.

☐ Taxation

Return on capital of an enterprise is usually calculated **before tax is taken into account**, first, because rates vary from year to year, and second, because special allowances and taxation rebates received in certain years influence the after-tax profit for those years in such a way that a realistic comparison is not possible.

☐ Investments and income from investments

When an enterprise's assets include investments not essential to the operating process, these investments should not be included in the total operating assets when the return on capital of the enterprise is calculated. If the investments are excluded the income therefrom should obviously also be excluded in determining the enterprise's return on capital.

For example, on 31 December 19.2 ZA Limited had investments of R10 000 which earned dividends of R1 000. In the calculation of ZA Limited's return on capital it was assumed that these investments were essential to the operating process. Consequently the investments and the income earned were included in the calculation.

Interpretation

ZA Limited's return on capital rose from 11,36% in 19.1 to 14,11% in 19.2. This increase was achieved despite an increase in the assets in operation; therefore there was a proportionately greater improvement in profits before interest and taxation. Further analysis is necessary to identify the exact causes of this improvement.

29.6.2 Net profit ratio and asset turnover

If meaningful conclusions are to be drawn from the return on capital, the ratio must be analysed into its two components, namely the **net profit ratio** and **asset turnover**. The enterprise's return on capital is influenced by the enterprise's ability to:

- ☐ make a profit on sales as expressed by the net profit ratio
- ☐ generate sales from assets as expressed by the asset turnover ratio.

$$\frac{\text{Net profit}}{\text{Sales}} \times \frac{\text{Sales}}{\text{Assets}} = \frac{\text{Net profit}}{\text{Assets}}$$

□ The net profit ratio

As has already been stated, the primary objective of a business enterprise is to make a profit. Profit is earned from sales and the profit that can be earned from every rand of sales, as reflected in the **net profit ratio**, is an important measure of return on capital.

The net profit ratio of ZA Limited will be calculated as follows:

RATIO	19.2	19.1
$\frac{\text{Net profit}}{\text{Sales}}$	$\frac{47\ 000}{480\ 000} \times 100$ $= 9{,}8\%$	$\frac{35\ 000}{410\ 000} \times 100$ $= 8{,}5\%$

Interpretation

The improvement of the net profit ratio from 8,5% in 19.1 to 9,8% in 19.2 contributed to the improvement in the enterprise's return on capital. This improved net profit ratio indicates that a proportionately greater profit was earned from sales in 19.2 than in 19.1. However, it is not yet known whether this improvement has arisen out of a larger gross profit or lower expenses.

Therefore it is necessary to investigate related ratios in greater detail. As was seen from the financial reports for ZA Limited, a typical income statement incorporates the following elements:

	19.2 (R'000)	19.1 (R'000)
Sales	480	410
Less: Cost of sales	360	300
Gross profit	120	110
Less: Operating costs	76	79
Net profit	44	31

The net profit and the net profit ratio are therefore influenced and determined by:

- □ gross profit on sales
- □ expenses which must be recovered out of gross profit.

□ Gross profit percentage

To determine whether or not the gross profit for any period is satisfactory, the **gross profit percentage** (gross profit in relation to sales) must be determined for comparative purposes.

The gross profit percentage for ZA Limited will be determined as follows:

RATIO	19.2	19.1
$\frac{\text{Gross profit}}{\text{Sales}}$	$\frac{120\ 000}{480\ 000} \times 100$ $= 25\%$	$\frac{110\ 000}{410\ 000} \times 100$ $= 27\%$

Interpretation

The two ratios above indicate that there was a decrease in the gross profit percentage.

It is now necessary to determine which factors influence the gross profit percentage and which of these factors was responsible for the decrease.

Closer scrutiny of the following factors is needed to determine their influence:

- ☐ Lower selling prices.
- ☐ Higher discounts.
- ☐ Higher purchase prices.
- ☐ Incorrect inventory counts.
- ☐ Inventory losses and, if so, for what reason – drop in value, damage, evaporation, theft, etc.

Changes in the gross profit from one period to the next may also be analysed in terms of the influence of changes in the average selling and cost prices per unit, and according to sales volume. Obviously, this type of analysis is possible only if unit selling prices and costs are known.

Assume that the following data relates to the cost of sales for ZA Limited:

Example 29.2

ZA LIMITED
TRADING ACCOUNT FOR THE YEARS ENDED 31 DECEMBER 19.1 AND 19.2

	19.1			19.2		
	Quantity	R per unit*	R	Quantity	R per unit*	R
Sales	109 008	3,76	410 000	120 546	3,98	480 000
Opening inventory	18 000	2,60	46 800	18 992	2,78	52 800
Purchases	110 000	2,78	306 000	120 000	3,025	363 000
	128 000		352 800	138 992		415 800
Closing inventory	18 992	2,78	52 800	18 446	3,025	55 800
Cost of sales	109 008	2,752	300 000	120 546	2,986	360 000
Gross profit			110 000			120 000

*All calculations have been rounded off to two or three decimal places. Thus, in the determining of the variances below, differences will be encountered.

(1) Sales variances

Using 19.1 as a basis, the change in gross profit from R110 000 in 19.1 to R120 000 in 19.2 can be analysed as follows:

☐ **Sales volume variance:** This indicates the degree to which changes in quantity (at base year selling prices) have influenced the total income from sales. The sales volume variance is calculated using the following formula:

Difference between quantities sold in basic year and in current year			×	Average selling price per unit in basic year			=	Sales volume variance
19.2 120 546	–	19.1 109 008	=	Difference 11 538	×	R3,76	=	R43 397 (favourable)

☐ **Selling price variance:** This indicates the degree to which changes in selling price have influenced the total income from sales. The selling price variance is calculated as follows:

Difference in average selling price per unit between basic year and current year			×	Quantity sold in current year			=	Selling price variance
19.2 R3,98	–	19.1 R3,76	=	Difference R0,22	×	120 546	=	R26 603 (favourable)

Therefore the total difference of R70 000 between sales of R480 000 in 19.2 and R410 000 in 19.1 can be attributed to:

Additional quantity sold	43 397
Higher selling price	26 603
	R70 000

(2) Cost of sales variances

The cost of sales variance also comprises a volume and a cost element.

☐ **Cost of sales volume variance:** This indicates the degree to which changes in the number of units sold influence total cost of sales (calculated on base year cost price). The cost of sales volume variance may be calculated as follows:

Difference in quantities sold in basic year and in current year			×	Average cost price per unit in basic year			=	Cost of sales volume variance
19.2 120 546	–	19.1 109 008	=	Difference 11 538	×	R2,752	=	R31 752 (favourable)

☐ **Cost of sales price variance:** This indicates the degree to which changes in the cost price per unit during the base year influence the total cost of sales for the current year. The cost of sales variance can be calculated thus:

Difference in average cost price per unit in basic year and in current year	×	Quantity sold in current year	=	Cost of sales price variance

19.2 R2,9864	–	19.1 R2,7521	=	Difference R0,2343	×	120 546	=	R28 248 (favourable)

The total difference of R60 000 between cost of sales of R300 000 in 19.1 and R360 000 in 19.2 can therefore be attributed to:

Additional quantity sold	31 752
Higher cost price	28 248
	R60 000

Interpretation

In 19.2 average cost price per unit was R0,234 higher than in 19.1, while the average selling price rose by only R0,22. This difference, although small, was nevertheless sufficient to influence the gross profit percentage.

Average cost price of purchases is calculated by taking into account the cost price of opening inventory which is lower than that at which the goods were purchased during the current year. The acquisition price of R3,025 in 19.2 is actually R0,245 higher than the acquisition price of R2,78 in 19.1.

☐ Expense ratios

Operating expenses may be evaluated with reference to the ratio of each expense item to the volume of activity generating that cost. Therefore operating expense items are frequently expressed as a percentage of total sales.

The expense ratios of ZA Limited for 19.1 and 19.2 may be determined as follows:

Example 29.3

ZA LIMITED
COMPARATIVE INCOME STATEMENTS FOR THE YEARS ENDED 31 DECEMBER 19.1 AND 19.2

	19.1		19.2	
	R'000	%	R'000	%
Sales	480	100	410	100
Less: Cost of sales	360	75	300	73,2
	120	25	110	26,8
Less: Operating costs				
Salaries and wages	31	6,4	32	7,8
Rental	10	2,1	12	2,9
Transport costs	8	1,7	10	2,4
Advertising	6	1,3	5	1,2
Municipal services	3	0,6	2	0,5
Communication services	2	0,4	2	0,5
Printing	3	0,6	4	1,0
Other	1	0,2	1	0,2
Interest	2	0,4	3	0,7
Depreciation	10	2,1	8	2,0
	76	15,8	79	19,2
Net profit before dividends received and taxation	44	9,2	31	7,6

Interpretation

Total operating expenses as a percentage of sales dropped from 19,2% in 19.1, to 15,8% in 19.2. Savings on salaries, rental and transport costs were mainly responsible for this drop. Advertising and municipal services showed a small percentage increase and should be monitored.

☐ Cost-volume-profit relationships

An understanding of the influence of fixed and variable costs on the relationship between cost, volume of activity and profit is essential in the analysis and interpretation of income statements.

The gross profit and expense ratios discussed above are based on the assumption that the expense items concerned are variable, that is they change in relation to the volume of activity. If a cost has a fixed element this assumption is not valid.

Assume, for example, that ZA Limited is a manufacturing company and that production costs (instead of costs of purchases of merchandise) are as follows:

Example 29.4

ZA LIMITED
PRODUCTION COSTS FOR THE YEARS ENDED 31 DECEMBER 19.1 AND 19.2

	19.1		19.2	
Units produced	110 000		120 000	
	Total	Per unit	Total	Per unit
Variable costs:				
Material consumed	99 000	0,90	120 000	1,00
Fuel consumed	22 000	0,20	30 000	0,25
	121 000	1,10	150 000	1,25
Fixed costs:				
Factory rental	10 000		10 000	
Salaries	30 000		35 000	
Wages	130 000		150 000	
Maintenance	8 000		10 000	
Depreciation	7 000		8 000	
	185 000		213 000	
Total production costs	R306 000	2,78	R363 000	3,025

ZA LIMITED
COST OF SALES FOR THE YEARS ENDED 31 DECEMBER 19.1 AND 19.2

	19.1		19.2	
Opening inventory finished products	18 000 @ 2,60	46 800	18 992 @ 2,78	52 800
Add: Production costs	110 000	306 000	120 000	363 000
		352 800		415 800
Less: Closing inventory finished products	18 992 @ 2,78	52 800	18 446 @ 3,025	55 800
Cost of sales	109 008	R300 000	120 546	R360 000

(1) Variable cost variances

☐ **Variable cost volume variance:** This indicates the degree to which total variable costs, at base year prices, change as a result of fluctuations in the volume produced. It is calculated as follows:

Difference in quantity produced in base year and in current year			×	Variable cost per unit in base year			=	Variable cost volume variance
19.2 120 000	–	19.1 110 000	=	Difference 10 000	×	R1,10	=	R11 000 (favourable)

☐ **Variable cost price variance:** This indicates the degree to which changes in the unit prices of the base year influence total variable costs. It is calculated as follows:

Difference in variable cost per unit between base year and current year			×	Quantity produced in current year			=	Variable cost price variance
19.2 R1,25	–	19.1 R1,10	=	Difference R0,15	×	120 000	=	R18 000 (favourable)

The total difference of R29 000 between the variable costs of R121 000 for 19.1 and R150 000 for 19.2 is made up as follows:

Additional quantity produced	11 000
Unit price increase	18 000
	R29 000

(2) Fixed cost variances

The changes in fixed costs, from R185 000 in 19.1 to R213 000 in 19.2, may be due to one of two causes. They could have changed as a result of management decisions to expand production capacity. Scrutiny of the balance sheet shows, for example, that fixed assets increased by R18 000, from R170 000 on 31 December 19.1 to R188 000 a year later. This increase in capacity resulted in additional depreciation.

The increase in fixed costs could also be due to an increase in prices or tariffs. Note, for example, that salaries increased from R30 000 in 19.1 to R35 000 in 19.2: this rise could be due purely to salary increases and not to any increase in the number of employees.

☐ Asset turnover

This ratio indicates how effectively the enterprise's assets are being used by comparing them with the volume of sales that they generate. The ratio also expresses the turnover rate of assets, in other words the number of times assets are 'turned into' sales. From this it is possible to deduce whether there was an over or under-investment in assets: whether the enterprise invested too much or too little in assets in relation to the scope of its activities.

Based on the financial statements of ZA Limited, the ratio is calculated as follows:

RATIO	19.2	19.1
Sales / Average assets	480 000 / (350 000 + 316 000) ÷ 2 = 1,44	410 000 / (316 000 + 300 000) ÷ 2 = 1,33

Interpretation

The asset turnover showed only a small improvement, from 1,33 in 19.1 to 1,44 in 19.2. The average assets in operation increased from R308 000 in 19.1 to R333 000 in 19.2. Therefore we may deduce that the additional assets were reasonably well utilised.

The asset turnover may be further divided into turnover ratios for the different types of assets, according to the nature of the enterprise's activities.

□ Fixed asset turnover ratio

The fixed assets of a business enterprise largely determine the enterprise's capacity. In a manufacturing enterprise the nature and scope of machinery and equipment determine the potential production capacity, while in a trading enterprise the nature and extent of the premises and shopfittings largely determine the turnover that the enterprise can achieve.

The acquisition or expansion of fixed assets is usually the result of carefully considered management decisions; usually investment in fixed assets is not made arbitrarily. It is good policy, when changes in the investment of fixed assets are necessary, to evaluate the utilisation of the assets in relation to the activities they generate.

Consider, for example, the situation of ZA Limited. The cost price of assets increased from R170 000 in 19.1 to R188 000 in 19.2. To what degree was this additional investment utilised?

The fixed asset turnover ratio provides an indication:

RATIO	19.2	19.1
Sales / Average investment	480 000 / (170 000 + 188 000) ÷ 2 = 2,68	410 000 / (160 000 + 170 000) ÷ 2 = 2,48

The fixed asset turnover must be analysed carefully, taking into consideration the various factors which may influence the significance thereof.

First, often fixed assets are acquired over a long period. This means that, with inflation, assets acquired earlier will have cost relatively less than assets acquired later. This may mean that the fixed asset turnover on the newer and more expensive assets will be lower than on the older, cheaper assets with the same physical capacity.

Second, since depreciation is written off on fixed assets, the much lower book value of older assets cannot always be compared meaningfully with the relatively higher book value of assets acquired more recently. In the example above this incomparability is partly eliminated by using the cost price and not the book value of fixed assets when calculating the fixed asset turnover figure.

Interpretation

The fixed asset turnover improved from 2,48 in 19.1 to 2,68 in 19.2. This indicates a more intensive use of fixed assets in 19.2.

☐ Current asset turnover ratios

The two most important current assets in any trading enterprise are inventory and debtors.

In contrast to fixed assets, which usually change only as a result of management decisions, current assets change in relation to changes in the volume of activities. These assets are also strongly affected by the degree of control exercised over them. Therefore it is essential that the position of current assets is determined and evaluated regularly.

The debtors position is measured by the **debtors collection period**, while the inventory position is measured by **inventory turnover**.

(1) Debtors collection period

The credit granted by an enterprise to its debtors is generally limited to a specific period – usually 30 days in the retail trade and 60 to 90 days in the wholesale trade. Therefore the total debtors outstanding is evaluated in terms of the average number of days that debts are outstanding. This is calculated by means of a formula which embodies the following three elements:

- ☐ Credit sales.
- ☐ Average debtors.
- ☐ The number of days or months in a year.

The calculation is as follows:

$$\frac{\text{Credit sales for year}}{365} = \text{Credit sales per day}$$

If the average debtors is divided by the average daily credit sales, the result obtained is the number of days' credit sales tied up in debtors.

The formula for determining the debtors collection period is as follows:

$$\frac{\text{Average debtors}}{\frac{\text{Credit sales}}{365}} \quad \text{OR} \quad \frac{\text{Average debtors} \times 365}{\text{Credit sales}}$$

Debtors Turnove rate.

Debtors settlement peroid: →

The debtors collection period for ZA Limited will be calculated as follows:

RATIO	19.2	19.1
$\dfrac{\dfrac{\text{Average debtors}}{\text{Credit sales}}}{365}$ OR $\dfrac{\text{Average debtors}}{\text{Credit sales}} \times 365$	$\dfrac{(88\ 000 + 68\ 000) \div 2}{440\ 000} \times 365$ $= \pm 64$ days	$\dfrac{(68\ 000 + 70\ 000) \div 2}{360\ 000} \times 365$ $= \pm 69$ days

Interpretation

During 19.1 debtors were allowed an average of 69 days to settle their debts. During 19.2 the average period allowed was 64 days, which indicates a slight improvement in credit control emphasised by the fact that credit sales in 19.2 increased by R80 000 or 22% in comparison with sales in 19.1.

Analysts often calculate this ratio by using the debtors figure at the end of the financial year rather than the average debtors figure, for example:

RATIO	19.2	19.1
$\dfrac{\text{Net debtors at the end of the year}}{\text{Average daily credit sales}}$	$\dfrac{88\ 000}{440\ 000} \times 365$ = 73 days	$\dfrac{68\ 000}{360\ 000} \times 365$ = 68 days

(2) Inventory turnover

The inventory turnover ratio gives an indication of the number of times a year that inventory is changed either into sales or, in the case of a manufacturing process, into material consumed. Therefore the ratio indicates the degree to which ageing in inventory has occurred, or the relative decrease in inventory.

The **inventory turnover ratio** of a trading enterprise is calculated by dividing the cost of sales for the period by the average inventory for the same period. Regarding inventory used in a manufacturing process, the turnover is calculated by dividing the cost of material consumed in a specific period by the average inventory for that period.

The inventory turnover ratio of ZA Limited can be calculated as follows:

RATIO	19.2	19.1
$\dfrac{\text{Cost price of sales}}{\text{Average inventory}}$	$\dfrac{360\ 000}{(114\ 000 + 106\ 000) \div 2}$ = 3,3 times	$\dfrac{300\ 000}{(106\ 000 + 90\ 000) \div 2}$ = 3,06 times

The average age of inventory is often calculated in the same way as the average age of debtors. This ratio may be usefully applied especially when management's inventory policy is expressed in terms of the number of days' sales or consumption. The number of days' inventory on hand can be calculated as follows:

RATIO	19.2	19.1
$\dfrac{\text{Average inventory}}{\frac{\text{Cost of sales}}{365}}$	$\dfrac{(114\,000 + 106\,000) \div 2}{\frac{360\,000}{365}}$ = 111 days	$\dfrac{(106\,000 + 90\,000) \div 2}{\frac{300\,000}{365}}$ = 119 days

Interpretation

The inventory turnover rate improved from 3,06 times in 19.1 to 3,3 times in 19.2. This trend is reflected by an improvement in the number of days' inventory on hand.

29.6.3 Rate of return on owner's equity

The enterprise's rate of return gives an indication of the earnings yield on total investment of assets in operation. The total investment of assets in operation is generally financed from two types of source – equity capital and loan finance.

ASSETS = EQUITIES

=

Equity capital

\+

Credit financing

The interest on loan finance and tax on the remaining net income must be recovered from the gross earnings on total assets in operation. The remaining net income after tax accrues to owner's equity. The rate of return on owner's equity is extremely important to the owners, since it represents the earnings yield on capital invested by owners in the enterprise.

The primary criterion for return on owner's equity is the ratio of net income after tax to total owner's equity.

Non-incorporated enterprises are generally not liable for tax; the owner to whom the income accrues is the tax entity in such a case. The return on owner's equity for enterprises which are not liable for tax is determined by the ratio of net income to owner's equity.

The return on owner's equity of ZA Limited can be determined as follows:

RATIO	19.2	19.1
$\frac{\text{Net income after taxation}}{\text{Average owner's equity}}$	$\frac{32\,000}{(188\,000+100\,000)\div 2}$ =22,22	$\frac{22\,000}{(100\,000+80\,000)\div 2}$ =24,44

Interpretation

Despite an improvement in the enterprise's return on capital (14,11% in 19.2 and 11,35% in 19.1 – see para 29.6.1), the return on owner's equity deteriorated.

☐ **Debt equity ratio and the leverage effect**

The **return on owner's equity** is influenced primarily by three factors, namely:

- ☐ the enterprise's return on capital
- ☐ the debt equity ratio
- ☐ the average interest cost of loan finance.

The debt equity ratio is the ratio of total debt to total capital employed, and is expressed as a percentage.

The debt equity ratio of ZA Limited is calculated as follows:

RATIO	19.2	19.1
$\frac{\text{Total debt}}{\text{Total capital applied}}$	$\frac{162}{350}$ =46,3%	$\frac{216}{316}$ =68,3%

For a given return on capital of an enterprise, the return on owner's equity will increase as the debt equity ratio increases provided the interest cost on the debt is lower than the return on capital of the enterprise. The converse also applies: the return on owner's equity will decrease when the debt equity ratio increases if the average interest cost on the debt is higher than the enterprise's return on capital. This is called the **leverage effect**. The greater the difference between the enterprise's return on capital and the average interest cost on the debt, the greater the leverage effect.

Management can adjust the return on owner's equity for a given return on capital of the enterprise and a given interest cost of loan finance by adjusting the debt equity ratio, in other words by making more or less use of loan finance. However, there is a limit to the extent to which the leverage effect may be applied to raise the debt equity ratio to improve the return on owner's equity. The greater an enterprise's loan finance in relation to equity capital, the lower its creditworthiness, in other words financiers will be less likely to grant additional loans and interest on any such additional loan capital will be higher.

Interpretation

The debt equity ratio decreased from 68,3% in 19.1 to 46,3% in 19.2, mainly because share capital increased from R70 000 to R140 000. Due to the leverage effect the improved debt equity ratio caused the return on shareholders' equity to remain fairly constant despite the increased return on capital of the enterprise.

☐ Earnings per share

A shareholder's interest in a company is embodied in the shares he holds. Both the **market value of his shares** and the **dividends** earned by his investment in those shares are important to him.

The market value of shares is influenced by many factors, probably the most important being the supply of and demand for a share on the stock market.

The net income per share earned by the company is, however, one of the primary factors influencing the value of a share.

The price that a person is prepared to pay for a share is determined to a large extent by his expectation of earnings from that share, that is, the expected earnings per share. Therefore a shareholder of a company finds it meaningful to determine the earnings per share and to monitor the trend.

The earnings per share for ZA Limited are calculated as follows:

RATIO	19.2	19.1
$\frac{\text{Net income}}{\text{Number of shares}}$	$\frac{32\ 000}{140\ 000}$ = ±23 cents per share	$\frac{22\ 000}{70\ 000}$ = ±31 cents per share

Interpretation

Although the net income after interest and taxation increased from R22 000 in 19.1 to R32 000 in 19.2, the earnings per share decreased from 31 cents to 23 cents. This decrease is attributable to the fact that 70 000 new shares were issued during 19.2.

☐ Price earnings ratio

The market value of a share is determined largely by the earnings per share, taking into account the risk the market attaches to a share. This risk is expressed in terms of the **rate of return** expected from a share. If a share is considered to be a high risk share, such as that in an enterprise which is performing badly, a shareholder will expect a high rate of return on his share investment in the company. Investors in low risk shares, on the other hand, will be satisfied with a lower rate of return.

> Assume that Company A, a company performing badly, earns an income of 30 cents per share. Because there is a high risk of the company floundering, a shareholder would require, say, a 20% rate of return on his share investment in the company. Therefore he would not be prepared to pay more than R1,50 for a share in A. Earnings of 30 cents per share represent a rate of return of 20% on the market price of R1,50.
>
> The price earnings ratio of A's shares is 150c ÷ 30c, that is, 5.
>
> Assume that Company B, a company performing well, also earns an income of 30 cents per share. Shareholders in B, however, are satisfied with a 10% rate of return since the risk involved is lower. Therefore a shareholder will be prepared to pay R3,00 for a share in B, which will give the desired rate of return of 10%.
>
> The price earnings ratio of B is 300c ÷ 30c, that is, 10.

Assuming that the market price of ZA Limited's shares was 230 cents and 310 cents on 31 December 19.2 and 19.1 respectively, the price earnings ratio can be determined as follows:

RATIO	19.2	19.1
$\frac{\text{Average market price per share}}{\text{Earnings per share}}$	$\frac{230}{23}$ = 10 (or 10:1)	$\frac{310}{31}$ = 10

☐ **Dividend per share**

A shareholder is especially interested in the **dividends** he may receive. The dividend per share is therefore an important criterion when buying shares.

This ratio may be expressed in four different ways:

☐ Total dividends divided by the total number of shares equals the dividend per share, for example 10 cents per share.

☐ Dividend per share as a percentage of the nominal value of the share. A dividend of 10 cents per share for shares with a par value of R1 represents a dividend yield of 10%.

☐ Dividend per share as a percentage of the price paid for the share. A dividend of 10 cents per share for shares bought for R2 each (regardless of the par value) represents a dividend yield of 5%.

☐ The dividend per share as a percentage of the market price of the share.

Clearly, the latter two calculations are more meaningful in that they relate the return to the actual amount invested, or to the price which would currently have to be paid to earn that dividend.

Dividend per share in ZA Limited is calculated as follows:

RATIO	19.2	19.1
$\frac{\text{Dividends}}{\text{Number of shares issued}}$	$R\frac{14\ 000}{140\ 000}$ = 10 cents per share or a 10% dividend	$R\frac{7\ 000}{70\ 000}$ = 10 cents per share or a 10% dividend

This ratio is calculated on the par value of the shares. As has already been mentioned, the individual owner/investor would find it more meaningful to use either the purchase price or the present market price as a basis.

29.7 LIQUIDITY ANALYSIS

The liquidity of an enterprise is reflected in its ability to meet current obligations from available funds timeously. This entails settlement of current liabilities as they become payable, from current assets as they are converted into cash. Liquidity is measured according to two approaches, namely the **static** and the **dynamic** approaches.

29.7.1 The static approach

In the static approach, liquidity is evaluated according to the ratio of current assets to current liabilities. Two ratios are applicable – the **current ratio** and the **acid-test ratio**.

☐ The current ratio

The current ratio is expressed as follows:

Current assets : Current liabilities

The current ratio measures only the extent to which current liabilities are covered by available current assets at a specific time. Current liabilities comprise creditors who must be paid in cash in the short term. Current assets consist mainly of inventory, debtors and cash. However, inventory must be sold and the credit allowed to the resulting debtors collected before cash becomes available.

If current assets are converted into cash at a rate slower than that at which creditors demand payment, the enterprise may experience liquidity problems. The current ratio gives no indication of this rate.

The larger the ratio of current assets to current liabilities, the better the enterprise's ability to meet its short-term obligations (see remarks below). This is a crude ratio, since the liquidity of each current asset is not analysed individually.

The **current ratio** for ZA Limited can be determined as follows:

RATIO	19.2	19.1
$\frac{\text{Current assets}}{\text{Current liabilities}}$	$\frac{212\ 000}{106\ 000}$ = 2:1	$\frac{186\ 000}{156\ 000}$ = 1,2:1

☐ The acid-test ratio

The acid-test ratio is calculated on the same basis as the current ratio, however **inventory is not taken into account since it is less liquid** than other current assets.

The **acid-test ratio** for ZA Limited is calculated as follows:

RATIO	19.2	19.1
Current assets – Inventory / Current liabilities	(212 000 – 114 000):106 000 = 0,92:1	(186 000 – 106 000):156 000 = 0,51:1

Clearly, the enterprise's liquidity position improved considerably in 19.2. The poor acid-test ratio in 19.1 was dangerous and indicated that liquidity problems could have been experienced. Even in 19.2 the acid-test ratio is not entirely satisfactory: a ratio of 1:1 is the minimum requirement.

As has already been stated, these two ratios must be viewed with caution. A sizeable increase in the investment in debtors and inventory could bring about favourable current and acid-test ratios. This does not mean that such an investment is desirable. An unfavourable acid-test ratio may be the result of poor credit control and/or an excessive investment in inventory which is not justified by the enterprise's activities.

29.7.2 The dynamic approach

In the dynamic approach to measuring **liquidity** the enterprise's net cash flow for a certain period is estimated to determine as accurately as possible the availability of funds in relation to the need for funds.

This approach is discussed in greater detail in chapter 26.

29.8 SOLVENCY ANALYSIS

Solvency may be described as the extent to which the enterprise's assets exceed its liabilities in the long term. Therefore solvency pertains not only to the current state of an enterprise's affairs, but also to its ability to maintain solvency in the long term. Solvency differs from liquidity in that liquidity pertains to the settlement of short-term liabilities, while solvency pertains to the excess of total assets over total liabilities.

If solvency declines to the point where liabilities exceed assets, the enterprise is *prima facie* insolvent and its continued existence is in jeopardy. Therefore solvency is extremely important to both owners and creditors, especially long-term creditors.

Solvency can be expressed as the ratio of total assets to total liabilities. The **solvency ratio** of ZA Limited can be calculated as follows:

RATIO	19.2	19.1
Total assets / Total liabilities	350 / 162 = 2,16	316 / 216 = 1,46

Long-term creditors are also interested in the extent to which the enterprise's interest obligations are covered by available income.

Interest cover is the ratio between net income before interest and taxation and the interest liability.

ZA Limited's interest cover can be determined as follows:

RATIO	19.2	19.1
$\frac{\text{Net income before interest and taxation}}{\text{Interest}}$	$\frac{47^*}{2}$ = 23,5 times	$\frac{35^*}{3}$ = 11,6 times

*Net income before taxation plus interest added back.

The interest cover ratio must be evaluated in the light of possible fluctuations in available income. Interest cover which may be absorbed by a possible drop in income cannot be regarded as safe. If, for example, the interest cover is 2 and there is a possibility that the available income before interest and taxation may decline by 50%, the situation would be regarded as risky.

Interpretation

The interest cover improved from 11,6 in 19.1 to 23,5 in 19.2. With cover as high as this it seems unlikely that the enterprise will be unable to meet its interest obligations. The solvency ratio also shows that the enterprise's assets have increased in relation to its liabilities.

Summary of ZA Limited's position

ZA Limited's **return on capital** increased from 11,36% in 19.1 to 14,11% in 19.2. This was due to the combination of an increase in the net profit ratio from 8,5% to 9,8% and an improvement in asset turnover from 1,33 in 19.1 to 1,44 in 19.2.

The improvement in the **net profit ratio** may be attributed chiefly to greater efficiency, apparent from the improved expenses ratio of 15,8% in 19.2, compared with 19,3% in 19.1. The net profit ratio improved despite a drop in the gross profit percentage from 27% in 19.1 to 25% in 19.2.

The **utilisation of fixed assets** improved, as did the fixed asset turnover, which increased from 2,48 in 19.1 to 2,68 in 19.2. Current assets were also applied more effectively: the average collection period for debtors decreased from 69 days in 19.1 to 64 days in 19.2, while inventory turnover increased from 3,06 to 3,3.

Despite an improvement in the return on capital of the enterprise, the **return on owner's equity** deteriorated to 22,22. This was partly due to the doubling of share capital during the year. For the same reason, earnings per share decreased from approximately 31 cents in 19.1 to approximately 23 cents in 19.2. The dividend, however, remained at 10 cents per share.

The **liquidity** of ZA Limited improved considerably during the year: the current ratio improved from 1,2:1 in 19.1 to 2:1 in 19.2, and the acid-test ratio from 0,51:1 to 0,92:1.

The issue of 70 000 new shares was largely responsible for an improvement in the **debt equity ratio** from 68,3% in 19.1 to only 46,3% in 19.2. In addition, interest cover increased from 11,6 in 19.1 to 23,5 in 19.2, which is most satisfactory.

30

DEPARTMENTAL ACCOUNTS

An undertaking can subdivide its activities internally by making use of **departments**. The **AIM** of this chapter is to explain departmental accounts.

30.1 INTRODUCTION

In earlier chapters the concepts managerial and internal control, determination of profit in order to communicate the annual operation result to interested parties, and reporting on the enterprise's financial position, are referred to repeatedly.

Thorough planning and control are prerequisites for expansion and diversification. An important organisational aid is to divide the enterprise into **segments** or **departments** and to design the accounting system in such a way that separate results are available for each segment. The objective of segmentation is to ensure effective planning of and control over the subsections of a larger entity. Segmentation and expansion may be applied **internally** or **externally**.

Internal segmentation entails dividing the enterprise into departments or sections. **External segmentation** refers to expanding an enterprise beyond its existing limits. This can entail establishing branches or forming subsidiaries and groups. It can also entail expansion via third parties, for example agents.

30.2 DEPARTMENTAL ACCOUNTS

30.2.1 Introduction

When an enterprise engages in various activities, or markets various products or services, or organises its activities into different departments, the financial result thereof must be determined and reported on separately for managerial purposes.

A trading enterprise, for example, will want to determine the gross profit percentage and the inventory position of each product line separately. An enterprise functioning departmentally will want to determine the expenses and net profit of each department separately. It may also be desirable to evaluate departmental return in relation to the capital invested in each department.

There are three approaches to measuring and evaluating departmental performance.

First, the **net profit** of each department can be determined by taking into account in the reporting process **all** income and expenses relating to a department. This approach is problematic in that it is not always possible or easy to allocate general expenses to different departments. For example, what portion of a general manager's salary should be allocated to each department?

The **second** approach is to bring into account in the reporting process only the income and expenses directly related to a department. In this case reference is made to the **contribution** and not the net profit of the department.

The **third** approach is to bring into account in the reporting process only the income and expenses which can be **controlled** by the management of the department.

Thus it is important that the accounting system is designed in such a way that whichever approach is followed, the information regarding transactions in different departments can be recorded and reported separately.

30.2.2 Source documents

The principal requirement of a system is that the source documents should indicate the department or section to which a particular transaction relates. This allows a transaction to be identified and recorded separately by its original entry. Often columnar bookkeeping methods are used in manual systems, the books of prime entry having separate columns for each department. Each transaction is recorded in a total column together with all the enterprise's other transactions, and separately in a special column together with the other transactions of that particular department. Only the totals of each column are posted to the accounts of the various departments.

In computerised systems it is important that all the data needed is coded separately on the source documents. Therefore the accountant who designs the system should design the required departmental reports first in order to determine which data will be needed. This will give him an indication of which data in the source documents should be coded and how the code should be compiled.

30.2.3 Departmental records

If the operating results of different sections or departments are to be determined separately, it is necessary that each department's transactions are sorted and recorded effectively by means of a system which provides maximum information at minimum cost. In a conventional bookkeeping system this is most easily achieved using columnar journals and ledger accounts. Some large enterprises keep separate subsidiary books for each department.

Example 30.1 illustrates columnar (departmental) subsidiary books.

Example 30.1

SALES JOURNAL
APRIL 19.9

Date	Debtors	Invoice	Folio no	Sundries	Departments A	B	C	D	Total
19.9 Apr 6	A Sanders	314	53		100				100
8	F le Roux	315	67			50			50
10	R Jones: Sale of old shop fittings	316	11	40					40
12	B Sydney	317	59				60		60
14	T Arundel	318	A5					80	80
16	S Warwick	319	W1			30			30
20	R Botha	320	B6		40				40
25	R Stolmeyer	321	S14				70		70
30				R40	R140	R80	R130	R80	R470
						410			120

Debtors ledger
These items are posted to the individual accounts of each debtor in the debtors ledger

GENERAL LEDGER

DEBTORS CONTROL 120

19.9 Apr 30	Sales	470		

SALES 410

			A	B	C	D	Total
	19.9 Apr 30	Debtors	140	80	130	80	430

SHOP FITTINGS 11

	19.9 Apr 1	Debtors	40

The sales journal need not necessarily show only the sale of merchandise; the sale of sundry items can be recorded on an ordinary invoice and shown in a separate column in the sales journal. Items in this 'sundries' column, as is the case with the 'sundries' columns in the cash journals, are posted individually to the accounts concerned.

Similar columns will appear in the other books of prime entry such as the purchases journal and the returns journal. Columns may also be provided in the purchases journal for items which, although not merchandise, are purchased regularly.

Figure 30.1

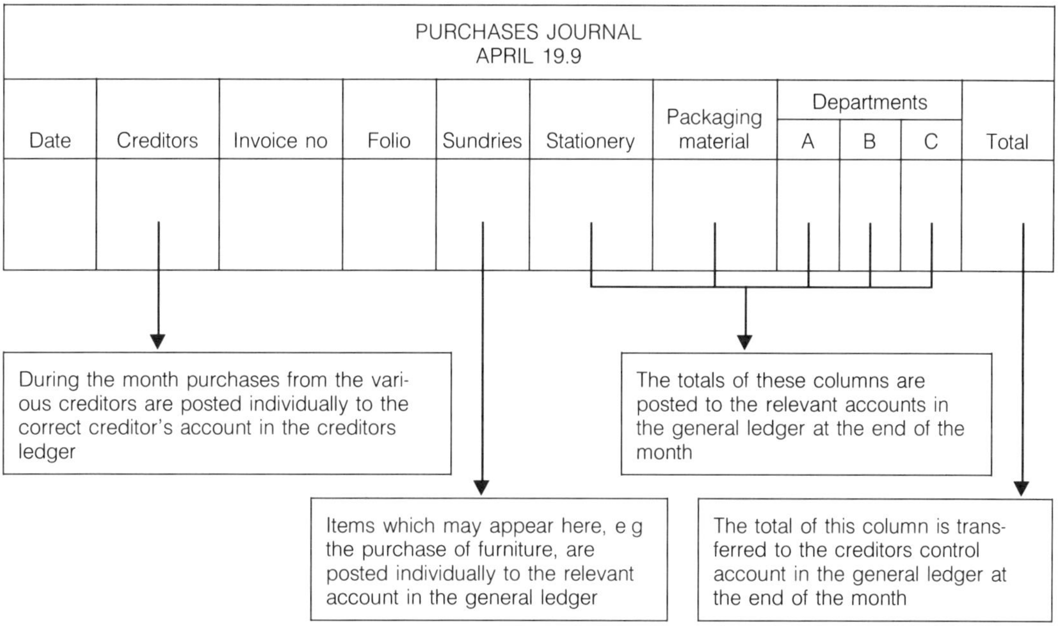

Providing additional columns in the purchases and sales journals for the purchase and sale of non-trade items eliminates the necessity of entering each of these transactions separately in the general journal.

In a **computerised system** the input data from the coded source documents is sorted into any desired classification. It is usually possible to process the same data into different classifications. For example the sales statistics can be provided per department, per product or per salesperson, or any combination thereof.

30.2.4 Inter-departmental transfers

In enterprises comprising different departments, goods are often transferred from one department to another. If accurate departmental profit is to be determined, the particulars of such transactions must be recorded correctly. In most enterprises these transfers are recorded at cost, as they are regarded simply as inter-departmental transfers and not sales. Transfers are usually recorded on inter-departmental transfer invoices or statements which constitute the source documents for the adjustment journal entries. The same applies in computerised systems.

The purchases account of the department transferring the goods is credited and the purchases account of the department receiving the goods is debited.

Example 30.2

During August 19.9, the following inter-departmental transfers took place (at cost) within an enterprise:

		R	Transfer invoice no
August	6 Dept A sends goods to Dept D	40	A10
	10 Dept B sends goods to Dept C	60	B36
	14 Dept B sends goods to Dept D	80	B37
	20 Dept C sends goods to Dept A	20	C13
	25 Dept B sends goods to Dept A	10	C14

The transactions can be recorded as follows on an inter-departmental transfer statement:

INTER-DEPARTMENTAL TRANSFER STATEMENT
AUGUST 19.9

Date	Transfer invoice no	Receiving department				Despatching department			
		A	B	C	D	A	B	C	D
Aug 6	A10				40	40			
10	B36			60			60		
14	B37				80		80		
20	C13	20						20	
25	C14	10					10		
		R30	—	R60	R120	R40	R150	R20	—

A comprehensive journal entry for the above statement would be as follows:

19.9			
Aug 31	Dr Cr		
	Purchases: Dept D (120 – 0)	120	
	Purchases: Dept C (60 – 20)	40	
	Purchases: Dept A (30 – 40)		10
	Purchases: Dept B (0 – 150)		150
	Recording of inter-departmental transfers for August at cost price		

30.2.5 Allocating departmental expenditure: Net profit approach

In order to determine the net profit of each department, the expenses must be allocated to each department. The expenses relating to each department can be divided into:

- ☐ direct departmental expenses
- ☐ indirect departmental expenses.

Direct departmental expenses are expenses relating to a specific department and which can be allocated to the relevant department without being apportioned arbitrarily, for example the salary of a saleslady working in a specific department.

Indirect departmental expenses are general expenses which relate to numerous departments and therefore must be apportioned to each department on an equitable basis, for example rent paid for the building as a whole.

The **basis of allocation** will depend on the **nature** of the expense and/or the activity to which is relates. Whatever the means of allocating expenditure, the columns necessary for each department must be provided in the subsidiary books.

A distinction is generally made between **fixed costs (expenses)** and **variable costs (expenses)**.

☐ Fixed costs

Fixed costs remain constant per period, irrespective of the volume of activity during that period. Fixed costs generally represent the cost of the capacity available to an enterprise for production or other activities, irrespective of whether the capacity is utilised. A good example is the rental of shop premises, which constitutes a capacity cost in the form of trading space. Rental remains constant from one month to the next, regardless of the monthly turnover. Therefore, before fixed costs can be allocated to the relevant departments, the nature of the capacity giving rise to those costs must be determined. Second, it must be determined how that capacity should be divided among the different departments, for example the surface area occupied by each department could be used as a basis.

☐ Variable costs

These costs vary directly or indirectly with the volume of related activities. For example, raw material or power consumption in a factory will increase with increased production, and *vice versa*.

The following methods are generally used to allocate common expenditure and costs to departments:

☐ Allocation of expenditure according to turnover: Certain expenses, such as sales commission and freight, vary directly in proportion to turnover and thus can be allocated according to departmental turnover.

☐ Allocation according to floor space utilised: Expenses which relate to the floor space utilised by a department, such as rental or cleaning services, can be allocated on this basis.

☐ Allocation according to average value of inventory on hand in each department: Expenses which are directly related to the value of inventory on hand, such as insurance thereon, can be allocated on this basis. The calculation is similar to the previous two calculations.

☐ Allocation according to an estimated percentage or ratio: This method of allocation, although somewhat unsatisfactory, is often used for allocating fixed sales, delivery or administrative expenses. The percentage (or ratio) allocated to each department is predetermined by management.

☐ **Allocation of expenses according to the number of units produced or sold:** This basis is used if the number of units produced or sold can be determined from the records of the enterprise, and can be applied to both fixed and variable costs.

☐ **Allocation according to time:** This basis is used *inter alia* where an employee is employed in more than one department. Allocation per department can be in terms of actual hours recorded or according to estimated hours.

☐ **Allocation of expenses according to the purchases in each department:** Certain expenses which are directly related to purchases, such as freight in, can be allocated in the same way as departmental turnover – according to the purchases of the relevant department.

Example 30.3

Excelsior Traders is a retail organisation which is divided into two departments namely Hardware (20 000 m^2) and Haberdashery (30 000 m^2). Using the following particulars, compile the operating accounts of the enterprise:

	Hardware	Haberdashery
	R	R
Sales	60 000	40 000
Salaries of sales staff	8 000	6 000
Purchases	30 000	20 000
Inventory 1/7/19.3	10 000	8 000
Depreciation	1 000	800
Inventory 30/6/19.4	15 000	12 000
Expenses to be allocated:		
In relation to turnover		
Bad debts		800
Printing and stationery		600
Delivery expenses		2 000
General expenses		400
Travellers' expenses and commission		3 000
In relation to purchases		
Freight in		1 000
In relation to average inventory		
Insurance		225
In relation to floor space		
Assessment rates		1 200
Expenses not allocated		
Interest received on investments		700
Accounting fees		1 200

The departmental trading and income account is prepared before the combined general income account for the two departments is prepared.

EXCELSIOR TRADERS
DEPARTMENTAL TRADING AND INCOME ACCOUNT
FOR THE YEAR ENDED 30 JUNE 19.4

	Hardware	Haberdashery	Total	Basis of allocation
Sales	60 000	40 000	100 000	Actual
Less: Cost of sales	25 600	16 400	42 000	
Inventory 1/7/19.3	10 000	8 000	18 000	Actual
Purchases	30 000	20 000	50 000	Actual
Freight in	600	400	1 000	Purchases
	40 600	28 400	69 000	
Less: Inventory 30/6/19.4	15 000	12 000	27 000	Actual
Gross profit	34 400	23 600	58 000	
Gross profit % to turnover	(57,3%)	(59%)		
Less: Expenses				
Bad debts	480	320	800	Sales
Printing and stationery	360	240	600	Sales
Delivery expenses	1 200	800	2 000	Sales
General expenses	240	160	400	Sales
Salaries	8 000	6 000	14 000	
Depreciation	1 000	800	1 800	
Travellers' expenses and commission	1 800	1 200	3 000	Sales
Insurance*	125	100	225	Average inventory
Assessment rates	480	720	1 200	Floor space
	13 685	10 340	24 025	
Net profit	R20 715	R13 260	R33 975	
Net profit % to turnover	(34,53%)	(33,15%)		

GENERAL INCOME ACCOUNT

Net departmental profit	33 975
Add: Interest received on investments	700
	34 675
Less: Accounting fees	1 200
Net profit	R33 475

*Insurance is allocated as follows:

	Hardware	Haberdashery
Opening inventory	10 000	8 000
Closing inventory	15 000	12 000
	R25 000	R20 000
∴ Average inventory	R12 500	R10 000

Insurance is apportioned:

Hardware $\frac{125}{225} \times 225 = R125$

Haberdashery $\frac{100}{225} \times 225 = R100$

30.2.6 Eliminating less profitable departments

Statements like those in the previous example compiled on a departmental basis may indicate that certain departments are not as profitable as expected, or even operate at a loss. Management may consider closing unprofitable departments with the purpose of maximising profits by keeping expenses to the minimum. However, the decision to close a department is a complex one. Although closure of the department will decrease certain costs, it will not eliminate all costs allocated to that department. Management must take both **avoidable** and **unavoidable costs** into consideration. Avoidable costs are those which will be eliminated by closing the department, while unavoidable costs are those which cannot be eliminated, even if the department is closed.

Example 30.4

XY TRADERS
INCOME STATEMENT FOR THE YEAR ENDED 31 DECEMBER 19.6

	Department A		Department B		Total	
Sales		84 200		189 300		273 500
Cost of sales		62 800		100 130		162 930
Gross profit on sales		21 400		89 170		110 570
Less: Operating expenses		23 040		38 470		61 510
Sales expenses		17 180		29 580		46 760
Salaries of sales staff	12 000		20 000		32 000	
Advertising	1 200		1 800		3 000	
Depreciation	780		1 380		2 160	
Rental	3 200		6 400		9 600	
General and administrative expenses		5 860		8 890		14 750
Insurance on inventory	400		700		1 100	
Bad debts	300		450		750	
Share of office expenses	5 160		7 740		12 900	
Net profit (or loss)		R(1 640)		R50 700		R49 060

The management of XY Traders is considering closing Department A. An analysis of the department's expenses reveals the following:

	Avoidable costs	Unavoidable costs
Salaries of sales staff	12 000	
Advertising	1 200	
Depreciation		780*
Rental		3 200
Insurance	400	
Bad debts	300	
Share of office expenses		5 160*
	R13 900	R9 140

*It is assumed, for the purpose of this example, that these two items will not decrease on closure of Department A.

If Department A is closed, R9 140 of its costs (unavoidable) will have to be borne by Department B. In other words, despite the closure of Department A there will be a continuing cost of R9 140 which will decrease the profits of Department B.

Certain less profitable departments are often retained simply because they cater for the needs of established clients who also patronise the more profitable departments.

30.2.7 Departmental contributions approach

Evaluation of a department's performance according to its net income can be criticised, criticism being directed principally at the assumptions made in allocating costs to the various departments. Critics of the departmental net income approach advocate that the method should be replaced by a **departmental contribution to overheads approach** as a means of evaluating a department's performance.

A department's contribution to overheads is that amount by which its income exceeds its **direct costs**, in other words a department's contribution to overheads is the amount of its income remaining after all direct items have been debited, but before indirect and service costs have been allocated thereto.

This approach is illustrated in the departmental income statement in example 30.5.

Example 30.5

EXCELSIOR CLOTHING STORE
DEPARTMENTAL INCOME STATEMENT FOR THE YEAR ENDED 31 MARCH 19.4

	Men's department	Ladies' department	Children's department		Total
Sales	50 000	20 000	10 000		80 000
Less: Cost of sales	32 500	12 000	6 000		50 500
Gross profit	17 500	8 000	4 000		29 500
Less: Direct expenses	10 000	4 800	2 100		16 900
Salaries of sales staff	9 000	4 250	1 750		15 000
Advertising	500	250	150		900
Depreciation	500	300	200		1 000
	R7 500	R3 200	R1 900		12 600
Less: Indirect expenses					
Rental				3 000	
Power consumption				400	
Assessment rates and insurance				600	4 000
Net profit					R8 600

30.2.8 Controllable costs approach

The viewpoint of a third approach to evaluating departmental performance is that, because many of the costs taken into account in the previous two approaches are beyond the control of the departmental management, they should not be taken into account in evaluating a department's performance.

According to this approach, only **controllable costs** should be taken into account in the evaluation of a department's performance.

Controllable costs are those costs over which the departmental manager can exercise some control. Controllable costs must not be confused with direct costs. Certain direct costs cannot be controlled by the departmental manager. He has, for instance, little or no control over the equipment (and corresponding depreciation thereof) in his department. However, he does have a reasonable degree of control over the employees in his department and the extent of their duties.

31

BRANCHES

The **AIM** of this chapter is to explain certain aspects of the accounting responsibility of enterprises which have branches.

31.1 INTRODUCTION

An entrepreneur may expand and diversify his business by opening **branches** which are geographically separated from the central enterprise. Branches function independently, but remain part of the central organisation. The concept **branch** implies that there is a central organisation with a **head office**.

The central organisation provides the capital to establish the branch, determines policy and generally supplies all the merchandise and also certain services to the branch. The branch, in turn, is accountable to the head office. The assets of the branch belong to the head office, which is entitled to all profits generated by the branch's trading activities. The head office, in turn, is responsible for all liabilities and obligations of the branch. The branch usually submits periodic reports of its financial and other activities to the head office.

As a company grows and expands into new markets, it may be necessary to establish branches with some degree of autonomy in order to provide a better service to clients. The degree of autonomy granted to the managers of such branches by the head office, and the accounting records maintained by these branches, differ considerably from one enterprise to the next.

This chapter deals with the problems encountered in branch accounting. It is impossible to cover all possibilities, so a general system is discussed and illustrated in sufficient detail for the basic procedures to be understood and applied to most of the systems which are found in practice.

31.2 INTERNAL CONTROL

Internal control procedures at a branch depend on various factors such as the relative size of the branch and the ease in communicating with the head office. In the case of smaller branches there may not be sufficient personnel to implement the division of duties necessary for good internal control. Therefore the head office will be obliged to exercise maximum control over the branch.

There are various control procedures, some aspects of which are discussed below:

☐ Sales

Although invoices are generally issued by the branch, they can be made out in the name of either the head office or the branch. In computerised systems the invoices are usually despatched by the head office as a follow-up to delivery notes sent by the branch to the head office.

Maintenance of debtors records and responsibility for collections is usually undertaken by the head office. In such cases cash sales as well as payments by debtors are not deposited in the branch bank account, but directly into the head office account.

☐ Purchases

Purchases for both the head office and the branches are usually centralised, the advantages being that over-investment in inventory can be avoided and bulk discounts can be obtained. Goods are invoiced from the head office to the branches. Obviously the head office will keep detailed inventory records. The branches, on the other hand, maintain records of quantities only and not of prices.

This applies particularly where goods are invoiced by the head office to the branch at a percentage mark-up.

Branches may have limited direct purchases, especially in the case of urgent orders. For accounting purposes such purchases must be distinguished from the goods received from head office.

☐ Cash and bank

A minimal bank balance is generally sufficient unless the branch buys and sells independently of the head office. Such an account could function on the imprest system: a balance of, say, R1 000 could be restored periodically by the head office when the branch presents the necessary supporting documents for expenses incurred. The branch could use the imprest account to pay wages, make small purchases and pay for repairs, maintenance, motor and other expenses. The only receipts that should be recorded in this account are cheques received from head office, since cash sales and payments by debtors are deposited directly into the head office account. The branch usually also maintains a petty cash account on the imprest system in order to pay for smaller items such as refreshments.

31.3 ACCOUNTING RESPONSIBILITY FOR BRANCHES

The accounting system used to record branch transactions can vary from a completely **centralised system**, where processing is done entirely by head office, to a basically **decentralised system**, where most of the processing of the branch transactions is done by the branch itself. In other cases the accounting function can be shared, some of the data being collected and processed by the branch while other information is maintained by the head office. Whichever system is chosen, it must be designed to satisfy management's information needs.

If the branch is big enough it may have a complete accounting system independent of that of the head office. These two extremes are referred to as situations where (i) **branch accounts are kept by head office** and (ii) **the branch keeps its own books**. In practice, accounting for branches usually falls somewhere between these extremes. However, both cases will be described for illustrative purposes.

The decision as to whether a branch should do its own bookkeeping is based on the extent of its transactions, its distance from head office, the degree of control which can or must be exercised, the ability and independence of branch personnel and security considerations. The chief criterion, however, is always efficiency.

Where an organisation has branches, two types of entity can be distinguished. First, the undertaking can be considered as a separate entity. The financial result and position of the undertaking as a whole is the combined result and position of the head office and its branches.

It is important to distinguish between **internal transactions**, that is transactions between branches and between branches and the head office, and **external transactions**, that is transactions with **third parties**. Internal transactions are eliminated in the combined financial statements of the enterprise as a whole, that is the head office and its branches. If this is not done there will be a duplication of the results of these transactions. Recording the internal transactions between branches and between each branch and head office is, however, essential for obtaining a complete picture of the operating result of each branch. Therefore mutual or internal purchases and inter-branch sales are recorded separately from external transactions.

31.3.1 Books kept by head office (centralised system)

In a centralised system the accounting records are maintained completely by head office. Supporting documentation is sent to head office by the branches and serves as a basis for recording transactions.

Inventory purchased by head office and sent to branches for them to sell can be invoiced to the branch:

- ☐ at cost price
  or
- ☐ at an amount above cost (usually a fixed retail selling price).

Invoicing the goods sent by head office to the branches at cost **reduces head office inventory** by the same amount as that at which the inventory was originally recorded in its books. The transfer is **not considered to constitute sales** and therefore does not result in gross profit for the head office. Branches receive the goods at cost price and earn gross profit when the goods are sold.

☐ Branches invoiced at cost

Where branch records are kept by head office the information from head office's own documentation is supplemented by the information obtained from branch returns. In practice the **branch returns** will be summarised monthly and recorded in the relevant branch account in head office's books.

Where various branches exist, a separate account should be kept for each, although in a manual system this can be done in columnar form for the sake of simplicity. In head office's books, the sales and various other accounts will be distinguished by the name of the branch.

The following are typical accounts provided for in the books of head office:

- ☐ Branch inventory account. Despite the name of this account, it will be seen in the examples below that it is actually a branch trading account.
- ☐ Branch debtors account (if the branch sells goods on credit).
- ☐ Branch bank and petty cash or cash accounts.
- ☐ Branch profit and loss account.

When the head office trading account is prepared the cost of goods sent to the branch is deducted from head office purchases. If this is not done, head office purchases will comprise head office and branch purchases. This overstatement of purchases will result in an overstatement of head oiffice's cost of sales, and consequently an understatement of the head office's gross profit percentage.

Since inventory is usually valued at cost in the financial statements of an enterprise, the method of invoicing goods to the branches at cost is the easiest to apply, as both head office and branch inventory are shown at cost. Therefore no further adjustments are required.

Example 31.1

The following information is taken from the books of Zazep Traders:

☐ **Balances**	1 May 19.5	31 May 19.5
	R	R
(1) Branch inventory (at head office cost price)	12 600	(17) 9 600
(2) Branch debtors	5 420	to be determined
(3) Branch bank account (favourable)	3 640	to be determined
☐ **Mutual transactions between head office and branch during May 19.3**		R
(4) Goods sent to branch (at head office cost price)		25 800
(5) Goods returned to head office		480
(6) Cash transferred from branch to head office		34 780
☐ **Transactions by head office on behalf of branch**		
(7) Salaries paid to branch personnel		1 500
☐ **Branch transactions**		
(8) Cash sales deposited		5 040
(9) Credit sales		32 480
(10) Goods returned by branch debtors (at selling price)		120
(11) Payments by debtors, deposited in branch bank account		34 020
(12) Discount allowed to debtors		300
(13) Bad debts written off		60
(14) Rental paid per cheque		440
(15) Wages paid per cheque		160
(16) General expenses paid per cheque		140

Required:

Record the above transactions in the head office general ledger.

Solution

Remarks

1 In recording the transactions, head office will follow the usual dual entry procedures. The return received from the branch at the end of the month will serve as the source document for recording the branch transactions in the books of head office.

2 In practice, a separate branch expenses account can be opened for each type of expense. For the sake of simplicity, a single branch profit and loss account is used in all the examples.

3 The head office bank account is not reflected in the solution.

BRANCH INVENTORY ACCOUNT

(1) Opening balance	12 600		(5) Branch goods: Returns	480
(4) Branch goods	25 800		(8) Branch bank: Cash sales	5 040
(10) Branch debtors: Returns	120		(9) Branch debtors: Credit sales	32 480
			(17) Closing balance (given)	9 600
	38 520			
(18) Branch profit and loss: Gross profit (note 1)	9 080			
	R47 600			R47 600
Balance	b/d	9 600		

BRANCH GOODS ACCOUNT

(5) Branch inventory: Returns	480	(4) Branch inventory	25 800
(19) Head office trading (note 2)	25 320		
	R25 800		R25 800

BRANCH DEBTORS ACCOUNT

(2) Opening balance	5 420		(10) Branch inventory: Returns	120
(9) Branch inventory: Sales	32 480		(11) Branch bank: Payments	34 020
			(12) Branch profit and loss: Discount	300
			(13) Branch profit and loss: Bad debts	60
				34 500
			(20) Balance	3 400
	R37 900			R37 900
Balance	b/d	3 400		

BRANCH BANK ACCOUNT

(3) Opening balance	3 640		(6) Head office bank	34 780
(5) Branch inventory: Cash sales	5 040		(14) Branch profit and loss: Rental	440
(11) Branch debtors	34 020		(15) Branch profit and loss: Wages	160
			(16) Branch profit and loss: General expenses	140
				35 520
			Balance	7 180
	R42 700			R42 700
Balance	b/d	7 180		

BRANCH PROFIT AND LOSS ACCOUNT

(7) Head office bank: Salaries	1 500	(18) Branch inventory: Gross profit	9 080
(12) Branch debtors: Discount	300		
(13) Branch debtors: Bad debts	60		
(14) Branch bank: Rental	440		
(15) Branch bank: Wages	160		
(16) Branch bank: General expenses	140		
	2 600		
(21) Head office profit and loss (note 3)	6 480		
	R9 080		R9 080

Notes

1 The branch's gross profit percentage is determined by balancing the account after closing inventory is posted to the branch inventory account:

Credit total	47 600
Debit total	38 520
∴ Gross profit	R9 080

2 The amount of R25 320 balances the branch goods account and is credited to the head office trading account or purchases account.

3 In the above example the branch gross and net profit (which is eventually reflected in head office profit and loss account (21)) is determined separately in order to illustrate the nature of branch bookkeeping. In practice the individual amounts of sales and expenses will be incorporated with the corresponding head office figures.

□ Branches invoiced at selling price

Head office can exercise stricter control over branch inventory if it is invoiced to the branch at selling price. Head office keeps a record of goods invoiced at selling price and the monetary value should correspond with the monetary value recorded in the branch's inventory records. Therefore control is exercised via monetary values. The branch usually sells the goods at the price at which they are received from head office.

Consequently, the value of the branch's inventory on hand at any time should correspond with the monetary value of the inventory received from head office, less any sales.

However, the branch inventory must be included at **cost price** (**to head office**) when head office prepares the financial statements. Branch inventory on hand at the end of the accounting period obviously represents the value at selling price where the goods-to-branch-at-selling-price system is in use. The profit factor included in this amount is **unrealised profit** as far as head office is concerned and must be eliminated from the financial statements. This profit made by head office is only of an internal nature. The profit is realised only when the branch inventory is sold to third parties.

There are two alternative methods of recording transactions in head office's books if goods are invoiced to branches at selling price, namely:

- □ the **branch gross profit method** (also known as the branch trading account or branch adjustment account method)
- □ the **memorandum column method**.

In the first method the despatch of goods to or the return of goods from the branch is recorded at selling price. To complete the double entry:

- □ the cost price of goods is recorded in the branch goods account, and
- □ the profit portion of each transaction is recorded in the branch gross profit account.

The **branch inventory account** should always have a **debit balance**, which represents the branch's inventory on hand at selling price. The **branch gross profit account** should always have a **credit balance**, being the profit element included in the inventory on hand. This credit balance must be deducted from the balance on the branch inventory account at the end of the accounting period in order to reduce branch inventory on hand to its cost price. The branch goods account will always have a credit balance, which represents the cost price of the goods in the hands of the branch. This amount must be deducted from head office purchases when the head office trading account is prepared.

Example 31.2 Illustration of goods invoiced at selling price (gross profit method)

If the records are kept by head office the following typical transactions will be recorded (narrations are omitted):

(1) Goods which cost R9 000 are invoiced to the branch at R12 000

Branch inventory	12 000	
Branch goods account		9 000
Branch adjustments account		3 000

(2) R2 500 of the goods in (1) are sold on credit at the price at which they were invoiced by head office

Branch debtors	2 500	
Branch inventory		2 500

(3) Goods to the value of R1 000 are returned to head office for credit

Branch goods account	750	
Branch adjustments account	250	
Branch inventory		1 000

(4) The price of goods with a selling price of R1 600 is reduced by 10%; half are sold for cash

Branch adjustments	160	
Branch inventory		160
Cash	720	
Branch inventory		720
½ (R1 600 – 10%)		

(5) Goods with a selling price of R400 are returned by a customer

Branch inventory	400	
Branch debtors		400

Note that all profits and losses are recorded in the branch gross profit account, which serves as the branch trading account. The estimated gross profit from the sale of goods despatched to the branch is credited to the branch gross profit account at the time the goods are despatched, in other words, before any sales have taken place. This profit is realised only when the branch sells the goods. In the example above the R3 000 will be earned only after all the inventory is sold. In the interim, price reductions can reduce the profit (see entry 4). At any time the inventory should be reflected in the branch inventory account at selling price. At the end of the accounting period the closing inventory must be reduced to cost price by deducting the relevant mark-up. This mark-up is incorporated in the branch gross profit account. A physical stock-take should be done in order to identify shortages timeously.

Example 31.3

This example illustrates (a) the gross profit account and (b) the memorandum column methods, whereby goods are despatched to the branch at selling price.

Refer to example 31.1 and assume that the same information is applicable, except that the goods are sent to the branch at selling price, which is cost price plus $33^1/_3\%$.

Before the solution(s) is shown, it is important that the concept percentage mark-up is understood.

If goods are invoiced to the branch at cost price plus $33^1/_3\%$, this means that goods which cost R100 are invoiced to the branch at R$133^1/_3$. To convert the latter figure back to cost price if only the selling price (R$133^1/_3$) is known, the **percentage mark-up on selling price** must be calculated, viz:

$$\frac{\text{\% mark-up on cost}}{\text{Selling price}} = \text{\% mark-up on selling price}$$

$$= \frac{33^1/_3}{133^1/_3}$$

$$= 25\%$$

If 25% is deducted from R$133^1/_3$ (i e $33^1/_3\%$) then the original cost price (R100) is arrived at.

This type of calculation is encountered frequently and therefore must be understood thoroughly.

The ratio between the percentage mark-up on cost and selling price is easy to understand if it is expressed as a fraction:

Mark-up on cost = $33^1/_3\%$ or $^1/_3$ on cost price is equivalent to 25% or $^1/_4$ on selling price (refer to calculation above)

Similarly:
If the percentage mark-up on cost is 50% (or $^1/_2$), it is $\frac{50}{150} = 33^1/_3\%$ (or $^1/_3$) on selling price.

Therefore there is a fixed ratio between the two percentages.

☐ Gross profit account method

BRANCH INVENTORY (at cost price)

(1) Opening balance (12 600 + 33⅓)	16 800	(5) Branch goods: Returns (480 + 33⅓)	640
(4) Branch goods (25 800 + 33⅓)	34 400	(8) Branch bank: Cash sales	5 040
(6) Branch debtors: Returns	120	(9) Branch debtors: Credit sales	32 480
		(17) Closing balance (9 600 + 33⅓)	12 800
			50 960
		(x) Branch gross profit: Inventory difference	360*
	R51 320		R51 320

*The purpose of invoicing inventory to branches at selling price is illustrated by determining an 'unexplained' inventory loss of R360 which must be brought into consideration in the branch inventory account in order to balance the account. Inventory differences and adjustments will be discussed in greater detail later on.

BRANCH GOODS (at cost price)

(5) Branch inventory: Returns	480	(4) Branch inventory	25 800
(19) HO purchases	25 320		
	R25 800		R25 800

BRANCH GROSS PROFIT

(5) Branch inventory: Returns (33⅓% × 480 or 25% × 650)	160	(1) Opening balance (33⅓% × 12 600)	4 200
(x) Branch inventory: Inventory difference	360	(4) Branch goods (33⅓% × 25 800)	8 600
(7) Closing balance (25% × 12 800)	3 200		
	3 720		
Branch profit and loss	9 080		
	R12 800		R12 800

The other accounts – branch debtors, branch bank and branch profit and loss – will appear exactly as in the example. Note that the gross profit in both the cost price and the selling price methods is exactly the same (R9 080), but that the latter method identifies a 'loss' of R360.

This loss should also be revealed by means of a physical stock take, irrespective of the method applied.

☐ Memorandum column method

In this method the branch gross profit account is eliminated by adding an extra (cost price) column to the branch inventory account. Using the same information as before:

BRANCH INVENTORY

	Memorandum selling price	Dr		Memorandum selling price	Cr
(1) Opening balance	16 800	12 600	(5) Branch goods	640	480
(4) Branch goods	34 400	25 800	(8) Branch bank	5 040	5 040
(10) Branch debtors	120	120	(9) Branch debtors	32 480	32 480
(18) Branch profit and loss		9 080	(17) Closing balance	12 800	9 600
			(x) Inventory difference	360	
	R51 320	R47 600		R51 320	R47 600

31.3.2 Books kept by the branch (decentralised system)

In a decentralised system, transactions between head office and the branch are recorded in the books of both. Where the branch keeps its own books, the accounting entries will be similar in many respects to those made by a sole trader. However, the branch capital is provided by head office and is therefore usually recorded by the branch as a credit to the 'head office account', with a corresponding debit in head office's books to 'XX branch account'.

The head office account in the branch's books and the 'branch account' in head office's books are therefore reciprocal accounts, that is equivalent accounts which are maintained in different sets of books and which have identical, but opposite, balances.

After all transactions, adjustments and closing entries have been recorded in both sets of books, the head office account balance in the branch's books should be the same as the branch account in the head office's books (unless any transactions between the head office and the branch have not been recorded in one set of books).

In addition, head office may supply the branch with inventory and also pay various expenses on behalf of the branch. On the other hand, the branch may transmit cash to head office periodically. These transactions must be debited to the branch and credited to head office in the books of head office and the branch respectively. Sometimes separate accounts are used – the 'head office current account' in the branch's books and the 'branch current account' in head office's books. The reason for keeping accounts separate from those in which the initial capital is recorded is that the latter account represents the initial fixed investment, while the 'current account' is used to record the daily transactions. The distinction is not so important, and henceforth the term 'current account' will be used for all transactions between head office and the branch, although, as far as the initial capital is concerned, this is actually an incorrect designation.

Head office can **invoice** goods to the branch at **an amount above cost**, as in the case where the branch records were maintained by head office. The principle of **eliminating unrealised profit** which is included in unsold stock still applies. In practice there are various methods whereby goods sent to a branch can be recorded, and the method used to eliminate the unrealised profit will depend on the entries which have been made in the books of head office and the branch. The methods discussed below, therefore, are not necessarily comprehensive.

Some typical transactions are explained below by means of journal entries.

Example 31.4 Illustration of a decentralised system of branch accounting

(1) A Durban head office opens a branch in Pinetown, deposits R15 000 in its bank account and transfers to it furniture and fittings with a cost price of R4 000, on which R2 200 depreciation has already been written off.

HEAD OFFICE			BRANCH		
Branch current account	16 800		Bank	15 000	
Accumulated depreciation	2 200		Furniture and fittings	4 000	
Bank		15 000	Accumulated depreciation		2 200
Furniture and fittings		4 000	Head office current account		16 800

(2) The Pinetown branch buys a motor vehicle for R4 900 cash

No entry			Motor vehicle	4 900	
			Head office current account		4 900

(3) Head office sends goods with a cost price of R10 000 to the branch and invoices it at R14 000

Branch current account	14 000		Inventory from head office	14 000	
Goods to branch		10 000	Head office current account		14 000
Unrealised profit in stock		4 000			

(4) The branch sells R1 000 goods for cash and R5 800 goods on credit

No entry			Bank	1 000	
			Debtors	5 800	
			Sales		6 800

(5) Head office pays rental of R1 200 for the Pinetown premises

Branch current account	1 200		Rental	1 200	
Bank		1 200	Head office current account		1 200

(6) The debtor pays his account and takes 2,5% cash discount

No entry			Bank	5 655	
			Discount allowed	145	
			Debtors		5 800

(7) The branch transmits R5 000 to head office

Bank	5 000		Head office current account	5 000	
Branch current account		5 000	Bank		5 000

(8) The branch provides depreciation of R245 on the motor vehicle and R100 on the furniture, and pays salaries of R600, wages of R200 and general expenses of R120

No entry			Depreciation	345	
			Provision for depreciation		
			Furniture		100
			Motor vehicle		245
No entry			Salaries	600	
			Wages	200	
			General expenses	120	
			Bank		920

Note that head office records only transactions between itself and the branch; other transactions are recorded only in the branch's books. When required the branch will close its books, determine its profit or loss, and credit or debit it to head office. Based on (1) to (8) above, and assuming that inventory on hand amounts to R9 100 at selling price, the branch trial balance will appear as follows:

PINETOWN BRANCH
TRIAL BALANCE

Head office current account		27 000
Motor vehicle	4 900	
Furniture and fittings	4 000	
Accumulated depreciation		
Furniture and fittings		2 300
Motor vehicle		245
Sales		6 800
Inventory from HO	14 000	
Salaries	600	
Rental	1 200	
Wages	200	
General expenses	120	
Depreciation	345	
Discount allowed	145	
Bank	10 835	
	R36 345	R36 345

In order to close off the branch's books the following entries will have to be made (narrations have been omitted):

ix	Trading account Inventory from head office	14 000	 14 000
x	Sales Inventory on hand Trading account	6 800 9 100	 15 900
xi	Trading account Income account	1 900	 1 900
xii	Income account Salaries Rental Wages Depreciation Discount allowed General expenses	2 610	 600 1 200 200 345 145 120
xiii	Head office current account Income account *Loss debited to head office account*	710	 710

Head office will incorporate the branch results into its books by means of a journal entry as follows:

xiv	Unrealised profit in inventory Branch income account *$^{40}/_{140}$ × (14 000 – 9 100) being that portion of the price mark-up realised by means of branch sales*	1 400	 1 400
xv	Branch income account Branch current account *Recording branch loss*	710	 710

A profit of R690 (1 400 – 710) will be reflected in head office's books in respect of the branch's activities. The branch, however, will reflect a loss of R710, since it did not record the entry in respect of the mark-up on goods received from head office.

The financial statements of the branch will appear as follows:

PINETOWN BRANCH TRADING ACCOUNT AND INCOME STATEMENT FOR THE PERIOD . . .		
Sales		6 800
Cost of sales: Inventory from head office	14 000	
Less: Closing inventory	9 100	4 900
Gross profit		1 900
Salaries	600	
Rental	1 200	
Wages	200	
Depreciation	345	
Discount allowed	145	
General expenses	120	2 610
Loss for the period		R710

BALANCE SHEET AT . . .			
CAPITAL EMPLOYED			
Head office current account			
Amount advanced			27 000
Loss for the period			710
			R26 290
EMPLOYMENT OF CAPITAL	Cost price	Accumulated depreciation	
Fixed assets			
Motor vehicle	4 900	245	4 655
Furniture and fittings	4 000	2 300	1 700
	R8 900	R2 545	6 355
Current assets			
Inventory		9 100	
Bank		10 835	19 935
			R26 290

This information is obtained from the branch trial balance. Head office will also combine the branch result with the result of its own activities. This can be done by means of a worksheet. The purpose of combining the results is to reflect the total result of the entity's transactions with third parties. Consequently, accounts containing transactions between head office and the branch will be eliminated. These accounts will usually reflect equal but opposite balances and are simply contra'd against each other by means of a worksheet adjustment. The most important accounts are the following:

- ☐ The branch current account (debit balance in head office's books) and the head office current account (credit balance in the branch's books).
- ☐ The goods to branch account (credit balance in head office's books) and the inventory from head office account (debit balance in the branch's books).

A rearrangement of the branch trial balance and the incorporation of the head office trial balance will be done as follows on a worksheet:

	Balances		Adjustments		Income statement		Balance sheet	
	HO	Branch	Dr	Cr	Dr	Cr	Dr	Cr
DEBITS								
Land and buildings	20 000						20 000	
Motor vehicle	7 000	4 900					11 900	
Furniture and fittings	8 000	4 000					12 000	
Opening inventory	5 000				5 000			
Bank	2 000	10 835					12 835	
Branch current account	27 000			27 000(1)				
Purchases	56 000				56 000			
Inventory from head office		14 000		14 000(2)				
Salaries	2 400	600			3 000			
Rental	3 600	1 200			4 800			
Wages	900	200			1 100			
General expenses	480	120			600			
Depreciation	720	345			1 065			
Discount allowed	150	145			295			
	R133 250	R36 345						
CREDITS								
Capital	40 000							40 000
Head office current account		27 000	27 000(1)					
Accumulated depreciation								
Furniture	3 820	2 300						6 120
Motor vehicle	1 900	245						2 145
Trade creditors	7 930							7 930
Sales	63 000	6 800				69 800		
Branch goods	14 000		14 000(2)					
Unrealised profit in inventory	2 600							2 600*
	R133 250	R36 345						
Closing inventory	12 900	9 100				22 000	22 000*	
			R41 000	R41 000	71 860	91 800		
Net income for the year					19 940			19 940
					R91 800	R91 800	R78 735	R78 735

*Net inventory figure in the balance sheet (22 000 – 2 600) = R19 400.

Note that the corresponding accounts between the branch and head office are eliminated. The combined financial statements are prepared from the information in the last four columns.

31.3.3 Mutual transactions between branches and items in transit

Often an enterprise has numerous branches. Usually the branches are supplied with goods by the head office, but branches may also conclude transactions between themselves. For example, a branch which has a temporary shortage of a particular item can obtain the item from the nearest branch if the head office itself it out of stock, or if transport costs can be minimised where the head office is far away. If the head office keeps the books, this will entail merely a transfer from one branch account to another. On the other hand, if the branches keep their own books the entries will be the same as when the head office sends goods to a branch (except that no mark-up will be recorded between the branches). The branches will debit and credit each other respectively, and the balances will be contra'd when the combined accounts are prepared.

☐ Items in transit

Items may be in transit between the branch and head office, or between branches, at the end of the financial period, for example the remittance of money or goods which will not have been received by the other party just before the close of the financial period.

Usually transactions with and between branches will be recorded in the books of each party by means of identical but opposite entries in the current account of the relevant party. Therefore it should be possible merely to contra the current account balances when the combined financial statements are prepared. However, when items are in transit or when a transaction has not yet been recorded by one of the parties, the current accounts will not agree.

The balances on the accounts will have to be reconciled and the adjustment journal entries made.

The account should be reconciled before the branch's books are closed off, since this enables the branch to make the necessary adjustment entries. If the branch's books have already been closed off, head office will have to make the adjustments. This situation is illustrated in example 31.5.

Example 31.5 Reconciliation of branch and head office accounts

Alpha Company has a branch in Athlone. The current accounts of the branch and head office have not been reconciled in the past, and at the end of the 19.9 financial year the acco unts were as follows:

(1) Books of Athlone branch

CURRENT ACCOUNT: HEAD OFFICE					
31/3	Cash remitted	5 000	1/1	Balance	15 000
30/6	Cash remitted	5 000	15/4	Equipment from HO	1 200
30/9	Cash remitted	5 000	30/6	Goods received	3 900
31/12	Cash remitted	5 000	31/8	Goods received	6 000
31/12	Balance	21 490	31/10	Goods received	7 190
			31/12	Profit for the year	8 200
		R41 490			R41 490
			1/1	Balance	21 490

(2) Books of Alpha Company

CURRENT ACCOUNT: BRANCH					
1/1	Balance	19 500	3/1	Cash received	4 500
31/3	Despatch to branch	4 000	3/4	Cash received	5 000
10/4	Equipment to branch	1 200	4/7	Cash received	5 000
28/6	Despatch to branch	3 900	2/10	Cash received	5 000
15/7	Repairs: Branch manager's motor vehicle	240	31/12	Balance	22 440
31/8	Despatch to branch	6 000			
31/10	Despatch to branch	7 200			
		R41 940			R41 940
1/1	Balance	22 440			

First, the opening balances differ by R4 500. However, head office received R4 500 on 3 January 19.9, which means that the balance on the branch current account agrees with the balance on the head office current account at that date. Apparently the cash was in transit at the end of the previous financial year. Since the difference was corrected automatically, it will not influence the reconciliation at the end of the year.

Second, it appears that at the end of the current year cash was again in transit, this time R5 000 remitted by the Athlone branch.

Third, there is a problem with goods sent to the branch. The branch has not recorded the R4 000 goods sent to it on 31 March and the despatch on 31 October is recorded as R7 190, while it has been recorded in the head office books as R7 100. Both these items will have to be investigated to determine the actual position. For example, the goods for R4 000 may have been sent to another branch, whose current account also does not balance with that of head office. Note that the terminology for the accounts is slightly different from that used earlier, but they serve the same purpose. This also happens in practice.

Fourth, it appears that the branch manager's motor vehicle was repaired by head office. The amount has been debited to the branch correctly, but the branch has neglected to make the corresponding entry.

Finally, the branch has already closed off its books and credited the profit of R8 200 to the head office account, but head office has not yet made this entry.

Therefore the reconciliation will be as follows:

Balance on head office current account in Athlone branch's books		21 490
Add: Cash remitted on 31 December and not recorded by head office	5 000	
Goods recorded by head office as despatched to Athlone branch, but not recorded in branch's books	4 000	
Repairs recorded in head office books, but not branch's books	240	9 240
		30 730
Less: Profit credited by branch to head office, but not shown in head office's books	8 200	
Goods reflected by head office as R7 100 on 31 October, but credited by branch as R7 190	90	8 290
Balance on branch current account in books of head office		R22 440

Since the branch has already closed its books, head office must make the entries. It is assumed that head office's books are correct as regards the goods despatched. The following adjustments will have to be made by head office:

i	Athlone branch current account Income: Athlone branch *Branch profit for the year as calculated in note (1)*	4 050	 4 050
ii	Cash in transit Athlone branch current account *Cash remitted by Athlone on 31/12/19.9 not yet received by head office*	5 000	 5 000

Explanatory note:

Branch profit for the year, as calculated	8 200
Less: Unappropriated receipt of goods on 31 March	(4 000)
Repairs on 15 July not recorded by branch	(240)
Add: Goods received 31 October, recorded as R7 190 instead of R7 100	90
	R4 050

The result of these entries is that the current account of the branch is adjusted to a debit balance of R21 490. This is cancelled by the credit balance of R21 490 in the branch's books. In other words, when a branch keeps its own books the profit or loss must be recorded in head office's books, the result must be combined, and the current accounts must be reconciled.

32

CONSIGNMENTS

The **AIM** of this chapter is to explain the accounting procedures applicable to consignments.

32.1 INTRODUCTION

A consignment is made when a principal forwards goods to an agent who will sell them on his behalf.

The dealer does not sell the goods to the agent, nor does the agent buy the goods from the dealer. The agent merely undertakes to sell the goods on behalf of the dealer at the best possible price. For these services he receives compensation in the form of commission on the sales. Until the goods have been sold they remain the property of the dealer and not of the agent. This means that the dealer is entitled to the proceeds from the sale of the goods he despatched, so the agent is obliged to pay the dealer the proceeds after deducting his commission and expenses.

In South Africa consignments occur especially in the marketing of agricultural products. Even where the marketing is controlled by marketing boards, the principle remains the same. Farmers seldom sell directly to the consumer, except in very small quantities. Their products such as wool, sugar-cane, citrus fruit, livestock and crops are usually sold by an agent, market or co-operative on their behalf. Agents are also used where a dealer wants to introduce a new product or to find new markets for his products.

32.2 TERMINOLOGY

The following terminology generally applies to consignment transactions:

- **Despatcher (or consignor):** This is the person who despatches the goods for sale, that is the owner of the goods.
- **Agent (or consignee):** This is the person to whom the goods are sent for sale.
- **Commission:** This is the term used to describe the compensation payable to the agent for his services in selling the goods.
- ***Del credere* commission:** An agent who stands surety for the debts of persons to whom he has sold goods on credit receives **commission over and above his usual compensation** on sales. This compensation is known as *del credere* commission. If, by agreement with the consignor, an agent is entitled to ***del credere* commission**, he (the agent) is personally responsible for any bad debts arising from credit transactions.
- **Pro forma invoice price:** The consignor may be unwilling to reveal the cost price of goods to the consignee. Therefore goods are usually invoiced to the consignee at a price higher than cost. This does not imply that the consignor is charging the agent, nor that the price on the **pro forma invoice** has any bearing on his immediate bookkeeping. The **pro forma** invoice price simply indicates to the consignee **the minimum price for which he may sell the goods**. The pro forma invoice price has no accounting implications and therefore is not journalised. The prices used in the accounting system are the cost price and the selling price.

32.3 ACCOUNTING ENTRIES IN THE BOOKS OF THE CONSIGNOR

Usually each consignment is usually identified separately by the opening of an independent account for it, and the profit (loss) per consignment is determined as soon as the result is known.

Goods sent to a consignee remain the property of the consignor until they are sold, and in the case of a perpetual inventory system the consignment is journalised as follows at cost:

32.3.1 Recording of inventory despatched

Consignment account Inventory *Recording of goods despatched to agent K (details)*	xx	 xx

In the case of a periodic inventory system, the purchases account will be credited.

The consignment account has a twofold purpose: it serves as an **inventory account for goods held by agents** and also as a **consignment income account**.

Consignment goods may be obtained in one of two ways: they may be purchased especially for consignment, or they may be taken from the enterprise's trading inventory.

If goods are purchased especially for consignment, the journal entry is as follows:

Consignment account Cash (supplier) *Goods purchased and sent to agent K (details)*	xx	 xx

32.3.2 Consignment-related expenses

Costs such as rail or sea freight or insurance will be incurred on each consignment. **These additional costs form part of the cost price of the consignment inventory**, and must be debited to the appropriate consignment account.

32.3.3 The account sales

As soon as the consignor receives details from the agent regarding the sale of goods, he (the consignor) is able to determine the profit or loss on the consignment.

The notice or report received from the agent is known as an **account sales** and provides full details about goods received by the agent, goods sold, costs incurred by the agent, a debit for his compensation (commission), and the balance of unsold goods.

When the account sales is received the consignor must journalise the details as follows:

Consignment account (costs incurred plus commission payable) Agent *Costs incurred by agent K as per account sales (details)*	XX	XX
Agent Consignment account *Selling price of goods sold by agent as per account sales (details)*	XX	XX

Thus the consignment account contains all the details concerning the consignment transactions. Therefore a profit (loss) can be determined and transferred to the general income account. The balance on the account represents the **cost price of the unsold inventory** and is shown, together with other inventories, in the financial statements.

The balance on the agent's account represents the amount he owes, in other words the sales, less his expenses and commission.

32.3.4 Cost price of unsold consignment inventory

The cost price of unsold inventory consists of the initial purchase price plus the proportional portion of all costs related to the consignment, but excluding commission. Commission is a function of sales and is therefore a selling expense which must be written off against the profit (loss) arising from the particular sales transaction.

Example 32.1

On 2 January 19.1 AB company despatched 150 tons of iron ore to CD Agents Limited at a pro forma price of R8 per ton. The cost price of the iron ore was R2,90 per ton and railage amounted to R104.

On 1 April, CD Agents Limited forwarded a cheque and the relevant account sales to AB company, showing that the ore was sold at R9 per ton, that shipping charges were R2 per ton and harbour dues amounted to R160, and that insurance amounted to R120.

Sales commission is calculated at 6% and *del credere* commission at 2%.

The journal entries will be as follows:

19.1 Jan 2	Consignment account Inventory *Despatch of 150 tons of ore, cost price R2,90 per ton, to CD Agents Limited*	435	 435
	Consignment account Cash *Railage freight on consignment to CD Agents Limited*	104	 104

Apr 1	Consignment account
	  Shipping freight
	  Harbour dues
	  Insurance
	  Commission (6%)
	  Commission (2%)
	    CD Agents Limited
	Costs incurred by CD Agents Limited, per account sales no . . .
		
		300
		160
		120
		81
		27
			
			688

	CD Agents Limited Consignment account *Proceeds from sale of 150 tons of ore at R9 per ton*	1 350	 1 350
	Cash CD Agents Limited *Cheque received from CD Agents Limited (1 350 – 688)*	662	 662
	Consignment account Income *Profit on consignment to CD Agents Limited (1 350 – 435 – 104 – 688)*	123	 123

The consignment account in the ledger will appear as follows:

CONSIGNMENT ACCOUNT: CD AGENTS LIMITED					
19.1 Jan 2 Apr 1	 Inventory Railage freight Shipping freight Harbour dues Insurance Commission Commission Profit on consignment (to income account)	 435 104 300 160 120 81 27 123	19.1 Apr 1	 CD Agents Limited	 1 350
		R1 350			R1 350

Example 32.2

Assume that at the end of AB company's financial period only half of the goods have been sold for R675. Therefore the agent has unsold inventory on hand.

The consignment account in the ledger will appear as follows:

CONSIGNMENT ACCOUNT: CD AGENTS LIMITED					
19.1			19.1		
Jan 2	Inventory	435	Apr 1	CD Agents Limited	675
	Railage freight	104	Dec 31	Closing inventory	560
Apr 1	Shipping freight	300			
	Harbour dues	160			
	Insurance	120			
	Cost of goods despatched	1 119			
	Commission 6%	41			
	Commission 2%	13			
	Profit on consignment for the period	62			
		R1 235			R1 235
19.2					
Jan 1	Inventory (balance)	560			

Since half of the consignment has not been sold, the value of the closing inventory is calculated at 50% of the cost of goods despatched, namely 50% × R1 119 = R560.

32.4 ACCOUNTING ENTRIES IN THE BOOKS OF THE AGENT

When the agent receives the goods he does not usually make a formal accounting entry,* since he did not purchase the goods nor do they belong to him. However, he will keep an **inventory record** to record the receipt and sale of the goods.

Expenses incurred by the agent in respect of the consignment will be recorded in his books as follows:

Consignor	xx	
Cash/Creditors		xx
Expenses i r o consignment no . . .		

The journal entry for each sales transaction is as follows:

Cash/Debtors	xx	
Consignor		xx
Sale of consignment goods		

Commission owing is recorded as follows:

Consignor	xx	
Commission received		xx
Commission on consignment goods sold		

*An alternative would be to debit a consignment received account with the invoice price, and to credit the consignor. When the goods are sold the amount will be credited to the consignment received account.

Example 32.3

Using the same data as in example 32.1, the journal entries in the books of CD Agents Limited will be as follows:

AB Company		580	
Cash			580
Shipping freight	300		
Harbour dues	160		
Insurance	120		
Expenses paid on consignment			
Cash		1 350	
AB Company			1 350
Proceeds from sale of 150 tons of iron ore			
AB Company		108	
Commission received (6%)			81
Commission received (2%)			27
Commission on sale of 150 tons of ore			
AB Company		662	
Cash			662
Payment to AB Company for balance owing on consignment			

The account of AB Company will appear as follows in the ledger of CD Agents Limited:

AB COMPANY			
Cash: Expenses	580	Cash: Sales	1 350
Commission	108		
Cash	662		
	R1 350		R1 350

32.5 FINANCING CONSIGNMENTS BY MEANS OF BILLS

Bills are used, especially in transactions with overseas agents, in order to obtain a part of the proceeds in cash as quickly as possible.

The procedure is as follows: On shipment of the goods the consignor draws a bill on the consignee covering a large portion of the cost of the consignment, for example two-thirds thereof. The consignor tenders this bill to a bank for discounting after attaching to it the bill of lading, the insurance policy, the pro forma invoice and all other relevant documents. This bill is known as a **documentary bill**. Since all these documents are endorsed in favour of the bank, it has complete security over the consignment and is able to discount the bill without delay. The consignor therefore obtains the money immediately.

The bank forwards the documentary bill to its branch or correspondent overseas, requesting that the bill be presented to the agent for acceptance. If the agent accepts the bill the bank hands him the relevant documents and he is free to effect the necessary clearances and sell the goods. By the time he has to pay the bill he will already have sold the goods, and should not encounter any problems. If the proceeds from the goods are higher than the amount of the bill, the agent is also obliged to pay the balance to the consignor.

A point to be noted is that if the agent neglects or refuses to accept the bill, he may not take possession of the goods and the bank has the right to sell the goods at the best possible price and use the proceeds to cover the bill, which has already been discounted. If the proceeds exceed the amount of the bill the bank is obliged to pay the balance to the consignor after deducting all expenses. If the proceeds are insufficient to cover the bill, the bank may recover the difference from the consignor.

On acceptance of the bill the following entry is made:

Bills receivable Agent *Acceptance of bill receivable no . . . by agent K (details)*	xx	 xx

On discounting of the bill the transaction is journalised as follows:

Cash Consignment account (discounting costs) Bills receivable *Discounting of bill receivable no . . .*	xx xx	 xx

The remaining balances represent the value of unsold inventory in the consignment account and the value of the bill as a credit on the agent's account.

This credit on the agent's account represents a liability in that the money has already been received although the goods have not yet been sold. The consignor is responsible to the bank for this liability.

If the agent fulfils the agreement by selling the goods, redeeming the bill at the bank and forwarding an account sales to the consignor, the following journal entry will be made:

Consignment account (agent's costs and commission) Agent *Agent K's costs and commission per account sales (details)*	xx	 xx
Agent Consignment account (sales) *Sales by agent according to account sales and cash paid into bank to redeem bill (details)*	xx	 xx

33

JOINT VENTURES

The **AIM** of this chapter is a brief discussion of joint ventures in order to explain certain principles and practices applicable to them. The more advanced aspects of accountability by joint ventures are beyond the limited scope of this book. (In this regard refer to Exposure Draft 71, published in June 1987 by the Accounting Practices Committee.)

33.1 INTRODUCTION

It is obvious from the discussions of the different forms of undertaking that business people often combine their physical, financial and entrepreneurial ability in order to conduct business. In continuing operations this results in the formation of (permanent) partnerships, close corporations and companies.

In contrast they may need to combine their abilities for only a limited period, or only for carrying out a specific project. Because of the relatively short duration of such an association a permanent arrangement such as a partnership would be unsuitable and unnecessary.

In such cases parties often enter into a more informal type of association known as a **joint venture**. A joint venture is an association similar to a partnership, but which is entered into for a limited and specific objective.

In a joint venture, which like a partnership is usually entered into on the basis of a written agreement, each joint venturer will make a specialised contribution. For example, one party to the undertaking may provide the manufacturing facilities, another the technical skill and yet another the financial or marketing expertise. Joint ventures are encountered in all spheres of business. These days they are frequently used in large construction projects.

32.2 ACCOUNTABILITY

As a result of this latter development, large companies have become involved in 'long-term' joint ventures and suitable accountability of their interests in such ventures has become essential. Relevant guidelines and statements have been issued on this topic. In this chapter, however, the discussion is limited to smaller undertakings which enter into short-term joint ventures.

Two possible methods of accounting can be used for such joint ventures:

- ☐ A **separate set of accounting books** is provided, in the same way as for a partnership. In this case no particular accounting problems exist. All transactions are recorded according to the double entry system and an income statement and balance sheet are prepared in the usual manner.
- ☐ A **separate set of books is not provided**. Because of the relatively short duration of many types of joint venture, separate books are often not provided.

In a joint venture each party, by mutual agreement, assumes responsibility for certain specified tasks in order that the objectives of the joint venture may be achieved. For example, one party may purchase certain goods on behalf of the joint venture and send them to another party who is responsible for sales. At specific times (e g when the venture has been concluded or at other specified times) each entrepreneur must provide the other parties with a complete financial report of all his transactions on behalf of the joint venture.

In order to do this, each entrepreneur records the transactions that he concludes on behalf of the joint venture in his own books, in a **special account** in the ledger, 'Joint venture with X'. The report that a joint venturer provides the other joint venturers will be a summary of the transactions recorded in this account. When all the parties have submitted their reports to each other a **joint statement** is prepared from this information to determine the result of the venture. This joint statement is also known as a **memorandum statement** and is prepared separately from the relevant reports. It does **not** form part of the double entry system in any particular set of books.

The **profit or loss** of the venture as determined from the memorandum statement will be **divided** in the statement between the entrepreneurs, according to their mutual agreement.

Each entrepreneur will record his **portion of the profit or loss** from the venture, as determined in the memorandum statement, in the joint venture account in his own books. The debit or credit balance on the account at this stage will represent the amount due by (if a debit balance) or due to (if a credit balance) the other parties in the venture.

Since each entrepreneur records only those transactions that he concluded on behalf of the joint venture and his portion of the profit (loss) in the joint venture account in his books, these accounts in the separate sets of books will have **the same balance but be on opposite sides**. This indicates that one entrepreneur owes the others that amount.

The following table summarises the recording of typical transactions in a joint venture where no separate books are provided for the venture.

	IN THE BOOKS OF A VENTURER	
TRANSACTION	DEBIT	CREDIT
1 Goods bought on behalf of the venture	Joint venture with . . . account	Bank/Creditors
2 Expenses incurred on behalf of the venture	Joint venture with . . . account	Bank/Creditors
3 Cash/Credit sales	Bank/Debtors	Joint venture with . . . account
4 Payment *to* fellow joint venturer	Joint venture with . . . account	Bank
5 Payments received *from* joint venturer	Bank	Joint venture with . . . account
6 Transfer of goods between joint venturers	NO ENTRY	
7 Assets (e g inventory) taken over by joint venturer	Asset account	Joint venture with . . . account
8 Portion of profit of the undertaking as determined in the memorandum statement	Joint venture with . . . account	Profit and loss account

Example 33.1

Tony and Sam enter into a joint venture to repair electronic equipment on 1 January 19.7. Business will be conducted on a cash on delivery basis.

They agree that Tony will obtain the orders for repairs, collect the equipment from customers and deliver it to Sam, who will effect the repairs. Tony will then deliver the equipment to the customers and collect the outstanding amounts.

Each person will charge the expenses incurred in this respect to the venture and the parties will settle any amounts due on a quarterly basis. Profits or losses will be shared between them as follows:

Tony $^{2}/_{5}$
Sam $^{3}/_{5}$

The following transactions were concluded on behalf of the joint venture during the three months ended 31 March 19.7:

1 Tony sent Sam a cheque for R6 000.
2 Sam purchased spares and other materials for R7 000 cash. On 31 March 19.7 items with a cost price of R4 000 were on hand.
3 Tony spent R1 000 on advertising and collected R49 000 from customers.
4 Wages paid to employees:
  Sam R19 500
  Tony R5 500
5 Motor vehicle expenses paid by Tony amounted to R5 000.
6 Sundry expenses paid:
  Tony R2 000
  Sam R2 000

Required:

Prepare the joint venture accounts for the three months ended 31 March 19.7.

Solution

First the joint venture accounts of each party's transactions in his own books are shown:

In Tony's books

JOINT VENTURE WITH SAM					
1 Bank: Cheque to Sam		6 000	3 Bank: Payments by customers		49 000
3 Bank: Advertising		1 000			
4 Bank: Wages		5 500			
5 Bank: Motor vehicle expenses		5 000			
6 Bank: Sundry expenses		2 000			
		19 500			
Balance	c/d	29 500			
		R49 000			R49 000
			Balance	b/d	29 500

In Sam's books

JOINT VENTURE WITH TONY					
2 Bank: Spares and materials		7 000	1 Bank: Cheque from Tony		6 000
4 Bank: Wages		19 500	Inventory of spares on hand	c/d	4 000
6 Bank: Sundry expenses		2 000			
					10 000
			Balance	c/d	18 500
		R28 500			R28 500
Balance	b/d	18 500			
Balance: Inventory	b/d	4 000			

At this stage each party will provide the other with details of transactions recorded in his books. The memorandum statement and the result of the activities of the joint venture will be prepared as follows from the complete information:

TONY AND SAM
MEMORANDUM JOINT VENTURE STATEMENT
FOR THE THREE MONTHS ENDED 31 MARCH 19.7

Income from repairs		R49 000
Expenses:		38 000
Spares purchased: Sam	7 000	
Less: Inventory on hand	4 000	3 000
Advertising: Tony		1 000
Wages: Tony	5 500	
Sam	19 500	25 000
Motor vehicle expenses: Tony		5 000
Sundry expenses: Tony	2 000	
Sam	2 000	4 000
NET INCOME		R11 000
Allocated as follows:		
Tony $^2/_5$	4 400	
Sam $^3/_5$	6 600	R11 000

Thereafter each party will record his portion of the net income in his books by means of a journal entry. For example, in Tony's case:

19.7 Mar 31	Joint venture with Sam Profit and loss *Being $^2/_5$ of net income of joint venture with Sam*	4 400	4 400

After the applicable portions of the net income have been recorded, the relevant accounts for the three months can be closed off and balanced as follows:

In Tony's books

JOINT VENTURE WITH SAM							
19.7				19.7			
Mar 31	Profit and loss		4 400	Mar 31	Balance	b/d	29 500
	Balance	c/d	25 100				
			R29 500				R29 500
				19.7			
				Mar 31	Balance	b/d	25 100

In Sam's books

JOINT VENTURE WITH TONY							
19.7				19.7			
Mar 31	Balance	b/d	18 500	Mar 31	Balance	c/d	25 100
	Balance: Inventory	b/d	4 000		Balance: Inventory	c/d	4 000
	Profit and loss		6 600				
			R29 100				R29 100
19.7							
Mar 31	Balance	b/d	25 100				
	Balance: Inventory	b/d	4 000				

Note that excluding the inventory of the joint venture which is still in Sam's hands, the joint venture accounts in the respective books of the two entrepreneurs have the same balance (R25 100), but on opposite (debit and credit) sides. In other words, on 31 March 19.7 Tony owed Sam R25 100.

33.3 INVENTORY ON HAND

The example above illustrates interim profit determination by a joint venture. This is usually necessary where the financial year of one or two of the entrepreneurs closes before the joint venture has been finalised. The usual principle of matching income and expenditure always applies in an interim closure.

Special attention should be paid to the inventory on hand when interim statements are prepared for a joint venture. The usual inventory valuation principles, viz the lowest of cost or net realisable market value, still apply.

Inventory is recorded according to one of two methods:

- When the inventory (as in the previous example) has been bought and financed by one party exclusively, it will be reflected in his joint venture account only.
- If the inventory has been **financed** by the parties in their **profit sharing ratio**, the total inventory is shown in that ratio in the books of each party.

33.4 TAKING OVER INVENTORY AND OTHER ASSETS

When a member of the joint venture takes over inventory or goods from the undertaking for his own account, it is treated as a 'sale' by the joint venture. Depending on whether he is taking them for his own use or absorbing them into his own inventory, the party taking the goods will record the transaction as follows:

Purchases (or drawings) Joint venture with . . . *Inventory taken over from joint venture*	xx	 xx

The same principle applies where the joint venture has fixed assets (e g equipment) which are taken over by one of the parties, for example when the joint venture is dissolved. Again the entry in the relevant party's books will depend on whether he is taking the equipment for his own use or retaining it as an asset in his business.

Equipment (or drawings) Joint venture with . . . *Asset taken over from joint venture*	xx	 xx

34

NON-PROFIT ORGANISATIONS

The **AIM** of this chapter is to explain certain specific concepts, accounts and financial statements applicable to accounting by non-profit organisations.

34.1 GENERAL

34.1.1 Definition

A non-profit organisation can be **defined** as an economic entity which, without gain, provides a service to the community and has an equity interest that cannot be sold.

The concept 'non-profit' in the definition does not imply that such an organisation cannot budget for, and indeed realise, a net income for any financial year. The nature of this type of enterprise implies that any increase in net assets arising from the activities of the undertaking must be applied to improve the community services rendered by the specific organisation. The increase in the net assets of the entity does not accrue to the persons supporting the organisation (e g the members).

Depending on the type of undertaking, equity is usually furnished by grants from the State or authorities, donations or membership fees. These contributions to equity do not confer the same rights as contributions to the equity of a limited company confer on shareholders.

If the above definition is analysed it can be seen that any organisation which operates solely for the benefit of those persons who contribute to its equity must be excluded from classification as a non-profit organisation, because although these undertakings are not carried on with a view to making a profit, they function primarily for the benefit of the members. Strictly speaking, therefore, private clubs, mutual benefits etc (i e organisations which do not serve the 'general' community) should be excluded from the concept 'non-profit organisations'. In practice, however, they are considered as non-profit organisations.

34.1.2 Organisational and management characteristics

Since there is no individual equity in this type of undertaking, the management of the organisation is usually entrusted either to persons having a particular interest in the type of service provided by the organisation, or to persons appointed by the members. Therefore, these entities are controlled by persons who do not have a recoverable interest in the organisation. They also do not run the risk of personal investment losses in this regard.

Often these organisations are organised on an informal basis and there is not always proper control over management. Therefore it is even more important that the financial statements of such organisations provide useful information to interested parties. These parties (financial supporters, supervisory government institutions, etc) have to use the information contained in the financial statements at least partly to evaluate the activities of the relevant organisation.

34.1.3 Underlying accounting philosophy

Bearing in mind the typical characteristics of a non-profit organisation, the question arises which particular requirements of accounting systems and financial reporting procedures apply to this particular type of organisation.

Financial statements must provide economically interested groups with a comprehensive review of what the particular organisation achieved during a specific period. The accounting records and system developed for an economic entity must be logical and consistent and must be related to the objectives of the entity, as well as the circumstances in which it conducts its activities.

Because of the typical characteristics of non-profit organisations, the primary aim of accounting reporting should be to provide control over sources by means of accounting responsibility. Seeing that the function of stewardship is basic to this type of organisation and because responsibility for profit is not associated with this type of entity, most non-profit associations and organisations use the so-called **funds accounting procedures** for financial reporting.

34.1.4 The concept funds accounting

Funds accounting requires that the sources of finance of an organisation are divided into various funds. A **fund** can be defined as a sum of money or other source which is set aside for specific activities designed to achieve specific objectives and which is regarded as a **separate accounting entity**.

The difference between this definition of a fund and the usual meaning thereof is obvious: the concept fund implies an amount of money from some other source which is intended for a specific purpose. The concept fund in a non-profit organisation embraces the additional principle of a separate accounting entity. Thus the accounting system will provide for a number of self-balancing 'fund units' utilised in accordance with the limitations placed on the use of the funds. The funds procedure is designed to prevent sources intended for a specific use from being applied for any other purpose.

Funds can generally be divided into two categories:

☐ Revenue funds

The primary use of accounting records for this type of fund is to disclose the source of the fund and the manner in which it was applied. These funds are typical of those encountered in non-profit organisations.

☐ Self-sustaining funds

These are fund entities which, once an initial contribution has been made to them, are intended to be self-sufficient. Such funds can be considered as small profit oriented enterprises within the framework of a non-profit organisation.

34.1.5 The accumulated or general fund

In addition to the specific funds (entities) which may exist in a non-profit organisation, it will also have a **general (or accumulated) fund**. This is a fund through which all funds pass in the general course of the activities of the organisation (and therefore excludes special funds).

The accumulated fund is synonymous with shareholders' equity in a company with share capital.

34.1.6 Funds for special projects

If an organisation such as a college, for example, has a special fundraising campaign in order to finance a specific project (e g building a hall), the monies collected for this purpose must be credited to a separate fund and invested separately until such time as the project has been completed.

Income from this investment will also be credited to the specific fund and will be reinvested. Once the desired amount has been collected and applied to the project the asset becomes the property of the college and the project fund is transferred to the accumulated fund (see remark (2) in example 34.3).

34.1.7 Budgetary control

The preceding discussion is a brief explanation of the most important characteristics of generally accepted accounting practice for non-profit organisations. In practice each such organisation will have its own particular objectives and circumstances which may require certain adaptations to its accounting records, systems and financial reporting. Thus the accounting practices of a municipality will differ from those of a hospital, university or church association.

In all these organisations it is vital that control is exercised over funds by means of budgets and by ensuring that the various funds are allotted to the specific purpose for which they were intended. Then actual expenditure may be compared with prior allocations and in this way control over expenditure can be exercised.

The funds accounting concept is always applied in recording gifts and bequests received by non-profit organisations. The beneficiary organisation must adhere to the conditions of a gift or bequest and account for it financially in an appropriate manner.

34.1.8 Examples of the treatment of funds

The following examples illustrate different types of funds and their accounting treatment.

Example 34.1 Income of a fund to be used for a specific purpose

On 31 December 19.0 the Johannesburg College received a bequest of R15 000 from Mr R Cohen on the express condition that the income from the fund be used for study bursaries for students of the college. The fund was invested in a fixed deposit at XY Building Society at 10% p a. Interest is received annually on 31 December. Allocations are also made annually on 31 December. In 19.1 no allocations were made. Any income not used is reinvested in a fixed deposit at the same building society for another year. The following allocations were made:

31/12/19.2	R2 700
31/12/19.3	R1 800

The following transactions were recorded in the general ledger of the Johannesburg College:

COHEN BURSARY FUND

		Income	Capital			Income	Capital
		R	R			R	R
19.1 31/12	Balance	1 500	15 000	19.0 31/12	Bank: Capital donation	—	15 000
				19.1 31/12	Bank: Interest on investment	1 500	—
		1 500	15 000			1 500	15 000
19.2 31/12	Bank: Bursaries awarded	2 700	—	19.2 1/1	Balance	1 500	15 000
	Balance	450	15 000	31/12	Bank: Interest on investment (1)	1 650	—
		3 150	15 000			3 150	15 000
19.3 31/12	Bank: Bursaries awarded	1 800	—	19.3 1/1	Balance	450	15 000
	Balance	195	15 000	31/12	Bank: Interest on investment (2)	1 545	—
		1 995	15 000			1 995	15 000
				19.4 1/1	Balance	195	15 000

Calculations

1 $(10\% \times R15\ 000) + (10\% \times 1\ 500) = R1\ 650$.
2 $(10\% \times R15\ 000) + (10\% \times 450) = R1\ 545$.

Remarks

1 The income from interest on the fund does not increase the 'general' assets of the college and therefore is not reflected in the general funds of the college.
2 A separate Cohen bursary fund income statement will be presented together with the general income statement of the college.
3 The relevant items will be reflected as follows in the balance sheet at 31 December 19.3:

		R
FUNDS		
Cohen bursary fund		15 195
Capital	15 000	
Retained income	195	
ASSETS		
Other investments		
Cohen bursary fund		
Fixed deposit at XY Building Society		15 195

Example 34.2 Income of a fund which must be employed for the purchase of a specific asset

On 31 December 19.1 the Johannesburg College received a bequest of R10 000 from the estate of the late Dr A Katz on condition that the income from the fund be used to purchase laboratory equipment. The amount was invested in a fixed deposit at S Bank on the same date at 10% p a. On 31 December 19.2 equipment amounting to R800 was purchased. The balance of the income was reinvested for a further year at the same interest rate. On 31 December 19.3 the total available funds was used to purchase equipment.

The transactions will be recorded as follows in the books of the college:

DR KATZ LABORATORY FUND

		Income	Capital			Income	Capital
		R	R			R	R
19.2				19.1			
31/12	Accumulated fund (1)	800	—	31/12	Bank	—	10 000
	Balance	200	10 000	19.2			
				31/12	Bank: Interest	1 000	—
		1 000	10 000			1 000	10 000
19.3				19.3			
31/12	Accumulated fund	1 220	—	1/1	Balance	200	10 000
	Balance	—	10 000	31/12	Bank: Interest	1 020	—
		1 220	10 000			1 220	10 000
				19.4			
				1/1	Balance	—	10 000

Remarks

1 The college can treat the purchase of equipment in two ways:

(a) Consider it as a **replacement** of assets, in other words consider it as an operating expense, in which case only the above (debit) entry is made in the fund account.

(b) Consider the equipment as an asset and thus capitalise each purchase. In this case **assets of the college will increase** by R800 on 31 December 19.2 and by R1 220 on 31 December 19.3. Therefore the increase in assets (debit equipment, credit bank with purchases) represents an increase in the general or accumulated fund of the college. This requires a **transfer** from the **income account** of the special fund to the accumulated fund (as shown above). Note, however, that the capital of the special fund is not affected.

2 It will be noted that in both the above examples the use of income from the special fund was **limited** to the income for that year (including surpluses carried forward from the previous year).

If the amount used exceeds the amount available in the income account of the special fund, the balance must be settled from the general fund of the organisation.

3 Balance sheet presentation at 31 December 19.3: The fund will be treated as follows in the balance sheet if the purchase of equipment is treated as the acquisition of an asset:

FUNDS	
Accumulated fund	
Balance 31/12/19.2	xx
Add: Transfer from Katz fund i r o purchase of equipment 31/12/19.3	1 220
Special fund	
Katz laboratory fund	10 000
ASSETS	
Other fixed assets	
Laboratory equipment (at cost price)	2 020
Less: Depreciation	xx
Other investments	
Katz laboratory fund: 10% fixed deposit at S Bank	10 000

Example 34.3 Bequest for general use

During 19.3 the college received R2 000 from Mr A Jones, who stipulated that this amount must be invested and the income utilised to settle general operating expenses.

This donation can be treated in two ways:

- ☐ Since the income from the fund must be used to defray the general operating costs of the college, the capital bequest can be credited directly to the accumulated fund. The investment will appear as a separate item, but will be classified under investments representing a portion of the accumulated fund.
- ☐ In acknowledgement to the donor it can, as in previous examples, be shown as a separate fund with its corresponding investment. The income from the investment will be shown in the general income and expense account of the college.

34.2 FINANCIAL REPORTING BY CLUBS AND SOCIETIES

34.2.1 The receipts and payments statement

The **receipts and payments statement** is often the only financial statement presented at the annual general meeting of small clubs and societies which have no assets other than cash funds. This statement is merely a classified summary of the cash book for the particular financial period and is the simplest type of financial report that can be presented.

All receipts are shown on the debit side of the statement and all payments on the credit side. The opening and closing balances of the cash fund are shown in the usual way. Where a receipts and payments statement is presented this is usually an indication that a cash book in some form is the only accounting record and that the double entry system is not being used.

Example 34.4 Receipts and payments statement of a sports club

The following details relate to XY Golf Club for the financial year ended 31 December 19.8:

	R
Cash on hand 1/1/19.8	200
Entrance fees received for 19.7	100
Entrance fees received for 19.8	150
Annual membership fees received:	
19.7	300
19.8	400
19.9	50
Green fees received	700
Operating expenses paid	1 300
Cost of additions to building	4 000
Loan received from Town Council	4 500

Operating expenses of R70 must still be paid on 31 December 19.8. The operating expenses shown above include R40 in respect of arrear expenses for 19.7.

The receipts and payments statement of the club will be reflected as follows:

XY GOLF CLUB RECEIPTS AND PAYMENTS STATEMENT FOR THE YEAR ENDED 31 DECEMBER 19.8			
Cash balance	200	Operating expenses	1 300
Entrance fees:	250	Additions to building	4 000
19.7	100	Cash balance 31/12/19.8	1 100
19.8	150		
Membership fees:	750		
19.7	300		
19.8	400		
19.9	50		
Green fees	700		
Loan: Municipality	4 500		
	R6 400		R6 400

An analysis of the above statement shows the typical characteristics of a receipts and payments statement, namely:

- ☐ It includes all receipts and payments, that is prepaid and accrued amounts, capital and operating expenses and income.
- ☐ No surplus or shortfall is determined for the year. Obviously this cannot be done because capital items are included in the statement, while prepaid and arrear income and expenses are excluded (e g the arrear operating expense of R70 for 19.8 is not included).
- ☐ The financial position of the club is not reflected because, other than cash funds, the assets and liabilities are not shown.

34.2.2 Financial reporting by larger clubs and societies

From the preceding it is obvious that a receipts and payments statement is not a fair presentation of a society's affairs. A more sophisticated set of financial statements is necessary. In the case of clubs and societies this will normally consist of an **income and expenses statement and a balance sheet**.

☐ The income and expenses statement

The income and expenses statement is equivalent to the income statement encountered in ordinary trading enterprises. It performs the same function as the income statement (it determines the result of the activities of a financial period which is not described as a net income or loss, but as a **net surplus** or **shortfall**), and is prepared according to exactly the same principles and practices.

☐ The balance sheet

Similarly, the balance sheet of a club or society is prepared according to the same principles as an ordinary trading undertaking, the difference (as has already been stated) being that owner's equity is replaced by accumulated funds.

☐ Trading activities

Most larger clubs trade with their members, usually by providing restaurant and bar facilities. In such cases the club will prepare the usual operating (trade) accounts.

Example 34.5 The financial statements of a club

The following balances appear in the books of Sunrise Social Club on 31 December 19.5:

	R
Furniture at cost 31/12/19.4	5 000
Accumulated depreciation: Furniture 31/12/19.4	1 000
Additions to furniture 30/6/19.5	500
Crockery at valuation 31/12/19.4	2 000
Restaurant inventory at cost 31/12/19.4	800
Bar inventory at cost 31/12/19.4	2 500
Restaurant sales for the year	7 000
Bar sales for the year	15 000
Billiard room receipts for the year	500
Membership fees received	1 070
Entrance fees received	2 400
Interest on investment received	300
Purchases: Restaurant	5 000
Bar	8 000
Rental of premises	4 000
Salaries and wages	7 000
Replacement of crockery	500
Electricity and water	1 200
Cash on hand 31/12/19.5	100
Cash in bank 31/12/19.5	1 320
Investment: Fixed deposit at 10% p a at XY Building Society	3 000
Trade creditors 31/12/19.5	700
Accumulated funds 31/12/19.4	13 000
Membership fees in arrears for 19.4	50

Additional information:

(1) Depreciation on furniture must be provided for at 10% per annum on cost.
(2) Crockery is valued at R1 800 on 31 December 19.5.
(3) Inventory on hand, at cost, on 31 December 19.5:

Bar	R2 700
Restaurant	R500

(4) An extract from the members' register shows the following:

Year	No of members	Membership fees received (at R10 per member)	
19.4	100	R950	
19.5	110	30	for 19.4
		1 000	for 19.5
		40	for 19.6
		R1 070	

The committee decided to terminate the membership of the two members who did not pay their 19.4 membership fees and to write off their fees as irrecoverable.

(5) Twelve new members were admitted to the club in 19.5 at an entrance fee of R200 per member. It is the club's policy to transfer entrance fees directly to accumulated funds.

The relevant financial statements for the club will be prepared as follows:

SUNRISE SOCIAL CLUB
TRADING ACCOUNT FOR THE YEAR ENDED 31 DECEMBER 19.5

	Bar	Restaurant	Total		Bar	Restaurant	Total
Inventory 1/1/19.5	2 500	800	3 300	Sales	15 000	7 000	22 000
Purchases	8 000	5 000	13 000				
	10 500	5 800	16 300				
Less: Closing inventory	2 700	500	3 200				
	7 500	5 300	13 100				
Gross profit	7 200	1 700	8 900				
	R15 000	R7 000	R22 000		R15 000	R7 000	R22 000

INCOME AND EXPENSES STATEMENT FOR THE YEAR ENDED 31 DECEMBER 19.5

Rental		4 000	Gross profit		8 900
Wages and salaries		7 000	Bar	7 200	
Crockery		700	Restaurant	1 700	
Replacements	500		Billiard room receipts		500
Scrapped	200		Interest on investment		300
Water and lights		1 200	Membership fees (1)		1 100
Membership fees written off (1)		20	Net shortfall for the year		2 645
Depreciation (2)		525			
		R13 445			R13 445

SUNRISE SOCIAL CLUB BALANCE SHEET AT 31 DECEMBER 19.5		
FUNDS AVAILABLE		
Accumulated funds		12 755
Balance 31/12/19.4	13 000	
Add: Entrance fees 19.5	2 400	
	15 400	
Less: Net shortfall 19.5	2 645	
Current liabilities		740
Creditors	700	
Prepaid membership fees	40	
		R13 495
EMPLOYMENT OF FUNDS		
Fixed assets		5 775
Furniture	3 975	
At cost price	5 500	
Less: Depreciation	1 525	
Crockery at valuation	1 800	
Investment		3 000
Current assets		4 720
Membership fees owing	100	
Inventory	3 200	
Bar	2 700	
Restaurant	500	
Cash on hand	100	
Cash in bank	1 320	
		R13 495

Remarks

1 Notes in respect of the accounting policy have been left out of account.

2 Entrance fees are not usually shown in the income and expense statement because they are once-off receipts and not of a recurring nature. In practice, therefore, they are 'capitalised' by being added to the accumulated funds.

Calculations

1 Membership fees

MEMBERSHIP FEES					
19.4	Owing	50	19.4	Received	30
				Written off	20
19.5	Income and expenses	1 100	19.5	Received	1 000
				Owing (10 × R10)	100
			19.5	Prepaid for 19.6	40

2 Depreciation
$(10\% \times R5\ 000) + (10\% \times R500 \times 1/2) = R500 + 25 = R525$.

Example 34.6 Financial statements of a college

The financial statements of Excelsior College at 31 December 19.3 can be prepared from the following trial balance and additional information:

EXCELSIOR COLLEGE TRIAL BALANCE		
Restaurant sales		12 000
Tuition fees		30 000
Interest received		
General reserve fund		200
Jansen bursary fund		1 000
Excelsior library fund		600
Building fund		1 500
Special funds		
Jansen bursary fund		10 000
Excelsior library fund		6 000
Building fund		15 000
Creditors (restaurant)		2 000
Accumulated fund		136 450
Restaurant		
Inventory 1/1/19.3	200	
Purchases	8 000	
Replacement of crockery	150	
Light and water consumption	300	
Salaries and wages	3 000	
Education department		
Salaries and wages	20 000	
Printing and stationery	600	
Administration costs	400	
Maintenance		
Equipment	200	
Furniture	100	
Library at cost price 1/1/19.3	20 000	
Books purchased during the year	900	
Fixed property at cost price	100 000	
Furniture at cost less depreciation 1/1/19.3	5 000	
Equipment at cost less depreciation 1/1/19.3	3 000	
Equipment purchased at beginning of year	400	
Vehicles at cost less depreciation 1/1/19.3	7 000	
Vehicles: Fuel and repairs	1 300	
Crockery at valuation	1 000	
Investments in 10% government debentures 1/1/19.3		
General reserve fund	2 000	
Jansen bursary fund	10 000	
Excelsior library fund	6 000	
Building fund	15 000	
Debtors (tuition fees)	1 500	
Cash in bank	8 700	
	R214 750	R214 750

Additional information:

(1) The committee of the college has decided to award the total available amount from the bursary fund as bursaries and to credit the relevant amount to the outstanding fees of the students in question.
(2) The income from the library fund is available to finance the purchase of books.
(3) The restaurant inventory amounted to R400 on 31 December 19.4.
(4) Depreciation must be calculated as follows on the closing balances of the various assets:
Furniture: 10%
Equipment: 15%
Vehicles: 20%
Seeing that the vehicles are for general use, the relevant expenses are not debited to a specific department.
(5) The income from the building fund as well as half of the net surplus in any one year must be invested in the fund until it reaches R50 000. This investment has not been made for the current year.
(6) Crockery on hand is valued at the same amount as the previous year.

EXCELSIOR COLLEGE
RESTAURANT INCOME AND EXPENSES ACCOUNT FOR THE YEAR ENDED 31 DECEMBER 19.3

Inventory 1/1/19.3	200	Sales	12 000
Purchases	8 000		
	8 200		
Less: Inventory 31/12/19.3	400		
Cost of sales	7 800		
Gross profit	4 200		
	R12 000		R12 000
Replacement costs: Crockery	150	Gross profit	4 200
Lights and water consumption	300		
Salaries and wages	3 000		
	3 450		
Net surplus transferred to general income and expenses account	750		
	R4 200		R4 200

EDUCATION DEPARTMENT INCOME AND EXPENSES ACCOUNT FOR THE YEAR ENDED 31 DECEMBER 19.3				
Salaries and wages		20 000	Tuition fees	30 000
Printing and stationery		600		
Administration costs		400		
Maintenance		300		
Equipment	200			
Furniture	100			
Depreciation		1 010		
Furniture (10% × 5 000)	500			
Equipment (15% × 3 400)	510			
		22 310		
Net surplus transferred to general income and expenses account		7 690		
		R30 000		R30 000

GENERAL INCOME AND EXPENSES ACCOUNT FOR THE YEAR ENDED 31 DECEMBER 19.3				
Depreciation			Net surplus	
Vehicles (20% × 7 000)		1 400	Restaurant	750
Fuel and repairs		1 300	Education department	7 690
		2 700	Interest received	200
Net surplus		5 940		
Allocated as follows				
Building fund	2 970			
Accumulated fund	2 970			
		R8 640		R8 640

BALANCE SHEET AT 31 DECEMBER 19.3		
FUNDS AVAILABLE		
Accumulated fund		136 450
Balance 31/12/19.2		
Add: 50% of net surplus for 19.3	2 970	
Transfer from income of library fund (1)	600	3 570
		140 020
Special funds		35 470
Jansen bursary fund		10 000
Excelsior library fund		6 000
Building fund (2)		19 470
Creditors		2 000
		R177 490
EMPLOYMENT OF FUNDS		
Fixed assets		134 890
Fixed property at cost price		100 000
Library at cost price		20 900
Furniture at cost price less depreciation		4 500
Equipment at cost price less depreciation		2 890
Vehicles at cost price less depreciation		5 600
Crockery at valuation		1 000
Investments in 10% government debentures		33 000
General reserve fund (3)		2 000
Jansen bursary fund		10 000
Excelsior library fund		6 000
Building fund		15 000
Cash in bank for investments in building fund		4 470
Current assets		5 130
Inventory: Restaurant		400
Debtors: Tuition fees (4)		500
Cash in bank (5)		4 230
		R177 490

Remarks

1 Since R900 was spent and capitalised on books during the year (see 'library' in balance sheet), the full income of the fund (R600) must be transferred to accumulated funds, as the books increased the assets of the college.

2 Building fund

Balance 31/12/19.2	15 000
Add: Interest (reinvested)	1 500
50% of net surplus reinvested	2 970
	R19 470

3 General reserve fund investment
Note that this investment is not represented by a specific reserve under 'special funds' in the balance sheet. Therefore it is part of the accumulated fund which is invested. Obviously it is possible to credit the allocation from accumulated funds to a specific 'general reserve fund'.

4 Debtors: Tuition fees

Per trial balance	1 500
Less: Bursaries allocated out of income from bursary fund	1 000
	R500

5 Cash in bank

Per trial balance	8 700
Less: Amount reserved for investment	4 470
	R4 230

35

INCOMPLETE RECORDS

The **AIM** of this chapter is to illustrate the conversion of incomplete records to a double entry system.

35.1 BACKGROUND AND INTRODUCTION

The essence of the double entry accounting system is the analysis of each transaction in terms of the basic accounting equation: assets = liabilities + owner's equity. Many smaller undertakings and organisations maintain only minimal accounting records and do not have a system whereby transactions may be analysed and recorded within the framework of the double entry system. Such a system is often referred to as a **single entry system**.

The accounting records of many smaller non-profit organisations such as clubs, cultural societies and small undertakings are often kept by means of a single entry system. Nevertheless, details of the financial activities of such organisations and undertakings are available in different documents such as bank statements, invoices, accounts, wage sheets and minute books.

There are two major disadvantages to such incomplete (non-double entry basis) accounting records:

- A great deal of useful information may be lost. It is possible to prepare financial statements from the available information, but this may be more difficult than when complete records are available. Certain transactions may not be accounted for and there is also no continuity in the recording of financial and other useful information.
- The advantages of the controls inherent in a double entry system are lost.

A discussion of the treatment of incomplete records is useful for various reasons. First, it emphasises the advantages of a comprehensive double entry system. Further, it is practical because accountants often have to prepare financial statements from such incomplete records, chiefly for income tax purposes. In practice, therefore, the conversion of single entry information to a double entry basis is an analytical exercise. It may also happen that the double entry records of an enterprise are lost (e g as a result of damage by fire) and that the accountant must reconstruct them from incomplete records.

Consequently, attention is given to certain aspects and practical procedures which arise as a result of keeping incomplete records.

35.2 DETERMINING OWNER'S EQUITY IN AN ENTITY

Assume that a trader has been in business for some time and that he wants to determine his interest in the undertaking at a specific date. In order to do this he must determine the total interest in the business and against this, bring into account any external interest. This can be done by constructing an **equity statement**. (This is a statement which contains basically the same information as a balance sheet, but because it is not prepared from balances of accounts in a double entry system, it is usually not known as a balance sheet.)

The equity statement must be prepared by referring to any applicable information available. It has already been stated that even undertakings which do not have formal accounting systems will find it necessary to keep records of certain basic information in order to conduct their business.

For example, records of cash received and paid and of amounts owing, both to and by the undertaking, are essential. Cash on hand can be determined by a cash count, cash in bank from the bank statement, and amounts owing to and by the undertaking from invoices. Stock can be counted physically and then valued. The cost of fixed assets purchased can be determined from the supporting documentation. Owner's equity will be the difference between the values allocated to assets and liabilities.

Since the owner is trying to establish the extent of his interest in the business undertaking, his **personal assets** and **funds** must be excluded from this equity statement.

35.3 DETERMINING INCOME FROM INCOMPLETE RECORDS

The most practical method of determining net income or loss from incomplete records is to analyse the change in owner's equity during any specific period. Obviously, owner's equity increases if a profit is made and when the owner makes additional investments in the undertaking. Conversely, owner's equity decreases as a result of losses and drawings by the owner. If the opening and closing balances of the owner's equity is determined as described in paragraph 35.2 and the additional capital introduced and drawings are known, then the change in owner's equity is attributable to the profit or loss arising from business operations.

The procedure for determining the profit can be illustrated schematically by means of the following example:

Example 35.1 Determining a net profit or loss from incomplete records

	Case A (net profit)	Case B (net loss)
1 Determine owner's equity in the undertaking at the end of the period by preparing an equity statement	40 000	30 000
2 Determine owner's equity in the undertaking at the beginning of the period by preparing an equity statement	28 000	35 000
Increase (decrease) in equity	12 000	(5 000)
3 Deduct any new funds introduced into the undertaking by the owner in whatever form (cash, assets)	(2 000)	(1 000)
Apparent profit (loss)	10 000	(6 000)
4 Add (deduct in the case of an apparent loss) any withdrawals by the owner from the undertaking in whatever form (cash, assets)	4 000	4 000
Profit (loss) for the period	R14 000	(R2 000)

This can also be represented in account form:

CASE A

Drawings (4)	4 000	Opening balance of equity (2)	28 000
Closing balance of equity (1)	40 000	New funds introduced (3)	2 000
			30 000
		∴ Profit	14 000
	R44 000		R44 000
		Balance	40 000

CASE B

Drawings (4)	4 000	Opening balance of equity (2)	35 000
Closing balance of equity (1)	30 000	New funds introduced (3)	1 000
	34 000		36 000
∴ Loss	(2 000)		
	R36 000		R36 000
		Balance	30 000

Example 35.2 Incomplete records in the case of a partnership

A and B entered into a partnership on 1 January 19.7 by contributing the following assets respectively:

	A	B
Cash in bank	5 000	3 000
Inventory	4 000	2 000
Vehicles	10 000	—
Equipment	—	8 000
	R19 000	R13 000

The partners share profits in the ratio 3:2 after allowing for interest of 10% p a on initial capital and interest of 5% p a on average annual drawings.

The partnership did not maintain a complete set of financial records, but the following information can be extracted from the existing records and notes:

	R
Stock 31/12/19.7	10 000
Debtors for goods sold on credit 31/12/19.7	15 000
Creditors for goods purchased 31/12/19.7	7 000
Cash in bank 31/12/19.7	3 000
Vehicles at valuation 31/12/19.7	9 000
Equipment at valuation 31/12/19.7	7 000
Drawings during the year: A	6 000
B	4 000

The partnership profit for the year must be calculated and allocated to the partners. Finally, an equity statement must be prepared:

PARTNERSHIP A AND B
EQUITY STATEMENT AT 1 JANUARY 19.7

Vehicles	10 000	Capital introduced		32 000
Equipment	8 000	A	19 000	
Inventory	6 000	B	13 000	
Cash in bank	8 000			
	R32 000			R32 000

EQUITY STATEMENT AT 31 DECEMBER 19.7

Vehicles	9 000	Creditors	7 000
Equipment	7 000	Closing balance of equity	37 000
Inventory	10 000		
Debtors	15 000		
Cash in bank	3 000		
	R44 000		R44 000

Determination of profit

Closing balance of partners' equity		37 000
Opening balance of partners' equity		32 000
Increase in equity		5 000
Less: New investments by partners		—
		5 000
Add: Drawings by partners		10 000
Profit for the year (before interest on capital and drawings)		15 000
Add: Interest on drawings		250
A ($\frac{5}{100} \times \frac{1}{2} \times 6\ 000$)	150	
B ($\frac{5}{100} \times \frac{1}{2} \times 4\ 000$)	100	
		15 250
Less: Interest on capital		3 200
A (10% × R19 000)	1 900	
B (10% × R13 000)	1 300	
Profit available for allocation		R12 050
Allocated as follows		
A ($^3/_5$)		7 230
B ($^2/_5$)		4 820
		R12 050

PARTNERSHIP A AND B ADJUSTED EQUITY STATEMENT AT 31 DECEMBER 19.7					
			A	B	Total
Vehicles	9 000	Capital			37 000
		Introduced 1/1/19.7	19 000	13 000	
Equipment	7 000	*Add:* Share of profit	7 230	4 820	
Inventory	10 000	Interest on capital	1 900	1 300	
Debtors	15 000		28 130	19 120	
Cash in bank	3 000	*Less:* Interest on drawings	(150)	(100)	
		Drawings	(6 000)	(4 000)	
			R21 980	R15 020	
		Creditors			7 000
	R44 000				R44 000

35.4 CONVERTING INFORMATION FROM INCOMPLETE RECORDS TO A DOUBLE ENTRY BASIS

The determination of a single net income amount, as discussed in the previous paragraph, is naturally not suitable for most purposes. For example, it would be unacceptable for income tax purposes. Therefore it is often necessary to convert the information obtained from incomplete accounting records to a double entry basis and to prepare comprehensive financial statements from this information.

The following 'conversion procedure' can be employed to introduce a double entry system where previously it did not exist:

☐ Prepare an initial equity statement from the available information. Draw up a nominal ledger and open the relevant asset and equity accounts.

☐ If no form of cash book exists, the cheque books, deposit books, cash sales and cash purchases invoices, and other evidence of monies received (e g receipts) and monies paid (e g wage sheets), must be used to construct a detailed columnar statement of receipts and payments. (Often a complete cash book is drawn up.) This will be an important source of information which will include the following:

Receipts:
- cash receipts from sales and other income, for example interest
- collections from debtors
- proceeds from the sale of assets
- proceeds from borrowed funds
- cash introduced by owners.

Payments:
- cash and cheque payments relating to purchases of goods and operating expenses
- payments to creditors
- repayments of loans
- cash drawings by owners.

This information is analysed, recorded in columns and posted to the nominal general ledger.

- ☐ The most important components of other items can be reconstructed from various other sources (credit sales and credit purchases invoices, transfer deeds and lawyers' statements), and then the relevant subsidiary books (including a general journal) can be drawn up. The transactions for the period are recorded in the subsidiary books and then posted to the nominal and other relevant ledgers, such as debtors and creditors ledgers.
- ☐ Finally a trial balance is compiled, the necessary adjustments are made and the financial statements are prepared.

In practice, the amount of work necessary to convert a single entry system to a comprehensive double entry system will depend on the completeness or otherwise of the existing records. The success of such a conversion will depend on the accountant's knowledge of the particular type of enterprise. He should have an in-depth knowledge of the type of transactions which usually occur in the particular type of enterprise.

The following example shows how the different income and expense figures can be calculated using the information in single entry records.

Example 35.3 Determination of income and expense figures from single entry records

J SMYTHE EQUITY STATEMENT AT 31 DECEMBER 19.1			
ASSETS		EQUITY	
Equipment at cost price less depreciation	5 000	Capital: J Smythe	58 000
Fixed property at cost price	20 000	Trade creditors	12 300
Investments	10 000	Salaries accrued	200
Inventory at cost price	20 000	Prepaid rental receivable	500
Debtors	5 000		
Bills receivable	6 000		
Interest accrued	400		
Prepaid insurance	600		
Cash in bank	4 000		
	R71 000		R71 000

Summary of activities during the year ended 31 December 19.2 (prepared from cash and other supplementary records):

	R	R
Cash payments		56 700
To creditors for merchandise	30 000	
Insurance premiums	700	
Salaries	15 000	
Other operating expenses	4 000	
Drawings by owner	7 000	
Cash receipts		77 800
Rental received	4 000	
Interest received	800	
Cash sales	40 000	
Collections from debtors	33 000	
Sales returns and allowances		2 000
Discount allowed to debtors		500
Debtors written off as irrecoverable		600
Discount received from creditors		1 000
Purchases returns and allowances		800

Balances of items at 31 December 19.2 determined by analysis:

Bills receivable	10 000
Debtors	8 000
Interest receivable	500
Inventory at cost price	4 000
Prepaid insurance	300
Creditors	9 000
Salaries accrued	1 500
Prepaid rental receivable	400

Additional information:

(1) There was no change in fixed assets.
(2) Depreciation on equipment must be calculated at 20% on cost.

□ Reconstruction of the sales figure

In order to calculate missing figures for an income statement, a thorough understanding of the relationship between cash flow and income and expense items is necessary.

Sales are generated from two sources: cash received from customers and from a gross increase in debtors and bills receivable. Since the opening balance of debtors represents income realised in the previous period, collections from debtors are irrelevant to the income in the current year. Therefore the opening balance of debtors and bills receivable must be deducted from the total cash receipts from debtors in order to determine the sales (to debtors) realised in cash in the current period. Conversely, at the end of the period debtors represents sales in the current year which are not reflected in the cash collected and which must thus be included to convert the cash collected figure to the amount of credit sales for the year.

In addition, further appropriate adjustments relevant to debtors and credit sales (e g discount) must be brought into account. Collections and debtors taken into account in this calculation should include only those arising from trading activities.

The calculation of the gross sales figure can be determined by one of the following two methods:

Method 1: Vertical statement

CREDIT SALES FOR 19.2		
Collections from debtors	33 000	
Less: Debtors and bills receivable 31/12/19.1	11 000	22 000
Add: Irrecoverable amounts	600	
Sales returns and allowances	2 000	
Discount allowed	500	
Debtors and bills receivable 31/12/19.2	18 000	21 100
∴ Credit sales for 19.2		43 100
Add: Cash sales for the year		40 000
Total gross sales		R83 100

Method 2: T-form statement

The account is constructed from the given information according to the usual double entry procedure. (The numbers indicate the sequence of the calculations.)

DEBTORS AND BILLS RECEIVABLE

(1)	Balance 31/12/19.1	11 000	(2)	Cash collected	33 000
	Debtors	5 000	(3)	Sales returns	2 000
	Bills	6 000	(4)	Discount allowed	500
(7)	Credit sales (balancing figure)	43 100	(5)	Irrecoverable amounts	600
			(6)	Balance 31/12/19.2	18 000
				Debtors	8 000
				Bills	10 000
		R54 100			R54 100

□ Reconstruction of the purchases figure

The purchases figure is determined in the same manner from the cash payments records and returns of creditors outstanding at the beginning and the end of the period. The relationship between the present cash flow and the relevant expense must be borne in mind.

The creditors balances at the beginning of the year represent purchases from the previous period; they are irrelevant to the determination of the operating result for the current period. Therefore the creditors' opening balances must be deducted from the total payments to creditors in order to determine the cash payments for goods during the year. In contrast, creditors at the end of the period represent credit purchases for the period which have not been reflected in any cash payments and which therefore must be added to cash purchases to determine total purchases from suppliers. Other suitable adjustments relating to creditors' accounts (e g discount received) must also be taken into account in determining purchases.

CREDITORS AND PURCHASES

(2)	Cash payments	30 000	(1)	Balance 31/12/19.1	12 300
(3)	Discount received	1 000	(6)	Purchases (balancing figure)	28 500
(4)	Returns and allowances	800			
	Balance 31/12/19.2	9 000			
		R40 800			R40 800

□ Reconstruction of operating expenses and income

In the determination of operating expenses and income during the conversion process, the relationship between cash flow and the expenses or income for the relevant period must again be borne in mind. In addition, the related asset and liability items (i e prepaid and accrued amounts) must be brought into account.

These aspects are obvious from the following:

	Insurance	Salaries	Other operating expenses	Depreciation
1 Cash payments during 19.2	700	15 000	4 000	—
2 *Less:* Amounts included which do not pertain to 19.2				
Prepaid expenses 31/12/19.2	(300)	—	—	—
Accrued expenses 31/12/19.1	—	(200)	—	—
3 *Add:* Amounts not paid which pertain to 19.2				
Prepaid amounts 31/12/19.1	600	—	—	—
Arrear amounts 31/12/19.2	—	1 500	—	—
4 Depreciation for the year	—	—	—	1 000
Total expenses for the year	R1 000	R16 300	R4 000	R1 000

These figures may also be determined by using T-accounts:

(a) INSURANCE

19.2			19.2		
1/1	Prepaid amounts b/f from 19.1	600	31/12	Prepaid amounts c/f to 19.3	300
31/12	Bank	700		Expenses to income statement	1 000
		R1 300			R1 300

(b) SALARIES

19.2			19.2		
31/12	Bank	15 000	1/1	Arrear amounts b/f i r o 19.1	200
	Arrears balance c/f i r o 19.2	1 500		Expenses to income statement	16 300
		R16 500			R16 500
			19.2		
			31/12	Balance	1 500

Similarly, the relevant amounts for income items are determined by either of these two methods:

(c) RENTAL RECEIVED

19.2			19.2		
31/12	Prepaid amounts i r o 19.3	400	1/1	Prepaid amounts i r o 19.2	500
	Income to income statement	4 100	31/12	Bank	4 000
		R4 500			R4 500

After all items have been posted to the general ledger, the reconstruction of certain accounts has been done, and a trial balance has been prepared, the relevant financial statements can be prepared:

J SMYTHE
INCOME STATEMENT FOR THE YEAR ENDED 31 DECEMBER 19.2

			Remarks
Sales	83 100		Reconstruction 1
Less: Returns	2 000	81 100	
Less: Cost of sales			
Inventory 31/12/19.1	20 000		
Purchases less returns (28 500 – 800)	27 700		Reconstruction 2
	47 000		
Less: Inventory 31/12/19.2	4 000	43 700	
Gross profit		37 400	
Add: Other income		6 000	
Rental received	4 100		
Interest received	900		Reconstruction 3(c)
Discount received	1 000		Note (1)
		43 400	
Less: Expenses		23 400	
Insurance	1 000		Reconstruction 3(a)
Salaries	16 300		Reconstruction 3(b)
Other operating expenses	4 000		
Depreciation (20% × 5 000)	1 000		
Bad debts	600		
Discount allowed	500		
Net profit		R20 000	

Note

1 Short method of reconstruction:

Interest received 19.2 (cash)	R800	
Add: Receivable 31/12/19.2	500	1 300
Less: Receivable 31/12/19.1		400
Due for 19.2		R900

J SMYTHE BALANCE SHEET AT 31 DECEMBER 19.2		
CAPITAL EMPLOYED		71 000
Capital: J Smythe	58 000	
Balance 31/12/19.2	20 000	
	78 000	
Less: Drawings	7 000	
Current liabilities		10 900
Creditors	9 000	
Salaries accrued	1 500	
Prepaid rental receivable	400	
		R81 900
EMPLOYMENT OF CAPITAL		
Fixed assets		24 000
Fixed property at cost price	20 000	
Equipment at cost price less depreciation	4 000	
Investment		10 000
Current assets		47 900
Inventory	4 000	
Debtors	8 000	
Bills receivable	10 000	
Interest receivable	500	
Prepaid insurance	300	
Cash in bank (4 000 + 77 800 − 56 700)	25 100	
		R81 900

36

THE INFLUENCE OF CHANGING PRICES ON ACCOUNTING

The **AIM** of this chapter is to explain certain problematical aspects of accountability in times of changing price levels.

36.1 THE HISTORICAL COST PRINCIPLE

The historical cost principle stipulates that the price actually paid for assets and operating expenses must be brought into account in the accounting process.

The price of an item is the amount asked or paid for it. Price reflects the value sacrificed for the acquisition of an item at the moment of purchase; therefore price paid is a historical fact and does not necessarily reflect the value of the item after the transaction, since this may change. Value changes when supply or demand changes. If the value of an asset which was acquired at a specific cost changes in the course of time, the accounting records will no longer reflect its value.

When recording accounting transactions at **historical cost** it is assumed, by implication, that **prices** remain **stable**. This is obviously **not** so in practice and consequently **profit determination in a period of rising price levels** poses a problem. The price of the acquisition or expense is not necessarily a reflection of the value sacrificed.

36.2 TYPES OF PRICE LEVEL CHANGES

Price level changes can be general or specific in nature. **General price level changes** reflect increases or decreases in the value of the monetary unit. Prices are expected to show a specific trend. If the cost of an item was R10 three years ago and the same item now costs R20, it may be concluded that the price level has risen, the buying power of money has decreased, and that there is inflation.

Specific price level changes can result from technological advances, changes in consumer demand, etc.

If the value of money changes, measuring transactions in terms of stable monetary units is obviously not a suitable method. **Financial statements should be adjusted** for the following reasons:

- ☐ To create a more accurate basis for the evaluation of the investment in an undertaking.
- ☐ To enable meaningful comparisons between the results of different years.
- ☐ To make comparisons between undertakings more meaningful.

36.3 ADJUSTING FOR PRICE LEVEL CHANGES

Adjustments for changing price levels can be one of the following types:

- ☐ partial adjustments
- ☐ general adjustments
- ☐ specific adjustments based on current replacement value.

36.3.1 Partial adjustments

Price level changes especially affect:

- ☐ assets having a relatively long lifespan, for example fixed assets subject to depreciation
- ☐ acquisitions where there is a lapse of time between the time of acquisition and the allocation of that cost to the income account for a specific period, for example inventory.

In order to counteract the effect of inflation to a certain extent, an undertaking may revalue its fixed assets periodically and use the LIFO (last-in-first-out) method of inventory valuation.

☐ **Revaluation of fixed assets**

If assets which are used and consumed are revalued to their current cost periodically, the depreciation written off every year is more realistic than if it were based on historical cost.

The fixed assets concerned are also reflected at a more realistic value in the balance sheet. It is generally accepted accounting practice to disclose the method of valuation of fixed assets.

☐ **The LIFO method of inventory valuation**

Inventory valuation, including the last-in-first-out method, is discussed in detail in chapter 15. One of the methods used to determine a realistic profit under inflationary conditions is to value inventory according to the LIFO method, which means that the cost of sales is reflected at the latest purchase price.

A disadvantage of this method is that the inventory on the balance sheet is also valued on the LIFO basis, that is the cost of sales is shown at a relatively high price while inventory on hand is shown at a relatively low price.

36.3.2 General adjustments

In some countries the financial statements of an undertaking are adapted to reflect the **general purchasing power** of money as at the last day of the accounting period. Usually an index, such as the consumer index, is used to convert historical amounts to current purchasing power equivalents. The purpose is to convert all amounts in the financial statements to a common accounting unit with the same purchasing power.

☐ **The difference between current cost and historical cost financial statements**

The basic difference between general purchasing power and historical cost financial statements is the unit of measurement used in the statements.

In historical cost financial statements amounts are shown at historical cost, while in general purchasing power financial statements historical costs are adjusted for changes in price levels. In the latter financial statements the unit of measurement is defined in terms of a single specified price level, viz the current cost of the monetary unit on a specific date. Although the amounts are adjusted, the cost principle, on which the historical cost statements are based, still applies to general purchasing power statements, viz the amounts still represent costs and not current values.

In the process of adjusting historical costs to specific current costs, current cost changes are the only factors taken into account. The amounts reflected in general purchasing power financial statements are not intended to represent valuations, replacement costs, or any other form of current value.

☐ **Monetary and non-monetary assets and liabilities**

For the purposes of current cost accounting, **monetary** assets and liabilities are those where the amounts are determined contractually or by statute in terms of a number of monetary units, irrespective of changes in the buying power of those units. A fixed sum of money will buy progressively fewer goods and services during a period of inflation; therefore money loses general purchasing power as a result of inflation. A debt repayable in the future will become a smaller liability during a period of inflation because it is repayable in money having reduced buying power. Examples of monetary assets and liabilities are cash, debtors, bills receivable and payable, and loans.

Non-monetary assets and liabilities (viz assets and liabilities not included above) generally tend, subject to changes in demand and technological improvements, to retain their purchasing power as price levels increase. Examples of non-monetary items are land, installations, equipment and inventory.

If a change in the price of a non-monetary item is equal to the rate of change in the general price level, there will be no increase or decrease in general purchasing power.

☐ Current cost accounting

Another method of accounting for the influence of inflation on the financial statements is to show some (or all) of the items in terms of their **current cost**.

The most popular method is to prepare a distinct and separate statement which reflects the financial result as restated by the following adjustments:

- ☐ **Depreciation:** An adjustment for the difference between depreciation based on the current cost of fixed assets and depreciation determined on the historical cost.
- ☐ **Cost of sales:** An adjustment for the difference between current cost of inventory at the date of sale and the amount used to determine the historical cost.
- ☐ **Leverage:** The leverage adjustment must be made in the following cases:
  - Where the total liabilities (including preference share capital) exceed the total monetary assets. In this case a portion of the operating capacity is effectively financed by net monetary liabilities. In order to calculate the portion financed by shareholders, an adjustment must be made showing the extent to which depreciation and cost of sales adjustments need not be fully provided for.
  - Where total monetary assets exceed total liabilities. In this case an adjustment must be made to reflect the increase in net monetary assets needed to maintain the operating capacity of the undertaking.

A current cost balance sheet may also be prepared, but at present this is not general practice in South Africa.

It must be noted that these adjusted financial statements do not replace the historical cost financial statements, but are supplementary thereto.

36.4 CONCLUSION

Consistent inflation has shown that the traditional historical cost accounting system has serious limitations. These limitations have already resulted in deviations from the strictly historical cost conventions. For example, many undertakings have revalued their fixed assets and adopted the LIFO basis of inventory valuation in order to determine a more accurate measure of cost of sales.

Exhaustive debates as to which type of system should replace or supplement the historical cost system have been going on for many years. To date no consensus has been reached.

The two main approaches which have been proposed are general purchasing power accounting and current cost accounting. General purchasing power accounting considers inflation generally and current cost accounting considers inflation specific to the entity. Current cost accounting is presently preferred in determining the income of an entity.

SCHEDULE A

PRESCRIBED INFORMATION TO BE INCLUDED IN THE ANNUAL STATEMENTS OF COMPANIES

This schedule provides an overall view of the requirements of the Companies Act, 1973 (Act 61 of 1973) regarding the minimum information which must be included in the annual financial statements of companies (see also chapter 18). Not all the required information is necessarily applicable in each case. The funds statement is not included here, as it has already been discussed in chapter 27.

In the second section of this schedule the minimum information is summarised in an example of annual company financial statements.

PART I: BALANCE SHEET: SHAREHOLDERS' EQUITY AND LIABILITIES

Relevant paragraph (P) of schedule 4 of the Act or article (A) of the Act	*Particulars*		
P9	The liabilities shall be summarised with such particulars as are necessary to disclose their general nature and shall be classified under headings and sub-headings appropriate to the company's business.		
	SHARE CAPITAL	R	R
P5 *(a) (b)*	*Authorised*		
	Par value shares: Classes (preferential, ordinary, unclassified, etc). Number *and* nominal value of shares in each class		
	No par value shares: Classes (preferential, ordinary, unclassified, etc). Number of shares in each class		
A74	Any particular class must consist *exclusively* of par value *or* no par value shares		
P5 *(a) (c) (d)*	*Issued*		
	Number of issued shares *and* the amount of issued share capital for *every* class of par value shares	XX	
P5 *(d)*	Number of issued shares and declared capital account for every class of no par value shares	XX	
P5 *(e)*/A76	Shares premium account (par value shares only) *(see notes)*	XX	XXX
P6, 4	NON-DISTRIBUTABLE RESERVES*		
A98	Capital redemption reserve fund	XX	
	Pre-incorporation profit	XX	
	Appreciation on revaluation of fixed assets	XX	
	Excess of net asset over purchase price, on takeover of a going concern	XX	XXX
P6, 4	DISTRIBUTABLE RESERVES*		
	General reserve	XX	
	Reserve for increased replacements cost of fixed assets	XX	
P4 (3)	Excessive 'depreciation' provisions	XX	
	Retained profits	XX	XXX
	SHAREHOLDERS' EQUITY		XXXX
P9	LONG-TERM LIABILITIES		
P8	Debentures (amounts and classes)	XX	
	Mortgages	XX	
P10 *(b)*	Secured/unsecured loans *(see notes)*	XX	XXX

*Show movements on reserves and disclosable provisions during accounting period, according to P7.

Relevant paragraph (P) of schedule 4 of the Act or article (A) of the Act	*Particulars*	R	R
P12 *(a)*	INDEBTEDNESS TO SUBSIDIARIES*		xxx
P12 *(b)*, 4(1)	HOLDING COMPANIES AND FELLOW SUBSIDIARIES*		
	Debentures	xx	
	Other debts	xx	xxx
P9, 6	CURRENT LIABILITIES AND PROVISIONS		
P10 *(a)*	Bank overdrafts	xx	
P10 *(b)*	Short-term loans	xx	
	Sundry creditors	xx	
	Provision for income tax (less provisional tax)	xx	
P10 *(c)*	Dividends paid and recommended	xx	xxx
			Rxxxx

NOTES RE SHARE CAPITAL

P5 *(f)* 1 *Redeemable preference shares:*
- (a) Earliest and latest redemption dates
- (b) Whether redemption is obligatory
- (c) Premium (if any) on redemption.

P5 *(g)* 2 *Convertible preference shares:*
Conditions of conversion (or a note where these conditions may be inspected).

P30 3 *Options and preferential rights to shares:*
- (a) Number, description and amount of shares under option, etc
- (b) Option price
- (c) Option period.

P31 4 *Directors' authority to issue shares:*
- (a) Number or amount of shares
- (b) Terms and period of authority.

P29 5 *Company's shares (debentures) held by subsidiary:*
Details of beneficial holdings.

P32 6 *Arrear dividends on cumulative preference shares:*
Amount according to class of share and period in arrear.

NOTES RE DEBENTURES

P8 *(a)* 1 *Convertible debentures:*
Convertibility and conditions of conversion (or a note where these conditions may be inspected).

P8 *(a) (c)* 2 *Redeemable debentures:*
- (a) Date of optional or compulsory redemption
- (b) Particulars of redeemed debentures which the company has power to re-issue.

*May also be shown under long-term liabilities or current liabilities, according to circumstances.

Relevant paragraph (P) of schedule 4 of the Act or article (A) of the Act	*Particulars*
P8 *(b)*	3 *Debentures of companies held by its trustee or nominee:* Nominal amount and book value.
P29	4 *Debentures of company held by subsidiary:* Details of beneficial holding.
	NOTES RE LONG-TERM LIABILITIES
P11	1 *Secured liabilities:* Where secured otherwise than by operation of law, state the liability and the assets by which secured.
P 10*(b)*	2 *Loans:* Where the date of repayment is more than one year after the accounting date, note the— (a) interest rates (b) repayment dates (c) instalments in which repayable.

PART II: BALANCE SHEET: ASSETS

P13	The assets shall be summarised with such particulars as are necessary to disclose their general nature and shall be classified under headings and sub-headings appropriate to the company's business.
P14	The following must be separately identified and classified under appropriate headings: fixed assets, current assets and assets which are neither fixed nor current.

		R	R	R
P15	FIXED ASSETS	*Cost price or valuation*	*Accumulated depreciation*	*Balance*
P16 (1) (3) P16 (6)	Land and buildings at cost price (give description, date of acquisition and purchase price)	xxx		xxx
P16 (1) (3)	Plant at cost price less depreciation	xxx	x	xxx
P16 (1) (3)	Other fixed assets at valuation less depreciation (give year of valuation, etc)	xxx	x	xxx
		Rxxx	Rx	xxx
P16 (2), 20	Goodwill, patents and trade marks at cost price less amounts written off			xxx
P16 (2) (4)	Other fixed assets at cost price, replacements debited against income (or provision for renewal)			xxx
				xxxx

Relevant paragraph (P) of schedule 4 of the Act or article (A) of the Act	*Particulars*			
P15, 17	INTEREST IN SUBSIDIARIES	R	R	R
	Shares at cost price		xx	
	Debt		xx	xxx
P15, 18	HOLDING COMPANY AND FELLOW SUBSIDIARIES			
	Debentures at cost price		xx	
	Other debt		xx	xxx
P15, 21	INVESTMENTS*			
	Listed at cost (market value Rxx – where different)		xx	
	Unlisted at cost (in all cases, directors' valuation Rxx or according to P22) *(see notes)*		xx	xxx
	INCOME TAX LOAN LEVY			xxx
P19	LOANS AND CREDIT TO DIRECTORS AND EMPLOYEES			
A295	Loans to directors and managers		xx	
A296	Loans to directors and managers before appointment		xx	
A38 (2)	Loans to directors and employees for the purchase of shares		xx	xxx
P25 (1)	CURRENT ASSETS			
P25 (2) (3)	Inventory			
	Raw materials			
	Finished goods	x		
	Merchandise	x		
	Consumable stores	x		
	Work/contracts in progress	x	xx	
	Debtors less provision for doubtful debts		xx	
	Cash *(see notes)*		xx	xxx
P26	PRELIMINARY EXPENSES			
	Particulars re P26			xxx
				Rxxxx

NOTES RE INVESTMENTS

P23 1 *List of names* of companies in which investments are held, and extent of investment in each company.

*May be shown, where circumstances warrant, under current assets, e g in the case of a company trading in shares; in this case P25 (5) is also applicable.

Relevant paragraph (P) of schedule 4 of the Act or article (A) of the Act	*Particulars*
P24	2 Give amount of *profit made on realisation* of any investment applied to write down the book value of remaining investments (if not already shown in income statement).
	NOTES RE INVENTORY
P25 (3)	1 *Method of valuation:* (a) Whether it is consistent with the method of the previous year (b) Whether it is the lowest of (i) cost or (ii) net realisable value, etc (c) Whether it is the LIFO, FIFO or average cost method (d) Whether overheads were included with cost of uncompleted work/contracts (e) Methods used to provide for obsolescense of spares kept for maintenance purposes.
P25 (4)	2 *Additional information* required to fairly represent the value of inventory.
	ADDITIONAL INFORMATION TO BE PROVIDED
P27	1 *Comparative figures*, where applicable.
P28	2 *Notes to balance sheet.*
P33	(a) *Contingent liabilities:* (i) Particulars of any encumbrance of company's assets to secure the liabilities of any other person (ii) Any other contingent liabilities.
P34	(b) *Contracts for capital expenditure:* (i) Contracts for which no provision had been made (ii) Capital expenditure authorised by directors but not yet contracted for (give the source of funds to meet such capital expenditure).
P35	(c) *Basis of translation for foreign currency.*

PART III: THE INCOME STATEMENT

		R	R
	Operating income for year before taking into account the items listed below		xx
P36 *(a)*	Profits on share transactions (showing their application to write down the book value of remaining investments, if this is not given in the balance sheet)		xx
P36 *(b)*	Income from investments:		
	Listed	x	
	Unlisted	x	xx
P36 *(c)*	Income from subsidiaries:		
	Dividends	x	
	Interest	x	
	Managerial and other fees	x	
	Other specified income	x	xx

Relevant paragraph (P) of schedule 4 of the Act or article (A) of the Act	*Particulars*		
		R	R
P36 *(e)*	Profits on disposal of fixed assets		xx
P36 *(f)*	Withdrawals from provisions, not applied for the purpose thereof		xx
P43	Income of an exceptional or non-recurrent nature, eg devaluation profit		xx
P36 *(a)*	Losses on share transactions		xx
P36 *(e)*	Losses on disposal of fixed assets		xx
P36 *(f)*	Provision for depreciation, etc, of fixed assets (including disclosable provisions)		xx
P36 *(k)*	Interest on loans		xx
P36 *(l)*	Interest on share capital, paid out of capital		xx
P36 *(m)*	Payment of leasing charges for depreciable moveable property		xx
P36 *(n)*	Remuneration (other than to *bona fide* employees) for all managerial, technical, administrative or secretarial services		xx
A297	Directors' remuneration *(see notes)*		xx
P37	Auditor's remuneration:		
	Audit fee	x	
	Fee for other specified services	x	
	Expenses	x	xx
	Net profit (loss) for year		xx
P36 *(g)*	Provision for tax specifying the type of taxation (whether local or overseas, normal company taxes, undistributed profits tax, etc) re *(a)* the accounting period and *(b)* any other financial year		xx
	Net after-tax profit for the year		xx
	Balance of retained profits brought forward from previous year		xx
P36 *(g)*	*Add:* Excess provision for tax (specifying type of taxation and accounting period)		xx
P36 *(j)*	Credit due to an event in a preceding accounting period		x
P36 *(j)*	*Less:* Debit due to an event during a preceding accounting period		x
			xx
P36 *(i)*	Withdrawals of distributable reserves		xx
P36 *(h)*	Amounts reserved for redemption of, respectively *(a)* shares and *(b)* loans (including debentures)		xx

Relevant paragraph (P) of schedule 4 of the Act or article (A) of the Act	*Particulars*	R	R
A98 (1) *(c)*	Provision for premium on redemption of redeemable preference shares		xx
A98 (1) *(b)*	Transfer to capital redemption reserve fund		xx
P36 *(i)*	Transfer to other non-distributable reserves		xx
P36 *(i)*	Transfer to distributable reserves		xx
P36 *(d)*	Dividends paid and proposed (stating dividends which are provided partly or wholly from capital profits)		xx
	Balance on retained profit (loss) at end of year		Rxx
	NOTES RE DIRECTORS' REMUNERATION		
A297	The following information re directors' remuneration must be presented either in the income statement or in a note:		
	(a) Directors' fees*		
	For services as directors	x	
	Other fees	x	xx
	(b) Pensions for directors or former directors*		
	For services as directors	x	
	Other pensions	x	xx
		Loss of directorship	*Loss of other office*
	(c) Compensation to directors or former directors for loss of office		
	Paid by or receivable from the company	x	x
	Paid by or receivable from subsidiaries	x	x
	Paid by or receivable from other persons	x	x
		Rxx	Rxx

ADDITIONAL INFORMATION TO BE PRESENTED

P39 1 *Comparative figures*, where applicable.

P38 2 *Turnover*

(a) The following to be shown as a general rule—
   (i) either the total amount of turnover
   (ii) or the percentage increase or decrease of total turnover during the preceding accounting period.

(b) State any change in the method for calculating turnover.

(c) Where, by virtue of nature of the company, there could be doubt as to what is meant by turnover, indicate by way of a note the basis upon which turnover has been determined.

*Payments, etc, of controlled subsidiaries must be included in the subtotals under both headings (a) and (b), but need not be shown separately.

Relevant paragraph (P) of schedule 4 of the Act or article (A) of the Act	*Particulars*
P40	3 *Notes to the income statement*
P41	(a) (i) State if provision for depreciation replacement or depreciation of fixed assets is made by some method other than by a depreciation charge or provision for replacement or dimunition in value, *or* (ii) The fact that provision has not been made for depreciation, etc, on assets.
P42	(b) The fact, reason and relevant accounting period, in cases where provision was not made for tax.
P43	(c) Material respects (and the amount in each case), in which any items in the income statement were affected by— (i) transactions or circumstances of an exceptional and non-recurrent nature, including amounts paid as fines consequent upon contraventions of the Act (ii) any change in the accounting basis or the methods used to determine assets.

PART IV: THE DIRECTORS' REPORT

The directors' report accompanies the balance sheet and income statement, serving as a supplement and guide to these statements wherever necessary. This report covers, at least, that information prescribed by schedule 4. Any further matter not stipulated by schedule 4, but material to an understanding of the company's affairs, must be covered by the report (A299(2) and P59).

CONTENT OF THE DIRECTORS' REPORT

1 GENERAL REVIEW

A general insight must be given into:

P60 (1) (a) The company's business and operations during the accounting period, and the results thereof.

(b) Every fact or circumstance material to a clear view of the company's affairs by its members must be taken into account, including a statement of the proportion of profit and loss attributable to the various classes of the company's business.

(c) The report must deal with any material fact or circumstance which occurred between the accounting date and the date of the report.

2 SPECIFIC MATTERS TO BE COVERED

P61 (1) The *nature of the business* of the company (and of its subsidiaries, if any) as well as any major change therein during the accounting period.

(2) In aggregate figures the amounts and particulars of any *shares and debentures issued* during the accounting period, including the purpose for and circumstances in which such shares and debentures have been issued.

(3) Any *major change in the company's fixed assets* (and those of its subsidiaries, if any) during the accounting period, or any change in policy relating to the use of fixed assets.

(4) The amount (if any) already paid, or declared, or proposed to be paid by way of *dividend for each class of share.*

(5) The fact that the company's business, or any part thereof has been *managed* (if that is the case) *by a third party*, under any agreement (a management contract), as well as the name of such third party.

(6) The names of the *directors* and the *secretary*, the secretary's business and postal address, and any changes to such names and addresses during the accounting period.

(7) If the company is a subsidiary the name of the holding company and its ultimate holding company and, if the latter has been incorporated in a foreign country, the name of that country.

PART V: THE AUDITOR'S REPORT

Article 282 stipulates that the auditor of the company is to report to the members in the manner and on the subject matter as prescribed by the Act. He must also execute all other duties incumbent upon him through the Act and through any other legislation.

The auditor's report forms an integral part of the annual financial statements. Article 300 defines the auditor's particular duties.

The auditor, having complied with the stipulations laid down in article 300, and having acquainted himself with all the matters contained therein, and having carried out his audit without restriction of any nature, then reports to the members of the company to the effect that he has examined the annual company statements (and the group financial statements or the group report) and that these, in his view, fairly present the company's financial position (and that of its subsidiaries) and the results of its activities (and those of its subsidiaries), in the manner prescribed by the Act.

Should the auditor be unable to make such a report, or to do so without reservation, he should *include* in his report a statement to this effect setting out the facts or circumstances preventing him from making such a report, or from doing so without qualification (article 301).

INDEX